The Nightmare of Reason

THE

NIGHTMARE

OF REASON,

A Life of Franz Kafka

by Ernst Pawel

FARRAR · STRAUS · GIROUX

NEW YORK

Second printing, 1984

Printed in the United States of America
Published simultaneously in Canada
by Collins Publishers, Toronto
DESIGNED BY HERB JOHNSON

Library of Congress Cataloging in Publication Data
Pawel, Ernst.
The nightmare of reason.
Bibliography: p.
Includes index.
1. Kafka, Franz, 1883–1924—Biography.   2. Authors,
Austrian—20th century—Biography.   I. Title.
PT2621.A26Z8155   1983   833'.912 [B]   83–25376
ISBN 0–374–22236–3

The following photographs were reproduced with the kind permission of the Archiv Klaus Wagenbach Berlin: Kafka (age ten) with his sisters, Kafka as a high-school student, Kafka and Ottla, Kafka at thirty, the Workmen's Accident Insurance Institute, Kafka and Felice Bauer, Dr. Siegfried Löwy and Ottla, Dora Diamant, the last picture of Kafka.

The photographs of Kafka and Hansi, and of Max Brod, were reproduced with the kind permission of Mrs. Ilse Ester Hoffe.

TO THE MEMORY OF

Ottla Kafka and Milena Jesenská

Contents

PREFACE   xi

KEY TO ABBREVIATIONS   xiii

THE NIGHTMARE OF REASON   3

BIBLIOGRAPHY   449

INDEX   457

Illustrations

FOLLOWING PAGE 210

Kafka's parents
The Kinsky Palace
Kafka's birthplace
Kafka (age ten) with his sisters
Kafka's grammar school
Kafka as a high-school student
Kafka's high-school class
Kafka and Ottla
Kafka and Hansi
Max Brod
Oskar Baum
Prague's Old Town Square
Kafka at thirty
The Workmen's Accident Insurance Institute
Kafka and Felice Bauer
Envelope of a letter to Felice
Dr. Siegfried Löwy and Ottla
Golden Lane
Schönborn Palace
Maisel Street and the Jewish Town Hall
Milena Jesenská
Puah Ben-Tovim
Dora Diamant
Bergmann, Brod, and Israel's President Shazar, 1967
The last picture of Kafka
Oppelt House
The tomb of Kafka and his parents

MAP OF PRAGUE   456

Preface

No life of Franz Kafka could have been written—or, for that matter, would have been written—had it not been for the vision and courage of Max Brod. It was he who twice rescued Kafka's work, first from physical destruction, later from indifference and oblivion. To Brod we also owe the first biography of Kafka, a profoundly personal document published in 1937. That the biographer, in this instance, also happened to be his subject's closest friend, a witness to his life and times, may not have been an unmixed blessing; familiarity breeds blind spots, and the view from up close tends to distort one's perspective. But while Brod's opinions and conclusions may be open to challenge, no one now living can hope to match his intimate, firsthand knowledge of Kafka's world. Like all Kafka biographies, the present one is therefore a tribute to Max Brod's dedication, loyalty, and to his singular generosity of spirit.

In the intervening half century, however, much new material relating to Kafka has emerged which Brod either chose to ignore or could not have known about. The bibliography lists the most relevant publications, but the work of Klaus Wagenbach and Hartmut Binder is in a class by itself and must be acknowledged as such. Their decades of research yielded an abundance of vital details and documents that would have been irretrievably lost without their efforts. I am greatly in their debt for many of the facts, even where I differ in my reading of them.

Many individuals in Europe, Israel, and the United States have generously shared their personal recollections or helped in the far-flung search for source material. I want to express my special thanks to Marianne Steiner, to Dr. Puah Menczel, Miriam Singer, and Moshe Spitzer, to Ruven Klingsberg, to Margot Cohn and the staff of the Israel

National Library at Hebrew University, and to the librarians of the Leo Baeck Institute in New York. David Rieff's sensitive guidance and editorial support have been both exemplary and invaluable. I am immensely grateful to all of them.

E.P.

Key to Abbreviations

Brod, bio.   Max Brod. *Franz Kafka—Eine Biographie*. Frankfurt am Main: Fischer Verlag, 1963 (*Franz Kafka—A Biography*. Translated by G. Humphreys Roberts and Richard Winston. New York: Schocken Books, 1963).

Brod, St. L.   *Streitbares Leben*. Munich: Herbig Verlag, 1969.

DI   *Tagebücher 1910–1923*. Frankfurt am Main: Fischer Verlag, 1973 (*The Diaries of Franz Kafka, 1910–1913*. Translated by Joseph Kresh. New York: Schocken Books, 1965; *The Diaries of Franz Kafka, 1914–1923*. Translated by Martin Greenberg. New York: Schocken Books, 1965).

FA   *Brief an den Vater*. New York: Schocken Books, 1953 (*Letter to His Father*. Translated by Ernst Kaiser and Eithne Wilkins. New York: Schocken Books, 1953).

FEL   *Briefe an Felice*. Frankfurt am Main: Fischer Verlag, 1976 (*Letters to Felice*. Translated by James Stern and Elisabeth Duckworth. New York: Schocken Books, 1973).

L   *Briefe 1902–1924*. Frankfurt am Main: Fischer Verlag, 1975 (*Letters to Friends, Family and Editors*. Translated by Richard and Clara Winston. New York: Schocken Books, 1977).

MIL   *Briefe an Milena*. Frankfurt am Main: Fischer Verlag, 1966 (*Letters to Milena*. Translated by Tania and James Stern. New York: Schocken Books, 1962).

O   *Briefe an Ottla und die Familie*. Frankfurt am Main: Fischer Verlag, 1974 (*Letters to Ottla and the Family*. New York: Schocken Books, 1982. Translated by Clara and Richard Winston).

WAG.   Klaus Wagenbach. *Franz Kafka. Eine Biographie seiner Jugend*. Bern: Francke Verlag, 1958.

All quotes are my own translations from the original sources. Equivalent English versions, where available, are listed here merely for the convenience of readers unfamiliar with German. Page numbers refer to the original, but in the case of diary entries and correspondence, dates have been substituted for easier reference wherever possible.

E.P.

The Nightmare of Reason

One

In Prague, he is always present but never mentioned, and it comes as a shock suddenly to find oneself face to face with him in the heart of the city—Kafka's brooding features, life-size, cast in black bronze and mounted above eye level on the wall of a drab building on Maisel Street. On this spot, so a small plaque proclaims, stood the house in which the writer Franz Kafka was born.

It is a modest memorial, conceived in ambivalence and therefore singularly fitting in its way. Commissioned by Communist authorities, designed by the sculptor Karel Hadlik, and unveiled in 1965, at a time when the human face of socialism began to rise above the parapets of Stalinoid concrete, it was intended as the initial stage in Kafka's metamorphosis from decadent nihilist into a revolutionary critic of capitalist alienation. In the summer of 1968, Soviet tanks put an end to liberal illusions, and further efforts at rehabilitating Kafka were suspended. But his presence, once acknowledged, is hard to exorcise in a town where every moment of the day and night recalls his nightmares. The bronze sculpture was left in place, so was the marker on his house in the Alchemists' Lane—concessions to tourism, or one of those Schweikian triumphs of cunning that have kept the Czech cause alive through the ages. Either way, they bear witness to one all-important, fundamental fact of Kafka's existence: that he was born in Prague, was buried in Prague, and spent almost all forty-one years of his life in this citadel of lost causes, the "little mother with claws" that never loosened her grip on him and shaped his vision of the world.

An uncanny world in which to grow up, still solidly embedded in the Middle Ages, walled in by mystery and legend turned to stone. The view from the Kafka windows stretched back over the centuries, and every walk, every errand took the child through the vaulted archways and twisting alleys of a vengeful past. This was to be his life's stage.

Friedrich Thieberger, a renowned Jewish scholar with whom Kafka later studied Hebrew, recounts that "once, as Franz and I were standing at the window looking down on Old Town Square, he pointed at the buildings and said: 'This was my high school, the university was over there, in the building facing us, my office a bit further to the left. This narrow circle . . .' and his finger described a few small circles, 'this narrow circle encompasses my entire life.' "

But long before the town became a concept in the child's mind, long before the physical reality of even his most immediate environment began to register in meaningful and coherent images, he had to find his way in the far more bewildering shadow world of very large, powerful human beings and learn to deal with the dual threat of both their presence and their absence. What Kafka chose to remember about his childhood is highly revealing, though no more so than what he chose to forget. Even a "memory come alive," as he once described himself in one of his last diary entries, tends to be selective in ways determined by beginnings beyond memory—by a real-life mother who unwittingly betrayed him long before her image fused with the symbol of his quest for love, just as the real-life father, with his waxed mustache and drill-sergeant temper, preceded the image of divine omnipotence.

* * *

Posterity has come to know them only as "Kafka's parents"—such are the perils of raising a writer in the family, especially a writer devoid of conscious hypocrisy. Yet Herrmann Kafka was already thirty-one years old when he became Kafka's father, a demanding role at best, for which he happened to be particularly ill equipped. The very qualities that had enabled him to claw his way out of grinding poverty into middle-class respectability and relative affluence—unself-conscious egotism, brute drive, and a single-minded concentration on money and status—did not make for grace, warmth, and sensitivity in his contacts with people in general. As a parent, however, he suffered from an additional handicap: he himself had never had a childhood.

His own father, Jakob Kafka, born in 1814, was the second of nine children—six boys and three girls—raised in a one-room shack in the Czech village of Wossek. Under the laws then in force, he was not permitted to marry; a 1789 decree promulgated to curb the growth of the Jewish population barred any but the oldest son of Jewish parents from obtaining a marriage license, and Jakob had a stepbrother older by a year. What saved him from dying without legitimate progeny—death twice over, in the context of his faith—was the revolution of 1848, or rather its savage repression. By the sort of ironic paradox that crops up with predictable unpredictability throughout Jewish history, the new constitution, designed to strengthen the hand of the autocratic government, brought Jews the very freedoms which the French Revolution and its aftershocks had promised but largely failed to deliver.

In granting full citizenship rights to the roughly 400,000 Jews within the empire—including the right to marry at will, to settle in the cities, and to enter trades and professions—the Habsburg bureaucracy was moved not by humanitarian impulses but by political and economic considerations. The business skills and energy of peddlers, money-lenders, and craftsmen were an untapped resource invaluable to a country on the verge of industrialization, and the Jews' peculiar, co-hesive, but supranational allegiance made them a potential counterforce to the radicalism of contending nationalities that threatened the survival of the multinational state. But all that mattered to Kafka's grandfather Jakob, in 1848, was that at last he could marry, and he proceeded to do so at once, taking as his wife the daughter of his next-door neighbor.

A kosher butcher by trade, Jakob Kafka was a surly giant of a man, reputedly able to lift a bag of potatoes with his teeth, but all his back-breaking labor never netted him more than the barest subsistence. His wife, Franziska Platowski, already thirty-three when she married, had an outgoing and cheerful disposition that, under the circumstances, should have qualified her for sainthood. Between 1850 and 1859, she gave birth to six children and raised them all in that one-room shack, in abject poverty; for long stretches, the family's diet consisted of little more than potatoes.

Somehow they survived—the parents as well as all six of their children—itself a rare feat in its day, and evidence of robust genetic equipment. (The shack itself, though, still inhabited after the Second World War, outlasted them all.) The children were put to work as soon as they were strong enough to pull a cart. Summer and winter, in any kind of weather, they had to make the rounds delivering slabs of meat to Jakob's far-flung clientele. The frostbites and footsores that Herr-mann, the second-oldest, suffered as a result became his battle scars; he kept regurgitating the inventory of his childhood privations with a mix-ture of pride and self-pity which his own son in turn found singularly revolting. In fact, the perennial paternal litany, half boast and half accusation, of "You don't know how well off you are . . . When I was your age . . ." loomed large on the list of grievances Kafka hoarded against his father.

This sniping across the generation gap is common enough. But in contrast to so many fathers licking their imaginary wounds, Herrmann did not have to invent or exaggerate the hardships of his youth in order to score points, and no one saw this more clearly than the target of his scorn. In "Josephine, the Singer," Kafka's last story, written on his deathbed, he evokes the world in which his father came of age:

> Our life [he wrote, referring to Josephine's "nation of mice"] simply happens to be such that a child, as soon as it can get about a little and is to some extent able to find its way in the world, must take care of itself just like an adult. We are, for economic reasons, scattered over too large an area, our enemies are too numerous, the dangers that everywhere lie in wait for us are too unpredictable—we simply cannot afford to shield our children from the struggle for existence; to do so would doom them to an early grave. But one additional reason should be cited, this one hopeful rather than depressing: the fertility of our tribe. One generation—and each is immensely populous—crowds the other; the children have no time to be children . . . no sooner has a child made its appearance than it is a child no more; other children's faces press in from behind . . . rosy with happiness. Yet however charming this may be, and however much others may rightly envy us for it, the fact remains that we cannot give our children a true childhood.

The ancestors of both Jakob and Franziska had for at least a century lived in Jewish enclaves surrounded by a Czech peasant population. Unlike most of their coreligionists, forced by a 1787 decree to adopt German surnames, they had—presumably by special dispensation—chosen Slavic names; the Kafkas, at any rate, always assumed that their family name derived from *kavka,* the Czech word for "jackdaw," although *Jakovke*, a Yiddish diminutive for Jakob, is another and not unlikely derivation.

The Kafkas spoke Czech at home but, like all Jews, sent their children to the Jewish school—schools were denominational, a six-year attendance compulsory for boys—where, by law, German was the language of instruction. Herrmann did his compulsory stint, the full extent of his formal education, and became fluent in spoken German, though he never quite mastered the intricacies of the written language and, to the end of his life, evidently felt more at home in Czech.

At fourteen, one year into manhood under Jewish law, he left home for good to make his way in the world. Despite stiff competition, the young peddler survived on his own. Retail distribution in rural areas was still in its infancy, while the increasing volume and variety of manufactured goods—especially in Bohemia, cradle of the nascent industry—required domestic outlets. The Jewish peddlers thus filled a growing need, and many of them laid the foundations for what in later years became respectable fortunes. Some switched to manufacturing; Franz Werfel's father came to own the largest glove factory in Bohemia, Freud's father had a textile plant in Moravia. Others progressed from moneylending to high finance or, like Herrmann Kafka, expanded into the retail and wholesale business.

Altogether, the economic position of Austro-Hungarian Jewry in the second half of the nineteenth century improved rapidly. The manifest success of the "founding fathers," however, ought not to obscure the merciless struggle it took to rise from well below bare subsistence to even the relatively modest heights eventually scaled by a Herrmann Kafka. The attitudes and opinions shaped by this experience came to dominate Jewish middle-class life to the end. But even more significant was the preponderance of certain personality traits favoring survival in the ruthlessly competitive world of emerging capitalism, a natural selection that made for a remarkable degree of uniformity in the pattern of their family relations.

No one defined and explored that pattern more creatively than Sigmund Freud, himself a child of that same time and place—born at Pribor, Moravia, the son of a textile merchant who went bankrupt as a result of the Czech anti-German and anti-Jewish boycott and moved his family to Vienna in 1859, when Freud was three years old. The world that shaped Freud's vision, the rising Jewish middle class in nineteenth-century Austria, was also the world of the Kafkas, and the almost paradigmatic nature of the oedipal conflict in that family, the often startling literalness with which Kafka himself seemed to be acting out the Freudian script, no doubt owes much to these common antecedents.

Psychoanalysis, not least for that very reason, has contributed highly pertinent insights to an understanding of Kafka's character and work.

But our ultimate concern is not so much with the ways in which he typified all sons locked in mortal combat with their fathers as with the ways in which he was different and unique: how he came to be Franz Kafka.

* * *

For six years, young Herrmann traveled the byways of rural Bohemia and Moravia. In 1872, at the age of twenty, he was drafted into the Austrian army, served the prescribed two years, during which he was promoted to sergeant, and after his discharge headed for Prague to seek his fortune.

The removal of residence restrictions in 1848 had triggered a mass migration of Jews from country to city. To a landless population, subsisting on the margins of an impoverished agricultural economy, the city was the new Jerusalem, the promise of the good life. To the Jews, moreover, increasingly victimized by anti-Semitism, the city also offered such safety as lies in numbers and in anonymity. Within mere decades, the rural ghettoes were deserted, and villages such as Wossek had to close their synagogues for lack of a minyan.

Herrmann settled in the decaying slums of the Josephstadt, Prague's teeming medieval ghetto, with its string of bordellos and sleazy dives. It was not the most propitious of times for a young man without funds or connections. The Vienna stock-market crash of 1873 closed out two decades of unprecedented boom and signaled the onset of what turned out to be a tenacious and long-lasting depression. But the twenty-two-year-old army veteran, accustomed to hardship and frugal in his habits, was determined to find ways of starting a business of his own. It took him eight years. He got his chance in 1883, when he married the daughter of a wealthy brewery owner.

* * *

His bride, Julie Löwy, was born on March 23, 1856, in Podebrady, a predominantly Czech town on the river Elbe. Her ancestry included an unusual array of remarkable or at least unconventional characters, deeply religious for the most part and far more concerned with metaphysical pursuits and spiritual values than with the accumulation of worldly goods—Talmudists, miracle rabbis, eccentric troublemakers,

Christian converts, and visionaries. In a brief autobiographical sketch written in 1911, Kakfa alluded to this exotic heritage:

> My Hebrew name is Amschel, after my mother's maternal grandfather, whom my mother—she was six at the time of his death—remembers as a very pious and learned man with a long white beard. She remembers how she had to hold on to the toes of the corpse while asking his forgiveness for whatever wrongs she may have done him. She remembers her grandfather's many books lining the walls. He bathed in the river every day, even in winter, when he had to chop a hole in the ice. My mother's mother died before her time of typhoid fever. Her death so affected the grandmother that she became melancholy, refused to eat, spoke to no one, and, one year after her daughter's death, went out for a walk and never returned; they pulled her corpse out of the Elbe River. Even more learned than my mother's grandfather was her great-grandfather, equally renowned among both Christians and Jews. Once, during a conflagration, his piety worked a miracle; the flames spared his house while devouring all the others around it. He had four sons; one converted to Christianity and became a physician. All of them died young, except for my mother's grandfather. He had one son, whom my mother knew as Crazy Uncle Nathan, and one daughter, my mother's mother. [DI, 12/25/11]

The extent to which personality traits are inherited may be a matter of controversy, but Kafka himself never had a doubt about the mother's bloodline being the dominant strain in his makeup. It was one of the very few issues on which, after a fashion, he saw eye to eye with his father; Herrmann, too, blamed the constitutional taint endemic among his wife's maternal ancestors for his son's unworldliness and lack of drive.

They were, nonetheless, the only ancestors whom Kafka acknowledged as such. The sainted great-grandfather and namesake Amschel, or Adam, Porias was born at Podebrady in 1794 and died there in 1862. A rabbi and Talmudic scholar, he had the reputation of a holy man among both Jews and Gentiles. Unfortunately, the odor of sanctity is frequently toxic to those too close to its source. His son Nathan, born in 1824, was considered mad; his wife, Sarah, committed suicide in 1860; his daughter Esther, born in 1839, was married off to the textile merchant Jakob Löwy and died of typhoid fever at twenty-nine, after having given birth to three children—Alfred, Joseph, and Kafka's mother, Julie.

Julie was three when her mother died. Her father remarried with unseemly haste and had three more children, Julie's half-brothers Richard, Rudolf, and Siegfried; the panoply of ostentatiously Teutonic names suggests the distance Jakob Löwy had already put between himself and his Orthodox upbringing. He was a typical member of the new Jewish middle class, resolutely assimilationist, staunchly German in language and outlook, pro-emperor in politics. Already quite wealthy in Podebrady, he sold his brewery at a profit and moved to Prague, where he again prospered in the same business.

But despite the relative affluence of her home, Julie's childhood was also a difficult and unhappy one. Her stepmother, a distant Porias relative, was no replacement for a real mother, and Julie, as the oldest of six children and the only female, grew up as a Cinderella of sorts, maid to her father's wife and surrogate mother to the five boys, hardworking and competent in everything she did. It earned her trust and affection from everyone but her parents; she was, however, modest in her expectations, never complained, and altogether learned to keep her feelings to herself.

Yet hiding behind this screen of brisk competence was an enormously warmhearted woman, capable of giving much love and equally desperate to receive it. Long before she was married, the five brothers she had helped to raise had flown the clammy coop and scattered all over creation: Alfred eventually became director general of the Spanish railways in Madrid, Joseph founded a colonial trading corporation in Paris, Richard settled in Prague as a clerk, Siegfried—Kafka's favorite uncle—spent his life as a country doctor, and Rudolf, an accountant in a Prague brewery, converted to Christianity. Only Joseph and Richard ever married; the others remained lifelong bachelors. But though they drifted apart and later had no use for one another, all of them remained in close touch with their only sister and mother substitute.

Affectionate and generous she was, from all accounts. But what her firstborn needed, by way of affection, far exceeded the demands of even the closest relatives and friends. As a mother, Julie no doubt did her best; but having never been mothered herself, her best was a kind of corseted tenderness that must have felt like ice to the touch.

She was already twenty-six at the time of her marriage, still living with her parents in the stately Smetana Mansion on Old Town Square,

a challenge to every matchmaker and meddling relative
There is no record of how she and Herrmann Kafka got t
like most marriages in their circles, theirs was probably n
heaven but put together as a business deal. That Julie, unlik
mother, had a say in the choice is likely; the emancipation ᴏ   ...,
though lagging behind that of the Jews, had made some slow progress.
Whether she loved Herrmann, on the other hand, was hardly the sort
of question she would have asked herself; you did not marry the man
you loved, but loved the man you married. Marriages endured, because
women endured marriage. Julie endured. Every so often she lapsed
into "weeping spells and melancholy"—bouts of probably clinical depression—but she endured.

Socially, Herrmann was not her equal. The line between the
German-speaking, urbanized, middle-class Jews and their Czech-
speaking, semiproletarian country cousins, while still fluid, already
marked a gap defined by considerable snobbery. But Herrmann, at
thirty, had assets that made up for lack of money and social standing:
a broad back and a nimble if uneducated mind, the proven capacity
to take care of himself in a rugged world, and, above all, a strident,
irrepressible, infectious vitality.

That they were also two very lonely people deprived of their childhood, scarred orphans in search of a home, may not have been apparent to them, then or later. But it probably accounts for their lifelong
intimacy in a partnership that defies the paltry stereotypes of a happy
marriage.

The wedding took place in Prague on September 3, 1882, at the
elegant Hotel Goldhammer on Old Town Square, just a few steps from
the historic 500-year-old building in which the newlyweds began their
married life.

"*Na Věže*" (At the Tower) straddled the border between two
worlds. A massive structure at the corner of Maisel and Carp Streets,
it formed the extreme tip of the Jewish ghetto, jutting out into the heart
of Hussite Prague, its back against the Russian Orthodox St. Nicholas
Church, its front facing a notorious underworld bar and a string of
bordellos. Originally the residence of the town scribe, it was acquired
in 1629 by the Strahov monastery, turned into a theater in the
eighteenth century, and, in the late 1870s, subdivided into a warren of
small apartments, in one of which Herrmann Kafka and his bride spent
the first two and a half years of their marriage. "*Na Věže*," along with

most of the medieval ghetto slums, was razed around the turn of the century in one of the few large-scale urban renewal projects ever to be carried out in Prague. One of its portals, however, survived and has been incorporated into the otherwise nondescript building that now displays Kafka's bronze likeness.

By the end of the year, Herrmann had opened his first dry-goods store, and Julie was pregnant. On July 3, 1883, at home and with a midwife in attendance, she gave birth to a healthy boy. He was named Franz, in honor of the Emperor Franz Joseph, and a physician performed the circumcision on July 10.

*   *   *

As a setting for the birth of Franz Kafka, the ancient mansion-turned-tenement crumbling in a wedge-shaped no-man's-land between hostile cultures could hardly have been more appropriate, though this was certainly not the way his young parents felt about the place. Bent on getting ahead, rising up in the world, and giving their children a better start in life, they saw in the Tower not a romantic abode but a dilapidated dump in a disreputable and noisy neighborhood from which they were eager to escape as soon as they could afford it.

Franz spent the first two years of his life in this eerie place; what, if anything, it contributed to the infant's inchoate awareness of the outer world is anybody's guess. In all likelihood, those first images merged with the pervasive gloom of the family's later habitations in somewhat less disreputable but none too dissimilar vestiges of medieval monumentalism, prison-like structures with dank walls and dark hallways, with primitive plumbing, musty rooms, coal-burning tile stoves, the smell of cabbage and unaired bedding, and the skitter of ghosts beyond the circle of candlelight sounding suspiciously like rats on the warpath.

A depressing environment, but quite the norm in Prague's Old Town. The Tower itself was officially condemned soon after Kafka's birth, along with most of the Josephstadt. The crime-ridden slums of the ancient Jewish ghetto were undoubtedly an unhealthy place for ordinary human beings; yet one suspects that what finally prodded the bureaucracy into uncharacteristically decisive action was the threat to public order rather than to public health. Even so, the actual demolition was deferred for a number of years, and the Tower did not come down till the turn of the century.

In May 1885, meanwhile, the Kafka family had move(
las Square. Now the very heart of Prague, it was even th(
thoroughfare of a tense provincial capital and, as such, th(
stage for mass protests and demonstrations. Whether this
troubled the Kafkas—many of the demonstrations tended t(
of hand and turn into anti-Jewish riots—or whether they had simply
overreached themselves is not known. But in December of that same
year, the restive couple moved back to the familiar surroundings of the
Old Town. They were to change residences four more times before
settling at last, in June 1889, in the House Minuta, again off the Old
Town Square, where Kafka, about to turn six, was to spend the next
seven years of his childhood.

The House Minuta—"Minute" in Czech, though the derivation may
be Latin; for once, neither history nor legend offers a clue to the significance of the name—juts out at a right angle to the Old Town Hall
and separates Old Town Square from the Little Square. Built during
the sixteenth-century Bohemian Renaissance, the essentially Gothic features of its original architecture were gradually submerged in successive
renovations. But a more expert attempt at historical restoration, undertaken some years after Kafka's death, uncovered a series of wall frescoes,
elaborate Florentine graffiti that now once again grace the two façades.
They have become a landmark feature of the tourist circuit, just a few
steps from the famous Town Hall Clock, with its hourly procession of
the Twelve Apostles, followed by a fittingly grim reminder that the
Reaper, scythe in hand, has gained yet another hour on the living.

*   *   *

To the end of his days Kafka felt that his childhood had crippled
him, rendered him unfit for life among the living. Objectively, the circumstances in which he grew up did not materially differ from those
generally prevailing in most of Prague's Jewish middle-class homes.
But unhappiness, for one thing, is a profoundly subjective experience
linked only tenuously to objective reality. And for another, the fragmentary facts known about Kafka's life during his preschool years, from
1883 to 1889, offer at least some clues to the dread and anguish of a
childhood which he never quite outgrew.

From the very beginning, life in this family, as organized by, around,
and for the benefit of the Lord and Master, focused not on the home

but on the store. Within a few years, and in the midst of a severe and persistent recession, Herrmann managed to expand the small retail haberdashery he had opened at the time of his marriage into a thriving wholesale dry-goods business. His own childhood had taught him what he could never hope to teach his children—that money is the root of all success. He knew that man doesn't live by bread alone; but without bread he does not live. And if money cannot buy happiness—a startling discovery made by the next generation—it does buy bread as well as butter, decent clothes, shelter, and even books. What is more, money—given enough of it—will not only buy creature comforts but transform the creature into a man of substance and social significance.

Herrmann set out to succeed, with a single-minded, driving determination that left no room and little time for anything else in his life. This was particularly true during the difficult first years in a new business, which coincided with the infancy of his son. Franz seldom got to see his father, though he heard him more often than he cared to, then or later. The booming parade-ground voice of that distant divinity, its ear-splitting vulgarity and thunderous threats, helped to stoke fantasies that never quite yielded to the prosaic image of the real-life father. It also left Franz with a lifelong morbid sensitivity to noise.

Since everything in the Kafka household revolved around the struggle to get ahead, it seemed only natural for Julie also to be devoting herself to the business. With thousands of peasant girls flocking to the cities, household help and baby nurses were no problem. But Julie did more than just help out. A rare combination of competence and tact soon made her indispensable to a husband who was astute and indefatigable in his work but uncouth and quick-tempered in his dealings with both customers and employees.

The fact that the children were essentially brought up by maidservants and, later on, governesses again merely followed a common pattern. Julie, however, was not just physically absent; she was unavailable to Franz in much more fundamental ways. She served her husband with the same obedient devotion with which she had helped her stepmother run the household, and for much the same reasons. Being helpful, being needed, a helper, a helpmate, had early on become her way of reaching out for love or at least approval—hardly the sort of response to be got from an infant. In fact, in later years, with her children come of age, this same trait proved admirably suited to her role of matriarchal peacemaker, dispenser of common sense, chamomile tea, and emotional support, who defused and defanged paternal wrath and meddled with discreet motherly concern in the affairs of her children. But as long as they were small, she kept her distance and instead hired help to provide for their physical care.

In the early years of marriage her maternal instincts must, in any case, have been severely strained by her husband's ceaseless demands for attention and sympathy. She worked for him during the day, she listened to his grumbling and grousing, and she played cards with him almost every night throughout their forty-nine years of married life. They met each other's needs, as solid a foundation for marriage as any. Unfortunately, neither quite met the needs of their children. Since these needs varied greatly, the consequences were quite different for each of them, but it seems clear that Franz, the firstborn, was by far the most deprived and the most severely affected.

Having to choose between rival demands on her time and attention —which, for Julie, was what love came down to, at that stage—she never gave her husband reason to complain, then or later.

> She loved you too much [Kafka wrote to his father years later, picking at the scabs of his childhood], she was too loyally devoted to you to act for any length of time as an independent spiritual force in the child's struggle. The child's instincts in this matter proved correct, by the way; over the years, Mother became ever more closely tied to you. Where she herself was concerned, she always maintained her independence, strictly within the narrowest of bounds, but beautifully and delicately, without ever basically hurting you. Yet as the years passed, she came to adopt your judgments and condemnations of the children ever more blindly and completely, a matter not so much of reason as of feeling.

What the adult could not recapture was the helpless rage of the abandoned infant spilling over into fear and hatred, directed not at the mother who failed him but at the rival who was stealing her and beating him out in an unequal struggle. At age thirty-six, he could still complain that "as a young child I lost the battle against my father, but all through these years, ambition wouldn't let me leave the battlefield even though he still keeps beating me time and again" (DI, 12/2/21).

The image, here, of the stereotypically oedipal constellation, that once revolutionary concept long since ossified into a schematic platitude, is almost too pat for comfort. But the basic triangular relationship in the Kafka household soon evolved into a much more complex configuration with the births, at two-year intervals, of Franz's two brothers. Georg was born in September 1885; he died of measles in the spring of 1887. In September of that same year, Julie again gave birth to a boy; half a year later—in April 1888—Heinrich died in turn, the victim of otitis.

*   *   *

Curiously little attention has been paid to these deaths and their effect upon the surviving child. The reason, no doubt, is the manifest attitude of the survivor himself, whose few glancing references to what must, after all, have been a major tragedy in his home and in his childhood are consistently flat, factual, and devoid of affect.

Kafka was four the year Georg died and Heinrich was born, almost five at the time of Heinrich's death, an age at which an intelligent and uncommonly sensitive child would have to be aware of his parents' reaction, if nothing else. That the effect on the young mother was devastating can be taken for granted; but the loss, within a year, of two of his three children—male children, at that, the times and attitudes being what they were—must have been a severe blow for the father as well. It seems inconceivable that the grief of his parents, barely recovering from one death only to be struck by a second, could have been lost on the five-year-old and, once again, only child. And the fact that this particular tragedy never became part of the "memory come alive" makes it not less but, on the contrary, potentially far more significant than any conscious recollections.

Repression is an effective but highly dangerous mechanism of defense, a slow-acting poison. Like any firstborn and still-dependent infant, Kafka must have been wildly resentful at the intrusion of two more rivals for his mother's attention. No angel yet in anyone's book, gifted with more than his share of turbulent intensity, he must have wished them out of his life, done away with them in primitive fantasies of murder by magic, and struggled with the guilt and fear which, in the normal course of events, mark the genesis of human conscience.

But events did not take a normal course. His fantasies came true, so that the death of his two baby brothers left him with a burden of guilt too heavy ever to acknowledge.

Two

" "I was the oldest of six children," the then twenty-nine-year-old Kafka wrote to his fiancée, Felice Bauer, in December 1912. "Two brothers, somewhat younger, died in infancy, through the fault of the doctors. Then came a period of quiet, through which I was an only child, until some four or five years later my three sisters arrived at intervals of one and two years respectively. Thus for a very long time I was all alone, forever battling nurses, aging nannies, snarling cooks, morose governesses, because my parents spent all their time in the shop."

To the end of his life, Kafka retained an acerbic vision of childhood untouched and unretouched by nostalgia or piety—a hard-edged recollection of what it was like to be a child in a world ruled, run, and, for all he knew, created by the Father. The underpaid and overworked servants vented their rage, in time-honored fashion, upon the most defenseless member of the enemy tribe, while the mother, depressed, mourning the loss of two of her children, busy in the shop, and, above all, unswerving in her wifely devotion and loyalty, had little to offer the child by way of warmth and affection.

In fact, the most enduringly human presence in that emotional desert may have been Marie Werner, never referred to as anything but *slečna*—the Miss. A timid and mousy Jewish spinster, she had joined the household shortly after the parents' marriage and remained to raise, if that is the word, not just Franz but also his three sisters. The reverential awe in which she held the Father made her yet another exponent of paternal power, offering neither protection nor even a neutral refuge. One distinctly positive attribute, however, was *slečna*'s total ignorance of German, Kafka's first language. And though he never developed any affection for the woman, his diffident contact with her gave him an early grasp of colloquial Czech.

At one point during those early years—just how early is unclear—Herrmann also hired a French governess for the boy, this being the mark of cultural refinement in the upper-middle-class circles to which he so diligently aspired. Mlle Bailly's titillatingly suggestive corpulence, however, seems to have been far more inspiring than her qualities as a teacher. Some ten years of private French lessons yielded markedly meager results; and although Kafka characteristically blamed his own lack of talent, both his knowledge of Czech and his later Hebrew studies demonstrate an at least average aptitude for languages. On the other hand, Mlle Bailly served as the first object of his conscious erotic fantasies. Whether she factually attempted to seduce the boy, as he intimated years later in a cryptic diary entry, would seem far less important than her role in providing an acceptable focus for the diffuse and still largely incestuous sexuality of preadolescence.

The most sustained account of Kafka's childhood as seen by himself is contained in the fifty-page "letter," which, at the age of thirty-six, he wrote to his father. In it, he summons up an incident which he obviously considered not only emblematic of relations with his father but of lasting significance in the evolution of his self-image:

> As for those early years, there is only one episode of which I have a clear recollection. You may also remember it. One night I kept constantly whimpering for water, certainly not because I was thirsty but partly, no doubt, to make trouble, partly just to amuse myself. When repeated and emphatic threats failed to work, you snatched me out of my bed, carried me out onto the *pavlatch* [balcony], and left me there alone for a while in my nightgown, with the door locked. I am not saying that what you did was wrong; there may have been no other way for you to get some peace and quiet that night. But I am bringing it up as a typical example of your child-rearing methods and their effect on me. I subsequently became a rather obedient child, but I suffered inner damage as a result. Something in my nature kept me from ever making the proper connection between the pointless whining for water—which seemed perfectly natural to me—and the monstrous terror of being carried out of the room. For years thereafter, I kept being haunted by fantasies of this giant of a man, my father, the ultimate judge, coming to get me in the middle of the night, and for almost no reason at all dragging me out of bed onto the *pavlatch*—in other words, that as far as he was concerned, I was an absolute Nothing.

Whether it all happened the way Kafka remembered it—for that matter, whether it happened at all—is irrelevant. Screen memory or fact, it worked on his imagination, and the unrelieved bitterness with which he invoked it some thirty-odd years later testifies to its symbolic significance even if Kafka, in line with early Freudian notions of "traumatic neuroses," may have greatly overestimated its importance as a causative factor. It is only within a family relationship already at the flash point that a factually trivial episode—Herrmann was mostly bark and no bite, basically incapable of real cruelty—could assume the proportions of a major trauma. But to a child hating his father to the point of murder, those memorable moments of terror out on the *pavlatch* were fire and brimstone well deserved, just punishment for evil thoughts, and further proof of his dread rival's omnipotence.

There is thus good reason, on the whole, to credit Kafka's account of his early childhood as stultifying and oppressive, spent among uncomprehending strangers manipulated by the whims of an absolute power beyond appeal. And just when the delicate youngster with the dark, burning eyes had begun to master the basic rules of survival and become familiar with the landscape to the point of feeling reasonably safe in it, the rules changed and the ground shifted under his feet. What he had taken for the world turned out to be no more than a fenced-in patch of back yard at the edge of the wilderness. In the vast silence beyond, the divine thunder came to sound increasingly thin and plaintive, the voice of a rooster whose rule gave way to the rule of the law, no less baffling and capricious for being wholly anonymous and impersonal. The full force of its gravity would only make itself felt later; its initial purpose was no more than the methodical transformation of the obedient child into an obedient subject.

By law, school attendance—at least in theory—was compulsory for all children throughout the Habsburg empire, starting at age six. Franz Kafka, having passed his sixth birthday on July 3, 1889, was enrolled in the Deutsche Volks- und Bürgerschule—the German National and Civic Elementary School; the school year, following the summer recess, began on September 16, 1889.

* * *

It was Protestant Prussia, in its day the most advanced model of the nation-state, with the most efficient army and bureaucracy on the

Continent, that first introduced universal compulsory education. In 1763, the "soldier king" Frederick II decreed at least four years of schooling for all the children of his realm. In promoting universal literacy, the absolutist admirer of the French *encyclopédistes* no doubt saw himself as putting into practice some of their most revolutionary ideas. But enlightenment translated into peremptory orders, enforced with Prussian discipline and efficiency, turned out to have far less to do with freedom of thought than with the need for a minimally literate citizenry, able to function in a postfeudal society.

Essentially the same reasons of state led to the introduction of compulsory education in Austro-Hungary in 1774. The system, in fact, derived straight from the Prussian model; Maria Theresa had no compunction about stealing her archenemy's ideas and educational experts. But two specific problems greatly complicated the situation in the empire.

The first was the still unresolved power struggle between Church and state, which in the Protestant lands to the north had been decisively settled some two centuries earlier. In the Habsburg monarchy, the conflict remained perpetually suspended in a volatile mixture of confrontation and accommodation. The rulers themselves, though personally unswerving in their piety and devotion—none more so than Maria Theresa—never hesitated to assert their seniority in what they conceived of as a mutually useful and profitable partnership. Education, however, such as it was, had until the middle of the eighteenth century been the exclusive preserve of the Catholic Church; non-Catholic communities within the empire—Hungarian Calvinists, Lutheran Saxons—were obliged to maintain their own schools to the best of their limited financial abilities.

But practical considerations compelled drastic reforms, and Maria Theresa was nothing if not practical. Untouched by the spirit of the enlightenment, encased in an armor of bigotry and prejudice, she nonetheless had no qualms about doing what, for the increasingly centralized bureaucracy of her autocratic government, had become imperative. The ideological underpinnings for this radical step were provided by one of those gifted demagogues whom Austria seems to have spawned in peculiar profusion. Josef Sonnenfels, son of a converted Moravian rabbi and author of the country's first penal code, had already become one of the most influential members of the empress's entourage when, in a series of philosophical treatises, he codified the doctrine of the state's absolute control over the spiritual and intellectual life of its subjects, the Church being relegated to a secondary and purely supportive role. And although Sonnenfels's personal influence eventually waned, his ideas became the guiding principles of the monarchy's educational system. The Church, too weak as well as too wise to risk a head-on collision, demonstrated instead a flexibility that assured its continuing influence and became a permanent ingredient of Austrian politics.

An ultimately far more disruptive issue had to do with the complex mix of nationalities that found themselves lumped together in the haphazard improvisation referred to as Austro-Hungary but that contained numerous minorities neither Austrian nor Hungarian, such as Czechs, Slovaks, Croats, Ruthenes, Slovenes, Rumanians, and Poles. The main thrust of the 1774 General Education Act was, in fact, the cultural homogenization of these diverse populations, whose linguistic separatism posed growing political as well as administrative problems. Consequently, German was to be taught as a compulsory subject in all elementary schools, and mandated as the exclusive language of instruction at the secondary level and beyond. The ostensible rationale was utilitarian: since the state and its organs of government conducted all business in German, familiarity with the language was part of becoming a properly responsive and responsible subject. The practical effect of this policy would have amounted to forced Germanization of all ethnic minorities, but initially there seemed to be no alternative, the choices being mass education, albeit in German, and mass illiteracy, in whatever language. Even in Bohemia, most advanced of the non-Austrian provinces, only about half of all school-age children received any kind of instruction, while in districts such as Dalmatia, Galicia, and the Bukovina, schooling for the population at large was, in effect, nonexistent.

But the old order, with its timeless patterns and steady pace, was rapidly disintegrating. The rural community, where a man's roots reached back for generations, and where he was both trapped and protected by an intricate network of lifelong entanglements, crumbled under the onslaught of industrialization and urbanization. The rise of nationalism in the early nineteenth century had multiple and complex causes, but its dynamic passion and quasi-religious fervor ultimately derived from the same deep-felt human needs as the faith it replaced.

In the age of anonymity, of urban exile and meaningless labor, the search for identity acquired a new and desperate urgency. Ethnic origins, once taken for granted, became of transcendental importance; and no single aspect of this quest proved more decisive, more emotionally charged than the fight to preserve the native tongue. Instinctively, the alienated and uprooted victims of bureaucracy and progress clung to the community of language as a fixed point of reference, a link to both past and future. Language is the essence of being, the matrix of perception. To rob a man of his language is to rob him of his first, most basic sense of self; and the last-ditch defense of the native tongue became the rallying point in what began as a struggle for ethnic and cultural identity and culminated in the movements for national liberation that eventually doomed the Habsburg monarchy.

Inevitably, the in many ways most decisive confrontation over language rights involved the schools. "A Czech child belongs in a Czech school"—the slogan coined early in the seventeenth century by John Amos Comenius, last bishop of the Moravian Brethren and author of the first illustrated Czech primer—became both battle cry and plan of action for the Czech nationalists, leaders of the opposition to the central government. And as industrialization combined with population growth to provide the movement with an ever more substantial power base— the textile industry alone, in Bohemia and Moravia, employed some 600,000 workers by 1810, while the Czech population increased from 4.5 million in 1781 to 6.5 million in 1846—the school system, rather than serving its original purpose of Germanizing and unifying the empire's heterogeneous populations, became a major factor in raising their distinct national consciousness.

*   *   *

The Jews were different; for neither the first time nor the last, they found themselves impaled on the point of a dilemma. The secular schooling imposed and enforced by the state was meant to lead their children out of the ghetto—and straight into oblivion.

Throughout the Middle Ages and until well into the eighteenth century, they had suffered the indignities of enforced segregation. But whatever the problems of ghetto survival, defining the nature of Jewishness was not among them. Anti-Jewish laws and persecution aside, the religious traditions of Judaism continued to structure an entire way of life that created clear lines of demarcation between them and their Gentile surroundings. That both Judaism and anti-Semitism transcend purely religious categories was to become apparent later on, when blood, nation, and revolution came to replace Christianity as the dominant social myths. But as long as the survival of the Jews as Jews rested on the integrity of their religious traditions, and on the transmittal of those traditions down the chain of generations, the uncompromisingly Jewish education of the young remained one of the community's most vital concerns. It was an all-encompassing formative process that began in earliest childhood and, at least in principle, continued for life, literacy being an integral part of Jewish identity and the minimum requirement for participation in religious ritual. No male could lead a life Jewish in the traditional sense without the ability at least to read the Torah. Both the extreme intellectual tensions and the broad-based, essentially populist participation in the spiritual as well as the political aspects of communal life among the Jews, even before the Christian era, are rooted in this unique and troublesome emphasis on universal literacy.

In this dense, self-contained universe, the *Toleranzpatent,* or Edict of Toleration, issued in 1782 by the Emperor Joseph II, had the effect of a bombshell. The blast shook prison walls; in theory, most physical and legal barriers segregating Jews from non-Jews were to be abolished, although it took another seventy years to reach even nominal equality.

Nevertheless, the edict contained a promise—whether good or bad for the Jews has been hotly argued ever since; there are those who insist that the price of freedom is always higher than the value received. But freedom—for Jews or for anyone else—was certainly not what the ultrareactionary emperor had in mind when he signed the *Toleranzpatent;* his goal, defined by economic and political considerations, was nothing less than the conversion of the Jews, the obliteration not just of legal restrictions but of the entire ethnic, linguistic, and religious heritage that made for Jewish separatism.

The task inspired a veritable paroxysm of bureaucratic ingenuity on the part of the Habsburg government, but in its basic thrust the legislation aimed straight at the heart of the problem. Along with a drastic reorganization of community affairs, it mandated the adoption of German names and surnames, required the use of German in all legal documents such as birth and marriage certificates, and—a first in Europe —made Jews subject to compulsory military service. Each of these measures provoked considerable resistance, yet none was to have more far-reaching consequences than the imposition of compulsory secular schooling.

While the *Toleranzpatent* opened secondary schools and universities to Jewish students, it required every Jewish community in Bohemia and Moravia to organize its own elementary school, with German as the language of instruction. Where this proved impractical, Jewish children were to attend Christian schools. (The measures were eventually extended to other parts of the empire, but it was in the Czech-language areas that it had its most significant impact.)

Ironically, it was Bohemia's chief rabbi, Ezekiel Landau, "the Renowned One of Judah," fierce antagonist of Jewish enlightenment as personified by Wessely and Mendelssohn, unyielding in his hostility to any form of secular education, who found himself constrained to preside at the opening of the first German-Jewish school in Prague on May 2, 1782. The Hebrew poem he composed for the occasion may have been meant as an act of defiance, and his faithful flock, in what amounted to a mass boycott, simply chose to ignore what they regarded as a den of heresy. But once again, Austrian bureaucracy proved bureaucratically creative; a 1786 decree, which made the issuance of a marriage license conditional on possession of an elementary-school certificate, led to an immediate and dramatic increase in the number of both schools and students, though full compliance with the law was probably not achieved until the mid-nineteenth century.

By then, however, the character of these schools had undergone a profound transformation, from basically Jewish institutions to outposts of Germanism in a largely Czech and increasingly hostile environment. At first, the original four hours of instruction in secular subjects had served merely to supplement the much more extensive program of the traditional Talmud-Torah schools. But as the latter began to lose their vitality and their students, Jewish subjects were incorporated into the secular school curriculum, where they progressively dwindled in importance as the emphasis shifted to an all but exclusively German orientation. As a result, the schools began to attract growing numbers of non-Jewish students and teachers; their links to Judaism grew ever more tenuous, and in 1869, many were taken over by the state.

The German-Jewish schools were, of course, merely one aspect of the prevailing assimilationist tide. But they helped to channel its force and, on balance, achieved most of the results the Habsburg bureaucracy had hoped for. If the vast majority of Jews never quite became Germans, or anything else, they had nonetheless been most effectively induced to shed their past, their traditions, and their language. In

Bohemia and Moravia, at least, German had totally supplanted Yiddish, ample reason in itself to further exacerbate Czech antagonism toward the Jews, who in the absence of viable alternatives tended more and more to identify politically as well as culturally with the German minority, without thereby being accepted by it on equal terms.

*   *   *

The German National and Civic Elementary School was a grim and forbidding structure on what was still called the Meatmarket, although by that time the picturesque display of bloody carcasses had yielded to the wholesale trade in fish, dead and alive. Still, it seemed a singularly appropriate name for a street flanked by two institutions, one German, the other Czech, dedicated to the education of children.

It was the family cook who, on the morning of September 15, 1889, escorted little Franz to the Meatmarket; his mother was in her last month of pregnancy and gave birth a week later—on September 22—to Elli, Franz's oldest sister.

Earlier that year, in the not too distant Austrian town of Braunau, one Clara née Plözl, wife of the customs inspector Alois Hitler, had given birth to another of the emperor's subjects, a sickly infant whose survival seemed doubtful. He survived.

Three

To the end of his life, Kafka persisted in denouncing school as a "conspiracy of the grownups," the lapidary half-truth still charged with the despair of the six-year-old. The squat, four-story bunker on the Meatmarket, barracks architecture crossed with bureaucratic monumentalism, loomed as the entrance to a maze of tunnels, their every juncture guarded by fierce Minotaurs armed with Authority. Sneaking past these monsters, one by one, constituted the crucial test of survival; test-passing became the all-absorbing obsession of the child seeking daylight and a breath of fresh air.

He hated school. So did most of his contemporaries; they feared their teachers and were scarred for life by an ordeal that simply has no parallel in the post-colonial America of coed schools and prissy schoolmarms. And they were meant to; fear and hatred make for law and order. But Kafka lacked even the initial grace of innocence; child though he was, he felt defeated in advance by the mere prospect of a struggle for which he knew himself to be hopelessly ill equipped.

> Never, I thought, would I make it through first grade; but I did, I even got a prize. I certainly won't pass the high-school entrance examinations; but pass I did. I'll definitely fail in my first year in high school; but no, I didn't fail, I succeeded in passing, time and again.
>
> Success, however, did not inspire confidence; on the contrary, I was always convinced . . . that the more I accomplished, the worse off I would be in the end. In my mind's eye I often saw a terrifying conclave of teachers (the Gymnasium merely provides the most cogent example, but they were all around me) meeting to discuss this unique, this absolutely outrageous case, to wit: how I, the most incompetent, certainly the most ignorant of all, had managed to sneak from first into the second Gymnas-

ium grade, then into the third, and so on up the line. But now that I had at last aroused their attention, I would of course be immediately thrown out, to the immense satisfaction of all righteous men delivered from a nightmare. It isn't easy for a child to live with such notions. What, in the circumstances, could I have got out of my lessons? Who would have been able to spark even a glimmer of interest? [FA]

And so, unsurprisingly, each weekday morning signaled the start of another battle. The way from the House Minuta to the Meatmarket, though it led through the heart of centuries, was hardly more than a ten-minute walk. Yet every morning for at least a year the reluctant scholar had to be dragged every inch of the way by one of those monsters-turned-myth who haunted his childhood and left poisoned stings to fester in delicate tissue.

Some thirty years later he recalled how

our cook, small, desiccated, thin, with pointed nose, hollow cheeks, yellowish but firm, resolute and superior, took me to school every morning. We lived in the house that separates the Old Town Square from the Little Square. First, we crossed the square, then we took the Teingasse, and on through a kind of archway into Meatmarket Lane to the Meatmarket. And every morning for about a year, the same scene was replayed: As we left the house, the cook would threaten to tell the teacher how naughty I had been at home. Now while I probably wasn't very naughty, I was in fact spiteful, lazy, sad, bad-tempered, from all of which no doubt something suitably nasty could have been concocted for the benefit of the teacher. Since I knew this, I did not take the cook's threat lightly. But at first, I felt that the road to school was, after all, enormous, that a lot could happen along the way (and because roads are, in fact, never enormously long, such apparent childish improvidence gradually turns into timidity and dead-eyed seriousness). Moreover, at least as long as we were only on the Old Town Square, I still had serious doubts whether the cook, an authority figure of merely the home-grown variety, would dare even to address an authority figure such as the teacher, who commanded the respect of the whole world. I may even have said something to that effect, whereupon the cook with her thin, merciless lips would curtly tell me that I didn't have to believe her, but that she'd tell the teacher just

the same. Somewhere around the entrance to Meatmarket Lane
fear finally gained the upper hand. . . . School was in and of itself a horror, and now the cook was trying to make it even worse.

I began to plead, she shook her head; the more I pleaded,
the more vital seemed the object of my pleas and the greater the
danger. I stopped, begged her forgiveness, she dragged me on.
I threatened her with retaliation by my parents, which made
her laugh: here *she* was all-powerful. I clung to the storefront
gates, to curbstones, refused to go on until I'd been forgiven. I
pulled her back by her skirt (she didn't have an easy time of it,
either) but she dragged me on, all the while assuring me that
this, too, would be told to the teacher. It got late, the Jacob
Church clock struck eight, other children began to run. I was
always in utter terror of being late; now we, too, had to run,
with me still wondering all the way if she would or wouldn't
tell. Well, she didn't, she never told. But she always could have;
in fact, the probability seemed to increase every day (yesterday
I didn't tell, but today I am definitely going to), and this threat
she never relinquished. [MIL, p. 47]

And in a diary entry of July 1910, the by then Doctor of Jurisprudence drew up another indictment:

Whenever I think of it, I must say that in some respects my
education has done me a great deal of harm. This reproach aims
at a great many people: my parents, some relatives, several
visitors to our home, various authors, a certain cook who took
me to school for a year, a whole group of teachers (compacted
in my memory to one tight lump, lest one or another elude me,
yet the lump itself crumbling time and again), a school inspector . . . [DI, 7/10/10]

So much for nostalgia and adventures of the mind. Yet while
Kafka's rancor may have been justified or at least justifiable, the menace
of those monsters embalmed by memory and stuffed with grievances
lacks conviction. Not that his fears were less than real; but he was not
altogether helpless in dealing with their sources.

The little lamb being offered up for sacrifice on the altar of authority
would seem to have been nowhere as vulnerable and defenseless as he
tended to believe, then or later. A formal photograph taken about that
time shows a fine-boned child with strikingly sensitive features, prettified
for the occasion, watching the birdie with a mixture of diffidence and
contempt, his dark-eyed intensity troubling as well as troubled. "After

all, I was an obedient child," he insisted, in the famous letter to his father. Obedient he was, indeed, often to the point of self-effacement; obedience paid for the leisure to daydream, for the luxury of being left alone, and for occasional scraps of affection from the grownups around him. The distinctly truculent silence, on the other hand, into which he withdrew even as a preschooler put a safe distance between him and his parents, his teachers, all the *Respektspersonen* duty-bound or paid to run his life for him and make him what he did not want to be. Across that distance, contacts were as rare as confrontations.

One consequence was his profound mistrust of the very authority figures whom the child in him wanted desperately to be able to trust. He was respectful toward his teachers, not because he respected them, but because they were entitled to it by virtue of being *Respektspersonen*. In school, five mornings and four afternoons a week, they were the guardians, interpreters, and enforcers of the law, the ultimate power beyond appeal, devoid of any discernible human weakness.

Such, at least, they appeared to their victims. In actual fact, these terrifying ogres were no more than low-grade civil servants mired in a job which, aside from modest pay and lifetime security, offered the cachet of semiprofessional status and the prospect of a small pension. There were many among them who abused their authority, who vented their frustrations on the backs of children or squelched any manifestation of natural curiosity, and the voluminous recollections of badly traumatized classroom survivors testify to widespread incompetence, stupidity, and outright sadism on the part of petty bureaucrats charged with the task of stuffing knowledge into boys' heads. (The education of girls was deliberately confined to the barest minimum lest it interfere with women's natural destiny; it was not until 1891, largely on the initiative of Tomáš Masaryk, that a secondary school for girls—one of the first in the empire—opened in Prague.)

Much more surprising, in the circumstances, was the number of teachers who tried to do as good a job as possible within the limits of the system, and who cared about the children as well as about the subject matter. Most of Kafka's own teachers, in fact, seem to have belonged to that category—relatively decent human beings who believed in the value of what they were doing and took an active interest in their pupils. Prague's German schools, to be sure, with their largely Jewish student body within a predominantly Czech environment, were hardly representative of the school system as a whole. In Austria proper, as in Germany, the overwhelming majority of teachers, like their fellow bureaucrats in other branches of government service, were arch-reactionaries whose approach to education reflected the rigid conservatism of their politics. Yet even there, one could find idealists who attempted to foster growth and individuality in their pupils.

What in the end defeated even the best and the most dedicated among them was a system whose main purpose was to bolster and perpetuate the spirit of autocracy. Within the elaborate hierarchies of class and power, each subunit institutionalized its own inequities, all but precluding human contact across the lines of demarcation. In Kafka's case, no doubt, his diffident hostility toward a succession of teachers who, on the whole, appear to have been rather uncommonly gentle and well-meaning, had more to do with the inner self than with the outward climate. Nevertheless, even this relatively benign institution, crowded, with no outdoor play space, drab walls defaced by the framed pieties of mindless moralistic slogans, reeked of fear, force, and boredom.

The perpetual state of war between teachers and pupils had some distinctly healthy consequences. Hating one's surrogate father, the un-civil servant appointed *in loco parentis,* made it easier to repress the far more dangerous hatred of one's real oppressor. Moreover, fear of the common enemy tended to further a rudimentary sense of group solidarity; the atmosphere of the classroom bred intense, even passionate friendships that often lasted a lifetime. On the other hand, it forced the teacher into an adversary role all but impossible to transcend; with the best of intentions, few succeeded in communicating with their charges across the mine fields of hostility crisscrossed with barbed suspicion. Fraternization between natural enemies was an act of treason, and reasoned dissent or even a frank exchange of ideas between unequals as rare in the classroom as it was in the home, the office, or the government. Kafka's relations with his father may have been unique in their specific complexity; but the ways in which their hostility manifested itself, the sullen contempt, the spluttering rages, and the refusal ever to hear one another were the rule rather than the exception. So, too, was Kafka's lifelong difficulty in face-to-face dealings with authority figures.

At that, the particular schools he attended were probably the most liberal institutions of their kind, beleaguered outposts in largely alien territory, but far from certain whom and what they were defending. Prague's German-speaking minority was rapidly dwindling in proportion to the fast-growing Czech majority, from 14.6 percent in 1880, when the first language census was taken, to 13.6 percent in 1889, Kafka's first school year. The city's population totaled 303,000 at the time; of these, 41,400 gave German as their first and principal language. (By 1910, the percentage had dropped to 7.3, or 32,000 out of a total of 442,000.)

This minority, however, comprised both Christian Germans and German-speaking Jews. And while common goals and a common language initially favored a measure of political cooperation as well as business contacts between these two influential segments of the middle class, the spread of pan-German nationalism, with its anti-Semitic cast, soon drove a wedge between them. By the 1890s, they had split into distinctly separate and mutually antagonistic camps, though the differences between them were largely lost on their Czech fellow citizens. To the Young Czech nationalists, the Jews were Germans. To the Germans, the Jews were Jews; the racial doctrines which an Austrian corporal was to translate into genocide half a century later were already sprouting in the subsoil of Austro-Hungarian politics.

Caught between the lines, trapped in the shrinking no-man's-land between crusading armies headed for a showdown but both equally committed to their Jew-baiting extremism, Bohemia's Jews found themselves in a unique quandary that was to shape the attitude of Kafka and his generation in fatally decisive ways. It spared them some of the illusions to which other Western Jews, notably in Germany and Austria proper, had avidly surrendered. In Prague, unlike in Vienna, baptism was rare; Jews remained Jews, even if their Judaism generally amounted to little more than showing up four times a year at the synagogue to demonstrate their loyalty—to God on the three High Holidays, and to the House of Habsburg on the emperor's birthday.

The very circumstances, however, that made assimilation so obviously problematical from the outset also left the secularized, culturally uprooted Jewish middle class no practical choice other than to identify with either the Czechs or the Germans. The language census first introduced in 1880 was, in effect, nothing less than a forced confession of faith open to public inspection, and it illustrates one aspect of the dilemma. In response to the initial questionnaire, only one-third of Bohemian Jews gave Czech as their principal language; ten years later, their number had risen to well over 50 percent. Much the same trend was evident in Prague itself. In 1890, only one-fourth of the capital's approximately 25,000 Jews—the figure remained virtually constant all the way to the end in 1939—professed to be speaking Czech at home; by the turn of the century, Czech had officially become the principal language of over 55 percent of Prague's Jews.

Rather than suggesting a shift in the cultural attitudes of the Jewish community, these figures merely reflect its vulnerability to outside pressure. A great many Jews were, in fact, bilingual, Kafka's father being a typical example. Herrmann Kafka opted for Czech from the very beginning; as a businessman dealing with a large Czech clientele, he presumably felt it prudent to do so, and the subsequent boycott mounted by Czech nationalists against enterprises owned by "German" Jews bore out the timeliness of his decision. The switch in self-proclaimed allegiance on the part of Bohemian Jews between 1880 and 1914 seems to have been mainly a pragmatic response to the rapidly growing economic and political power of Czech nationalism; it certainly did not involve a true change of heart. Although a small, consciously and self-consciously Czech Jewish movement—in which Herrmann Kafka appears to have briefly participated—rallied to the cause of Czech independence, the increasingly outspoken anti-Semitism of the dominant Young Czech faction precluded any large-scale rapprochement. In its overwhelming majority, the Jewish bourgeoisie remained committed to German culture and language; and though the ugly manifestations of German anti-Semitism would have been hard to ignore, they were willfully being dismissed as marginal phenomena. Moreover, for all their ambivalence about the Habsburg rule, most Jews—whether or not they acknowledged it—saw the Vienna government as the sole if rather rickety support of law and order, at least to the extent of protecting them from mob violence. The repeated intervention of Austrian troops, called out to quell massive anti-Jewish riots in Prague and in the provinces, certainly justified that attitude.

The most sensitive gauge of their true allegiance, however, was the fact that throughout the Habsburg era, and regardless of professed language preferences in the family, fully 90 percent of all Jewish children in Bohemia received their education in German, from primary grades through graduate studies. The proportion of Jewish children enrolled in the Czech school system never rose much above 10 percent until well after independence and the consolidation of Masaryk's liberal government.

*   *   *

The school on the Meatmarket was thus a paradox within an anomaly—an outpost of German culture largely staffed and attended by Jews, defiantly facing a Czech elementary school whose pupils made it a regular practice to waylay and beat up the kids from across the street in the cause of Slav militancy. The principal, Franz Fieger, was a mild-mannered German; his teaching staff included Czechs as well as Jews, none of whom indulged in the calculated cruelties so prevalent in the schools of Austria and Germany proper. Kafka's own grade-school teachers certainly exemplified the enlightened spirit of resigned liberal-ism conscious of its isolation: the German Hans Markert in first grade, his unseemly kindness camouflaged by a majestic beard styled after the ubiquitous image of the Emperor Franz Joseph; the Czech Karl Netuka in second grade, easygoing and informal, with a lively sense of humor; and in third and fourth grades the Jew Matthias Beck, a first-rate teacher genuinely devoted to his pupils.

Whatever misgivings Kafka may have had about his scholastic abil-ities, the evidence of his grades suggests both ample talent and applica-tion. He was, in fact, a star pupil throughout the first four years, popular among his classmates and exceedingly well liked by his teachers. But the constant struggle to conform and perform left him drained to the point where, in his memory, the whole experience boiled down to a viscous mixture of boredom and fear, in which the teachers floated as so many faceless figures, *Respektspersonen* indistinguishable from one another as, day in and day out, they sat in judgment over him.

Reading and writing gave him no trouble. He memorized the multi-plication tables. He learned to swallow facts and bring them back up on demand, undigested, bypassing the brain. But the most valuable lesson he absorbed was not part of the lesson plan at all: he learned to make friends. And one of the friendships struck up in the very first grade was to last a lifetime; although Kafka and Hugo Bergmann, class-mates all through elementary and high school, eventually went their separate ways, they remained friends to the end.

This was the prison in which he served four years of his life, a crumbling ruin under siege. The weight of the past pressed in slowly, as yet indistinguishable from the burden of the future.

Four

T HE boy, though academically gifted, seemed delicate and shy to Matthias Beck, and the teacher therefore urged the parents to keep him in grade school for the optional fifth year. "Rushing these things is liable to take its toll," he is quoted as having told Kafka's parents. Kafka later came to feel that the teacher had been right, though there is nothing to suggest that the additional year would have made any difference in his adjustment. At any rate, Beck's advice was duly ignored, and in the spring of 1893 Kafka presented himself for the high-school entrance examinations, first in a series of public trials in which ignorance, confusion, or a mere lapse of memory was punished with inexorable finality. As a process of unnatural selection, the method seems to have worked; thus of the eighty-three students comprising Kafka's first high-school class in 1893, only twenty-four remained at the end of the eighth year to take the *Matura*, or final comprehensive examinations—not necessarily the fittest but, by prevailing standards, probably those most adept at meeting the demands for which the rigors of the system had prepared them.

To the high-strung youngster desperately lacking in self-confidence, every examination, from first to last, was a dress rehearsal for the Day of Judgment. Nor did passing a test bring relief; all it meant was that he had succeeded one more time in hoodwinking his judges and thus added to the sum total of his transgressions ultimately to be accounted for.

But though always anticipating failure, he never did fail. Even the vestigial brain cells not jellied by panic proved more than equal to the crude challenges designed to test the ability to pass tests. He had no serious difficulties demonstrating the requisite mastery of German grammar and spelling, religion—whatever that meant—and arithmetic to qualify for admission to one of the high schools in his district, the choice being between a "Humanistic Gymnasium" and a "Realschule." The Humanistic Gymnasium, distinguished by its grinding emphasis on Greek and Latin, served as breeding ground for future academics and administrators, while the Realschule, which concentrated on French and other mundane subjects, with just an obligatory sprinkling of Latin to create the illusion of a well-rounded education, was designed to prepare its students for a career in business and the lower echelons of the civil service. The actual difference may, however, have been more aptly defined by contemporary critics, who maintained that while the Humanistic Gymnasium taught nothing real, the Realschule ignored everything human.

It was, of course, taken for granted that Herrmann Kafka, upward-mobile and by now increasingly prosperous, would choose to enroll his son in the German National Humanistic Gymnasium, a high school that occupied the third floor of the Kinsky Palace on Prague's Old Town Square. "Right in the heart of the city is where I was brought up, in the heart of the city."

True, in a way. Few buildings could have been more authentically part of old Prague than this ornately baroque eighteenth-century showpiece. Yet the high school on its premises—the students were made to use the servant entrance and back stairs—had scant contact with either the city or the world beyond. Like a hilltop monastery in the days of the Black Death, it strove to isolate the inmates from the plague by immuring them in discipline, strict rules, and the relentless pursuit of passing grades.

In the long run, no walls could provide shelter, and the fossilized grammar of dead languages failed to exorcise the virulence of the present. Kafka was ten years old when he entered the Gymnasium, eighteen when he graduated—eight crucial years in his life, shaped to no small extent by major upheavals beyond the range of his vision and awareness. But though he did not know much about them—did not want to know, an adolescent more preoccupied than most with his own elusive self—the ominous rumblings gradually seeped into his consciousness and forced him to take notice. In the long run, it is difficult to ignore an earthquake.

In the short run, however, it may be equally difficult to understand just what it is that makes the ground shake under one's feet. Kafka's school years more or less coincided with the final decades of a century in which technology and ideology—the French and the

Industrial Revolution—fused in an explosive mix culminating in unprecedented and relentless progress. Between 1880 and 1913, manufacturing production worldwide rose at three times the rate of population growth of roughly 1 percent a year. Europe's population during that same period, despite declining birth rates and the loss of some 30 million to overseas emigration, increased from 340 to 475 million, a rise that in most advanced countries was outstripped in turn by the rise in the gross national income. Industrialization, creating vast new wealth along with vast new poverty, turned masses of peasants into an urban proletariat increasingly conscious of its power. The quest for new markets and new sources of raw material became the manifest destiny of the nation-states.

Yet while these trends accelerated throughout Western Europe, the pace and specifics varied widely. And in Austro-Hungary, social destabilization and the emergence of new power centers endangered not only the still essentially feudal order but the very survival of the multinational state as such. Economic progress and industrialization dramatically exacerbated the internal conflicts that like a web of fault lines veined the foundations of the empire, posing a threat which the Vienna government countered by bureaucratic improvisations, in the hope that stuffing enough paper into the crater's mouth would keep the volcano from erupting.

It didn't. By the second half of the nineteenth century, the Habsburg monarchy had become an anachronism suffering from arrested development. Its feudal structure, paternalistic politics, and imperial pretensions precluded the implementation of whatever realistic measures might have staved off disaster and led instead to frantic efforts designed to block social change; their manifest futility did not lessen the zeal with which they were being pursued. And though they failed to prevent political disintegration, they were at least partially successful in hampering economic development, frustrating modernization, and delaying industrial progress, all of them rightly perceived as threats to the established order. On the eve of the First World War, Austro-Hungary was by surface area the second-largest state in Europe and, with 50 million inhabitants, the third largest by population. Yet it did not, by any definition of the term, qualify as one of the advanced industrial nations, and the per capita income lagged by about 40 percent behind that of Germany.

It would no doubt be equally valid to ascribe the political under-development of the empire to its economic difficulties. Even in the most unambiguous model, the interplay between politics and economics defies simplistic analysis, and the case of the Danube monarchy, with its eleven nationalities spread over a vast territory differing widely in the distribution of natural resources, raises the problem to a high order of complexity. Its most intractable feature was the centrifugal force of nationalism, linked in turn to regional growth patterns that, in many instances, far outpaced the sluggish economic development of the country as a whole. The most prominent trouble spots, in this respect, were Bohemia and Moravia, heartland of the empire's three most important growth industries—textiles, metallurgy, and sugar—and hot-bed of Czech irredentism.

* * *

Between 1848 and 1890, Bohemia's share in the total industrial output of the monarchy rose from 46 to 59 percent. By 1890, Bohemia and Moravia accounted for 65 percent of Austria's industrial labor force, with only about one-third of the population still employed in agriculture. But while the Czechs constituted a majority of roughly 65 percent in the two provinces—the relative Czech-German propor-tions had stabilized around 1848 and remained more or less constant thereafter—it was the German-speaking minority, specifically including the Jews, which continued to exercise dominant control over most commerce and industry.

Class warfare, superimposed upon ethnic antagonism, adds up to far more than a double dose of hatred, and there is no doubt that exploitation and discrimination greatly spurred the rise and radicaliza-tion of militant Czech nationalism. At the same time, the true dimen-sions of the struggle far transcended the simple scheme of confrontations between the haves and have-nots, between enslaved natives and their foreign oppressors. For one thing, although the rural and urban pro-letariat remained the numerically largest element among the Czechs, the lower middle class expanded with astonishing rapidity throughout the second half of the nineteenth century. In ever-increasing numbers, Czech shopkeepers, artisans, small businessmen, and clerks encroached upon what had been German or Jewish spheres of interest. But it was the depression, triggered by the Vienna stock-market crash of 1873, that heated up the interethnic competition to the point of economic warfare.

Europe's feverish *Gründerjahre*—the years of the founding fathers —ended in a spectacular bust followed by a period of stagnation, the result of sustained overproduction far beyond the absorptive capacity of existing markets. And although the more advanced nations re-covered rapidly, Austro-Hungary had a much more difficult time coping with the consequences. The Austrian economy, in fact, never fully hit its stride again throughout the remaining Habsburg decades.

The social consequences were predictably severe, and neither stick nor carrot, neither brutal repression nor progressive social legislation— the most progressive, for its day, anywhere in Europe, at least on paper —could significantly mitigate the damage. On the one hand, they led to the rise of a militant labor movement for which the Social Democratic Party, founded in 1878, strove with somewhat indifferent success to provide spiritual guidance; the deep-seated mistrust between Czechs and Germans soon split both organized labor and its political institu-tions along ethnic lines which, as often as not, ended up fighting each other rather than the common enemy. The middle class, on the other hand, turned ethnic conflict into a destructive, and often self-destructive, economic crusade; "Each to His Own," "Buy Czech," or "Don't Patronize Czech Traitors" became not only injunctions enforced with rocks but the very touchstone of one's patriotism.

*   *   *

Yet any strictly rational approach to history distorts it much as a road map distorts reality. The most sophisticated theories of why what happens suffer from a flat-earth syndrome; missing are the dimensions of fear, centuries of hate gathering in poisoned pools, the darkness of bigotry, ignorance, despair. The irrational, by definition, eludes the reasoned unraveling of causal connections, slips through the mesh of logic, and locks men into its own version of the truth. Hunger is the result of maldistribution and economic inequities; being hungry is a rage in the belly.

The struggle between Czechs and Germans spanned well over half a millennium, from the first Hussite rebellion in 1378 to the mass expulsion of ethnic Germans in 1945, interludes of peaceful oppression, random slaughter, and inquisitional murder alternating with more formal military confrontations. Time and again the Czechs were defeated by superior forces, their leaders hanged, beheaded, or exiled, yet in the end they survived, masters in the art of survival. By mid-nineteenth century, the thrust of their militancy had shifted away from armed insurrection toward much broader goals. But if they now chose to marshal their growing strength in politics and trade rather than dissipating it in futile adventures, the blood of those past centuries still colored every conflict and aroused passions whose intensity bore scant relation to the concrete issues at hand.

In Kafka's time, it was the struggle for language rights, no longer for equal status, but for the preeminence of the Czech language in Bohemia, that provoked the most furious clashes between Czechs and Germans. The replacement, in 1891, of Prague's German street signs by all-Czech ones was a triumph of small substance but of vast emotional impact. On July 6, 1915, in the midst of World War I, with Austria vainly struggling to hang on to her possessions, a somber and imposing monument to Jan Hus was dedicated on Prague's Old Town Square; chiseled into the pedestal was the reformer's famous motto: "The Truth Shall Prevail." In true Hussite hearts, however, it did not prevail until three years later, when the adjacent St. Mary's column, erected in 1648 in honor of the Virgin, was toppled by way of celebrating the birth of the independent Czechoslovak republic.

Since then, Prague has been through many equally dubious moments of truth—Nazi troops marching down Wenceslas Square, the murder of Jan Masaryk, a giant monster Stalin towering like a vengeful golem over the city and being hauled off his pedestal six years later, smashed to bits, only to be replaced by Soviet tanks in the Old Town Square, and the dead winter silence that followed the brief jubilation of a Prague spring. Every one of them was the result of complex socio-economic and political concatenations amenable to rational analysis. Yet each contains an immeasurable quantity of totally irrational components—the collective weight of memory and madness. Truth prevails —occasionally, and seldom for more than one brief moment in time.

* * *

The post-Holocaust resurgence of anti-Semitism in countries such as Poland and Czechoslovakia, *judenrein* to all intents and purposes, provides an appropriately absurd illustration of the extent to which this quintessential manifestation of the irrational has, in the course of its 2,000-year history, become an integral part of the Western heritage. Jew-hatred, in the absence of live Jews, feeds upon dead ones or invents its own—a murderous myth whose origins are inextricably intertwined with the origins of Christianity.

The heart of the myth itself has remained inviolate and can be fully understood only by those able to understand how an unremarkably ordinary, respectable, and conscientious family man, fond of his wife and children, can smash the skull of a six-year-old little girl, dump the body into a lime pit, and pride himself on having done his duty as a patriot and soldier. What changed, however, was the manifest content of the myth as it spread through the substratum of Western tradition and fused seamlessly with the fears, superstitions, and realities of everyday life. And as the myth evolved, so did the image of the Jew, from Christ-killer, vampire, rapist, and poisoner to usurer, crooked merchant, capitalist exploiter, Bolshevist menace. The gun-slinging Zionist imperialist is merely the latest version of the portrait, the Jew as storm trooper, embodying the salient traits of all previous exhibits in this gallery of paranoia.

It is impossible to grasp the meaning of anti-Semitism in Kafka's time without a clear awareness of these roots buried deep within the mythology of evil. There was, of course, no shortage of precipitating causes; there seldom is. Poverty, unemployment, and frustration provided substantial incentives for organized Jew-baiting. The Czech boycott soon put an end to most Jewish-owned businesses in the towns and country districts of Bohemia. Industrialization pitted Czech workers against Jewish bosses.

That social tensions fuel anti-Semitism is banally self-evident; yet the fact remains that, feared as competitors, fought as exploiters, the Jews were still being hated as Jews, even though the new creed of nationalism had blurred the meaning of a term once unequivocally defined by religion. And where, in the pre-enlightenment age, a Jew could cease being Jewish by virtue of becoming a Christian, no baptism could convert him into an authentic Czech or German. The ghetto walls had been razed, the age-old traditions were rapidly eroding, but the newly emancipated citizens of the nation-state still found themselves accused of being Jewish—and increasingly unable to understand the nature of the accusation. The harder they tried to defend themselves by being more Czech than the Czechs, more German than the Germans, the harsher the ultimate sentence.

Throughout the last two decades of the century, inspired demagogues among both Czech and German extremists learned to exploit the elemental dynamics of hatred with a skill and efficiency that foreshadowed the "final solution." The earliest efforts to politicize mass hysteria, in fact, date back to 1883, the year of Kafka's birth, when Czech, German, and Hungarian extremists met to organize an empire-wide movement based exclusively on anti-Semitism. As a program, the sentiments they shared did not quite suffice to reconcile conflicting chauvinist aspirations, and the "united anti-Jewish front" died aborning. But a trial held that very year in the small Hungarian town of Tiszaeszlar made it abundantly clear that causing an explosion in a gas-filled sewer takes no organizing talent and less than minimal intelligence.

In this revival of the medieval "blood libel," the town's Jews were accused of having abducted and killed a young girl in a gruesome orgiastic ritual. The sensational charges, substantiated by no known facts other than the girl's disappearance, provoked a wave of anti-Jewish violence throughout the country, thanks in no small measure to the testimony of the expert witness for the prosecution, one August Rohling, professor of theology at the University of Prague, who solemnly and authoritatively declared that "the Jew's religion bids him to exploit all non-Jews in every way possible, to destroy them physically and morally, to despoil their life, honor, and property by overt violence and secret cunning; in fact it commands him to do so whenever possible." Rohling's book, *The Talmud Jew*, subsequently went through many editions and became one of the basic texts of Austrian Nazism.

The case itself, like so many similar ones, eventually fell apart for lack of evidence; not only did the body never turn up, but the supposed victim was reportedly seen very much alive by several later witnesses. Just the same, it left a great deal of damage in its wake, not least to Jewish dreams of freedom and equality in the nascent secular state. "The illusion was brief," wrote a pro-Czech Jewish politician; "in Tiszaeszlar it vanished like mists before the wind. Rational opposition can be vanquished by reason, but no power will prevail against evil instincts; they spread like the plague, and no quarantine will contain them. Twenty years of political education, destroyed in that one single day when Esther Solymossy disappeared."

The illusion was not only brief but also limited to a rather small circle. The overwhelming majority of Bohemian Jews, no matter how great their capacity for self-deception, would have been hard put to ignore the virulent rhetoric of Czech demagogues or the endemic anti-Semitism of their fast-growing constituencies in the capital as well as in the provinces. And at the very time when Czech nationalists indiscriminately attacked all Jews as being pro-German, Hitler's forerunners in Austria proper, for their part, registered their first major electoral successes. Illusions, under the circumstances, would have been difficult to sustain; and those who managed to cling to them out of whatever hidden strength or perversity must have been definitely disabused by the Prague pogrom of December 1897.

The infamous "December storm" was triggered by yet another of the almost weekly street battles between Czech and German students. But tensions over new language laws and recent government changes had reached a boiling point, and what started out as a banal incident quickly escalated into citywide riots skillfully orchestrated by the leaders of the Young Czech movement. The violence spread rapidly outward from the center to the suburbs; having first sacked the more conspicuous German cultural and commercial institutions, roving mobs turned against the Jews and, for three days running, systematically looted Jewish-owned shops and business establishments, smashed thousands of windows, broke into several synagogues, and assaulted whomever they took to be a Jew. The government finally saw itself forced to declare martial law in the city and bring in the troops to restore order.

The Kafka establishment appears to have been one of the few Jewish businesses spared by the mob; legend has it that its leaders, on passing the store, told their men to "leave Kafka alone; he's Czech." The story, though unverifiable, sounds plausible; the robust Herrmann, fluent in Czech, certainly did not conform to the anti-Semitic stereotype.

Time and again, though, the psychotic core of anti-Semitism exploded in orgiastic mass hysteria. And none of the factual conflicts—social, political, or economic—so roiled the murky depths of atavistic superstition as did the Hilsner case, Eastern Europe's equivalent of the Dreyfus affair. On April 1, 1899, the day before Easter Sunday—a fact that of itself was to acquire a sinister significance—the body of nineteen-year-old Agnes Hruza was found by the roadside near her native village of Polna. In the rural atmosphere rife with suspicion and hate, the murder instantly roused age-old primitive passions; word went out that once again a Christian virgin had been raped and ritually slaughtered, her body drained of blood to be used in the preparation of Passover matzos.

Sixteen years, however, had passed since the Tiszaeszlar trial; and in the turbulent interval that separated these two emblematic cases— Kafka's childhood and adolescence—anti-Semitism had coalesced in a network of extremist movements led by a phalanx of aggressive and highly skilled propagandists. The editor of a Prague anti-Semitic rag, appointing himself both prosecutor and judge, publicly denounced the Jewish shoemaker Leopold Hilsner as the actual killer, aided and abetted by the entire Jewish community of Polna. At the same time, he took pains to alert the chief spokesman for the German anti-Semitic faction in the Vienna parliament; as a result, the case was tried in the press by the most extravagantly obscene techniques of yellow journalism long before judicial proceedings had even begun. A swill of anti-Jewish pornography flooded the country, from picture postcards and gruesomely illustrated pamphlets to dioramas and wax museum exhibits.

The trial itself starred the Jew-baiting leader of the Young Czechs— later to become Lord Mayor of Prague—as lawyer for the victim's family. Karel Baxa's formidable histrionic talents turned the supporting role into the main attraction as he projected his prurient fantasies of lust, murder, and dark ritual. It was a masterful appeal to the worst instincts of his audience, which thanks to extensive and sensational press coverage included not only the entire country but also a good part of Europe. The accused, of course, did not stand a chance and was promptly sentenced to death.

At that point, however, the ideals of truth and justice embodied by Jan Hus found an articulate champion; almost singlehanded, he turned the tide.

No statesman in this century can match the unique combination of uncompromising probity, moral courage, and shrewd mastery of practical politics that distinguished Tomáš Garrigue Masaryk. (A firm believer in women's rights, he added the name of his American-born wife, Charlotte Garrigue, to his own.) The short-lived promise of a truly democratic Czechoslovakia, aborted at Munich in 1939, was almost entirely his creation and remains his monument, albeit neither visible nor mentionable in the current People's Democracy. At the time of the Hilsner trial, however, Masaryk was still a professor of philosophy at the Czech university in Prague and leader of the numerically insignificant Realist Party.

In a pamphlet meticulously tracing the countless legal errors, obfuscations of fact, and evidence of bias on the part of the court, he called for a reopening of the case. The cool, dispassionate tone of his plea—in marked contrast to the passionate eloquence of Zola's *J'accuse*, published around the same time in not too dissimilar circumstances—outraged his radical compatriots almost as much as the substance of his charges. Student demonstrations were organized to demand his ouster, the university canceled his lectures, the pamphlet was banned, and practically overnight he found himself branded a traitor to his people. Years later he was to recall "the timid faces of so many of my acquaintances who suddenly gave me a wide berth, while others tried to justify anti-Semitic clericalism—memories that to this day burden my by now tired soul."

In due course, however, Masaryk won cautious support from the Social Democrats. Liberal and leftist students rallied to his cause. Jewish organizations, mindful of the fact that Jewry as a whole was on trial, provided legal assistance. The appeal was granted, and though the second Hilsner trial again ended in a guilty verdict, it failed to generate the pervasive hysteria of the first one; Masaryk's example had had a bracing effect on the conscience and backbone of the more rational elements among both Czechs and Germans.

Hilsner's death sentence was eventually commuted; pardoned in 1918, he died a few years later in inconspicuous poverty. The murder itself was never solved, in spite of several promising leads; pressure from the increasingly influential anti-Semitic faction in parliament prevented any reopening of the investigation.

*   *   *

This was the atmosphere of Kafka's world, dense with hate. But he had never known any other, and it took time for him to understand why he had trouble breathing.

Understanding, when it came, turned out to be as toxic as the air itself.

Five

KAFKA had started grade school as an only child; by the time he entered the Gymnasium, four years later, he was the oldest of four children in the family. Elli (Gabriele) was born on September 22, 1889, exactly one week after the memorable first trip to the Meatmarket. Two more girls followed in rapid succession—Valli (Valerie), born September 25, 1890, and Ottla (Ottilie), on October 29, 1892.

These rather closely spaced additions—the result, one suspects, of some grimly determined efforts to make up for the loss of the two boys —permanently altered the family structure and climate, if not the balance of power. From the parents' point of view, girls obviously did not warrant the sort of investment, emotional and financial, to which boys were entitled in the immutable order of the universe. By the same token, they presented far fewer problems. Loving, lovable, or insufferable, they were destined to marry and to procreate, the parents' chief concern being to keep them from getting pregnant until they were safely out of the house. Their education, for the most part, was confined to practical subjects deemed helpful in preparing them for their natural destiny; if, along the way, they picked up a smattering of foreign languages, music and art appreciation, no harm done.

As it happened, the women of Kafka's generation rebelled against their parents in ways even more fundamental, if far less dramatic, than their brothers. Some of the more fortunate among them, in fact, benefited from a decidedly superior secondary education simply because the Czech and German high schools for girls were private rather than government-sponsored institutions and, as such, not hamstrung by state-imposed curricula. Moreover, they paid well and had their pick of the best teachers, who could be fired for incompetence without regard to any civil-service status. Kafka's own sisters still received a more traditional upbringing; yet each of them, in due course, broke away and asserted her independence far more effectively than their brother ever did.

Given the age difference, however, relations in the early years were necessarily tenuous and distant, though in his diary he alludes to the "sensuality unconsciously aroused by the sight of infants wrapped up in swaddling clothes and tied up in ribbons as if to satisfy desire." The three girls no doubt kept the mother busier than ever, a time-tested method of combating the bouts of depression to which she was prone, though it probably reinforced the sense of abandonment from which her oldest had been suffering since his own infancy. By this time, however, he must—at least at the conscious level—have come to terms with his mother's emotional distance, and it seems doubtful whether her involvement with the new rivals made any significant difference.

On the contrary, their arrival had certain salutary consequences. For one thing, it took some of the pressure off the only child and provided Herrmann Kafka with additional targets for his choleric outbursts and scattershot sarcasm around the dinner table. For another, it necessitated larger quarters; and in the spacious apartment on Celetna Street, to which the Kafkas moved in the spring of 1896, just before Franz's bar mitzvah, he for the first time had a room of his own.

*   *   *

The Austrian Gymnasium of Kafka's day was a singularly depressing institution, something of a cross between monastery and reform school. Although Church control of education had officially ended in 1866, priests and monks continued to be heavily represented at both instructional and administrative levels, assuring a perpetuation of clerical influence which, all things considered, was probably no more pernicious than the state's own contribution to the school system. Thus, one of Kafka's most dreaded—and most brilliant—teachers happened to be a Piarist brother. The Piarist order, in fact, ran a school of its own, regarded as the socially most exclusive in town and attended by an ethnically mixed but economically cohesive upper-middle-class elite, among them Max Brod and Franz Werfel. From their accounts, it appears that discipline at the Piaristenkollegium was considerably more relaxed than at Kafka's Altstädter Gymnasium, either because the children of the rich are less easily intimidated, or because the Piarists, rather notorious for their worldliness—*Piaristen, schlechte Christen* was a much-quoted and not necessarily pejorative assessment of their doctrinal fervor— lacked some of the militant pedantry of their colleagues in government service.

In contrast to the Piaristenkollegium, located in one of the most modern and prosperous parts of town, the Altstädter Gymnasium—the Old Town Gymnasium, as it was commonly referred to—served an area largely populated by middle-class Jews who, for one reason or another, had not yet left the ancient central precincts adjacent to the ghetto for more prestigious residential districts. Inevitably, the student body reflected both the ethnic composition and the fluid status of that group—almost exclusively Jewish, ranging from the relative affluence of the Kafkas to children poor enough to qualify for a full state scholarship. But what the Altstädter Gymnasium lacked in social cachet, it more than made up for by its reputation as the strictest and most demanding school in Prague. Commenting on Kafka's lifelong boast of having been a poor student, Max Brod remarks that there simply were no poor students at the Altstädter Gymnasium, and that it took excellence merely to have lasted through the eight grades of that particular institution.

But whatever the differences in spirit and atmosphere, schools varied little as to teaching methods and subject matter. Systemwide uniformity was being rigidly enforced by a vast and top-heavy bureaucracy in which the classroom teacher constituted the lowest echelon; the operatic costumes, complete with plumed helmet and sword, which they were constrained to wear on national holidays, symbolized both their primary allegiance and the creaky pomposity that infested every hierarchical institution of the monarchy. A faceless, distant authority fussed with the most minute details of lesson plans, time allocation, promotion policies, reading material, and disciplinary procedures; the implementation of its often floridly insane regulations was enforced by regular on-the-spot inspections. Every year, the ukases and memoranda from "higher authorities" filled several volumes of the school's annual report.

Thus the curriculum of the Altstädter Gymnasium was determined by administrative fiat, the teacher's responsibility—at least in theory— being limited to uncrating the prescribed material in the classroom and policing its dutiful memorization. In practice, the task left some room for individual initiative. But given the nature of most subjects, and the requirement that students be able to regurgitate them on demand, rote learning reinforced by punishment and threats of failure necessarily made for the most common as well as the most effective method of indoctrination.

The school year consisted of ten months, with twenty-five hours of classroom instruction a week and between two and four hours of homework daily for the average student. Roughly one-third of that time was devoted to classical languages—eight hours of Latin every week through third grade, reduced to five hours through the remaining five grades; it was obviously deemed the one subject of paramount importance to the proper formation of the humanistic mind. Three hours of Greek were added in fourth grade, leading up to heroic feats of memorization in which huge lumps of undigested Homer had to be absorbed. The four hours initially allotted to German grammar in the lower grades shrank to three, starting in fourth grade, when the focus shifted to what passed for literature. Here, too, the emphasis was chiefly on the memorization of uplifting verse governmentally certified as poetry.

Geography, Kafka's favorite subject, received three hours, one of which was in later years devoted to the study of history—a plausible pretext for memorizing the dates of every battle fought between Thermopylae and Waterloo, as well as the sequential list of rulers for every hereditary Western dynasty from the Caesars to the Habsburgs. Mathematics, Kafka's least favorite subject, was considered of equally marginal importance; in eight years of three hours weekly, students did not progress beyond logarithms and analytic geometry. Science received understandably short shrift, since it involved actual contact with ideas and frequently infected students with decidedly subversive notions. By way of prophylaxis against just such heretical trends, all students had to submit to two hours of religious instruction every week.

In addition to these mandatory subjects, Czech, French, and physical education were being offered as optional enrichment, and at one time or another, Kafka tried them all. He enjoyed rowing on the Vltava as part of the sports program and, in fact, later acquired a rowboat of his own—one of the least ambiguous and most positive results of his formal schooling.

*   *   *

This, then, was the intellectual content of secondary education under the Habsburgs—institutional fare of scant nutritional value, and often spoiled to boot. Its deficiencies were glaringly obvious to most of its victims. The physician and novelist Ernst Weiss, later one of Kafka's closest friends, insisted that "school in no way prepares a student for the real world. . . . It is an institution where the power of money is never even alluded to, where one studies math and Greek but is taught nothing about communicating with other human beings." The prominent philologist Fritz Mautner was more specific; he charged that Austrian humanistic education failed even within the terms of its own purported goals and perverted the spirit of the ancient world into an instrument of torture. "Of the forty students in my class," he wrote in his auto-biography, "some three or four finally reached the point where, with infinite pains, they could just about handle a syllable-by-syllable trans-lation of some ancient classic. . . . This certainly did not convey to them even the remotest notion of the spirit of the antique, its incom-parable and inimitable strangeness. . . . As for the rest, the remaining 90 percent of the class, they managed to pass the finals without ever deriving the slightest pleasure from their tag ends of Greek and Latin, promptly forgotten in any case right after graduation."

On the other hand, humanistic education—at least in the form offered at the Altstädter Gymnasium—had its ardent defenders among the alumni. The legal scholar Guido Kisch and the historian Hans Kohn both felt that it had been an enormously enriching experience, and that criticism of nineteenth-century education in terms of twentieth-century attitudes simply missed the mark. And Kafka's oldest friend, Hugo Bergmann, the perennial star pupil in every subject, came to regard his schooling as a gift for life; in the climate of contending chauvinistic extremes, the monastic isolation that marked the spirit of the Gymna-sium seemed to him a positive blessing, and the abstruse complexities of Latin grammar provided a sense of abiding values and immutable order at a time when both of these were breaking down in the real world.

Such divergent views obviously tell more about those who held them than about the objective reality. Hugo Bergmann's enthusiasm, for instance, is understandable enough. While his parents' precarious financial situation would not normally have permitted him to pursue any kind of secondary education, sheer brilliance and unremitting hard work won him a full scholarship to this most prestigious of schools, where throughout all eight grades he consistently placed first in every single subject while managing, on the side, to earn pocket money by giving private lessons. That he saw in his accomplishments a cause for gratitude rather than pride reflects the same mixture of conservatism, pedantry, and faith that accounted for his inordinate love of Latin grammar and foreshadowed his subsequent career as scholar, archivist, and librarian.

Yet Bergmann, when reminiscing rather than rhapsodizing about his school days, recounts a story of his near-fall from grace, whose implications he obviously refused to acknowledge. *Primus* and undisputed favorite of the forbidding Piarist Brother Gschwind, Bergmann in fifth grade was granted a three-day leave of absence to attend a family wedding in the country. Traveling with his parents, he was delayed on the return trip and reported back to school two days late. Gschwind, an eminent classicist who not only taught Greek and Latin but, for the entire eight years, ruled over the Bergmann-Kafka class as *Ordinarius*—classroom teacher in the widest sense of the word, i.e., endowed with the full powers of both judge and executioner—was so incensed by this unintentional breach of discipline that, for the remaining three months of the semester, he refused to even so much as acknowledge his former favorite. Moreover, he declared that in his view a scholarship student who violated any rule or regulation thereby automatically forfeited his right to public funds, and that he would therefore have to take appropriate action. For what seemed like an eternity, Bergmann floated in a nightmarish limbo, haunted by fears of damnation, disgrace, and toil in the innards of some dank ghetto sweatshop. At the end of the school year, however, a beaming Gschwind offered his congratulations and informed Bergmann that, while his conscience had made him vote against renewal of the scholarship, he had been overruled by higher authority and was sincerely happy about it.

The anecdote, of course, was meant to illustrate the multifaceted and contradictory character of Friar Gschwind. But it also affords a chilling glimpse of the smug, self-righteous cruelty, the arbitrary terror and ever-present fear of punishment that poisoned the atmosphere of the school and to which even a Hugo Bergmann, gifted far above average and immune to the day-to-day tortures suffered by mere ordinary pupils, proved vulnerable in the end.

It would indeed be fatuous to view that atmosphere, by-product of much broader and more ominously destructive trends, in terms of our own cultural bias. Few valid parallels, in fact, can be drawn between the free, locally controlled, coeducational American public-school system and the narrowly elitist, state-controlled, all-male institutions of an autocratic nineteenth-century monarchy bent on maintaining the status quo. But what often has been—and never ought to be—forgotten is that, by and large, children in American public schools are not made to feel afraid. The upper-middle-class children of Kafka's generation, on the other hand, paid dearly for their transient mastery of the Latin subjunctive.

Both critics and defenders, however, missed one vital point: whatever the purported ideals of a classical education, the Humanistic Gymnasium was essentially a vocational school designed to prepare bureaucrats for life in a bureaucracy. As such, it did a workmanlike job. It accustomed the students to doing vast amounts of utterly pointless work. It trained them to fear their superiors and disdain their inferiors. And it conditioned them to the stupefying boredom of endless days spent shuffling papers in dim and dreary offices.

Still, the fact remains that many teachers sabotaged their state-imposed mission, that many students successfully resisted indoctrination and ended up as rebels rather than bureaucrats, and that genuine curiosity and independent thought frequently survived all carefully plotted efforts to kill them. Both teaching and learning can zoom out of control and develop a momentum of their own; neither takes place in a vacuum, not even in the vacuum of formal education.

That Kafka seldom alluded to his Gymnasium years is no true measure of their significance. Eighteen years after graduation, in the *Letter to His Father*, he still clung to the self-image of the marginal student who just barely managed to scrape through, in part because of poor memory and generally inadequate endowment, in part because "I was about as interested in school—and not only in school but in my surroundings altogether, at this decisive age—as a larcenous bank clerk would be in the petty routine of his job while trembling with fear of being found out."

Even that retrospective assessment, however, is not to be taken at face value. For one thing, it conflicts with Kafka's factual classroom performance; his grades as well as the testimony of his schoolmates clearly show that with the exception of mathematics—one subject that consistently gave him trouble—he was an average student at the very least, certainly never in danger of failing. For another, it is obviously part of that attitude expressed in his diary: "At a time when I was still content, I wanted to be discontented and strained toward discontentment with all the means of time and tradition at my disposal; now I want to turn around and go back. In other words, I am always discontented, even with my contentment."

Yet the reality was grim enough, even if his vision of it magnified the senseless drudgery and oppression beyond mere human proportions. Whether the fear it engendered warped him for life, or whether it merely gave body and flavor to what he brought with him from home is beside the point, the more so since the two hypotheses are not mutually exclusive. Much more significant is the fact that, at least in this respect, Kafka's experience was far from unique; most Europeans of his generation remember their school years as a nightmare. His own feelings are eloquently described in a 1920 letter to Milena Jesenská:

> And of course we also share the death wish, the wish for an "easy" death; but that, after all, is a child's wish, rather like myself back in school, during math, as I watch the teacher leaf through his notebook looking for my name, the very image of strength, terror, and reality as against the total insignificance of my knowledge. And, half dreaming with fear, I wish that I could rise like a ghost, as insubstantial as my knowledge of math, make my way ghostlike among the school benches, pass through the door somehow, collect myself outside and be free in that beautiful air which, in all the world known to me, did not contain as much tension as that room. Yes, that would have been "easy." But it was not to be. Instead, I was called up to the blackboard and given a problem, whose solution required a logarithm table which I had forgotten at home. I told a lie, said that I had left it in my desk—thinking that the teacher would just hand me his own. Instead of which he sent me back to my desk, whereupon I discovered to my horror—genuine horror; when it came to being scared in school, I never had any need to pretend—that it wasn't there, after all. The teacher (I just met him the other day) called me a "crocodile" and immediately gave me an "unsatisfactory," which actually was very good, being after all a mere formality and, beyond that, an injustice (it was true that I had told a lie, but nobody could prove it; is that unjust?). Above all, however, I didn't have to demonstrate my shameful ignorance. Thus, on the whole, this too was rather

"easy"; given favorable circumstances, one could "disappear" even in the classroom itself, the possibilities were endless, and one could also die in life.

There is ample reason to believe in the subjective authenticity of that fear in an environment which programmatically fostered it as an educational principle. As such, however, it probably missed its mark. What Kafka was afraid of, even as a ten-year-old, went far beyond strict teachers or bad grades, and even the almighty father merely lent his face and voice to something much more terrifying. The didactic intimidation to which he was exposed in the Gymnasium must have struck him as the natural if incomprehensible order of things, the logical sequel to grade school and home. And while it no doubt kept him in a constant state of apprehension, its effect on his intellectual and emotional development—as distinct from his nerves—proved remarkably slight. He could be frightened into inarticulate silence, but never bullied into thinking thoughts other than his own.

Moreover, he was already perfecting the art of "disappearing"—not of just being "out of it," as any daydreaming adolescent will, but of vanishing behind that "glass wall" which all those who knew him eventually ran up against. That he sincerely believed himself to be incompetent, lazy, forgetful, clumsy, badly dressed, incoherent—the list is long, grew longer as self-disdain yielded to self-hatred—can scarcely be disputed; yet there is a curious undertone of perverse complacency, almost of pride, to the strident insistence with which he flaunts his faults. Self-flagellation is a not uncommon form of self-abuse, and the sinner lustfully wallowing in his guilt was known to perceptive inquisitors, grand and petty, long before Freud and Dostoevsky. But Kafka's self-deprecation, unconsciously gratifying or not, served a clearly defensive purpose: it removed him from the contest, put him out of danger's reach, and enabled him to "disappear" at the crucial moment of confrontation just as he had "disappeared" in the classroom. The strategy of dying in life, shaped in those early years, became a compulsion difficult to overcome in the later ones, when living with death necessitated drastic readjustments and the defiant complacency gave way to despair.

*   *   *

The eight Gymnasium years spanned a developmental stage of crucial significance, and what Kafka actually learned in school bore only the most incidental relationship to what he was made to study. In the classroom, under unremitting pressure from the instruments of power, he acquired an impressive body of esoteric and largely useless knowledge. But school extended far beyond the classroom. It was a society—primitive, transitory, an ice floe adrift between home and the world. And whatever real growth and learning took place in these chill surroundings had far less to do with memorizing verb tenses or dynastic dates than with a growing awareness of that outside world, its menace, its promise, and of his own place in it.

He was a timid and lonely child when he entered the Gymnasium, still timid and lonely—at least by his own account—but a child no longer when he graduated eight years later. No child anymore, not yet a man, trapped *entre deux âges* as between a rock and a hard place. Timid, lonely—and Jewish. The hardest rock of all.

Had Kafka not been born and raised a Jew, he would not have been Kafka, any more than Joyce, reared among the Eskimos, could have written *Ulysses*. Though the point seems blatantly obvious, its significance has all too often been missed, distorted, or willfully ignored. He has been hailed as a crypto-Christian, unveiled as a pseudo-Marxist; the absence of explicitly Jewish references in the surviving texts has made literary pedants feel justified in dismissing his "religion" as an incidental biographical detail.

All these simpleminded approaches, whatever their motives or causes, suffer from the same basic failure of the imagination. To grow up as a Jew in Kafka's Prague was a matter not of choice but of destiny. What Kafka made of that destiny at different points in his life, the manner in which collective fate shaped his individual vision and conduct, is part of the larger story; moreover, his attitude toward Judaism—and far more is involved here than religion as such—underwent significant changes over the years. Yet who he was, and what he did, cannot possibly be understood without a clear realization that his being Jewish—not faith, to begin with, not observance, but the mere fact of being Jewish in turn-of-the-century Prague—was at least as vital a component of his identity as his face or his voice.

Both parents belonged to the first generation of assimilated Jews. Though no longer observant in any meaningful sense, they retained a tenuous and largely sentimental attachment to the traditions in which they were raised, while at the same time straining to become the sort of non-Jewish Jews—Austrian citizens of the Mosaic faith—that would assure their full acceptance as equals in the social strata to which they aspired. Implicit, of course, in this wishful fantasy was a defensive ambivalence toward Judaism; what the assimilated Jew assimilates, among other things, is the anti-Semitism of his role models—one source of the corrosive self-hatred so widespread among Western Jews in the pre-Holocaust era.

In the circumstances, the child's initial awareness of himself as a Jew could scarcely have made for a happy discovery. In the *Letter to His Father*, Kafka assays this aspect of his development with a critical detachment which, despite its polemical tone, conveys a vivid sense of the situation at home:

> As a child, goaded by your reproaches, I reproached myself in turn for not attending services often enough, for not fasting, and so on. It was you whom I thought I had wronged, rather than myself, and I felt crushed by the ever-present burden of guilt.
>
> Later, as a young man, I failed to understand by what right you, with that farce of a Judaism you indulged in, could reproach me for not making an effort (at least out of a certain sense of reverence, as you put it) to act out a similar farce. It really was a big nothing, as far as I could see, a joke. Not even a joke. Four times a year you took yourself to the synagogue, where you certainly were closer to those indifferent than to those who took the matter seriously. Patiently you went through the formalities of prayer, sometimes you amazed me by being able to point to the passage in the prayer book that was just being read. As for the rest, just so long as I was in the temple—the only thing that mattered—I could do as I pleased. And so I yawned and dozed away countless hours (I've never again been so bored in my life, I believe, except later on at dance lessons) and did what I could to enjoy the small distractions that were being offered, such as the opening of the Ark, which always reminded me of a shooting gallery where, when you hit a bull's-eye, a door flips open the same way, except that out there something interesting popped out, while here it was only the same old dolls without heads. . . . Otherwise my boredom was not seriously interfered with, except perhaps by the bar mitzvah which, however, required just some ridiculous memorizing and amounted to no more than passing a ridiculous test . . . also by some minor incidents of no great significance, such as . . . when you stayed in the temple for the memorial service while I was being made to

leave. For a long time . . . this evoked a barely conscious suspicion of something indecent about to take place. This is how
it was at the synagogue. At home things were, if possible, even
more meager, confined to the first Seder night, which increasingly turned into a comedy, with wild fits of laughter, admittedly
instigated by the growing children. (Why did you have to give
in to their influence? Because you provoked it.) This, then, was
the faith that was passed on to me; at best, one might add to it
the outstretched finger pointing at "the sons of the millionaire
Fuchs," who attended synagogue with their father on the High
Holidays. I failed to understand what better use I could possibly
put this faith to than to get rid of it as fast as possible; getting rid
of it seemed to me precisely the most reverential of acts.

Still later, I saw things again in a different light and realized
what could lead you to believe that in this respect, too, I had
malevolently betrayed you. You had actually managed to sal-
vage some scraps of Judaism from that small, ghetto-like village
community. They didn't amount to much, to begin with, and
crumbled some more in the city and in the army. Still, the impressions and memories of your youth just about sufficed for
some Jewish life of sorts, especially since you were not too
demanding in that area, having come of robust stock; religious
scruples were unlikely to affect you personally unless mixed
with social scruples. At bottom, your guiding faith in life consisted of the belief that the opinions of a certain Jewish social
class were unassailably correct; since these opinions were also
part and parcel of your own personality, you actually believed
in yourself. Even this still contained enough Judaism, but not
enough to pass on to the child; it dribbled away altogether in
the process. Part of the problem was the impossibility of passing
on the memories of one's youth, the other was the fear you inspired. Also, a child hyperacutely observant out of sheer anxiety
could not possibly be made to understand that the few insipid
gestures you performed in the name of Judaism had some higher
meaning. For you, they had their meaning as token reminders
of an earlier time; that was why you wanted to pass them on to
me. But since even for yourself they no longer held any intrinsic
value of their own, you could do so only by threats or persuasion.
On the one hand, this could not possibly work. On the other,
since you didn't even see the weakness of your position, my apparent obstinacy was bound to infuriate you.

What Kafka here describes was a situation common to most middle-class families of that generation, the only unrealistic touch being his need to bend what he himself lucidly recognized as an irresistible evolutionary process ("The whole phenomenon is, of course, far from being an isolated case; much the same applies to a large segment of this transitional generation of Jews, who flocked to the cities from a still relatively devout countryside") into an *ad hominem* accusation, nothing less than an indictment of the father for being what he was and could not help but be.

The child's first impressions of the sort of Judaism kept alive in the Kafka home—and in the homes of most of his friends and acquaintances—were thus hardly calculated to inspire anything but bored indifference at best. "I still remember," he wrote to his fiancée (FEL, 9/16/16), "how as a child I quite literally drowned in the horrible boredom and mindlessness of the hours spent at the synagogue. They were the preliminary sketches made in hell for planning the subsequent organization of life in the office." Like the exotic rites, incomprehensible gibberish, and plaintive caterwauling to which, along with the dance lessons, he was being dutifully exposed by way of social conditioning, the parental *Pietät*—sentimental ethnicity—may initially have seemed merely ridiculous and incomprehensible. In later adolescence, however, it took on a more ominous tint, emblematic of that "otherness," that sense of being different, which for many of Kafka's generation came to be the sum and substance of Judaism. Though hardly a creed to live by, it still turned out to be enough of a one to die or to be killed for.

There is no way of tracing the evolution of that awareness in Kafka, for the simple reason that his early and earliest years were spent almost exclusively among Jews, within the invisible ghetto that had taken the place of what, a generation or two before, had still been a tangible entity. His small if expanding universe was still predominantly Jewish: his parents' circle of relatives and friends, to begin with, later on 90 percent of the pupils in his elementary school, thirty out of the thirty-nine students in his section of first grade at the Gymnasium, and seventeen out of the twenty-four survivors in the graduating class. Limited contact with non-Jews, sporadic and guarded, took place only across the well-defined borders of that closed universe. High above its upper margins loomed authority, power, and privilege, a bureaucracy which still barred Jews from all but its lowest ranks. Down below lurked the servant class, the Czech maids and cooks at home, the clerks and laborers in Herrmann Kafka's shop—his "paid enemies," as he persisted in ranting about them in front of the impressionable child.

In all likelihood it was the dawning perception of this dual threat—on one side the vast and mysterious powers that reduced even the omnipotent father to groveling and scraping, and on the other the murderous hatred of the "paid enemies" toward their paying enemy—that crystallized into a siege mentality reinforced, in due course, by the inevitable encounters with overt anti-Semitism.

> Out of fear alone, if nothing else, I couldn't understand how one could be so abusive toward a stranger [Kafka wrote in the *Letter to His Father*], and out of fear I wanted somehow to effect a reconciliation between your employees, on the one hand —wildly angry, as I believed them to be—and you and your family, on the other, if for no other reason than my own safety. This required not merely ordinary decent comportment toward your help, or even modesty, but outright humility; I had not only to be first to greet them but also to discourage any acknowledgment of my greeting. And even if I, worm that I was, had licked the soles of their feet, it still wouldn't have made up for the way you, the master, kept hacking away at them from up above. The attitude I thus came to form toward my fellow man persisted well beyond the shop, and on into the future.

An outcast, that is, long before he even became conscious of the tribal exile. The womb-like shelter of the prototypical Jewish family—close-knit, fetid, all-embracing, a mutant organism evolved to provide life-sustaining warmth in an arctic night—had cast him out. Or so he felt, and spent a lifetime trying to make up for what he had never known. The father, with his crude selfishness, parvenu mentality, and mindless vulgarity, bore a large if unwitting share of responsibility for his son's troubled childhood. But with the best will in the world, Herrmann Kafka could never have passed on to his children a sense of what it meant to be Jewish, for the simple reason that what it meant to him was the very specter he had struggled all his life to get away from: degrading poverty, social discrimination, the dead-end street of the shtetl, and the dead hand of tradition. The father had suffered because he was a Jew. His children were Jews because they suffered, but it was certainly not within his power to provide them with clues as to the cause of their suffering or the meaning of their Jewishness.

That the state-sponsored religious instruction in school could not make up for this failure goes without saying. Nevertheless, as in every school throughout the realm, all students twice a week dutifully divided into religious groupings and attended classes taught by clergymen of their respective faiths. (Though non-believers abounded, atheists formally registered as such were rare; the tax laws made this overt manifestation of subversive principles rather expensive. In any event, atheist students were kept busy with edifying assignments during religious instruction.)

Since Jews at the Altstädter Gymnasium formed the overwhelming majority, it was the Catholics and Protestants who filed out of the room, leaving their Jewish classmates to the ministrations of Rabbi Nathan Gruen. It is conceivable that a more imposing figure could have made an impression on this group of aggressively intelligent, intellectually curious, and articulate students; it is equally conceivable that students more firmly rooted in Jewish tradition might have learned to disregard Gruen's sloppiness, distracting mannerisms, and disjointed discourse to discover a man of apparently quite formidable learning. But somehow the confrontation was a disaster from start to finish, though probably no worse than what went on in most schools. While Kafka himself never referred to it, Max Brod reported from the Stefansgymnasium that religious instruction there was literally regarded as a joke; and while this attitude reflected a profound identity crisis within the Jewish community at large, the manner of instruction and the selection of instructors undoubtedly played a part. The lesson plan called for a capsule survey of Jewish history, essentially a mindless reading of select passages from the Old Testament in German, without commentary or amplification, alternating with a travesty of Hebrew lessons limited to little more than teaching the alphabet and mouthing the prayers, without regard to any sense or content. In the absence of grammar or vocabulary drills, the language was in fact reduced to pure gibberish, to the point where most students never even suspected any meaning in the convoluted sounds they were made to extract from these weird notations.

Preparations for the bar mitzvah proceeded in the same vein and consisted of memorizing a passage from the Torah, to be mumbled at the synagogue, and the obligatory "Thank you, dear parents" speech to be delivered at the party that followed. To the proud father—having sired a male was what entitled him to his pride—the occasion was, like his conspicuous High Holiday temple attendance in frock coat and top hat, merely another ostentatious display of Judaism converted into a status symbol; the engraved invitations referred to it as a "confirmation." To the boy, it was just another test. Under Jewish law, Amschel, alias Franz Kafka, became a man on the morning of June 13, 1896, at the Zigeunersynagoge—the Gypsy Synagogue, so called because of its location on a street formerly known as Zigeunerstrasse, though the strange name contains a chilling hint of things to come; a few decades later, the gypsies were to share the fate of the Jews.

But the relative isolation of that voluntary ghetto offered no long-range protection. Kafka undoubtedly met up with street-level anti-Semitism even in grade school, certainly on the way to it. In any event, he would have had to be deaf and blind not to be aware of what to the grownups around him was a constant preoccupation. But a year and a half after his bar mitzvah, in 1897, the "December storm" broke in Prague, an anti-German protest against new language laws that turned into a three-day anti-Jewish riot. Although property damage was high, no fatalities were recorded; in the light of what was to follow, these now seem storm warnings rather than a full-blown hurricane. Nonetheless, the damage to Jewish self-esteem, to the Jews' sense of citizenship, and to Czech-Jewish relations was enormous, and it seems inconceivable for the incident not to have left its mark on a hypersensitive and guilt-ridden adolescent. He was not, then or later, given to abstract sociological or political generalizations; whatever touched him touched him personally. The mob that for some days took over the streets of the city and beat up anyone who looked like a "dirty kike" must have given him clues to his identity that were hard to miss.

Again, Kafka's dilemma was far from unique. Apart from a handful of youngsters from a strictly Orthodox background, most of his schoolmates—most of his generation, in fact—grew up in homes much like his own. They were Jews rather in spite of themselves, defined as such by shrewd demagogues or demented lunatics. And, unlike their fathers, content to be tolerated as long as they were left to prosper, the sons expected equality rather than tolerance, only to discover that the real world did not admit Jews as equals. Some thereupon decided to change the world; others turned Jewish with the same fervor with which the Czechs and Germans flaunted their national allegiance. It was no accident that in 1896, just around the time of Kafka's bar mitzvah, the prominent Viennese journalist Theodor Herzl published his utopian vision, *The Jewish State;* a thoroughly assimilated Jew, he had been shaken to his depths by the Dreyfus trial, and by the riptides of anti-Semitism in its wake sweeping across a supposedly enlightened Europe.

Any generalization about Jews, even about the relatively small, homogeneous group of young Prague intellectuals, is bound to be deceptive. The leading spirits among them were precociously original and independent-minded individuals; Brod and Werfel, for instance, published their first writings while still in high school. They each had to find their own way, and for most of them it turned out to be a lifelong struggle.

Nevertheless, they basically faced two choices: socialism or Zionism; the brotherhood of man that knew no more distinctions of class, race, nationality, or religion, and in which Jews would simply merge with the rest of humanity in one big, happy family, or the other extreme, the rebirth of Jewry as a nation in a land of its own. Many young Jews rejected both these choices with equal vehemence and sought salvation instead in a return to traditional Judaism, conversion to Christianity, literary or political nihilism. But the overwhelming majority moved in either of these general directions, and the adolescent Kafka was no exception.

* * *

Marxist-oriented socialism had already become a significant factor in the politics of the Austrian empire. The Czech Social Democratic Party, founded in 1878, quickly attained a leading position in the fast-growing Czech labor movement, and the 2.8 percent of the vote it obtained in the 1891 elections, the first in which it participated, did not reflect its true strength. The Austrian party, founded in 1888, elected its first parliamentary deputy in 1893; by 1911, it had become the largest party in parliament, with 88 deputies out of a total of 533.

But if the party as such derived its political power from an increasingly class-conscious labor movement, the spread of Marxism among disaffected intellectuals as well as among the Jewish bourgeoisie, especially in Bohemia, had little to do with the movement's strictly economic goals and a great deal to do with its professed larger ideals. The appeal of a classless society, purged of clerical influence and national rivalries, is easy enough to understand, especially when viewed against the actual conditions prevailing in the Danube monarchy. Jews were, in fact, heavily represented in the leadership of the Austrian Socialist Party, and even the Prague bourgeoisie tended to vote for socialist deputies, less out of enthusiasm than for lack of alternatives. Although this, in turn, helped to undermine socialist credibility in both the Czech and the German labor movements and encouraged the growth of rival "national socialist" factions, it must be said that the Austrian party never submitted to incipient anti-Semitic tendencies within its own ranks.

The real clash between theory and practice, however, took place in a different though related area and foreshadowed the disaster of August 1914, when the socialist mass parties throughout Europe surrendered all pretense at international solidarity and rallied to the defense of their respective flags and ruling classes. This primacy of national interests and primal allegiances was already implicit in the bitter conflicts which, in 1896, led the Czech Social Democrats to split the movement and form their own faction. The Czechs felt patronized, not without reason. The Austro-Marxists, on the other hand, considered all "Slavs" politically retarded and culturally underdeveloped. Since this particular bias came down to them directly from their in some respects rather preposterously blinkered prophet himself, it is hardly surprising that even the Jews within the Vienna party leadership proved far from immune to this sort of Teutonic arrogance.

To the youngsters of Kafka's circle, however, such arcane controversies would have been meaningless even had they been aware of them. Rebelling against the philistine materialism of their elders—or against their elders, *tout court*—many of them found in socialism not just a plausible system of ideas and ideals to live by but, more important, a surrogate family; the conspiratorial intimacy with open-minded adults and like-minded peers provided support and a sense of belonging at a time in life when these were of vital significance.

The gravitational pull of radical ideas, greatly enhanced by developmentally conditioned rebelliousness, thus became a palpable influence in the upper grades of the Gymnasium. Kafka first drifted into its orbit around the age of fifteen; his fumbling, tentative approach toward what at best may be qualified as vaguely socialist attitudes rather than any clear-cut commitment to socialism in either word or deed followed the common pattern of intellectualizing emotional needs, even if in his case both the intellect and the emotions were far from common.

The symbiotic entanglement with his family, the haunted pursuit of a mother lost to him along with two rivals killed by his own lethal fantasies, the obsessive struggle against the omnipotent father, spawned a rage so overpowering that it all but crippled his instincts and left him firmly locked in guilt beyond understanding.

The rage, had he let it explode, would have called the vengeance of the gods down on his head. Instead, from infancy to the onset of adolescence, he did as he was told, obeyed parents and teachers—a quiet, cooperative child who dutifully went to school and synagogue, did his homework, received respectable grades, and never caused trouble. He read omnivorously: fairy tales, for which he never lost his passion, adventure stories, Sherlock Holmes, the Leatherstocking tales, Sven Hedin's accounts of polar expeditions and voyages to distant lands. And though far from gregarious, he made friends.

His friendship with Hugo Bergmann never quite reached the passionate intensity of some of his later and more fleeting attachments. Yet that very failure enabled the two of them to maintain their lifelong affection and contact even in spite of often widely divergent views. And there is no doubt that Bergmann's ideas and personality exerted a considerable influence on Kafka. Above all, Bergmann was the first to force Kafka into confronting his own Jewishness and its implications.

Their mothers were already on friendly terms; the two first met as preschoolers and remained classmates through all twelve grades and into the first year at the university, during which Bergmann consistently headed the class in every subject. Conscientious, gifted with an extraordinary and many-faceted intelligence that enabled him to handle languages, math, and natural sciences with equal ease, he yet had nothing of the grind about him. On the contrary, he was popular among his classmates, always generously shared his knowledge, helped others with their homework, and Kafka, for one, may well have owed many a passing grade to Bergmann's precocious pedagogic talents.

In his reminiscences, published on the occasion of the 1969 Kafka exhibit at the Hebrew University in Jerusalem, Bergmann described the early years of their friendship as lighthearted and untroubled. They constantly visited back and forth, did their homework together, and the fact that Franz had not only a room but even a desk of his own so impressed Bergmann that some eighty years later he still felt impelled to mention it, with awe rather than envy. He recalled Julie Kafka's "kindly, rather melancholy smile" and had vivid recollections of the father: "I did not, however, see him with his son's eyes, as portrayed in the *Letter to His Father* (which letter, I hope and trust, he was never given to read), but as a Jewish businessman of that era, with both feet firmly planted in the physical reality of his business."

They were in their first or second year of high school when Kafka announced, at the Bergmann house, that he was going to be a writer; the proclamation struck Hugo's older brother as hilarious. And Bergmann's scrapbook, filled with greeting-card prose and doggerel contributed by friends and schoolmates over the years, preserved Kafka's earliest surviving literary effort, in his own handwriting, dated November 20; the missing year, according to Bergmann, was probably 1897:

> *Es gibt ein Kommen und ein Gehn,*
> *Ein Scheiden und oft—kein Wiedersehn.*
> *Prag, den 20. November*

One comes and goes,
One parts—oft not to meet again.

A rather odd selection for the scrapbook of one's closest friend, at age fourteen. Whether spontaneously inspired or self-consciously hoarded for the occasion, it strikes an authentically "kafkaesque" note and clearly prefigures the intense ambivalence that soon was to mark Kafka's relations with Bergmann, whom he loved, whom he never ceased to love, and whom he could never permit himself to hate for being a paragon of all virtues, for being a dazzling all-around bloody genius, for being able to meet every challenge, in school or out, with an unflappable ease that must have seemed downright obscene to one for whom getting up in the morning sometimes seemed a near-insurmountable task.

But the onset of biological puberty just around that time led to a sudden growth spurt, both physical and emotional. Within the year, the fifteen-year-old found himself, at five foot nine, the tallest boy in his class—considerably above the then average for his age, freakishly gangling in his own eyes. His grades took an abrupt and precipitous nose dive. The routines and rituals of childhood, painstakingly and painfully evolved to protect him from himself, proved suddenly useless in coping with the turmoil of adolescence. Timidity and obedience had, to some small extent, given him space to dream his own dreams; to be his own self was a task of a different order. It presupposed finding out who he was, in relation to others; and the process of defining his identity began, understandably enough, by his staking out the distance between himself and his closest friend.

Kafka's teenage revolt against God can hardly be regarded as a crisis of faith; the tepid religiosity of his early years lacked conviction, and his concept of the Almighty Himself could, at best, have been no more than a suitably retouched enlargement of Herrmann Kafka. Instead, the burgeoning interest in ideas and issues, his shifting enthusiasm for Darwin, Nietzsche, and Spinoza, and his wildly fluctuating political sympathies were more in the nature of a quest than a rebellion, groping efforts to make contact with others, to find a way of living in the here and now, and a clue to the riddle of life.

But the angel he wrestled with in the flesh, at this stage in his search, took on the very human features of Hugo Bergmann, with whom he began to engage in typically circular but all the more impassioned arguments about heaven, hell, and points in between. Some rather basic personality conflicts fueled their intellectual skirmishes, but for the hitherto timid and self-effacing youngster they represented a vital first step toward self-assertion and independence. And Bergmann was, in this respect, a near-ideal foil—informed, articulate, and absolutely unbending in his commitment to Judaism, to the ideal of Jewish life in a Jewish land, and to political Zionism as its practical realization. Moreover, having once found the path to righteousness, he never once strayed from it, at least not in the sphere of politics. Unlike most of the early Zionist converts, he lived up to his commitment and went to Palestine in 1920, later to become rector of the Hebrew University and founding what is now Israel's National Library.

Years later, in a diary entry of December 31, 1911, Kafka looked back on those verbal duels:

> I remember, for instance, how in high school I often—though not exhaustively; even in those days I probably tired easily— used to argue with Bergmann about God and His existence in a Talmudic manner either borrowed from him or discovered within myself. At the time, I liked to enlarge on a theme I had come across in a Christian magazine—*The Christian World,* I believe —which compared a clock and the world to God and a watch-

maker. This, I thought, I was well able to refute vis-à-vis Bergmann, even though my counter-argument lacked solid foundations and, for purposes of practical exposition, had to first be put together like a jigsaw puzzle. One such argument took place as we kept walking around the Town Hall tower; I remember it exactly, because some years ago we reminisced about it together.

In his memoirs, Bergmann in turn refers to what was probably the same episode:

> Franz at the time was passing through an atheist or pantheist phase and absolutely wanted to deprive me of my Jewish faith. He was a very good debater. This happened one spring, just before the Passover holidays and the Seder night, which I loved very much for my parents' sake. I fervently wanted to hold out against him, at least until the Seder, and on that occasion I succeeded; Franz's debating skill failed to defeat me. Much later on, he himself sought the faith he had vainly tried to take from me.

In certain respects the—rather qualified—radicalization of the still shy, very proper, meticulously dressed, and unfailingly polite young Kafka was a far more age-appropriate and normal development than Bergmann's somewhat prissy and conservative stance. Bergmann was, however, much more attuned to the true spirit of the times than most of the middle-class rebels around him; while they still dreamed of assimilation and universal brotherhood, he believed in nationhood for the Jews and became as uncompromisingly nationalist in his way as the Czechs and Germans were in theirs. What is more, he was a very practical, down-to-earth idealist, endowed with much the same boundless energy that distinguished the earlier generation of founding fathers, including Herrmann Kafka, "with both feet firmly planted in the physical reality of his business," except that Bergmann's business happened to be Zionism. The first Zionist in his Gymnasium, he soon made converts. And as more and more Bohemian Jews, hemmed in by contending nationalist extremists, themselves turned toward a nationalism of their own to sustain their pride and identity, Bergmann became one of the movement's outstanding spokesmen and organizers.

In the circumstances, the gradual estrangement between him and Kafka was inevitable and probably began around 1898, though Bergmann in his memoirs places it later:

In the final school year, 1900–1901, our friendship appears to have cooled somewhat. Presumably I was unable to share his interest in literature to the same extent as other classmates; moreover, his socialism and my Zionism may have been too strong, and the subsequent fusion of these two ideals in a "socialist Zionism" was yet to come. When, on April 24, 1899, the Prague Zionists held their first meeting at the Commodities Exchange, it was the Jewish socialists who broke it up.

For Kafka, the estrangement was a liberating move toward both intellectual and emotional independence. Bergmann's religious and ideological commitments certainly played a role; so did his manifest lack of interest in what had already become Kafka's main passion in life. But beyond that, the very qualities that Bergmann shared with Herrmann Kafka—sheer energy, competence, self-assurance, a firm footing —were bound to strain the relationship in adolescence. Toward the end of his life Kafka looked to Bergmann, by then already established in Jerusalem, for help in realizing his dream of settling in Palestine. But in late adolescence and early adulthood, he deliberately moved away from his friend, and an unpublished 1902 letter from Bergmann to Kafka illuminates their relationship in some rather startling ways:

> Why did I become a Zionist? Once again your letter contains the by now obligatory mockery of my Zionism. I really ought to stop being surprised, yet I keep wondering, time and again, why you, my schoolmate for so long, cannot understand my Zionism. . . . To you, my Zionism is no more than an obsession. You simply don't seem to realize that it is also part of my life, and yet that is what it is. I can see your smile. And yet, you would understand if you could but know me—and know yourself. Subconsciously you have since childhood been in search of life's meaning, and so have I. But you grew into a different kind of person. You could soar aloft in solar regions and span the skies with your dreams. What was there to sap your strength? You have always relied only upon yourself and thus built up the strength to be alone. As for myself, I never dreamed much. And even when I did, my dreams didn't take me very far; rugged reality soon stopped them in their tracks and made sure I didn't lose touch with it. I kept searching and searching, but I could never muster the strength to stand alone, the way you did.

Quite aside from its anguished affirmation of faith, Bergmann's letter offers a rare glimpse of the youthful Kafka radically different not only from the self-image but also from the etiolated visionary haunting the hagiographies. That the outwardly sturdy, competent, and consistently overachieving Bergmann should portray himself as weak and ineffectual may be a sign of either neurosis or modesty carried to hyperbole. But the counterpart to this self-portrait, the picture of the solitary dreamer as strong and self-reliant in his loneliness, provides a much-needed corrective to Kafka's perception of himself and may well be the most trustworthy picture of him at this stage by an outsider. Although far from objective—a close relationship of such intensity and duration hardly lends itself to detached objectivity—Bergmann unquestionably remains the sole reliable informant about those early years.

Once he entered the university and drifted into what Max Brod later dubbed the "Prague circle," Kafka acquired a measure of visibility if not prominence. But much of the information about his childhood and school days remains highly suspect. The spread of his posthumous fame suddenly jogged the memory of quite a few of his contemporaries to whom, at the time, he could hardly have been more than a name, a quiet presence, at best a more or less memorable face. Most of their reminiscences, eroded by time and distorted by all the human frailties to which memory is subject under the best of circumstances, do not inspire much confidence.

To Bergmann, on the other hand, Kafka had been friend, schoolmate, soulmate as far back as he could remember, and there is an indisputable authenticity about his rather uncommon vision of a Kafka armored, aggressive, and slightly larger than life. What spills out in this letter—especially in the tone, the note of exasperation just this side of outrage—suggests characteristics which, while not negating Kafka's self-image, complement it in ways that make the later influence of both the man and his work a great deal more comprehensible. Kafka, weak and incompetent, was also strong in his solitary dreams, infinitely determined and well defended in his loneliness. He was gentle, kind, considerate, and he could use words as weapons, draw blood with a glancing phrase. He could embrace opposite extremes in his work and in his life—and suffer the consequences.

*   *   *

Whatever the significance of the adolescent's intellectual rebellion, there is no hard evidence to suggest that it had much to do with what

Bergmann referred to as "socialism," at least not in any meaningful sense of that term.

At a rather advanced age, and after his own belated conversion to Communism, Kafka's classmate Emil Utitz claimed to remember what he had curiously enough failed to recall in his earlier reminiscences, published in 1946: that the sixteen-year-old Kafka, together with several of his friends, joined the anticlerical Free School Association, dedicated to radical school reforms. This perhaps well-meant attempt at a revisionist view of Kafka, part of the aborted effort to "rehabilitate" him, seems unconvincing, not least because the Free School Association was only founded in 1903, and the first local chapter in Bohemia was formed in 1907.

It is nonetheless true that the surge of adolescence sensitized Kafka to a broad range of more or less radical ideas, and there is something stunningly apt about his choice of Spinoza as his first spiritual mentor. The appeal of that gentle yet uncompromising heretic, drummed out of the Amsterdam Jewish community some 250 years earlier, obviously derived from an unconscious identification; moreover, Spinoza's pantheism may have helped Kafka to rationalize his own break with both the vestigial pieties of his father and the religious nationalism of Hugo Bergmann.

The influence of Spinoza was soon superseded by Darwinism. Kafka is reported to have shared the enthusiasm that greeted the appearance, in 1899, of *Die Welträtsel* (*The World's Mysteries*) by the German biologist and philosopher Ernst Heinrich Haeckel, who mounted Darwin's theories into the framework of a mechanistic monism that left no room even for Spinoza's monistic deity. If so, it was short-lived on Kafka's part, lasting just long enough to propel him into a more outspoken atheism, a brief flirtation with German nationalism, an impassioned identification with the cause of the Boers, the discovery of Nietzsche, and, later on, a somewhat diffident interest in the anarchism of Tolstoy and Kropotkin.

Such exploratory forays are hardly unusual in an adolescent trying to find his bearings, but in Kafka's case they seem to have been markedly superficial. Abstract ideas, whether in philosophy, politics, or religion, were at best of marginal and passing interest to him. He was never a systematic thinker; the very notion of a closed system, in fact, must have seemed repellent. Neither formal logic nor synthetic dogma offered any meaningful clues to the mysteries of the universe that preoccupied him, and he had yet to discover his own proper way of dealing with them. In the meantime, he avidly fished in the main currents of nineteenth-century thought and used whatever seemed helpful to the precariously emerging self. Yet the very skepticism which rendered him receptive to these ideas—and was reinforced by them in turn—also inevitably led him to question their validity and reject them in short order.

On the other hand, this inner ferment seems to have opened him up at last to broader and more intense human contacts; and while his choice of friends, too, was necessarily determined by his needs of the moment, such teenage friendships tend to develop their own momentum, something of the spontaneous comradeship of the guerrilla band fighting regular forces. Whatever the influence of specific individuals, Kafka's peers as a group unquestionably helped to shape many of his attitudes in significant ways.

First came the friendship with Ewald Felix Přibram, clearly a turning away from Hugo Bergmann and all he stood for. Přibram, a bright and amiable youngster, was said to have been held in awe by his classmates because he had carried his atheism to its logical conclusion: he was the only one among them to have formally resigned from the Jewish community. Since this step was taken by Přibram Senior in the name of the entire family, Ewald may have deserved less credit than he ostensibly got. By a curious coincidence, however, this act of defiance was eventually to have rather unexpected consequences for Kafka and his career; the elder Přibram became chairman of the Board of Directors of the Workmen's Accident Insurance Institute, a position to which no Jew could have aspired, and as such made it possible for Kafka, in turn, to obtain the job he held for the final sixteen years of his life.

Přibram, Kafka once remarked in a letter to Brod (L, 1904) had "reasonable views about almost everything but art," a shortcoming which does not seem to have detracted from what remained a relatively close if low-keyed friendship. This levelheaded rationalist, on the other hand, had one passion which Kafka in turn found totally incomprehensible: he loved flowers.

> Ever since childhood [Kafka explained to his fiancée in 1912 (FEL, 3/10/12)], there have been times when I was almost unhappy about my inability to appreciate flowers. This seems to be related in some way to my inability to appreciate music; at least I've often sensed a connection. . . . I might not have been so acutely aware of being a stranger among flowers had it not

been for a good friend I had toward the end of my Gymnasium years and at the university (his first name was Ewald, itself almost the name of a flower, don't you think?). He was not particularly sensitive to aesthetic impressions, didn't even have an ear for music, yet he loved flowers so passionately that when, for instance, he was looking at them, cutting them . . . watering them, arranging them, carrying them, or giving them to me . . . this love literally transformed him, to the point where he even talked differently . . . in spite of a slight speech defect. We often used to stand in front of flower beds, he lost in rapture while I looked on in utter boredom.

Kafka's attitude toward flowers, and toward nature in general, was to undergo profound changes in later life. But his early indifference does not seem to have harmed his friendship with the easygoing Ewald, who drowned in 1940, trying to escape from the Germans.

In addition to Ewald, Kafka moved closer to several classmates more specifically socialist in outlook. The degree of Kafka's involvement with them—and with socialist politics—must remain open to question, largely because the sources cannot be considered reliable. Aside from Emil Utitz, they include Hugo Hecht, later a specialist in venereal diseases and first German Communist deputy to the Prague municipality. As a refugee in the United States, where he practiced dermatology in Cleveland until way into his eighties, Hecht published his reminiscences about the twelve years he spent with Kafka in elementary and high school; they offer no basis for gauging the substantive depth of their relationship. Kafka's only extant allusion to him is in a letter to his sister Elli and seems to indicate that it was Hecht who took it upon himself to enlighten him about the facts of life. The man obviously preached long before he practiced.

Another classmate said to have influenced him in the direction of radical politics was Rudolf Illový, whose subsequent career progressed —or descended, depending on one's point of view—from editor of *Pravo Lidu,* organ of the Social Democratic Party, to bank executive, and from proletarian poet to editor of proletarian anthologies. Illový, two years older than Kafka, dropped out of school in 1898, which would make any closer ties between them highly unlikely. In his *Conversations with Kafka,* Gustav Janouch, the son of one of Kafka's colleagues at the insurance company, quotes a contemptuous remark of Kafka's made around 1920 to the effect that "Illový was the parlor pink in our class.

Now he is a bank clerk, getting a salary from the capitalists so that he can fight capitalism more effectively." The quote sounds at least plausible, as does much else in Janouch's book. Unfortunately his memoirs, though purportedly based on notes made at the time, were never submitted for publication until well after World War II and must be accepted entirely on faith.

But one can certainly postulate an interest in socialism on Kafka's part, or at least a break with the Jewish middle class and its values, though that break turned out to be not nearly as radical as he may have believed at the time. For one thing, his reticence and skepticism were incompatible with blind enthusiasm; he remained the detached and critical observer, a metaphysical anarchist with no talent for party politics. And for another, Jewish middle-class values were far too deeply embedded in his consciousness. And insofar as they were Jewish rather than middle class, they also proved considerably more complex and dynamic than what he took them to be at the height of his adolescent rebellion. In short, what his "socialism" amounted to, in the end, was little more than a lifelong identification with the underdog—"the party of the personnel," as he put it.

* * *

In Kafka's view, the formal part of his high-school education contributed next to nothing to his intellectual development. It seems hard to argue the point, yet eight years of intensive exposure to even the fossilized fragments of culture could not entirely fail to leave an impression. The staff of this elitist school included an unusual number of above-average teachers, some noted for uncharacteristically broad scholarship in their respective fields, others for progressive teaching methods and equally uncharacteristic rapport with their students.

The man who loomed largest in Kafka's schedule, if not his life, was Dr. Emil Gschwind—Jupiter astride Mt. Olympus, remote but never absent, and deadly on target with the lightning. As *Ordinarius*, Brother Gschwind was for eight years in absolute administrative charge of the class. In addition, he taught Greek and Latin, including ancient history, and in the final two years also lectured twice a week on something that went under the impressive label of "Philosophical Propaedeutics," essentially a survey course in elementary philosophy and psychology.

The short-necked, heavy-set monk had the face of a bulldog topped, above bushy eyebrows, by the high forehead of a sage. The mismatched features quite accurately reflected the clash between obsessive pedantry and profound scholarship, between sadistic pettiness and an incorruptible sense of justice so strikingly evident in the incident described by Hugo Bergmann. Gschwind, author of several studies in linguistics, was rightfully regarded as an eminent classicist, and one can only speculate on the reasons that led him to waste his scholarly gifts and encyclopedic knowledge on a gang of recalcitrant teenagers who, as a group, progressed in classical philology with all the speed and enthusiasm of a mule team being driven up a mountain. As a mule driver, however, Gschwind was uncommonly effective: the challenge implicit in the task may well have been part of the inducement. On a day-to-day basis, the high-school teacher certainly wielded far more authority and power than the reclusive scholar in his monk's cell.

Many years later, Kafka referred to this strange character in a letter to his fiancée:

> I am reminded of a teacher who, on reading the *Iliad* with us, often used to say: "Too bad one has to read this with the likes of you. You cannot possibly understand it, and even when you think you do, you don't understand a thing. One has to have lived a great deal in order to understand even a tiny snippet." This remark—the tone, let it be said, characterized the whole man—made more of an impression on the callous youth I was than all of the *Iliad* and *Odyssey* put together. Too humbling an impression, perhaps, but a substantial one nonetheless.

This reference, apparently the only direct one, scarcely exhausts the influence of Brother Gschwind. In an excess of zeal, he demanded—and got—far more than even the prescribed lesson plan called for, assigned staggering amounts of homework as well as extracurricular reading, and insisted on translations not only into German but also from German into Greek and Latin, at a time when this tricky feat had already been dropped as an official requirement.

In spite of these extraordinary efforts, however, the vast majority of students still managed cheerfully to forget all their Greek and Latin as soon as it had served its purpose of enabling them to graduate. Kafka was no exception. Under the influence of Max Brod, he later did read some Plato in the original, but there are practically no references to ancient authors or, for that matter, the world of ancient Greece and Rome in any of his work or later correspondence. Yet what he may well have absorbed from this exceedingly knowledgeable pedant in matters stylistic was his fanatical devotion to verbal and grammatical accuracy—nothing more or less than the right word in the right place.

In this respect, neither the German lessons nor the men who taught them provided much inspiration. Kafka's first German teacher, Ferdinand Deml, specialized in fairy and folk tales; the Gymnasium's twenty-fourth annual report for 1896 quotes him to the effect that "whosoever absorbs the language and spirit of the fairy tale is forever armed against any perversion in thought and writing." Truth may lurk even in pomposity, but the link to Kafka, and to Kafka's lifelong passion for fairy tales, seems doubtful. At best, Deml deserves credit for having failed to squelch an enduring fascination with these profoundly ambiguous collective dreams and nightmares, fed by sources painfully close to Kafka's own creative inspiration.

The upper grades were subjected to a perfunctory sampling of mostly mediocre prose and verse, including skimpy selections from the standard classics. By that time, however, Kafka's taste in literature was already too well formed to be in serious danger of corruption. When it came to literature, his judgment matured early. There was never anything ambivalent or hesitant about it, and no amount of treacle could keep him from discovering Kleist or dampen his enthusiasm for Goethe.

The situation was quite different in the natural sciences, in which, with ample justification, he considered himself hopelessly untalented. Yet during his adolescence he for some years developed a lively interest in the subject, testimony to the seductive potential of a true teacher. Dr. Adolf Gottwald, who covered whatever science the syllabus called for—natural history, botany, physics, chemistry, zoology, astronomy—had an impressive academic background, including medical studies and ten years as a university lecturer; why he had slipped back into the lower echelons of high-school teaching is unclear, but some decidedly subversive opinions, openly proclaimed, may have played their part. Gottwald was an atheist, a Darwinist, a follower of the Prague positivist Ernst Mach. He was also a spellbinding teacher with uniquely easy and informal manners, to whom the teenagers in his charge responded with passionate devotion. Their feelings for the man quite naturally kindled their interest in the subjects he taught, and even Kafka seems to have succumbed to the Gottwald spell. At any rate, he did engage in a passing flirtation with science, even to the point of actually contemplating chemistry as a field of study after graduation. He also converted to

Darwinism and discovered that God, if not dead, was certainly not where he was supposed to be. And while these adolescent postures and posturings derived in part from developmental needs, chances are that they owed more to Gottwald than Kafka was ever ready to acknowledge, even to himself. Fear made him keep his distance from fathers and father figures; fear, not only of closeness itself, but of discovering in close encounters that fathers have clay feet and no teeth to bite with. It was a discovery he could not yet afford to make.

The net result of twelve formative years invested in attending distinctly superior schools was definitely not what it might have been. But the discrepancy between the children's ability to learn and the school's ability to teach, between what children want to know and what the school is determined to make them learn, is not peculiar to Kafka's time and place. The objective reality was clearly nowhere as dismal as he saw it, and much the same applies to his scholastic career—far from brilliant, but nothing like the disaster he described. He was tongue-tied in class and often mortified by his inarticulate stammer. Years later, remembering his classmate Emil Utitz, who disposed of "a boundless supply of big words, veritable boulders," he confessed that "it made me despair to watch the ease with which he tossed them about. The feat seemed utterly beyond me, and I took a vow never again in my life to be as envious as I was then." That he lacked a natural aptitude for math was a fact of life, though less than fatal in a humanistic Gymnasium, where the subject was relegated to minor status.

Whether that deficiency relates to what Brod, among others, has described as Kafka's paralyzing incompetence in the presence of abstractions and abstract formulations, however, seems far less certain. In a 1913 letter to Felice, Kafka mentions a weighty philosophical treatise just published by his friend Felix Weltsch, and confides that he had to force himself to read and understand it. "My attention strays too easily when there is nothing there to grab hold of." One suspects that his aversion was not to abstract thought so much as to its formulations, the vaporous verbosity and "veritable boulders" tossed about by his erudite friends. His deep mistrust of big empty words came in good stead later on. But in his teens, the inability to reel off what Brod referred to as "abstract logical arguments" must have proved a humiliating handicap at the Gymnasium, and most particularly in a class in which glibness was commonplace to the point where over half its members later deemed themselves writers, philosophers, or both.

The long ordeals of testophobia and rote learning came to a climax in the summer of 1901 with the *Matura,* the comprehensive finals qualifying for admission to the university. The written part included math, translations from German into Latin, from Greek and Latin into German, and an essay on a topic in German literature, with orals covering these as well as most of the remaining subjects. The prospect of those apocalyptic trials turned the final school year into a frenzied last-ditch effort to shore up the crumbling ramparts of knowledge, retrieve eight years of facts and figures, and prepare for a bloodbath. It is easy enough, in this instance, to credit the recollections of Kafka's schoolmates to the effect that he was desperately afraid.

The polymath Hugo Bergmann helped him review math in one last frantic attempt to comprehend the incomprehensible, but the vision of those venerable bearded men sitting in judgment over him and discovering to their horror, but still just in time, what all through the years he had so shamefully managed to conceal from them must have kept him awake many a night.

In the end he passed, again not brilliantly and, according to him, "partly by cheating." Two of his classmates, in fact, claim to have bribed the Greek teacher's housekeeper and obtained an advance copy of the finals; Kafka, according to them, was in on the plot. The anecdote seems out of character but, given the all but unbearable pressure, not altogether impossible. If true, it must have added another brick to his already overburdened conscience.

Six

Looking back on his adolescence, Kafka always insisted: "As a boy I was innocent, and as uninterested in matters sexual as I now am in, say, the theory of relativity (and I would have remained so, had they not been forcibly thrust upon me). Only trivial things struck me . . . such as that the very women in the street who to me seemed the most beautiful and best-dressed were supposed to be bad" (DI, 4/10/22).

Such innocence is suspect, and far more likely to be a defense against rampant anxiety than genuine lack of interest in what, for most boys of whatever age, constitutes a topic of inexhaustible fascination, nowhere more so than in the overheated atmosphere of *fin-de-siècle* Europe, with its pervasive sexuality and tension between extremes of license and repression. Sex, the fateful duality between Eros and Thanatos, was the sinister leitmotif dominating literature, drama, and the arts of the period. And beyond the poetic metaphors loomed the brutal real-life affinity of sex and death—botched abortions, childbed fever, syphilis, suicides.

In the event, the published reminiscences of friends and schoolmates tend to confirm Kafka's image of himself as slow, if not downright retarded, in his sexual development. This probably meant no more than that, as a high-school student, he was afraid to pick up prostitutes, and that he masked his embarrassment at dirty jokes and smutty stories by a convincing aloofness that provoked guilt and outrage. In fact, this pose so infuriated his classmates that "for his own good" they finally took it upon themselves to reveal to him the facts of life, whether or not he wanted to know them. In a 1921 letter to his sister Elli, he described this assault:

> The two boys, for instance, who enlightened me undoubtedly know no more today than they did then; they were, however, as it turned out, particularly sturdy and determined characters. One to my right, one to my left, they jointly taught the lesson; the

one on the right jolly, paternal, man of the world, with precisely the kind of laugh which I was later to hear from men of all ages, myself included (I am sure there must also be a different and free way of laughing about these things, but I have yet to hear it from among the living), the one on the left matter-of-fact, didactic, which was far more disgusting. Both got married long ago and remained in Prague; syphilis maimed the one on the right years ago beyond recognition, I don't know if he is still alive. The one on the left [Hugo Hecht] is professor and specialist for venereal diseases and chairman of a society for the prevention of VD. I don't want to weigh them one against the other; in any case, they were by no means friends of mine. At the time, they merely happened to band together for the express purpose of enlightening me. [L, Fall 1921]

This ostentatious innocence was obviously symptomatic of much more than hormonal insufficiency or retarded development, nor was it merely defensive in nature. Kafka could be downright aggressive about his professed inadequacies, and while as a rule he turned his fury back upon himself, he was not above using weakness as a weapon against others—unwittingly, perhaps, but to often devastating effect. A passage in the *Letter to His Father* recalls a striking example:

I recall going for a walk with you and Mother one evening on Joseph Square, near what today is the Agricultural Bank. I began to talk about those interesting things, stupidly boastful, superior, proud, detached (that was faked), cold (that was genuine), and stammering, much the way I usually talked to you. I chided the two of you for having left me in ignorance, so that my schoolmates finally had to come to my aid. I told you that I had skirted grave dangers (here I was brazenly lying, in my customary fashion, so as to prove my courage; for as a result of my timidity, I had no clear idea of what these "grave dangers" were all about), but I finally hinted that by now I fortunately knew everything, no longer needed advice, and that everything was all right.

I had begun to talk about this mainly because it gave me satisfaction at least to be talking about it; then again, also out of curiosity, and finally, because I wanted to get even with the two of you for something or other. You took it without fuss, quite in keeping with your nature, only said something to the effect that you could give me advice on how to do these things without danger. Perhaps that was just the kind of answer I wanted to lure out of you; that would have been consistent with the prurience of a child overstuffed with meat and all good things, physically inactive and forever preoccupied with his own self. Nevertheless, my outward sense of modesty was so deeply offended—or at least I believed that it ought to have been so deeply offended— that in spite of myself I could no longer talk to you about it and abruptly ended the conversation with arrogant impertinence.

It isn't easy to evaluate the answer you gave me at the time. On the one hand, there is something shockingly candid about it; on the other, as far as the lesson itself is concerned, it seems harmless by modern standards. I don't know how old I was at the time, certainly not much over sixteen. For such a boy it was nonetheless a rather curious answer; and the fact that this was actually the first direct lesson bearing on real life that I ever received from you also highlights the gap between us. Its real meaning, however, which impressed itself on me even then, but of which I became half aware only much later, was the following: what you advised me to do was in your opinion—not to mention my own opinion at the time—the filthiest thing in the world. That you wanted to make sure I wouldn't physically bring any of this filth into the house was beside the point—was merely your way of protecting yourself, your house. Rather, the main point was that you yourself remained beyond the scope of your own advice, a married man, a pure man, aloof from such things—a percep- tion on my part probably further intensified at the time by the fact that marriage itself seemed to me equally obscene, and that I therefore found it impossible to apply to my parents that which I had generally picked up on the subject. You therefore loomed all the more pure and superior. The thought that, before your marriage, you might have given yourself similar advice seemed utterly unthinkable. Thus almost no trace of earthly filth stuck to you; and yet it was you who, with a few frank words, pushed me down into this filth as if this had been my destiny. And if the world consisted only of you and me—something I found very easy to imagine—then the purity of this world ended with you, and the filth began with me, by virtue of your advice. In and of itself it seemed rather incomprehensible why you would thus condemn me; the only possible explanations were ancient guilt and a profound contempt on your part. This again struck at my innermost being—and struck hard, indeed.

The episode is both moving and profoundly absurd, a blend of incongruities in which Kafka excelled to perfection. But its least curious aspect is the father's frank if insensitive vulgarity. No prude, he, and no Victorian hypocrite, the ex-sergeant had unquestionably sown wild oats aplenty in his day and learned to take care of himself in the swampy combat zones of provincial garrison towns. He saw nothing remarkable, let alone immoral, in prostitution. Quite to the contrary: the chastity of respectable women was in large measure safeguarded by the ready availability of commercial sex. To blur the line between sex for money and sex for fun—as the younger generation seemed increasingly inclined to do—spelled danger to the integrity of the family and led to libertinage, adultery, and divorce. Seen in this light, Herrmann's offer—repeated at later stages in his son's life—was unremarkable enough, its brutal formulation merely of a piece with the father's lifelong contempt for the son's squeamish sensibilities.

For Kafka, at sixteen, to be repressing his rational awareness of parental sexuality was equally normal, even in the face of some fairly blatant reminders—"the sight of the double bed at home, the rumpled sheets, the nightgowns carefully laid out, can almost make me want to vomit, can turn me inside out as though my birth had not been final, as though I were doomed to emerge time and again out of the musty life in this musty room" (FEL, 10/19/16). All the more baffling, therefore, this provocative outburst on the part of a morbidly reticent youngster, this strange eagerness to engage his parents, of all people, in a discussion of subjects so highly charged that he avoided them even with his closest friends.

He himself, however, supplies part of the answer: he wanted to get even. Consciously, no doubt, the point of the picador's lance was aimed at the father, who responded on cue and in character to give the son yet another chance to despise him. It was a pattern to be repeated time and again, the angry rebellion of the surly adolescent, followed by an orgy of self-flagellation before the internalized image of merciless omnipotence which bore only a remote and ever more tenuous relation to the mere mortal onto whom it was grafted. If Herrmann's blunt answer shocked him—as no doubt it did—he had clearly asked for it.

What it did to his mother, on the other hand, silent witness to this as to so many other pitched battles between father and son, he pointedly fails to record, though it is easy enough to imagine the depths of her embarrassment and humiliation. Yet there is reason to believe that this, above all else, was the unconscious purpose of the unprovoked attack, that she rather than the father was the real target of his savage anger, that he never forgave her for having abandoned him and seldom missed an opportunity to humble his rival in her eyes.

Twenty years later he drew up the brief against his father, which contains the account of the episode. But once again, it was the mother on whom he served it. The fact that she never passed it on to the accused does not seem to have disturbed Kafka; he knew that it had reached the person for whom it was intended.

*   *   *

In the oedipal triad, the two contenders square off at the base of a pedestal on which the mother, the object of their struggle, passively awaits the outcome. Though Freud's original scheme, with its focus on the father as the key actor in the passion play, has undergone some refinements, it retains the essentially patriarchal view rooted in his society and its myths.

In Freud's case, one suspects wishful thinking as well; his mother, twenty years younger than his kindly but ineffectual father, was clearly the dominant parent by far. In Kafka's case, the emphasis was equally misplaced. Julie Kafka was no mere object but rather an active party to the continual warfare between husband and son. She had betrayed her firstborn, failed him not by deliberately withholding what he needed but because it simply was not there for her to give. There is no doubt that she cared deeply for her son. But especially in her younger years, before repeated tragedy and depression had eroded her defenses, she herself was far too rigid and deprived to express love in ways that would have made it possible for him to take it for granted. On the other hand, she was a good wife to her husband, because what he, in turn, needed she was indeed able to supply. She provided the dowry that got him started in business; she worked with him and for him, kept his books, kept his house, stoically bore him six children, stoically played cards with him every night, and her knowing silence left much deeper and more lasting traces than the vapid blather and bluster of the titular head of the family. Her son, who loved her, hated her for it.

He blamed his father for having robbed him of his childhood, flailed at him for the rest of his life, knowing full well—and repeating time and again—that Herrmann bore no blame for being what he could

not help but be. Yet with all his articulate anger, the damage he inflicted on his father was minimal. His unthinking cruelty toward his
mother, on the other hand, must have drawn blood time and again,
though he himself failed to perceive either weapon or wound. Julie
Kafka bled in silence, a not uncommon habit of women in her time.

All parents fail their children, and all children weave their parents'
failure into the texture of their lives. This was Freud's grim message—
rewritten since by his disciples as a cheerful greeting card, which is what
happens to prophets.

Kafka grew up hating his body. He dreaded physical intimacy. Sex
to him was the quintessence of filth, the antithesis of love. For the adolescent to be craving both filth and love with equally avid intensity is normal enough, but Kafka never quite succeeded in outgrowing the terrible
acuity of his childhood vision. He could neither overlook nor overcome
the irreconcilable antagonism between beauty and beast, and a diary
entry of August 14, 1913, sums up his defeat in one single, terrible
sentence: "Coitus as punishment for the happiness of being together."

Puberty did not create his conflicts; it merely fed the demons and
infused them with hormonal energy. And in trying to cope with them,
Kafka was hobbled not only by what nature and nurture had made him
but also by the rites and realities of the jerry-built world in which he
came of age.

In the "soft beds and overheated rooms of a Prague childhood" to
which he alludes, there lurked the temptations that led to insanity or
paralysis. The pretty creatures in the streets spread lingering death.
Fear crippled lust, and where lust won out, guilt followed inexorably.
Women were evil and had to be kept in their place—kitchen, church,
whorehouse, or factory.

The fear of women was pervasive in a social order that institutionalized their status as inferiors. For men—and in this, as in so many other
respects, Kafka was far from unusual—to overcome this fear and to
outgrow a bias legitimized by law and sanctified by tradition took a
long and arduous struggle toward self-awareness that involved feelings
as well as reason and was therefore seldom wholly successful.

*   *   *

Kafka's first documented romance took place in the summer of 1900,
his seventeenth, which he spent with his parents on a holiday in the

village of Rostok near Prague. His flirtation with Selma Kohn, daughter of the local postmaster, was a platonic affair consummated in high-minded talk about literature and life, and climaxed by Kafka's effusive farewell contribution to Selma's scrapbook:

> How many words there are in this book. They are meant to re-mind. As if words could stir memory. Words are poor moun-taineers, and poor miners. They retrieve neither the treasures from the peaks, nor those from the heart of the mountain. But there is a living memory that softly strokes what is memorable, like a gentle caress. And when the flames arise out of these ashes, glowing and hot, and you gaze into them as though spell-bound by their magic, then . . . But one cannot impose oneself on these chaste thoughts with a clumsy hand and crude tools; one must make do with these undemanding white sheets. And this is what I did on September 4, 1900. [L, 1900]

Though they apparently never saw each other again, a footnote to this summer idyll affords an intriguing glimpse of Kafka as a teenage suitor. In 1955, Selma Robitschek née Kohn, in a letter to Max Brod, validated Kafka's faith in the spellbinding power of memory:

> . . . and in the midst of it stood a very, very old oak tree. We often sat beneath that tree, Franz and I, two children, and he read Nietzsche to me, oblivious to whether or not I was able to make anything of it. Fifty-five years have passed. . . . We flirted with one another the way one did in those days; I was pretty, he was very smart, and both of us were so divinely young. The Kafkas had rented the second floor of our house for the summer. Our garden opened onto a hill, with a bench at the top. In the eve-nings, we often walked up to that bench, Franz with a burning candle in his hand, trying to talk me into sticking to my intention of enrolling at the university. Well, nothing came of it. My father wouldn't permit it, and in those days children obeyed their par-ents. That was how we parted. [L, p. 495]

Nietzsche was soon to be superseded by other idols. But if the read-ing list changed, the basic pattern of Kafka's invariably crab-like ap-proach to women he respected—women he felt he ought to respect, act responsibly toward, yearned to be spiritually intimate with, and was deadly afraid of—remained remarkably consistent. He urged them to pursue their studies, to educate themselves, helped to guide their read-ing, later on ardently supported efforts by several of his women friends, including his youngest sister, to work as farmhands in preparation for life in a Palestinian kibbutz. He never shared the mordant, pseudo-urbane if sometimes elaborately masked contempt for women that afflicted most of the men in his circle, and in later years he became even more overtly critical of these fashionable attitudes. But whether the often almost comically earnest eagerness on his part to foster women's intellectual growth was prompted by progressive ideas or by the mere unconscious need to desexualize them is hard to say. Chances are that, as with most good intentions, the motives were mixed. One thing, however, seemed impossible for him to contemplate with women he respected.

His visceral disgust for the physical aspects of sex may have somewhat delayed his sexual initiation, at least by prevailing Prague standards. But by the time he was twenty, in 1903, sexual needs, fears, guilt, confusion, and curiosity combined to propel him into his first adventure —another test he felt sure he would flunk. Opportunities abounded, as readily available as a glass of beer, but he was fastidious enough that first time to eschew the commercial establishments and pick a shopgirl from across the street, who was freelancing on the side. As always, he passed the test, and found the experience exactly as he had expected he would—dirty, degrading, depressing; hence stirring and tremendously exciting.

That wallowing in dirt and guilt can offer satisfactions of a special kind, and that the stench of brimstone, unwashed bodies, and excremental slime—both metaphorically and literally, sanitary facilities in nineteenth-century Prague being what they were—enormously enhances the sexual experience for those so disposed is no recent discovery. The epidemic *nostalgie de la boue* was, and remains, very much part of the mother-versus-whore syndrome, and the young Kafka, in frequenting bordellos or "seducing" underpaid working girls, merely followed the conventions of his class and time. Many years later, in a 1920 letter to Milena Jesenská, he described that first experience:

> I remember the first night. We were living at the time in Celetna Street, across from a dress shop, where a shopgirl always used to stand in the door. There I was, up in my room, just a little past my twentieth birthday, incessantly pacing back and forth, busy cramming for the first State Boards by trying to memorize material that made no sense to me whatsoever. It was

summer, very hot at the time, altogether unbearable. I kept stopping at the window, the disgusting Roman law clenched between my teeth, and finally we managed to communicate by sign language. I was supposed to pick her up at eight o'clock that evening, but when I came down, another man was already waiting for her. Well, that didn't make much of a difference. I was already scared of everybody, anyway, and he was just one more to be afraid of. If he hadn't been there, I would still have been afraid of him. But the girl, though she took his arm, motioned me to follow. . . . The fellow took his leave, the girl ran into the house, I waited till she came out again, and we went to a hotel in Malá Strana. Even before we got to the hotel, everything was charming, exciting, and disgusting; in the hotel itself it was no different. And when, toward morning—it was still hot and beautiful—we crossed the Charles Bridge on the way home, I was in fact happy, but happy at finally having some peace from my ever-complaining body; happy, above all, that the whole experience hadn't been even filthier and more disgusting. I was with this girl one more time, two nights later, I believe. Everything was as good as the first time. Right after that, however, I left on a summer vacation, where I played around a little with a girl; when I got back to Prague, I simply could no longer stand the sight of that shopgirl. From my point of view, she had become my bitter enemy, and yet she was, in fact, a good-natured and friendly girl who kept haunting me with her uncomprehending eyes. I won't say that the sole reason for my hostility could have been (it surely wasn't) a tiny repulsive something the girl committed in all innocence in the hotel (not worth mentioning), a trifling obscenity (not worth mentioning). But the memory lingered— that very instant I knew I would never forget it, and at the same time I knew—or thought I knew—that while outwardly this smut and obscenity were not necessary, inwardly they were indeed an indispensable part of the whole experience, and that it was precisely this smut and obscenity (of which her little gesture and her little remark were the only little signs) that had drawn me with such mad force into this hotel, which otherwise I would have shunned with my last remaining strength.

It was, as these things went, a remarkably untraumatic initiation, quite in line with prevailing customs, and Kafka's attitude was equally conventional. The humiliation of these working-class girls by middle-class males of all ages became a ritual phenomenon so widespread and common as to be taken for granted, a law of nature rather than a perversion of its spirit. Some of the most sensitive souls and keenest intellects of Vienna and Prague failed to see it for what it was: a brutal degradation of human beings that humiliated both parties and did much lasting damage. The fact that all Kafka's close friends led conspicuously stormy sex lives, complicated by many of the same problems that bedeviled him, would suggest a general malaise of which his own difficulties were merely a greatly exacerbated version. Kafka's lucidity was his own, and he paid for it in guilt many times over. Men like Brod and Werfel sugarcoated their guilt in sentiment and let it melt on the tongue.

*   *   *

By now, however, there were three young women who, one by one, had entered Kafka's life in late adolescence and claimed their respective places in it. "With my sisters—this was especially true in the early days—I was often an altogether different person than with other people," he noted in his diary, and witnesses bear him out. "Fearless, vulnerable, powerful, surprising, moved as I otherwise only am when I am writing" (DI, 7/21/13).

He was already six when his oldest sister Elli was born in 1889. Valli came next, in 1890, and Ottla, the youngest, in 1892. The age gap was thus significant enough to attenuate normal sibling rivalries and to invest him with a natural prestige and authority further enhanced by his stature as the only male. During the very early years, he had little contact with the girls, who were largely cared for by servants; but as they grew older, he entered into their games, led them in noisy processions through the apartment, instigated raids on their mother's wardrobe for dramatic disguises, and started what became a long-standing tradition in the Kafka household: he wrote and staged short plays for the girls to enact on special occasions, notably the parents' birthdays. Unfortunately, all that survives of these fledgling literary efforts is a few titles—"The Juggler," "Talking Photographs," and "George of Podebrad," the latter referring to the fifteenth-century Hussite hero-king of Bohemia, an intriguing choice of subject matter for this particular dramatist.

Inevitably, these initially remote if amiably incestuous relationships grew increasingly more complex as the girls themselves reached adolescence, and as each in turn faced many of the hurdles that the older brother had never quite managed to clear. As it happened, they turned out to be a good deal sturdier than he. Although Elli in many ways took after her brother and for years withdrew turtle-like into her shell, ignoring the father who kept viciously pecking away at her, she eventually emerged wholly intact, affectionate, and efficient in her multiple roles as wife, mother, daughter, and sister, and thoughtful enough not to be entirely at ease in any of them. Valli, the second, more pliable on the surface, accomplished the same feat in a less dramatic transformation. Only Ottla, the youngest and by far the most spirited of the entire clan, turned openly rebellious in her teens and defied not only the father but everything he stood for. She had no use whatsoever for *Respektspersonen* and no fear of the family drillmaster who, inevitably, came to be afraid of her instead. "All I do is say one word to her, and right away she jumps at me." Not only did Ottla's habit of hanging out with "social inferiors" offend Herrmann Kafka's fastidious sense of status, but he also rightly suspected her close relations with the household help, the whispered exchanges with the untrustworthy son, and the endless gossiping with the girls in his shop to be in the nature of a conspiracy against him.

The deep and lasting bond between Ottla and her brother had many shadings and, over the years, underwent many transformations as she passed through her own stages of growth, from impish baby of the family to rebellious teenager, practical visionary, wife, and mother. What she offered him was intimacy without risk, a belated mothering of sorts. What she received from him, or at any rate shared with him, was a tragic sense of responsibility for good and evil. Throughout her rebellion and search for self—defying the father, working the land, breaking away from home, marrying a non-Jew—she in fact acted out her brother's wildest and most impossible dreams. Yet nothing she did with her life was as much in his spirit as her final decision to sacrifice it.

In 1941, German occupation forces began the roundup and deportation of Czechoslovakia's Jews. In October of that year, Elli, Valli, and their husbands were deported to the Lodz ghetto, where they subsequently perished. Ottla, as the wife of an "Aryan," was exempt from Nazi orders affecting the Jews, an exemption that violated everything she believed in and, in her eyes, corrupted the very essence of her marriage. She therefore formally divorced her husband and, a Jew once more, was deported to the Terezin ghetto in August 1942. On October

5, 1943, she volunteered to escort a children's transport to Auschwitz. Her husband and their two daughters survived the war.

*   *   *

The experience of growing up with—or at least next to—these young women had a discernibly humanizing influence on Kafka's development. For one thing, their mere presence during his adolescence gradually succeeded in transforming the tribal barracks into something resembling a bourgeois home—no cozy nest by a long shot, but livable and alive. As they grew up and married in turn, they provided him with fragments of a conventional family, practical help, and unconditional acceptance, asking for nothing in return. "My youngest sister (already over twenty) is my best friend in Prague," he wrote to Felice in 1912, "and the other two are also kind and full of sympathy" (FEL, 11/11/12).

They were good to him, he was fond of them, but at bottom the mirror-smooth harmony of these blood relations, so seldom ruffled by even the merest wisp of rivalry or jealousy, points to cold blood and vast distances. Very much part of his day-to-day life, often perhaps central to it, the sisters were never even marginal to the struggle that consumed his nights. In the petrifying garden of his fantasies there is the occasional bland, would-be helpmate, pale echo of sisterly benevolence. But the women of his nighttime self are, by and large, anything but sisterly or benevolent. Kafka's rational views about women, as about so many other issues, were eminently sensible, far more so than was common in his circle. But what the work records, the bedrock of his inner truth uncensored by reason, is a demonic vision of woman eerily consistent with the fanged monsters that hovered in the poison fumes of a twilight culture—Weininger's syphilitic vampire, Nolde's Death as a Woman, Wedekind's Lulu, and Freud's hysterical virago seeking to avenge her loss.

Far more insistent than sex, in his late adolescence, was the need for friends, for spiritual and intellectual companionship. The loosening of childhood bonds with Hugo Bergmann and the tentative flirtations with radical classmates and their radicalism were part of the initial phase. But his first truly passionate friendship began for Kafka around 1899 with an adolescent crush on his classmate Oskar Pollak.

Though exactly Kafka's age—born in Prague in 1883—Pollak was by far the more mature; his contemporaries describe him as years ahead of his age in self-assurance, sophistication, and intellect, a highly temperamental character of conspicuous brilliance, enormous vitality, and a broad range of interests way beyond any of his peers. That it was Kafka who this once overcame his shyness and made the initial advances is to be taken for granted, given Pollak's prestige and exalted status at school. It showed good sense and sound instincts; Pollak was precisely the sort of mentor he needed to help him break out of the stultifying sterility of the classroom and give his brain something more exciting to feed on than the grit and gravel of the curriculum.

Even at that time, Pollak's interest in art, his knowledge of art history and partisan involvement in aesthetic theory appears to have been objectively impressive, and along with it went a near-Faustian drive for omniscience. The luxuriant black beard he already sported at age nineteen was probably meant to symbolize that quest, not confined to the arts and sciences; Pollak was an outstanding athlete, and one of the pioneers of downhill skiing in Bohemia. He initially chose chemistry as his major at the university, went on from there to philosophy, archaeology, and art history, wrote his doctoral dissertation on medieval Prague architecture, and settled in Rome with the intention of producing the definitive work on the age of the Baroque. He quickly established himself as one of the up-and-coming authorities in the field, but long before his far-flung researches into the Vatican's abundant source material could bear fruit, Austria slid over the edge and dragged the rest of the world with it. Rather than waiting to be drafted, Pollak enlisted at the outbreak of the war, presumably out of misguided adventurism, *pour le sport*; a fanatical Italophile, he was certainly not motivated by chauvinism, nor was he the only one who, despite political indifference or even outright opposition to the war, indulged in romantic delusions about its nature as a test of manhood and transcendence of self. Whatever his motives, Pollak paid for them with his life; he was killed fighting the Italians on the Isonzo River in June 1915. His preliminary studies on the Roman Baroque were published posthumously in several volumes.

During the later student years, around 1903, the ties between Pollak and Kafka began to loosen; but the very differences in outlook and temperament that eventually led to their estrangement proved enormously stimulating in the early days of their friendship. It was the range of Pollak's interests that led to Kafka's first serious concern with style in art and language, made him aware of the constricting parochialism of their native environment, and opened his eyes to what was happening in the wide world beyond. "Prague," Kafka wrote to Pollak in 1902, "doesn't let go. Neither of us. This little mother has claws. We ought to set fire to it at both ends, on the Vyšehrad and on the Hradčany, and maybe then it might be possible to escape" (L, 12/20/02).

It was probably through Pollak that Kafka discovered the *Kunstwart,* a pretentious German "bi-monthly review of poetry, the theater, music, fine and applied arts," which for the first time put him in touch with contemporary intellectual currents, even if it had some distinctly noxious side effects. The *Kunstwart* did, in fact, offer a fairly comprehensive survey of at least the German cultural scene, though it hardly ever deigned to cast a glance beyond the borders of the Reich. Its whole tone and orientation—derived originally from Nietzsche and scrupulously maintained by its eruditely pedantic editor, the folklorist Ferdinand Avenarius—was rather emphatically Teutonic. Not only the choice of material but also the style of most contributions clearly prefigured the "blood-and-soil" romanticism of the Wagner-George axis. Nevertheless, its quest for "authenticity," however defined, the earnest effort to come to terms with contemporary works of art, and the persistent if biased search for neglected poetic masterpieces of the past were themselves a revelation to the provincial high-school student. He surrendered to Nietzsche, succumbed to the craggy virility of homespun "Aryan" poetry and prose, but also began to show a growing interest in the visual arts and, above all, sharpened his own critical faculties.

On balance, the *Kunstwart* influence was overwhelmingly positive simply because it shocked Kafka out of his intellectual isolation. The magazine's factual content soon lost much of its importance as he learned to trust his own judgment, and in this respect he was neither shy nor retarded. When it came to literature, he had absolute pitch.

Even so, the stylistic poison of the *Kunstwart,* with its cult of long discarded words, regional turns of speech, and *echt* simplicity of heart, not to mention simplicity of mind, took a while to work its way out of his system. Specifically, it showed up for years in his correspondence with Pollak, presumably because those charming archaisms and coyly stilted phrases enabled him to dissimulate a tenderness increasingly inappropriate. Max Brod cites an example of Kafka's Teutonic folklore phase:

> Just across from the vineyard, by the highway deep in the valley, stands a tiny little house, the first and last in the village. Not much

to it. Worth, among brothers, a hundred miserable guilders at most. . . . I am probably the only one, not excluding the owner, who loves it and weaves it into his dreams. Small it is, and low; not even old, either, some fifteen little years at most . . . and in front of the door a broad and heavy stone bench that almost looks old. And one day three journeymen appear, canes in hand and all-too-light little packs on their backs—all of this I watch from above, and it is like a dear old quiet German fairy tale.

Nothing "kafkaesque" about that passage, but one would suspect that at that point his feelings about Pollak still blunted Kafka's better judgment. What these feelings were is fairly obvious even on the strength of the very fragmentary correspondence that survives, and there seems to be no reason to doubt that he himself was perfectly aware of the candidly romantic adulation and its roots.

What is more, he felt sufficiently uninhibited and at ease with these feelings to more or less declare his love—*Ich habe Dich sehr lieb*—to express jealousy and disappointment along with tenderness and admiration. It takes no great perspicacity to discern strong homoerotic impulses at work in this relationship; far more significant is the fact that Kafka had no problem acknowledging them for what they were. Yet this in no way justifies any rash assumptions about either Kafka's or Pollak's sexual orientation.

To say that, like all of their contemporaries, they grew up without any meaningful contact with the opposite sex is an understatement. They in fact inhabited an all-male preserve, segregated not only through twelve years of elementary and secondary schools but well into the student years and beyond, down to the famous cafés and beer gardens of Mitteleuropa, where the most conspicuous and consistent female presence was the waitress. It was a system that strongly encouraged boys to be boys and never run the risk of growing up.

The system was effective; much of what, among Kafka's unstable friends, passed for masculine charm, artistic temperament, and reckless passion was simply infantile behavior. And the emotional intensity that marked so many of their male friendships had far less to do with homosexuality than with immaturity, with arrested development, with the split vision that cannot perceive the link between sex and sentiment. What you love, you don't sleep with; what you sleep with, you don't love. One loved one's friends, one's mother, and one's wife.

It seems clear that Kafka, at the time of his relationship with Pollak, was still only just emerging from a rather prolonged adolescence, with its characteristic sexual ambivalence. That he retained his normal share of that ambivalence is to be taken for granted; on the other hand, nothing in his later life or work justifies any sweeping conclusions about latent or overt homosexuality—which has not kept certain zealously simpleminded interpreters from advancing definitive theories on the subject.

In any event, what counts is the degree of intimacy rather than the extent of physical involvement. Even later, in letters to Brod and other correspondents, Kafka was often affectionate, sending love and kisses, not at all out of line with contemporary customs and certainly no indication of homoerotic practices. The physical components, if any, of Kafka's friendship with Pollak would in any event seem of very minor importance compared to the enormous significance that Pollak's friendship in its early stages had for Kafka's emotional and intellectual growth.

"Among all those young people," he wrote to him in 1903, "I really spoke only to you; and whenever I did speak to others, it was only incidentally, or on your account, or because of you, or in connection with you. Among many other things, you were also something like a window for me, through which I could look out into the street. Left to myself, this would have been impossible, for despite my height, I still don't reach up to the windowsill."

It was Pollak's spirit that gave Kafka the strength, in his twentieth year, to finally crack the shell of his adolescence; drawing up the balance sheet of that summer, he wrote:

> I've grown healthier, I've grown stronger, I was out a lot among people, I can talk with women . . . and someone, standing behind a tree, says to me quietly, "You will do nothing without others"; but I now record, with emphasis and ornate syntax: the life of a recluse is repulsive; lay your eggs honestly in front of everybody and let the sun hatch them out; it is better to bite into life than to bite one's tongue; honor the mole and his kind, but don't make them your patron saint.

This letter of June 1903 marks an important turning point. For in denouncing the recluse and the mole, Kafka for the first time in his life resolves to bare the most closely guarded secret of his life—in fact, his secret life itself:

I am going to get a package ready for you. It contains everything I have written up to now, out of my own self and out of others. Nothing will be missing, except for the childhood things (misfortune, as you can see, has been haunting me since early in life), some that I no longer have, some that I consider worthless in this context, furthermore the outlines, because they are countries for those familiar with them and mere sand to the rest, and finally those things that I cannot show even to you, because it gives one the shivers to be left completely naked and have someone palpate you, even if you begged for it on your knees. . . . What I want you to do is read these pages, be it with indifference or revulsion. Because some of it is also indifferent and revolting. Because—and this is why I wanted it—that which to me is most dear and difficult is only cool, the sun notwithstanding, and I know that the eyes of a stranger will make everything warmer and more dynamic by merely looking at it. . . . Well, why all the fuss. . . . I am taking a piece of my heart, wrapping it up cleanly in a few written sheets, and giving it to you.

*   *   *

Chances are that Kafka never remembered a time in his life when he did not want to write. Long before his quasi-public announcement to the Bergmann brothers, in the early high-school years, he had already embarked on some fairly ambitious projects. None of these precocious efforts survived his destructive self-critique, but a diary entry provides an oblique view of the child novelist at work:

I once planned a novel in which two brothers fought one another, one of whom ran off to America, while the other remained behind in a European prison. I never wrote more than a few lines at a time, because it quickly tired me. One Sunday afternoon we were visiting my grandparents; as always, we had eaten their special kind of soft bread with butter, and I started to write about my prison. It is quite possible that I did it mostly out of vanity and that, by shifting the paper on the tablecloth, tapping with the pencil, and looking about me from under the lamp I wanted to tempt someone to take what I had written, look at it, and admire me. My few lines mainly described the hallway of the prison, its chilling silence above all; there were also a few kind words for the imprisoned brother, because he was the good one. I may have had a passing notion of how worthless this description was; but up to that afternoon I had never paid much attention to such feelings when seated at the round table in the familiar room among relatives whom I was used to (my timidity was so great that it turned mere familiarity into near-happiness) and would not let myself forget that I was young and destined to rise beyond the present tranquillity to future greatness. An uncle who liked to make fun of people finally took the page from me against my mere token resistance, cast a brief glance at it, handed it back to me, didn't even laugh, and said to the others, who were watching: "The usual stuff." To me he said nothing. I remained seated and again bent over my now worthless page; but with one single blow I was in fact banished from the community; my uncle's judgment echoed in me in its now almost real significance, and even within the bosom of the family I caught a glimpse of the cold space of our world, which I had to warm with a fire I first had to seek. [DI, 1/19/11]

The episode foreshadows in uncanny detail much of the ambivalence that characterized Kafka's later attitude toward fame, criticism, and the suffocating intimacy of the family. Even more revealing, though, is the subject matter itself—the rivalry between brothers, and the escape of the bad one to that mythical land beyond the seas, to a freedom at once infinitely terrifying and alluring; years later, these inchoate visions of guilt, punishment, and redemption took shape in the novellas Max Brod published after Kafka's death under the collective title *Amerika*.

There is, of course, something quaintly appealing about a time and place where little boys dreamed of becoming writers rather than of streaking on horseback across the wide prairies or of leading cavalry charges against the heathen Turks, but even within Kafka's narrow circle he was probably something of an exception. The primitive daydreams of a normal childhood simply did not afford room enough for the savage violence of inadmissible fantasies, and with somnambulant assurance he resorted instead to a more powerful medium. What later became a "form of prayer" began, logically enough, as a form of magic, to be practiced in stealth and awed solitude.

By the time they reached their late teens, many of his classmates had themselves begun to dabble in verse or prose with the avowed intention of becoming writers. Aside from its tantalizing combination of middle-class respectability and bohemian self-indulgence, writing was one of the few occupations in which neither native intelligence nor nationality presented insuperable obstacles to success even in Austro-Hungary. About half the class eventually produced printed matter of one sort or another, but some of the more precocious and gifted members of Kafka's generation, such as Werfel and Brod, published remarkably polished work while still in high school.

Kafka, on the other hand, withdrew into silence during those formative years; he shared his writing with no one and protected this secret life of his to the point of not even hinting at it to anyone outside the family, until the intensity of his feelings for Oskar Pollak led him to risk baring his soul. At nineteen, having thus far written exclusively for himself, Kafka finally transcended the encapsulated solipsism of his adolescence and, for the first time, at least envisaged the possibility of a dialogue.

Shortly after alerting Pollak to the arrival of "a piece of my heart," he followed up on the announcement with another letter, unpublished but partly excerpted by Brod:

> Among the few thousand lines that I am giving you, there may perhaps be ten that I could still stand listening to. The trumpet blasts in the previous letter were uncalled for; what is headed your way is not the Revelation but a child's scribbles. . . . Frankly, I find most of it repulsive ("The Morning," for instance, and some other things), impossible to read in its entirety, and I'll be satisfied if you can stand a few samples. Bear in mind, though, that I started at a time when one "created works" and wrote bombast; there is no worse time for a beginner. And I was so infatuated with big words.

In this particular instance, Kafka's self-deprecation, though no doubt genuine, also contained a manifest plea: what he needed was not a critic but an audience. This becomes even more obvious in the next letter:

> What I lack is discipline. Your skimming these notebooks is, at this point, the least of what I want you to do for me. You have a beautiful room. The little lights in the shops below twinkle with furtive zeal. This is where I want you to let me read to you for half an hour every Saturday, starting the one after next. For three months I want to work hard. One thing above all I now know: art needs craftsmanship more than craftsmanship needs art. I realize, of course, that one cannot

force oneself to give birth; one can, however, force oneself to raise the children.

There is no record of how, or even whether, Pollak responded to his friend's work. The brash nineteen-year-old with his Van Dyke beard and reputation for omniscience was a radical critic in matters relating to art, people, and causes; but literature apparently interested him not at all, and it was this very indifference that made him the ideal first reader of Kafka's collected works. Pollak, to Kafka, must have seemed the very essence of indefatigable zeal and dedication in pursuit of esoteric passions, a striking contrast to what the worshipping young devotee perceived as his own sloth and lack of direction. But when it came to judging the merit of his work, Kafka neither sought nor needed help, then or ever. He had to satisfy a far more implacable and merciless judge, and he seldom succeeded. As his powers matured, the judge grew ever more demanding, and the trial dragged on with no hope of settlement or resolution short of death, because writing—so he believed—was his sole reason for living, and his sole means of keeping alive. A belief no more susceptible to logic than any other act of creation. I write, therefore I am. Therefore I am like God.

Being a child not of God but of Herrmann Kafka, and of the Age of Reason, he tortured himself and those close to him by constantly trying to justify and rationalize what defies explanation. All his writing, so he told Brod and repeated, much later, in the famous *Letter*, was an attempt to escape from the father; which, even if it were true, says nothing about why he chose this particular road to redemption. Perhaps the closest he ever came to touching on the sources of both his needs and his art was in a letter to Milena Jesenská: "I am constantly trying to communicate something incommunicable, to explain something inexplicable, to tell about something I only feel in my bones and which can only be experienced in those bones. Basically it is nothing other than this fear we have so often talked about, but fear spread to everything, fear of the greatest as of the smallest, fear, paralyzing fear of pronouncing a word, although this fear may not only be fear but also a longing for something greater than all that is fearful."

What he felt in his bones was a reality beyond appearances. As a writer, he was a realist.

*   *   *

Nothing expresses Kafka's innermost sense of self more profoundly than his lapidary definition of "writing as a form of prayer": he was a writer. Not a man who wrote, but one to whom writing was the only form of being, the only means of defying death in life.

The difference involves fundamentals: the radical distinction between genius and talent, among others, but above all the approach to writing as a holy vocation, a sacred service rather than a means to many ends, a way of life as sternly self-contained as the daily Talmud study of Kafka's legendary sainted ancestors on his mother's side.

The attitude at least partly accounts for the vast distance that separates the mature Kafka from most of his contemporaries. It is certainly not the only reason why he remained relatively unknown in his lifetime, nor why his posthumous fame has all but eclipsed that of Prague's entire literary establishment; the luminaries of his day are dead and, whether burned or buried, no longer have the power to haunt us. If Kafka does, it is due in no small measure to the obsessive passion he brought to writing as a holy office.

This is not to impute to him the furtive conceit of a divine mission, humbly unavowed. The irresistible compulsion to write seemed to him part of a dark, utterly personal fate, and there is no doubt that much of the time he felt more driven than chosen.

> Writing sustains me [he wrote to Brod in 1922]. But wouldn't it be more accurate to say that it sustains this kind of life? Which does not, of course, mean that my life is any better when I don't write. On the contrary, at such times it is far worse, wholly unbearable, and inevitably ends in madness. This, of course, only on the assumption that I am a writer even when I don't write—which is indeed the case; and a non-writing writer is, in fact, a monster courting insanity. But what about this being a writer as such? Writing is a sweet and marvelous reward, but a reward for what? In the course of the night it became clear to me, as plain as a children's show-and-tell lesson, that it is a reward for serving the devil. This descent down to the dark powers, this unleashing of ghosts by nature bound, these questionable embraces and whatever else may be going on down there, none of it remembered as one writes stories in the sunlight up above. Perhaps there are also different ways of writing, but I only know this one; at night, when fear keeps me from sleeping, I only know this one. [L, 7/5/22]

But however unique Kafka's feelings about the vocation that chose him, they also reflect the spirit of an age in which literature had taken the place of faith, ritual, and tradition and itself become a form of religion. The phenomenon was not confined to Jews; Flaubert speaks of literature as *la mystique de qui ne croit à rien*. But both their past and their present had rendered Jewish intellectuals particularly vulnerable. Jewish communal life was all but dead; the founding fathers believed in money, progress, and the Emperor Franz Joseph rather than the God of Israel, and read the *Prager Tagblatt* instead of the Torah. But their sons turned on them and, in devious and unorthodox ways, rather in spite of themselves, restored the ancestral links to the Talmud sages, mystics, pious yeshiva pupils, and learned shlemiels of the ghetto: they wrote.

In terms of sheer volume, the productivity of Jewish writers in Austro-Hungary was truly staggering; and relative to the size of their respective communities, Prague's literati and litterateurs outnumbered even the Vienna contingent, though in any case the circles overlapped and intersected. The capital obviously offered greater scope and more challenging opportunities, but in Prague, the Jews remained a cohesive and numerically dominant majority within the German-speaking minority—some 85 percent of the roughly 35,000 German speakers out of a total population of around 420,000 in 1900, whereas in Vienna they accounted for a mere 10 percent of the city's approximately 1.5 million. And if Vienna had a great many Jewish writers, it must have seemed at times as though every Jew in Prague, whatever his ostensible trade or profession, was busy churning out books. "If people hear you're from Prague," reported Egon Erwin Kisch, one of Kafka's schoolmates who himself went on to fame and notoriety as a prolific journalist and champion of the left, "it is simply taken for granted."

The quality of this massive output ranged from a few enduring works to a daily torrent of ephemeral trash, with the bulk of it clustered on the soggy middle ground somewhere between these two extremes. Talent varies as much as motives, and there are as many reasons why people write as there are people; quite a few of them, though highly motivated, lacked any shred of talent whatsoever. But collectively, what fueled this outburst of frenzied self-expression was the dilemma which at that juncture faced most Western Jews: the awareness, however dim, that assimilation was a failure. The fathers, smugly content with having overcome piety and poverty, groomed their sons for roles they could never hope to play. The sons, however, found themselves locked out of the show altogether; and trapped between promise and reality, they drifted into literature as a way out of the impasse.

It was a return to tradition, in its way. But whereas, to their ancestors, words were the building blocks of faith, they themselves used words to demolish faith, to bewail their loss of it, and ended up with literature taking its place. God was dead, but the running argument with his chosen people—who chose whom, and why?—continued unabated, and with no loss of stridency.

The spirit of that timeless quarrel lived on in the ruthless polemics, the quest for absolutes of truth and justice, the pitiless criticism, sardonic self-critique, black humor, and blazing despair which distinguished and pervaded the work of every major German-Jewish writer, from the first to the last, from Heinrich Heine to Kurt Tucholsky, from Karl Marx to Karl Kraus. What kept them—whether formally converts, agnostics, or tepid non-Christians—from becoming fully assimilated was neither blood nor race nor lack of patriotic sentiment, but the ambiguities of everything the host tribes took for granted and did not wish to have questioned.

This was not a fashionable view, the less so since to simple minds it seemed to echo racist sentiments. Kafka was among the very few who not only saw the pointed horns of the dilemma but also did not deceive themselves about their thrust.

"Most of those who started to write in German," he wrote to Brod in June of 1921, "wanted to get away from their Jewishness, usually with their fathers' vague consent (the vagueness of it was what made it outrageous). They wanted to get away, but their hind legs still stuck to the fathers' Jewishness, while the forelegs found no firm ground. And the resulting despair served as their inspiration."

Even Brod, by then a committed Zionist, protested against what seemed to him far too drastic a formulation. But when it came to writing, his sacred vocation, Kafka knew no compromise—in this, too, he was flesh and blood of the old Talmudist from Podebrady.

"All of this literature is an effort to breach the frontier," he added, in a 1921 diary entry (DI, 1/16/21). "But for the intervention of Zionism, it could easily have developed into a new mysticism, a Cabala. Incipient trends in that direction exist. What is needed, however, is something like an inconceivable genius who either sends out roots into the ancient centuries or else re-creates them all over, yet does not spend himself in the task but only now begins his work."

Whether he caught a glimpse of that genius in himself is uncertain. In any case, to be chosen was not, as he saw it, a cause for rejoicing. But to read him as a latter-day Kleist, to trace his inspiration back to primordial *Angst* or Kierkegaard, and to invoke Goethe, Dickens, and Dostoevsky is to confuse form and substance, is to miss the essence of who he was and what he was struggling to discover within himself. Kafka's true ancestors, the substance of his flesh and spirit, were an unruly crowd of Talmudists, Cabalists, medieval mystics resting uneasy beneath the jumble of heaving, weatherbeaten tombstones in Prague's Old Cemetery, seekers in search of reason for their faith. He was their child, last in a long line of disbelieving believers, wild visionaries with split vision who found two answers to every question and four new questions to every answer in seeking to probe the ultimate riddle of God.

Seven

A T the graduation ceremonies of the Altstädter Gymnasium in July
1901, twenty-two members of Kafka's class received the coveted
Reifezeugnis, the certificate attesting to their ostensible maturity,
though in actual fact it amounted to no more and no less than a ticket
to privilege. Aside from providing access to higher education, it also
meant deferment, exemption, or, at worst, a mere token form of military service.

Bergmann and Utitz graduated with honors. (The third honors
graduate, one Karl Steiner, joined the Austrian National Railways upon
graduation but left no tracks of his own.) As for Kafka, he no doubt
considered it a major miracle merely to have made it at all, to have
served out the first part of his sentence, the initial twelve-year stretch
at hard labor, to have hoodwinked judges and jailors. No dramatic
last-minute catastrophe, as he had feared, no cabal of hooting teachers
unmasking him as the fraud he felt himself to be. He had slipped
through the meshes, ingloriously but inconspicuously, and reaped his
reward: another six years in the adjacent prison, a few blocks down the
street.

Even Kafka, though, must have had a few moments of unambiguous
triumph, or at least satisfaction and relief at never again having to
creep up the back stairs of the Kinsky Palace, never again to be trapped
for hours on end on a school bench much too small for his near-six-foot
frame, a sinner in the stocks forced to undergo trial by arithmetic and
torture by boredom.

Worse tortures lay ahead, although early in July they may have
seemed remote; the winter semester at Prague's German Ferdinand-
Karls University did not start till mid-November. Kafka had officially
opted for philosophy as his field of study, a choice little short of

grotesque, given his conspicuous lack of aptitude for the subject. Perhaps he for once got carried away; in the light of his unexpected success, the impossibility of the impossible might have loomed less forbidding. Far more likely, though, was the intent—conscious or otherwise—to stage-manage another dramatic confrontation between the self-made, loathsome, status-conscious, penny-pinching, vulgar, feared, adored bourgeois oaf of a father and the high-minded, sensitive, impractical son determined to pursue the one career practically guaranteed to leave him forever financially dependent on his lifelong antagonist as a way of perpetuating and institutionalizing their struggle.

If so, the attempt was a failure. The real-life Herrmann Kafka, as distinct from the bloated monster dominating his son's imagination, didn't bite; in fact, he seldom did more than grumble. Like any totally self-centered parent, he considered his son an appendage of himself, and this particular one turned out a bitter disappointment. Herrmann hadn't much liked the child; he decidedly disliked the man. Yet at the same time, the brooding and sardonic stranger with his dark gray eyes and eloquently ironic silences mocked and taunted him in his very own house, made him feel uneasy, awkward, and inferior even in the absence of open hostilities. And whenever the truce between them broke down, it was the son who ruthlessly attacked, and the father who withdrew—into his room, his shop, or his cardiac palpitations. That those same dark and probing eyes could be totally blind to such self-evident realities, that they saw in him not an aging, harried, and confused workhorse but an invincible, omnipotent foe, was something he could not possibly have imagined and was certainly not equipped to understand.

Herrmann grumbled about the "Herr Sohn"—His Lordship the Son, as he referred to Franz—thinking of himself as too good for business. At the same time, he would no doubt have been even more upset if the Herr Sohn had not gone on to acquire his doctorate. Philosophy? Completely *meshugge,* a fancy way to starve to death. On the other hand, this butter-fingered dreamer would probably never amount to much, anyway. So let him philosophize, if that's what it takes to make him happy . . .

The Herr Sohn, however, was a past master at the art of losing, and he deftly managed to twist even this seemingly sensible attitude on his father's part into a disastrous dilemma for himself, for which again he blamed his reprehensible progenitor.

For instance, take the choice of a career [he lamented, in the *Letter to His Father*]. True, here you gave me complete freedom, in your own generous and, in this instance, even indulgent manner. At the same time, though, you were also conforming to the commonly prevailing norms of the Jewish middle class in dealing with its sons; these norms, or at any rate the values of that class, set the standards for your behavior. . . . [And after a few pages of berating himself for his weakness, indolence, ignorance] This, then, was the situation in which I was given the freedom to choose a profession. But was I still capable of making use of such freedom? . . . Even at the Gymnasium, despite all constraints, I was solely preoccupied with myself; how much more was this true now that I was free. Real freedom to choose a career, therefore, did not exist for me.

Whether these retrospective ruminations at age thirty-six accurately reflected the nineteen-year-old's state of mind is at least open to question. There is a good deal of evidence to indicate that in his post-adolescent period Kafka was nowhere near as despondent and unhappy as he subsequently chose to remember. At any rate, by way of a graduation present, the parsimonious but proud papa, in a rare—quite possibly unique—burst of generosity, treated his son to a three-week vacation at the seashore, and in August, Kafka set out for Norderney, a romantic North Sea island some seven miles off the German coast, generally popular as a resort and of special appeal to Prague's Jewish bourgeoisie. For Shakespeare notwithstanding, Bohemia was not a "desert country near the sea," and Norderney happened to be one of the few German seaside resorts not aggressively hostile to affluent Jews, even if they were foreigners.

It was Kafka's first trip abroad, and the long train ride clear across Germany seems to have left far more lasting impressions than his first encounter with an unfamiliar, ominous, and unpredictable element. He was, and remained, a "child of the city," at home in the dark alleys of memory and mind shaped by his singular vision of Prague. The sea, in its vastness, gave him nothing to respond to, and even its menace—he witnessed a violent storm and got seasick on the crossing to the neighboring island of Helgoland—lacked meaning within the exquisitely human dimensions of his fears. Nature on whatever scale was an uncanny universe to him at this stage in his life; he was still the quintessential urban Jew, who couldn't tell a flower from a vegetable.

It became a handicap of sorts which in later years he conscientiously sought to overcome. Zionism, hypochondria, a quasi-Tolstoyan idealization of the peasant as "the true nobleman—the true citizen of the earth," radical rustics à la Hamsun, and Goethe's naturalist passion, along with the living example of his sister Ottla, all combined to inspire earnest efforts on his part to cultivate a healthier, more open attitude toward nature. He took up gardening, hiking, rowing, reported with some enthusiasm on his success in pitching hay and herding sheep, and, by 1916, could assure his fiancée that he had "changed from a city person to a country person."

Yet one suspects that two years earlier, in a letter to Grete Bloch of April 1914, he had been much closer to the truth: "I've always been depressed in the country. What strength it takes to absorb the sight of so broad a landscape. With a Berlin street I can do it in a flash." He taught himself to pay attention to nature, because attention must be paid, for reasons of mental and physical health, moral purity, and Jewish renewal. But true sensitivity cannot be generated by an act of will, and he never really managed to acquire it, on the evidence of his work, where it remains a largely hostile and intrusive element, to be ignored whenever possible. Which, no doubt, was why he "didn't like to live either in the mountains or by the sea—they're both too heroic for my taste."

*   *   *

Some time in the course of that summer, Kafka seems to have had second thoughts about the wisdom of his defiant career choice. By the time he got back to Prague, he had changed his mind and switched his matriculation to chemistry, of all things.

For anyone but Kafka, however, this was not of itself an unreasonable choice. As Hugo Bergmann explains in his memoirs:

> In those days, the situation was such that a Jewish graduate, unless he accepted baptism in order to enter government service, had in fact no other choice but law or medicine, the two professions that offered self-employment. Since these did not interest either Kafka or myself, we looked around for other possibilities and were advised to study chemistry, because there seemed to be employment opportunities for Jews in the chemical industry. We therefore went to the Chemical Institute of the

Prague German University, had an interview with its director, Professor Goldschmied, a baptized Jew, and were duly admitted. Unfortunately, neither of us had given any thought to the fact that chemistry is studied not in books but in a laboratory. We both had trouble with the lab work, because our hands were too clumsy to cope with the glassware. Kafka didn't last long. Shortly after the start of the semester, he switched from chemistry to law, the very subject he had initially despised, though in fact he mainly audited August Sauer's lectures on German literature. I did manage to finish out the year before giving up chemistry and turning to mathematics, physics, and philosophy.

The short-lived revolt against reason, realism, and the mores of the Jewish middle class had thus come to an end, and by November 1901, the future author of *The Trial* was, appropriately enough, busy studying the "Institutions of Roman Law" in the first of his eight semesters at the law school of Ferdinand-Karls University. This rather picturesquely moldy institution had its origins in the University of Prague, founded in 1348; in 1882, the year before Kafka's birth, it was split into parallel Czech and German faculties—a concession to the growing strength of Czech nationalism which, if anything, merely exacerbated the underlying problems. The Czech and German institutions, while still sharing the same medieval buildings, split into opposing camps, two hotbeds of ultranationalist extremism, creating an atmosphere scarcely conducive to high academic standards. In fact, the general level of teaching at the law school was authoritatively described as scandalous.

The student body of the German university, drawn mainly from German enclaves in Bohemia, was predominantly reactionary, with a majority of the 1,350 students organized in patriotic dueling fraternities. Prancing about in flashy uniforms and proudly showing off their facial hashmarks—dueling scars deliberately left unsutured—as proof of tribal loyalty and manly courage, they did their boozy best to provoke street brawls with their young Czech rivals.

Reactionary militancy among students was certainly not unique to Prague. Though briefly in the vanguard of democratic forces, the student movements in Germany and Austria had been brutally and decisively crushed in 1848. Throughout the century that followed, rightwing extremism dominated academic life in both those countries. In stark contrast to the leftist radicalism endemic in much of the world among the privileged and educated young, whose idealism tends to make them rebel against the values and institutions of their parents and their class, German and Austrian students were inclined to honor their fathers and mothers by hating foreigners and Jews.

The situation in Prague, however, was even more acutely exacerbated by the triangular nature of the ethnic conflict, in which political ideology became an integral part of one's personal identity. The "patriotic" German fraternities, linked in an umbrella organization bearing the imaginative name of Germania, largely set the tone in the German half of the university, just as the militant Young Czechs did in the other half.

Though officially forbidden to do so, these fraternities made it a practice to recruit pledges among the graduating high-school seniors and to invite likely prospects to their beer parties. According to Hugo Bergmann, he and Kafka, during their last year at the Gymnasium, once found themselves attending such a meeting, staged by the Altstädter Kollegientag, an ultra-nationalist dueling fraternity, and were forcibly ejected when they refused to rise as the brethren intoned the "Watch on the Rhine," the sacred hymn of Teutomania. What prompted the presence of these two youngsters—both Jewish, one calling himself a Zionist, the other a socialist—at the meeting of a formally anti-Jewish organization is hard to fathom, and Bergmann supplies no clue. Yet, apocryphal or not, the story aptly illustrates social life and student activities at this venerable institution.

By the time classes actually began, however, in the fall of 1901, both Kafka and Bergmann had followed the lead of most German-Jewish students by joining that peculiar and characteristically Prague institution, the Lese- und Redehalle der deutschen Studenten in Prag—the Hall of Lecture and Discourse for German Students in Prague. Founded in 1848 to foster German culture at the university, the Hall, as it was referred to, underwent an involuntary liberalization in 1892, when the pan-German nationalists banded together to found the anti-Jewish and antiliberal Germania, leaving the Hall in a paradoxical situation. On the one hand, it was by all odds the most dynamic and effective center of German culture in Prague, with a library second only to that of the university itself, regular weekly readings by prominent German literary figures, and organized concerts, art exhibits, and discussion groups on various cultural topics. At the same time, its membership—around 450 students in Kafka's day—had become overwhelmingly Jewish.

This may not have been of much concern to the ordinary student member, who joined up mainly for the Hall's social and cultural activities, and for such essential services as subsidized eating clubs, housing, and job contacts. But these innocent and indifferent foot soldiers had no real say in running the affairs of the Hall, even though some of them—including Kafka, Brod, and Pollak—eventually headed certain purely cultural committees. The organization as a whole was tightly controlled by its Board of Governors, a close-knit clique of aspiring politicians bent on establishing a power base for personal advancement. Most were upper-middle-class refugees from Judaism—either converts or vociferous assimilationists prevented by their "tainted" origins from overt identification with the pan-German reactionaries who were their natural constituency, but all the more determined to preserve some semblance of the Teutonic, or at least non-Jewish, character of an organization they had come to regard as their personal fiefdom. On two occasions—in 1904 and again in 1907—the Hall's Board of Governors petitioned the university to ban the Zionist student organization Bar Kochba as detrimental to the German spirit of the institution.

The paradox of the Hall is further compounded by a piquant irony: during the very years in which Franz Kafka participated as a lowly member, the Board of Governors was headed by another member of the family—his second cousin Bruno Kafka, whose ruthless, abrasive, but highly effective stewardship of the Hall foreshadowed his subsequent rise as one of Prague's outstanding lawyers and politicians.

The genetic link between the two was a common great-grandfather, Joseph Kafka. Bruno's father, Moritz, moreover, for many years represented Herrmann Kafka's legal interests. But despite these family connections and undoubtedly frequent encounters at the university and the Hall, Franz and Bruno apparently never had the slightest contact with one another. There is no evidence that Bruno, two years older than Franz, ever deigned to so much as acknowledge the younger cousin's existence, while Franz, in turn, referred to Bruno with the awed respect he invariably reserved for any manifestation of aggressive energy and competence in a man's world.

Yet at some deeper level, the common ancestor clearly lived on in both of them, split into antagonistic opposites of remarkable symmetry. There was the striking family resemblance, to begin with: the same dark eyes and dense, jet-black hair, though Bruno's features were of a much coarser cast, with a mouth frozen in permanent disdain. They were of about equal height, but Bruno's six-foot frame was fleshed out, the corpulent embodiment of vast arrogance and boundless ambition. The subtle self-hatred and complex ambivalence toward Judaism with which Franz struggled all his life were mirrored in Bruno's imperious self-assurance, his baptism, and his scathing hostility to anything relating to Judaism or the Jews.

Bruno Kafka's dazzling display of brilliance undoubtedly cloaked intelligence of a high order; above all, however, he was the consummate manipulator and opportunist. He had whatever talent it takes to teach law and compile a commentary to the criminal code, but his rapid rise in the world owed far more to an instinctive grasp of the link between power and money. His baptism opened the way to a prestigious academic position; his marriage to the daughter of Bohemia's "copper king," Max Bondy, subsequently baptized and born again as Maximilian Bondy, Elder von Bontrop, gave him access to a vast fortune. When this freshly minted knight and father-in-law acquired the German-language newspaper *Bohemia,* Bruno became its editor and publisher, and from this position of strength launched a political career that culminated in his leadership of the German National Democrats, a party he later represented in the Czechoslovak parliament. He died in 1931 at the age of fifty; longevity does not seem to have been among the gifts that great-grandfather Joseph passed on to his descendants.

The ubiquitous and ever-busy Max Brod crossed swords with this mutant Kafka on more than one occasion, starting with Bruno's ascension to the Hall throne, where he used his stranglehold on the organization's finances to curb the activities of Brod's cultural committee, and ending with a confrontation in the first Czech parliament, in which the German National Democrats, heavily dependent on the German-Jewish vote, accused Brod's Zionists of divisive tactics in the cause of racial fanaticism.

The skirmishes of Brod versus Bruno Kafka were in the nature of a duel between a gnat and an elephant, as Brod himself readily acknowledged, moral outrage and romantic idealism being no match for the icy sarcasm and supreme manipulative skills of his opponent. But if history is written by the victors, it is the novelists who rearrange it to suit their needs, and avenging past defeats ranks high among the spurs to creativity. Brod got even in the end by lampooning Bruno Kafka in a *roman à clef,* and by living long enough to see him consigned to oblivion.

Bruno Kafka's contemptuous dismissal of Brod was typical of relations generally between the Hall's politicians and its intellectuals, a distinction based on aspirations and pretensions rather than achievement or ability. The contempt, though cordial and reciprocal, was tempered by a degree of mutual interdependence; it was the intellectuals who, after all, accounted for the Hall's reputation as a center of German culture. The Board of Governors, on the other hand, while proficient at rigging elections, also proved remarkably adept at raising funds and running an organization that deftly combined ward-style politics and student welfare with an Old Boys network. Tangible evidence of Bruno Kafka's own managerial talents was the acquisition, during his reign, of an imposing new building, the expansion of the library, and the sort of prosperity that took the pain out of subsidizing cultural and educational programs.

Given the particular Prague ambience, with its surfeit of actual or self-styled literati of one sort or another, the Hall's "Section for Literature" inevitably became the focal point of its intellectual life, a club within a club dedicated to the worship of literature and the promotion of critical blasphemy. For Kafka, however, it was more than that: a refuge and a revelation, discovered just in the nick of time. The uncharacteristic and rather one-sided intensity of his tie to Oskar Pollak expressed a late-adolescent hunger for contact, the need to break out of his isolation and risk exposure, both as a writer and as an adult human being. In addition to the social aspects, moreover, the Hall also loomed as an oasis in an academic desert infinitely more arid and forbidding even than anything Kafka had experienced at the Gymnasium.

Four of the seven courses for which he registered in his first semester dealt with basic concepts of Roman and German jurisprudence and took up sixteen out of a total of twenty-four weekly lecture hours. The remainder was devoted to a mandatory course in "practical philosophy" and an introduction to the history of German art. Inspired teaching can presumably make even the elementary study of law yield some uplifting results; but Kafka's teachers, from all accounts, were desiccated pedants whose total indifference to their students was surpassed only by their lack of interest in the subject matter itself. Kafka, whose own interest in the legal theories of Roman imperial or Catholic philosophers was minimal at best, felt himself once again drowning in academic miasma; boredom closed in on him like a cloud of poison gas. In the circumstances, the lectures and discussions at the Hall provided much-needed air.

The casual socializing in a benignly civilized atmosphere did a great deal to mitigate the pressures of the law curriculum and contributed to making Kafka's student years relatively bearable. What, if anything the Hall contributed to his intellectual development is much more difficult to assess. The cultural offerings were lively and varied, and he took an active part in organizing the almost weekly readings from, or by, an eclectic group of authors ranging from home-grown talent such as Meyrink, Leppin, Salus, and Werfel to prominent luminaries from abroad. There is no doubt, however, that it was his spirit rather than his intellect that benefited most from these common efforts in congenial company, and that these casual, undemanding contacts did much to lure him out of himself. He never quite overcame his shyness, but he stopped being awkward about it, and his frank vulnerability tended to put people at ease. They felt they could trust him.

The most significant impact, however, the Hall was to have on Kafka's life, his work, and our knowledge of it grew out of one seemingly casual encounter. On October 23, 1902, he attended a lecture on Schopenhauer, given by an eighteen-year-old *Wunderkind*—law student, musician, composer, poet, and embryonic novelist—by the name of Max Brod, who in the course of the discussion referred to Nietzsche as a "fraud." Kafka's objections to this rather intemperate characterization led to a lengthy argument that was to be the beginning of a lifelong friendship quite possibly unique in the history of literature.

*   *   *

Kafka's posthumous fame has all but eclipsed that of the man who was so largely responsible for it. In the English-speaking world, in particular, Brod today is mainly known as Kafka's biographer, faithful friend, and literary executor.

There is, in this one-sided image of him, a melancholy irony which he again lived long enough to appreciate. Kafka, when he died in 1924, was known only to a small circle of friends, whereas Brod, who eulogized him at the graveside, was by then the internationally prominent author of no less than thirty-seven volumes of fiction, poetry, essays, and plays. Himself a composer and performer of some competence, he worked as music critic and feature writer for the *Prager Tagblatt*. Increasingly active in Jewish affairs, he represented the Zionist faction in the Czech parliament. But perhaps the most important services he rendered to the arts transcended his own creative contribution. Brod's most singular talent, in fact, lay in an almost unprecedented combination of critical acumen and generosity of spirit. Jaroslav Hašek's *Švejk* and Leoš Janáček's operas, for instance, owe their worldwide fame largely to Brod's enthusiastic efforts on their behalf. He discovered and promoted the then little-known Carl Nielsen, and his exceedingly practical help to poets and writers he considered unjustly neglected probably has few parallels in the literary cliques and circles of Central Europe, where as a rule one man's success was another man's poison. But forty-four years later, by the time Brod himself died in Tel Aviv in 1968 at the age of eighty-four, his main claim to fame was his link to Kafka—the devoted disciple who, by a breach of faith, had saved his master's work from destruction.

Yet this frail, sickly man had led an amazing life. In addition to his countless articles, essays, translations, and far-flung correspondence, he managed to produce a staggering total of no less than eighty-three books, one for nearly every year of his life. An awe-inspiring feat, even if the quality varied greatly; many were lightweight entertainment, while the theological tomes of his later years had a certain earnest pretentiousness about them; he had discovered God in general, the Jewish God in particular, and he was promoting Him with much the same enthusiasm with which he had once worked on behalf of the likes of Werfel, Janáček, and Hašek. Among an older generation, though, he was still remembered for early works of substance and merit, such as *Tycho Brahe's Path to God, Reubeni, Prince of the Jews,* and his chatty postwar memoirs.

To the world at large, however, he was above all the man who knew Kafka, the man who had twice rescued what became *The Trial* and *The Castle*—once from the author himself, the second time from the Nazis. It was he who edited all the manuscripts unpublished in Kafka's lifetime, i.e., the bulk of what now constitutes the Kafka *oeuvre,* including the diaries and novels, and who wrote the first Kafka biography. (Although several of Brod's novels were translated, this biography, originally published in 1937, has long been the only one of his books available in English.)

The uncertain flame which Brod had so carefully nursed and nurtured thus eventually burst into a conflagration that all but consumed his own original work. And even he, proud though he had every right to be of what he had done for Kafka—a pride of ownership edged, in later years, with prickly contentiousness as the vultures out of academe descended upon what he alone had kept alive—must at times have felt outrage at the wayward tricks of fate and fame. The golem had usurped the place and role of his creator.

Brod had the vision to recognize Kafka's genius long before anyone else had even begun to suspect it. Moreover, at a vulnerable age—barely past adolescence, yet already a published author, gadfly, and celebrity on the culture scene—when condescension or jealousy of a potential rival would have seemed far more likely reactions, he had the grace and moral stature not only to see but to acknowledge Kafka's superiority. He early on came to believe, instinctively and on as yet very slender evidence indeed, that Kafka was to be the most important writer of his time. And as a man who, for better and for worse, always acted on his instincts, impulses, and convictions, he made the friend's success and recognition one of the foremost concerns of his own life.

Chances are that, without Brod, the bulk of Kafka's work would have been lost to the Night and Fog that settled over his world. This was Brod's singular achievement, and one which no critical reservations about his evolving views on Kafka, or his editorship of the posthumous publications, should ever be allowed to obscure.

*   *   *

In a 1938 review of Brod's Kafka biography, Walter Benjamin asserts that "there is little chance of Brod's *Kafka* one day finding its place among the great biographies of poets. . . . But it is the more remarkable as testimony to a friendship which is far from being one of the lesser enigmas of Kafka's existence."

Much as he was at home in the realm of ideas, Benjamin knew next to nothing about live human beings, a total stranger even unto himself. He judged Brod, with merciless rigor, by exalted intellectual standards and inevitably missed the essential truth about him, which happened to be a purely human trait: a zest for life. Brod's perennial optimism was, in fact, an outgrowth of that passionate enjoyment of life, or the capacity for enjoyment in which Kafka, by contrast, was so woefully deficient.

At that, the objective circumstances of Brod's early years seem scarcely conducive to extravagant good cheer. With a mother whose rampant hysteria was inexorably deteriorating into clinical paranoia, and a kindly but ineffectual father who slowly rose from bank clerk to branch office supervisor, home life was certainly more strained, both emotionally and financially, than in the Kafka household. The most tragic blow came with the diagnosis of a life-threatening curvature of the spine when Brod was four years old. Abandoned by the luminaries of the local medical establishment, who considered the case beyond help or hope, his frenzied mother whisked the child off to a miracle healer in Germany's Black Forest. For one entire year, the five-year-old lived with this sullen sorcerer, a shoemaker by trade, who built him a monstrous harness into which he was strapped day and night. The horse cure, though effective to a degree, left Brod with a permanently deformed physique, whose apparent frailty seemed accentuated by the strikingly massive head. That the deformity made for a troubled adolescence may be taken for granted; but if his subsequent promiscuous generosity as a lover was inspired by the need to reaffirm his wholeness, he should have been reassured well into old age by an impressive roster of attractive women who succumbed to his charms, presumably including his wife.

Somehow Brod emerged from all this with the sort of militant optimism which is commonly taken as a measure of faith but which, in his case, clearly preceded it. It was hope—a genetic endowment, a gift from heaven, or the youngster's magic formula for exorcising the evil spirits of the Black Forest—that led him to his special brand of faith, and ultimately to his vision of God. And it was hope that, no doubt, largely accounted for this long and fruitful life in the face of heartbreak, tragedy, and exile. The price he paid for it—with interest and pleasure, one assumes—was a willful avoidance of those murky depths of spirit and soul in which Kafka took up permanent residence.

In insight and outlook, those two young men were, in fact, different past any point of contact, and to that extent Benjamin's bridled disapproval of what he saw as a peculiar friendship seems at least understandable. What he failed to understand, or at any rate to appreciate, was that in their complex totality as human beings, Brod and Kafka were almost exact opposites, and that this very contrast, though it led to friction and, in later years, to a more formal and distant relationship, also formed one of the strongest bonds between them. It certainly accounts for the uncharacteristic spontaneity and openness with which the young Kafka responded from the very beginning to Brod's outgoing personality and combustible enthusiasms, though it took several years before he trusted him enough to confess that he, too, was of the holy order of "writers."

After Kafka's death, however, these same differences began to assume an altogether more problematic significance as Brod undertook the monumental twin tasks of editing and explicating the friend's work. He found in Kafka precisely that which he needed to find—hope for the Jews, hope for the world, and hope for himself. In the wake of a man-made cataclysm that invalidated any and all rational grounds for hope, faith alone could still justify the sort of hope that had always enabled him to live. And in constructing what he regarded as a satisfactory basis for this life-sustaining faith, he drew on Kafka as a source.

*   *   *

At the time of their initial contacts, in the fall of 1902, they were both still in their teens—Kafka, at nineteen, one year older and two semesters ahead of Brod, who was entering law school just as Kafka, in turn, came slinking back into it after another unsuccessful escape attempt.

The inglorious failure of his experiment in chemistry had been punished by six months of legal theory and history, undiluted and indigestible, at the end of which his parched brain seemed to him in danger of crumbling altogether. By the spring of 1902, therefore, having again built up some minimal reserves of courage and despair, he decided to drop the law and switch once more, this time to Germanistics and art history. The choice was again provocatively impractical and met—was perhaps designed to meet—with predictable and indignant opposition on the part of his father, by now volubly distressed at the prospect of having to support an impecunious scholar for the rest of his life. Nonetheless, Kafka's impulse was basically sound— that of a trapped, starving animal wanting to claw its way out and sink its teeth into solid food.

Soon, however, Germanistics also turned to sawdust in his mouth. For one thing, the faculty's most distinguished member, Professor August Sauer, proved a bitter disappointment, though the reasons can only be guessed at; the relevant passages in Kafka's letters to Oskar Pollak were excised by Brod at the time of their publication and must be considered lost. Sauer proclaimed the supremacy of German culture with an aggressive vigor which, given the volatile atmosphere of ethnic tensions, inevitably politicized his lectures and electrified his audiences, the more so since he was also a spellbinding orator. This of itself should have sufficed to antagonize Kafka, ever suspicious of leaders and their followers, and constitutionally incapable of blind devotion. And while, at the time, he probably still shared the prevailing parochial overestimation of German *Kultur,* he was already resolutely opposed to its political manifestations. Above all, though, it was Sauer's intellectualized literary racism and anti-Semitism that must have stirred Kafka's first serious doubts about his place in a language and culture not merely alien but outright hostile.

These doubts were bound to make him reconsider once again what he had let himself in for with this latest change of direction, the more so since his schedule that summer included courses such as New High German syntax, German grammatical and stylistic exercises, the Middle High German poetry of Hartmann von Aue, and the letters of the eighteenth-century critic Gerstenberg—recondite subjects, all of them, and no doubt of scholarly interest, but which must have struck Kafka as not much of an improvement over Contracts or Church Law. He nonetheless briefly contemplated pursuing his studies at the University of Munich, presumably to escape not only Sauer but Prague altogether.

It was to be the second of numerous unsuccessful attempts to flee, to tear himself away from the claws of "the Little Mother." The first one also took place that summer of 1902 and centered on hopes of help from Julie Kafka's brother, Alfred Löwy, the legendary "uncle from Madrid," an affluent and well-connected bachelor who had risen to the post of director general of the Spanish railways. It, too, failed, as Kafka reported in a letter to Oskar Pollak:

> The uncle from Madrid (director of railways) was here; that is why I also returned to Prague. Shortly before his arrival I conceived the odd, unfortunately very odd idea of asking him to help me find a way out of this mess, to direct me somewhere where I could finally make a fresh start. Well, I began cautiously; no need to go into details. He started unctuously to pontificate, though he is normally a rather nice person, offered his sympathy, well, well. Forget it. I shut up at once, actually without quite wanting to; and although we kept company throughout the two days which I was spending in Prague for his sake, I never again alluded to the subject. He is leaving tonight. I am still going to Liboch for a week, then for another week to Triesch, then back

again to Prague, and on to Munich to study. Yes, to study.
[L, 8/24/02]

Triesch was a Moldavian village near the town of Iglau, Kafka's peaceable kingdom, where his favorite Uncle Siegfried, another of Julie Kafka's brothers, practiced as a country doctor. (He killed himself on the eve of his deportation to Terezin in 1942.) An eccentric, diffident, book-loving bachelor, Dr. Löwy was the only relative beyond the immediate family with whom Kafka maintained lifelong close ties. The crusty Uncle Doctor, with his broad range of interests, rational skepticism, and wayward sense of humor was himself, one suspects, in hiding from a world he found less than alluring; and though he struck others as cold and aloof, he was perhaps the only adult figure in Kafka's childhood who, in his undemonstrative way, conveyed something akin to paternal sympathy and understanding.

Kafka to the end of his life was to spend many of his vacations in Triesch, whose landscape imperceptibly merged with an idyllic vision of rural tranquillity forever beyond his grasp. In the course of time, he undoubtedly came to realize that a deadly undertow lurked below the deceptively tranquil surface, and that Uncle Siegfried, too, was caught up in it, another complicated urban Jew who did not know how to live. Nonetheless, the immense peace of the countryside in the days before electricity and internal combustion, combined with the undemanding presence of the closest he ever came to an accepting and competent father figure, never failed to restore his spirits.

The stay in Munich, however, lasted only a few days. For whatever reasons—Uncle Siegfried's advice, his father's objections, the atmosphere of the city itself, or his fatal involvement with Prague and everything it represented—Kafka dropped the original plan, gave up on Germanistics, and, for his third semester, returned home, resigned at last to his fate and settling down in earnest to the task of becoming a lawyer, as befitted a prospective member of the Jewish middle class not otherwise endowed with marketable skills.

Eight

IF resignation connotes growth, Kafka had matured by the fall of 1902. It was obvious by then that his attempts to get away from Prague, to put some distance between himself and his parents, and to escape the mortification of the Law in all its gruesome variants, had ended in failure. They were halfhearted attempts lacking conviction, though stage-managed with a somnambulist aplomb bordering on genius. In any event, he accepted these failures as somehow pre-ordained and, during the remaining five semesters, settled down to the dreary struggle of getting his law degree.

It proved a challenge, at least to his nerves and his powers of memory. The intellectual and academic level of what, at the time, was a minor provincial law school seems to have fallen considerably short of even the far from exalted standards prevailing in the more prestigious institutions of the empire. Contemporary critics characterized them as shocking, a judgment concurred in by several of its more illustrious alumni, who eventually managed to rise above the handicap of their inauspicious debut.

An institution, however, is shaped by its function. The purpose of this German law school, operating in an alien and increasingly hostile environment, was to turn out cadres of bureaucrats equipped to enforce centralized power in peripheral outposts of the empire. And in this task, which imposed no great strain on mediocre minds, it appears to have been reasonably successful.

Minds other than mediocre, on the other hand, were bound to suffer; memorizing a telephone directory would probably have seemed less of a torture to Kafka than tangling with the mummified abstractions of canon law or the civil code, embalmed in glutinous legalese. Instruction consisted exclusively of formal lectures, with few seminars or discussions. Attendance was mandatory, the more so since the inevitable finals necessitated copious and continuous note taking in every course.

International law, in Kafka's third semester, was taught by one Josef Ulbrich, whose claim to immortality rests on his having compiled an *Austrian Encyclopedia of Administrative Terms*. Kafka's fellow student Guido Kisch, later an eminent jurist, left a portrait of this luminary in action: "I can still see him sitting on the dais, with his chalky, bloodless face forever unshaven, sloppily dressed, head bowed, eyes glued to the top of his desk and never once looking up. What little one might have picked up in his excruciatingly boring lectures was even further reduced by his disconcerting habit of simply not showing up for class, without advance notice or formal cancellation." (The most likely explanation for Professor Ulbrich's unkempt appearance, distracted manner, and frequent unexplained absences seems never to have occurred to Kisch or any of his fellow students; in their generation, alcoholism was virtually unknown among Jews.)

It was during the spring semester of 1903 that Kafka had his first sexual encounter. Sheer reckless despair may have been what finally drove him over the edge to which he had so long been clinging in a state of petrified panic; syphilis or death by lightning must have seemed vastly preferable to slow suffocation by Roman law, which happened to be the subject of a comprehensive examination marking the midpoint of the four-year program. He passed the tests with rather high marks, but the effort was alleged to have left him spent to the point of necessitating a two-week "nature cure" at the White Deer Sanatorium near Dresden, Germany.

There is, on the face of it, something faintly absurd about a physically healthy twenty-year-old choosing to recuperate in a sanatorium from the rigors of an exam. Whether this particular "nervous breakdown"—there were to be many more such episodes later on—could actually be ascribed to overwork and fear of failure, or whether it was triggered by deep-seated conflicts related to Kafka's sexual initiation, remains an open question. But the headlong flight back into childhood, into a voluptuous infantilization made respectable by bearing the label of therapy, set a pattern; long before actual illness validated his lurid hypochondria, Kafka time and again sought refuge from friends, family, and demons in these emotional hothouses, where sickness both real and imaginary was cultivated as a way of life.

He spent the rest of that summer vacationing with his family in southern Bohemia and, in a letter to Oskar Pollak, admits to having had a reasonably happy time: "I've grown healthier (today I'm not feeling so well), I've grown stronger, I spend much time among people, I can talk to women—all this must be said here. But as for miracles, the summer didn't bring any."

* * *

The second half of his studies, beginning with the winter semester of 1903–4, produced no miracles, either. The subject matter, however, seemed less dull. He had competent instructors in economics, statistics, commercial and constitutional law; but the two figures dominating that segment of his academic career were Horaz Krasnopolski and Hans Gross.

Krasnopolski was an influential legal scholar who believed in the unchallengeable supremacy of the Austrian Civil Code as a sacred text and guide to daily living. No mental giant he, but an obsessive collector of legalistic snares, traps, and fishhooks, to one of which he, in fact, owed his professorship. When Franz Brentano, the ex-priest and Vienna professor of philosophy, began to attract unwelcome attention with theological doctrines deemed subversive by the imperial authorities, he was exiled to the University of Prague, where he continued his work and again acquired a devoted and enthusiastic following. It was young Krasnopolski who provided the sanctimonious justification for removing the troublemaker permanently from the scene: the chastity vows of priesthood, in his interpretation, were legally binding for life, regardless of subsequent defection from the calling or even outright apostasy; as an ex-priest, Brentano had violated both canon and civil law by getting married. However dubious a piece of legalistic legerdemain, it earned Krasnopolski a full professorship in Prague, where he was eventually succeeded by Bruno Kafka. Brentano, who spent the rest of his life in Florence (he died in 1917), became the object of a budding cult and, in Kafka's day, was still being venerated in Prague by a devoted group of disciples.

Nevertheless, in spite of his defects, or perhaps because of them, Krasnopolski turned out to be an inspired if thunderous lecturer, probably the only member of the law faculty who took his job seriously.

This, however, also made him a fierce and dreaded examiner. At Kafka's finals in civil law, three out of four professors voted for a passing grade; Krasnopolski was the lone dissenter.

A more complex and fascinating character was Professor Hans Gross, who after years of practical experience as an investigative judge in Graz took over the chair of criminal justice and legal philosophy at Prague University in 1902. Gross was considered one of the founders of scientific criminology; his *Handbook for Investigative Judges, Policemen, and Gendarmes*, first published in 1893, remained for decades the standard bible of police work, translated into every European language. But while he also pioneered the use of police dogs, his most innovative contribution was an emphasis on the criminal rather than on the crime; legal education, in his view, had to transcend mere knowledge of the law and concern itself with the psychology of the criminal.

It was this perspective, dramatized by examples from Gross's extensive practical experience, that made him one of the few truly popular and effective lecturers. Kafka himself devoted the major share of three semesters to courses taught by Gross. They offered fascinating glimpses of detective work and investigative procedures, and several critics claim to have discovered not only traces of these lectures but features of the professor himself in both *The Trial* and *The Castle*. True or not, Gross was to leave a very personal though indirect impression that may have been even more significant.

Whatever his psychological sophistication in matters criminal, the Herr Professor as a father proved to be no less vulnerable and obtuse than most, with one important difference: here was one authoritarian who, when it came to his own son, had the means to enforce his authority and did not hesitate to do so.

His son Otto, six years older than Kafka, had been a brilliant student of psychology. But instead of embarking on an academic career in conformity with his father's wishes, he went to Vienna and, in 1904, gained entrance to Freud's inner circle with what Ernest Jones referred to as a "remarkable paper on psychoanalysis." Freud himself, according to Jones, at one point expressed the opinion that Gross and Jung were the only original minds among his followers. Gross's originality, however, soon developed bizarre features and, by 1908, had tipped over into florid schizophrenia complicated by morphine addiction. Jung, in a burst of messianic energy, dedicated himself to curing his colleague; the results, palliative at best, were constantly being undermined by the outraged father, who time and again exploited his standing with the courts and the police to have his son committed to mental institutions. This paternal concern degenerated into a process of extended brutalization and became a *cause célèbre* among libertarians, left-leaning politicians, avant-garde writers and artists, who saw in it an abuse of power symbolic of the generational conflict between authoritarian repression and intellectual freedom.

It was not until 1917 that Kafka actually met the son of his former teacher. By then, Otto Gross flaunted the twin halos of martyr and revolutionary, more wildly original—and far more unstable—than ever. Nevertheless, he was a fascinating companion, and their at one point fairly close contact must have added substantially to Kafka's information about Freud, however tainted the source. For a while Gross, Kafka, and Werfel seriously planned the joint publication of a magazine, but financial difficulties aborted the project. Gross Senior died in 1915, unforgiving and unforgiven; his son committed suicide three years later.

*   *   *

Despite better teachers and more interesting material, Kafka's grades during the last four semesters underwent a spectacular downward slide that came close to ending in disaster, real this time rather than imaginary. Inner conflicts contributed their share to this as to all his problems, but there were some obvious and, on the whole, positive reasons for his progressive slippage as a test-taker and budding legal scholar. Thanks to his membership in the Hall and to his friendship with Brod and Přibram, he was being drawn into a rather active and extensive social life, which took up a sizable portion of his time and energy. This, in turn, served to stimulate his interest in a range of subjects light-years removed from the "sawdust" he was obliged to masticate by way of preparing for the mandatory examinations. In addition, he quietly, surreptitiously, but persistently continued to struggle with his own writing.

The predictable result was another *crise de nerfs,* or rather, a failure of nerve. In July 1905, some weeks before the end of the semester, he once again sought refuge in a sanatorium, and this time the month-long cure at Zuckmantl, in Silesia, evidently met needs deeper than mere physical rest. Though he forever after remained resolutely discreet about his affair with an older woman—Max Brod deciphered her signature on a picture postcard as something like

"Ritschi Grade"—the memory of that fleetingly unambiguous happiness, derived from what was probably a quasi-maternal affection more than anything else, remained with him for life. Years later—in 1916—he was to write: "Actually, I was never on intimate terms with a woman, except for those two times—in Zuckmantl (but she was a woman, and I was a boy), and in Riva (but there she was half a child, and I hopelessly confused, sick in every sense conceivable)." The relationship was resumed the following summer, when Kafka again spent a month in Zuckmantl, and its echo, though already muffled by ambivalence, sounds the basic theme of "Wedding Preparations in the Country," written in the spring of 1907.

*   *   *

With his return to Prague in the fall of 1905 began the final assault on the uppermost ramparts of futility: preparation for the comprehensive orals—the *Rigorosa*—constituting the qualifying test for the doctoral degree. (The Doctor of Laws required no written dissertation.) It was a period of relentless cramming, months in which "under considerable nervous strain" Kafka "intellectually fed on sawdust which, moreover, had already been pre-chewed by thousands of other mouths." After passing the first trial—*Rigorosum II*—on November 7 with three votes out of four, he again lost his nerve and toyed with the idea of getting a medical dispensation. But with the aid of Brod's meticulous notes, he managed to scrape by *Rigorosum III* on March 13, 1906, with three votes out of five. The concluding *Rigorosum I* (the numerical sequence honored tradition rather than common sense), for which he studied daily from six in the morning until late into the night, took place on June 13, and his zeal was rewarded: all five examiners unanimously passed him. At the graduation ceremonies on June 18, 1906, Kafka was awarded the degree of Doctor of Laws.

It was, on the whole, an undistinguished and inconspicuous academic career, rather in keeping with the intellectual level of the doctoral program itself. "Even conservative academic circles," noted an anonymous contemporary commentator in the *Prager Tagblatt,* "can no longer deny the fact that in Austria today no particular qualifications are required to obtain the degree of Doctor of Laws, and that these requirements have for the most part become empty formalities, so that the newly created doctor remains largely innocent of knowledge in any subject."

The observation, though probably accurate, was also irrelevant in that for most students—Kafka included—the doctorate simply signified a modest means to a modest end, i.e., the prerequisite for medium-level entry into governmental or semiprivate bureaucracies. Kafka, for one, never had any intention of practicing law; at the same time, it is intriguing to speculate on the extent to which those four years of relentless exposure to legal prose and legalistic thinking left their stamp on his later work.

But if unrewarding intellectually, the university years were also relatively untraumatic as the omnipotent ogres who had ruled the Gymnasium gave way to remote, self-important, often rather ridiculous mortals, and the sharp terror of the high-school classroom yielded to the impersonal boredom of the lecture hall. (Creative boredom, in a way, to which we owe most of Kafka's sketches that have been preserved. Tossed off in the margins of his lecture notes, these doodles were avidly collected by Max Brod, moving testimony to the intensity of Brod's admiration for Kafka even in those early days of their friendship.)

The fact is that Kafka's student years, roughly between the ages of eighteen and twenty-five, coincided with another spurt in his emotional and intellectual development; and if the studies as such contributed little, they also did not—despite the occasional crises—significantly inhibit his growth or interfere with his private pursuits.

It was a time, to begin with, when he seemed determined to break down some of the walls of what he perceived as his prison—the parental lair, the suffocating parochialism of Prague, the penitentiary routines of formal schooling, the cash-register mentality of middle-class Jews, and above all his own crippling fears and what he felt to be a lack of spontaneity, an inability to make contact with the expanding universe around him. In short, he wanted to be, not quite like everybody else— he always knew better than that—but enough like them to feel at ease in his own skin. An acceptable role model eluded him, as it had since earliest childhood; his lifelong passion for biographical and confessional literature, from straight biographies and autobiographies to memoirs, diaries, journals, and collected letters, probably derived from that hopeless but never-abandoned quest.

Yet it is also true that he was at least partly successful. By the time he met Brod, at the start of the third semester, his friendship with Oskar Pollak had already cooled considerably. The two were beginning to draw apart and go their separate ways; but the adolescent ardor and intensity of Kafka's initial attachment had been a vital first step beyond the periphery of self-involvement, and it enabled him to outgrow both his shyness and his jealousy. Though his inner picture of himself remained unchanged, it began to diverge significantly from the impression he made on most of those who met him at the university and in the intersecting social circles he came to frequent with increasing regularity.

Even discounting the pungent odor of incense that inevitably tends to infest hagiographic eulogies, all descriptions of Kafka by his contemporaries unanimously stress a quality as irresistible as it was difficult to define—a striking combination of innate nobility and tact. It was a blind man, the novelist Oskar Baum, who may have seen it most clearly. In describing their first meeting in the fall of 1904, he recalls the profound impression made on him by Kafka's first gesture as he entered the room.

> He knew he was in the presence of a blind man. Yet as Brod was introducing him, he silently bowed. A pointless formality in my particular case, one would have thought, since I was after all unable to see it. But because I bowed in turn, somewhat too abruptly, his smoothly parted hair fleetingly touched my forehead. And I felt moved in a way which at that moment I could not immediately account for. Here was the *first* of all human beings I had ever met who, rather than making allowances for my disability by being considerate or in any way departing from his normal behavior, treated it as something that regarded no one but myself. That was what he was like. That was the effect of his simple and natural remoteness from conventional formalities. The human depth of his severe, cool reserve far transcended kindness of the conventional sort, such as the pointlessly emphatic cordiality in words, voice, and handshake which otherwise I regularly had to put up with on being introduced to people for the first time. [Brod, bio., p. 96]

The peculiar magic by which, with no apparent effort on his part, he earned the instant respect of even casual acquaintances and, in not a few instances, the lifelong devotion of dedicated friends, stands out in stark contrast to the assiduously cultivated self-image of the un-attractive, brooding loner. Yet the apparent contradictions are largely a matter of perspective. Thus what he experienced as inarticulate awk-wardness—"never, never shall I be able to toss big words around like giant boulders"—was seen by others as cool reserve; in a crowd of logorrheic intellectuals, Kafka stood out as the one man who spoke only when he had something to say. The rare considerateness, empathy, and tact so universally praised not only by friends but also by col-leagues, servants, cleaning women, children, grew out of his ritualistic defense against the accursed shyness, the fear of strangers, the ever-present sense of guilt toward any social inferiors, and toward all non-Jews generally. Finally, the nagging and recurrently overwhelming sense of failure made for conspicuous modesty in an environment in which vanity, ego inflation, and opportunism were notoriously endemic. For instance, it took Brod, already a published author and surrounded by pretentious literati of every ilk and variety, over two years to find out, more or less by accident, that this remarkable new friend of his also happened to be writing stories.

Of course, there was more to it; Kafka had assets of which he was seldom, if ever, aware—striking good looks (he hated the sight of himself in the mirror, was ashamed of his tall, slender body, that rattling pile of bones with no trace of living flesh), boyish charm (in his mid-thirties, at the beach, people still mistook him for a gawky teenager), an offbeat sense of humor, and vast reserves of down-to-earth common sense, rarely invoked on his own behalf but of inestimable help to many a friend in need.

Most of all, though, it was his unworldliness to which people re-sponded—with awe, love, irritation, but always out of an awareness of hidden depths, an uneasy sense of his having strayed into their own time and place by some accident or miracle that baffled him as much as anyone else. The cavernous solitude of his secret existence, though hardly suspected, made itself felt in the most trivial gesture of his public persona. He was struggling to live, or at least to survive, in two worlds at once: the middle-class Jewish law student in turn-of-the-century Prague, and the underground hermit pursued by the timeless mystery of his inexplicable existence. And as a student he still clung to the belief that these two worlds were distinct and separate places, that the differ-ence between heaven and hell was more than just one of words and that, given the strength, he could escape from one to the other.

Nine

" WHEN one was with him, one had a strong feeling that nothing common and vulgar really existed. Saints and founders of religions are said to have had a similar effect on people, and my association with Kafka has convinced me that such reports have a basis in fact" (Brod, bio., p. 50).

Thus Brod, commemorating the dead friend. What he found in the living Kafka, however, was a father figure, to begin with, and despite the apparent incongruities, it is easy enough to see how the volatile nineteen-year-old coffeehouse celebrity succumbed to an authentically independent mind. Their very first encounter, in a sense, foreshadowed their subsequent relationship: the brash, bright, diminutive teenager denouncing Nietzsche as a fraud, and the earnest, ironic apprentice lawyer, impeccable no doubt as always in dress and demeanor, politely but firmly demolishing such juvenile bombast.

Reciprocal needs forge powerful bonds between people. What Kafka, for his part, sought—and in large measure found—in Brod was both simpler and more complicated at once: a link to the real world, in the here and now. (That Brod would eventually turn out to be his link to the future as well was something he could hardly have foreseen or hoped for, if hope it was.) This frail and deformed youngster with his demonic energy and indestructible optimism seemed to possess the secret not only of how to survive but of how to celebrate survival. He loved people, loved to surround himself with people, be at the center of things, ever ready to admire, yet craving admiration in turn.

There was a dark side to Brod, to his frenzied activity, his relentless exuberance and compulsive sociability. Precocious, brilliant, and facile, he spread himself thin, forced the growth of his many talents, and gave none of them a chance to ever fully mature. He dazzled by his versatility as a writer, critic, musician, organizer, politician, lover, philosopher, performing well enough in all these roles yet ultimately falling short of his potential in most of them.

He had, however, trained himself to look strictly at the bright side, and his scrupulous avoidance of introspection was among the traits that most endeared him to the compulsively introspective Kafka. Far from blind to what Brod so stubbornly chose to ignore about himself, Kafka nonetheless loved him for his spontaneous generosity, his lively mind, and his unstinting admiration. And it was largely Brod who lured Kafka out of a solitary confinement from which he had struggled to escape without quite knowing how to go about it. For one thing, he introduced Kafka to his friends, with initially rather ambiguous results. Aside from being jealous, diffident, afraid of strangers, Kafka was also in many ways hopelessly clear-eyed, and many of the epigones with whom Brod had surrounded himself struck him as dubious company. "In part they depend on you, in part they are independent. To the extent to which they are dependent, they surround you like a responsive mountain range with an ever-ready echo. . . . But to the extent to which they are independent, they hurt you even more in that they distort you, put you into a false situation" (L, p. 24).

A plea and protest as well as an accurate observation; but Brod had no talent for monogamy in any form. And by including Kafka in his circle—in the innermost of many concentric circles, in fact—he enabled him to meet a great many people close to him in age and interests, and to form the kind of casual relationships that drew him out of his isolation but stopped short of threatening intimacy.

The group initially comprised several of Brod's classmates from the Piarist Gymnasium, but the only figure of more than transitory interest was the English teacher Emil Weiss, Brod's somewhat older relative and ardent admirer. Weiss, a fierce-looking redhead, was a temperamental Anglophile with an infectious enthusiasm for English literature and the English language, subjects which at the time in German-oriented Central Europe were regarded as strictly esoteric. He gave dramatic readings of Shakespeare, Byron, and Shaw, and it was probably his influence that led Kafka at one point, around 1906, to study English. That is to say, he acquired a textbook edition of Macaulay's *Lord Clive of India*, enough to deter even a linguistically more gifted student; nevertheless, on his job applications in 1907, Kafka listed a "fair" knowledge of English as one of his qualifications.

Of far more lasting importance, however, were Brod's friends Felix

Weltsch and Oskar Baum, both of whom Kafka first met in 1903. The foursome soon formed a tight nucleus within the larger grouping and, for a number of years, became inseparable companions, meeting regularly at least once a week to read, discuss, and criticize one another's work, going on long hikes together in the environs of Prague, patronizing some of the reputedly more hygienic *établissements,* and intrepidly tackling the ultimate questions of life and of art.

Beyond a common background and a broad range of common interests, all four shared an awareness of being handicapped, hence different—Brod and Baum in outwardly obvious ways, Weltsch and Kafka in less apparent but perhaps more crucial ones. Each derived emotional support and creative stimulus from this quadrilateral comradeship, none more so than Kafka, until the marriages of first Baum, then Brod, and finally Weltsch transformed the easy camaraderie of their bachelor days into more formal relations.

In his memoirs, Brod piously insists that the wives came to be included, and so indeed they were—vying with each other as to who could bake a better cake for their get-togethers. His condescending gallantry is one of the more irritating manifestations of his essential misogyny. In this, however, he was not alone. The sexual myths and social realities of his time, which victimized men as much as women, made unambiguous friendships between them exceedingly difficult, almost as rare in this particular class as a genuine and lasting marital relationship. All three of these marriages, in fact, were in trouble almost from the start, but this merely placed further strain on the ties among the men.

Nevertheless, the four remained close friends for life, and there is little doubt that, during Kafka's student years, these friendships provided the strength that allowed him to come out of his shell and lead what, at least in his companions' view, resembled a normal existence. They, too, lived with their parents, as did most grown children until marriage, no matter how rebellious or disdainful of the older generation. Unlike Kafka, though, they were all three of them prolific writers rapidly gaining recognition, a fact that initially must have seemed rather depressing to him. It took him nearly three years before he could bring himself to let the friends in on his own addiction to writing; by then, however, he felt sufficiently at ease with this audience to read regularly from work in progress. What he received in return was precisely the sort of enthusiastic response, informed criticism, and intelligent encouragement he needed at that stage in his creative development.

Brod's role has been discussed. It underwent major changes over the years, but during that early period of their friendship, his quick sympathy, practical proposals, and sheer exuberant vitality pulled Kafka time and again out of the recurrent depressive episodes which, in his case, assumed the agonizing form of total creative paralysis.

Weltsch and Baum, however, each in his own way, were hardly less important to him in his erratic, desperate, but persistent quest for the kind of hope, redemption, and peace from which he felt that he alone among men had been excluded. Although Weltsch, one year younger than Kafka, had also attended the Altstädter Gymnasium, the two had never met; a one-year gap in a German high school was a distance between planets. Extraordinarily gifted, many-faceted, and conscientious, he was by far the most broadly knowledgeable and most rigorously logical of the four. He subsequently came to be one of the outstanding personalities in contemporary Judaism, yet he remained modest and shy to the point of self-effacement, not unlike Kafka in his pseudo-timidity, and with much the same wry humor that masked the often savage ferocity of self-destructive impulses.

Weltsch, too, was a law student rather in spite of himself, and after obtaining his law degree in 1907, he spent another four years getting his doctorate in philosophy—proof of tenacity, but also an exercise in futility when it came to earning a living. After collecting his second doctorate in 1911, he was forced to take a subordinate job as librarian at Prague University, which he held until his emigration to Palestine in 1938. In Jerusalem, he worked at the Hebrew University library until his death in 1964 at the age of eighty.

The quiet, methodical efficiency with which he managed every aspect of his life, both private and public, made him an ideal librarian; in fact, he made a major contribution to the esoteric art of cataloguing and eventually became head of the bookbinding department. Despite a miserable salary—barely enough to support a wife and daughter—and the inveterate anti-Semitism of his superiors, the undemanding job allowed him to concentrate his energies in more vital areas. The publication, in 1913, of *Perception and Concept* signaled the start of a substantial philosophical *oeuvre* that included titles such as *Grace and Freedom, The Riddle of Laughter, The Venture of the Middle*, and *Religion and Humor in the Work of Franz Kafka*. They reflect, on the one hand, an unswerving but increasingly unpopular commitment to the vulnerable center equally opposed to all radical extremes and, on the other, his growing preoccupation with Judaism and Zionism.

Despite a generally respectful reception, however, his books failed to elicit the response he had hoped for from professional philosophers, whose monumental indifference left a deep and lasting hurt. For all his ironic detachment, the note of bitterness is hard to miss in this 1922 letter to Hugo Bergmann:

> Philosophy—I don't like to touch on that wound. My job and my family life make it absolutely impossible for me to work in the realm of philosophy, and yet I am dying to do so. Among the Czechs, all sorts of people get to be professors, yet for me it would have been impossible even had I tried to go that route. It would have been hopeless. Above all, one has to earn money, and philosophy offers no chance for that. *Grace and Freedom* received some nice notices, but I now realize that a philosophical book can have an impact on the world of philosophy only if it was written by a "disciple," or by one who himself has disciples. . . . I am waiting for a miracle that would once again free me to work. A fragment of my critique of Brentano's *Sanction of Ethics* may be published in the Czech *Journal of Philosophy*. Altogether, as a philosopher I am better known among the Czechs than among the Germans.

What Weltsch failed to achieve among the world's philosophers he more than made up for among the Jews of Prague, where after World War I he became one of the leading figures. In terms of his innermost aspirations, the growing influence he exerted between 1918 and 1938 as editor of the *Selbstwehr—Self-Defense,* the German-language Zionist weekly published in Prague—may have been a booby prize of sorts, scant compensation for the standing that eluded him among his professional colleagues. But this in no way detracts from the immense practical importance of his work during the critical last phase of European Jewry.

*   *   *

There was a resemblance even in their physical appearance. Both Kafka and Weltsch were gangling near-six-footers, with a gait so similar that from a distance they were often mistaken for each other.

More to the point, though, was the easy, comfortable intimacy that developed between them, a rare luxury for both those otherwise so diffident and distant individualists. Kafka never laughed as much as he did with Weltsch, and it was Weltsch who first stressed the role of humor in Kafka's work—gallows humor spiked with desperation, but liberating for them both.

Their relationship to Oskar Baum, however, whom they both met through Brod, was of a different nature altogether. Congenitally blind in one eye, Baum—born, like Kafka, in 1883—lost the sight in the other eye at the age of eleven in his native Pilsen, in one of the routine street brawls between patriotic Czech and "German" high-school pupils. Shortly after this tragic accident, he was shipped off to the Vienna Jewish Home for the Blind, a residential institution where he spent his entire adolescence getting the kind of training deemed suitable for the visually handicapped.

He came out of that experience with a blazing hatred of all coercive institutions, professional philanthropists, and self-appointed guardians of the blind, an attitude which—as he noted in one of his novels—merely confirmed said guardians' a priori conviction that all blind people were by nature ungrateful. They certainly had ample reason to feel that way about Baum, who, in addition to the regular training in Braille and other survival skills, also received a thoroughly professional musical education in keeping with his special gifts. But in his view, the smugness of his benefactors far outweighed their competence. His early novels were a powerful protest against the condescension and—at best —pity with which the helpers treated the helpless and robbed them of their dignity.

Baum was a fighter by nature, tall and well built, extraordinarily good-looking, and, in marked contrast to his three friends, totally devoid of self-pity, not a blind man, but a man who happened to be blind, yet otherwise far more secure in his masculine self-confidence than his sighted companions. Women quite literally fought over him; he achieved financial independence, got married, and fathered a child while the others were still living with, and off, their parents.

Baum's early writings made him a leader in the movement to reform the treatment of the blind; but his demand for justice in place of pity, for equality instead of institutionalized philanthropy, led him further afield, and for the rest of his life he remained an exemplary spokesman for human rights in general. He wrote a number of sensitive, reasonably successful novels and made his living first as a piano teacher and an organist, later as one of Prague's outstanding music critics. After the Nazi occupation in 1939, he helped to organize the escape of Czech Jews and anti-Nazi refugees. He died in March 1941 in a Prague hospital; his wife was deported shortly thereafter and killed at Terezin. Their son reached Palestine, only to be killed there in a Jewish terrorist attack.

*   *   *

Kafka's relationship to Baum, however, was far more circumspect than the comfortable familiarity he at times achieved with Weltsch and Brod. It took some ten years before he dropped the formal second person plural and switched from *"Sehr geehrter Herr Baum"* to "Dear Oskar," a clear indication of the need or desire to maintain a certain distance. Baum, he once told Brod, frightened him, and the reasons are not hard to guess; the blind prodigy not only made it awkward for Kafka to feel sorry for himself but also set a consistently depressing example of discipline and strength. It was only in his novels and occasional poetry that one catches undertones of the immense pain and stark desperation so admirably kept under control but which, in the final analysis, may have made Baum more subtly responsive to Kafka's troubled being and troubling work than his more intimate friends.

What [Baum wrote in his reminiscences (*Almanach, 1902– 1964*)] can I tell strangers about Kafka? Those who did not know him may never be able to imagine a human being so singular in his ultimate essence. Even his most trivial reflex contained something of this most personal quality. He never condemned, he merely noted the facts. Without hatred or squeamishness, but also without romanticizing sentimentality, he went right to the skeletal frame of every soul, every event, every situation. . . . With unequaled vision he examined, demystified, revealed the authentic core of the inner life—his own, and that of others. By nature he was a fanatic full of luxuriating fantasy, but he kept its glow in check by constantly striving toward strict objectivity. To overcome all cloying or seductive sentimental raptures and fuzzy-minded fantasizing was part of his cult of purity—a cult quasi-religious in spirit, though often eccentric in its physical manifestations. He created the most subjective imagery, but it had to manifest itself in the form of utmost objectivity.

Early in 1918 I spent eight days with him in Zuerau, a village snowbound at the time, where his courageous sister was managing a farm. During those long nights, in talks lasting into the early morning, I learned more about him than in the ten years before, and in the five that remained. Perhaps I may some day succeed in conveying a picture of his bitter and morbid state of mind at the time. Of the many plans and projects he talked about in the course of those nights—without any hope, without even any intention of ever realizing them—I want to mention only one fantastic little story: a man wants to make it possible for people to get together without being formally invited, just to see others, to talk to them, observe them without getting involved in any close relationships. Anyone can come and go as he pleases, with no obligation, and is yet made to feel welcome without any hypocrisy. And in the end, the reader realizes that this attempt to conquer the loneliness of human beings is nothing more or less than the invention of the first coffeehouse.

* * *

Many were the nights [wrote Brod (bio., p. 103)] we spent together in theaters, cabarets, or in wine taverns in the company of pretty girls. For as it happens, the picture of Kafka as some sort of desert monk or anchorite is totally misleading; at least, it most certainly does not apply to his student years. And later? Later on, what he wanted out of life was too much rather than too little—either perfection, or nothing at all. This, it is true, led him to steer clear of casual love affairs and to take all matters erotic with the utmost seriousness. Thus he would never tell a dirty joke or even tolerate one being told in his presence. Not that he would ever stop anyone; it was simply that no one would ever have thought of doing it in his presence. His whole being was a quest for purity.

In those early years of his youth, however, this stern attitude had not yet crystallized quite so explicitly. Thus I remember his passion for a barmaid named Hansi, about whom he once said that entire cavalry regiments had ridden on her body. Franz was quite unhappy in this liaison, a fact patently evident on a photograph that shows him together with Hansi, and on which he looks as if he wanted nothing so much as to run away. A diary entry of mine notes: Trocadéro Tavern. That's where Franz has fallen in love with the "Germania" on the German postal stamp. *Chambre séparée.* But he is so weirdly reticent. When he tells her that he'd set her up in a place of her own, he laughs as though he meant it ironically.

The characteristically dithyrambic tone that marks Brod's reminiscences of those early years with Kafka probably owes a great deal to nostalgia and piety.

I admired Franz's skill in swimming and rowing; he was particularly good at handling what we called the "soul-drowner." He always outdid me in dexterity and daring, and he had a special knack for leaving people to their own devices just in particularly tricky situations—this with an almost cruel smile meant to convey something like "God helps those who help themselves." How I loved that smile, which also contained so much confidence and encouragement. Franz, it seemed to me, was indefatigable when it came to inventing new athletic feats— this, too, an aspect of his personality pursued, as he pursued everything else, with total dedication.

One suspects that Brod's own personality and rust-resistant good cheer may have somewhat colored his recollections of the youthful Kafka's demonstrative normality. Typical of both style and mood is Brod's rhapsodic diary entry of January 1, 1906: "With Kafka. How beautiful life is. We were in a downright divine mood. Later with Přibram. Then we tossed snowballs at Weltsch's window, and at midnight he came down to join us."

Brod remains one of the most authentic witnesses to Kafka's life, his testimony backed by abundant documentation. Yet the picture he gives us is fragmentary at best, and Kafka himself was acutely sensitive to the vulnerability that made Brod shy away—wisely or instinctively —from uncharted depths and contagious depression. In Brod's presence he therefore made every effort to be witty, worldly, and related; whenever he couldn't muster the requisite strength, he simply stayed away, sometimes for weeks at a time. But it is to Brod's credit to have inspired those efforts to the point where they eventually acquired a momentum of their own.

For it is certainly true that Kafka in his twenties did not act or behave like a recluse or outcast. Whatever his innate handicaps or reservations, he managed for quite some time to participate with apparent conviction in the extracurricular rites of academe and the rituals of the German-Jewish middle class. He spent many a night carousing till dawn, frequented bordellos, tried dutifully to seduce waitresses, shopgirls, and other ladies of presumed easy virtue—"My dear Max, seeing as the little lady, whose aunt for the time being prevailed over her talents, has escaped us, when do we go to see the Hindu dancer?" (L, p. 34).

In his last semester, Kafka also renewed his friendship with the flower lover Ewald Felix Příbram. They took their finals together; unlike Kafka, the sober and sensible classmate of his high-school days had emerged as a brilliant law student—later a brilliant lawyer—who passed all his exams with flying colors. More important, Příbram had also blossomed out into an elegant and sophisticated socialite, junior member of the *haute bourgeoisie,* without compromising either his integrity or his robust common sense. His father, Dr. Otto Příbram, was president of a major industrial enterprise as well as chairman of the Board of the Workmen's Accident Insurance Institute, and a prominent figure in the centers of influence. Through Ewald, Kafka came into at least superficial contact with this alien and exclusive world of money and manners—no doubt a distant, diffident observer as always, but sufficiently intimidated by his lack of savoir faire to acquire a copy of Oscar Bies's standard work on proper manners, *Der gesellschaftliche Verkehr,* the Emily Post of his day.

It is also to be presumed that for all his unworldliness, Kafka was not unmindful of the potential usefulness of proper connections. And in fact it was thanks to Příbram's father that, a few years later, the Workmen's Accident Insurance Institute was persuaded to relax its policy against hiring unconverted Jews just enough to make an exception for Dr. Kafka.

Ten

PRAGUE, the little mother with claws that Kafka once proposed to put to the torch, is a vision of time frozen in space, lopsided and full of sloping planes; the past predominates, distorts all other dimensions, blunts the sharp angle between day and night, and warps the solid coordinates of reality.

Even so, it was the world, created by Kafka, or creating him. And in exploring it, he ventured out of himself—alone, with cautious daring, heart in mouth, or sheltered by the youthful exuberance of familiar company. No recluse, to be sure, but certainly not one of the boys, even if "boys" like Brod, Baum, and Weltsch hardly qualified as the norm. The most objective clue to Kafka in his postadolescent phase may well be the marvelously ludicrous snapshot that caught him with Hansi, the toast and trollop of the Royal Imperial cavalry alluded to by Brod. His neck clamped into the high, starched neck brace of a choker which the Germans, with apt symbolism, refer to as a *Vatermörder*—parricide—and balancing a Chaplinesque derby on his head, he looks out at the camera in quizzical self-contempt while the plastic Brünnhilde next to him caresses her dog with a smirk of terrifying vapidity. The Talmud Torah pupil, got up to look like a man-about-town.

This town—his town—was an ancient battleground, with no defeats or victories ever acknowledged as final, and the struggle continuing without surcease. Where guns and politics had failed, culture became the weapon of choice, and intellect a matter of self-defense. In 1880, the "Germans" still accounted for 15.5 percent of Prague's 228,000 inhabitants; twenty years later, with the population almost doubled, the German component had shrunk to 7.5 percent. Moreover, the overwhelming majority were Jews, although Paul Eisner's estimate of 85 percent has been questioned. Yet, as if to compensate for the steady erosion of its political and economic power bases, this shrinking minority of about 34,000 people supported a network of cultural activities qualitatively as well as quantitatively out of all proportion to its size.

In addition to an educational establishment comprising no fewer than eleven high schools, Prague had two major German-language dailies, *Bohemia* and the *Prager Tagblatt*. The *Tagblatt* was more liberal—or less reactionary—than *Bohemia*, but both were run by competent staffs, maintained uncommonly literate standards, and could draw on the talents of a network of prominent contributors from all over Europe. The financial section of the *Tagblatt* was, in fact, considered by far the best informed and most informative in the entire country.

Much more important, though, in the light of their role as standard-bearers of *Kultur* among the Slavic hordes, were the abundant space and attention both papers lavished on literature, music, and the arts. They regularly featured reporting on the cultural scene at home and abroad, reviews, articles by scholars noted in their field, and above all a great deal of fiction by some of the best—and, inevitably, some of the most forgettable—writers of the day. Through no accident, Heinrich Teweles, editor in chief of the *Tagblatt* and himself a poet of sorts, also headed the German Authors League Concordia and, in this capacity, for many years ran the local literary mafia as its undisputed godfather. The *feuilleton*, in effect, was the heart and soul of any newspaper, in Prague as throughout most of Europe, in the days when the primacy of the printed word still went unchallenged; and it was in the *feuilletons* of their hometown papers that Kafka and his friends first published many of their shorter pieces.

The other great instrument of enlightenment, intellectual cross-fertilization, and cultural imperialism was the theater. Aside from the Rudolfinum—the monumental concert hall put up in 1882 by the Bohemian Savings Bank to celebrate its fiftieth anniversary and now the House of the Artists—there were three German theaters in Prague, determined to mount not just entertainment but a challenge to the superb Czech stage productions that had become a prominent symbol of the Czech revival and drive for cultural identity.

The oldest of these, in the Old Town, was built in 1781 by Count von Nostitz. It saw the world première of Mozart's *Don Giovanni* in 1787 and peacefully hosted both Czech and German repertory companies throughout much of the nineteenth century, until national rivalries transformed it into the Deutsches Theater. The classical building with its small, intimate stage is currently known as the Tyl Theater; in the city's landmarks, nothing much changes but the names. In 1886, the German community funded construction of the modern, 2,000-seat Neues Deutsches Theater near the center—known since 1950 as the Smetana Theater—and imported Angelo Neumann, a friend of Wagner and leading wizard of the stage, as its director. Neumann turned Prague, already one of the great musical centers of the Continent, into a showplace for opera as well. He was among the first to promote Verdi and Caruso, without thereby neglecting contemporary dramatists such as Ibsen and Hauptmann. After Neumann's death in 1910, the polydextrous Heinrich Teweles added the directorship of the Neues Deutsches Theater to his numerous other conquests.

Inevitably, the very success of these two institutions engendered smugness and provoked opposition. Around 1900, an avant-garde theater in the suburbs—the German Summer Theater, defunct since 1910—began to stage experimental productions by what were then still controversial modernists such as Tolstoy, Strindberg, Schnitzler, and Wedekind.

Plugged permanently, as we are today, into the whole world's multimedia madness, brainpan dented by continuous bombardment with hard-sell electronic garbage, it takes imagination to appreciate the rare power of the unamplified human voice, the enormous influence wielded in their time—in Kafka's time—by institutions such as newspapers and the theater. They carried messages, garbled but exciting, from the mysterious universe beyond city limits. And in the still unpolluted quiet, the few who cared had a chance to hear what was being said.

*　　*　　*

A German-Jewish student in Prague read the *Tagblatt*, went to the theater several times a month, attended lectures, dances, and the annual carnival-cum-marriage market billed as the Spring Festival at the Casino Club, went swimming in summer at the Militär- und Civilschwimmschule—the famous bathing establishment on the Vltava, scene of some of Kafka's most memorable childhood traumas—and ice skating in winter on Jews' Island (long since rebaptized Children's Island), played tennis at the German Lawn Tennis Club beneath Charles Bridge, and several times a week, in the absence of more pressing obligations, spent the evening with his regular cronies in his regular café. It was a relatively civilized and civilizing routine which, without making exorbitant demands on the individual, allowed him painlessly to slip into the mainstream of a larger community defined by its common enemies as much as by its common roots. Kafka, too, observed the ritual, though it no doubt took an effort, simply because what came easily and naturally to most people was precisely that which to him seemed most hopelessly unattainable. Yet to all appearances, he succeeded; the only one he failed to convince was himself.

The theater may well have been one part of this routine that prompted no self-confrontation. Whether he loved or hated it depends on what sources one is inclined to trust; he himself was not effusive on the subject. But acting, as such, always fascinated him, and the first literary effort of his that we know about was the "historical" drama about George of Podebrady, Czech folk hero and Hussite King of Bohemia. Written at about age nine and unfortunately lost to posterity, it foreshadowed an enduring interest in the stage easy enough to understand in one who is himself a permanent resident in the twilight zone between dream and reality. Though he is known at various times to have worked on dramatic material, his active career as a playwright and director came to a close with the series of one-acters he wrote for his parents' birthday parties and produced by enlisting the entire household as his actors. Of his later efforts, only one fragment—part of the "Grotto" or "Guardian of the Tomb" has survived. Several attempts to stage it, notably in France, met with modest acclaim; Kafka himself adamantly refused to read it to his friends, asserting that this categorical refusal constituted "the only thing about the play that was not dilettantish."

His often grotesquely hypertrophied criticism may have aborted whatever else he specifically wrote for the stage, and the posthumous dramatizations of *The Trial* and *The Castle*, like most attempts by less than masters to meddle with masterpieces, do violence to the originals. But there is clearly a dramatist's vision at work in the stark settings, confrontations, and dialogue of much of his fiction.

He was, in any event, a regular theatergoer in his student days, and fortunate in that, for a provincial city of its size, Prague offered a theatrical fare exceptional in both range and quality. And largely in deference to his friends—both Baum and Brod were, after all, musicians of more than routine competence—he occasionally made himself attend concerts, although he had absolutely no ear or feeling for music.

Given his near-native fluency in Czech, it would seem reasonable to assume that he also went to see Czech stage productions, either at the Czech National Theater—a national shrine built between 1868 and 1881, financed entirely by small individual contributions and to this day bearing on its façade the legend *Národ Sobě* (From the People to the People)—or at the numerous lively, irreverent back-alley stages and cabarets that were beginning to mushroom around this time. If so, there is no mention of it anywhere, although Kafka was rather exceptional in his familiarity with that mysterious "other half" of Prague, the world of the Czechs, shunned or sedulously ignored by most of his own companions and compatriots. The Czechs repaid the compliment by busily studying and translating countless fourth-rate French authors while totally ignoring the Rilkes, Werfels, and Kafkas in their midst. Even during the interludes of armed truce in the Czech-German conflict—there were relatively few open clashes in the decades preceding the war—the abyss dividing the two cultures was bridged only by a few individuals on either side.

In later years Kafka had less and less time for diversions, less psychic and physical energy available for casual indulgence. The theater as mere entertainment, or for that matter entertainment of any kind, with the exception of the early movies, lost much of its appeal. Instead, his interest in the stage became that of a discriminating and incisive critic, and on his trips abroad he seldom missed a chance to take in a performance by some of Europe's great repertory companies. One of his most memorable theatrical experiences, however, turned out to be a series of mediocre plays performed in the fall of 1911 by a less than mediocre troupe of peripatetic Yiddish actors in a sleazy Prague café, and in a language he could barely understand. Their artistry was minimal, their lives a sequence of miserable improvisations, but what they brought him were the first authentic glimpses of Jewishness as an integral part of everyday life, a vague response to questions yet unasked.

*   *   *

When it came to organized student activities, however, Kafka's enthusiasm was restrained, to say the least. The student body as such was, in any case, dominated—at least numerically—by the roughly seven hundred rabidly nationalistic *Volksdeutsche* from the provinces, whose chief interest was to provoke clashes with the Czechs by heroically parading up and down the Graben—the Moat, one of Prague's main thoroughfares—every Sunday morning. Moreover, the inflated sense of self-importance with which organizational politics rewards the movers and shakers was not among Kafka's secret ambitions. For some years he belonged to the Lesehalle, notably its literary section, which under the chairmanship of Brod—a mover and shaker *par excellence*—ran a particularly aggressive and stimulating program of lectures and discussions; he at one time even officiated as "reporter on the arts." But his interest quickly waned, and by 1905 he had dropped out altogether.

Far more congenial to his nature was the loose, uncommitted and noncommittal sociability afforded by a different and much older institution, the café. Kafka's fairy-tale version of its origins, which he later outlined to Baum but probably never got down on paper, poignantly evokes the magical appeal of this "attempt to conquer the loneliness of human beings": a possibility "for people to get together without being formally invited, just to see others, to talk to them, observe them without getting involved in any close relationships. Anyone can come and go as he pleases, with no obligation, and is yet made to feel welcome without any hypocrisy."

The social and symbolic aspects of Central European coffeehouses can hardly be overstressed; what they offered, beyond atmosphere and sociability, were warmth and shelter from noon to five in the morning, not to mention the usual reading racks filled with newspapers and magazines, all for the modest price of a cup of coffee. These were tangible benefits, and far from negligible in the overcrowded cities of the industrial age, whose dilapidated housing stock had fallen way behind the explosive population growth. At the same time, most cafés had long since acquired a distinct ambience of their own, a cross between club and corner bar, catering to a specific clientele and salvaging some communal sense of belonging within the arid landscape of urban anonymity.

Prague's coffeehouses numbered in the hundreds; they served as nerve centers of its culture, politics, business, and crime. Some of the most popular, of course, had nothing more going for them than the elegance of their decor and the quality of their pastry, cozy establishments to which respectable bourgeois families would repair of a Sunday afternoon to gorge themselves on gossip and whipped cream. Far more typical, though, were the less respectable and less-than-respectable places scattered throughout every section of town—home to the home-less, refuge to errant souls, con men, politicians, artists, and book-keepers; smoke-filled, noisy rooms that served as party headquarters, lecture hall, battleground, or neutral zone where friends and enemies—the lines were fluid—would regularly get together to settle scores, accounts, or problems, plot seduction or a coup d'état, and for a few hours be made to feel a little less futile, a little less insignificant, or simply a little less lonely.

Among the most conspicuous products of this subsurface fermenta-tion were the literary cafés, each with its own hard core of *Stammgäste* or habitués—regulars who set the tone and determined the specific factional allegiance of their respective tree houses. By far the best known were the Arco and the Louvre, which between them neatly defined the ideological polarities. The Arco's local reputation as a headquarters of the avant-garde went back to before the turn of the century, when the ornery headwaiter of the originally rather staid old Café Arco in an exclusive section of town had a fight with the owner and spitefully proceeded to open an Arco of his own in a much less fancy neighborhood near the Prague Central railroad station. The specialty of this illegitimate offshoot was a reading rack stocked with radical and avant-garde literature from all over Europe; but it was Kafka's generation that put the Café Arco permanently on the map as one of the great literary centers of the Continent. During its most vital period, which crested around 1912, its regulars included most of Prague's artistic and literary elite—actors, painters, a surfeit of German-Jewish writers, along with a not insignificant component of Czechs. In fact, the cautious *rapprochement* between the Czech and German avant-gardes, promoted by bilingual authors such as Brod, Kisch, Pick, and Fuchs, lent a special flavor to the Arco that may partly account for the venomous attack on the "Arconauts" with which Karl Kraus immortalized the establishment in one of his characteristically un-translatable diatribes: *"Es werfelt und brodet und kafkat und kischt"*— Werfel, Brod, Kafka, and Kisch constituting, in his eyes, a Jewish cabal besmirching the purity of the German language of which he was the self-appointed guardian and high priest.

There were, of course, many more such literary cafés, packed from midday on with argumentative literati, poetizing anarchists, prolix pornographers, and otherwise reputable doctors, lawyers, and real-estate brokers who also wrote fiction and poetry of often considerable merit. But the Arco, by virtue of its size and clientele, had become the most conspicuous symbol of a phenomenon that survived in Prague long after it had vanished from the more cosmopolitan centers of the Continent—a community of intellectuals. Like all such intimate, often incestuously parochial enclaves within which all knew one another and knew all about one another, it generated claustrophobia and creative ferment in about equal proportions. But despite sharp internal divisions, this subculture, rooted in common hostility or at least indifference to the crass materialism of the times, maintained a remarkable degree of cohesiveness all the way to the beginning of the First World War.

Though he came to experience this cohesiveness as increasingly oppressive, Kafka in the early years showed up fairly regularly at the Arco, from all accounts an inconspicuous and taciturn patron determined to "observe without getting involved." This defensive stance was much more difficult to sustain at the elegant Café Louvre, where Prague's Brentano disciples gathered twice a month to pay tribute to their spiritual leader by studying his scriptures.

Franz Brentano's relatively brief tenure at Prague University had been abruptly terminated back in the 1880s with the aid of Horaz Krasnopolski's imaginative interpretation of canon law. He thereafter settled in Florence and devoted the rest of his life—he died in 1917 at the age of seventy-nine—to the elaboration of his theories, which laid the groundwork for Husserl's phenomenology and played a role in the development of the original Gestalt school of psychology. His influence in Prague, however, continued undiminished, as did the undying enmity between the faculties of law and philosophy. The latter remained firmly in the hands of committed "Brentanists," whose proprietary control over staff and curriculum was no less authoritarian for being exercised with urbanity and a grudging concern for due process in education. This did not, however, include tolerance for philosophical heresies or heretical philosophers, a category which took in a broad sweep of ancient and Western thought.

In his first two semesters, Kafka had evidently been interested—or felt obliged to show an interest—in academic philosophy. He took a course with Anton Marty, venerable dean of the faculty, who out-brentanoed Brentano; his equally venerable lecture series on "Fundamental Questions of Descriptive Psychology" was delivered to generations of students in a verbally identical version, down to a limp joke about "Kant's Critique of Pure Nonsense" that marked the Herr

Professor's once-a-year concession to vulgar levity. The two courses taught by Christian von Ehrenfels on "Practical Philosophy" and "The Aesthetics of the Musical Drama" may have proved more stimulating; the much younger Ehrenfels, still under Brentano's influence but already striking out in new directions, was an independent thinker who subsequently formulated some of the basic concepts of Gestalt psychology.

These tentative incursions more than satisfied Kafka's curiosity; he showed no further interest in the field. Nevertheless, he was apparently deemed worthy of admission to the "Brentano circle," which for over a decade met regularly at the Louvre to explicate the Brentanist canon and to debate broader philosophical topics in the light of Brentano's *Weltanschauung*. Initially an adjunct to the academic seminar and attended mainly by students and professors, it evolved into a bimonthly display of intellectual fireworks as well as a breeding ground for doctrinaire orthodoxy. In due course, a few outsiders infiltrated this exclusive circle; one of them, the redoubtable Berta Fanta, eventually managed to crack the narrow Brentanist orientation by founding another intersecting but far more eclectic circle, which was to play a significant role in the city's cultural life.

Berta and her sister, Ida Freund, had been among the first women in Prague to fight their way into the university, at least to the extent of being allowed to audit certain courses. Married to the affluent and eccentric owner of the medieval Unicorn pharmacy on Old Town Square, who himself at one time came close to converting to Islam, Berta Fanta spent her life in both the indefatigable pursuit and the dissemination of culture. She lectured widely on a broad range of topics and ingested new ideas, doctrines, and prophets with an indiscriminate rapacity that led her from an early worship of Nietzsche and Wagner, via Brentano, on to spiritualism, Mme Blavatsky's brand of theosophy, and Rudolf Steiner's anthroposophy. In all fairness, this drift into occultism tells less about the quality of her mind than about her emotional maturity; moreover, it was peculiarly in tune with the mood of a time and place in which neither traditional faith nor rational politics held out much hope anymore of personal fulfillment or universal salvation. In this city of alchemists and wonder rabbis, of heretics and Hussite martyrs, where clocks ran backward or proclaimed the immanence of death every hour on the hour, where legend clung like moss to every stone, it seemed natural enough to be dabbling in the supernatural.

Even Kafka, in fact, let himself be dragged along to spiritualist séances by his supersophisticated cronies—something of a lark, perhaps, but one cannot help feeling that many of his friends, for all their public display of skepticism, were privately as eager to believe in ghosts as later on they wanted to believe in Stalin, Jehovah, or Jesus Christ. Kafka, on the other hand, had no talent for facile self-deception and no use for bargain-basement faith; his final opinion is tersely summed up in a remark recorded by the writer Willy Haas (in *Die Literarische Welt*), who once attended a table-rapping séance with him in the company of Brod and Werfel: "The fact that the sun will rise in the morning is a miracle. The fact that the table moves after it has been pushed around long enough is not a miracle."

Seen against this background, Berta Fanta's esoteric proclivities did not seriously reflect on her intelligence, which in any case seems to have been far less of a factor in the success of her varied endeavors than her energy, ebullience, and personal magnetism. Her Tuesday evening at-homes soon outgrew their Louvre connections; and as she herself moved on beyond Brentano, the Fanta salon in the Old Town Square became the meeting place of a cosmopolitan elite which, in later years, included figures such as Einstein, at the time a young professor at Prague University, the mathematician Gerhard Kowalewski, and the physicist Philipp Frank. The moving spirits in what gradually evolved into an extracurricular postgraduate seminar—at one time, two years were devoted to a study of Kant—were Hugo Bergmann and Felix Weltsch. Bergmann's growing attachment to his hostess, or vice versa, eventually culminated in his marriage to her daughter Else.

All the sources agree that Kafka for some years attended the Brentanist meetings at the Café Louvre. But whether he did so reluctantly or enthusiastically, whether he was politely bored or profoundly influenced by what went on there became the subject of an acrimonious dispute between Brod and later German biographers. Brod maintains that by the time he himself joined the Louvre circle in 1903, Kafka, who had been inducted a year earlier, had already lost all interest, not only in Brentano, but in speculative philosophy altogether, and that it was only at Brod's insistence that he sporadically consented to attend meetings until the fall of 1905.

At that time, Brod published a novella that contained what the Brentanists considered a slighting reference to their idol. It was an incidental aside of no major significance, but quite sufficient to rouse the hackles of fellow student Emil Utitz, self-appointed watchdog of the holy grail and even then as rigidly doctrinaire in his Brentano phase as he was later to be in his devotion to Stalin and Gottwald. On a motion from Utitz, Brod was formally expelled from the Louvre circle, whereupon Kafka promptly resigned in protest.

Klaus Wagenbach, on the other hand, maintains that Kafka faithfully attended these meetings for many years, took a lively part in the discussions, and shared the prevailing philosophical bias. His main source for this information is Emil Utitz, who after Kafka's short-lived 1963 rehabilitation in the East disgorged a host of fond and largely unverifiable reminiscences about his erstwhile schoolmate. Brod, in this version, stands accused of having suppressed Kafka's Brentanist past out of his own injured vanity; and though it is acknowledged that Kafka never and nowhere refers to Brentano, some creative textual critics have, with no great effort, been able to adduce what seems to them convincing evidence of Brentano's enduring impact on Kafka's work.

The factual side of the dispute is rather easily resolved. Brod, being human, may have been guilty of error, distortion, forgetfulness, or unconscious bias, but he was not a liar. Utitz, on the other hand, earned the rare distinction of being one of the few people whom Kafka almost permitted himself overtly to despise as a phrasemongering opportunist—and this way before his hyperarticulate schoolmate had carried opportunism to extremes. The controversy, however, cuts deeper; it illustrates the persistent efforts being made to magnify what at best were peripheral influences out of all proportion to their specific gravity so as to turn Kafka into a German classic, a socialist realist, an embryonic Christian—in short, anything but what he was, for better and for worse: a Jew from Prague.

*   *   *

The break with the Louvre crowd also led to a temporary chill in relations with the Fanta circle. Both Brod and Kafka stayed away for some time, but in the end Hugo Bergmann's diplomacy and Berta Fanta's apologies succeeded in mollifying Brod, who quit pouting and returned to the fold, for many years thereafter a regular and zealous participant at the Tuesday evening gatherings: "Never in my life did I study and learn with as much thoroughness and joy as at the Fanta house" (Brod, St.L.).

Kafka, too, resumed relations, but with a marked lack of enthusiasm, a rare and distant visitor who usually showed up only in response to Brod's urgent entreaties—"I dislike going to the Fantas' " (L, 6/2/14). In part, of course, the dislike was generic; he felt ill at ease among strangers, and the brief spurt of self-inflicted sociability had spent itself rapidly in the transition from "carefree" student life to the rigors of mandatory adulthood. Moreover, the tortuous pathways of these earnest truth-seekers must have seemed ever more remote from where he was headed. He could hardly have been expected to work up much passion for an in-depth study of Kant, Fichte, and Hegel; and never having been able to penetrate the mysteries of simple algebra, he was unlikely to appreciate the learned lectures on Cantor's transfinite numbers or Einstein's theory of relativity that added so much luster and distinction to the Fanta salon.

But there was something else that may have helped to fuel his dislike: a gut reaction to the high-minded piousness and academic pomposity, the ostentatious spirituality and crass social pretentiousness that were an integral part of this culture circus, its performers and audience carefully hand-picked by the two anthroposophical sisters according to criteria in which snobbery, plain and fancy, ranked high on the list. It was an atmosphere scarcely compatible with the rigorous search for truth which, by the end of his student years, had become Kafka's all-encompassing goal—the writer's search for his own truth, pursued in stealth and solitude.

Eleven

For nearly a century, voices dark with foreboding had predicted the end of the monarchy. Yet the ramshackle structure of this imperial bureaucracy had withstood quakes and upheavals of every kind, and time and again the prophets of doom had been made to eat their words or take more potent poison. In any event, the bulk of the population, which by 1910 had reached nearly 50 million, were far less concerned with politics than they were with survival—and as yet only dimly aware of the connection.

Material conditions in Austro-Hungary had, in fact, improved considerably. Between 1903 and 1913, agricultural productivity increased by 85 percent, and industrial output rose by about 77 percent. The rise in industrial wages outstripped the increase in the cost of living. The currency was stable, and remained so until 1914; the 1907 Austrian budget closed with the biggest surplus in the nation's history.

Progress was, of course, uneven, and large pockets of both rural and urban poverty persisted in every part of the empire. Agriculture, despite the marked rise in productivity, continued to suffer from obsolete farming methods perpetuated by landlords far more eager to raise prices than to increase production; the output still lagged behind that of most Western countries, repeatedly forcing the government to contract for large-scale food imports from abroad. Rapid industrialization led to major dislocations, to the explosive growth of an often brutally exploited working class on the one hand and, on the other, to an enormous concentration of wealth and power.

But the economy as a whole, during what turned out to be the terminal phase of the empire, appeared quite sufficiently robust to inspire confidence in the future, and the rising standard of living rendered the vast majority of the emperor's subjects monumentally indifferent to both the gloom of the intellectuals and the oratory of the politicians. And yet, material progress not only failed to translate into political stability but, on the contrary, seemed to exacerbate the strains and stresses that eventually led to the collapse and dismemberment of the multinational state.

It had been the Emperor Franz Joseph's not unreasonable conceit to defuse national rivalries by abolishing suffrage restrictions based on property. He was convinced that the militant independence movements merely reflected competing economic interests and therefore regarded the property-owning middle classes as the most dangerous and disruptive element. But his attempt, in 1896, to neutralize the non-German, anti-German bourgeoisies—chiefly the Czechs, by far the most advanced —through universal male suffrage failed on two counts. At the practical level, the large non-German minorities in the more or less democratically elected national parliament, the Reichsrat, persistently sabotaged proceedings to the point where no meaningful legislative power could be exercised, while German minorities in the provincial parliaments, the Landräte, retaliated in kind, so that autocratic rule by the emperor, his cabinet, and the tentacular government bureaucracy continued virtually unchanged. Equally important, though, the link between nationalist extremism and economic self-interest, while real enough, turned out to be a great deal more complex than Franz Joseph's curiously Marxist concept allowed for.

For, contrary to the emperor's expectations, it was not the irredentism of the oppressed but the nationalism of the oppressors, German nationalism in Austria proper, that first boiled over into extremism of primitive malignancy. As far back as 1885, Georg Ritter von Schönerer, a brilliant demagogue who drew his inspiration from the Teutonic racism of Gobineau, Wagner, Nietzsche, and Stoecker, founded the vehemently anti-Semitic and xenophobic Pan-German Nationalist Union. Industrialization triggered massive population shifts; and with Czechs and Jews pouring in ever-increasing numbers into many previously all-German towns and cities, Schönerer's racist slogans— *Religion ist einerlei, Rasse ist die Schweinerei* (Whatever their religion, it's their race that makes them pigs)—appealed powerfully to the paranoid siege mentality of the Austrian middle class. The language ordinances promulgated by Prime Minister Badeni in 1898, which gave Czech equal status with German, were followed by bloody riots that forced the emperor to fire Badeni and abrogate the new laws. Predictably, this in turn set off equally riotous protests on the part of the Czech nationalists and gave further impetus to what, in many ways, may be considered the first authentic Nazi movement; by 1901, its representation in the national parliament had risen to twenty-one deputies. As a leader, Schönerer was soon eclipsed by emotionally less unstable and politically more effective personalities, such as the volubly anti-Semitic rabble-rouser Karl Lueger, Vienna's popular mayor from 1897 till his death in 1910. Nevertheless, Schönerer is rightly regarded as the spiritual father of that greatest of all Austrian demagogues, Adolf Hitler; the Third Reich was spawned on the fetid subsoil of Habsburg Austria.

In its own time, of course, this embryonic radical extremism was still perceived as a fringe phenomenon, an irrational undercurrent within the essentially rational struggle between competing interests and rival nationalities. Even those actually engaged in it continued, for the most part, to believe in an eventual resolution through legitimate political processes. But there were notable exceptions.

* * *

What makes them appear so eerily prescient in retrospect was, in its day, the very opposite—monumental egocentricity, deliberate blindness, and indifference to organized rescue efforts. The writers and artists who transformed the agony of the Austro-Hungarian empire into a stunning burst of creative energy—Rilke, Schnitzler, Musil, Broch, Klimt, Kokoschka, Mahler, Schönberg, Loos, Wittgenstein, and Freud, to name but some of the most prominent—were men of little faith and much skepticism to begin with, and no faith at all in politics and politicians. If, on the whole, they were no more able to see the shape of things to come than anyone else, the greatest among them had a prophetic vision of their own time unobstructed by delusions of hope. The dark despondency that haunts so much of their work had its source, not in the mundane conflicts of impersonal forces, but directly in the tragic sense of what accounted for the despair of human beings floating weightless in the night of time, seeking new gods in place of those who had abandoned them.

What was true of Vienna and its hinterlands applied with twofold force to the milieu in which Kafka came of age as a writer. The German-Jewish artists and intellectuals of Prague, as a group, were encapsulated in their impotence, foreign bodies rejected by all the mutually hostile factions, effectively isolated from the power struggles in which they stood to lose no matter what the outcome. Even the outlets open to emancipated Jews elsewhere in the West—egalitarian utopias, Marxism, Christianity—were largely closed to them by an endemic anti-Semitism too pervasive to be ignored by even the most dedicated idealists. Many nonetheless refused to accept the role of apathetic bystanders; they joined German liberal or left-wing causes, threw in their lot with the Czech nationalists or social democrats, or embraced their own freshly minted brand of nationalism, a politicized version of the age-old dream of Zion eloquently promoted by the Austro-Hungarian journalist Theodor Herzl. Some felt attracted to anarchism, or at any rate to that motley collection of picaresque eccentrics, militant pacifists, libertarians, vegetarians, and practical jokers who professed an often highly qualified allegiance to the ideas of Bakunin, Kropotkin, and Tolstoy. Though rather conspicuous in Prague, the membership of their organization—to the extent to which anarchists can ever be said to organize—never exceeded a few hundred, no doubt including a substantial number of police informers. Their blasphemous lampooning of powers divine or imperial, and the barbed ridicule with which they skewered soldiers, priests, and bureaucrats, may not have been a threat to the institutions of the state, but it certainly punctured their pomposity. One of the movement's most inspired leaders was the immensely gifted though rarely sober Jaroslav Hašek, whose *Good Soldier Švejk* embodies the very essence of Czech passive resistance in all of its madness, cunning, and humanity. In the parliamentary elections of 1912, Hašek ran an uproariously funny campaign as the sole candidate of his own Political Party of Modest Progress within the Confines of the Law. Though closely watched and harshly persecuted, the revolutionaries were hardly taken seriously by anyone, themselves included, the sole exception being Inspector Karel Slaviček, the ever-vigilant chief of the Prague police department's antisubversive squad.

It is thanks to the archives of his organization, compiled with diligent pedantry and preserved with worshipful respect by his equally zealous successors, that one specific Kafka myth can safely be laid to rest: he may have been an *intellectuel engagé*, but the *engagements* of his intellect transcended pranks and politics; the legend of Kafka as a backroom conspirator active in the Czech anarchist Club Mladych (Club of the Young) is just that, for better or for worse. It was sparked by the imaginative reminiscences of the ex-anarchist Michal Mareš published in 1946, in which he describes Kafka as a friend and comrade who participated in anarchist meetings and demonstrations. After a clash with police in 1909 that led to the arrest of Mareš and several of his comrades, Kafka supposedly accompanied them to the police station and personally posted bail for their release.

The Mareš story, subsequently embroidered by Gustav Janouch, found its way into several Kafka biographies, from which he emerged as a youthful conspirator and fellow traveler of the Czech liberation movement. The account, however, is wholly inconsistent with everything known about his life, his friends, and his character. A most unlikely plotter to begin with, he would scarcely have been willing or able to conceal his involvement from the close friends with whom he had almost daily contact. Moreover, it is inconceivable for a quasi-government employee—notably one as conspicuous in dress and appearance as the towering Dr. Kafka would have been at an anarchist meeting—to have escaped the attention of the ubiquitous police informers, who regularly accounted for a sizable portion of the audience. Yet the files of a police department that not only kept but forever preserved detailed records of the most trivial transgressions, down to a dog owner's failure to restrain his pet from defecating on public property, contain not a single reference to Kafka, Franz. In fact, on at least five occasions, even in the midst of war, the police routinely granted him the certificate of good conduct required for employment or travel abroad. The only anarchist with a somewhat similar name embalmed in those file cabinets is one Anton Kafka or Kavka, a schoolteacher and occasional versifier born at Sedlice; one may charitably assume that the similarity in names caused some confusion.

The truth is more prosaic. Kafka did indeed know Mareš, an apprentice some eight years his junior, but only casually, as a neighbor on the same block. He also met Hašek a number of times, and may well have attended a few public meetings or demonstrations as an interested observer. His own socialist leanings are attested to by Bergmann and Brod. He continued platonically to empathize with the exploited and oppressed, and he on occasion displayed definite pro-Czech sympathies. In later years, he also seems to have been intrigued by the non-violent philosophical anarchism of Kropotkin and Alexander Herzen. This was probably as close to radical activism as Kafka ever got.

*   *   *

All these sporadic attempts to break out of the invisible ghetto—the visible one, Prague's notorious Fifth Quarter, was finally being razed—were essentially doomed. The Jewish intelligentsia on the whole remained isolated, inbred, and inward-looking, for want of any effective ways of influencing the course of events. And in tearing into themselves and each other, they unwittingly re-created a ghetto not unlike the one which their grandparents had so exuberantly left behind and which was now being leveled, block by block. Theirs was a paradoxically communal "shtetl" of cantankerous individualists huddled in the warrens of their self-absorption, with literature their religion and self-expression their road to salvation. A good many were puling infants wallowing in excremental self-indulgence; the best, in probing the chill within themselves, sensed the approach of the ice age. To that extent, their vision proved prophetic.

By the time Kafka edged toward its margins, the literary scene, like everything else in Prague, had split into hostile camps, essentially the sons versus the fathers once again, but more formally categorized as Young Prague versus the Old Guard. The Old Guard presented a still formidable target, firmly ensconced in the social structure and literary sensibilities of the German middle class, but effectively reduced by then to two masters bereft of disciples. Moreover, these two—Hugo Salus and Friedrich Adler—cordially detested each other, for reasons they themselves could no longer remember.

Salus (1866–1929) was the acknowledged pope of the establishment, and he looked the part—a strikingly handsome gynecologist and obstetrician with a thriving practice, whose novels and poetry, tinged with autumnal *Weltschmerz*, had achieved a measure of success not only in his hometown but also in Germany proper; in 1901, one of his poems—*"Das einfältige Lied"*—was set to music by Arnold Schönberg. The rare cachet of international recognition, so avidly coveted by the claustrophobic natives, further bolstered his autocratic tendencies and lent wholly unwarranted authority to his ex-cathedra pronouncements. For some decades, Salus reigned as the arbiter of literary taste, uncompromising in his hostility to young rebel upstarts. That they offended his taste, shaped by the bucolic romanticism of the early nineteenth century, is understandable; more important, though, they savaged the moral principles and political convictions that made Salus so representative of his entire generation.

Though born a Jew and never converted, he nonetheless considered himself a German first, last, and always, ultraconservative in his views and rabid in his defense of continued German cultural and political dominance. Typical of his feelings, if not of his talent, is a doggerel he saw fit to publish when, for the first time, the Prague Zionists entered their own slate in the municipal elections, thereby threatening to siphon off some votes from the German bloc: *Heute gibt es nur Deutsche/ Wer nicht deutsch wählt, verdient die Peitsche.* (Today there are only Germans. He who does not vote German deserves the whip.) He died in 1929, thus missing out on the free trip with which the Germans, a mere thirteeen years later, rewarded his kind of loyalty to their *Kultur,* on the other hand, he still lived to see his son Wolfgang, a gifted poet, turn into a dedicated Communist.

The cardinal and second-in-command was another superassimilated Jew, Friedrich Adler, who in spite of the perennial bad feelings between them shared Salus's Teutonic fervor as well as his sedate literary tastes. Raised in abject poverty in an all-Czech village, Adler (1857–1938) managed to study law and ended up as Secretary of the Prague Chamber of Commerce; when it came to the intrigues of intraorganizational politics, however, he was no match for the adroit Salus, even if he happened to be the better poet by far. His major contributions were masterful translations from the Czech, which made this staunchly pro-German traditionalist one of the first—and one of the best—of the cultural mediators who attempted, at rather lofty heights, to build bridges across the chasm.

The gap between these problematical father figures and their youthful antagonists involved fundamental attitudes in which age, as such, played a mere subordinate role. Rilke, born in 1875, the first authentically new voice of his generation, was only nine years younger than Salus, and most of the Young Prague rebels were born in the 1870s. Yet it seemed as though, within that decade, they had passed a point of no return: the orderly universe of progress and enlightenment had suddenly closed in on them and turned into a maze without exit. They were on their own. *Sauve qui peut.*

And it was not much they had in common as a group: the influence of Rilke, perhaps, which persisted long after the poet himself left Prague in 1890, and a familiarity with Czech and the Czechs rare among the older generation. Goethe and Schiller, though still on their pedestals, had turned into pigeon perches; Rimbaud was the new Faust incarnate, Verlaine his Mephistopheles, and the stench of the Flowers of Evil inflamed the imagination. They despised Vienna—*Los von Wien*—and instead turned worshipful faces toward Munich and Dresden, where bohemians of a different sort were in open rebellion against genteel romanticism and bourgeois smugness.

But in their panic, it was each man for himself, a wild stampede of gregarious loners grappling with monsters spawned in their own bellies. What mattered to them was not the decline and fall of the Habsburg empire but rage at life unlived, and fear of death anonymous. Known but to God. And, possibly, to their immediate superiors; for most of these *enragé* writers worked for a living, petty bureaucrats or struggling professionals "in civilian life" caught in the gears of senseless routines, self-styled martyrs who passed unnoticed in the crowd, with murder in their hearts. A few—including some of the most seriously unstrung among them—were highly gifted and original, many more were glibly competent, and their collective output covered the entire range from sublime to unreadable.

In fact, often the selfsame individual exemplified both extremes. The syphilitic post-office clerk Paul Leppin, uncrowned king of that Bohemian *bohème*, wrote stunning poetry along with mushy-core pornography of opulent absurdity and syntactic incoherence. Decadence had its day, or rather, its night—moonlit graveyards, haunted castles, necrophilia in dank dungeons, rape, incest, vampires, and ghosts. The wedding of Eros and Thanatos turned into a costume ball, an orgy of masturbatory phantasmagoria larded with rhetoric and ersatz Poe, but the fear behind the carnival masks was genuine enough, and it showed up even in the ornate prose of their towering gothic platitudes.

Or in mysticism, that indigenous product of Prague, shelf-worn and neglected during the decades of economic progress and liberal enlightenment, but now back in style. Its best-known exponent was Leppin's mentor Gustav Meyrink, who, having failed as a banker, changed his name from Meyer to Meyrink and switched to pursuits less occult than finance. He dabbled in spiritualism, cultivated an air of omniscient mystery, and became guru to a coven of sorcerers' apprentices who convened regularly at the Café Continental for witchcraft with *Schlagobers*, until the enormous popular success of his *Golem*, published in 1915, afforded him the means to exorcise his demons and retire happily to a Bavarian mountaintop. Whether or not the devil had a hand in this triumph of matter over mind we'll never know; the fact remains that this best-selling shlock novel about Jewish Prague was written by perhaps the only writer of his time and place who happened to be neither Jewish nor a native of Prague, but the illegitimate son of a German count and a Viennese actress, born in Vienna in 1868.

Most of the Young Prague rebels, writers such as Oskar Wiener, Otokar Winicky, Victor Hadwiger, Camill Hoffmann, left little of substance. Even within their own lifetime they were, in fact, rapidly being outpaced by what may loosely be classified as the next generation, though again less than a decade separated Leppin and his crowd from Kafka, Brod, Werfel, and their respective circles. (Rilke, the obvious exception, was eight years older than Kafka; but while he served as a model, he was never a Prague poet in any meaningful sense.) Yet their achievements, however ephemeral, were real enough; they broke with the mannered parochialism and ethnocentric complacency of their mid-century predecessors, they at least acknowledged the existence of their next-door neighbors, and along with sainted relics from the past, they smashed enough windows to let in a few breezes from distant corners of the earth which, if they didn't quite clear the air in smoke-filled Prague cafés, at least created some turbulence.

Ultimately, though, the onslaught did considerably less damage to romanticism, emperor worship, or the venerable Old Guard than it did to the German language itself, which emerged badly bruised and battered from the encounter, abused, maltreated, and grotesquely bloated. The stylistic vandalism—florid rhetoric, ghoulish erotomania, fake sentiment, and glutinous *Kitsch*—that so luxuriantly proliferated in the writings of that transitional generation may have been a necessary evil; it leveled the ground and made room for what followed. But in its own time it was a plague infesting the language, and thus the very consciousness, of many younger and far better writers, who faced a long and hard struggle to overcome the effects of their exposure at a tender age to this portentous stylistic elephantiasis. And some—Brod and Werfel among them—never fully recovered.

* * *

It was isolation as much as genius that rendered Kafka so remarkably immune to this contagion. For even during his, to all appearances, most gregarious student days, he was ever alone in a crowd rather than part of it; and though he genuinely suffered from this sense of separation, this punishment for sins unknown, the fact remains that it also fostered a precocious independence in those areas in which he did not doubt his competence. Thus when it came to reading and writing, he stood his ground—an interested observer once again, thoroughly familiar with the fads and fashions of his day but ever determined to preserve enough distance for a strictly critical perspective. Even his late-adolescent flirtation with Oskar Pollak and the *Kunstwart* may be seen in this light, a determined effort to transcend the influence of his immediate environment. And although the coyly archaic *Kunstwart* style briefly corrupted his own, he outgrew it rather quickly and, in so doing, greatly strengthened his self-assurance. This precocious intellectual independence, so striking in its contrast to his otherwise rampant self-doubts, shows up in Brod's account of their first encounter in October 1902. Following some inconclusive arguments about Nietzsche, the talk shifted to their Prague contemporaries, whom the eighteen-year-old Brod admired with his usual effusive ardor; Meyrink in particular was his favorite of the moment:

> In the Gymnasium I had been weaned on the classics and rejected everything that was "modern." But already in the upper grades a change had set in, and now, in my storm-and-stress phase, I welcomed everything that was weird, unbridled, shameless, cynical, extreme, hyperbolic. Kafka responded calmly and wisely. Of Meyrink he thought less than nothing. . . . I proceeded to quote from memory some "beautiful passages," one of them from Meyrink's *Purple Death*, in which he compares butterflies to open books on magic. ("Glittering butterflies, the size of a hand, weirdly marked, sat with wings outspread like open magic books on quiet flowers." Meyrink: *Der Violette Tod*.) Kafka turned up his nose. That sort of thing seemed to him farfetched and much too blatant. He rejected anything that seemed contrived for effect, intellectual, synthetic, though he himself would never have used such threadbare clichés.

Be it said that Brod, though he eventually outgrew Meyrink, never quite shed his own predilection for soaring sentiment and purple prose, and the calm wisdom he ascribes to his then nineteen-year-old friend is probably an example of this penchant. But what Kafka evidently did possess already was sound judgment and an instinctive feel for the authentic that owed nothing to prevailing currents.

Yet if he kept his inner distance from people, he nonetheless was seldom alone; it would be impossible to overestimate the role that reading played in Kafka's life. Books were his true teachers, his most intimate companions, at times his most dangerous antagonists. "Many a book is like a key to unknown chambers within the castle of one's own self," he wrote to Oskar Pollak in 1903 (L, 11/9/03). He loved books, the feel of books, the sight of books on display. Brod reports that he had never seen Kafka borrow books from the extensive library of the German Reading Hall; but the town's dingy old bookstores were among his favorite haunts, and all his life he faithfully checked out publishers' catalogues for items of possible interest. Frugal in other ways, often to the point of stinginess, he could be outright extravagant when it came to books and not even feel guilty about it. With friends he was notoriously generous, fond of giving some thoughtfully chosen novel or volume of poetry as a present. Yet he was in no sense a "collector"; what aroused his cupidity were not antiquarian rarities or fine bindings but, above all, the text between the covers. He not only loved and bought books—he read them.

> Altogether, I think we ought to read only books that bite and sting us [he wrote to Pollak in 1904]. If the book we are reading doesn't shake us awake like a blow to the skull, why bother reading it in the first place? So that it can make us happy, as you put it? Good God, we'd be just as happy if we had no books at all; books that make us happy we could, in a pinch, also write ourselves. What we need are books that hit us like a most painful misfortune, like the death of someone we loved more than we love ourselves, that make us feel as though we had been banished to the woods, far from any human presence, like a suicide. A book must be the ax for the frozen sea within us. That is what I believe. [L, 1/27/04]

And that was how he read, starting with the fairy tales of his childhood, going on to the standard teenage fare of suspense, adventure, and exploration—Conan Doyle, Knut Hamsun, Sven Hedin, James Fenimore Cooper, Jules Verne—and constantly branching out without ever quite abandoning the early favorites. At seventeen, he had already read Nietzsche, at forty he still read fairy tales and the Czech Boy Scout magazine. Books were the drug of choice against the unbearable childhood, the difficult adolescence, the frustrations of any age; books were the opium of the intellectuals, and Kafka's addiction was as common in his circles as teenage acne.

Brod mentions some of Kafka's early favorites: Goethe, Thomas Mann, Hamsun, Hesse, and Flaubert, along with a number of nineteenth-century German classics such as Hebbel, Fontane, and Stifter. His list, compiled from memory many years later, was probably neither reliable nor comprehensive; in any event, Kafka's tastes, the profound fascination and identification with individual writers such as Flaubert, Hofmannsthal, Dickens, Dostoevsky, and later on Goethe, Kleist, and Kierkegaard, underwent many shifts and changes. Moreover, many authors long forgotten played some part in his growth simply because at one time or another he loved and admired them, either for aspects of their work or because they in some way helped him to gain access to "unknown chambers within the castle of his own self."

But amid the eclectic diversity of his interests, one constant stands out: his intense curiosity about the facts of other people's lives. What seemed to fascinate him almost more than anything else were the life stories of the famous, the infamous, and the merely literate, in all their intimate and unabridged detail, the whole stew of lofty thoughts and banal accretions, the clutter and trivia fermenting in the huge, multi-volume biographies, autobiographies, diaries, journals, and collected letters that were always among his favorite reading. What they may have proved to him, who trusted the word more than the thing itself, was that there were people able to put one foot in front of the other and thus progress at their own pace from birth to death. To one who time and again found himself paralyzed by fear and indecision, this must have provided a measure of comfort.

* * *

Tracking the inspiration behind Kafka's work back to a host of secondary sources may be intriguing as a parlor game but yields little of practical use. Beyond the incontrovertible fact that he was the sum of his life experience, and that the books he read were very much part of it, lies a trap for arrogance or ignorance. What the creative unconscious chooses to transmute into art is totally unpredictable, subject to its own logic and reason; it seems as sterile an academic exercise to factor out traces of Kleist, Dickens, or Kierkegaard as it is to identify the characters in Kafka's stories with real-life counterparts.

Much more pertinent, in his case, are the early manifestations of authentic originality nurtured in solitary self-confinement, his readiness to see the world through his own eyes. As a twenty-year-old student, still in his outwardly sociable phase, he in complete secrecy wrote the first version of "Description of a Struggle," a piece of prose sharp as an ice pick, forged in the very struggle which the story itself attempts to dramatize.

The earliest of Kafka's stories to have survived, it was never published in his lifetime, mainly because he was himself keenly aware of the flaws most later critics point to with more or less tolerant indulgence. The first version seems to have been written in the winter of 1903–4. One brief section, published in 1908 in the first issue of the literary magazine *Hyperion,* marked Kafka's debut in print—a rather respectable one, in the company of Rilke, Hofmannsthal, and Heinrich Mann. Two further chapters appeared in *Hyperion*'s final issue of March/ April 1909, and several more fragments were subsequently incorporated in Kafka's first book, the *Meditations,* published by Kurt Wolff in 1913.

The "Description" contains, in as yet inchoate form, many of the themes of his later work, and it was obviously his struggle—and failure —to articulate them to his own satisfaction that, time and again over the years, sent him back to just this novella. The excerpts he did consent to publish—reluctantly, or at least with a show of reluctance— were polished and revised over and over, and after fussing with the piece for years, he in 1909 set out to rewrite it from scratch. The manuscript of this second version breaks off after 58 handwritten pages, as against the original 110; it is impossible now to determine whether the rest was lost, or whether he gave up the attempt.

Made gun-shy by his experience with Pollak, he took another two years before he trusted Brod sufficiently to own up to the unspeakable practices that everyone else around him indulged in with such uninhibited exhibitionism. Only around 1905 did he finally bring himself to confess that he, too, was a writer, by letting Brod read the "Description of a Struggle."

Brod appears to have been genuinely stunned, and his response merits admiration for both its generosity and its perspicacity. Prague's literary lion cub was given to somewhat facile enthusiasm, but he knew genius when he saw it and would let neither envy nor egotism stop him from revealing his discovery to the world at large. On February 9, 1907, therefore, in reviewing a play by his friend Franz Blei in the literary weekly *Die Gegenwart,* he ended on a note of typical fustian and rather atypical slyness: "It is a token of the high level reached by German literature that we now have several authors able to meet its exalted standards and who grace the most diverse aspects of existence by their art and cruelty. Heinrich Mann, Wedekind, Meyrink, and Franz Kafka, together with the author of this play, belong in this sainted company."

Considering that Kafka at that point had yet to publish a single line, the statement may have struck those who knew him as somewhat premature. Nonetheless, it was the first mention of Kafka's name in print, and he accepted it with tact and good grace. "Yesterday I read the *Gegenwart,*" he wrote to Brod. "It is a prank, a real prank, but a most kindly one. Well, at least I'll have taken one dance step this winter. . . The only sad thing about it—and I know this was not your intention—is that for me to be publishing anything later on will be construed as an indecent act, for the delicacy of this first appearance would be damaged beyond repair. And never could I hope to produce an effect to rival that with which your sentence has endowed my name."

Blei, a versatile hack, also published and edited a succession of slick, highbrow magazines—*Amethyst, Hyperion, Die Opale*—renowned as much for their exotic eroticism as for their literary quality, in spite of which each of them, after a few years, invariably slipped into the gap between Blei's ambitions as an editor and his lack of resources as a publisher. Brod at that time was still on friendly terms with him, and his insistent pleas finally convinced Kafka to submit the two fragments of the "Description" that appeared in *Hyperion*'s maiden issue.

By 1910, Kafka had evidently given up on trying to describe his struggle and made Brod a present of the manuscript. "What pleases me most about the novella, dear Max, is that it's out of the house" (L, 3/18/10). Brod rediscovered it among his papers in 1935 and published a combined version as part of Kafka's posthumous work. The decision may have made sense at a time when he was still striving to build his friend's reputation, but it blurred significant differences between the earlier and later versions that cast light on Kafka's growth as a writer and have only recently become accessible through a parallel edition.

Brod insists that, in contrast to most posthumously published Kafka material, to which he himself assigned more or less appropriate titles, the "Description of a Struggle" was Kafka's own choice. It was slow to attract attention even after it finally came out in 1937, and it never yielded much, by way of commentary, beyond the received wisdom and unsolicited platitudes of Marxist alienation, metaphysical uprootedness, inadequate ego integration, and the quest for God. Even here, the text is already dense enough to support any number of free-floating hypotheses. Where it falls short is in transcending its fragmentary nature and in transforming flashes of lightning into a steady source of light.

In its skeletal outline, this *voyage intérieur* is a nocturnal pilgrimage to the Laurenziberg, now Petřin, a hill overlooking Prague and, as we know from his journal, of special significance to Kafka as the scene of an adolescent epiphany:

> Many years ago, I sat on the slope of the Laurenziberg, in a sad enough mood, to be sure. I tried to sort out what it was I wanted from life. The most important, or the most attractive wish turned out to be a vision of life (and—this was a necessary part of it—the ability to convince others of it by my writing) in which life, while retaining its natural full rise and fall, can be seen at the same time, and no less clearly, as a nothing, a dream, a state of suspense. A beautiful wish, perhaps, if I had wished it right.

Features of the narrator's antagonist have variously been attributed to Ewald Přibram and Oskar Pollak, a point of scarcely more than anecdotal relevance in the context of this struggle between self and world, between the two halves of the split self, both equally incapable of selfhood but described, in their externalized embodiment, with that nightmare precision that became one of the most effective elements of Kafka's technique. Only to the extent to which Přibram and Pollak, at one time or another, embodied aspects of Kafka himself is his perception of them reflected in the anonymous, instinct-ridden alter ego with whom the narrator is locked in mortal combat.

The somnambulist journey through slippery streets and frozen fear toward the heights that dominate the city—this is the only one of Kafka's stories suffused with graphically detailed images of Prague—is flight and struggle against both life and death, against the promise and menace of life as much as against the awareness and temptation of death—a preliminary sounding of the depths that later drained him, and from which he derived his strength. In the "Description of a Struggle," his powers were clearly not yet up to the challenge; the often scintillating fragments, dense with arcane messages, simply would not fit together, despite years of polishing and filing. Yet its early version is of more than mere biographical interest. Themes, texture, and technique foreshadow the great works of Kafka's mature period; "Diversions, or Proof That It Is Impossible to Live" reads the title of the second chapter, a preface of sorts to his entire legacy, which proves that *not* to live is equally impossible. Already in this early effort, the opposites coexist, suspended in permanent paradox, relentlessly exerting their gravitational pull on mere humans trapped in the field of contending forces. His vision, trained like a microscope on minute details, amplifies reality far beyond the real; not "surrealist" in the accepted sense of the then as yet unknown term, but miraculous to the point where it slides imperceptibly, without transition, into fantasy, into the reality of the waking dream.

But above all it was Kafka's language that signaled the break with the past. Even at this early stage, the glacial prose with which he probed his nightmares was like a knife aimed at the heart. Hard-edged, stripped of fustian, fashion, and artifice, it fully justified Brod's belief that Kafka's talents were of an order altogether different not only from his own but from those of anyone he had ever known before.

Twelve

IN the spring of 1906, with graduation imminent and claims on parental support running out, Kafka could no longer avoid facing the
responsibilities of adulthood, more specifically, the need to find a job.

There was never any doubt in his mind about his true vocation, or
at least less doubt than about almost anything else in his life. But
precisely because he saw writing as a sacred vocation, an irresistible obsession—"God doesn't want me to write, and still I've got to write"—
he was determined not to have it tainted by material considerations.
Besides, he was worldly enough by now to know that his own agonizingly
slow process of creation offered little hope of ever providing for even
his minimal needs; never could he expect the kind of popular success
that Brod and so many of his friends were already achieving. At twenty-
three, he had not yet published a line, never yet earned a penny of his
own, and was still wholly dependent on his parents—a common enough
situation in middle-class families, but one that lends itself to emotional
blackmail in the best of circumstances. And circumstances in the Kafka
home were not the best; Herrmann, for one, never tired of reminding
the Herr Sohn of his own deprived childhood—"at seven they made me
drag a cart from village to village . . . with sores on my feet because I
didn't have shoes. It was a feast day when we had potatoes. . . . We all
slept in a single room . . ."—and having subsidized a doctor of sorts, he
was not about to go on subsidizing an impecunious scribbler. Nor would
the scribbler, accustomed as he was to see himself through his father's
eyes, have expected him to.

That was presumably one reason why, on April 1, 1906, with still
another six weeks to go before his third and final set of examinations,
Kafka volunteered for a six-month clerkship in the law offices of Dr.
Richard Löwy, an attorney on Old Town Square, "only to put the
time to some use," as he later put it in his job applications, "since from

the very beginning I intended not to practice law." Kafka was too careful a writer for this peculiar construction to have been wholly accidental; if he did not yet know what he wanted, he definitely knew what he didn't want. At any rate, the unpaid position, which entailed little work and few obligations, enabled him in good conscience to take two months off during the summer. It also presumably served to placate his father, while at the same time disabusing him of any lingering hopes of involving his son in the family business.

Not that Kafka could ever really keep clear of what, after all, was the very core of his parents' life, the object of their unremitting struggle, symbol and substance of their rise in the world. That very spring, Herrmann had moved his business to Celetna Street and did not hesitate to call on his son for help whenever help was needed—ever more often, as it happened, because both parents were now subject to frequent bouts of illness. Julie suffered from stomach trouble and "female complaints," possibly related to recurrent depressions; Herrmann's palpitations, with which he tyrannized his family and employees, were diagnosed as a weakness of the heart muscle. (He died at age seventy-seven, Julie at seventy-eight.) In May, Kafka wrote to Brod: "It's been a long time since I saw you (been lugging and dusting boxes, because we're moving the store, little girls, very little studying, your book,* whores, Macaulay's *Lord Clive*, and so it all comes together). Well, since I haven't been to your place for so long, I'll be coming today, so as not to disappoint you, and because I think today is your birthday" (L, 33).

On June 13 he passed his finals in Roman and German law with a grade of "satisfactory," and on June 18 he was awarded the Doctorate of Laws. (His formal sponsor was Max Weber's younger brother Alfred, who had just joined the Prague faculty and later became a prominent sociologist and economist in his own right. Brod studied with him, but Kafka's contact with him seems to have been confined to this one ceremonial occasion.)

July and August were once again spent at the Zuckmantl Sanatorium, where he resumed his affair of the previous year with the anonymous inspiration for Betty, the "aging, pretty girl" of "Wedding Preparations in the Country." The story obviously reflects aspects of the Zuckmantl experience, even beyond manifest surface details such as the train ride from Prague and certain identifiable features of the local

* Brod's *Death unto the Dead*.

topography. It seems most unlikely that Kafka ever seriously contemplated marrying "Betty," as has been suggested. Rather, what until then had been an abstraction looming, like death, in some remote future had suddenly leaped into focus for him as a concrete threat, an imminent and inexorable challenge. And some of the obsessive ambivalence with which Kafka, in later years, struggled to reconcile the irreconcilable —the need to be what he was, and the need to be what he felt he ought to be—is already sounded in this brittle, unfinished novelette.

On October 1, 1906, shortly after his return to Prague, he began a one-year clerkship in the court system, first in the county court and later in the court of criminal justice, mandatory requirements for government service. Since Kafka had no remote intention of applying for a government post and, moreover, as a Jew had next to no chance of obtaining one, the move can only be construed as yet another attempt to stall for time and delay the inevitable showdown. And to a degree it succeeded; he gained a precious year, and one which in many ways turned out to be among the few relatively happy ones of his short life.

He was still half hoping against hope for a last-minute miracle and at the same time desperate at not being able to put this interval between verdict and sentence to better use. "My path is a bad one," he wrote to Brod in May 1907, "and this much I can see—I am bound to end up like a dog. I, too, would like to give myself a wide berth. This being impossible, I can only rejoice that I feel no pity for myself and have at last become selfish to that extent."

The bleak mood of that spring imparts a further note of muted despair to the "Wedding Preparations in the Country," written during these months. (The title itself was later supplied by Brod, who edited the original 58-page manuscript, along with two later revisions of sixteen and eight pages respectively, for posthumous publication in 1951.) Nevertheless, this once again fragmentary work represents a marked advance in both conception and technique over the earlier "Description of a Struggle." Here, the self-lacerating conflict of the protagonist Raban —the same two vowels as Kafka, the same number of letters, *Rabe* the German for raven, Kafka the Czech (*kavka*) for jackdaw; the pseudonyms will later be pared down to the initial K., an amputated consonant with phantom-limb pains—assumes a focused intensity that parallels Kafka's own progression from anxiety to fear, from diffuse self-involvement to a growing awareness of manifest threats. The threat of marriage, for one, punishment for growing up:

. . . but why can't I deal with it the way I used to handle danger when I was a child? No need even for me to go to the country myself; that isn't necessary. I'll send my body, all dressed up. If it staggers out of my room, its stagger reveals not fear but nothingness. Nor is it excitement that makes it stumble on the steps, travel sobbing into the country, and eat its evening meals there in tears. For all this time I myself lie in bed, cozy under my yellow-brown blanket, exposed to a breeze wafting through the seldom-aired room. . . . And while I lie in bed, I assume the shape of a giant insect, a stagbeetle or a cockchafer, I think. . . . The shape of a large beetle, yes. I could then pretend it was a matter of hibernating and press my little legs to my bulging belly. And I would whisper a very few words, instructions to my dreary body standing close by, its back bent. I have soon finished; it bows, leaves swiftly, and will get everything done to perfection, while I have my rest.

The vivid fantasy of depersonalization contains a germ of "The Metamorphosis," written five years later. But a threat even more imminent than marriage was the prospect of a ritual to which he knew he was about to be sacrificed. "You work so hard at the office that you're too tired even to enjoy your vacation properly. And all that work still doesn't entitle you to loving concern from people. Instead, you're alone, a total stranger, a mere object of curiosity." Though he had never yet worked in an office, he was obviously already worn out in anticipation and terrified by the certain knowledge that even the utmost zeal would not earn him the human warmth and closeness he longed for, at least in the abstract.

The visual realism of the "Wedding Preparations"—the second paragraph alone, for instance, contains five distinct references to people's hands in motion or at rest—further intensifies that amplification of reality which, by its relentless concentration on the microscopic detail, pushes vision far beyond conventional limits. It was the time of Kafka's fascination with Flaubert, and his own pseudo-realism—the opulent dreamscape chiseled out of icy language—has been ascribed in part to the influence of the great French realist, whose *Sentimental Education* remained one of Kafka's all-time favorites. But the parallels are deceptive, and influence in any event presupposes the readiness to be influenced. What Kafka found in Flaubert, by way of a model, were hard-edged images of small worlds, sharply defined by a style more closely related to visual perception than to inner vision. It was during this very period that he also developed a sudden passion for art and socialized rather extensively with a number of young Prague artists, who professed great admiration for his own fluid line drawings, masterful in their stripped-down simplicity, and urged him to get professional instruction. (One of them, his former classmate Friedrich Feigl, left a well-known sketch of Kafka reading from his own works.) In May, Kafka designed a cover for Brod's forthcoming volume of lyrics, *The Path of the Lover,* which for technical reasons, however, could not be used.

He seems, in fact, to have briefly toyed with the idea of giving up writing for art altogether—less, one assumes, out of any compelling inner need than out of an understandable dissatisfaction with his literary accomplishments as measured against the prolific outpourings of contemporaries such as Brod, Werfel, and Baum. The impulse, however, did not outlast the few art lessons to which he subjected himself against his better judgment, and which he later blamed for having permanently ruined whatever little talent he may have had to begin with.

* * *

On June 20, 1907, the Kafka family moved from Celetna Street 3, near the old Powder Tower, to the fourth floor of a modern apartment house on Nikolas Street (now Parižska) 36. The building, aptly named the Ship, stood on the south bank of the Vltava, overlooking the river. Erected as part of a major complex designed to replace the razed ghetto slums, it was one of the first in the city to boast an elevator.

Shortly after the Kafkas' move, construction got underway on a new bridge (the present Svatopluh Čech Bridge) spanning the Vltava from the foot of Nikolas Street to the Letna Gardens on the north bank; its southern access ramp took off right in front of the Ship. The project called for a direct link between the new bridge and the Old Town Square, a mindless piece of bureaucratic planning that involved the destruction of a number of old buildings in the historic city center. The Ship itself eventually fell victim to an even more ruthless foe of historic charm: it was leveled in 1945 by the retreating Germans.

The sweeping view from Kafka's room—"elbows propped on the table, he looked out of the window at the river, the bridge, and the heights on the other bank with their hint of green," as he described it in "The Judgment"—may have been an improvement over the dank and crepuscular quarters on Celetna Street. But in his father's house there were always too few mansions. The new apartment, though more spacious, was still a tight fit for eight people—the parents, Kafka, his three sisters, a maid, and the household factotum, Marie Werner—in addition to a cat and two canaries. In the circumstances, privacy was nonexistent. No one could sneeze, cough, use the single bathroom, or so much as stir in bed without alerting the rest of the family; Herrmann, in particular, imposed no restraints on his persistent urge to let the world know how he felt, or felt about it.

The three girls ended up sharing a room. Kafka's own room with a view formed the only passage between the living room and the parents' bedroom, an arrangement that would have been distressing enough to any ordinary adult; given Kafka's near-pathological sensitivity, it became a cause of continual martyrdom, one possible reason why he subjected himself to it for some seven years. "When the breakfast noise dies down to the left of me, the lunch noise starts up on the right. Everywhere doors are being opened as though people wanted to come crashing through the walls" (L, 12/15/10). Hardly, one would think, a propitious environment for creative work, and yet Kafka's own choice, which obviously met deep inner needs. For the stubborn fact remains that, except for the last nine months of his life, he never really left his parents' house. Even during the two years, from 1915 to 1917, when he worked and slept in rented rooms—a tentative first step toward independence to which his illness put a decisive and disastrous end—he regularly took his meals at home.

* * *

On July 3, 1907, Kafka celebrated his twenty-fourth birthday. He had paid his debt to parents and society by painfully squiggling through the multidimensional mazes of formal and informal education and emerged, bloody and far from unbowed, but come through just the same—certainly more than he ever expected, though he never once saw a rational alternative to plodding ahead in obedience to the inscrutable laws that seemed to govern his existence. But he had now reached an end and a beginning. Ahead of him, beyond open waters, lay a world of seemingly boundless opportunities, something like the mythical "Amerika" of his fantasies. He at last had his chance to make good his escape from his parents, from Prague, from himself. The prospect terrified him.

In the meantime, however, there was one last, long summer, the definitive end of childhood, timeless, lazy, with no responsibilities other than to enjoy himself. And, somewhat to his own surprise, he almost succeeded.

His father, having once treated him to a trip abroad, saw no cause for further extravagance. Kafka therefore spent most of August with Uncle Siegfried at Triesch. His relations with the shrewd and compassionate country doctor were affectionate, yet distant enough to impose no strain, two lonely people who obviously enjoyed each other's company up to a point but also knew how to keep out of each other's way. Uncle Siegfried never pried, never offered advice unless asked, but always made himself available when needed.

It may well have been this solid and uniquely uncomplicated relationship that partly accounts for the uncharacteristic exuberance with which Kafka drifted through that summer, and for the insouciance, if not—for him—downright bravado with which he seemed to be facing the coming season in hell. But there was another reason, briefly alluded to in his mid-August reply to a report about job prospects from Max Brod, who had conscientiously remained in Prague to hunt for mindless work that would leave him time and strength enough for his own writing:

> Coming home from the hike last night (fun, great fun) I found your letter. It threw me, even though I was tired. Because when it comes to indecision, now there is something I know all about; in fact, I know nothing else. . . . That is why it would scarcely be appropriate for me to even try and change your mind.
>
> Your circumstances and my own are totally different. It therefore doesn't matter that, when I came upon your "decided not to accept," it gave me a scare like a bulletin from the battlefield, and I had to catch my breath before I could go on. . . . I told myself that you, for your part, had to keep busy. I am sure of your needs in this respect, even if I find them incomprehensible. You would not be happy spending a whole year hiking in the same woods. Besides, isn't it almost certain that during your clerkship you'll find some literary position that will obviate the need for anything else?
>
> As for myself, on the other hand, I would have run all the way to Komotau like a lunatic. [Brod had been offered a post-office job at Komotau, which he eventually accepted.] I do not,

however, need activity, the less so since I am incapable of it. And while the same woods may not always satisfy me, either, it seems quite clear that I have accomplished nothing during my clerkship year. . . .

No, if my prospects haven't improved by October, I am going to take a diploma course at the Mercantile Academy and study Spanish in addition to French and English. It would be splendid if you'd join me. What you have over me, when it comes to learning, I'll make up for by my impatience. My uncle would have to find us a job in Spain, or we could go to South America, to the Azores, Madeira. . . .

In the meantime, however, I am still allowed to live here till August 25. I ride around a great deal on the motorcycle, I swim a lot, I lie naked in the grass by the pond, I stay out in the park till midnight with a girl who has awkwardly fallen in love; I've cut hay in the meadow, set up a quoit game, nursed trees after a storm, herded cows and goats and driven them home at nightfall; I've shot pool a lot, taken long walks, drunk much beer, I've even been to the temple. But most of my time here—six days so far—has been spent with two little girls, very bright, students, very social-democratic. They have to keep clenching their teeth so as not to be continuously forced to proclaim some principle or conviction. One is A. The other, H.W., is small, with cheeks eternally and transcendently red. She is very nearsighted, and not only on account of the graceful motion with which she places the pince-nez on her nose—whose tip, by the way, is composed of truly beautiful facets. Last night I dreamed about her foreshortened fat legs; such are the byways that lead me to recognize a girl's beauty and make me fall in love . . . [L, mid-August 1907]

*   *   *

Hedwig Weiler, the H.W. of the letter, commonly rates no more than a footnote in Kafka's biography, and unlike most other women in his life, she seems to have drifted out of it without leaving any discernible traces in his surviving work. Their affair, which lasted about a year, certainly lacked the self-torment, fustian, and high drama of Kafka's subsequent involvements. Nonetheless, to judge from the very few letters of his that have been recovered, it seems to have been a relationship that combined genuine mutual affection and concern, shared interests, and sexual attraction frankly avowed and presumably acted upon. At least during the early stages when, however indecisive, he still thought, or deluded himself into thinking, that life offered choices—Paraguay, Madeira—he managed to sound spontaneous and responsive, open to his own feelings as seldom before or after, in love with a real-life woman rather than with a disembodied image of his needs and fears. That there were narrow limits to his ability to love a real-life woman—or his ability to love altogether—may have been a major factor in their apparently abrupt but undramatic breakup some time in the fall or winter of 1908.

Hedwig Weiler, at any rate, was far too substantial a person in her own right to lend herself to immolation by fantasy. Five years younger than Kafka, the then nineteen-year-old—on a visit to her grandmother in Triesch—had already completed two semesters of philosophy at the University of Vienna. A rabid socialist, at once down-to-earth and idealistic, she was hugely endowed with that worldly wisdom and driving energy that inevitably inspired Kafka's awe, admiration, and ultimately self-contempt.

An early, chatty letter, written from Prague right after their separation on August 19, suggests considerable intimacy but also strikes the first note of anguish:

> I have no social life, no distractions. I spend my evenings on the little balcony overlooking the river. I don't even read the *Workers' News*, and I am not a good person. . . . I just don't have that interest in people that you demand. You see, I am a ridiculous person. And if you love me a little, it is out of pity; my share is fear. How pointless are meetings by mail, the splash of waves on the shores of a lake that separates two people. The pen glides over the tops of the letters, and this is the end. It is cool, and I must lie in an empty bed.

Yet the ties were still strong enough for him to decide, early in September, to join Hedwig in Vienna and spend a year studying at the Mercantile Academy. Whether this was mere wishful thinking, or whether it was vetoed by his increasingly disgruntled father, is unclear; Herrmann's business had, in fact, suffered some serious reverses just then as a result of the renewed Czech boycott of German and Jewish firms. Hedwig, in any event, suddenly made up her mind to leave Vienna. On September 15, Kafka wrote to her: "I know you have to get away from Vienna, just as I must get away from Prague—which means that we could spend the year in Paris, for instance. But the following is true: we'll start by doing what we each have to do. And if we go on doing that, won't we inevitably find the way to one another?"

A mere four days later, however, the real world had come crashing down on him.

"Yes," he wrote to her on September 19, "the decision has been made, but only today. Other people only rarely make decisions and then enjoy them during the long intervals in between. I, on the other hand, incessantly make decisions, like a boxer, except that I don't box. . . . I am staying in Prague and, in a few weeks, will probably get a job with an insurance company. Until then, all my time will be devoted to studying the insurance business, which, however, is very interesting" (L, 9/19/07).

The decision had indeed been made, but made way back in the dark ages of childhood, made for him rather than by him, and most of his efforts to unmake it, to shape his own destiny rather than have it cast in the standard mold, were at best delaying tactics, shadowboxing, as he himself knew even while going through the motions. He wanted to break away precisely as he had contemplated suicide: had he really been capable of striking out on his own, there would have been no point in his so doing. In announcing that "the decision has been made," he was, in effect, telling Hedwig Weiler that the trap had been sprung. And the note of relief, if not of downright triumph, is unmistakable.

* * *

In his 1937 biography of Kafka, Max Brod left a vivid description of their joint search for a suitable job, and of the problems they faced:

> Now when it came to the point of having to make a living, Franz insisted that the job have nothing to do with literature; that would have seemed to him a debasement of literary creativity. The bread-and-butter job had to be kept strictly separate from his writing; he would accept no commingling of the two, such as for instance in journalism. . . . For years those views of his also influenced me and my choice of profession. Like him, out of respect for art I suffered the tortures of the damned in the most hideous, boring, and uncreative law offices until finally, years later, I found my way as a music and theater critic. Today I regard Kafka's intransigence on this point as a noble error and regret the many hundreds of joyless hours it

made me waste in near-despair in offices similar to those in which Kafka now began his martyrdom, killing time, God's most precious gift.

What we were both desperately looking for was a job with a "single shift"—working hours, that is, till two or three in the afternoon . . . with afternoons free. Commercial firms had both morning and afternoon office hours, which left no substantial block of time for literary work, walks, reading, the theater, etc. . . . The 2:00 p.m. closing time, however, was confined to only a very few enterprises, most of them government offices, which even at that time, under the old Austrian empire, hired Jews only if they were backed by powerful sponsors.

Brod's notion, which he goes on to develop at some length, of the genius forced to dissipate his creative energy in senseless toil and drudgery is the conventional view, and obviously not devoid of foundation. But Kafka's situation, as he himself pointed out, was quite different from that of his friend; different, in fact, from that of anyone else in his circle.

That he was determined jealously to guard the purity of his "writing as a form of prayer" and resisted every temptation, if such it was, to prostitute his gifts by writing for a living, is true. This, moreover, whether or not he knew it at the time, placed him squarely in the tradition of the Talmud sages—and of Spinoza—who practiced a trade for a living because it was forbidden to profit from teaching the Torah. It is also true, however, that he was far more keenly aware of the nature of these gifts than anyone else around him, Brod included. He knew perfectly well that he could never conceive of writing the kind of popular novels with which Brod made his reputation, or produce reams of marketable journalism à la Egon Erwin Kisch.

In fact, given his uncompromising approach to both life and art, his attempt to keep these two strictly separate and find a job that involved minimal demands on his time, energy, and emotions made perfectly good sense. That he was not entirely successful, that even his work for the insurance company eventually turned out to demand a great deal beyond mere routine attendance, was partly his own doing and undoing: he was constitutionally incapable of tackling any task, no matter how trivial, with the indifference and contempt it deserved.

Whether, as Brod suggests, Herrmann Kafka could have staked

his son to a few years of creative freedom is a question not only rhetorical but nonsensical as well; a generous and understanding father would presumably have raised an altogether different son. Such speculations, moreover, ignore an even more vital point: Kafka's job, while imposing an onerous routine, also provided a structure and status on which he came to depend for a large measure of identity and self-respect in the otherwise baffling and incomprehensible world of ordinary people. He turned out to be not only an overly conscientious but also a reasonably effective functionary—far more effective, certainly, than he ever gave himself credit for. But though he hated the monster bureaucracy to which he felt indentured, just as he hated his family and his living arrangements, these were the lifelines that forced him to get out of bed in the morning, that enabled him to come up for air; and he—or something within him—knew better than to cut them, even if one end was always looped around his neck.

The initiation, however, turned out to be considerably more traumatic than even he had anticipated and came close to aborting his career in the insurance business.

Partly as a result of Kafka's less than brilliant academic record, the job search presented even more than the usual difficulties, and in his desperation he turned for help to the "uncle from Madrid," the director of the Spanish railways. Kafka had always more or less counted on him, anyway, for a glamorous job abroad, and in the end Uncle Alfred came through, though not quite in the manner expected. A self-made, experienced, and highly successful executive, he had much too much common sense and family loyalty to indulge the romantic fantasies of his unworldly nephew by shipping him off unprepared to some remote outpost of civilization. Instead, he used his connections to obtain for him a foothold with the Prague branch office of the Assicurazioni Generali, with prospects for an eventual transfer to more exciting locales.

The Assicurazioni Generali, with headquarters in—then—Austrian Trieste, was founded in 1831 as a transport, marine, and fire insurance company and later branched out into life insurance. In Kafka's day, new staff members were routinely assigned for training to this increasingly lucrative but technically less demanding field.

For all its progressive and aggressive business practices, the Assicurazioni Generali's personnel policies remained obdurately medieval, a relic of Austrian feudalism at its sanctimonious worst. As it happened,

Kafka's application, completed in his own hand on October 2, 1907, has been preserved in the company archives; the printed preamble, with its litany of rules and regulations—unconditional promptness, overtime without compensation, fourteen days vacation every second year at the convenience of the company, no resignation without three months' notice, no private property in office desks, etc.—suggests something of the tone that prevailed. In his replies to the questions, Kafka stated that, except for the usual childhood diseases, he had always been in good health, that he was exempt from military service "due to weakness," that he knew German stenography, that aside from German, his mother tongue, he was fluent in Czech and familiar with French and English but lacking in practice, and that he had thus far been supported by his parents.

The application was forwarded to the head office at Trieste with a covering letter requesting approval at a monthly salary of 80 crowns, hardly more than a token gratuity. A postscript adds that "we intend to give Dr. Kafka special training in life insurance operations so as to use him later for assignments abroad. He came to us highly recommended by the U.S. Vice Consul in Prague, Mr. Weissberger, father of your representative in Madrid. Dr. Kafka's family enjoys an excellent reputation." (Arnold Weissberger, who at his son's request had interceded on Kafka's behalf, hardly knew him. He was an officer of the Union Bank, famous as a discriminating collector of antiques, who had emigrated to the United States in 1868, acquired U.S. citizenship, and, after his return, been appointed honorary U.S. vice consul.)

Also on file is the six-page protocol of Kafka's pre-employment medical examination by one Dr. Wilhelm Pollak, who described the applicant as delicate but in good health, 1.88 meters tall (just a trace under six feet), weighing 61 kilos (134 pounds), slender, graceful, appearing younger than his age, definitely fit for employment in insurance. The only positive finding was a slight dullness of the upper pulmonary apex "due to rachitic deviation" (WAG, p. 141).

Sixteen years of continuous exposure to the autocratic pedantries of the Austrian school system had obviously inured Kafka to bureaucratic pettiness, and in spite of the ridiculous salary, he started out with high hopes and expectations. It was, after all, a first step toward independence, and he seems to have found the technical aspects of the insurance business of considerable, if baffling, fascination. In a remark attributed to him by Brod (bio., p. 70), he once aptly compared insurance to the religion of primitive man, who "believes in warding off evil by all sorts of manipulations." The mysteries of primitive religion can obviously be intriguing.

At the end of his first week on the job he still managed to sound relatively upbeat. Writing to Hedwig on October 8, 1907, he tells her that

> my life is now totally disorganized. True, I have a position with a tiny salary of 80 crowns and an immense eight to nine hours of work, but I gobble up the hours outside the office like a wild beast. I have never, until now, been in a position of having to cram all my daily living into six hours; besides, I am also studying Italian and want to spend these beautiful evenings out of doors. Now as to the office. I am with the Assicurazioni Generali, and there is at least hope of my someday gracing an armchair in some faraway country and gazing out of the office window upon sugarcane fields or Moslem cemeteries. The insurance business as such interests me very much, but my present work is dreary. [L, 10/8/07]

A month later, he already sounded considerably less positive.

> How soon and how far I'll be transferred I do not as yet know. Probably not until I've put in a year. The nicest thing would be a transfer out of the company altogether, which is not entirely impossible. What I resent is not the work as such so much as the indolence of swampy time. The office hours, you know, are indivisible; even during the last half hour one feels the pressure of the preceding eight as keenly as during the first one. . . . I am studying Italian, since I'll probably first be sent to Trieste. To those who are sensitive to such things, I must have looked pathetic during the first few days. As indeed I was. I felt déclassé. People who haven't idled away at least part of their life till age twenty-five are much to be pitied; the money you earn you can't take with you into the grave, unlike—and of this I am convinced—the time you lazed away. I am in the office at eight in the morning and leave at 6:30 at night. [L, 11/07]

In the circumstances, there could be no hope of accomplishing any creative work of his own, of doing the one thing he was meant to do— "writing, this horrible occupation of which I am now deprived, and whose loss is my whole misfortune" (L, 11/07). By year's end, the lure of distant lands and Moslem cemeteries had wilted altogether in the heat of the ten-hour "normal" workday, with two hours for lunch and frequent mandatory overtime, six days a week minimally, plus additional Sunday work—also unpaid—whenever required. Moreover, the Assicurazioni Generali was a decidedly profit-making enterprise bent on competing in the international market; its aggressive management had no intention of putting up with the famous Austrian *Schlamperei,* the sloppy indolence and amiable inefficiency so widely prevalent in both the public and private sectors of the empire's sprawling, interlocking bureaucracies. Employees were treated like raw recruits conscripted for life and wholly owned by the company, chewed out in public, barked at, and dressed down irrespective of status or age, in a manner more suitable to an army barracks than an insurance office. And although Kafka happened to have an exceptionally civilized superior with wide-ranging literary interests—the two, in fact, subsequently remained on friendly terms—he found the unremitting pressure, hysteria, and humiliation unbearable. "My home life had already made me all too sensitive in this respect." After a mere few weeks he therefore began to look for a more congenial job.

The search had to be conducted with the utmost discretion. Job hopping generally was frowned upon, a sign of shiftlessness, disloyalty, and lack of character. And the Assicurazioni, in particular, considered quitting tantamount to treason and dealt with it accordingly. The last thing Kafka needed, at this stage, was yet another black mark on his record. A switch was also bound to place him in an awkward position vis-à-vis his sponsor; and since Arnold Weissberger happened to be a colleague of Brod's father, and Brod himself was not given to undue discretion, he had reason to worry. "Under no circumstances should your father mention that I am dissatisfied, or that I am going to quit the job, work for the post office, or anything like that. It would upset me very much, because Mr. Weissberger went to no end of trouble to get me into the Assicurazioni, and I was insanely grateful to him, as seemed appropriate enough after my earlier despair" (L, 12/07).

* * *

The search, however, became more and more difficult and discouraging—"you will forgive my miserable self if I tell you that I spent Sunday morning and early afternoon applying for jobs, though by no more than my bodily posture, an exercise in total, dreadful futility."

In the meantime, pressures at work continued to build up.

> I had a miserable week [he complained to Hedwig]. Much too much work at the office. Maybe that is the way it's always going to be, from now on; one has to earn one's grave. . . . They chased me all over the place like a wild beast, and since I don't happen to be one, you can imagine how I felt. Last week I was a truly fit candidate for the street where I now live and which I've dubbed a "launching ramp for suicides," because it leads to the river, where they are now building a bridge. On the other side is a series of hills and gardens called the Belvedere; they're going to tunnel through them, so that one can walk along the street, across the bridge, and underneath the Belvedere. So far, however, only the skeleton of the bridge has been erected, and the street ends at the river. All of this is just a joke, anyway, because crossing the bridge to the Belvedere will always remain more attractive than going to heaven via the river. [L, Spring 1908]

Allusions to suicide crop up several times during that period, their self-conscious jocosity no true measure of the depth of his despair. "The handiest way out, beckoning perhaps already since childhood, was not suicide itself, but the thought of suicide. In any case, what kept me from killing myself was no special cowardice but a reflection that again added up to meaningless futility: 'You, who can do nothing, want to do this, of all things? If you were capable of killing yourself, you would no longer have to do it, so to speak' " (L, 11/07).

He was unable to write; so far as is known, he produced nothing between September 1907 and September 1909, with the exception of a single book review. And feeling like a beast of burden for most of the day, there was more than logic to his devouring the few remaining hours "like a wild beast," as he confided to Hedwig. The metaphor seems somewhat overblown, unless—as Kafka undoubtedly did, or at least was disposed to feel—one categorizes all sexual activity as inherently beastly. The more prosaic truth, however, was that he simply conformed to the lugubrious patterns of hormonal politics that ruled male conduct in his class and time. Like most of his contemporaries, he for years quite regularly frequented whorehouses, slept with freelance prostitutes, and picked up weary semipros in sleazy all-night cafés, such as the Trocadéro, the Eldorado, or the London. (According to the *Prager Tagblatt* of November 18, 1906, Prague had thirty-five public brothels, about five hundred full-time and some six thousand part-time prostitutes. Prague also had an inordinately high rate of illegitimacy—44 percent of total births in 1912, as against 16 percent in Berlin; the discrepancy is interesting, though certainly open to any number of interpretations.)

At any rate, unless one insists on imputing early sainthood or precocious wisdom to the youthful Kafka, there was nothing incongruous or even remarkable about his behavior; he merely observed the age-old customs sanctioned by tradition, hallowed by class privilege, and codified by society as a means of simulating man's superiority; Max Brod, for instance, probably never outgrew his predilection for chambermaids and waitresses. Kafka's letters of the period tell of numerous affairs, decidedly not of the heart, with a Joszi, a Maltschi, a Hansi, scornfully referred to as *Weiber,* a term of collective disdain loaded with sexual antagonism.

But if these liaisons scarcely qualify as "beastly," they were also singularly devoid of human content. The conscious degradation of woman is a potent defense against unconscious fear of the all-powerful, all-devouring female that haunts the arts and literature of the period; it shaped Freud's perception, and it clearly emerges in Kafka's own later work, notably *The Castle* and *The Trial.* But degrading woman to a sexual object reduces sex itself to an exercise in object relations difficult, repugnant, or downright impossible within the context of a relationship between human beings.

It was this crime against nature, the mother-versus-whore syndrome with its concomitant *nostalgie de la boue* and debasement of sex, that Kafka later called "a disease of the instincts, a fruit of the times" (L, 4/17). And though it afflicted practically all his friends to some degree, the fact that they were seldom even aware of it unless it happened to impair their "performance" was equally characteristic; when it came to marital relations and family life, the petulant selfishness and obtuse cruelty of these hypersensitive and cultivated intellectuals knew no bounds. Again Brod is a stellar example, though far from unique.

With weary despair, Kafka eventually came to recognize the problem: "Obviously, on account of my dignity, on account of my pride (never mind how humble he seems, the crooked Western Jew), I am able to love only that which I have placed so far above me that it becomes unattainable" (L, 11/21). Yet it seems more than likely that in his affair with Hedwig Weiler, relations deteriorated in the precise measure in which she ceased, in his eyes, to be a female with a pretty nose, fat legs, and irrelevant ideas and became a complex, ambitious, and vulnerable human being, while he, in turn, sought relief, release, and oblivion in the sexual jungle of Prague's whorehouses, wine cellars, and *cafés chantants*.

*   *   *

By midsummer 1908, the furtive job hunt finally yielded results, thanks to the aid of Kafka's old friend, Ewald Felix Přibram. Ewald's father, in spite of his Jewish origins—never denied but sedulously ignored—had risen to prominence within the most conservative inner circles of finance and industry, and served on the boards of several corporate enterprises. Thus from 1895 until his death in 1913, Dr. Otto Přibram also had a seat on the board of the Arbeiter-Unfall-Versicherungsanstalt für das Königreich Boehmen in Prag—the Workmen's Accident Insurance Institute for the Kingdom of Bohemia in Prague. This semigovernmental institution, as a matter of principle, did not employ Jews, although a Dr. Fleischmann—unconverted, three-quarters Czech, and a social democrat to boot—had breached the barrier some time before Kafka, in July 1908, was hired as a "probationary assistant" in industrial accident insurance. Throughout his tenure, the two remained the only Jews among the institute's approximately 250 employees—"he the first, I the second, last, and crumbling Jew in this place," Kafka wrote as late as 1917; and when asked to sponsor the application of an Orthodox Jewish friend, he categorically refused: "The institute is off limits for Jews. . . . It is incomprehensible how the two Jews that work there managed to get in (with the aid of the third Jew), but it will never happen again."

The deeper implications of this situation took time to sink in. For the moment, he felt immensely relieved. The work as such was far better suited to his background and interests, and while the starting salary of 3 crowns a day was not much of an improvement, the chances for advancement were good, even if they did not include the prospect of foreign intrigue. Yet in the final analysis, all these benefits were merely incidental to the all-important blessing of the "single shift," the straight six-hour working day from 8 a.m. to 2 p.m. A medical certificate attesting to "nervousness and cardiac excitability" made for a face-saving exit from the Assicurazioni, and on July 30, 1908, Kafka reported for the job in which he was to remain for the rest of his life.

Thirteen

THE Workmen's Accident Insurance Institute for the Kingdom of Bohemia in Prague was an integral part of the pullulating Austro-Hungarian bureaucracy that like a giant net of near-epic intricacy covered the entire Habsburg domain and, for all its rips, bulges, and frazzled strands, somehow managed to keep the disparate fragments from breaking loose. This particular mini-empire, founded in 1889, had been spawned by the comprehensive social legislation enacted by Parliament between 1885 and 1887 under pressure from the growing and increasingly militant labor movement.

The laws as such were ambitious in scope. Modeled on the reforms promulgated two years earlier by Bismarck in an effort to forestall the spread of socialism in Germany, they not only aimed at regulating relations between capital and labor but also marked an incipient attempt to define the state's responsibilities toward the individual worker. And although widespread corruption and inefficiency slowed their implementation, the ultimate effect was nonetheless substantial. No less militant a critic of the establishment than Viktor Adler, leader of the Austrian socialists, testified in 1895 that in its social legislation Austria ranked a close third, right behind Germany and Switzerland.

Mandatory coverage for industrial accidents, paid for entirely by employer contributions, was introduced as part of this legislative package in 1887, with health insurance added two years later. The system was to be administered through six regional headquarters, incorporated as "semigovernmental" institutes—subject, that is, to a degree of government regulation, including civil service status and pension rights for the employees, but autonomous as to the management of all business and financial aspects.

In the case of the Prague institute, at least, this ingenious notion of harnessing private enterprise to public welfare proved a disaster. Its district, the grandiosely named but, for all that, fittingly mythical "Kingdom of Bohemia," covered a territory nearly as large as the other five combined, and the number of its employees rose rapidly from the original 52 in 1889 to about 250 by the time Kafka arrived on the scene. This, of itself, seems scarcely excessive, considering that the office was by then responsible for well over 35,000 industrial enterprises ranging in size from toolsheds to factories.

Yet however efficient the clerical staff at the paper-shuffling level, the institute's original management team seems to have been strikingly innocent of actuarial experience or even ordinary business sense, although deficiencies in the empowering legislation also played a part. Premiums for this compulsory accident and health insurance were not related to risk factors but based solely on the number of employees in a given enterprise. And since the employers alone were responsible for the entire amount, they not unsurprisingly tended to report as few employees as plausibility would permit. Nor were they taking much of a risk; the institute employed a total of only seven inspectors for the entire district, a fact far from secret, which, in turn, led to a rash of fraudulent or grossly inflated claims. The inevitable result was a deficit that, starting in 1893, mounted annually at an alarming rate and, by 1908, had reached a point where even Viennese bureaucrats felt moved to overcome their natural indolence long enough to take corrective action.

As luck would have it, therefore, Kafka's entry coincided with a sweeping reorganization which, in effect, amounted to a fresh start and quite coincidentally provided him with some serendipitous opportunities. The senile chief administrator, persuaded to take his long-overdue retirement, was replaced by Dr. Robert Marschner, an energetic young professor of insurance at the Prague Institute of Technology, with whom Kafka had already taken several specialized courses. It was presumably this earlier contact that explains why, with a mere few weeks of service to his credit, he was the one chosen to deliver the welcoming speech at the ceremonies formally marking Marschner's appointment. And while this maiden effort of his professional career adds nothing to his literary luster, it turned out to be a creditable enough performance, appropriate to such occasions unto our own day, complete with the obligatory upbeat ending: "Complaints against the institute, both justified and unjustified, have piled up in the course of the years. One thing can henceforth be taken for granted: we shall do good work. Whatever may be useful or necessary by way of reforms, within the bounds of existing laws, will be done."

What is more, the new administration actually lived up to his platitudes. Marschner quickly put into place a whole new system of controls, from internal audits to the rigorous investigation of suspect claims. Premiums were adjusted to reflect varying risk factors in different industries, and routine checks on employers, along with gentle persuasion or threats of legal sanction, dramatically raised the level of compliance with the law and, not incidentally, the institute's annual premium income. At the same time, Marschner initiated what was to become one of the most progressive innovations in the field—a heavy stress on the institute's active and systematic involvement in occupational safety measures and in the prevention of industrial accidents which, with the rapid mechanization of the workplace, had become a problem of epidemic proportions.

Marschner's decisive moves brought almost immediate results: the annual report for 1910, his first full year in office, was also the first in seventeen years to show a positive balance sheet. The excess of income over expenses amounted to nearly 3 million crowns, an impressive achievement, even if it still left a deficit of well over 37 million accrued since 1893.

Kafka himself wrote several sections of that report dealing with accident prevention. More interesting, though, and indicative of Marschner's quick grasp of his protégé's special talents, is a lengthy press release published in the *Tetschen-Bodenbacher Zeitung* of November 4, 1911. Although unsigned, it can definitely be ascribed to Kafka, not only on the basis of a diary entry of October 10, 1911—"Wrote a sophistic article for and against the institute for the *Tetschen-Bodenbacher Zeitung*"—but also because certain passages fairly mock the flatfooted pedantry of the customary bureaucratese:

> We readily concede that the institute's annual reports up to 1909, with their figures documenting a downright organic growth of the deficit, offered scant reason for enthusiasm. On the contrary, these reports succeeded in scuttling all hope for the future of the institute, which seemed to resemble nothing so much as a dead body sprouting an ever-proliferating deficit as its sole surviving limb. . . . Now things have changed . . . but nothing short of broad-based public support can make sure that these promising changes will become permanent.

And touching on the institute's campaign for accident prevention, he goes on to remark that

> such innovative efforts will unavoidably give rise as well to a few puerile inanities. Thus for instance, employers are urged to view the institute's exhibit of safety devices—which, by our count, contains a total of six items. Silly, no doubt; yet this, too, something to be grateful for. After all, how often in the past has the Prague institute offered the public a chance to laugh at its excess of youthful zeal?

*   *   *

In the light of Kafka's stubborn resolve not to profane the sanctity of his vocation, one would have expected him to be crushed by this ironic twist of fate. Yet oddly enough, there is no record of his ever having complained about these frequent writing assignments in the line of work. On the contrary, he made it a regular practice to send copies of the annual report to many of his friends, always careful to note his personal contributions. It would be difficult to perceive this as anything other than a touch of pride in a job well done.

He had reason to be proud. His articles, for the most part highly technical in nature, combine an astonishing grasp of abstruse detail with a lucidity of presentation seldom encountered in writings of this sort, least of all in German. They quite incisively refute the caricature of Kafka as a bumbling fool forever sleepwalking in broad daylight and incapable of tying his shoelaces—an impression to which he himself so copiously contributed.

As a matter of fact, his superiors almost immediately recognized what, in their consistently glowing job evaluations of Kafka throughout the years, crops up time and again as his "exceptional faculty for conceptualization," presumably referring to his deviant talent for summing up complex subject matter in straightforward and simple German prose. "Combines outstanding zeal with sustained interest in all assignments," wrote his superior at the end of the first year; and six months later: "Dr. Kafka is an eminently hardworking employee endowed with exceptional talent and devotion to duty" (WAG, p. 149).

After keeping an eye on him for a few months, during which Kafka got his bearings in the statistical and claims departments, Marschner seems to have been sufficiently impressed by his new assistant to put him in charge of the institute's pioneer venture into aggressive accident prevention. It is most unlikely that this hard-driving and immensely competent executive would have picked a man who struck him as an unworldly and fumble-fingered dreamer for a challenging new assignment on which he had staked so much of his reputation.

And Kafka fully justified this confidence. Accident prevention in the workplace required a thorough familiarity with production methods in various industries, down to the specific tasks involving the individual worker. Kafka's sharp eye for minute details, his hyperacute perceptivity and pedantic thoroughness, no doubt stood him in good stead; much more remarkable, though, is the speed with which he was able to assimilate a vast body of knowledge in what, up until then, had been totally alien territory—clear proof of an intellectual potential radically at odds with his relatively poor scholastic showing. His initial contributions to the institute's 1907 and 1908 reports still dealt mainly with legal issues concerning mandatory coverage in the construction industry, and with the novel problem of motor vehicle operations. The sections he wrote for the 1909 and 1910 reports, on the other hand, dwell at length on the technical details of specific safety measures, such as the modifications of a mechanical jointer plane that eventually were to save the lives and limbs of hundreds of workers, especially in the various branches of Bohemia's dominant lumber industry.

Effective action along these lines, aside from specialized knowledge, also required familiarity with actual working conditions in factories and shops. Over the years, Kafka audited a number of engineering courses at the Technical Institute; his graphic description of the torture machine in *The Penal Colony* may owe something to this enforced expansion of his cultural horizons. Far more important, however, were the numerous trips he undertook on behalf of the institute. Beyond their narrow professional purpose, they provided intimate glimpses of life and work in the industrial towns of Bohemia, which even Kafka—ever inward-looking, incapable of traveling without the heavy baggage of his self-absorption—could not fail to take in. These impressions, amplified by his subsequent experience in handling disability and death claims on behalf of workers maimed or killed on the job, served to reinforce the instinctive identification with the underdog that defined his manifest political orientation. Brod reports how Kafka once remarked, in utter amazement: "How modest these people are. Instead of storming the institute and smashing the place to bits, they come and plead" (bio., p. 76).

That, given his position, such sentiments were bound to confront him with serious moral dilemmas is to be taken for granted. According to Gustav Janouch, whose father also worked for the institute, Kafka resolved such quandaries on a case-by-case basis; where he felt that workers had been victimized by bureaucratic excesses, he surreptitiously sabotaged the institute's case in court, on occasion even going so far as to pay the plaintiff's legal expenses. There is no independent confirmation of such devious generosity on his part, nor does he himself ever allude to it. In any event, these moral conflicts were probably submerged in later years by the growing tension between job and writing, which drained off compassion for victims other than himself.

But if his initial zeal on the job gradually gave way to boredom, indifference, and, ultimately, despair, the change apparently did not impair his proficiency. He was promoted within the year, granted full civil service tenure in 1910, advanced to Junior Secretary in 1913, Secretary in 1920, and Senior Secretary in 1922, shortly before his retirement on full disability. Throughout World War I, he was draft-deferred as essential at the institute's request. His superiors persistently remained enthusiastic in their periodic evaluations and always endorsed his requests for salary increases. Chief Inspector Eugen Pfohl, his immediate superior until 1917, insisted that "without Kafka, the whole department would collapse." Kafka, in turn, referred to Pfohl as a man whom he loved like a father. And in 1913, he was the only staff member to accompany Marschner and Pfohl to a conference on accident prevention held in Vienna.

Relations with colleagues and subordinates, down to the janitors and cleaning women, were equally cordial. Brod, who often visited him in the office, was told that "Kafka didn't have a single enemy." Generous to a fault, he was always ready to help out with small loans, as likely as not refusing to accept repayment. Something of an odd bird, to be sure, but his often startling candor and gentle manners were generally perceived as an appealing streak of naïveté. "Our office baby," one of his colleagues said of him. "Once he came into my room just as I was eating a bread-and-butter sandwich. How can you gobble up all that greasy stuff, he asked me; the best food is a lemon." And a cleaning woman fondly remembered how Dr. Kafka never just passed on to her his little presents of candy or flowers but always begged her to do him a favor by accepting them—"so different from the other gentlemen."

Even discounting the dash of piety that inevitably tends to color such reminiscences, it seems clear that Herr Doktor Kafka was highly esteemed as a staff member and universally popular as a person. Unlike Raban, the protagonist of his "Wedding Preparations," he himself did earn the "loving concern" of his fellow workers, though one cannot be sure to what extent he even let himself be aware of it.

* * *

An objective view of Kafka's situation at the institute thus largely refutes Brod's view of him as a helpless victim trapped in the gears of a merciless brain crusher and condemned to mindless and inhuman toil. The bureaucracy in its ultimate ramifications—of which he had an incisive grasp, as shown in both *The Trial* and *The Castle*—was indubitably monstrous, in an impersonal way. At the personal level, however, the representatives with whom Kafka had his day-to-day dealings proved consistently humane; in later years, when his illness necessitated long leaves of absence and finally forced him to retire, they treated him with exquisite consideration. The work as such was obviously not devoid of challenge but, except for the occasional crises bound to arise in any office, hardly taxing in terms of either volume or hours, as he himself quite readily acknowledged in his more sober moments. And far from being a nameless cog in a giant engine run amok, he was from the very beginning in decision-making positions and contributed his share toward a significant reduction of crippling and fatal accidents in some of Bohemia's major industries.

At the same time, this strictly objective view from the outside, though more consistent with the facts than the shopworn romantic cliché of genius in thrall, is equally misleading, or at the very least irrelevant.

To begin with, Kafka was a writer, not an insurance executive. His disguise happened to fit rather well, as disguises go, and at times made him look deceptively like a career bureaucrat. But the job nonetheless represented a makeshift compromise between mundane duties and inner needs that was bound to fail in the long run, if for no other reason than that the rhythms of creative inspiration are intrinsically incompatible with the regular clockwork routine of even a six-hour daily stint.

At best, what the job offered him was a footing of sorts, much like a tightrope strung between the two poles of his existence, on which every morning he performed a somnambulist balancing act. Nor did his seeming proficiency offer much satisfaction in the long run. On the contrary, recognition, success, promotions were all bought at enormous expense in energy and time stolen from his true task in life. Or so, at least, he felt; and the fact that in later years, during long leaves of absence, he frequently produced nothing at all is no argument to the contrary. After a few years—certainly by 1912, when, on the one hand, the novelty of the job had worn off and, on the other, his powers as a creative artist had begun fully to assert themselves—he came to regard the demands of the job as a major cause of the crushing depressions that sapped his creativity and at the same time precluded any rational solution.

> As I was getting out of bed this morning [he wrote to Pfohl in February 1911] I simply collapsed, and for a very simple reason: I am badly overworked. Not in the office, but because of my other work. The office plays an innocent part only to the extent that, if I didn't have to report there, I could peacefully live for my work alone and wouldn't have to spend those six hours a day on the job. They tormented me to a degree you cannot possibly imagine, especially this past Friday and Saturday, because I was so full of my own things. I realize that this is nothing but blather; I am guilty, and the office has the clearest and most justified claims upon me. To me, however, this means leading a horrible double life, from which madness probably offers the only way out. I am writing this in the bright light of morning, and I would certainly not be writing it at all if it weren't so obviously true, and if I didn't love you like a son. [DI, 2/19/11]

Madness did indeed offer a way out, one of several; except that in his case, what he so blithely referred to as such took the form of an excruciatingly clairvoyant lucidity. That Kafka, for most of his life, suffered from recurrent depressions is banally self-evident. He displayed all the classic symptoms of an overweening aggression turned inward: suicidal self-hatred, agonizing indecision, hypochondria, manipulative self-pity, insatiable demands for love beyond any hope of satisfaction, and, in addition, the perennial somatic complaints, from chronic headaches and insomnia to lassitude and digestive disturbances. But symptoms describe an illness, not a person, and the often dubious value of diagnostic tags is limited at best to clinical practice; moreover, the distinction between sickness and health, in these murky borderline areas, implies a measure of arbitrary judgment. To designate Kafka's despair as a depression is not an explanation but merely a label for what is abundantly self-evident. Here again, as in his relations with his father, the family, the women in his life, what counts is not what he had in common with millions of others so much as what made him unique, the ways in which he alone was able to transform his struggles into an act of supreme creative fulfillment.

* * *

The escape from the Assicurazioni Generali must have felt like a last-minute reprieve, and the prisoner was, for once, suitably exuberant. The new job promised to satisfy all his modest material needs—financial independence, respectability, and three-fourths of every working day to himself. It was summer when he started at the institute, an unusually hot summer stretching into autumn. For the first time since childhood Kafka had missed out on his summer vacation; would not, in any case, have been entitled to one, under Assicurazioni rules. But still his luck held out. Early in September 1908, the promising new candidate was sent on a ten-day orientation trip to the industrial centers of northern Bohemia; whatever the educational value of the tour, Kafka clearly relished this late-summer journey through the Bohemian forests. To Brod he reported, on September 2, that life, while boring on occasion, was not all bad; it offered, among other things, "very good food morning, noon, and night, and living in hotel rooms. I like hotel rooms. I always feel immediately at home in hotel rooms, more so than at home, really." The freedom of anonymity, with roast duck and dumplings on the side. He obviously liked the fare, and in the first flush of triumph was even able to digest it. And four days later: "What I want to tell you is that I am very happy, and that I'd like you to be here, because there are things in the woods that one could spend years thinking about, while lying in the moss" (L, 9/08).

High spirits before the fall, a brief surge of manic exaltation that collapsed right after the prodigal's return to Prague and provoked the judge in him to savage retribution.

> After eight happy days in the Bohemian forest—where the butterflies soar as high as the swallows back here—I have now spent four days in Prague, and I feel so helpless. Nobody likes me, and I don't like anybody, but the second is merely the consequence of the first. Your book,* which I am finally read- ing straight through, does help. As long as I am reading, I cleave to it, even though it certainly isn't meant to be a cure for unhappiness. But otherwise I feel so desperately in need of just a friendly caress that yesterday I took a whore to a hotel. She was too old to still be sentimental, but nonetheless sorry— though not surprised—that one is not as nice to a whore as to a lover. I offered her no comfort, since she didn't comfort me, either. [L, 9/08]

It was the onset of a precipitous slide into depths lower than any he had previously known, and it continued for nearly a year. There was, on the face of it, no cause rational or even plausible to account for it, other than the office, and that struck even him as rather unconvincing. On the contrary: he had gained his independence, earned unexpected recognition and welcome respectability. Seventeen years of mindless memorizing, of fear and trembling before inquisitorial examiners, of degrading dependence on parental generosity were at long last behind him. He was free to do as he pleased—leave the perennial uproar of his parents' home, leave Prague altogether. The taste of it, like the taste of roast duck, turned to ashes in his mouth.

For what it all added up to was what he had always suspected yet managed, until now, to dilute with hope against hope, a few illusions, and some valid excuses: that the obstacles in his path had very little to do with outward circumstances.

The prisoner pining away for his freedom who, when at last the gate swings open, refuses to leave is a far from rare phenomenon. Yet no matter how much he had anticipated it, the shock of recognition left him defenseless and naked to himself. What kept him from living, he now knew, was what had kept him from dying.

The full awareness of his situation may have overwhelmed him

---

* Brod's *Castle Norrepygge.*

quite abruptly and precipitated his withdrawal into protective isolation, but it had certainly been building up for some time. In December 1908, he wrote to Brod that "for the past two years I have been desperate, and only the upper and lower limits of this despair determine my current moods" (L, 12/10/08). The affair with Hedwig Weiler had run its course; at her request, he returned all her letters. His own last known letter to her was written in April 1909, and its ending conveys an inkling of despair's lower limits: "Just in case you'd like to know something about me. . . . My mother is going to be operated on next week, my grandfather had a severe fainting spell today, and I myself am not in the best of health, either" (L, 4/09).

Throughout this period of bleak misery, however, his performance on the job remained consistently impressive, at least in the eyes of his superiors. The discipline may have forced him to face the days, one at a time, and diverted some of his self-absorption, but the therapeutic value of keeping busy has its limits. Given his state of mind, the results that so impressed his superiors also took a great deal more out of him than was objectively warranted. Most important, it left no energy for his own writing—or so he believed. There was certainly more to his creative stasis than mere lack of energy or time, but whatever the causal relationship, it made the crisis that much more painful.

He began increasingly to withdraw into himself, into the serpentine routine of paperwork, seldom went out in the evening, turned down most invitations, and might have cut himself off from his friends altogether had it not been for Max Brod.

* * *

Brod at this time was himself going through a difficult period. For one thing, he was desperate in his dreary drudgery at the Prague post office, where he had transferred from Komotau at a sizable cut in salary. For another, he had just lost his oldest and closest friend, Max Baeuml, who had suddenly died in November. Grief, agonizing boredom, and a not insubstantial capacity for voluble self-pity made him turn to Kafka for sympathy, and their mutual vulnerability gave rise to a far more intimate friendship than before. But Brod, as was his nature, bounced back quickly, and what in due course he was able to offer Kafka was nothing short of life support.

Although he could not keep the friend from wallowing in misery,

Brod did everything in his power to keep despair from dragging Kafka into total isolation. They began to meet daily after work, walking home together, and Brod never grew tired of trying to coax and cajole the reclusive companion into joining the social activities and mundane distractions of their immediate circle. And having mediated Kafka's public debut in Franz Blei's *Hyperion* the previous year, he now—ever alert to the etiquette of literary politics—persuaded Kafka to return the favor by reviewing Blei's novel, *The Powderpuff,* in a German literary magazine. He had certainly nothing but Kafka's best interests at heart; above all, he wanted to jar him out of his creative lethargy. But in this instance, the strategy misfired. What Kafka came up with was a piece of painfully convoluted prose that totally obfuscated the contents of the book under review, while making it abundantly plain that the reviewer simply could not bring himself to say one sincere good word for it. That Kafka himself had misgivings after the fact is attested to by his letter to Blei, one week after the review appeared in *Der Neue Weg* of February 22, 1909: "Please don't take offense at the manner in which I presented *The Powderpuff.* . . . And since I know of your great interest in matters Czech, I am sending you, under separate cover, the just published annual report of my institute, which up to page 22 was written by me."

Whether this offbeat sample of his own unadorned prose was meant to mollify, edify, or instruct Blei is hard to tell. The very idea of submitting it to a man notorious for the elliptic preciosity of his taste and style, however, not only underscored Kafka's initial pride in the fruits of his forced labor, but also suggests something of that incongruous naïveté his office colleagues found so appealing.

Nevertheless, the job took its toll. "You have no idea how busy I am," he wrote to Brod, turning down yet another of his invitations. "In my four districts—quite apart from my other work—people tumble off scaffolds and into machines as if they all were drunk, all planks tip over, all embankments collapse, all ladders slip, whatever gets put up comes down, whatever gets put down trips somebody up. And all those young girls in the china factories who constantly hurl themselves down whole flights of stairs with mountains of crockery give me a headache." (L, Summer 1909)

Moreover, the inescapable gregariousness of office life must have all but exhausted Kafka's scant reserves of sociability. He found it more difficult than ever pretending to be part of a crowd; typical is this note to Brod—defensive, ironic, perhaps merely apologetic: "I have one question I'd like you to answer right away: if, for instance, eight people take part in a conversation, when do you speak up in order not to be considered taciturn? It surely cannot be done deliberately, the less so if one is about as remote from the subject as a red Indian. I wish I'd asked sooner" (L, 10/25/08).

Alone, he was at ease with his loneliness; in a crowd, it made him feel an outcast. The convivial get-togethers of argumentative and self-important intellectuals, Brod's natural habitat, bored him to distraction —red Indian at the Rotary luncheon—and feigning interest for civility's sake took an effort he found increasingly strenuous and distasteful.

Then again, he had seldom ever been able to relax his guard except in one-on-one encounters. All his meaningful friendships, those in which he truly invested himself, had always been highly exclusive. And if the jealousy that so roiled his adolescent passion for Oskar Pollak no longer seemed appropriate or admissible, he still continued to seek from friends and lovers alike what he had failed to receive as a child. Latent for the most part, swaddled in layers of self-effacing kindness and genuine concern, a fierce possessiveness burned on and every so often erupted in all of its flagrant egotism. And Brod, from 1909 at least until his marriage to Elsa Taussig in 1913 ("a married friend is no friend") was the main target of these unarticulated and largely unconscious demands, which by their very nature were beyond his, or anyone else's, power to meet. To his credit, Brod handled the situation with consummate skill and exquisite tact. That is to say, he mostly ignored it, either deliberately or because he failed to gauge the true scope and nature of Kafka's needs, and instead made it his business to help the friend as best he knew how—by goading him to work and saving him from drowning in his loneliness. No small accomplishment. Without his patience and devotion, the almost total paralysis of Kafka's creative energies, and with it the crisis itself, would almost certainly have persisted much longer.

* * *

As it was, spring came, and with it the first glimmer of hope. Kafka discovered, or rediscovered, the healing power of nature and the grim joy of driving this troubled and troubling body of his to the limits of endurance. He acquired a rowboat, kept it tied up in a slip near his house, and regularly went rowing on the Vltava. And it was his turn now to be the moving spirit in the all-day hikes he organized nearly every Sunday through the then still wholly rural environs of Prague— the Karlstein fortress, the Vltava Rapids, the spectacular Sazava Valley —with Brod and Felix Weltsch as his regular companions. Here again he knew no compromise. "Somehow the number of kilometers we covered (every Sunday) assumed an importance which today I am no longer quite able to appreciate," Brod relates in his autobiography, going on to explain how, at the time, Kafka and he "lived in the curious belief that in order to take possession of a landscape, one had to establish direct physical contact by swimming in the vital flow of its waters. Thus we later also explored Switzerland by practicing our strokes in every accessible body of water" (Brod, St. L., p. 22).

It was on one of these excursions, in the summer of 1909, that Brod brought along a precocious youngster still in his last year of high school by the name of Franz Werfel, whom he introduced as a budding genius; it was an opinion which the young poet himself had long since come to take for granted. Rotundly handsome at nineteen, carefully unkempt, vestigial baby fat turning into incipient flab, Werfel had all the self-willed poise and manipulative charm of a child blessed by fortune and spoiled by his parents. The son of a wealthy industrialist, he had been raised in the lap of luxury or, more accurately, in the lap of his adoring mother, whose smothering devotion probably accounted for his happy disposition but also kept him from ever growing up. What saved Werfel was, quite simply, genuine talent and enormous vitality; what ultimately wrecked him was the frenzied quest of the never-weaned infant which, long before Lourdes, led him to Alma Maria Mahler-Gropius-Werfel née Schindler, an iron maiden of bloated pomposity whose strange appeal to an assortment of culture heroes makes one suspect a strong streak of perversity in either the culture or its heroes.

At this time, however, the *Star of the Unborn* was still in its ascendancy, the *Song of Bernadette* happily uncrooned. Instead, poised naked by a babbling brook, the prospective new member of Brod's Secret League of Happy Nature Worshippers declaimed the stirring verses which, thanks to Brod's customary aggressive and selfless promotion, were soon to be published under the collective title of *Weltfreund* —Friend to the World—and gained Werfel instant acclaim as the golden voice of the new generation.

Rereading Werfel's youthful effusions at this remove, it takes a major effort of the imagination to account for the sensational impact that this banal rhetoric, mindless optimism, and sentimental bombast had on his contemporaries. Part of the explanation, no doubt, lay in the personality of the man himself—witty, urbane, and with a formidable histrionic talent and stage presence that made his readings an unforgettable experience. Even Kafka, poles apart from Werfel in every conceivable sense, and moreover sharply critical of his later work, was sufficiently captivated to note as late as 1911 that Werfel "early, easily, and with true musical feeling wrote some very good things; the happiest part of his life is behind him and ahead of him, while I keep struggling with weights I cannot get rid of" (DI, 12/18/11). Envy, perhaps, of fortune's child, but also a tribute to Werfel's charismatic recitals, which left a residue of unexamined awe.

Kafka's subsequent relations with Werfel were problematic and contradictory; the more he came to like the person, the less he liked the work, thus boxing himself into another of those dilemmas in which he seemed to specialize; to criticize Werfel was to lose him. Werfel, for his part, sneered at his first reading of the Kafka fragments in *Hyperion*: "Beyond Tetschen-Bodenbach [the Czech-German border] no one will be able to figure out what this is all about." He was wrong, and quick to acknowledge it. He praised Kafka's writings, offered generous help during the difficult final days of Kafka's illness, visited him in the hospital, and paid fulsome tribute to him after his death as one of God's elect, a messenger from heaven. Which did not prevent him from furiously lacing into his close friend, the critic Willy Haas, for having ranked Kafka higher than Werfel in the hierarchy of immortals.

The contrast between these two—between the chubby, cheerful *Weltfreund* splashing in lukewarm pieties, and the tortured ascetic pursuing doubt to its ultimate paradox—sharply defines the uniqueness of Kafka. Werfel, in his bubble bath of colorful illusions, was a representative of his time, as Kafka is of ours. Which says a great deal more for Kafka than it does for our time.

*   *   *

Young Werfel's initiation into the nature-loving trio's Sunday ritual had an absurd but symbolic aftermath. The following Monday morning, an irate Mama Werfel came storming into Brod's apartment and accused him of criminal negligence in allowing her fair-skinned darling to expose his tender bottom to the brutal midsummer sun, contracting so painful a sunburn that he might not even be able to sit for his high-school finals. After all, he was a mere child, whereas the Herr Doktor was supposed to be a responsible adult . . .

Alma herself couldn't have put it more aptly.

Fourteen

IN August 1909, having completed a year at the institute, Kafka asked for a raise as well as for a week's leave of absence because of nervousness and fatigue; both were granted within days. Max and his younger brother, Otto Brod, had wanted him to join them on a ten-day vacation at Lake Garda, and after blowing hot and cold for a week— "If anybody were to carry on all evening long the way I did last night, I'd give some serious thought to whether I'd really want to saddle myself with him" (L, 9/09)—he set out with his two companions as scheduled on September 4. Even granting the suasive force of Brod's relentless enthusiasm, it seems unlikely that Kafka—stubborn, when he felt the need, beyond all argument or reason—would have risked ten days of enforced sociability in alien surroundings if the murky depression had not already begun to lift.

Technical arrangements were wisely left to the youngest of the three. When it came to coping with the intricacies of low-budget, or near-no-budget travel, Otto Brod, though only twenty-one at the time —four years younger than his brother—already displayed all of the competence and initiative that later made for a battlefield hero and successful executive, with enough energy left over for two thoroughly respectable novels and a biography of Voltaire, half finished at the time of his deportation by the Nazis in 1942. He was gassed at Auschwitz, together with his wife and only daughter, at the age of fifty-four.

Otto had already been to Riva on his own and come to love the picturesque little town at the northern tip of Lake Garda in what was then still Austrian territory. Sheltered by the steep cliffs of the Monte Rocchetta, it had been a cultural center of some importance during the Renaissance—an edition of the Talmud printed locally in 1558 is still on display in the Civic Museum—as well as a vacation spot for the discriminating few; in 1786, Goethe worked on the final version of his

Iphigenie in nearby Torbole. If Kafka and his friends were aware of these historic associations, they failed to mention them; in any event, they had come to soak up sun rather than culture.

Nor did they need to make excuses for their escapist zeal. Otto, of course, was still a student at the time, but the other two had for over a year been trapped in dingy offices, spent themselves in dull routine, and struggled to balance the conflicting demands of job versus art. Ten days of complete freedom, of intimacy untroubled by intruders and intrusions, seemed paradise. They stayed at the more than modest Pension Bellevue but luxuriated in the warmth and unforced idleness of endless days, which magically transformed the world, or at least their view of it. "The hostel . . . at first glance seems to us the filthiest we've ever seen," wrote Kafka, normally fastidious to the point of phobia, "but soon it doesn't look nearly as bad. Dirt that simply exists, that is no longer being talked about, that doesn't change anymore and has become indigenous, dirt that in a sense renders human life more solid and earthbound . . . who, one asks, could object to this kind of dirt?" ("The Aeroplanes of Brescia").

Brod, in turn, insists that never in his life was he so cheerful and at peace with himself as during vacations spent with Kafka. "We left all our cares and worries behind us in Prague and turned into happy children, inventing the most absurdly lovely jokes—it was a great happiness to have Kafka around and to relish firsthand the constant flow of lively ideas; even his hypochondria was still imaginative and amusing" (bio., p. 90). And Kafka obviously reciprocated Brod's sentiments. "Never were we as close to one another as on our travels," he later confided to his fiancée.

They were, in fact, well matched as travelers in other ways as well. Eager, deliriously happy to get away from Prague, they obviously never really left the place, especially when in each other's company. Their three joint trips abroad, aside from offering scenic delight and a temporary break in the routine, left them curiously untouched by any real awareness of the myriad ways in which life in the Italian campagna, or in a Paris *quartier,* differed from what they were accustomed to and took for granted. They had little contact with ordinary people: both were poor linguists, and although Kafka had studied Italian along with French and was able to read both with some proficiency, their combined mastery of the spoken vernacular was barely up to asking for directions to the men's room. Yet even where they dutifully did the sights, even where they spoke the language—in Zurich, Munich, or Berlin—they seldom made an effort to enter into the spirit and atmosphere of the place. Ultimately, in reading the accounts of these two innocents abroad, one comes to suspect that Brod was nowhere at home but in Prague. When he had to flee, in 1939, he took his hometown with him to Tel Aviv, along with his Kafka manuscripts; left on the Vltava was a mere shell of a city under foreign occupation. Kafka, on the other hand, was simply nowhere at home. Could he, a tongue-tied stranger even among his own, be expected to be less of a stranger abroad?

*   *   *

If neither the Italian present nor the Roman past managed to arouse much interest—again, perhaps, a matter of language: eight dreary years of Latin verbs and Gallic wars, enough to snuff out any vestigial spark of curiosity—there was still the future to stir the imagination. News of its impending dawn came to them via the local press, which announced an international air meet on September 12 at Brescia, forty-six miles to the south across the Italian border.

None of them had ever seen an airplane, but it was Kafka, according to Brod, who was most eager to go, quite undaunted by the prospect of large crowds, overtaxed facilities, a miserable train ride, and their critical shortage of funds.

And go they did, in the end. But Brod, who for nearly a year had tried in vain to goad, coax, or lure Kafka back to writing, now tied their trip to the idea of a contest: they would each do an article, compare the results, and decide on the winner.

A childish enough ruse, to be sure, yet Kafka seems to have been partial to such games. The result was "The Aeroplanes of Brescia," a piece published on September 28, 1909, in the Prague *Bohemia,* which a month later also printed Brod's complementary account. On the whole, despite a few typical Kafka touches, it has a stiff and stilted feel to it, rather on the order of a "My Day at the Air Show" school assignment, though it retains the distinction of containing one of the earliest descriptions of an airplane in the German language.

Even so, it was the first piece of writing Kafka had done since the unfortunate book review a year and a half earlier, and it apparently did for him precisely what Brod had hoped it would. "I wanted to demonstrate to him, by concrete example, how one just had to pull oneself together. I wanted to prove to him that his fears of literary barrenness were unfounded, and that all it took to put his gifts back to work was willpower and concentration" (Brod, bio., p. 94).

It clearly took a good deal more than that, in Kafka's case, if not in Brod's. Still, the fact remains that after his return to Prague, he at last, and for the first time in years, began actively to fight his creative paralysis. And beyond merely helping him to overcome his writer's block, "The Aeroplanes of Brescia" may well have been of far greater significance to his development than its intrinsic value would suggest. These casual travel notes, more or less forced upon him, pointed the way toward a lifelong habit of recorded observations and self-observations that formally began with the first of his diaries a few months later.

Riva marked the end of suspended animation, of lethargy too debilitating even to mobilize despair. But as passive resignation gave way again to active misery and protest, the conflicts between the unhappy child and the unwilling adult in him made themselves felt with new vehemence. If Kafka, up to now, had been at odds with himself and the world, he was now at war. And one of the most desperate battles he fought was with his own body.

*   *   *

Fear, disgust, and rage were what this recalcitrant bundle of taut nerves, brittle bones, frail organs, and coddled flesh had aroused in him since earliest childhood, and it takes no great sophistication to trace these sentiments back to their poisoned sources. Kafka himself was in no doubt as to their origins; in recapturing the nascent self-awareness of early childhood in the *Letter to His Father,* he mentions how desperately he at that time would have needed encouragement of some sort.

> After all, I already felt oppressed by your mere bodily presence. I remember, for instance, how at the river pool we often used to undress together in the same cabin. I was skinny, weak, slight. You were strong, tall, massive. Even inside the cabin I saw myself as a miserable creature, not only in your eyes, but in the eyes of the whole world, because to me you were the measure of all things. But then we stepped outside to face the crowds, myself holding on to your hand, a little bag of bones,

skinny, barefoot on the wooden planks, scared of the water, unable to ape the strokes which you, with the best of intentions but actually to my profound humiliation, insisted on demonstrating over and over. And at that point I was absolutely desperate; all the bad experiences I had collected in every sphere of life came together in one perfect fit. I was probably happiest when you occasionally undressed first, enabling me to dawdle and postpone the ignominy of my public appearance until you finally came back to get me. I was grateful to you for not seeing my discomfort; I was also proud of my father's body. This difference, incidentally, persists to this day, and in much the same way.

Variations on a theme by Freud. The fact that Kafka was by then probably familiar with Freudian theory, at least in its broad outlines, does not make the particulars any less vivid; these childhood scars still bled on touch. And after childhood came puberty, the scrawny little runt turning into a grotesquely elongated worm painfully struggling to keep upright against the force of gravity, but with a heart too weak, so he believed, to pump enough blood up and down the vast distances between head and feet.

Shame he talked about all his life, indeed bragged about, with a vicious self-deprecation suspiciously akin to pride in his own freakishness—especially to women who threatened intimacy, and who failed to see him as he saw himself. What he seldom talked about, except for a few cryptic allusions, was the guilt induced by masturbation. Yet the dangers of self-abuse—blindness, paralysis, insanity—were commonly accepted in his day as scientifically established and validated by the incontrovertible authority of popular belief. The fear of cruel punishment for lack of self-control was, in fact, a major reason for regular whorehouse visits, regarded as a healthy alternative. It seems rather improbable that Kafka, of all people, should have escaped these struggles between lust and fear, or the guilt and anxiety engendered by the inevitable defeat.

There was one other area—not altogether unrelated—in which Kafka seems to have quite systematically repressed memories too highly charged to put into words. Virulent anti-Semitism in the streets of Prague, mob attacks on Jewish stores and passers-by who looked like Jews, the bloody 1899 pogroms in the wake of the Hilsner ritual murder trial, the anti-Jewish boycott, and the recurrent organized riots which, whatever the ostensible provocation, inevitably turned against the Jews and time and again led to the proclamation of martial law in the city—one instance was in 1908, just as Kafka started to work at the institute—were impossible to ignore, yet they remain virtually unmentioned in either his voluminous correspondence or the diaries. (One telling exception is a 1920 letter to the non-Jewish Milena Jesenská describing, with ironic detachment, a pogrom he was witnessing at the time.) Evidently it was only in his fiction that he felt both safe and articulate enough to give voice to his sense of terror.

It seems difficult to account in any other way for this rather startling reticence. Yet where, in the case of masturbation, the transgression was individual and specific, his being a Jew—hence, by definition, a chosen target—was his share of a collective guilt beyond absolution. And where, as a child, he had looked at himself through his father's eyes and despised what he saw, his self-image in later years was shaped in no small measure by hooligans and pogromchiks—a "typical" stoop-shouldered, weak-kneed, flabby, and timid Western Jewish intellectual who hated his body for, in his view, conforming to the anti-Semitic stereotype.

This was a burden shared by many young Jews of his generation, conditioned beyond conscious awareness by the myths, trappings, and claptrap of German romanticism and pan-Slav militancy. The cult of physical fitness, the idealization of athletic prowess, the strident emphasis on muscle over mind—and on paramilitary mass athletics over competitive sports—constituted an element basic to German nationalism since the post-Napoleonic era. By providing fit and hardened cannon fodder, it served the expansionist aims of first Prussian, and later German, militarism; at the same time, the pagan cult of the body became an integral part of all nineteenth-century racist, *völkisch* movements, finally culminating in the *Blut und Boden* mythology of the Hitler Youth and the Nazi storm troopers. Pan-Slavism, menaced and alarmed, launched its own gymnastic organization, the Sokol, in 1863. Though on the whole it lacked the purposiveness and drill-master mentality of its German counterparts, in Prague its function as essentially a paramilitary youth branch of the Czech independence movement assured it a solid mass base and considerable influence.

All of these trends left the young Jews of Kafka's generation in a difficult bind. On the one hand, they themselves subscribed, with varying degrees of enthusiasm, to the tenets of back-to-nature romanticism

and body worship as part of their own revolt against the money mentality of their fathers and the superstitious orthodoxies of their grandfathers. On the other hand, the political exploitation of these appealing
sentiments had spawned a racism that relegated all Jews to the status
of subhumans solely on the basis of their ancestry. Spurned and excluded from the club, they formed their own—quite literally so in
Prague, where around the turn of the century organizations such as the
Zionist Makkabi and the assimilationist Deutsche Turnverein—German
Gymnasts' Association in name, preponderantly Jewish in membership
—began to promote the cause of fitness among Jewish youth, and
within a much broader framework the whole secular Zionist movement, whose call for "normalization" through manual labor and return
to the soil echoed the mythologies of rival nationalisms, not excluding
their aggressively anti-intellectual stance. Thus in 1912 the Prague
Zionist *Selbstwehr,* later to be edited by Kafka's philosopher friend
Felix Weltsch, appealed to young Jews to "shed our heavy stress on
intellectual preeminence . . . and our excessive nervousness, a heritage
of the ghetto. . . . In our own interests and those of our people, we
need harmoniously balanced personalities. We spend all too much of
our time debating, and not nearly enough in play and gymnastics. . . .
What makes a man a man is not his mouth, nor his mind, nor yet his
morals, but discipline . . . what we need is manliness" (12/23/12,
quoted in Stoelzl, p. 134).

Given the programmatically anti-Semitic slant of the racist anti-
intellectualism from which these sentiments were borrowed or appro-
priated, they rather eloquently express not only Jewish self-hatred but,
more specifically, its impact on the individual: for your own sake, and
that of your people—stop looking like a Jew.

Kafka himself, to be sure, needed no outside help to make him
loathe his looks and his body, nor did he join in any mass movements
designed to foster biceps building or Prussian ideals of manliness among
the Jews. Nevertheless, in their own insidious way, these trends and
currents had a direct influence on him greater than he realized. Many
different reasons account for his daily calisthenics, for the avid pursuit
of outdoor sports, the forced marches in the country, the conspicuous
idiosyncrasies ranging from vegetarianism to going without coat or
gloves even in the dead of winter, and for his later attempts to take up
gardening and carpentry. Yet a pattern common to them all was the
grim resolve to punish the body for what it was or, more precisely, for

not being what some part of him felt it ought to be: a healthy animal in a happy herd.

*   *   *

The enmity, then, went back to beginnings.

Through the years, however, it had been a state more of sullen hostility, of himself watching himself with that hypochondriacal apprehension which—to Brod, at least—still seemed "imaginative and amusing," while the body responded in the ways of all bodies unloved. In addition to the transient and more or less normal adolescent hysteria about digestion, complexion, potency, hair loss, curvature of the spine, and underdeveloped biceps, he was already morbidly sensitive to noise and had developed a phobic fear of mice. But now, as the crushing reality of adulthood, with its shrinking options and vanishing illusions, started closing in on him, the body rebelled in turn.

The initial symptoms were stomach trouble, indigestion, constipation, "a partial break in the communications between stomach and mouth," as he so graphically described it (DI, 10/10/11), "with a lid the size of a guilder either sliding up and down or else resting at the bottom and radiating upward with pressure lightly spreading across the chest." The mobile metaphoric lid may have been an ulcer, brought on or exacerbated by unusual stress in the office; the large-scale reclassification of accident risks taking place at the time necessitated frequent travel and irregular meals: "What a time I've been having. . . . At half past six this morning I took the train to Gablonz, from Gablonz to Johannesberg, after that to Grenzendorf, now I'm off to Muffersdorf, after that to Reichenberg, then on to Röchlitz, in the evening to Ruppersdorf and back" (L, 1909). And again: "A good thing this trip is almost over. . . . I've been sick to my stomach the entire time, and having to rate risks from the time I have my milk in the morning to the time I rinse my mouth at night is no cure" (L, 12/21/09).

He mistrusted doctors. "I don't believe famous doctors," he wrote Felice Bauer. "I believe doctors only when they tell me that they don't know anything. And besides, I hate them" (FEL, 11/5/12). He rationalized this aversion partly by holding "the doctors" responsible for the deaths, in infancy, of his two younger brothers, an explanation that may have served to assuage some of his own guilt feelings in the matter but certainly fails to account for such an uncharacteristically simpleminded attitude. Basically, however, his quarrel was not just with doctors; he mistrusted *all* authority generally, even while spending his life searching for the one to which he could submit in good faith. And if his own father let him down by being what he was—flawed, fallible, capricious, dense—there was good reason to be wary of all those who would usurp his place, to scrutinize them carefully, and to find them wanting. Ultimately, none of the mere mortals whom Kafka came across in his quest passed muster. He sought perfection but uncovered only human frailty, and he utterly lacked the ability to compromise, with others as with himself. In that sense it is certainly true, as has been so perfervidly proclaimed by authoritative explicators whose authority seems every bit as flawed as any Kafka ever encountered, that his search for the perfect father was the search for God, doomed in advance by a skepticism, reverent yet radical, which he often decried as a heavy burden but was never able or willing to shed.

Kafka's mistrust of orthodox medicine, however, happened to be well-founded, no matter how irrational the feelings that inspired it. What most exasperated him was not the ignorance of doctors so much as their presumptuous refusal to acknowledge it, a stance of authoritative omniscience not unknown in our own day but even less warranted at a time when leeches were still a far more common remedy than the newly introduced aspirin. Nonetheless, he in the end felt compelled to consult a physician, who proceeded to pump out his stomach (L, 1/29/10); an expert reading of tea leaves or entrails would presumably have been equally helpful, but diagnostic X-rays were not yet available, and the standard treatment for ulcers, as for most chronic diseases, was liable to do more harm than good.

In any event, Kafka did not need any sophisticated technology or, for that matter, professional advice to know what ailed him. Many of his notions about health and disease were simply primitive superstitions, others were primitive truths that had been lost sight of by the mechanistic medicine men of his day—notably, the unity of body and mind. Kafka never doubted, nor ever ceased to believe, that what made him ill was the way he lived. The struggle to regain his health, which eventually escalated into desperate obsessions and fatal illness, began with seemingly rational enough attempts on his part to overcome relatively trivial complaints.

As early as 1908, he had already been converted to a systematic body-building program developed by the Danish author Jens Peter

Mueller, which involved cold ablutions and daily—or in his case, nightly —calisthenics by an open window, in winter as in summer. *Muellern*— "to mueller"—became a regular verb in his vocabulary, and a regular routine in his life for many years. But the digestive troubles that now began to plague him seemed to call for more specific measures, the more so since in addition to pains and nausea he had also been suffering from a related physical dysfunction that was to worry him obsessively for years. The fetish of bowel regularity, already in his day zealously promoted and exploited by the increasingly enterprising drug industry, seems consistent with the symptoms of emotional constipation that Kafka displayed in other spheres.

His first step, sensibly enough, was to eliminate from his diet anything he thought might disagree with him. But the list of forbidden items lengthened rapidly and soon began to encompass major food categories. Within a year, he had become a vegetarian and worked out for himself an intricately abstemious diet to which, barring exceptional circumstances such as travel or hospitalization, he faithfully adhered for the rest of his life. It consisted mainly of unprocessed natural foods —bread, fruit, and milk for breakfast, vegetables for lunch, yogurt, nuts, and fruit for dinner, a downright provocative departure from the dietary habits hallowed among the Jewish bourgeoisie in what was then the land of *Schnitzel* and *Schlagobers*. That he also abstained from alcohol, tobacco, and sweets goes without saying.

Worse was to come. In the course of his self-help researches, he had apparently come across the once popular writings of a nineteenth-century American food faddist, Horace Fletcher (1849–1919), who stressed careful mastication as the key to good health; and Fletcherism's new convert now began sedulously to apply the master's principles by chewing every bite a dozen or more times. The effect on the family gathered around the dinner table is not hard to imagine. Not only did the Herr Sohn turn up his nose at what was good for the Jews and for everybody else; this latest quirk of his made it virtually impossible for anyone to share their meals with him. "For months on end," as he told Felice, "my father had to hide behind his newspaper during dinner, until he got used to it" (FEL, 11/7/12).

The regimen revitalized his digestive system, or so he believed, with a fervor that itself probably contributed to the cure. And however bizarre it may have seemed to his contemporaries, ignorant as yet of vitamins and accustomed to gauge both health and prosperity by a man's girth, it was no doubt nutritionally far superior to the standard fare of the urban middle class. Unfortunately, it did not do much for him in the long run.

In the first place, a sound diet, while helpful, is no panacea. Kafka's stomach symptoms subsided, not so the conflicts that had given rise to them and which, in due course, manifested themselves in other afflictions, notably boils and the severe, almost daily headaches that plagued him until the onset of his eventually fatal illness. But more important, the whole dietary regimen, however rational some of the original precepts, derived its obsessive drive from sources deep within lost memory and quickly proliferated into a system of compulsive rituals that replicated the talismanic function of Jewish dietary law and served needs and goals far different from those of which he himself was consciously aware. The increasingly ascetic discipline he inflicted upon himself as punishment for transgressions beyond knowledge and atonement no doubt helped to repress inadmissible impulses but, in the end, itself turned destructive with a vengeance. There is an element of rising savagery in the way in which he progressed from the avoidance of certain foods to what amounted to a self-imposed starvation diet, rendered pathetically ironic by the fact that in the end the very nature of his final illness—tuberculosis of the larynx—made swallowing all but impossible, so that he quite literally starved to death.

That the grandson of a kosher butcher should turn vegetarian—first on ostensibly practical grounds, later as a matter of moral principle—is certainly no mere coincidence. But Kafka went much further. Like his pious ancestors, he committed himself to the strict observance of ritual law, with one all-important difference: where the observance of *kashrut,* of traditional Jewish dietary laws, linked the individual to the community, the rituals evoked by Kafka effectively cut him off from it and dramatized his alienation not only from the ancestral tradition but even from his own family. It was rather awkward to "fletcherize" in company; and in fact, he gradually got into the habit of taking all his meals by himself and intensely disliked eating in anyone else's presence.

* * *

Quite regardless of its ultimate ramifications, however, the struggle in the short run was not without its victories. Despite chronic complaints, relapses, and troubles both real and imaginary, Kafka in the months following his return from Riva was reasonably successful in shoring up his defenses and striking a balance of sorts between dreams and responsibilities. A precarious balance, to be sure, purchased at the cost of persistent anguish, which, like a layer of frozen rage, covered the surface of a seething cauldron. "My condition is not unhappiness," notes the diary, "but it isn't happiness, either, nor is it indifference, fatigue, or other interests. What, then, is it? The fact that I don't know probably relates to my inability to write. And this, I believe, I understand even though I don't know the reason" (DI, 1911).

Nevertheless, he "functioned," as current jargon would have it, aptly enough in his case; there was indeed a distinctly mechanical quality in the way he went about the business of living during this transitional period. His health was improving. In addition to his other physical activities, he had taken up horseback riding and become a frequent visitor to the racetrack in suburban Kuchelbad. "I go rowing, horseback riding, swimming, I lie in the sun," records the diary, along with visits to bordellos undertaken in much the same spirit of self-improvement.

The feelings painstakingly bottled up would not, however, always stay capped. One embarrassing eruption marred Kafka's promotion to legal counselor in April 1910, an occasion which the institute's president, Dr. Otto Přibram, saw fit to honor personally with his presence. "It would be too involved to explain to you the importance of this man," Kafka wrote later, in describing the incident to Felice. "But believe me, it is enormous, so much so that an ordinary employee imagines the man as not of this world but residing up above. And since we generally don't get a chance to talk to the emperor—a situation common, of course, to all large organizations—this man inspires in the average clerk a sense of coming face to face with the emperor."

What it inspired in Kafka was a sense of desperate absurdity, a backward tumble into childhood hysterics. His rage—at himself, at this emperor without clothes to whom he was indebted for the job he loved to hate, at the whole ridiculous scene which, as usual, he watched from a distance even while being part of it—exploded in a fit of uncontrollable laughter that turned the pompous ceremony into a slapstick comedy. At first he tried to feign a coughing spell and merely

to grin respectfully at the president's delicate little jokes, but . . . soon I was laughing out loud. I saw my colleagues desperately

Franz Kafka's parents, Herrmann and Julie Kafka

TOP LEFT: *"The Tower," Kafka's birthplace in Prague*
TOP RIGHT: *Kafka's grammar school*

The Kinsky Palace

Kafka (age ten) with his sisters Gabriele and Valerie

THIS PAGE:

Kafka as a high-school student

Kafka's high-school class, with Principal Frank (left) and Ordinarius Emil Gschwind. Top row: Kafka, second from left. Second row down: Oskar Pollak, second from left. Third row: Hugo Bergmann, third from left; Ewald Přibram, extreme right

OPPOSITE PAGE:

Kafka as a student, with Hansi, the "Trocadéro Valkyrie"

Kafka and Ottla, around 1914

Max Brod in 1917

BELOW:
Felix Weltsch
Oskar Baum

Kafka at thirty

Prague's Old Town Square

The Workmen's Accident Insurance Institute, where Kafka worked from 1908 to to 1922. His office was on the fifth floor

The envelope of one of Kafka's letters to Felice

PREVIOUS PAGE:
Kafka and Felice Bauer at the time of their second engagement (1917)

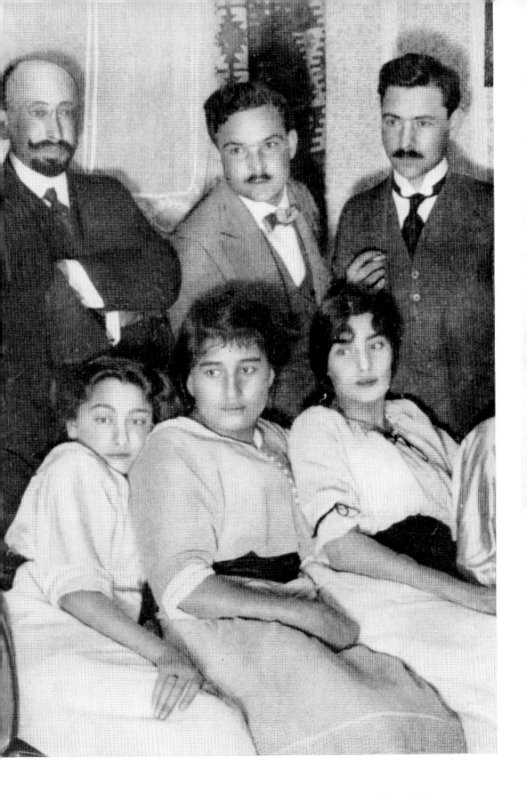

Dr. Siegfried Löwy (top left) and Ottla (bottom, second from left) with her cousins Trude (left) and Martha, daughters of Richard Löwy

TOP LEFT: *Puah Ben-Tovim*   RIGHT: *Dora Diamant*

Bergmann (left) and Brod (right) in conversation with Israel's President Shazar, May 1967

The last picture of Kafka, age forty

The Oppelt House, Old Town Square 5 (now No. 6), Kafka's last residence in Prague

OVERLEAF:
The tomb of Kafka and his parents at the Strasnice Cemetery in Prague

Dr FRANZ KAFKA
1883–1924

יום ג׳ לה סיון תרפ״ד לפ״ק
חלל הטהור דוקטאר מוהר אנשיל פה
בן הנעלה כ״ר וועניך קאפקא נ׳
ושם אמו יטל
ת נ צ ב ה

HERMANN KAFKA
1854–1931

JULIE KAFKA
1856–1934

afraid of getting carried away in turn and felt more sorry for them than for myself, but I just couldn't stop myself anymore. . . . And of course, once I got going, I laughed not only at the current jokes but at all the past and future ones as well, and by then nobody knew anymore what it was I was howling about. . . . And even this display of indecent behavior might still have been passed over and forgotten. . . . Unfortunately, another colleague, for reasons totally unfathomable, chose that precise moment to embark on a ponderous discourse of his own. And as he, hands aflutter, began to dispense his special brand of inanity, it got to be too much for me. The world, of which at least an illusory image had until then persisted in my mind's eye, simply vanished, and I exploded in gales of laughter as ruthless and hearty as perhaps only grade-school youngsters are capable of. . . . At the same time, of course, my knees were shaking with fear. . . . Thanks to a letter of apology I wrote to the president right after the incident, thanks also to the intervention of one of his sons, who happens to be a good friend of mine . . . the matter has now largely been smoothed over. Needless to say, I was not granted a full pardon, nor can I ever hope for one, but that does not matter seriously. [L, 1/8/13]

The brief regression of which he was so manifestly proud apparently did no lasting damage to his career. Three months later he felt justified in asking for another raise in his basic salary, from 1,800 to 2,400 crowns. He also, in view of the heavy work load, requested permission to postpone his summer vacation to late fall; an article in the *Gablonzer Zeitung* of October 2, 1910, sheds some incidental light on the scope of his activities at the time. It reports on a lecture by Kafka to an audience of employers in the north Bohemian town of Gablonz, followed by a rather acrimonious discussion of the newly revised risk assessments, the system of inspections, and the discrepancies between premiums and benefits. In a skillful defense of the institute, Kafka candidly admitted past shortcomings but stressed the need to convert what had been an adversary relationship into one of cooperation in the best interests of all concerned.

* * *

Then there was the other self, the sleepwalker chasing dreams out of time, and driven to writing as others are to murder, ecstasy, or drink.

The two were joined in the flesh, Herr Doktor Kafka, legal counselor, and his nighttime double, clawing at each other with murderous ferocity; the writer, if he wanted to survive or at least keep from ending up as the mummified appendage of a stuffed bureaucrat, had to defend himself in the only way in which writers can plead their case.

In the total overview, Kafka's diaries are the minutes of a fourteen-year trial in which he represented both the defense and the prosecution, with equal zeal and never a moment's doubt as to the guilt of the accused or the final outcome of the proceedings. But when he first began to keep these voluminous notebooks—many of them no doubt destroyed, mutilated, or lost—in the spring of 1910, they were above all a lifeline, a line tied to the center of his real life somewhere beyond the curvature of night; and he knew in his racked brain and aching bones that only by hanging on to it, by working his way hand over hand toward the fixed point of suspension, could he hope to save himself from drowning in the banality of his day-to-day existence. And hang on he did. "I'll never again give up the diary. This is what I must cling to, because it is the only place where I am able to do it" (DI, 12/16/10).

The diaries both forced and inspired him finally to develop the working methods best suited to his inner rhythms and outer eccentricities. For one thing, they tied him to what soon became a regular routine, which, like most of his habits, quickly rigidified into a compulsive ritual, faithfully observed for many years: the late-afternoon nap, followed by a "fletcherized" light snack in preparation for the nightly no-holds-barred wrestling match with language and himself that often lasted into the small hours of the morning and left him numbed through much of the next day. In part, no doubt, external circumstances dictated this weird schedule; in the crowded apartment he shared with seven other adults, even the barest minimum of peace and privacy was not to be had until the rest of the household had turned in for the night. Yet his constant complaints on this score, as on so many others, sound less than persuasive. Once he had attained financial independence, there was absolutely nothing to prevent him from leaving the uncozy parental nest, other than his own fear of flying.

Still, the discipline of putting words on paper religiously, night after night, soon yielded results, not least because the fiction of mere "diary" entries made it much easier to bypass the brutal self-censorship that had blocked his spontaneity in so many of the more self-consciously formal approaches to his writing. Not that all the material was necessarily allowed to stand; much of it subsequently fell victim to one or another of the periodic auto-da-fés with which he tended to express his editorial reservations, but not—and this is what matters—until it had first been allowed to spill out and left a trail of words on the blank page, clues to an inner reality far more substantive and coherent than the world in which he reluctantly went to work every morning. In the course of the fourteen years left to him, the whole of his adult life, these so-called diaries assumed many forms and functions, from the writer's version of the artist's sketchbook to a tool for self-analysis; they were a fetishistic instrument of self-mutilation, a glimpse of reason at the heart of madness, and an errant light in the labyrinth of loneliness.

Among other things, they tell a great deal about Kafka—but only if read with extreme circumspection. Self-portraits, as they emerge from diaries, are inherently suspect; the testimony of the observer observing himself can never be taken at face value, if for no other reason than that the angle of vision is constricted by bias both latent and conscious—"Every day at least one line shall be directed against myself." The portrait that Kafka, guided by such sentiments, drew of himself is as accurate and revealing as any caricature, and equally remote from a true life-size, life-like image. In fact, the most trustworthy witnesses in the proceedings of Kafka-versus-Kafka are the creatures of his imagination, the protagonists of his stories, raised from primordial depths and immune to manipulation. It is they who, in their complex diversity, reflect the essence of his life in its true dimensions and tell us more about his thoughts and feelings than all the anguished lamentations about the state of his body and soul put together.

On March 27, 1910, the newspaper *Bohemia* printed a brief feuilleton item, "Reflections of a Gentleman Jockey," Kafka's mildly ironic meditation on the perils of victory. But most of his writing during this crucial formative period remained confined to the pages of the diary and never saw publication in his lifetime; it includes fragments such as "The Wish to Be a Red Indian," "The Little Ruin Dweller," "Unhappiness," and finally "The Urban World," a stark dramatization of the war between father and son that clearly represents a tentative early version of "The Judgment." It was with that story, written in September 1912, in the course of a single night, that the creative forces nursed and nurtured through three years of agony finally asserted themselves in all their formidable and mature authority.

Fifteen

IN the fall of 1910, Kafka and the Brod brothers headed for Paris. They had been looking forward to the trip, their first glimpse of the *Ville Lumière*, indisputably the capital of Europe, if not of Western civilization, and had conscientiously prepared for the pilgrimage by reading up on the sights and taking refresher courses in conversational French. Moreover, all three were knowledgeable about nineteenth-century French literature; Kafka worshipped Flaubert and had a sentimental attachment to Napoleon, a tribal memory perhaps of the flawed hero who, in spite of his shortcomings, remained European Jewry's great emancipator. But when it came to life, letters, and the arts in the France of their own day, their ignorance was monumental.

An ignorance which, while partly rooted in the lack of temperamental affinities, also reflected the uncivil war raging on their native turf, where one's enemy's enemy was one's natural ally. The wholehearted, not to say blind, commitment to German culture on the part of Prague's German—and especially German-Jewish—minority in turn gave added impetus to the already profound French influence among the Czech intelligentsia. Young Czech artists and intellectuals were thoroughly at home in the hospitable cosmopolitanism of the Paris scene, and programmatically oblivious to the holy trinity—Vienna, Munich, and Berlin—from which their German-speaking compatriots drew their inspiration.

For Kafka, however, this first visit turned into pure misery. Constantly under pressure at the office during the weeks preceding the trip, he had also dislocated his big toe and already felt wretched enough when, right after his return from Gablonz, the three of them took off on October 8. They spent a night in Nuremberg, and by the time they reached Paris the following day, Kafka had broken out in painful boils, diagnosed as furunculosis by the French doctors he reluctantly decided to consult. This ancient biblical plague, a staphylo-coccus infection still difficult to control, was considerably more serious before the advent of antibiotics and always posed a risk of potentially fatal blood poisoning; in any event, it was demoralizing and painful, the treatment messy and palliative at best.

Kafka, feeling—not for the first time and not for the last—like a modern-day Job, made a few feeble attempts to do at least some of the obligatory sights, keeping mostly to himself so as not to spoil his companions' holiday mood. But with new skin rashes and eruptions continuing to sap his strength and morale, he soon gave up and returned to Prague by himself. What he took back, by way of impressions, is tersely summarized in a note to the Brods, oddly revealing in other ways as well:

> . . . arrived safely . . . but was cheated out of the pleasure of yelling at the doctor by a brief fainting spell that forced me to lie down on his couch, during which time—really curious, this—I felt so much like a girl that I tried to tug down my skirt with my fingers. . . . Now I am sitting here at home in the afternoon as though in a tomb. I can't walk around because of the tight bandages, I can't sit still because of the pain. . . . The first night in Prague I dreamed, all night long, I think (sleep hung about this dream like scaffolding around new construction in Paris), that I was lodged in a large building consisting of nothing but Paris cabs, automobiles, buses, etc., that had nothing better to do than drive within a hair's breadth of one another back and forth, over and under, and all anyone talked about was fares, transfers, connections, tips, *direction Perrier*, counterfeit money. . . . Please make sure I didn't cheat you. By my not wholly reliable arithmetic I spent so little that it looks as if I'd wasted all my time in Paris cleansing my sores. [L, 10/10]

Sexual ambiguity rather than ambivalence; not the rape fantasy of one wishing to be a woman but the realization that in a world which reduced male-versus-female to power-versus-submission, he was—with no manifest pleasure—on the female side of the equation.

The Paris fiasco did trigger a short-lived surge of interest in matters French, easy enough to satisfy back home. France, probably the first nation in the world to harness cultural export to political ends (few other nations had enough culture even for home consumption), had a long tradition of selecting distinguished intellectuals as her representatives abroad, and the choice of Paul Claudel as French consul in Prague was a particularly effective one. By appointing a poet and dramatist of his stature—and with over twenty years of diplomatic experience—to what would have appeared to the uninitiated a mere provincial backwater, the French government clearly signaled its intention to fish in this troubled brew with as alluring a bait as could be found. Kafka describes Claudel's impressive appearance at a lecture early in November but does not seem to have seen or read any of his works. (Years later, in a *Figaro* review of the Gide-Barrault adaptation of *The Trial*, Claudel wrote that "besides Racine, who for me is the greatest writer, there is one other before whom I doff my hat: Franz Kafka.")

Altogether, the weeks after his return were marked by frenzied activity, one of those aura-like preludes to stagnation and paralysis in which he drove himself with all the energy of imminent but still latent desperation. He attended lectures almost every night, read Goethe's *Iphigenie*, and vowed that "I will not let myself get tired. I am going to dive into my novel even if it ends up slashing my face" (DI, 11/15/10).

With two more weeks of vacation time to use up before the end of the year, he took himself to Berlin on December 3 and spent five days going to the theater and tracking down vegetarian restaurants. At least, he mentions nothing else, nor is this wildly surprising; the capital of the Wilhelminian empire, though comparable to Paris in size and population, had remained essentially true to its past as a dreary garrison town, combining the virtues of cleanliness with such vices as were legally sanctioned and supervised by the *Sittenpolizei*, the police morals squad. "The architecture is not impressive," he reported to Brod (L, 12/4/10), an extravagant understatement for one weaned on the splendors of Prague, "but what contentment one feels here. I only keep listening to my innermost self." To the end of his life he clung to the image of Berlin as an oasis of peace and tranquillity, an image as grotesquely at odds with reality as it was consistent with his fantasy of total freedom through total alienation. In Berlin he was a stranger among strangers, with no past or future to entrap him.

In the broad historic perspective, of course, the claws of the Little Mother were as nothing compared to the talons of the Prussian eagle. But he and the big bird ignored one another; on the whole, he had no more contact with life in Berlin, where he more or less spoke the language (the slangy native vernacular may have given him some trouble), than he had in Paris, but he managed to take in four plays in as many nights—Molière and Schnitzler, along with *The Comedy of Errors* and *Hamlet*: "Max, I've seen a Hamlet performance. Or rather, I heard Bassermann [Albert Bassermann, German actor, 1867–1952]. For whole quarters of an hour I really had the face of an entirely different person. From time to time I had to look away from the stage at an empty box in order to regain my composure" (L, 12/9/10).

The euphoria had spent itself by the time he got back to Prague. To begin with, he had to contend with a wedding in the family: his twenty-one-year-old sister Elli married—or rather was married to—Karl Hermann, a merchant from Zuerau exactly Kafka's own age. The attendant commotion at home and the disruption in his routine probably outweighed, at least for the moment, whatever deeper emotions the event may have stirred in a highly sensitive area. More important, he found himself incapable of putting together a single solid sentence; the final week of his precious vacation went to waste, compounding his horror of what once again lay ahead of him by way of deadly drudgery. "I had eight completely free days," he lamented, in a letter to Brod of December 15. "My parents at the moment are happy and satisfied, and we almost never quarrel. My father only gets annoyed when he sees me at my desk late at night, because he thinks I work too hard. I was in better health than I had been for months . . . the house was almost quiet. The wedding is over, the new relatives are being digested, and all these gifts were being bestowed upon me at the end of the fall season, a time when I have always felt strongest." Such blatant good luck was bound to attract disaster, as indeed it did: "The core of all my misery remains: I cannot write. I haven't managed a single line I'd care to acknowledge; on the contrary, I threw out everything—it wasn't much—that I had written since Paris. My whole body warns me of every word, and every word first looks around in all directions before it lets itself be written down by me. The sentences literally crumble in my hands; I see their insides and have to stop quickly" (L, 12/15/10).

Even more eloquent is the diary entry of the same date:

> I simply cannot accept my conclusions, based on my current state, which has now lasted for nearly a year; my condition is much too serious for that. I don't even know whether there is anything new about it, although I actually believe that it is in

fact new. I've been through similar states, but never one like this. I really am like rock, like my own tombstone, with not a fissure for doubt or faith, for love or revulsion, for courage or fear in general or in particular. Only vague hope still lives, but no more so than the inscriptions on the tombstones." [DI, 12/15/10]

The very next day, bleak despair and everlasting damnation had given way to "the sense of happiness I feel within me from time to time, as for instance right now. It is really something sparkling that fills me with a slight and pleasant prickle and lets me believe that I have abilities of whose lack I can convince myself with absolute certainty at any moment, even right now" (DI, 12/16/10).

* * *

Despite such brighter moments—far more numerous, no doubt, than the scrupulous itemization of his miseries would lead one to suspect—gloom and self-torment prevailed after his return from Berlin. In December he destroyed most of what he had written during the year. "It is really a mountain, five times as much as I've ever written, and by its mere weight it pulls everything I write out from under my pen" (DI, 12/17/10).

Monotonously, he rails against the office as the symbol of his self-enslavement. "Above all else, it is clear to me that I am simply lost until I can break free of the office. The only hope is to keep my head above water long enough not to drown" (DI, 12/17/10). Again there is the desperate sense of unreality: "Since I seem to be fundamentally at my wits' end—in the course of the past year I have not been awake for more than five minutes—I can only wish myself out of this world every day or else start all over again as a little boy, though it would not give me the slightest reason for hope" (DI, 1/19/11).

But no matter how obvious the parallels to earlier such cycles, the nature of this crisis differed significantly from previous ones. Where formerly he had simply withdrawn into his shell, plunged headlong into self-pity, and surrendered to a sense of infantile helplessness, the conflicts with which Kafka struggled through most of 1911 were basically aspects of growth rather than defeat and finally led to a degree of maturity that allowed both the man and the artist to fulfill himself, after a fashion.

Not, though, without agony and many a false step.

There is much about myself I haven't written down during these past few days [he noted at the beginning of the year]. Partly out of laziness (I now sleep so much and so soundly during the day, I have more weight when I am asleep) but also because I am afraid of distorting my self-perception. This fear is justified, because the perception of oneself should be fixed definitively in writing only if it can be done in its entirety, down to its most remote implications, and with perfect truthfulness. Because if this does not happen—and I, for one, am not capable of it— then what is written down will, in line with its own bias and by the sheer weight of its finality, overwhelm intuition to the extent of wiping out the true feeling and leave instead a written version recognized too late as being worthless. [DI, 1/12/11]

In resisting the temptation to embalm ripening insight in anesthetizing platitudes, Kafka showed an admirable restraint that invites imitation. The glib jargon of latter-day psychology and post-Freudian Freudianism was not yet common currency; even so, he clearly saw the dangers of reducing the intricately complex interplay between levels of consciousness, the source of his inspiration, to blunt and predigested banalities.

It was this process of crystallization and consolidation that introduced decidedly new elements into his writing. "The Urban World," a fragmentary story written at the beginning of March and incorporated in the diary, is more than a preliminary sketch for "The Judgment"; it also marks the first time that his fiction attempts openly to confront what he had come to see as the focal dilemma of his life—the struggle against the father, in which even victory spelled defeat.

This initial foray ran out of steam after a mere few pages, before it had ever properly got underway, and it took another year and a half for him to acquire sufficient mastery over both his feelings and his craft to do justice to the theme. At the same time, however, the acuity with which he had begun to focus on his life situation in all its interlocking contradictions raised anxiety to the boiling point. The time for miracles had passed. He was a clerk who wanted to be a writer, a man cheated of his past, devoid of a future, with no family, no community to define his place, and no role in the human order. And he was going on twenty-eight—old enough to know that he could count on no one but himself for a solution, not old enough to abandon hope altogether.

If the picture struck him as understandably depressing, it also shook him out of his lethargy. The inner turmoil accounts for the black moods that Brod, with heroic naïveté, sought constantly to dispel: "I forever kept telling Kafka to snap out of his depression," he announced in his diary (WAG, p. 227). Yet even Kafka's increasing reluctance to participate in the social rituals of his circle may have been motivated at least partly by the need to conserve energy at a time when the growing demands made on him by the office were further outpaced by those he made on himself. And though, as usual, he felt inadequate in either sphere, the fact is that he met the challenge quite successfully.

At the beginning of the year, he spent two weeks—from January 30 to February 12, 1911—on institute business in north Bohemia. This time, as if to equalize the opposing pressures, he made himself keep a travel journal that bears many touches characteristic of his later fiction—the deftly sketched rogues' gallery of fellow passengers on the train, a description of the seventeenth-century Friedland Castle, fief of Count Wallenstein during the Thirty Years' War, and a halfhearted pursuit of two young girls in the park. Whether it was the castle at Friedland or the one at Wossek, birthplace of Kafka's father, that served as model for the "castle" in Kafka's novel published post-humously under that title is one of those weighty questions that have greatly exercised certain critics—as if the castle in Kafka's mind did not have an infinitely more substantive reality than either. He also managed to take in no less than three plays at the Municipal Theater of Reichenberg, a textile center of about 70,000 inhabitants, and his speculative curiosity about their way of life contrasts sharply with the pervasive lack of interest he had evinced in Berlin barely a month earlier.

Right after his return, the Board of Directors appointed him one of the institute's legal representatives, with full powers of attorney, and sent him on another trip covering much the same territory; in fact, business travel took up a large share of his time throughout most of the year. Despite these disruptions, he grimly made himself stick to a disciplined writing schedule, read extensively, attended numerous plays and lectures, and for all his self-imposed constraints still had a fairly active social life. Unhappiness there was aplenty, bouts of despondency genuine and profound, but nothing like the earlier states of suspended animation. The old habits of breast-beating and self-deprecation persisted, but they sounded less convinced and convincing; the inverted arrogance had hardened into something like self-confidence —sporadic, limited as yet to narrow spheres, but unmistakable. He himself demonstrated this transformation—quite unwittingly, hence all the more persuasively—in his account of a meeting with Rudolf Steiner.

Steiner, a German ex-disciple of Annie Besant who had broken away to dispense his own brand of mysticism under the name of anthroposophy, had come to Prague in March of 1911 to found a local branch of his deviationist cult and to deliver a series of lectures on its secret doctrines at the by-now-famous weekly meetings of the Fanta circle. The reputation of transcendental wisdom and spirituality that had prompted the invitation in the first place no doubt reinforced the charismatic effect of Steiner's high-minded obscurantism, at least on the hostess and her sister, both of whom had long since abandoned Brentano in their quest for higher consciousness and cosmic truth. Steiner, suitably prophetic in looks and demeanor, seemed a promising guide to the mysteries of the occult and, with enthusiastic support from his hostesses, eventually recruited the necessary quorum of initiates for Prague's first anthroposophic congregation, the Bolzano Lodge.

His lectures on the "Awareness of Higher Worlds" apparently roused high expectations, and even Kafka was sufficiently curious to attend at least two of them, though he by that time had taken an active dislike to the Fanta salon and rarely ever went there. Else Bergmann, Berta Fanta's daughter, claims to remember that "at those lectures I noticed the sparkle and glow in Franz Kafka's eyes, and the smile that lit up his face" (WAG, p. 175). If so, it was no epiphany that prompted the beatific grin. The impressions of Steiner's public persona he recorded in his diary sparkle, if anything, with an irony the more devastating for its faint undertone of disappointment:

> Dr. Steiner is being kept terribly busy by the disciples that are absent. At his lectures, the dead keep crowding in on him—seeking knowledge? Do they need it? They evidently do, after all. Sleeps only two hours. . . . Was very close to Christ. . . . Produced his own play in Munich (you can study it for a whole year and still won't understand it), designed the costumes, wrote the music. May not be the greatest spiritual researcher of our time, but is the only one to have been entrusted with the

task of combining science and theosophy. That is why he knows everything. Atlantic apocalypse, lemuric apocalypse, now end of the world through egotism. . . . Dr. Steiner's mission will succeed, if only the Ahrimanic forces don't gain the upper hand. . . . Mrs. Fanta: "I have such a poor memory." Dr. Steiner: "Don't eat eggs."

But Kafka, nothing if not thorough, apparently would not let this first impression deter him from testing his skepticism in a personal consultation.

In his room I try to demonstrate the reverence I cannot feel by finding a ridiculous place for my hat. . . . He starts off with a few loose sentences: "So you're Dr. Kafka. How long have you been interested in theosophy?" But I proceed with my prepared speech: "While a large part of me feels drawn to theosophy, I am also deeply afraid of it because I fear further confusion. And this would be very hard on me, because confusion is the sum and substance of my present miseries. My happiness, my abilities, and whatever chance I may have of being of some use have always resided in the realm of literature. Here, I believe, I experienced states (not many) which in my opinion closely resemble the clairvoyant states described by you, Herr Doktor. . . . The problem is that, for a variety of reasons, I cannot wholly devote myself to literary pursuits. Aside from my family situation, the slow gestation of my work and its unusual character of themselves already preclude any possibility of my supporting myself by writing. Moreover, my health and my character also keep me from living in ways that are precarious under the best of circumstances. I have therefore become an official in a social insurance institution. Now these two professions can never be reconciled to the point of achieving a balance of happiness in both. The slightest good fortune in one becomes the greatest of miseries in the other. If I've had a good night of writing, I am on fire the next day in the office and can't get anything done. This back and forth is getting worse all the time. At the office I live up to my outward duties, but not to my inner duties, and those unfulfilled duties grow into a permanent torment. Should I now add theosophy to these two mutually irreconcilable fields of endeavor? Won't it cause more trouble on both sides and be troubled in turn? Shall I, an already so unhappy person, be able to prove myself in all three fields? This is what I've come to ask you, Herr Doktor, because I feel that if you think me capable of handling it, I could assume the burden."

He listened with the utmost attention, but without ever seeming to look at me directly, wholly absorbed in my words. From time to time he would nod, which he apparently considers an aid to total concentration. At first a quiet cold bothered him, his nose ran, all along he kept working his handkerchief way up his nose, one finger on each nostril. [DI, 3/28/11]

End of report, final comment on Steiner and on theosophy. Neither is ever mentioned again.

Given his earlier comments on Steiner's platform presence, it seems somewhat unclear just what it was that Kafka expected from the interview. "The notion that an adult could receive good advice is one of my biggest stupidities," he confessed a few years later (FEL, 11/10/13). But whether he was still hoping for miracles or merely verifying first impressions seems less significant than the driven search itself, of which this episode is but one example among many. He was still looking for final answers even as he began to formulate the very questions beyond answers that are the core of his legacy.

At the same time, there was a distinctly new tone of self-confidence about the way in which he presented his case to Steiner—the legal brief outlining his dilemma, and the authority with which he took his literary gifts for granted. Open to question—wide open, with blood oozing out of the gap—was only whether he would squander these gifts or put them to use, never their existence as such.

* * *

His "health" was among the reasons Kafka cited in explaining why he could not possibly contemplate a freelance writer's existence. Absurd as the claim would seem on its face—was the blind Oskar Baum or the hunchbacked Max Brod physically better equipped for the rigors of fluctuating royalties?—the very fact of his invoking it provides some provocative clues to the nature and function of his lifelong hypochondria. The child's use of illness as a means of gaining attention, sympathy, and love is universal, and Kafka, unloved and unwanted, learned to use it with a consummate skill that set the pattern for the ways in which the grownup went about, for the rest of his life, manipulating those close to him. In this, moreover, he had a stellar example on which to model himself: no one was more adept at extorting sympathy through illness than Kafka's father.

But the flight into illness served more immediate ends—it kept the demons at bay. And in clinging to the myth of his "constitutional frailty," the adult was still using the child's game plan against the same demons. The only thing that had changed was the object of their wrath: where once they had to be restrained from murdering the father, they were now after the son. As a defense against suicidal depression, the whole elaborate cluster of rituals and taboos that Kafka had evolved to monitor the functions and dysfunctions of his body, appropriate or not, made sense. But in resorting to it, he often reverted to childhood.

This, at least, seems the most plausible explanation for the pathetic gullibility with which this otherwise so discriminating skeptic was ever ready to bow to the authority of quacks, frauds, and faddists, and to swallow some of their most noxious snake oil. Fletcher was bad enough. But in April 1911, right after his encounter with Steiner, another business trip took him to Varnsdorf, in north Bohemia, where one Moritz Schnitzer, a local manufacturer, had established a lucrative reputation as naturopath and healer. Kafka took the opportunity to consult him and was told that all his troubles resulted from the accumulation of poisons in his spinal column, which had almost reached the brain and would have to be eliminated by drastic changes in his way of life, including a subscription to Schnitzer's magazine. And although the naturopathic exegesis of the Bible, according to which Moses deliberately dragged the weary Israelites through forty years of desert so as to wean them away from the fleshpots of Egypt and habituate them to vegetarian manna, may have left Kafka less than convinced, he took Schnitzer's therapeutic recommendations quite seriously and did his best to incorporate them into his ever more complex routine.

In fact, six years later, already hospitalized with tuberculosis, he still wrote to Schnitzer for advice about a fasting cure. And in response to a justifiably outraged protest on the subject from his friend Felix Weltsch, he wrote: "What you said about Schnitzer is very true, but one easily underestimates such people. He is wholly artless, hence magnificently sincere, hence where he has nothing to offer—as speaker, writer, even as thinker—not only simplistic, as you put it, but downright idiotic. But sit down with him, look at him, try to understand him and his effectiveness, try for a moment to approach his point of view—he cannot so easily be dismissed" (L, 10/17).

He may also not have been quite as much of an idiot as even Kafka, in his saner moments, apparently judged him to be. At least he was smart enough not to compound his manifest failure by offering further advice.

* * *

An intrinsically far more significant personality appeared that spring on the Prague scene; in March, Kafka notes—without further comment —that he had attended a lecture by Karl Kraus.

The emblematic role of that peculiar figure in prewar Austrian life and, above all, letters is hard to overestimate, and even harder to understand. Exalted claims on his behalf continue to be advanced. Yet the actual work, read in the present, makes one suspect that the passions he was able to generate reflected the temper of the times far more than any genius ascribed to him, and that what sustained the interest of an enormous and faithful readership—Kafka included—over the first two decades of the century was not the method so much as the madness of the man. Kraus considered himself the master and arbiter of the German language, an opinion widely shared at the time that still has its defenders.

There may even be some truth to it. But far more pertinent to his fame is a piece of exquisite irony: the most pernicious of Jew haters upset the stultifying complacency of imperial Vienna by introducing the polemical stridency of Yiddish journalism. What made him the prophet of the Austrian apocalypse was the convincing pose he struck of Mosaic sound and fury, rather than the contents of the lapidary communications he tossed down from his mountaintop at a truly impressive rate.

Kraus, nine years older than Kafka, was born in 1874 at Jičín, near Prague, but transplanted at age three to Vienna. The son of a well-to-do Jewish manufacturer, he abandoned his studies to follow the lure of the stage, failed as an actor, and, after some years as a freelance critic, founded his own monthly, *Die Fackel* (*The Torch*), in 1899. Conceived from the outset as a vehicle for polemical satire, *Die Fackel* initially published contributions by many well-known contemporaries but, from 1911 until Kraus's death and its own demise in 1936, was written exclusively by him alone, the more or less monthly eruption of a sulphurous geyser. The sheer scale of Kraus's energy continues to amaze, and would have been admirable if its source had not been tainted to the point of perverting his judgment beyond all bounds of reason and decency.

Kraus's major intellectual and ideological commitment was to language. He regarded language as the sole criterion of morality, and appointed himself its supreme defender, a position from which he conducted a lifelong crusade against the mercenaries of corruption, foremost among them being the press in general, and the Jewish-liberal *Neue Freie Presse* in particular. But his enemies were legion, and he flayed them, dead or alive, with a froth and fury that bore no relationship to reasoned argument. In the course of laying about him, he skewered many a target that well deserved it; wholesale idiocy, venality, and hypocrisy flourished then as now. Yet to elevate Kraus to the status of moralist, social critic, or Old Testament prophet means shutting one's eyes to the morbid bias that persistently inspired his most vicious attacks. He accused Heine of having perverted the German language, "unlaced its bodice so that now any fool can fondle its breasts." *Die Fackel* went to war against Dreyfus, Herzl, and Freud, and although in the course of the First World War Kraus eventually became an ardent and effective pacifist, he even here concentrated his fire mainly on the excesses of a superpatriotic press. In the twenties he supported the clerical autocracy under Dollfuss, and as for Hitler, he could simply "think of nothing to say."

By way of an early Freudian counterattack, Fritz Wittels, one of the original apostles, presented a paper on "The Fackel Neurosis" at a meeting of the Vienna Psychoanalytic Society. Discrediting the thought by discrediting the thinker is obviously not the most subtle of arguments, to begin with; and in any case, at issue here was not the psychopathology of Karl Kraus—blatantly typical of his generation—but the fanaticism, style, and paranoid energy with which he transmuted it into perhaps the best-known manifestation of a widespread and highly destructive cultural phenomenon: Kraus was the quintessential incarnation of Jewish self-hatred carried to extremes.

Though he officially severed his links to Judaism in 1899 and secretly converted to Catholicism in 1911, he was far too bright and eccentric an individualist to engage in primitive Jew-baiting (he left the Church in 1923 in protest against the tawdry commercialism of the Church-sponsored Salzburg Festival). What he held against the Jews was, essentially, that they were Jewish and, in many instances, not even ashamed of it. What he accused them of was that they corrupted the German language, that they inevitably polluted it with jargon, Yiddishisms, elements of Jewish thought that a hawk-eyed purist like himself was able to spot in even the seemingly most accomplished German prose. The Jew writing in German was misappropriating and misusing another people's heritage.

Stealing a stranger's baby out of the cradle, as Kafka put it. He had many reservations about Kraus, whose rantings on a wide variety of subjects were always pungent, sometimes entertaining, often tedious, but hard to take seriously until the insane brutality unleashed by World War I offered him subject matter worthy of his ever-spluttering indignation. The reputation for moral courage and rational sanity he earned during those years as publicist, and as author of the interminable pre-Brechtian antiwar drama, *The Last Days of Mankind*, survived his subsequent steep decline into fatuous crankiness. As to the relationship of Jewish writers to the German language, however, Kafka's own views in later years came remarkably close to those of Kraus, though he approached them from a different angle and drew from them radically different conclusions. Kraus himself struck him as a mixture of wit, pettiness, and insight, a prime example of the very spirit he denounced: "The wit mainly consists of *mauscheln*" (from *Moyshe*—a mixture of German and Yiddish, accompanied by expressive gestures); "no one can *mauscheln* the way Kraus does" (L, 6/21). Or, as he is reputed to have told Janouch, "it's the poacher who makes the best forest warden." But in seeing the German-Jewish writer confronted by "three impossibilities . . . the impossibility of not writing, the impossibility of writing in German, the impossibility of writing differently" (L, 6/21) he implicitly endorsed Kraus's attitude, though from the consciously Jewish point of view—as a tragic dilemma rather than a criminal assault by insolent barbarians on the Christian virtue of the German language.

This growing conviction on Kafka's part, which profoundly influenced the stark asceticism of his later style, was criticized as extreme even by his closest friends, notably Brod. Nevertheless, the notion as such had certainly long been a commonplace in the anti-assimilationist circles around the Zionist *Selbstwehr*, with whom Kafka in later years sympathized if not identified, even if no practical alternatives seemed as yet to suggest themselves. The possibility of reviving a language dead for over two thousand years would have struck even the author of the *Judenstaat* as a utopian dream.

* * *

Kraus himself was eventually to unleash the full fury of his punitive thunder upon Prague's "Arconauts," closest to him in origin and background, hence most typically representative of what he had most come to hate. But in the spring of 1911 he still championed young Werfel, had just published three of his poems in *Die Fackel*, and enjoyed the Werfel family's sumptuous hospitality, for which he repaid them ten years later with a vile piece of gossip dressed as satire.

Young Prague, in turn, was delighted with the cantankerous iconoclast—with one notable exception. Max Brod had the temerity and courage publicly to reprimand the great man for his scurrilous attack on the critic Alfred Kerr. In the ensuing polemic, Kraus summed up his side of the argument by the crushing dictum that "*Geist auf Brod geschmiert ist Schmalz*" (mind smeared on bread is lard)—a play on the identical pronunciation, in German, of Brod's name and the word for "bread" that is not atypical of Kraus's much-vaunted verbal pyrotechnics. Whether and how this controversy influenced Kafka's initial reaction to Kraus is not known, but he was at the time merely beginning to confront the whole problem of Jewish identity or, more precisely, of his own identity in a non-Jewish and anti-Jewish world, and he certainly had not yet attained a firm enough footing to assess Kraus's standard discourse on the pernicious influence of Heinrich Heine.

* * *

Of interest in this connection is Kafka's encounter, a few months later, with Kurt Tucholsky, a man often referred to as the Berlin counterpart to Kraus—a comparison about as apt as that between an organ grinder and a piano virtuoso; both make noise. Kraus made a lot more noise grinding his organ, but any superficial parallels between the effusive pan-hysteria of the mean-spirited Viennese egomaniac and the desperate wit of the brilliant Berlin satirist falsify Tucholsky's role and position. He was Heine's direct—and final—spiritual descendant, engaged like him in a love-hate relationship with his native land that ended in exile and death but inspired a relentless struggle against German militarism, lynch law, and the rise of Nazism in the 1920s as the militant *Weltbühne*'s star contributor, in his own name as well as under five pseudonyms. His weapon was humor of the blackest kind, distilled out of a despair and alienation far more akin to Kafka than to Kraus, down to the deep ambivalence about his Jewish origins, which had nothing in common with Kraus's insensate hate of the *Ostjude* in himself and others.

In the fall of 1911, Tucholsky, another law student in spite of himself, passed through Prague and met both Kafka and Brod. Though still young and unknown, he even then made enough of an impression to warrant a rather prescient portrait in Kafka's diary:

> . . . a rather well-integrated young man of twenty-one, from the controlled forceful swing of his cane, which gives the shoulder a youthful lift, to the thoughtful approval and dismissal of his own writings. Wants to become a defense attorney, sees only a few obstacles ahead, along with possibilities for overcoming them: his high voice, which after the manly sound of the first half hour's talk allegedly tends to rise to a girlish pitch, doubts about his ability to strike poses which, however, he hopes to acquire along with more worldly experience, and finally the fear of bogging down in *Weltschmerz*, a tendency he has observed among aging Berlin Jews of his background, though for the time being he feels no trace of it. Is going to get married soon. [DI, 9/30/11]

The attraction was mutual. The difficult and acerbic satirist, recalling the occasion, noted that while he disliked the already well-known Brod, he "loved Kafka at first sight, before he had ever read a single line of his" (Tucholsky, p. 473). He was also, among many other things, a most discerning critic, who, as early as 1920, hailed Kafka in one of his *Weltbühne* reviews as the greatest German prose writer since Kleist and, a year later, deplored the fact that this Prague author was still so little known in Germany: "He writes the most lucid and most beautiful prose that is currently being created in the German language" (Tucholsky, p. 866).

*   *   *

The two had even more in common than they realized. Banned, banished, and silenced, Tucholsky killed himself in Sweden on December 21, 1935—not because he lost the struggle against Hitler, but because he lost his faith in mankind. A few weeks before his death, meticulously planned and executed, he referred in a letter to "Kierkegaard's immortal page about the poet who wants to transcend himself but only gets as far as religious longing, not piety as such. . . . That is my case exactly: not yet, and no more."

Sixteen

ALTHOUGH guilt, fear, and despair remained constant companions, 1911 was, on the whole, a year of creative turmoil in Kafka's life, a year of restless intensity and a still unfocused search spurred by needs dimly sensed but as yet undefined. The dilemma he had so rationally outlined to Steiner justified a measure of self-pity, but he was beginning to realize that it represented merely one facet of much larger and more fundamental questions, whose very formulation still eluded him.

That summer he read *David Copperfield*, as well as a biography of Dickens, a challenge and inspiration which, all told, probably did more harm than good. (Some attempts have been made [notably by Mark Spilka in *Dickens and Kafka*] to yoke Dickens and Kafka in terms of similar oedipal maladjustments, childhood traumata, etc. The parallels, such as they be, are broad enough to cover almost any two writers one cares to pair.) It was probably Dickens's elemental—and inherently inimitable—narrative drive rather than any unconscious affinities that captivated Kafka, as it had Dostoevsky, and partly inspired the original version of *Der Verschollene*—"The Man Who Disappeared"—on which he started that winter and which has not been preserved. An apparently drastic revision was published in 1913 under the title *The Stoker—A Fragment* as the initial and only segment of *Amerika* to appear in Kafka's lifetime. On the evidence, he was even less capable of following in other writers' footsteps than Dostoevsky; the Dickensian influence, to the extent to which it still intrudes on the revised version of the story, remains a distinctly foreign object.

At the end of August, Kafka and Max Brod again took their vacation together and agreed that this time their separate journals were to include not only travel impressions but also their feelings toward one another. It had been Brod's suggestion, one that struck Kafka from the outset as a "decidedly poor idea," probably for the very reason that made Brod propose it in the first place—an undercurrent of hostility, normally discharged in passing squabbles and brief moments of irritation, but liable to be amplified in any written record. Unfairly so, as they both seemed to believe; for while Kafka could be an unmitigated pain—he was forever late, fussed about his vegetarian food and his digestion, agonized over the most trifling of decisions—and Brod often seemed pompous, pretentious, sex-obsessed, and fidgety to Kafka, they basically got along rather well with each other, certainly far better than two such disparate eccentrics had any right to expect.

It was during the trip itself that they decided instead to jointly write a novel about it. Brod at the time had a predilection for communal projects of this sort, and so, throughout the fall and winter of 1911, the two of them tinkered with "Richard [later renamed Robert] and Samuel," even though it quickly became apparent to Kafka that as writers they were infinitely farther apart even than as friends: "Max and I must be fundamentally different. Much as I admire his work . . . still every sentence he writes for 'Richard and Samuel' involves reluctant concessions on my part which I feel in the very depths of my being. At least I did so today" (DI, 11/19/11). A few opening paragraphs have been preserved in Kafka's diary, but the attempt as a whole was aborted after the first chapter, published in May 1912 in the Prague magazine *Herderblätter*.

The two-week trip as such was this time mainly to be devoted to sightseeing rather than rest, and Kafka's separate journal makes no attempt to more than fix the onrush of kaleidoscopic impressions in terse cues for later use; thus his notes on the Milan Cathedral, on which he obviously drew for the "Cathedral" chapter of *The Trial*. Starting out with a city tour of Munich on August 27, they went on to Zurich, Lucerne, and Lugano, where they ran into a barrage of scare news about a cholera epidemic raging in Italy. The categorical denial by Italian authorities merely served to confirm their worst suspicions, but they nonetheless pushed on as far as Milan, where Brod's own baroque obsessions got the better of him. He fretted about collapsing unconscious, felled by the plague, and being buried alive by panicky Italian authorities so anxious to dispose of apparent victims that they wouldn't bother to make sure of their actual demise. He quite seriously entertained this fantasy—a recurrent phobia, it turned out—to the point of exacting a formal promise from Kafka that the friend would administer a *coup de grâce* of sorts—stab him through the heart, rather like impaling a vampire—before closing the coffin. This request, according to Brod, moved Kafka to tears—proof, if true, that Kafka's sense of humor could fail him on occasion.

In any event, they decided at this point to get out of Italy as fast as possible and spend the remaining five days together in Paris. Unlike the year before, Kafka was in good form and made the most of his stay, spending much time in the Louvre, indulging his passion for the French Revolution and Napoleon by visiting Versailles, the Carnavale Museum, the Invalides, and other historic places, without neglecting either technical progress—the *métro*, motion pictures, a scientific exhibit—or those special attractions for which, deservedly or otherwise, Paris was famous in its time. Though greatly impressed by the rational organization and dignified atmosphere of the brothel to which Brod introduced him, something apparently triggered a fit of panic that made him rush out in a funk and fight his way back to the hotel through streets as crowded with *poules* as the parlor of the whorehouse itself. Whatever its cause, this sudden change of mind and mood seems to have killed his one chance for closer contact with the natives, even if they were likely to have been natives of Algiers, Lodz, or Buenos Aires rather than Paris.

*   *   *

Brod had only two weeks' vacation and went straight home from Paris. Kafka had an additional week, which he spent at a *Naturheilsanatorium*—a naturopathic sanatorium—at Erlenbach, near Zurich, a place chiefly patronized by "aging middle-class Swiss matrons" suffering from constipation and obesity, where each day was rigidly scheduled with "baths, massages, gymnastics, obligatory rest periods before and after," while the evenings were devoted to organized "social activities," notably gramophone concerts featuring military bands and the reading of homespun poetry in the native Swiss dialect. For all his sarcasm in describing this ludicrous ambience, Kafka obviously derived considerable satisfaction from being fussed over and taken care of, getting precisely the kind of attention to which at home even illness never quite seemed to entitle him, because the father had always preempted such claims.

Still did, in fact: on the very eve of Kafka's departure for Italy—

the timing hardly accidental—Herrmann had once again gone through his standard repertoire. "Tomorrow I'm supposed to be leaving for Italy. And tonight Father was too upset to fall asleep, completely destroyed by business worries and by the illness which they had exacerbated. A wet cloth on the heart, nausea, shortness of breath, heavy sighs as he keeps pacing back and forth. The frightened mother tries to comfort him" (DI, 8/25/11).

In the absence of a mother, a Swiss sanatorium will do. At least it did, so he reports, alleviate his constipation, a perennial concern which Schnitzer's instant diagnosis of "toxic accretions threatening the brain" may well have rendered more acute than ever. A week after his return he recorded, with markedly pregenital delight, that "the painter Kubin [Alfred Kubin, 1877–1959] recommends Regulin as a laxative, a pulverized seaweed that swells up in the gut and makes it quiver, thus acting mechanically, in contrast to the unhealthy chemical effect of other laxatives, which tear through the feces and leave them sticking to the bowel walls" (DI, 9/26/11). However morbid, there is something pathetically human about this conspicuous concern, an undigested sliver of infancy that for brief moments made all the world's terrors amenable to natural catharsis by pulverized algae.

*   *   *

The open struggle between father and son that broke out toward the end of that year crystallized around what seemed like a relatively neutral if not trivial issue—the founding of the Prager Asbestwerke Hermann & Co.—the Prague Asbestos Works Hermann & Co. Though incorporated under the nominal ownership of Kafka's new brother-in-law, Karl Hermann, the initial funding, and probably the basic idea as well, originated with Kafka Senior, who thereby wanted to kill several birds with one not very well aimed stone: invest Elli's dowry in a career opportunity for her husband, lay the foundations for a family-owned industrial empire in the more remote future, and, in the here-and-now, offer his disappointing failure of a son one last chance to make something of himself if he already wasn't going to take over the family business. As it happened, the last bird did indeed come perilously close to getting killed.

Whatever possessed Kafka to get involved in this scheme is not entirely clear. In his version, he was dragged into it by his father, who wore him down with constant complaints and dramatic rehearsals of imminent deathbed scenes. In everyone else's opinion, he was himself largely responsible for the project, a responsibility which, as he later asserted, "I must have assumed more or less in my dreams." Dreams or waking, the fact remains that he borrowed enough money from his father to participate in the venture as a silent partner, and he may well have dreamed, however briefly and naïvely, of being able to quit his job and live off his share of the factory profits in return for an occasional guest appearance.

This, however, was not what his father and his equally enterprising brother-in-law had in mind. The factory in suburban Žižkov started up in November 1911 with twenty-five workers, mostly female, and fourteen machines driven by one 35-horsepower gasoline engine. Karl Hermann was supposed to supervise operations, but since he also represented the total sales force and, as such, spent much time on the road, the factory often had to be left in charge of the German foreman. Herrmann Kafka, ever convinced that in the absence of visible constraints, all workers were out to steal him blind, demanded that Franz show the flag whenever Karl was not around and keep an eye on the "paid enemies"—not exactly what Kafka had envisaged by way of silent partnership. The result was a series of increasingly hysterical confrontations that soon turned chronic hostility into acute hatred.

The paternal nagging started within the first few weeks. Already in December, the diary reports that "at lunch my father accused me of not paying enough attention to the factory. I told him that I had participated because I expected profits, but that I could not actually work there as long as I had my job at the institute. Father continued to argue. I stood by the window and kept silent" (DI, 12/14/11).

A mere two weeks later, the tone had grown considerably more strident:

> This factory is turning into a purgatory. Why did I agree when they made me promise to work there in the afternoons? Actually, no one twisted my arm; what forces me to go there are my father's reproaches, Karl's silence, and my own guilty conscience. I know nothing whatsoever about the place. This morning, when the committee came to inspect it, I stood around useless like a whipped cur. I consider it utterly impossible for me to absorb all the details of the operations. But suppose I were able to do so by endless questioning and pestering of all concerned—

then what? What would I have accomplished? I could not imagine myself achieving anything real. I am fit only for the kind of make-believe work to which my boss's common sense adds the salt that makes it look like a truly good job. On the other hand, this paltry effort on behalf of the factory would deprive me of my chance to use the few afternoon hours for myself, which inevitably would lead to the total destruction of my existence, already more and more constricted. [DI, 12/28/11]

The factory itself was a primitive, noisy, filthy place thick with asbestos dust, which at closing time the women—"hardly human, one does not greet them, doesn't excuse oneself when bumping into one of them" —brushed off with the single available brush that "makes the rounds of the room and is impatiently being clamored for. . . . They wash their hands as best they can; they are women, after all, able to smile despite their pallor and poor teeth. . . . You hug the greasy cases to get out of their way, keep your hat in hand when they bid you good night and don't know how to act when one of them holds your overcoat for you to slip into" (DI, 2/5/12).

Hardly the thoughts of a budding captain of industry, and by March 1912, the extra-oedipal conflict had reached a new stage. "Day before yesterday reproaches on account of the factory. For an hour after that I lay on the couch and thought about jumping out of the window" (DI, 3/8/12).

By May the factory was losing money, the son-in-law badgered Kafka Senior for additional funds, and Herrmann, snapping for air like a beached flounder, blamed his son for the impending ruin of the family fortune. On October 7, 1912, in a letter to Max Brod, Kafka again toyed with the idea of suicide.

> After writing well on Sunday night—I could have written all through the night and the next day and night and the day following, and then flown away, and today I could no doubt also have written well—one page, really just a matter of exhaling after yesterday's ten pages, actually did get finished—I have to stop for the following reason: my brother-in-law, the manufacturer, left this morning on a ten-to-fourteen-day business trip, a fact to which, in my happy absentmindedness, I had scarcely paid any attention. In his absence, the factory is left to the mercy of the foreman, and no investor, least of all one as nervous

as my father, would doubt for one moment that fraud and swindle of the most heinous kind are now going to be perpetrated there. I myself, incidentally, share this belief, though not so much because I worry about the money but because I am uninformed and have an uneasy conscience. Even an impartial observer, however, inasmuch as I could imagine one such, might see a certain justification for my father's fears, although personally I cannot forget that in the final analysis I don't see why, even in my brother-in-law's absence, his *Reichs-German* foreman, infinitely superior to him in everything that concerns technology and organization, could not be relied upon to run the place with his usual efficiency. After all, we are human beings, not thieves. . . .

Tonight, when my mother again started in with her old complaints and, aside from blaming me for my father's bitterness and illness, also brought up this new argument of my brother-in-law's departure and the lack of supervision at the factory, and when my youngest sister, who normally takes my side, deserted me . . . I realized with utter clarity that for me there now remained only two possibilities: either I jumped out of the window after everyone had gone to sleep, or else I went to the factory and to my brother-in-law's office every day for the next two weeks. . . . I did not jump, and the temptation to make this a farewell letter . . . is not very strong. . . . It also occurred to me that my death would interrupt my writing more decisively than if I remained alive. [L, 10/8/12]

Despite this grimly upbeat ending, the letter struck Brod as sufficiently alarming to justify his intervention. He took it upon himself to send a copy to Kafka's mother, who replied at once: "I have just received your letter, and from my shaky handwriting you will know how much it upsets me. I, who stand ready to shed my blood for each and every one of my children to assure their happiness, am helpless in this instance. Nevertheless, I shall do everything in my power to see that my son is happy" (Brod, bio., p. 85).

There is no reason to doubt that Julie Kafka was genuinely shaken up, but her first loyalty, then as always, belonged to her husband, who "must not be upset on account of his illness." At the same time, she did love her son, in her own way and without having any remote understanding of who and what he was. "Today at breakfast I briefly talked to my mother about children and marriage—just a few words, but for the first time it became clear to me just how untrue and childish an image she has of me. She considers me a healthy young man, somewhat given to imaginary ailments. These delusions will disappear in time, although marriage and children would banish them more quickly. At that point, my interest in literature will also shrink to such modest proportions as may perhaps be necessary to an educated person (DI, 12/19/11).

But Julie was also the only member of the household who persistently exhibited a measure of common sense. And having—as a stepdaughter, as a woman of her time, and as Herrmann Kafka's wife—spent a lifetime mastering the art of avoiding confrontations, she was inordinately skilled at evasive schemes, compromises, and behind-the-scenes manipulations. In this particular instance, while leading her husband to believe that their son was now conscientiously attending to his duties at the factory, she at the same time secretly hired her son-in-law's brother for the job. This arrangement lasted for several years, until Karl's brother Paul Hermann officially became a partner in 1914.

With the outbreak of the war, however, both brothers were drafted, and the factory loomed once again as a potential threat to Kafka's existence—more so than ever, in fact, because his then-fiancée, Felice Bauer, actively urged his participation and thus precipitated a serious quarrel between them. But the growing scarcity of raw materials soon rendered the issue academic. Production had to be suspended, and with the official liquidation of the enterprise in September 1917, Kafka's inglorious career as a manufacturer came to an equally inglorious but welcome end.

*   *   *

Ultimately, however, Kafka's involvement in this misbegotten enterprise must be viewed against the larger crisis which, long overdue, was now finally coming to a head in this twenty-ninth year of his life.

That he himself had a fairly clear idea of this can be gathered from his comment on the preliminaries to the firm's incorporation: "When, during the reading of the contract, the attorney came to the paragraph that dealt with my putative future wife and my putative future children, I saw across from me a table with two large chairs and a small one. The thought that I shall never be able to occupy these or any other three chairs with my wife and child immediately precipitated so desperate a desire for this kind of happiness that out of aggressive rancor I interrupted the lengthy proceedings by raising my only question, which instantly revealed my total misunderstanding of most of what had just been read" (DI, 11/8/11).

The somnambulist dreamer who "hadn't been awake for more than five minutes" through the year had woken up at last to find himself quite literally a *Luftmensch*—precariously poised, as he depicted it, on the top rung of a ladder suspended in midair. There was an element of panic in his grim resolve to come down to earth and make a place for himself. But whatever this called for by way of heroic deeds—marriage, progeny, links to a body beyond the mortal self—he knew, or was beginning to realize, that making a place for himself meant, first of all, displacing his father. The long years of sullen, guilt-edged hostility had come to an end; the wrangling over the asbestos factory foreshadowed the first open showdown between father and son and unleashed furies that found their voice, a few months later, in "The Judgment."

And it was this same profound crisis that accounts for the seminal importance of what, under different circumstances, an ever-busy and self-involved Dr. Kafka might hardly have noticed—the arrival in Prague of a Yiddish theater troupe. In fact, a year earlier—in May 1910—another such little band of itinerant players from Eastern Europe had spent twelve days in Prague and staged a number of Yiddish plays at the Café Savoy. Kafka, mostly at Brod's insistence, attended one performance but showed little more than polite interest. A mere fifteen months later, another group of eight ill-assorted, beaten but spunky performers low on funds and high on hopes descended on Prague and got more or less stuck for months on end, unable even to raise the fare needed to move on. But to Kafka, their appearance at the sleazy Savoy, in the heart of the disreputable former ghetto district, this time came as a revelation.

The different reception he accorded the two groups had nothing to do with objective criteria but reflected, instead, a radical difference in his receptivity. What he saw in May 1910 were bizarre creatures screaming at one another in a near-incomprehensible "jargon" and draining the last dollop of *shmaltz* out of an absurd tearjerker. Whatever he had in common with them was precisely what, up to that point, he had been most determined to ignore. By October 1911, however, inner pressures had built up to a crisis point. Age, despondency, and his writing—that constant search for self—had opened him up to his own feelings and

sensitized him to an existential isolation far more profound and universal than the bitter loneliness of the rejected child. What he sought in
Judaism was not faith so much as a living community, one of which he
could himself be a living part. And therein resided the seductive magic
of Yitzhak Levi and his players: eight messengers from the world in
which his own father had himself been a son, kindred spirits to a spirit
that was stirring within him, speaking his own lost language, rooted and
secure in their unassailable identity as Jews, Jewish in the way the
Czechs were Czech, the Germans German—and he himself was nothing.

Jewish, above all, in stark contrast to the synthetic religiosity of his
father's generation—on October 1, four days before his first encounter
with the Yiddish theater, he noted the "churchlike" atmosphere of
Prague's Old-New Synagogue on Yom Kippur, and the "muffled stock-
exchange murmur" during the *Kol Nidre* (DI, 10/1/11)—and to the
equally synthetic Jewish nationalism of the Zionists, patterned after the
militancy of the very movements that excluded them for being what
they now strove programmatically to submerge in the "normalization"
of the Jews.

It goes without saying that, despite a kernel of truth, these were
highly romanticized notions which Kafka himself was to shed or revise
drastically as he grew more familiar with Judaism and with the real
world of Jews in his time. In fact, even a closer acquaintance with Levi
and his troupe already provided more realistic perspectives. For these
troubadours of *Yiddishkeit* were themselves in full flight from the ghetto,
their very calling a challenge to Orthodox tradition; and the humiliating
poverty of their nomadic existence nurtured a skeptical realism unforgiving toward both themselves and others. In his reminiscences of the
Prague engagement, which Levi published in 1934 (*Tsvey Prager
Dikhter*, in *Literarische Bletter*, pp. 557–58),* he refers to the
attraction which the "exotic and religious qualities" of the Eastern
European Jews held for the Prague writers. "I remember my agitation
when, in one of his conversations with me, Max Brod spoke of the
beauty of the fur hat and silken, long coat, truly Rembrandt-like. I
answered him heatedly, 'The fanatic Eastern Jew can impress you modern, cultivated Jews, but we are happy that we pulled ourselves out and
freed ourselves from that world.'" Though otherwise thoroughly un-

* Quoted in Evelyn Tornton Beck, *Kafka and the Yiddish Theater* (University
of Wisconsin, 1971).

reliable as to facts, Levi's recollections of that particular exchange, whether literally true or not, certainly express the prevailing views on either side of the argument.

Kafka himself soon realized that if the ghetto was in him, he himself was no longer of it and never would be, and that it took more than a dose of nostalgia to resolve the dilemma of the secularized, post-enlightenment Jew, at least to the extent to which it was amenable to resolution of any kind. One early result was a change in his attitude toward Zionism. Though he never became an active proponent of Jewish nationalism in its aggressive, political stance, his very first brush with these genuine, unself-consciously integral Jews induced in him a consuming interest in the revival of an authentic Jewish civilization with its own language and social structure. And although Zionist factionalism and bureaucracy repelled him, he recognized that given the world he lived in, Zionism represented by far the most dynamic force in the struggle for Jewish survival and revival. Typically, however, his own commitment remained strictly private and personal. Within weeks of seeing his first Yiddish play, he began what turned into a lifelong study of Jewish history, literature, and the sources of Judaism. From that point on, he never missed an issue of the Zionist weekly *Selbstwehr,* took Hebrew lessons for many years, and found as much hope as he could ever muster in the Jewish agricultural settlements of Palestine, whose egalitarianism and dedication to manual labor came closest to his own ideals. In later years, and until his illness precluded such plans, he seriously contemplated emigrating to Palestine, where Hugo Bergmann, along with a substantial number of Kafka's friends and acquaintances, had already established a Prague beachhead of sorts. And on June 6, 1924, three days after Kafka's death, the *Selbstwehr* devoted an entire page to his obituary.

This takes us ahead of the story but merits emphasis simply because Kafka's ambivalence toward Judaism and the Jews—"What do I have in common with the Jews? I have hardly anything in common even with myself"—like his ambivalence toward almost everything else, the dilemma of the paradox, certainly continued to persist. But it should not be allowed to obscure a commitment on his part basic to both his life and his work.

* * *

Between October 4, 1911, when he saw his first play at the Savoy, and the spring of the following year, when the troupe finally drifted on to Germany and rapid disintegration, Kafka by his own count attended about twenty performances, seventeen of which he described in often considerable detail in the diary, down to a summary of the, as a rule, highly intricate and wildly melodramatic plots .They included works by most of the popular Yiddish playwrights of the day—Josef Latteiner, Abraham Goldfaden, Abraham Sharkansky, Jacob Gordin, Moses Richter, and Siegmund Feinmann.

These entries document his eloquent enthusiasm—reason enough to postulate a definite influence on his work. But it is one thing to accept the total impact of this emotionally charged experience on the whole of his development and quite another to try and pinpoint specific analogies between what he saw and what he wrote. What aroused his enthusiasm from the very first moment was, above all, the Jewishness of the plays and the players: "Some of the songs, the expression *yiddishe kinderlach*, the sight of this woman on stage—who, because she is Jewish, attracts us spectators because we are Jews, with no desire for Christians or interest in them—made my cheeks tremble" (DI, 10/5/11). At the same time, neither the *haimish* charms of these performances nor his own voluptuous pleasure in their warmhearted vulgarity and high-pitched sentiment could ever blind him to their essential crudity. This does not necessarily preclude his having borrowed, consciously or otherwise, from the glut of plot devices. But most of the parallels discerned in pursuit of academic laurels suggest, at best, an endemic imbalance between scholarship and imagination; at worst, they tend to obfuscate rather than elucidate the true nexus between Kafka and the Yiddish theater.

Thus, for instance, in her book by this title, informative as to the Yiddish theater, naïve in its approach to Kafka, Evelyn Tornton Beck asserts that "the seminal scene of *The Trial*, Joseph K.'s arrest, corresponds to a brief but important sequence in one of the Yiddish plays, the arrest of Don Sebastian in Faynman's [Feinmann's] *The Vice King*. . . . Stripped of its particularity (i.e., the Inquisition and the secret Jews), Don Sebastian's arrest is a model for that of Joseph K. . . . The wording and the pace of the dialogue in the two scenes is remarkably similar. In *The Vice King*, the deputy announces 'I have been sent . . . to arrest you'; in *The Trial*, the warder informs Joseph K., 'You are arrested.'"

Stripped of their particularity, many things do indeed resemble one another. As it happens, Kafka himself, in referring to Feinmann's play, spells out quite explicitly the true significance of this whole experience:

> Yesterday *The Vice King* by Feimann [sic]. My receptivity to the Jewish aspects of these plays is beginning to desert me, because they are too monotonous and degenerate into a wailing that takes pride in isolated violent outbursts. The first plays I saw made it possible for me to think that I had come upon a Judaism which contained the beginnings of my own, that they would develop in my direction and thereby enlighten and advance my own bumbling Jewishness. Instead, the more I hear, the more remote they grow. The people, of course, remain; and they are what I cling to. [DI, 1/6/12]

Whatever his fascination with the plays as such—folklore, language, exoticism—tempered by an increasingly critical view of their artistic value, Kafka's feelings toward the performers themselves remained those of an affection-starved outcast who had suddenly stumbled upon blood relations: "By their very presence the actors convince me time and again, to my consternation, that most of what I have so far written about them is false. False because I write about them with unwavering love (only now, as I write this, it too turns false) but fluctuating strength, and because this fluctuating strength does not strike the clear and true note of the real actors but is lost instead and muffled by this love" (DI, 10/23/11).

This is not to say that love and affection ruled the lives of these newfound friends of his. On the contrary; they were contentious, vituperative, constantly at odds, pigheaded in the extreme; what is more, the demoralizing hardship of their hand-to-mouth existence did nothing to improve their mood, manners, or character. But what Kafka could never bear in his own real-life family struck him here as an enviable demonstration of that tough vitality and grit necessary to Jewish survival.

An added element was his infatuation with Mania Tshissik, a fast-fading married member of the troupe whose onstage sex appeal in his eyes more than made up for her fatuous incompetence as an actress. Their relations remained strictly formal and distant; in fact, he deliberately kept them that way, to the point of not even daring openly to look her in the eyes at offstage meetings in public—"because that would have shown that I love her. Even young Pipes in all his innocence would have been bound to notice. And that would have really been scandalous. I, a young man generally taken to be about eighteen years old, declares in front of the assembled patrons of the Café Savoy . . . that he is smitten by love for a thirty-year-old woman whom almost no one even considers pretty, who has two children ten and eight, and whose model of a husband is sitting by her side" (DI, 11/7/11). That this distance, respectful or otherwise, made it easier for him to indulge his sexual fantasies can only be surmised. The closest he came to a consummation were the flowers he sent Mme Tshissik after one of her performances. "I had hoped that the bouquet would somewhat appease my love for her. It didn't. Only literature or coitus can satisfy it. I am writing this not because I didn't know it but because it may do good to spell out warnings often" (DI, 11/5/11).

But it was Yitzhak Levi (alias Jizchak, Isaac, and later Djak—Löwy in Kafka's German transliteration), director, promoter, star and guiding spirit of the troupe, with whom Kafka formed an almost instant friendship as challenging as it was rewarding. Though only twenty-four at the time—four years younger than Kafka—Levi had already done in real life much of what Kafka still dreamed about. Born in Warsaw in 1887 into an ultra-Orthodox Hasidic family, he broke with his parents and, at seventeen, escaped to Paris, worked as a laborer while acting in Yiddish amateur productions, joined his first professional troupe in 1907, and toured the major Jewish population centers in both Western and Eastern Europe. Following the financially disastrous Bohemian tournée in 1912, Levi settled in Berlin but periodically turned up in Prague and kept in touch with his friend. "You were the only one who was good to me, the only one that spoke to my soul," he wrote Kafka from Vienna in 1913 (which did not prevent him, three years later, from accusing Kafka of not having done nearly enough for him). They last saw each other in Budapest in July 1917. In 1920, Levi went back to Warsaw and gradually turned from mediocre acting to flowery journalism, but gave his farewell performance in the already besieged Warsaw ghetto in 1942 and was killed at Treblinka shortly thereafter.

It is not difficult to appreciate Kafka's instant fascination with this colorful, impulsive, and temperamental character. Whatever his limitations as an artist, he had the courage of his commitment, along with a contempt for status, conventions, and the allure of middle-class comforts that Kafka shared in principle but lacked in practice. Most important, he was unself-consciously secure in the only kind of Jewishness that Kafka regarded as authentic. Finally, and far from incidentally, he was a spellbinding storyteller and gossip, familiar to the point of contempt with at least the atmosphere and furnishings of the almost legendary milieu of medieval Orthodoxy in which he had been raised. That his imagination far outstripped his knowledge as well as his respect for truth was not to be held against him; he was an entertainer, not a sage. As such, however, he conveyed, both on stage and off, the flesh-and-blood sense of being a Jew.

To Kafka, this human element was infinitely more intriguing than bloodless theory. Yet in this instance, the erratic glimpses of Judaism provided by Levi made him both curious and keenly aware of his near-ignorance on the subject. By November 1, he was already "greedily and happily" immersing himself in Heinrich Graetz's *History of the Jewish People,* and the following January he tackled Meyer Pines's *Histoire de la Littérature Judéo-Allemande,* a massive work of decidedly anti-enlightenment, pro-Hasidic slant, "500 pages, and greedily, too, with a thoroughness, speed and joy such as I've never before felt with a book of this kind. Now I am reading [Jacob] Fromer's *Organism of Jewry*" (DI, 1/24/12).

But if his attachment to Levi, whom he saw almost daily throughout this period, taught him a great deal about Jewish life in Eastern Europe, it also supplied a few lessons about Western Jews and their curious ways, the most instructive of which may have been those administered by his father. To the former kosher butcher boy from Wossek, the dead past was something he had no trouble forgetting, and no wish to revive. Genuine live, Yiddish-speaking *Ostjuden,* on the other hand, were a reminder he did not wish to be associated with, directly or indirectly; one had to safeguard one's status and reputation.

His son's regular cronies were bad enough, a bunch of no-account scribblers who could do nothing even for themselves, let alone for him or his career. His taking up with this pack of Jewish gypsies was worse. But to be openly and ostentatiously consorting with this wild Jew from Warsaw, and to go so far as to let him into the house, was a slap in the face to Herrmann Kafka, Wholesale and Retail, which he was not about to put up with.

> Lest I forget [notes his son], in case my father ever calls me a bad son again: I want to record that in front of several relatives, for no special reason, just to insult me or supposedly to save me, he called Max a *meshuggene ritoch* [crazy nut] and that yesterday, when Levi walked into my room, he gave himself

sarcastic shakes, cut grimaces, and started talking about how just about anybody was being let into the house, wondering out loud what anyone could find interesting about people like that, what the point was of such useless contacts, etc. [DI, 10/31/11]

And three days later:

My father, in reference to Levi: "He who lies down with dogs gets up with fleas." I couldn't contain myself and said something offensive. Whereupon my father, with studied calm (though after a long interval, otherwise occupied): "You know that I am not supposed to get excited, and that I have to be treated with consideration. All I still need is you coming at me like that. I've had it with all the excitement. More than had it. So don't you talk to me like that." I said: "I am making an effort to restrain myself," and as always in such extreme moments, I sense in my father the presence of a wisdom of which I can only grasp a trace. [DI, 11/2/11]

Nonetheless, Herrmann Kafka's attitude could scarcely have been much of a surprise. What did shake Kafka was the discovery that a large part of Prague's Jews, not excluding most of his own friends, seemed in varying degrees to share his father's feelings, even if, as a rule, they tended to be less candid about their bias. The cool indifference with which Zionist circles, in particular, distanced themselves from the Yiddish theater struck Kafka as "wholly incomprehensible," though in fact it did not seem all that difficult to comprehend. The Zionists of that generation were committed to the in-gathering of the exiles, redemption through labor, and the revival of classical Hebrew as the common tongue of the Jewish people. Everything about the Yiddish theater, on the other hand, from the subject matter of the plays to the very idiom, was seen as a degenerate product of the ghetto and of a ghetto mentality which they rejected in every one of its manifestations. One may assume that this ideological stance often concealed unconscious prejudices passed on to them by their assimilated parents. But if Kafka had somehow escaped this hereditary taint—and he seems to have been the only one in his circle—his bewilderment and frustration still testify to a rather touching naïveté on his part.

Naïveté, or a near-saintly innocence that for the first and last time in his life enabled him to mobilize wholly unsuspected energies on behalf of these strangers, his next of kin. He seemed determined, single-handed, if necessary, to shake the Jewish public out of its incomprehensible torpor. Right at the outset, he persuaded Brod to review a performance in the *Prager Tagblatt*; the article, which appeared on October 27, 1911, was guardedly favorable and described the troupe as representative of an exotic culture with "a natural bent for music, and a primitive pleasure in blatant effects" that should offer enjoyment "provided one simply ignores the to us odd-sounding flavor of the jargon." ("Jargon" refers to Yiddish.) The Zionist *Selbstwehr* published a far more critical review by Hans Kohn, in which the later historian found the program tasteless and the troupe amateurish.

Indignant, Kafka now used all his connections. He provided Levi with introductions to friends and acquaintances in the provinces, urged Hugo Bergmann to exert his influence on behalf of the players, and personally invited the membership of the Zionist Student Organization Bar Kochba to a performance of Abraham Goldfaden's play by the same name on November 5, 1911. He later described the evening as a fiasco, both on stage and in terms of the audience reaction. Nevertheless, the *Selbstwehr*, largely in deference to his personal prestige and friendship with the editors, changed its tone if not its tune and began to support the troupe by several appeals, most of them apparently written by Kafka himself.

On January 24, 1912, he notes among the reasons for having neglected his own writing that "I had a lot of work with the Jewish actors. I wrote letters for them. I got the Zionist organization to ask its provincial branches if they would support guest appearances by the troupe, I wrote the necessary memorandum and had it multigraphed" (DI, 1/24/12). "Day before yesterday I wrote a good letter to Trautenau about Levi's guest engagement. It made me feel calm and strong every time I reread it, because of its unspoken allusions to everything that is good in me" (DI, 2/4/12).

This flurry of activity culminated in an organizational feat of major proportions: a special evening of solo readings, songs, and recitations by Levi on February 18, 1912. Kafka talked the Bar Kochba into sponsoring the affair, chose the program, obtained the use of the auditorium in the Jewish Town Hall from the Community Board—for a nominal rental of sixty crowns, but on condition that all material be submitted for approval in advance—saw to "the tickets, the numbering of the seats, the keys to the piano, a raised dais, piano player, costumes, ticket sale, newspaper publicity, censorship by police and by the Jewish Community Board" (DI, 2/25/12).

Oskar Baum, who had originally agreed to introduce Levi, later changed his mind, giving Kafka himself a chance publicly to affirm both his leading role and his newfound convictions by delivering the introductory lecture, fortuitously preserved for posterity by Elsa Taussig, Brod's future wife, who took it down in shorthand. The "Speech on the Yiddish Language" is a small masterpiece that demonstrates the enormous distance toward self-definition Kafka had traveled in this relatively short span of time and contains in embryonic essence some of the thoughts about Judaism and about his own role as a "German" writer he was later to develop more fully. It also shows him as a remarkably effective speaker, poised, urbane, and superbly attuned to his audience:

> Before we begin with the first verses by Eastern Jewish poets, I would like to assure you, ladies and gentlemen, that you understand far more Yiddish [he used the then customary word "jargon" throughout] than you think. I am not at all worried about the effect of what we have prepared for you this evening, but I would like you to be free to properly appreciate it. And this you will not be able to do as long as some of you are so frightened by the sound of Yiddish that the fear is written all over your faces. [And after briefly summarizing the evolution of Yiddish, stressing its ambiguous relationship to German, and giving some details about the program itself, he concluded:] But you will already be quite close to Yiddish if you realize that, active within you, in addition to knowledge, are forces and junctures of forces that enable you to feel yourselves into an understanding of Yiddish. . . . And once Yiddish has taken hold of you—and Yiddish is everything: word, Hasidic melody, and the very essence of this Eastern Jewish actor himself—you will no longer recognize your former complacency. At that point you will so powerfully feel the true unity of Yiddish as to make you afraid—not of Yiddish any longer, but of yourselves. And you would not be able to bear the burden of this fear by yourselves alone if, at the same time, Yiddish did not also endow you with a self-confidence that resists this fear and is even stronger. Enjoy it as best you can. And should the memory of it fade . . . let us hope that you will also forget the fear. Because we certainly don't want to punish you.

Kafka himself was immensely pleased with his performance: ". . . proud, unearthly awareness during my speech (cool composure before the audience, only lack of practice inhibited free, enthusiastic gestures), strong voice, effortless memory, recognition. . . . All of this revealed forces to which I would gladly entrust myself, if they would only last." But the entry ends in a poison-tipped stinger: "My parents weren't there" (DI, 2/25/12).

*   *   *

What up to then he had experienced chiefly as a personal conflict had now emerged as a much broader issue, transcending the family and dividing the generations. And the haunting loneliness of his childhood and youth echoed the infinite loneliness of the Western Jew adrift on hostile seas, with no land in sight and neither hope nor faith to sustain him. The very language he spoke—and wrote—was not his own but "a stranger's child snatched from the cradle" that betrayed him at every turn, down to the very core of his being.

> Yesterday it occurred to me that if I didn't always love my mother as much as she deserved and as I am capable of loving, it was the German language that kept me from it. The Jewish mother is no *Mutter*. . . . *Mutter* to a Jew sounds particularly German; it unconsciously contains Christian chill along with Christian splendor. The Jewish woman referred to as *Mutter* therefore becomes not only comical but a stranger as well. I believe that only the memories of the ghetto are what still preserves the Jewish family, for even the word *Vater* is far from signifying the Jewish father. [DI, 10/24/11]

It was a posture far removed from doctrine or programmatic ideology. He had met up with human beings out of his own past, tried to make contact with them, and been changed by the effort. And if hope and faith loomed as unattainable as ever, if his anguish remained intractable, he had nonetheless come out of the encounter far more conscious of who he was. With a lucid resignation that could pass for the beginnings of wisdom, he accepted himself as an alienated Western Jew, a fate that has since become the near-universal condition of Western man.

Unfortunately, the practical results of these frenetic and, in the circumstances, downright quixotic activities were negligible. The "German" Jews did not revise their opinion of the "Polish" ones. The actors remained as stone-broke as ever, and Levi's solo evening, conceived by Kafka as a benefit in more ways than one, failed instead even to cover expenses, so that he and Weltsch ended up petitioning the Community Board to forgive half the rental fee for the hall.

Seventeen

IF the energy Kafka displayed throughout much of 1912 had a spur of driven frenzy at its core, it also developed a momentum of its own and cannot be dismissed as merely a tidal high following the trough of depression. Office, factory, Yiddish actors, Judaism—he somehow juggled all of it and still found time and strength for numerous other commitments. In his own eyes, he remained the inveterate loner—"After all, how do I live in Prague? This craving I have for people, which changes to fear the moment it reaches the point of fulfillment . . ." (L, 7/22/12)—but even the no doubt sketchy account of social engagements and cultural pursuits listed in the diary entries for that period seems awe-inspiring and rather out of line with this self-image. Aside from the nightly ritual of the café, he found time to act as guide to the Jewish actors, joined his office colleagues on an outing, attended the Spring Festival of the German Casino Club, and met several times a week with intimates such as Brod, Weltsch, Baum, Werfel, and the poet Otto Pick.

He resumed contact with local painters—Alfred Kubin, Willy Novak, Ernst Ascher, the last asking him to pose in the nude for a portrait of St. Sebastian. He seldom missed a movie, frequented whorehouses and cabarets, and at the same time took full advantage of the more uplifting opportunities offered by Prague's crackling, uneven, but ever lively culture scene. He saw plays by Hauptmann, Hofmannsthal, Gustav Freytag, Jaroslav Vrchlický, Gabriele D'Annunzio, Rachilde, Franz Wedekind, and attended countless lectures by both local and imported luminaries.

What is more, he read voraciously, and with a particularly focused intensity. Even while embarking on his study of Jewish source material, he went back to Goethe, worshipped but neglected since high school, as though wanting to strike a balance between Jewish tradition and

German classicism, equalize his distance from both their gravitational fields lest he be trapped in either.

Most clearly indicative, however, of the vitality that marked this period in his life was the disciplined tenacity with which he also managed to pursue his writing.

> In me one can easily see a concentration on writing [he noted at the beginning of the year, in a diary entry more revealing than he may have realized]. Once my organism recognized that writing was the most productive aspect of my being, everything surged in that direction and drained off all other capabilities relating to the joys of sex, of food, of drink, of philosophical meditation, and of music above all. I lost weight in all those areas. This was necessary, the total of my energies being so paltry that only in focused concert could they more or less hope to serve the goal of writing. I did not, of course, choose this goal consciously and independently; it chose itself and is now—albeit fundamentally—being obstructed only by the office. In any case, I have no right to complain that I cannot bear having a lover, that I know almost as much about love as I do about music and have to content myself with superficial casual effects, that on New Year's Eve I dined on comfrey with spinach and a pint of Cérès, and that I was unable to attend Max's reading of his philosophical treatise last Sunday; the compensatory balance is self-evident. And since my development is now completed and, so far as I know, there is no longer anything for me to give up, I only need to cut the office work out of this communality in order to begin my real life, in which my face will finally be able to age naturally as my work progresses. [DI, 1/3/12]

This vision of real life as an ascetic monasticism wholly devoted to the sacred calling may as yet have been at odds with at least the surface texture of Kafka's day-to-day existence. But he was prescient in his view of the future: if writing alone justified his life, it also justified his not living his life. It provided a sanctified purpose—and a plausible excuse for choosing priesthood over manhood.

At the same time, this sacralized conception of his calling also imposed a stringent ritual and exalted standards. In the midst of all his feverish activity, he had been working rather steadily. But in the spring of 1912 he again conducted one of his periodic purges and consigned piles of manuscripts to the ubiquitous tile stoves that heated every room.

Among the few short works deemed fit to survive were "Bachelor's Ill Luck," "Unmasking a Confidence Trickster," "The Sudden Walk," "Resolutions," and "The Wish to Be a Red Indian," all written in the final months of 1911 and early 1912, and later included in his first published book.

Even this, however, adds up to a substantial achievement, in relative terms; his creativity, governed by inner rhythms, was obviously far less affected by outward circumstances than he himself, in times of stress and distress, liked to believe. Outward circumstances, in fact, could hardly have been less propitious. Aside from all his onerous duties and diverse distractions, particularly acute during this period, he also had to put up with the constant turmoil, clamor, and confusion of a very large family cooped up in a rather small apartment, with a single bathroom. He complained about it with heartfelt conviction: "In the next room, my mother is talking to the L.s about vermin and corns. Mr. L. has six corns on every toe" (DI, 3/24/12). "The broom sweeping the carpet next door sounds like the train of a gown being dragged along by fits and starts" (DI, 3/25/12). "Another day gone. Office in the morning, factory in the afternoon, now in the evening they are screaming in the house to my right and to my left" (DI, 4/3/12). "Desolate evening at home. My brother-in-law needs money for the factory, my father is upset about my sister, about the factory, and about his heart; my younger sister is unhappy, my mother unhappiest of all, and I sit here scribbling" (DI, 5/9/12).

One particularly eloquent lament on this score was to create a minor family scandal. "I want to write. My forehead keeps twitching. I am sitting in my room, noise headquarters of the entire house. I hear every door being slammed. . . . I hear even the clang of the oven door being shut in the kitchen. My father breaks down the doors to my room and comes marching through, the tail of his robe trailing in his wake. The ashes are being scraped out of the stove in the next room. . . . Valli, addressing no one in particular, shouts through the foyer as though across a Paris street, wanting to know if Father's hat had been brushed. . . . Finally, Father is gone, and now begins the more delicate, more distracting, more hopeless noise, led by the voices of the two canaries." This diary entry of November 5, 1911, complete with names unchanged, was published in the October 1912 issue of the *Herderblätter*, a Prague literary monthly edited by Willy Haas, and caused some understandable consternation in the Kafka household.

Yet the question of why, if he felt that way, Kafka did not move out and find a room of his own is one he never even seems to have asked himself, for reasons sound enough even if unconscious; he obviously was not yet ready to deal with the answer. Even at a more superficial level, there must have been an element of reassuring constancy, if not pleasure, in the very din, clatter, and commotion he described with such feeling, a sense of still being among his own, child, brother, member of the clan. Besides, in good times he had little trouble rising above it all, focusing inward, and, by writing late into the night and the early hours of the morning, finding the peace and quiet he needed to hear the voices within. For a writer quarrying the dream, night was in any case the best part of the day, the time when he saw farthest.

But even though a fair number of these fragmentary pieces found grace in his eyes, he had begun to realize that if literature was to be not only his goal but also his battering ram, his means of unblocking the path to freedom and independence, something more substantial was called for than the succession of brief sketches he had thus far been able to produce. His friends—Brod, Baum, Werfel, among others— had long since risen beyond local fame and youthful promise while he, nearly thirty, was still largely unknown, and not above envying them their success. "Even making abstraction of all other obstacles (physical condition, parents, character), the following argument offers a very good excuse for my not confining myself exclusively to literature, in spite of everything: I can venture nothing for myself as long as I have not produced a larger work that wholly satisfies me. This is indisputable" (DI, 12/8/11).

Three months later, in March 1912, he set out to write his first full-length novel.

* * *

Actually, the germ of that novel had lain dormant since childhood. In a diary entry quoted earlier in a different context, he mentioned having started "a novel in which two brothers fought one another. One went to America, while the other remained behind in a European prison" (DI, 1/19/11). The incident recounted by Kafka in this connection— his humiliation in front of the assembled family—must have taken place in preadolescence and the original vision of what we now know as *Amerika* evidently went back all the way to that "glimpse of the cold space of our world" with which he had lived longer even than he could remember.

Still riding the wave of near-manic energy that had buoyed him since early in the year, he started out with enormous verve and, between the spring and fall of 1912, turned out over 200 pages of a manuscript which Brod and he always referred to as "the America novel" but which he intended to call *Der Verschollene*—"The Man Who Disappeared." In due course, however, his customary self-critique vigorously reasserted itself, and by late summer he had grown thoroughly dissatisfied with the work. He found it badly flawed, especially by a failure to integrate the individual sections into a cohesive whole—the very same failure which, with ample justification, continued to bother him about the "Description of a Struggle." Sometime in late 1912, his self-confidence bolstered by the epiphany of "The Judgment," he started on a second version of *Der Verschollene*, whose first chapter, *The Stoker*, was separately published as a book in 1913. The entire manuscript, unfinished and untitled, just like *The Trial* and *The Castle,* was posthumously published in 1927 under its present title of *Amerika*.

Kafka refused to show or read the original version, about half the length of the final one, even to his closest friends and eventually destroyed it. Nevertheless, it seems safe to assume that at least in conception, if not execution, it did not depart radically from the later manuscript, and that it was the first to sound the leitmotifs recurring in all three of Kafka's novels, that "trilogy of loneliness," as Brod later called them: guilt and punishment, the rebellion of the sons, the victory of the fathers, and their power to punish transgression by exile and the ultimate loneliness of death.

Yet even the published version of *Amerika* still falls short of that flawless mastery with which Kafka, at his best, was able to transmute reality into its metaphor and to trace myth back to the agony of being human. It was, as has often been pointed out, his most "optimistic" novel. But this perceived optimism—strictly relative, to be sure—may also explain his growing disenchantment with the story and his failure ultimately to complete it, despite the bursts of inspiration with which he worked on it intermittently for several years.

One problem was his having started the novel in perhaps the most upbeat phase of his entire life, a point at which the impossible still seemed not only possible but almost within reach. That the story of the prodigal son, seduced by a servant girl, banished by the father, abandoned by the mother, and bent on finding himself in the never-never land of Red Indians and unlimited opportunities rather literally projected both his personal conflicts and his initially sanguine view of the outcome seems blatantly self-evident. The autobiographical elements have, in any event, been tracked down to their most minute and mostly irrelevant particulars, as have the putative external influences on plot and structure. For instance, a family scandal involving two of Kafka's cousins, one of whom got the family cook with child, while the other ran away, or was shipped off, to America is believed to have suggested plot material; the influence of Dickens was repeatedly acknowledged by Kafka himself, and the action of a play he saw in December 1911 at the Yiddish theater takes place in the *Goldene Medina*, whose streets turn out to be awash with tears rather than paved with gold.

The extent to which such impressions molded or modified the original vision must remain conjectural. But one prominent and enduring aspect of that vision is its fairy-tale quality, starting with the "America" of Kafka's imagination and the preeminent role it plays in this fantasized and ultimately unsuccessful attempt to escape from "a European prison."

He had, of course, long since outgrown the childhood fantasies nurtured by stirring tales of the Wild West and by America's focal position in the mythology of nineteenth-century Europe. Distances had shrunk drastically, and by the time he came of age, a steady stream of two-way traffic had developed between Prague and the America of the immigrants, a far different place from the land of cowboys and Indians. Many former emigrants returned, some permanently, others on extended visits, among them several members of Kafka's immediate family. Their accounts conveyed an understandably far less romantic but, in its way, no less fascinating picture of what, to the captive residents of the disintegrating empire, was in fact a new world at this juncture in history.

Moreover, Kafka, bent on setting the scene with the "most up-to-date" realism, avidly collected background material, attended lectures on the subject, and based many of the novel's descriptive details on contemporary sources, especially Arthur Holitscher's thoughtful and informative travel reports, which were being serialized at the time. And though it would be difficult to discover any but the most superficial resemblance between the stage set of Karl Rossmann's picaresque adventures and the United States of America of circa 1910, the ominous anarchy of total freedom and the whiff of *Mitteleuropa* decadence with which Kafka invests it transform the brave New World into a continent of loneliness, a land of terrifying opportunities.

That is why *Amerika* can be, and has been, read as, among other things, a perceptive social commentary and a prophetic glimpse of the future. Even here, with the ambiguities still reined in, the range of possible interpretations challenges the interpreters. Overlooked, however, is the image of America as a fairyland at the heart of the novel—a fairyland teeming with bad fairies, with every form of corruption and every species of the corruptible and the corrupt, always slightly in advance of every other civilized country, but still the last and only place on earth where miracles could happen. According to Brod, Kafka assured him that in the "Oklahoma Open Air Theater" at the end of the novel, the hero would "recover, as though through paradisiac magic, his vocation, freedom, and integrity, even his parents and his homeland."

But in the eventful two years that Kafka took to write it, the fairy tale turned into a nightmare and shook its author's faith in fairy-tale endings. And having come to feel that nothing short of such an ending could save him or his hero, he abandoned the effort and left the manuscript unfinished.

* * *

In midsummer, Kafka and Brod again took their annual vacation together. Leaving Prague on June 28, 1912, they spent the following day in Leipzig, at that time the heart, soul, and entrails of the entire German publishing industry. Brod had not only arranged for his publishers to meet Kafka but also, unbeknownst to his friend, had submitted a collection of published and unpublished pieces by what he confidently proclaimed as the most important author of the new generation.

The publishers were, in fact, duly impressed, though rather in spite of Brod, as it later turned out. To a degree unusual even in those happier preconglomerate days, the two young founding partners of the Rowohlt-Verlag combined a flair for business with a genuine love of books, and their aggressive efforts to sign up promising young authors were beginning to pay off in the success of their attractive and reasonably priced editions. It was Ernst Rowohlt who first took the friends out to lunch and startled Kafka by offering to bring out a selection of his writings. "Rowohlt quite seriously seems to want a book from me," notes the travel diary, in unfeigned innocence and probable ignorance of Brod's arduous spadework. Later that afternoon, on a quick tour of the publishing house, he met the other partner, Kurt Wolff, who took over all further negotiations and, after breaking with Rowohlt a few months later and founding his own firm, became Kafka's sole publisher.

His relations with Kafka were marked, from first to last, by the human qualities that were to make Wolff so vital a force in publishing on both sides of the Atlantic. The son of a prominent Bonn musicologist, four years younger than Kafka, Wolff was a man of great culture, discriminating taste, and quick, spontaneous warmth that still spills over into his recollections of that fateful first encounter with his future author, "timid, gauche, delicate, vulnerable, frightened like a schoolboy facing his examiners. . . . While Brod was acting the impresario to a star he had personally discovered, the star himself would have just as soon had us give him back his manuscript rather than go ahead and publish it" (*Autoren, Bücher, Abenteuer*, p. 68).

The one-day Leipzig interlude was to have a decisive impact on Kafka's career and on the fate of his work, both in his lifetime and beyond. At the very least, the fact of his being published in Germany proper, and by a publisher of Wolff's fast-growing reputation, assured him access to the entire German-speaking public and, above all, far more serious and widespread critical attention than he could normally have hoped for as a parochial scribbler emoting, like so many others, along the swampy margins of civilization.

At the time, however, he clearly felt ambivalent about the whole project and simply put it out of his mind as they left the next day on the final leg of their pilgrimage to Weimar. As it happened, both Goethe and Schiller, the two giants of German letters, died in the town that was later to lend its name to the short-lived republic. But while Schiller only retired there shortly before his death in 1805 to be near his illustrious friend, Goethe joined the staff of the Duke of Weimar in 1775 and spent over half a century in the town, thus laying the foundation for one of its major industries.

The spirit of Goethe, like his garden and the beech tree in front of his study, continued to be carefully cultivated by the good citizens of Weimar. Kafka and Brod allotted themselves six days for a proper mix of rest and contemplation that would do justice to both Goethe and whatever else the town had to offer. The principal shrine, then as now, was the house in which Goethe spent the last decades of his life, its interior faithfully preserved as he left it at the time of his death in 1832. On the whole, the effect on Kafka was depressing—"a sad sight that reminds one of dead grandfathers." To link the idolized living Goethe with the dead relics of his prosaic day-to-day existence required ostentatious piety, of the sort which Kafka was constitutionally incapable of, though the eminently practical arrangement of Goethe's study seemed to fascinate him.

And yet, the mischievous ghost of that wisest of fools, of the poet-privy councilor who in his seventies, altogether unwisely but with consuming passion, fell in love with the seventeen-year-old Ulrike von Levetzow must still have been haunting his old house on Frauenplan Square, laying snares for kindred spirits; the reclusive, very formal poet-lawyer from Prague promptly got trapped and in turn proceeded to make a fool of himself.

The very morning following his arrival, on his first extended tour of the Goethe house, Kafka fell head over heels in love with Margarete Kirchner, the pubescent daughter of the resident custodian. That the flirtatious teenager, as pretty as she was shallow, showed not the slightest interest in the dignified elderly gentleman did not prevent him from spending much of his time in Weimar dogging her every step, trying to catch glimpses of her or to strike up conversations whose abysmal banality merely seemed to add to her charms. He plied her with presents, was stood up by her several times, and concluded with melancholy resignation that "she definitely doesn't love me, but she has a certain respect for me."

And in a postscript a month later, in a letter to Brod from the Jungborn Sanatorium, he announced that he would avoid Weimar on his way home "out of obvious weakness. I had a brief note from her . . . with three photos . . . and she is beautiful. And I am going back via Dresden, as though it had to be that way, and will visit the zoo, which is where I belong" (L, 7/22/12).

Kafka's combustible passion for very young girls, in conspicuous contrast to his tortured ambivalence toward mature women, was to flare up time and again; the last companion of the then forty-year-old was nineteen-year-old Dora Diamant. It takes no very profound insight to perceive in it both the brother's love for his sisters, especially the favorite youngest one, versus the son's rage and longing for a distant and ungiving mother. He himself, in fact, was far from unaware of the connections and, as the final sentence in the above letter demonstrates, always retained a keen sense of the incongruities, even when he let himself be carried away by them.

At the same time—this, too, no news to him—the romantic-pathetic interlude was yet another unsuccessful evasion. One does not overcome the father by winning the love of one's little sister.

*   *   *

Each following their own by now well-established routine, Brod returned to Prague on July 7, while Kafka went on to spend the remaining three weeks of his vacation—he had once again obtained an additional week because of "a pathological nervous condition manifesting itself in nearly continuous digestive disturbances and sleep problems" —at the Jungborn (Fountain of Youth) naturopathic sanatorium, a picturesquely far-flung establishment in the foothills of the Harz Mountains. In its emphasis on holistic health, natural life-styles, and Eastern religiosity, the Jungborn was way ahead of its time, a Teutonically organized Esalen, nurturing body and soul on a diet of raw vegetables and uncooked ideas, some of which Kafka laconically recorded in his travel diary:

> Last night lecture on clothing. The Chinese cripple the feet of their women to give them a big behind. . . . The doctor, an ex-officer, is a follower of Mazdaznan [a briefly fashionable Zoroastrian cult]; from his lecture yesterday: Even if your toes are completely crippled, you can straighten them out by taking deep breaths while tugging at them. . . . Overexposure to moonlight is harmful. . . . Diaphragmatic breathing contributes to the growth and stimulation of the sex organs, which is why female opera singers, who have to breathe from the diaphragm, are so lewd.

The day started with "ablutions, Mueller-style exercises, group gymnastics, circle games, and the singing of a few hymns" and, with periods of rest and meditation, continued in this exuberant vein until nightfall. Nudism was the rule, Kafka once again being the odd man out—"they call me the man in the swim trunks." Such prudish or prudent restraint notwithstanding, he socialized quite extensively with his fellow campers —most of them, given the nature of the place, being no less odd or out in their way—and grew fond of several among them: "Thinking about the people here, this afternoon, made me feel all warm inside. Some of them are really interesting." There were Bibles in every room, and he made what seems to have been his first serious attempt to read both the Old and the New Testament. Moreover, a depressingly earnest born-again Christian fundamentalist picked on him as a likely prospect for conversion and proceeded to shower him with tracts. "I read in them a little and then, made unsure by my respect for the man, went over and tried to explain to him why there was no prospect of grace for me at present. Whereupon he harangued me for an hour and a half."

The deadpan sarcasm that flavors most of his references to this peculiar institution is nonetheless good-natured, and not devoid of awe. Pale child of the city, suffering from every imaginable and imagined ill, he badly wanted to believe in the healing power of nature, and he felt a heady contentment in this atmosphere of pseudo-mystical nature worship. Freed, moreover, from the constraints of his native fauna, he found it easier to break out of his isolation, to put on a different face and make the sort of spontaneous and casual contacts that ordinarily seemed beyond his grasp.

But while, with all that, he still managed to do a fair amount of reading, he had little time and even less inclination to write. Part of the reason, no doubt, was his growing dissatisfaction with *Der Verschollene*; the novel had by now run into serious trouble and, in his opinion, was headed for disaster. Even so, he stubbornly plowed ahead with it for another few months, and it seems likely that the Jungborn experience—both in its physical setup and in its chiliastic pretensions—contributed in some measure to his conception of the paradisiac "Oklahoma Open Air Theater," with which he planned to conclude the final version of *Amerika*.

*   *   *

Returning to Prague on July 28, he at last had to face up to the task he had so successfully avoided up to that point: putting together a representative selection from his work for submission to Rowohlt. Unsurprisingly, his instincts proved correct; ever the master of indecision, he turned the process of editorial triage into an orgy of self-doubt. Even the pieces he finally settled on seemed to him totally inadequate, and deteriorating further with each reading. At the end of a harrowing week, bogged down in revisions, he was ready to give up. He informed Brod that the situation was hopeless, that he simply could not get the material in proper shape for publication and would have to drop the whole project.

But once again Brod rose to the challenge. With pleas, impassioned reasoning, and practical assistance he convinced Kafka to again change his mind, and by August 12 an adequate number of short pieces had been selected. On the evening of August 13, Kafka took them over to Brod's house for help in arranging their final sequence.

That same night, as it happened, the Brod family had a visitor from Berlin.

The twenty-four-year-old Felice Bauer, a cousin of Max's brother-in-law, was in Prague on business for her firm and had spent the evening with the Brods. Forthright and self-possessed, she kept out of the way while Kafka and Brod put the final touches to the manuscript. Later they all had a brief but fairly lively conversation, at least lively enough for Kafka to propose a joint trip to Palestine the following year. Felice, who had to catch a train in the morning, left early, escorted to her hotel by Brod and Kafka.

Nothing more, on the face of it, than a pleasantly casual encounter. Yet when Kafka woke up the next morning, he was panic-stricken at the thought that Felice's presence might in some way have beclouded his editorial judgment, and he implored Brod to go over the manuscript once again. Brod did, or said he did, and shipped it out forthwith to Rowohlt, together with a covering letter from Kafka that speaks for itself:

> I am enclosing the little prose pieces you asked to see; I think they should add up to a short book. In making my selection, I sometimes had to choose between living up to my sense of responsibility and indulging my greedy desire to see one of my own included among your beautiful books. The final decision may not always have been entirely unbiased. Now, of course, I would be happy if the material pleased you at least to the extent of wanting to publish it. Its flaws would not seem instantly apparent at first glance even to a thoroughly experienced and knowledgeable reader. And after all, the most common manifestation of individualism among writers consists precisely of the specific ways in which each of them conceals his own deficiencies. [L, 8/14/12]

Eighteen

M ARRIAGE was a subject Kafka would have been hard put to ignore that fall, under any circumstances. In September Valli, his second sister, got engaged—the result of a year's tortuous negotiations with assorted marriage brokers and amateur matchmakers. (Of the three sisters, only the headstrong Ottla insisted on a husband of her own choice.) "Love between brother and sister—a reprise of the love between father and mother" (DI, 9/15/12), was Kafka's laconic comment. In November, his oldest sister, Elli, gave birth to a daughter, her second child; the joyous occasion aroused "envy, nothing but furious envy of my sister, or rather of my brother-in-law, because I myself will never have a child" (FEL, 1/8/12). And finally, an even more traumatic reminder: Max Brod's engagement to Elsa Taussig, whom he married at the end of the year. "I am not happy about either of these engagements, although I strongly encouraged Max and may even have helped to make up his mind. As for my sister, I at least did not try to dissuade her from getting engaged" (FEL, 1/10/13).

Yet the idea of marriage as such can, in any event, seldom have been far from his mind, no further than the bedroom next to his, on the far side of a flimsy partition. The infant's incestuous entanglements had spawned a scary vision of unholy matrimony that survived in the adult's phobic aversion to noise, his nausea at the sight of his mother's nightgown on the double bed. Age, habit, and repression somewhat blurred the picture, leaving the dim after-image of wedlock as a dismal if inevitable part of grown-up middle-class existence.

For years, though, it had been of scant personal concern, a distant threat nibbling at the margins of a consciousness preoccupied with far more imminent disasters. As he groped his way, one by one, around all the other hurdles blocking his path, the threat began to move in on him. And by 1909, with his formal schooling completed, he faced a trial of a different sort—the comprehensive test of manhood leading to the certificate of marriage. As always, he foresaw disaster, and "Wedding Preparations in the Country," written around that time, convincingly celebrates the will to fail. But it was not until four years later, when he at last began to assert his independence and seek a place of his own in the world, that marriage assumed the sinister dimensions of a direct challenge to survival.

"The Talmud says: a man without a wife is not a man," he noted in late 1911, alluding in the same breath to his constitutional frailty; how could he envisage any kind of future for himself "with this wreck of a body salvaged from some storage attic" (DI, 11/29/11). The very thought of "marital duty" roiled a lifetime's accretions of horror, fear, disgust. And no matter how he later rationalized this dread of marital intimacy—physical weakness, emotional exhaustion, or, most important, the all-consuming demands of his writing—it gave rise to an unshakable conviction on his part that he would never have children.

Nothing of what is known about Kafka's virility with other than prospective marriage partners suggests any undue difficulties or physical problems. If nonetheless he consistently and provocatively proclaimed his inability to father progeny, the implied impotence—or refusal—clearly refers to much more than the mechanics of procreation. Not his fathering a child, but his being a father was what struck him as utterly beyond belief. Marriage meant ceasing to be his parents' child and taking instead his father's place as a man among men.

Yet if this seemed impossible, so did the alternative.

Kafka was only too familiar, from firsthand contact, with the arid misery of aging bachelors. Three of his uncles—all on the mother's side—had never married. His favorite, the country doctor in Triesch, was a melancholy loner. The second, Richard Löwy, with whom Kafka feared certain affinities, had converted to Christianity and become a cranky hermit. And even the third, the legendary "uncle from Madrid," for all his worldly success seemed increasingly dispirited; when Kafka brought himself to ask about it, the uncle explained that while he enjoyed certain aspects of his life, the whole did not measure up to the sum of its parts.

For instance, I frequently dine at a very exclusive French *pension.* . . . I sit between a secretary of the French embassy and a Spanish artillery general, across the table from some sort of duke and a top-level functionary at the Naval Ministry. I know them all very well, I greet them as I sit down, then lose myself in my own thoughts and don't say another word until I take my leave. At which point I am all alone out in the street and cannot, for the life of me, see the sense of having wasted my evening. . . . I go home and regret not having married. [DI, 9/5/12]

Exposure to these advanced cases no doubt intensified the terror of the threat. Man may be mortal, but a man without a wife is not a man, and instead of dying at the end of his life, he withers away in the midst of it. The alternative to marriage was the sort of death in life envisaged in the diary entries of November 14 and December 3, 1911, later published in a tightened version as "The Bachelor's Ill Luck."

These, then, were his choices. Bachelorhood . . . "never to have a wife by his side as he climbs the stairs to his home, to be ill and have only the view from his window to comfort him, to live in a room whose every door opens only on the rooms of strangers, to be a stranger to his own relatives, whose friendship can be preserved only through marriage—first the marriage of one's parents, and later, as its effect wears off, through one's own marriage" (DI, 11/14/11).

Or marriage: open defiance of the giant monster *in loco parentis* that ruled his conscience and his consciousness. The horror of intimacy, the invasion of his innermost space, the slow strangulation of his art. The writer chained for life to the routine of a wage slave and the ritual of copulation.

By the time he met Felice Bauer, Kafka had come to feel that his entire future hinged on the resolution of this terrifying dilemma. And it was his struggle to resolve it that set the stage for the drama of two mismatched lovers and that preordained its outcome.

* * *

The drama has survived in two versions: Kafka's letters to Felice, and his unfinished masterpiece, *The Trial*. They differ substantially in emphasis and perspective; where the letter writer is a defendant pleading his case, the novelist pleads guilty to being human.

But it would be grossly simplistic to read these two accounts in terms of fact versus fiction. While the autobiographical element undoubtedly played a seminal role in the genesis of the novel, it neither defines its scope nor exhausts the sources of its inspiration. The letters, on the other hand, have as little in common with ordinary love letters as Kafka does with ordinary lovers, and the cumulative image of what he called his "struggle for Felice" projected by these bulletins from the battlefront adds up to a fever chart tracking—often day by day—the state of soul of the implacable antagonists, all of them embodied by Kafka himself.

Merely as such, of course, they would be of considerable interest for the light they shed on a crucial five years in Kafka's life. But beyond their purely documentary value, they are literature above all, literature in the most comprehensive sense of that somewhat shopworn and elusive term. Like the songs of the medieval "minnesingers," whom Erich Heller invokes in his introduction to the printed edition, the letters celebrate idealized abstractions of love and the beloved. Except that the minnesinger in this instance is a child of the twentieth century living through the early stages of a war that has yet to end, and his songs include not only glimpses of hell in the here and now but also cruelty, self-loathing, posturings, rumblings of the apocalypse, and the persistent clatter of trivia.

At the same time, however, they were also simply letters addressed to, received, and read by a recipient who, whatever her role in Kafka's conscious or unconscious, also happened to be a living, vulnerable human being in her own right. The disparity between that human being and the Felice of Kafka's creative imagination certainly accounts for one of the more tragic aspects of this drama.

*   *   *

Felice Bauer was twenty-four years old when Kafka first met her. Born in Silesia in 1887, she grew up in Berlin, one of five children of the insurance agent Carl Bauer. For six years, from 1904 to 1910, her parents were separated; upon graduating from high school she immediately went to work and helped to support the family. Starting in 1909 as a stenographer-typist with the Carl Lindstroem Corporation, manufacturers of dictaphones and recording equipment, she advanced rapidly and, by 1912, had been promoted to executive officer, a remarkable achievement for a young woman in her time and place, and one which amply substantiates the unanimous testimony from all sources describing her as highly efficient, level-headed, outgoing, and endowed with a great deal of poise and practical common sense. These, needless to say, were the very attributes in which Kafka felt himself to be woefully deficient and which he always tended to admire with excessive awe.

In 1919, some fifteen months after her final break with Kafka, Felice married a Berlin banker, with whom she had a son and a daughter. In 1936, the family fled to the United States, where, after her husband's death the following year, she once again proved her resilience by establishing herself in business, successfully raising her children, and remaining self-supporting until incapacitated by a lingering illness. She died in 1960.

In this context, a word about her role in the publication of Kafka's letters seems in order, the more so since it highlights an integrity on her part for which she did not receive due credit.

With the exception of a very few items, Felice appears to have meticulously preserved the bulk of the over five hundred letters she received from Kafka in the course of their five-year courtship. She not only failed to destroy them after the breakup, as Kafka seems to have done with her share of the correspondence, but took them along on her flight to the United States. Since these love letters from an at that time—and for many years thereafter—all but unknown and seemingly quite dead novelist from Prague had little if any monetary value, she could only have acted out of purely personal sentiment. The depth of her feelings may be gauged from the fact that she never alluded to her relationship with Kafka, carrying discretion to the point of keeping it a secret even from her own children. It was not until after the end of World War II that Max Brod, as Kafka's literary executor, alerted the publisher Zalman Schocken in New York to the existence of these letters in the hope of arranging for their acquisition and publication, disregarding Kafka's testamentary instructions to destroy them unread.

For several years, Felice adamantly refused to part with a treasure whose profoundly personal and private nature she threatened to protect in perpetuity by carrying out what Brod was unwilling to do. Ultimately, however, the protests of friends and relatives, coupled with Kafka's spreading fame, led her to soften her stand, and when deteriorating health necessitated a series of lengthy and expensive hospitalizations, she was prevailed upon, in 1955, to accept Schocken's offer of $5,000 for the original letters, along with exclusive rights to their publication. Schocken subsequently also acquired Kafka's letters to Milena under a similar arrangement.

The letters to Felice are currently still in the possession of the Schocken family. The letters to Milena Jesenká were sold to the German Literary Archives at Marbach, at a price that reflects not only Kafka's soaring market value but also the prosperity of German connoisseurs determined to collect the manuscripts of the Prague Jew now undergoing his metamorphosis into a German classic. Their zeal, however creditable and sincere, can also be interpreted as an act of *Wiedergutmachung*— of making up for, among other things, the wanton destruction of Kafka manuscripts by the Gestapo in 1933 and the incineration of his three sisters and their families by an older generation who, without having read a word of his, proudly adopted Kafka's worst nightmares as their own fondest dreams and made them come true.

* * *

The same young man whose heart and head, a mere six weeks earlier, had turned to jelly at the sight of an insipid Weimar nymphet, described his first response to his future fiancée in terms that could hardly have been less inspired and inspiring:

> Miss F.B. When I went to see Brod on August 13, she was sitting at the table but looked to me like a maidservant. What is more, I was not at all curious to know who she was but simply put up with her. Bony, empty face that openly displayed its emptiness. Bare neck. Casual blouse. Looked very domesticated, though as it later turned out, she really wasn't. . . . Nose almost as though fractured, blond, somewhat stiff, unattractive hair, strong chin. As I sat down, I took a first close look at her; by the time I was seated, I had already formed an immutable opinion. Just as . . . [DI, 8/20/12]

The notation leaves off abruptly in mid-sentence. But whatever Kafka's "immutable" opinion of Felice, it surely was no *coup de foudre*. If anything, his initial impression was of a distinctly unattractive if not downright homely young woman—accurate enough, as far as it went, except for the choice of the adjective *"leer"* in reference to her face, which decidedly was neither vacuous nor vapid, two possible interpretations. The literal meaning of the word, however, seems peculiarly apt: an emptiness upon which, given time and distance, he imposed the improvisations of his own fantasy.

Yet something about the real Felice—the very lack of sex appeal, her unaffected, forthright poise and competence—must have snagged his instincts and stirred deeper feelings, not instantly accessible; it took another month before he could mobilize himself to act on them. By that time, the reality of her physical presence had been softened by memory and defused by distance. The distance between them, though a mere six hours by train, was to remain a heavily fortified and fortifying safety zone, seldom crossed—never with less than disastrous results —that made it possible for him to pursue his ambivalence to the edge of madness, to worship the bride of his own creation without having to share bed and board with her corporeal humanity.

Trapped again in a maze without exit, he resorted to the only magic he had mastered: writing, he hoped—sometimes with real conviction —would enable him to combine loving and living and make it possible for him to turn handstands on the horns of the dilemma.

For one tense month, simultaneously driven by fear and patricidal fury, yet oddly serene on the outside, expectant rather than resigned, he drew strength from his icon of the Berlin Madonna, faint replica of his own efficient, competent, and sensible mother. On September 20, 1912, he wrote his first letter to Felice, and two nights later, the gathering tension broke in a blinding storm of creative despair. In one single sitting, from ten in the evening to six o'clock the following morning, he wrote "The Judgment." Punishment to fit the crime.

* * *

His letter to Felice was also a masterpiece, but one of cunning and dissimulation. The pose he struck—urbane young lawyer with a literary bent, Jewish, good family—was designed to reassure rather than deceive:

> In the rather likely event that you no longer have the faintest notion of who I am, allow me to introduce myself once again: My name is Franz Kafka, I am the person you met for the first time that evening at Director Brod's house in Prague, who subsequently passed snapshots of a trip to Weimar to you across the table, one by one, and who finally, with the very hand now striking the keys, held yours in a handshake by which you affirmed your promise to join me next year on a trip to Palestine. Should you still be willing to go—at the time you

said that you were not fickle, nor did I notice any indications thereof—it would not only be wise but absolutely essential for us to start discussing this journey at once. . . . Pausing to feed a new sheet into the typewriter, I realize that I may have described myself as much more difficult than in fact I am. If so, it serves me right; why do I insist on writing this letter at the end of a six-hour stint in the office, and on a typewriter to which I am not accustomed. And yet . . . even if you had your doubts, doubts of a practical nature, I mean, about choosing me as a traveling companion, guide, excess baggage, tyrant, or whatever else I might yet grow into, there should be no objection in principle to your having me as a correspondent—which, after all, is the only point at issue right now—so that you might as well give it a try. [FEL, 9/20/12]

The casual tone did not come easily; he later confessed to Felice that after having debated for weeks whether to write at all, he had spent at least ten days, on and off, composing this epistle, weighed every word, and fretted endlessly about the correct address. But by finally mailing it, he accomplished a deed of heroic proportions and struck a first blow in the struggle for his liberation.

It was the monstrous daring of this deed that pushed him over the brink of circumspection and dragged him, two days later, into the maelstrom that boiled up in "The Judgment." The reasonable enough plea with which he had concluded his first letter to Felice may have accurately expressed his conscious expectations at that point; the unconscious ones, however, transcended all bounds of mere reason from the start. And as he sat down at his usual time, at 10 p.m. on the night of September 22, the tail end of a dreary Sunday, to "describe a war, a young man at his window was to watch a crowd crossing a bridge," the enormity of what he had done and the mortal danger to which it exposed him fused in a climactic outburst that, trance-like, caught him in its grip and swept away all conscious intent; "everything turned under my hands." The result was an eight-hour orgy of near-automatic writing, at the end of which "the story quite literally came out of me like a regular birth, covered with filth and slime" (DI, 2/11/13).

The parturient felt understandably spent, but wild exultation prevailed over fatigue, and like any proud new parent he, at six in the morning, burst into his sister Ottla's room to read her "The Judgment."

The ecstatic note still reverberates in his account of the experience, entered the following night:

> I wrote "The Judgment" in one sitting during the night of the twenty-second to the twenty-third, from ten at night until six in the morning. My legs were so stiff from sitting that I could hardly pull them out from under the desk. The horrible strain and joy as the story began to unfold before me . . . Several times during the night I was carrying my own weight on my back. . . . It confirmed my belief that the novel [*Amerika*] is stuck in the disgraceful troughs of literature. *This* is the *only way* to write, only with such cohesion, with such total opening of body and soul. . . . My emotions during the writing: pleasure, for instance, at being able to offer Max something good for his *Arkadia* [a literary annual edited by Max Brod, published by Rowohlt], thoughts of Freud, of course. [DI, 9/23/12]

It was a heady triumph that for once silenced even the ever-carping voice of self-criticism. It also made for some stylistic flaws, choppy transitions, and for some histrionic melodramatics suggesting strident echoes of the Yiddish theater. Yet while not unaware of these short-comings—Kafka objectively considered *The Stoker* a superior work —he always retained a special affection for "The Judgment" as having expressed his deepest and most contradictory emotions with the inevitability of true art. In marked contrast to his customary reluctance, he was anxious to read the story to all his friends and gave an emotional interpretation of it two days later at Oskar Baum's house: "Toward the end my hand moved to my face of its own accord; I had tears in my eyes. The inevitability of the story confirms itself" (DI, 9/25/12). And the following month, invited by Willy Haas to give a public reading, he responded with unusual alacrity: "Of course I accept your invitation on behalf of the Herder Society; in fact, it will give me the greatest of pleasure. I shall read 'The Judgment,' about to appear in the *Arkadia*; it should take about half an hour. What sort of audience will be attending? . . . Is an ordinary business suit sufficient? (Pointless question, seeing as I have no other)" (L, 11/25/12).

* * *

The intimately personal aspects of "The Judgment" as they relate to Felice certainly did not escape Kafka, who immediately decided to dedicate the story "to F.B." although the true significance of what he at first conceived as simply an act of knightly courtship did not dawn on him until some months later: ". . . in devious ways I owe the story to her. But Georg [the protagonist of "The Judgment] is destroyed because of his fiancée" (DI, 8/14/13).

At the same time he was, if anything, far too keenly aware of the gap between the act of conception and the miracle of birth not to credit his story with a life of its own, quite properly beyond his conscious grasp. Inspired perhaps by his superficial acquaintance with early Freudian techniques, he made some attempts at exploring the subconscious origins of certain names—" 'Frieda' has as many letters as Felice and the same initial, peace (*Friede*) and happiness (Felice) are closely linked; 'Brandenfeld' relates via *Feld* [field] to *Bauer* [peasant] and again shares the initial." But aside from such interesting if hardly enlightening associations, he found himself groping in the mystery of his own creation: "Can you discover any kind of meaning in 'The Judgment'—I mean some straightforward and coherent meaning that one could pin down? I can't, nor can I explain anything in it" (FEL, 6/2/13).

Perhaps not, though he was, of course, perfectly cognizant of the father-son conflict as the focal theme dominating not only "The Judgment" but also *The Stoker* and "The Metamorphosis." In fact, he initially wanted Wolff to publish the three pieces jointly in one volume under the title of "The Sons"; although Wolff agreed, the project was later dropped as impractical. But in taking this theme—or more accurately, being taken by it—through a dizzying spiral of rising abstractions, Kafka transformed the very essence of minutely observed reality into an allusive nexus of forces no less real for being largely beyond prosaic labels and subject to a logic unconstrained by the primitive syllogisms of cause and effect. Thus, if the father in "The Judgment" was Herrmann Kafka, he was also all of the Herrmann Kafkas proliferating in Prague, all the German-Jewish "founding fathers" of the post-emancipation generation, all mortal fathers crippling their sons, and, finally, the specter of the father as the reflection of divine omnipotence, just as their power over the sons derives from sources far more impenetrable and profound than the economic, physical, and emotional dependence in which they manifest themselves. And it is this multifaceted ambiguity, counterpointed as always by a rigorous realism of detail, that evokes a sense of the human predicament in all its baffling complexity and at the same time leaves the story wide open to a host of interpretations.

The dominant trend, here again, is the brand of psychological reductivism that laboriously traces plot, structure, and characters back to their purported inspiration. The discovery that Herrmann Kafka lurks behind Georg's father seems no more original or helpful than the manifest resemblance between Yitzhak Levi and Georg's mythical friend in Russia, whom Kafka himself conceived as symbolic of "the link between father and son, that which they most have in common" (DI, 2/11/13). Such banalities are the small change of academic pedantry, which tends to confuse knowledge of facts with understanding their meaning—a benign enough delusion compared to the militant idiocy of more aggressive revelators. (A prominent specimen is Ruth Tiefenbrun's *Moment of Torment.* The author explicates "The Judgment" as a secret code by means of which Kafka cunningly discloses, exhibits, and indulges his homosexual fantasies.)

But even the most sane and sensitive reading is necessarily tied to the subjective bias of the interpreter and, at best, can only illuminate whichever side he happens to be on. For what a critic like Walter Benjamin sees as "the unmasking of the corrupt and parasitical world of the fathers" is also the oedipal conflict, the struggle between freedom and authority, and the confrontation between God and man.

* * *

It was as though the breakthrough of that memorable September night had with explosive force uncapped the wellsprings of long-dormant reserves. A mere two days later, on September 25, Kafka started on the second version of his "America" novel with much the same frenetic concentration that had carried him through "The Judgment." Brod quotes his own diary entries of that period: "September 29: Kafka in ecstasy, writing through the nights. A novel with America as the background. October 1: Kafka unbelievably ecstatic. October 2: Kafka continues to be tremendously inspired. One chapter is finished. Am very happy about it. October 3: Kafka is extremely well. October 6: Kafka read me both 'The Judgment' and the first chapter of the America novel, entitled *The Stoker*" (Brod, bio., p. 113).

Small wonder, then, that the news of his brother-in-law's business trip, which he received at just that moment, hit him with the force of a death threat. For the next two or three weeks—an eternity, in terms of his creative process—he was to waste most of his free time and energy on the asbestos factory, rather than pouring it into his novel, a prospect that led to the near-suicidal episode already recounted. The clash between the two worlds he was still trying to straddle, the world of his art and the world of his father, had erupted with a violence that threatened to tear him apart. No longer just a would-be writer, but a recognized and published one in the throes of inspired creativity, he suddenly found himself confronted by a father no longer willing to settle for his pound of flesh but bent on devouring the whole son, hide and hair.

Through Brod's deft intervention with Kafka's mother, the acute crisis was more or less resolved, though not without leaving a solid sediment of rage and hatred in its wake— "I hate them all, each and every one of them" (L, 10/8/12). Yet if the incident upset his schedule, the anger it released also reaffirmed the inner truth of his novel and provided some of the motive and inspiration behind "The Metamorphosis," written the following month.

Moreover, in spite of these disruptions, work on the novel seems to have continued at a furious pace. Having completed *The Stoker* around the first of October, Kafka by the end of the month had already written four more chapters— "The Uncle," "A Country Mansion near New York," "The Road to Ramses," and "The Hotel Occidental." A fifth chapter, "The Robinson Case," was finished on November 12, though he was less than happy with the outcome: "Yesterday I finished the sixth chapter, but I forced the ending and it turned out crude and poor. I suppressed two characters that should have been included, and they kept running after me all the time while I was writing. And since in the story they were supposed to make threatening gestures with their fists, they did so against me. They were far more alive than anything I was writing" (L, 11/13/12).

Between November 17 and December 6, Kafka worked on "The Metamorphosis," so that Chapter 7, "An Asylum," was not completed until January 6, 1913. After that, however, the pace began to slacken markedly, for reasons clearly linked to the dramatic changes that had in the meantime taken place in his personal situation. During the first two months of his increasingly insistent courtship, Felice had been understandably elusive, her reserve fueling both panic and inspiration;

he wrote not only out of fast-rising inner tensions but also to prove himself worthy of her, in his own eyes, if not in hers. The receipt, on December 12, of the first bound copies of his *Meditations* from Rowohlt must have further buoyed his spirits and his hopes.

By the end of the year, however, Felice had succumbed to Kafka's epistolary ardor, and relations between them had turned into a torrid love affair on paper that seemed headed for a conventional denouement. It allowed him, protected as he was by distance, to envisage a more or less normal existence which would somehow resolve his conflicts, assure his independence, and enable him to function effectively both as a husband and as a writer. The illusion did not outlive the spring, but while it lasted, the obsessive drive to prove and to explain himself lost much of its force, the tensions abated, and a near-blissful serenity helped to erode his inspiration. For a few weeks in January 1913, he continued to work on the novel, but on January 26 he declared himself "utterly defeated. The novel is crumbling in my hands, I don't seem able to get hold of it . . . my trying to go on with it at this point would endanger the work more than if I dropped it for the time being" (FEL, 1/26/13).

And drop it he did, for a year and a half, until June 1914, when in growing despair and under vastly changed circumstances he attempted to pick up the thread once again. In October 1914, during another burst of crisis-induced inspiration, he wrote the last completed chapter while simultaneously working on both *The Penal Colony* and *The Trial*. It was to be followed by a concluding chapter which, as we saw, had been projected as a triumphant finale in the Oklahoma paradise, with the hero miraculously restored to his social position, his family, and his own country. By then, however, there was war, in his own soul no less than in the world at large; in the circumstances, he must have found it increasingly difficult to sustain a faith in miracles that had never been germane to begin with. Twice more, in 1915 and 1916, he briefly returned to the novel, but in the end it remained unfinished.

* * *

The Stoker, its first chapter, is the only segment edited by Kafka himself and published in his lifetime. On April 2, 1913, Kurt Wolff, alerted by Brod, urged Kafka to let him see the first chapter of his new work in progress with a view toward possible publication in book form. Kafka complied at once, though expressing his reservations: ". . . while one does not exactly feel the 500 totally bungled pages that follow, it does not by itself seem enough of an integral whole. It is and will remain a fragment; this prospect alone endows the chapter with whatever cohesion it may have" (L, 4/4/13). Four days later, Wolff proposed publication in his new Doomsday series. On April 16, the contract was signed; by April 24, Kafka had corrected the galley proofs, and on May 25 he received the first bound copies of the book. Less than two months had elapsed from submission of the manuscript to its publication, eloquent comment on the meaning of progress in the world of publishing where, with its present no-hands automation and no-minds bureaucratization, an analogous time lag would be regarded as something of a miracle.

The modern conglomerate is, of course, hardly conducive to the kind of author-publisher relations that existed between Kafka and Wolff, who four months before asking for *The Stoker* had brought out the *Meditations* entirely on the strength of his own convictions and, despite generally respectful reviews, lost a fair amount of money on it. Of the eight hundred copies comprising the first edition, more than half still remained in stock five years later. Kafka himself remarked that André's, a well-known Prague bookstore, had sold eleven copies in all; ten he could easily account for, having bought them himself, but he kept wondering who might have bought the eleventh. Such willful contempt for cost-efficiency, bottom lines, and the opinions of the sales staff could hardly be justified in the atmosphere of current publishing, but the resultant loss cannot be calculated in terms of dollars and cents.

The Stoker—A Fragment (Kafka insisted on the addition to the title) was received with considerably more enthusiasm. Robert Musil pronounced it "enchanting," and both the comparison with Kleist and references to Kafka's use of the "unconscious" cropped up for the first time in contemporary reviews. That Karl Rossmann's fall and decline, exile and rebellion, sprang from the same seed as "The Judgment" seems obvious. But it also marks a crucial shift, not away from, but beyond the narrow focus toward a much broader view of authority, one in which the father is eventually demoted to a mere functionary of the nameless powers that be. The lively descriptions and Dickensian turns have encouraged critics so inclined to read it as a work of social protest, the oppression of the sons by the fathers symbolizing the class struggle and oppression of the wage slaves. And there is evidence to suggest that these parallels were quite deliberately drawn: not only was Kafka thoroughly familiar with the lives of the working class, but it was his own father whose mistreatment of his employees had provided the first and never-forgotten lesson on human relations in a capitalist society. It is also true that this experience, amplified by an insider's firsthand knowledge of bureaucracy in its most malignantly dehumanizing aberrations, assumed an increasingly significant place in his vision and work, beginning with *Amerika.*

None of this, however, makes him a socialist realist, nor yet a realist or socialist *tout court.* His views on power and authority, of guilt, punishment, and on man's fate in an inhuman world turned out to be both vastly more simple and infinitely more complex. And if he kept his distance from what appeared to be the burning issues of his day, the fact remains that his very remoteness afforded him far more revealing perspectives on the future than the commitment of those among his peers who so confidently expected the triumph of socialism in Prague to render Kafka obsolete.

*   *   *

Still, *The Stoker* as published seemed to end on a hopeful note. The outcast on his way to exile stands up for justice and the underdog, and though the outcome of his righteous indignation remains in doubt, he finds himself welcomed on his arrival in New York by his maternal uncle, a father figure far more powerful and wise than the petty tyrant who had banished him for having broken the rules of the game.

But the subsequent adventures of Karl Rossmann, edited by Brod only after Kafka's death and published by Kurt Wolff in 1927 together with *The Stoker* under the collective title of *Amerika,* reveal the progressively ever more pessimistic nature of Kafka's vision. It is a vision that takes in a great deal of territory alive with native dreams and immigrant nightmares, some of it startlingly prescient in its fantasies about American reality. Yet this scenery remains peripheral to the core of Kafka's pursuit of guilt as punishment. And if Karl Rossmann, at the end of *The Stoker,* appears to have found grace and redemption, he was soon to be disabused of his illusions in a rapid downward drift that dragged him, in recurrent cycles of abasement, into a pit from which only God, a miracle, or a revolution could still rescue him. But salvation in whatever form requires a faith which Kafka may have wished for but decidedly lacked, a reason at least as cogent as his personal problems for finally giving up on Karl Rossmann and leaving him on a train, headed for an unknown destination.

Unknown to Karl Rossmann, alias Franz Kafka, that is; we have since found out where those trains ended up, some forty years later.

Max Brod, on the other hand, believed in God and in miracles, understandably so, given the evidence of his own charmed life. This still does not quite excuse his having lopped off a final segment of the manuscript in an attempt to give it the more hopeful slant he felt it ought to have. The cut, however, was restored in subsequent editions of *Amerika,* including the English version.

*   *   *

In terms of Kafka's work schedule at the time, "The Metamorphosis," written at intervals between November 17 and December 7, 1912, was a parenthetical interlude, a brief change of pace from the novel. But its impact rather dwarfs that of the more ambitious work and in one terrifying flash lights up both the pathetic fragility of his defenses and the solid black core of despair, quite unmoved by wishful thinking and extravagant illusions. "The Metamorphosis," like "The Judgment," was an eruption—triggered, incidentally, by a brief bout of depression over a trivial misunderstanding with Felice; in the best of times, it took very little to shatter his brittle euphoria and set off a blast of anxiety. Less dramatic, less orgasmic an experience, it left him more puzzled than exhilarated, but perhaps for that very reason better able to give shape and structure to his anguish in what may well be the most "kafkaesque" of all his shorter works.

What it says about him, with chilling detachment and in a prose of limpid, hallucinatory precision seldom equaled and never surpassed in modern German, is devastating in its intimations, hell's antechamber inventoried by a claims assessor. But what it says about Kafka, with a more slashing cogency than ever before, is merely one small facet in a gallery of mirrors reflecting the evolution of *Homo sapiens* from child to clerk to vermin.

The exegetical literature on "The Metamorphosis" already comprises hundreds of books and articles, few of them contributing much to the kind of understanding to which one's own effort and experience offer the sole guide. Like all of Kafka's work, "The Metamorphosis" defies and transcends the standard categories of literary criticism; it is a poisoned fairy tale about the magic of hate and the power of hypocrisy, a surreal *Bildungsroman* charting the transmogrification of a lost soul into a dead bug—Kafka's claustrophobic horror of life with father as the model of man's life with his gods, and yet infinitely more than an allegory studded with symbols which, once picked out and decoded, yield but one consistent and definitive meaning.

"*Die Verwandlung*"—the English translation of the title as "The Metamorphosis" with its Ovidian connotations seems needlessly pretentious and jarringly at odds with Kafka's own style—did not appear until October 1915, when it was first printed in the *Weisse Blätter,* a literary journal edited by the Alsatian novelist René Schickele. A month later, it was published as a volume in Kurt Wolff's Doomsday series. The unusual delay was largely Kafka's own fault; the affair with Felice had kept him too preoccupied to attend to the mundane business of copying a manuscript.

Nineteen

I F writing was his reason for being, it was also Kafka's most unequivocal way of being himself. *Le style c'est l'homme* applied to
him with more validity and force than to almost any other modern
writer. He despised ornate verbal pyrotechnics and never sought cover
behind his words but, on the contrary, honed them to a fine edge before
turning them against himself for exploratory butchery.

Such as he was, he invested himself in almost every line he ever
wrote, and the purity of his prose—largely lost in translation—is as
troubling, chilling, and revealing in his notebooks, diaries, and letters
as it is in his more formal work. Even the "lawyer's tricks" of which
he accuses himself, notably in reference to the famous *Letter to His
Father,* were arguments not for but with himself, the lucid ambivalence
of one who sees a gossamer of infinite ambiguity in every patch of the
concrete.

This made him both a great letter writer and an unsatisfactory
correspondent—unsatisfactory for many of the same reasons that kept
him an outsider even within his most intimate circles. True, at a distance he was able to take more of a risk than in personal contact at
close quarters: "I write differently from the way I speak, I speak differently from the way I think, I think differently from the way I ought to
be thinking, and so on into deepest darkness" (L, 7/10/14). But even
the most spontaneous self-revelation and self-flagellation remains centered on the self, its focus precluding any genuine exchange. With rare
exceptions, Kafka's correspondence, like the bulk of his work, is a
dialogue with himself. And in that sense the over five hundred letters
he wrote to Felice Bauer between September 1912 and October 1917
may well be regarded as his longest novel, the only one he ever completed.

Eight days after having written his first letter to her, he received

Felice's reply, no doubt fittingly polite and noncommittal, though the wording could hardly have mattered. "The Judgment" bears witness to the tension that had in the meantime built up around the subject, so that receiving any kind of answer was bound to spark an explosion.

Within minutes, therefore, "at 10 a.m. on September 28," he sat down and shot back a long, rather rambling epistle which, measured against the true state of his feelings, may have seemed to him light-hearted and suitably inquisitive, but whose quite breathless tone would have startled any dispassionate recipient. He suggested that instead of writing him formal letters—"a letter always takes an effort"—she keep a diary and simply mail it to him in sections. "Of course, you'll have to record more than would strictly be necessary for yourself alone, because I still don't know you at all. You would have to note at what time you arrive at the office, what you had for breakfast, the view from your office window, what sort of work you do there, the names of your male and female friends, why you are getting presents, who is trying to undermine your health by offering you sweets, and the thousand and one things of whose existence and possibilities I know nothing" (FEL, 9/28/12).

This consuming hunger for facts, his constant plea for the most detailed account of Felice's habits, dress, daily routine, everything connected with her outer life and environment, runs like a red thread through the entire correspondence. So does the notion that he could get "to know her" by knowing what she had for breakfast. Her thoughts and feelings, on the other hand—at least as they concerned subjects other than himself—were seldom of more than passing interest to him. She had a lively enough mind but no great depth or intellectual pretensions, and wholeheartedly shared the conventional prejudices and often atrocious taste of her German-Jewish—far more German than Jewish—middle-class background. And while Kafka made a few token moves toward helping her expand her cultural horizons, he basically remained as indifferent to her intellect in general as he did to her literary judgment in particular, an indifference tinged with some of the patronizing contempt with which the men of his tribe have treated their women since the days of Abraham and Isaac. ("The trouble with the family life of the Jews," notes the diary, "is that the woman is excluded from the study of the Talmud" [DI, 12/25/11]).

As to Felice, the destruction of her part of the correspondence makes it difficult to say just how articulate she was about her feelings in her letters, though some of his responses and, above all, Felice's later actions, point to recurrent crises of understandably intense turmoil and confusion. But aside from torturing himself with eloquent guilt at causing her so much unhappiness, he chose never to probe very deeply; he had trouble enough handling his own emotions. And the less willing he was to share her real troubles, the more he fussed and fretted over the most trivial mishaps in her everyday life. Let her complain of a headache or a sore throat and he was quick with buckets of anguished sympathy and elaborate therapeutic advice.

Still, it was this very obsession with the trivia of existence, this microscopic amplification of detail in its ultimate banality, that links the letters to his work; both affirm, time and again, and with scintillating precision, Kafka's unique perception of what passes for the real world as an unending series of miracles. No one, perhaps, understood this better than Milena Jesenská, who once described it in a letter to Max Brod:

> For [Kafka], life is something altogether different from what it is for ordinary people. Above all, things such as money, the stock market, foreign exchange, or a typewriter are utterly miraculous (as indeed they are, only not to the rest of us). . . . Is his work at the office, for instance, anything like an ordinary job? To him the office, including his own part in it, is as mysterious and wonderful as a locomotive is to a small child. Have you ever been to the post office with him? Watched him compose a telegram, shake his head while he picks a window he likes best and then, without the least notion of why and wherefore, starts wandering about from one window to the next? . . . No, this entire world is and remains a mystery to him, an enigmatic myth. . . . His books are amazing. He himself is far more amazing. [Brod, bio., p. 198]

And it was this primordial awe of the mystery of things, of the miraculous and the enigmatic inherent in every facet of what others took for granted, source of his genius and his agony, that made him so preternaturally sensitive to the visible, tangible aspects of reality. They formed the one tenuous link between his inner vision and the outer world. They enabled him to translate his private terror into the common currency of language, and to give voice and substance to the phantoms haunting his dreams. His bride-to-be was clearly one of them; that was why he had to know exactly what it was she wore to the office, what she said to whom, and how she stirred her coffee, had to be able to see, to draw, and to describe her to himself with the same meticulous realism with which he endowed all the disembodied characters emerging from the lower depths of his consciousness.

* * *

The reaction of this on the whole rather proper and conventional young woman was both sound and predictable. Bewildered, a little stunned perhaps by such aggressive ardor from an all but unknown admirer, she simply refrained from answering and thus initiated a pattern that was to characterize their relationship throughout its long and tortuous course. Whenever she withdrew, he lashed himself into a foaming frenzy of despair and flirted with suicide or madness. Whenever she yielded to the platonic passion of his epistolary entreaties, threatened to take him at his word, let herself fantasize about marriage with all the trimmings, and, ever practical, suggested the appropriate steps, he fled in sheer terror, swaddled himself in his frailty and ill health, pleaded the ascetic demands of his vocation, his total enslavement to literature, and threw up all sorts of roadblocks he regarded as impassable. And the most tragic aspect of this recurrent drama, at least as it affected Kafka, was that both the passion and the terror were equally genuine and equally devastating in their impact. Terror is no less real for lodging in the soul rather than in the muzzle of a gun, nor is passion diminished by being rooted in despair. His constant refrain, "I cannot live with her, and I cannot live without her," was a cry from the heart.

Having waited two weeks for her answer, he began to grow frantic. On October 13 he again wrote to Felice, asking, or rather demanding to know, why she had not written, speculating and dismissing every conceivable reason except the one most likely. At the same time, he mobilized Brod's sister Sophie in Berlin on his behalf; an eager matchmaker, she rushed to the rescue, and a week later Kafka had his coveted reply.

From that point on, all stops were out and nothing could hold him back. Over the six-month period that followed, he wrote to Felice as often as twice and even three times daily—not short *billets doux,* either, but long letters for the most part, running the gamut from hysteria to humor, filled with self-pity, special pleading, and soaring sentiment as well as with shrewd observations, acerbic comments, and brilliant sketches of his world in all its stuffiness and fascination. And if she, in turn, failed to keep up the pace, missed a beat, or did not provide sufficiently explicit answers to his insistent barrage of pointedly specific questions—"I must have an explanation for Sunday. WHY were you indoors all day long? And why were you still so tired on Sunday night that you were looking forward to Monday, a workday?"—he could be peremptory if not downright tyrannical in his reproaches and admonitions.

Already in his exuberant reply to her second letter, on October 24, he not only bombarded her with questions—"Do these questions seem ridiculous to you? My own face is serious, and if you must laugh, please let it be a friendly laugh and answer in detail"—but also announced that "The Judgment," about to appear in Brod's anthology, would bear the dedication "For Miss Felice B." A week later, on November 1, he switched from the formal *Gnädiges Fräulein* to the almost familiar "Dear Miss Felice," by way of introducing the confessional tone that now began to predominate.

> My life consists, and basically has always consisted, of attempts to write, most of them unsuccessful. But whenever I did not write, I was immediately down and out on the ground, fit for the garbage. . . . I am the thinnest person I have ever known (which is saying something, since I am no stranger to sanatoria) . . . yet if there is a higher power that wishes to use me, or does use me, then I am in its grip, a ready tool at least. If not, then I am nothing and will suddenly be left in a dreadful void. And now I have enlarged my life by thoughts of you. Hardly a quarter hour of my waking time passes without my thinking about you, and there are many quarter hours in which I do nothing else. Yet even this is related to my writing. [FEL, 11/1/12]

No jaded libertine could have mounted a more practiced assault. Felice, though obviously flattered and charmed, was also sober enough not to let his poetic hyperbole overcome her own prosaic realism. Like Kafka's mother, she no doubt convinced herself that given a caring wife, a peaceful home, and a sensible diet, her ardent suitor would outgrow his romantic streak, settle down to business, and pursue his writing as a hobby in his spare time. Accordingly, she preached moderation and realistic goals and urged him to get more sleep.

Maternal platitudes of this sort were hardly what Kafka sought or needed; human weakness all by itself, as he pointed out, imposed moderation and trimmed one's expectations. On the contrary, he raged against the preordained verdict of destiny and sought to nullify it by striving for absolutes, be they or not mutually exclusive. Courting the distant beloved with ever more passionate words, he at the same time raised all sorts of arguments designed to disabuse her of any illusions concerning his potential eligibility as a husband: his grotesque appearance, his "fletcherizing" vegetarianism, his idiosyncratic attire—"I wear the same suit summer and winter, in the office, in the street, at my desk. . . . Never a vest. I am the inventor of the two-piece suit. . . . And do not try to change me, but put up with me at this great distance." Trifling arguments, advanced in lieu of more cogent ones, and with more than a touch of coquettish pride. A mere week later, however, on November 11, he threw vestigial caution to the winds and went all out in simultaneously reaching for both horns of the dilemma. Addressing her for the first time by the familiar second-person *Du,* he openly declared his love while at the same time confessing his true reason for not simply taking the first train to Berlin: "In short, I am just barely healthy enough for myself, but not healthy enough for marriage, let alone fatherhood."

Felice, baffled and hurt, resorted to what in those days was still a rather radical step: she picked up the phone and called Max Brod to ask for his help. Whether it was his advice or her own common sense that did the trick, the fact is that her reply not only succeeded in calming Kafka's fears but also sent him into a rapturous euphoria which, with the usual fluctuations, lasted until well into the following spring. Even while working steadily on his novel and completing "The Metamorphosis" on the side, as it were—the inspiration for it came to him while he lay helpless in bed one morning, vowing not to get up until he had a letter from Felice—and despite an unusually heavy work load at the office, he found time and energy for at least one, often two or three long letters to Felice every day. The ardor of his verbal passion rose steeply, along with the intensity of his anguish and the petulance of his reproaches—"You spent the whole week in rehearsals, you were ill for a day and a half. Despite your illness you went dancing on Saturday night, got back home at 7 in the morning, stayed up until 1 a.m. the following night, and went to the company dance on Monday night. What sort of life is this? Explanations, please, explanations"—

followed by desperate pleas for forgiveness and lyrical passages of exquisite tenderness. He was clearly very much in love with love, almost confident that with Felice's help "everything will turn out all right—except for one indelible black spot."

In a long Sunday letter of November 26, 1912, he became more explicit in his allusions to what haunted him: "All these contradictions have one simple and natural reason, which I keep repeating because I myself also seldom manage to forget it: nothing more or less than the state of my health. I cannot talk about it in greater detail, but this is what robs me of my assurance toward you, what tosses me back and forth and ends up throwing you off balance as well."

There can be no doubt that the obsessive fear of sex, or more specifically of wallowing in lustful filth and degradation not with a paid hooker or lower-class shopgirl but with the virginal mother image he secretly worshipped and wanted to love, did, in fact, account for much of the tension in the relationship. Its multiple causes, from unresolved oedipal ties and latent homosexual tendencies to childhood upbringing and cultural bias, have already been discussed. But with the growing threat of marriage—after all, what else could all this have been leading up to—the nauseous prospect of "marital duty" made him feel dead certain that he would never be able to consummate it, though it took him until April 1, 1913, to come straight out with it: "My true fear—and surely nothing worse can ever be said or heard—is that I shall never be able to possess you, that at best I would be confined, like an insentient, faithful dog, to kissing your distractedly proffered hand, not as a sign of love, but merely as a token of despair on the part of an animal condemned to silence and eternal separation."

For once, though, he did not rummage in his own heart and soul for the root causes of this fear. Instead, he defensively, almost defiantly, blamed his "delicate health" and his "constitutional frailty." The true significance of these code words may be suspected from a curious aside to Felice concerning his hero, Napoleon Bonaparte: "Napoleon certainly had far less to do with women than would appear to an observer dazzled by his glory. . . . I once read a peculiar autopsy report on Napoleon's body, which fleetingly refers to his restraint toward women in a very persuasive context as though it had been a well-known fact. And in spite of the apparent contradiction, his lovesick letters to Josephine and the crude language he used when talking about sexual topics would tend to confirm this observation" (FEL, 1/26/13).

The post-mortem findings coyly alluded to without further explanation were undoubtedly those of the British army surgeon W. Henry, who concluded his official autopsy report on the imperial prisoner by noting that "the member and testes were exceedingly small, and the diminutive size of the genitalia would appear to explain the reputed chastity and absence of sexual desire ascribed to the deceased." The report was reprinted in a widely discussed book on Napoleon's death by Paul Frémaux, published in 1911; Kafka was familiar with the German translation.

The testimony of Hugo Hecht, his erstwhile schoolmate and later specialist in venereal diseases, to the effect that Kafka himself suffered from a similar case of underdevelopment can hardly be credited to factual knowledge. The two were far from intimate friends, and a Hemingway-Fitzgerald type of men's room consultation seems hard to imagine. On the other hand, concern about penis size is common enough and has little to do with facts; reinforced by a morbid aversion to sex, at least sex with Felice, it could easily have evolved into an imaginary "constitutional frailty" precluding marriage.

* * *

Felice, at least on the face of it, remained calm, sensible, and supportive. She had every reason to believe that a properly nourished Kafka, surrounded by wifely care and overstuffed furniture and leading the regular life of a respectable insurance executive with literary interests, would eventually overcome his neurosis at least to the extent of being able to father the requisite number of children. In any event, the most vital ingredient of a happy marriage was money. Sex, at best, enhanced the flavor; more often, it spoiled the broth.

This, at least to judge from Kafka's responses, seems to have been Felice's basic outlook. Fun-loving, outgoing, but herself the child victim of a bad marriage and already far too tough-minded to indulge in girlish dreams of romance and everlasting bliss, she had a down-to-earth approach to their common future that in the short run proved immensely comforting because it enabled Kafka, once his outbursts had been properly registered and minimized, to carry on as before. In the long run, it made him sick.

On the other hand, the fact that a marriage such as envisaged by Felice required financial security would have been obvious to him even without his father's endlessly laboring the point. He still retained some illusions about a possible income from the asbestos factory; Felice, once she found out about the project, was greatly intrigued and urged him to participate more actively. But while he never worried about finances the way he did about sex, he knew that with his then salary he could never hope to support Felice in the style to which she was accustomed, let alone the one to which she aspired. Accordingly, on December 11, 1912, emboldened perhaps by the receipt of the first bound copy of his first book—the *Meditations,* which he immediately passed on to Felice with a proper dedication—he petitioned the institute's Board of Directors for a "fundamental revision" of his rank and salary grade, based on his record and greatly expanded responsibilities. On March 1, 1913, he was promoted to Vice-Secretary, with a substantial increase in salary to a respectable 4,588 crowns annually.

In the meantime, the letters continued at their frenzied pace, shuttling back and forth twice a day, an epic of passion and despair, with melodramatic turns and flashes of self-irony. "Your photograph," he wrote on December 25, three months after the start of the correspondence, "gives me a chance to kiss your whole face, and that is what I am doing and will do again before I go to sleep and again when I wake up. And let it be said that my lips are yours alone; I never kiss anyone else, neither parents nor sisters, and implacable aunts are only assigned a spot on my averted cheek." By January 3, he reports having dreamed of their engagement; a week later he gives a Chaplinesque account of his sister's wedding, which reminded him of a funeral— ostensibly because the communal ceremonies of Prague's assimilated Jews had in essence shrunk to these two symbolically entwined occasions.

His creative vein, however, began to give out; the novel was in trouble and ultimately had to be abandoned. What was more, relations with Brod, his in many ways most solid link to the world, had undergone subtle changes, precipitated by Brod's marriage and exacerbated by his zestful conversion to Zionism, which Kafka at that time still resisted with more than his usual skepticism. To Felice, though, who sensed the shift, he vehemently denied any tension between himself and his closest friend. Brod's rhapsodic review of the *Meditations* had just appeared in the Munich literary journal *März*; while deeply moved and grateful, Kafka assured Felice that Brod simply loved and vastly overestimated him as a person, and that Brod's opinion of his writing reflected these feelings rather than his considered judgment. "And the most terrifying part of it is that . . . I have the same attitude toward his work, except that I am sometimes conscious of it, while he never is" (FEL, 2/14/13).

He was more discreet in his allusions to Judaism, their one truly common bond, and one whose deep and pervasive significance was such as to be tacitly taken for granted. Felice had vaguely Zionist leanings, even more vague than Kafka's own, but she apparently attended synagogue services with fair regularity, as noted by him with some astonishment (and in obvious ignorance of the fact that Sabbath services start at sundown, hence later in summer than in winter): "You write that in summer you go to the synagogue on Friday nights; do you have different office hours in summer than in winter? I myself during the past few years have been to the temple only twice, both times for my sisters' weddings" (FEL, 1/17/13).

Yet in ways that he had only just begun to probe, his Jewishness, or lack thereof, was close to the core of his conflict over Felice. Unmarried, he was neither a man nor a Jew—a non-Jew, non-German, non-Czech, none but his own naked self adrift in a cold and hostile world. At the same time, he was quite definitely more of a non-Jew than anything else. If he could but find the gate that would admit him, he too could rejoin the ancestral tribe, become part of humanity, sustained by faith and a sense of belonging that would at last make it possible to live and to die. The handwriting on the prison wall spelled out the choice as well as the price: Marry Felice, surrender your selfhood, and the gate will be flung open, the tribe will embrace, engulf, and swallow you, silence your anguish and your voice, and blind faith will supplant the clear-eyed vision of guilt.

A promise of bliss that, like the prospect of marriage itself, scared him to death.

> You go to the synagogue, though of late you probably haven't been there [he wrote to Felice in February]. And what is it that sustains you—the idea of Jewishness, or the idea of God? Do you feel—and this is the essential point—an unbroken tie between yourself and some reassuringly distant, possibly infinite, heights and depths? He who always feels this is not forced to roam about like a lost cur with a mute plea in his eyes, nor yearn to slip into his grave as though it were a cozy sleeping bag and life a frigid winter night. [FEL, 2/9/13]

But though rarely discussed in his letters, Kafka's attitude toward Judaism during that very period had outgrown the early stages of naïve enthusiasm, bogged down in the inevitable complexities of the subject and become more problematic. His closest friends, such as Brod, Bergmann, and Weltsch, defined Judaism—and themselves—through an increasingly militant Zionism that Kafka found at once appealing and appalling, either extreme being more a matter of mood and feeling than of ideological reasoning. He faithfully attended the meetings, lectures, and discussions organized under Zionist auspices and featuring an eclectic array of Palestinian pioneers, liberal rabbis, aspiring prophets, as well as a growing contingent of native talent. By 1913, the Zionist movement was well on its way to becoming a powerful factor in the lives of Prague's younger generation of Jews, not the least of its achievements being a radical break with traditional Jewish attitudes toward women. The Zionist Jewish Girls' and Women's Club, organized in 1912, had as its first president Lise Weltsch (a cousin of Felix Weltsch), with whom Kafka was on terms of close friendship until she left Prague late in 1913. Brod's and Bergmann's wives, as well as Kafka's sister Ottla, all devoted much time to the organization, most of whose members emigrated to Palestine between 1918 and 1920. At the last count, fifteen were still alive in Israel.

One of the early settlers was Irma—now Miriam—Singer, a founder-veteran of Kibbutz Daganya and a pioneer in kibbutz child-rearing methods, who attended Hebrew courses with Kafka during the First World War. She recalls how, when she returned from Palestine in 1919 for a brief visit to Prague, Kafka quizzed her in endless detail on life in the Jewish agricultural settlements and how, on parting, he gave her a signed copy of the just-published *Country Doctor* with the words: "You're much too healthy, Irma; you won't understand this." She still cherishes the book; and now, in her late eighties, she feels qualified to understand it.

Yet here again, though linked to them all by close personal ties, Kafka functioned mainly as an interested, even fascinated, but always detached and critical observer. Moreover, much of the fashionable Jewish revival, from petty Zionist factionalism to the sententious pieties of root-digging Jewish literati, struck him as absurdly inauthentic. On January 16, 1913, he told Felice about a lecture by Martin Buber on "the Jewish Myth": "It would take more than a Buber to get me to leave my room. I've heard him before and find him dreary; there is always something missing in everything he says. (True, he is also capable of a great deal. . . . He published *Chinese Ghost and Love Stories,* excellent, at least the ones I read.) I am only going on account of Eysoldt [German actress, 1870–1955], who will be reading after Buber." Three days later, he reported having met Buber in person and found him "refreshing, simple, and remarkable, as though he had nothing to do with the tepid things he has written" (FEL, 1/19/13). Rather mild censure, compared to the quite uncharacteristic virulence with which, five years later, he classified Buber's latest book as "odious and repulsive" (L, 1/18).

On February 16 he informed Felice of his intention to spend a week on the French Riviera in the fall. She immediately proposed to join him, an offer which suggests at least a certain indifference on her part to bourgeois conventions but which sent Kafka into a tailspin. Panicky, he replied that "given, for instance, my present state and the always conceivable possibility of a recurrence, I could never dare wish to be your traveling companion. I deserve to be all alone, dumped by myself in a corner of some train compartment; that's where I should be made to stay. My contact with you, which I am striving to maintain with all my strength, must never be jeopardized by such a journey together" (FEL, 2/20/13).

Understandably troubled by this response, Felice evidently asked for an explanation and was treated to a veritable flood of self-reproaches summed up in the flat assertion that "no two days could you ever live with me" (FEL, 3/6/13). But he also, perhaps by way of compensation, for the first time gingerly broached what had long been an unspoken question in her letters by suggesting a face-to-face meeting in Berlin, which after lengthy negotiations and anguished indecision finally took place on Easter Sunday, March 23, 1913.

It quite lived up to his expectations.

He spent the evening of his arrival and much of the following Sunday morning waiting at the Hotel Askanischer Hof for word from Felice. After he had notified her by messenger that he had to leave for Prague at 4 p.m., they finally met and spent a few painful hours walking around Grunewald Park, total strangers to one another.

* * *

Their brief encounter in a three-dimensional reality forced changes on both of them. The fictive Felice of his fantasy had come to life, asserted a mind of her own, and walked straight out of his novel, slammed the door on it, disrupted its rhythm, and disoriented his perspectives. She, in turn, numbed by the mute pleas of her would-not-be lover, who looked and acted like a moonstruck teenager, realized that left to his own devices he would forever go on wallowing in self-pity, unable to make a move in any direction. Her letters slowed down to a trickle. Though she remained distantly sympathetic and reassuring, even acknowledged that he had grown indispensable to her, she was also now obviously determined to force the issue, one way or another. "I don't believe in your complaints," she told him outright, "and neither do you."

Shaken and chastened, he in turn toned down his effusions, plaintively denied himself the right to offer long-distance kisses, and instead proposed another confrontation in Berlin at Whitsuntide. He also arranged, by way of self-prescribed reality therapy, to spend a few hours every week working for a gardener in suburban Nusle. "My main purpose was to stop torturing myself for a few hours by doing some dull, honest, useful, silent, solitary, healthy, strenuous labor, as opposed to the ghost-like office work which literally slips out of my grasp every time I want to grab hold of it. The true hell is right there in the office; the other one I no longer fear" (FEL, 4/17/13). (A month later, he wryly notes in his diary that "I, who wanted to cure my neurasthenia by gardening, had to find out that the [son of the nursery's owner], heir presumptive to old Dvorsky and himself already the owner of a flower nursery, poisoned himself two months ago in a fit of depression at the age of twenty-eight" [DI, 5/2/13]).

The second meeting in Berlin, on May 11–12, 1913, was predictably no more successful than the first. Kafka visited Felice at home and met her family, who "mounted a display of total resignation as regards myself. I felt so small, while all of them surrounded me like giants, a fatalistic look on their faces (with the exception of your sister Erna, to whom I immediately felt close). I must have made a hideous impression on them; I don't want to know anything about it" (FEL, 5/15/13).

Whether calculated or instinctive, Felice's hardheaded refusal to play any further agony games and her—albeit unspoken—insistence on a binding decision in the immediate future cut off all his escape routes.

He fell back on his fear of impotence, which she had managed eloquently to ignore. "I cannot bear the responsibility, because I regard it as too great. You, in turn, cannot bear it because you barely see it. Of course, miracles do happen, one of them being the fact that you care for me. Why, then, should not my cure be among the sequence of miracles bound to arise out of our life together?" (FEL, 5/23/13). And as a token of his faith in miracles, he proposed to write to her father, explain the nature of his problem, and ask him for the name of a competent physician whom he could consult.

Felice's answer was an icy silence that drove him even beyond the brink of despair to the point where he overcame his telephone phobia and called her long-distance in the office. But her sporadic notes were not designed to improve matters. "That was no letter but only the ghost of one. I almost know it by heart: 'We're sitting here in the zoo restaurant, after having sat in the zoo all afternoon.' Why, but why did you have to sit in the zoo?" (FEL, 6/1/13). Felice, obdurate and growing ever more impatient, finally told him that what she wanted was an "open and honest" showdown; and Kafka, cornered at last, had to make his choice. In a treatise painfully composed over a period of at least a week but mailed on June 16, 1913, he asked Felice to be his wife.

*   *   *

More precisely, what he actually did was draw up a list of impediments to their marriage.

> Standing between you and me, apart from everything else, is the doctor. What he will tell me is uncertain; such decisions depend not so much on a medical diagnosis . . . as on the personality of the unknown physician. My own family doctor, for instance, in his stupid lack of responsibility, would not see the slightest objection. . . . But the time for hesitation has passed. Therefore I am asking you: given the above and unfortunately irremediable conditions, will you consider whether you would want to be my wife?

The forthright question was immediately followed by an avalanche of self-abasement: "I am a nothing, an absolute nothing. I know a little bit about judging people and putting myself in their place . . . but I don't believe I have ever met a single person who in the long run, on the average, here in this life and in his human relations (and after all, what else are we talking about?) is more hopelessly inadequate than I." He goes on to describe his antisocial nature, his lack of family feelings, his incapacity even for simple friendship:

> All of which might lead you to believe that I was born to the solitary life . . . when actually I cannot even get along with myself, except when I am writing. . . . Now consider what changes your marriage to me would bring about, what each of us would stand to gain and to lose. I would lose my for the most part terrifying loneliness, and gain you. . . . You, on the other hand, would lose a life with which you are almost wholly satisfied. You would lose Berlin, the office you enjoy, the girl friends, the small pleasures, the chance to marry a healthy, cheerful good man, to have beautiful and healthy children. . . . And you would lose in all the minor departments as well. . . . My income is probably no higher than yours. . . . I can expect little from my parents, nothing from my books. Which means that you would have to live on a much more modest scale than now. [FEL, 6/16/13]

A less promising marriage proposal would be hard to conceive. But Felice, accustomed by now to Kafka's style, accepted it with the same somewhat mystifying determination with which she had pushed for this resolution in the first place. That she was fond of him seems likely; just how her own neurosis meshed with his must remain a matter of speculation. She was obviously anxious to get married—anything rather than being "left on the shelf"—eager to leave home and to break out of a tense and antagonistic relationship with her parents, but she was certainly not equipped to gauge the true scope and severity of Kafka's difficulties and therefore overestimated her own ability to deal with them on a rational basis. Patiently she set out to refute his arguments, disclosed that she had substantial savings, assured him that having a good husband was more important to her than anything else. As to his "constitutional frailty," her only comment was: "Let's just forget about it."

Trapped in a double bind of his own design, Kafka quite literally "lay on the ground writhing and twisting like a wild beast," deluging her with impassioned pleas not to make any hasty decisions, and coming up with yet another argument that in his view militated even more decisively against marriage than his frailty: "To this, too, dearest, and to this perhaps above all, you fail to give sufficient weight in your deliberations: that writing is the one good feature of my being. . . . How will you put up with a marriage in which the husband . . . comes home from the office around 2:30 or 3, eats, goes to bed, sleeps until 7 or 8 in the evening, has a quick snack, takes a walk for an hour, then starts writing and writes on until 1 or 2 in the morning. Could you really put up with that?" (FEL, 6/21/13). "What I need for my writing is seclusion, not 'like a hermit,' that would not be sufficient, but like the dead. Writing in this sense is a sleep deeper than death, and just as one could not and would not drag a corpse out of his grave, I cannot be made to leave my desk at night, either" (FEL, 6/26/13). "Simply rush through the nights forever writing, that is what I want. To go to hell because of it, or go mad, that too is what I want, because it is the inevitable and long-foreshadowed consequence" (FEL, 7/13/13).

Writing, however, was the very release that had now become all but impossible. The creative stasis added living torture to his agony, bound and gagged him precisely at the point at which his writing was at last gaining a measure of critical recognition. The fact that this emphatic non-joiner, for all his solitary ways and resolute aversion to literary cliques, benefited enormously from the growing influence and widely ramified connections of Prague's literary-industrial complex may be evidence of compensatory justice or a mere ironic quirk of fate. But Brod, as already mentioned, discussed the *Meditations* on February 15, 1913, in the Munich weekly *März* and again in the August 1913 issue of the influential *Neue Rundschau*, a Vienna literary weekly edited by Robert Musil, who himself also reviewed the book favorably, if with somewhat more restrained enthusiasm. Kafka's poet-friend Otto Pick, on the other hand, gave it an ecstatic review in the radical Berlin weekly *Die Aktion*, while Albert Ehrenstein, another Prague littérateur, published a highly laudatory review on April 16, 1913, in the *Berliner Tageblatt*, Germany's largest and most respected liberal daily.

Their efforts on Kafka's behalf, while they did little for the book's sales (400 copies in five years following publication, about half the first edition), generated critical interest. It was favorably reviewed in at least another half dozen literary publications and, above all, brought Kafka's name before the public. When *The Stoker* appeared half a year later, in May 1913, as Volume III in Wolff's Doomsday Library, it received immediate attention. Articles by Hans Kohn in the Prague *Selbstwehr* and by Otto Pick in the *Prager Tagblatt* were followed by a perceptive discussion in the Vienna *Neue Freie Presse*, in which the Prague poet Camill Hoffmann transcended the common critical platitudes to stress the unique note of authentic, childlike naïveté reflected in the flawless and translucent prose. (Hoffmann, later cultural attaché at the Czech embassy in Berlin, vainly attempted in 1933 to retrieve a number of Kafka manuscripts from the clutches of the Gestapo. He himself perished in a Nazi death camp.) *The Stoker* even went into a second edition in 1916, though Kafka's royalties could hardly have amounted to more than a token.

His attitude toward his critics stands out in its sharp contrast to the morbid vulnerability he displayed in so many other spheres. While far from indifferent to what others had to say about his work—he frequently asked friends and publishers for copies of reviews—he accepted both praise and blame with uncommon and genuine equanimity. When it came to writing, he knew that he had no choice but to follow the dictates of his own inner voice; and no outsider, well-meaning or otherwise, was qualified to point the way. The tributes of his friends moved him to gratitude, but he dismissed them—often unjustly—as mere acts of friendship; an occasional hostile review seldom elicited more than puzzlement or a sardonic remark. He was always, after all, his own most severe critic, and the relatively small portion of his total output he consented to publish represented a selection of what he considered his most authentic work. Such as it was—and he never ceased discovering new flaws and shortcomings—he stood by it, and the opinions of strangers could tell him little that was of help. The tidal wave of critical interpretation that swelled his posthumous fame would probably have drowned him in short order.

But whatever brief satisfaction he may have derived from the reception of his books in that summer of 1913 was overshadowed by the paralyzing conflict over his marriage. The surge of inspiration that had carried him through the early months of his courtship and in fact— as he persuasively argued—provided the energy for this desperate venture had dissipated and left him in a state of utter desolation, rendered all the more unbearable by a decision practically forced upon him and which he was now doing his utmost to unmake even while lacking the courage to do so.

On July 3, 1913, his thirtieth birthday, he informed his mother ("quite briefly; she is never home for long and always through eating by the time I show up") that he had a fiancée. The news came as no surprise to Julie, who being every bit as practical and *geschäftstüchtig* as her putative daughter-in-law, immediately extorted Kafka's permission to order an investigative report on Felice's family from a commercial credit-rating bureau. (A lapse on his part he came to regret, and for which he fulsomely apologized.)

His writing, now and for months to come, was almost exclusively confined to his diary and letters, in which, with almost voluptuous passion and in ever more inventive formulations, he exposed what had long since ceased to be mere ambivalence and become a choice between hanging and being hanged. He explained to Felice that if he married her, he could never quit his job: "My worries about the two of us are worries incident to living; they are part of life, and for that very reason ultimately compatible with my work at the office. Whereas writing and the office are mutually exclusive. Writing has its center of gravity in the deep, while the office floats on the surface of life. The perennial up and down is bound to tear me to bits" (FEL, 6/26/13). A week later, he is "alarmed by what you say about my father; it is as if you were switching sides and making common cause with him against me" (FEL, 7/8/13). In fact, he has "a definite feeling that marriage, our union, the dissolution of this nothingness that I am, will doom me, and not only myself alone but also my wife" (FEL, 7/10/13).

On July 21, he drew up a balance sheet for himself of "everything that speaks for and against my marriage," coming up with six reasons against, and one in favor. "Inability to support life by myself. . . . My relationship with F. will lend more power of resistance to my existence" (DI, 7/21/13).

In the end, prudent foresight or plain desperation inspired him to join a housing cooperative, and he informed Felice that the apartment he had selected for them would not be available until the following May. Therefore, there was no longer any great urgency about his writing to her parents, and he proposed that they "leave everything as is until Christmas, or January, or February. You'll have a chance to get to know me even better, there are still some horrid nooks and crannies within me that you don't know about" (FEL, 7/13/13).

"As is," of course, though it enabled Kafka to postpone a commitment, resembled nothing so much as a state of siege, a personal counterpoint to developments in the outside world to which he remained resolutely indifferent. The sixtieth anniversary celebration of the Emperor Franz Joseph's coronation provoked violent anti-Austrian riots in Prague, led by the pan-Slav, pro-Russian Czech National Socialists. Once again, the Austrians moved in the troops and declared martial law on June 25, this time, however, going to the extreme of suspending not only the Prague Diet but also the Bohemian constitution, along with all the appurtenances of provincial autonomy. The show of force, though temporarily successful in restoring law and order, exacerbated the enmity between Czechs and Germans past all hope of a rational settlement. The ominous tension continued to mount until the outbreak of the war a year later and played its part in hastening the ultimate breakup of the multinational state.

Whether out of fatalism or indifference—both widely shared by his friends—Kafka seems to have taken little notice of these events, to the point where it would be difficult to ascribe to him any clear-cut sympathies for either side, the less so since the extremist demagogues now prevailing in both camps were equally vocal in their common hostility to the Jews. In any case, his personal problems loomed considerably larger than any crisis of empire and left little strength for other concerns. He had given up on gardening and acquired a boat instead, which he kept tied up in the river at the foot of his house and used for Sunday outings. But rowing did no more for his peace of mind than gardening had done, and in due course he would no doubt have come across the tale or body of a melancholy oarsman who had drowned his sorrows and himself. The movies continued to fascinate him, and he seems to have seen every new film shown in town. The human scene, on the other hand, seemed particularly bleak that summer, what with Brod newly wed, Weltsch contemplating marriage, Werfel working in Leipzig as reader for Kurt Wolff, Oskar Baum not only married but a parent, and the extending Kafka family more unbearable than ever. The only new acquaintance, and one who was to exert a not insignificant influence on his relationship to Felice, was Ernst Weiss, author of *The Galley*, Jewish physician, and "typical Western European Jew, to whom one therefore feels instantly close" (DI, 7/1/13).

Weiss, though only a year older than Kafka, projected the authority of an already impressive life experience. The son of a Brno textile manufacturer, he had lost his father at the age of four, discovered Freud instead while studying medicine in Vienna, but ultimately specialized in surgery, probably for the same self-destructive reasons that dominated most aspects of his life, down to his tragic end in 1940. In 1911, during a nightmarish residency, he completed his first novel, *The Galley*, which Kafka thought "ardent and beautiful." Near-destitute, ill with tuberculosis, Weiss subsequently spent two years traveling as a ship's doctor in the Far East. On his return, just around the time Kafka first met him, he decided to drop medicine altogether and settle as a freelance writer in Berlin, convinced that creative work demanded absolute freedom and independence.

It is easy to understand the mutual attraction between these two in certain ways kindred spirits, though in the long run Weiss probably troubled Kafka a great deal more than he helped him, both by his implacable hostility to Felice and by the ruthless rigor with which he forced himself to confront head-on many of the same problems that constantly seemed to defeat Kafka. At the outbreak of the war, Weiss volunteered because "the world now needs healers, not poets," and in 1916 was stationed in Prague, where close personal contact with Kafka finally led to a complete break between them, though each continued to think highly of the other's work. A reconciliation of sorts was effected in the final years of Kafka's life.

A brilliant paranoiac, himself hopelessly mired in a lifelong hate-love affair with the actress Johanna Bleschke, alias Rachel Sanzara, Weiss went on to become a prolific poet and successful author of some twenty well-received novels. He fled to France in 1933; his last novel, based on a secret medical report concerning Hitler's hysterical blindness during the First World War, was written in 1939 and entered in a contest for German refugee writers held in New York. Weiss staked his hopes for both a prize and a U.S. visa on it. The prize went to somebody else; the visa was eventually obtained in 1940 through the efforts of Thomas Mann. By then, however, the Germans had occupied Paris, and Weiss, much like Walter Benjamin, killed himself just shortly before the papers could be delivered. His manuscript surfaced in New York long after the war and was published in 1962; an English translation came out in 1977 under the title *The Eyewitness*.

* * *

In response to Kafka's perennial vacillations, Felice again withdrew into a detached indifference which succeeded in completely unnerving him. He began to suffer from the severe headaches and bouts of insomnia that were to plague him for years. He assured her that he lived only through and for her letters, and in reply to her suggestion that "he talk things over with Max," he rather heatedly demanded what there was to talk about.

> For that which concerns only the two of us, no one can assume responsibility, nor therefore offer advice. But if I should let myself be guided by Max's example in matters of financial management, things would indeed be sad. Max has more money than I, also more of an income, he is neither stingy nor spendthrift—and yet, in his house there is more talk of money and the lack of it than is good for them. And this constant harping on the subject—for which probably his wife, though in all innocence, is to blame—lends it an exaggerated importance which one can easily refuse to attach to it even in the face of real penury. [FEL, 8/1/13]

In August, Felice took her vacation at the North Sea and rejected his suggestion to spend part of it in Prague. He, in turn, disclosed that for some time now he had been suffering from "heart pains" and palpitations, dismissed by the family doctor as not of organic origin and which he himself ascribed in part to too much swimming and vigorous walking, but "mostly, though not entirely, to the unbearable separation from you" (FEL, 8/4/13).

After a month of tormented and tormenting letters that came close to cracking even Felice's steadfast composure, he finally gathered up the courage to confront his father and announce his intention to marry —a momentous step in his own eyes, perfectly well aware though he was that Herrmann had been kept duly informed of developments all along. "Did I ever tell you that I admire my father? You know that he is my enemy, just as I am his enemy, an enmity determined by our respective natures. Yet aside from that, my admiration for him as a person is perhaps as great as my fear of him. I can get around him in a pinch, but roll over him, never" (FEL, 8/24/13). He also wrote to Felice's father, formally asking for her hand, while at the same time enumerating all the reasons why his proposal should not be accepted. And to Felice herself he wrote that "of the four men whom . . . I regard as my actual blood relations—Grillparzer, Dostoevsky, Kleist, and Flaubert—only Dostoevsky got married, and perhaps only Kleist found the right way out when, driven by inner and outer need, he shot himself at Wannsee" (FEL, 9/2/13).

Though repeatedly tempted to emulate Kleist, Kafka finally chose a less drastic escape route. On September 6, he left for Vienna to participate in an international congress on rescue techniques and accident prevention; the papers presented by his two immediate superiors, Marschner and Pfohl, had largely been written by him. As it happened, the Eleventh World Zionist Congress was also meeting in Vienna at the same time, so that the city, which he cordially detested under the best of circumstances, was swarming with his friends and acquaintances among the literati, Zionists, and insurance experts. He did his best to avoid socializing—"all I keep doing is run away from literature and congresses," though he went to see Weiss and accompanied Lise Weltsch to a session of the Zionist Congress, at which he felt a total stranger. "Zionist Congress. The type of people with small round heads, firm cheeks. Labor delegates from Palestine, constant shouting. Herzl's daughter. . . . Pointless speeches in German, much Hebrew, real work done in small committees. Lise W. just lets herself be dragged along by the whole thing without really taking part in it, tosses spitballs into the hall. Hopeless" (FEL, 9/10/13).

Having arranged his annual vacation in conjunction with the business trip, he went on to Trieste on September 14 and got seasick on the brief ferry ride to Venice, where he spent four utterly miserable days brooding over his fate. Though he had agreed with Felice on no letters until after his return, he could not refrain from sending her a few more wildly desperate notes ending with "We must say goodbye."

As usual, he concluded the trip in a sanatorium, this time at Riva, where he stayed from September 22 to October 13 and recovered to quite some extent from his depression, though the remarkable if temporary cure can scarcely be credited to the therapeutic ministrations of the institute's owner and resident shaman, a Dr. von Hartingen. What happened instead was that Kafka fell deeply in love.

Once again the object of his passion was a very young girl, younger even than his own youngest sister, "a child, about eighteen, Swiss but living in Italy, near Genoa, thus as alien to me by blood as can be, quite unformed but remarkable and, despite a morbid streak, a very real person with great depth" (FEL, 1/2/14). The affair, probably platonic (he later speculated that it might have cost him a chance to sleep with an interesting and interested Russian lady), lasted only ten days; the girl exacted a promise of total discretion and barred all further contact, including correspondence. It was no doubt this very hopelessness with its safeguard against future complications that enabled Kafka to give rein at last to his long-suppressed sexuality and led to a lyrical interlude which he was always to remember with considerable feeling. "Too late. The sweetness of mourning and of love. To have her smile at me in the boat. That was more beautiful than anything. Always the wish to die, and the still just-hanging-on, that alone is love" (DI, 10/22/13). Moreover, the exogamic nature of the relationship clearly added to it the piquancy of the forbidden: "My stay at Riva was of great importance to me. For the first time I understood a Gentile girl and lived almost completely within her sphere of action" (DI, 10/15/13).

On October 29, following his return to Prague and after six weeks of silence, Kafka again wrote to Felice. The tone of the letter was markedly more resolute; and though he told her that his yearning for her crushed him like the weight of unwept tears, he in effect broke off the unofficial engagement.

Twenty

END of story, or so it seemed, another project abandoned as hopeless, though a vast sense of relief clearly eased the pain. Kafka's season in hell, four seasons, in fact; an eternity of hysterical self-torment and creative impotence.

He had survived, always a major triumph in his eyes, come back from Riva chastened and subdued, older by far and almost at peace with himself. Nothing had changed; and yet, as the notably different tone of his letters reveals, everything had changed. If life—Felice, the office, the father—had lost none of its terror, he now was able to contemplate it with a measure of maturity and inchoate wisdom that carried over into his fiction.

As for the story itself: this was not to be the end, after all.

For one thing, though far more lucid now about his doubts and more decisive about his indecision, he had come no closer to resolving the basic conflict between wanting to get married, accomplishing "the supreme act of social integration," and wanting to remain free, in total isolation from the world, alone "with pen and lamp in the innermost room of a cave." And for another, the story once again developed a momentum of its own, opened on uncharted depths that defied neat endings, and dredged up murky creatures who took it out of his hands and left him no choice but to follow their lead. In this instance, it was a friend, sent by Felice to mediate between them, who turned up at precisely the point where Kafka seemed all but done with the final version and forced him to rewrite it once again, this time as a cruel fairy tale for grownups.

* * *

Grete Bloch, from what little is known about her, could in fact have been a vision straight out of Kafka's fiction, sharply delineated in meticulous detail, yet framed by a mysterious obscurity of sinister potential. It was on October 29, 1913—the very day, as it happened, on which Kafka wrote the first letter to Felice since his return from Riva and in which he once more spelled out his determination to end the relationship—that the emissary sent him a note explaining how she happened to be in Prague on business and asking to see him on behalf of Felice. And although reluctant—"Under ordinary circumstances I would have been happy to meet you; but I have come to realize that discussions, rather than helping me see more clearly, only tend to confuse me further; and as no doubt you can imagine, more confusion is hardly what I need"—he ultimately agreed. Instead of the "aging spinster" he had expected, he found a twenty-one-year-old woman whose precocious intelligence and forthright sympathy more than made up for her lack of physical attraction.

Grete and Felice had known each other for only about six months, but the manifold similarities between them favored a fast friendship which far outlasted their relations to Kafka. Born in Berlin in 1892, Grete graduated from a commercial academy in 1908 and started working as a stenographer-typist for a major manufacturer of office equipment, where she rapidly rose to the post of executive assistant. Like Felice, she was enormously hardworking, conscientious, and efficient, but emotionally far more brittle and withdrawn. In 1916, Felice informed Kafka of a dramatic crisis in Grete Bloch's life; its precise nature remained unspecified, but Kafka repeatedly expressed his concern—"How does Miss Bloch take it, and what does it mean to her?"—and urged Felice to be supportive: "I am much upset at the thought of Miss Grete's troubles, and I am sure you won't desert her this time as, incomprehensibly, you sometimes did in the past" (FEL, 9/1/16).

Grete Bloch never married. In 1935, escaping from Nazi Germany, she stopped off in Geneva and turned over to Felice the part of Kafka's correspondence with her that has been included in the published volume of his *Letters to Felice*. After a brief stay in Palestine, she settled in Florence, Italy, where in 1944 she was caught in a Nazi roundup of Jews and murdered en route to an extermination camp.

The tragic circumstances of her death probably make it impossible ever definitely to resolve the question of whether or not she was the mother of a child by Kafka.

This, at any rate, was the claim she made on the eve of the Second World War in Florence, where according to local acquaintances she had become obsessively loquacious about her romance with the late writer. In a letter of April 21, 1940, to the musician Walter Schocken in Palestine, she specifically asserted that she had had a boy, fathered by Kafka, who died in Munich in 1921 at the age of just under seven; she had kept the child's birth, brief life, and sudden death a strict secret from everyone, including the alleged father.

While it seems highly plausible to assume that "Miss Grete's troubles" alluded to by Kafka in 1916 may have involved a pregnancy, the available evidence speaks strongly against his paternity. For one thing, the dates conflict; a child aged seven in 1921 would have had to be born around 1914, and though some of Kafka's letters of the period have undoubtedly been destroyed, nothing in his surviving correspondence with Grete Bloch permits one to assume that they even had the opportunity for the requisite intimacy. In May 1915 Grete joined Kafka and Felice on a trip to the Bohemian mountains, an unlikely arrangement, given the background of all concerned, if at that point she had either carried or given birth to a child by her girl friend's fiancé. By 1916, on the other hand, Kafka no longer had any direct contact with Grete Bloch. Finally, it seems inconceivable that a man of his sensitivity and hypertrophied conscience would at any time have so casually referred to "Miss Grete's troubles" and mobilized his fiancée on her behalf had he had even the remotest reason to suspect himself of having any part in them.

None of this, of course, adds up to conclusive proof either way. The most persuasive hypothesis is the tragic self-delusion of a frightened and lonely woman, cracking under the strain of her increasingly precarious existence as a refugee without a refuge. Faced with impending and already clearly discernible disaster, she may have sought that refuge in the past and begun to confuse fact and fantasy. That she had a child is likely; that she was once in love with Kafka is certain. And in the growing darkness around her, those two crucial experiences may have fused in a myth that became part of her remembered life and gave it the meaning she so desperately wanted it to have.

Other Kafka biographers, Max Brod foremost among them, do not share this opinion. Brod, to whom Walter Schocken disclosed Grete Bloch's letter in 1948, unquestioningly accepted it at face value, just as he accepted Gustav Janouch's "minutes" of his conversations with Kafka. That Brod assumed everyone to be as scrupulously truthful as he was himself does him honor, though his relentless exuberance might have benefited from a dash of healthy skepticism. Less justifiable is the conclusion he drew, with characteristic bathos, from what he regarded as a sensational revelation: "It seems hard to imagine what a blessedly wholesome effect it might have had on Kafka's development for him to learn that he was the father of a son. There was nothing he more fervently desired than to have children. . . . Everyone familiar with his work can cite the relevant passages in which he speaks of his yearning to be a father sitting by the cradle of his child" (Brod, bio., p. 210).

This is sentimental twaddle, at best the aging, childless Brod's projection of his own pietistic feelings. His picture of a snugly domesticated Kafka in bathrobe and slippers rocking the cradle by the light of his own halo is one of those mythopoeic fantasies which led Kafka to declare that "Max does not understand me, and when he thinks he does, he is wrong" (FEL, 4/20/14). True, in the abstract Kafka did exalt marriage and fatherhood as a triumph over mortality and a ticket of admission to the tribal shrine from which he felt excluded. In practice, however, he not only clung to his exclusion but also held far less exalted and supremely realistic views of marriage and parenthood, amply substantiated by firsthand observations of their devastating effect on his parents, friends, and relatives. And if he freely indulged in wistful dreams of patriarchal bliss, he also had no use whatsoever for real live children. How he would have received the news of his paternity, and of the crushing responsibilities that went with it, is anybody's guess. One somehow doubts, though, that his reaction would have been one of unalloyed joy.

* * *

The role of confidante in a lovers' quarrel is delicate at best. The fact that the disputants in this case hardly qualified as lovers, and that the intermediary was herself lonelier and less mature by far than either of them, merely added to the ambiguities inherent in the situation. And whether or not these included sexual intimacy between Kafka and Grete Bloch seems almost beside the point; the fact is that the two very soon found themselves drawn to one another. To Kafka, Grete became the good fairy protecting him from the bad one, the maternal friend to whom he could freely pour out his heart in complaints about the treatment he received at the hands of the witch mother. In the first six months of 1914, he wrote far more frequently, and at far greater length, to Grete than to Felice. Grete, on the other hand, fell hopelessly in love with the aging gentleman she always addressed as "Doctor," apparently one in a succession of father figures to whom she formed attachments in the course of a lonely and tragic life.

The immediate result of Grete's intervention, however, was that Kafka, heeding Felice's request, took the weekend off and went to see her in Berlin. He had his doubts ahead of time—"Do you really expect our meeting to clarify matters? I, too, believe it to be essential; but as to clarity . . . ? Don't you remember that each meeting left you more unsettled than ever? That only in our letters were we able to rise above our doubts, those letters that contain the better part of me?" (FEL, 11/6/13)—but the actual experience turned out even more humiliating than he had anticipated. Having asked him to travel seven hours each way in two days, Felice could only spare him two hours, which they spent walking in the park on Saturday morning. He left on Sunday with no further word from her.

This time, however, he had a chance to unburden himself. Right after his return, on November 10, 1913, he sent Grete a detailed report on his Berlin fiasco, the first in a series of confessions in which, with practiced hand, he picked apart the bonds between him and Felice and dissected his own ambivalence. But as always, the act of writing quickly transcended its objective function and became his means of reaching out—for what, exactly, he may not yet have troubled to envisage. As the confessions grew more intimate, and relations with Felice seemed to deteriorate beyond hope of repair, the tone became markedly more affectionate. Grete at the time was working in her firm's Vienna branch office, cut off from her Berlin circle, as miserable on the job as in her dingy furnished room, and Kafka's by now almost daily letters full of warm, compassionate concern must have been a great comfort. His usual barrage of insistent and specific questions conveyed an intense personal interest no longer linked to Felice. He offered fatherly advice on everything, from books and authors to proper dental care and diet, subjects on which he had very authoritative opinions. Above all, he urged her to get out of Vienna, that "moribund super-village" he blamed for so much of her misery. She, in turn, was grateful, impressed, and above all responsive; by the end of February they were making plans for a meeting at Easter.

Kafka's relations with Felice, in the meantime, had entered a near-total eclipse. For six weeks following their Berlin encounter she answered none of his letters, triggering another of their cyclic role reversals. Now that it was she who rejected him, the loss was seen not only as a blow to his self-esteem but as a threat to his future existence altogether, and on New Year's Day, 1914 he once again asked her to marry him. In contrast to his first proposal, this one was a sober attempt to gauge their chances of at least minimal happiness in the light of everything that had transpired between them. He knew what she would stand to lose. "On my part, there was never any question of 'loss,' but merely of an obstacle. And that obstacle," he assured her, "no longer exists," unequivocal notice that for whatever reasons—the Riva affair, some other experience, or simply a newfound maturity—his "constitutional weakness" no longer seemed to worry him. (This remark could, of course, also be made to support the hypothesis of sexual relations between him and Grete Bloch.) "Marriage is the only form in which our relationship, so vital to me, can be maintained. . . . And now decide, Felice" (FEL, 1/1/14).

For over a month, Felice left him dangling and simply gave no sign of life. His family had in the meantime moved away from the river back toward the center of town, into a fourth-floor apartment in the stately Oppelt House at the very corner of Old Town Square, a few steps from the Kinsky Palace, where he had gone to school and where his parents' business was now located. He sounded rather pleased with the change: "Directly opposite my window . . . is the great dome of the Russian church with its two towers, and between the dome and the neighboring apartment house I have a distant view . . . of the Laurenzis Hill with its tiny church. On my left the Town Hall rises sharply in a perspective that perhaps no one has ever really seen before" (FEL, 12/29/13).

But the first few weeks of the new year were desolate and depressing, and Felice's failure to respond merely added tension to the silence around him. For months he had been unable to write. Relations with Brod had now cooled perceptibly; not only was "a married friend not a friend," but the friend's marriage had itself already entered its first crisis as Brod embarked on a stormy (and long-lived) affair with a would-be actress in Berlin. The most serious issue between them, however, was Brod's increasingly dogmatic Zionism; Kafka's oft-cited note of January 8, 1914, "What do I have in common with the Jews? I have hardly anything in common with myself," must be read in the context of their running argument on the subject, though it also no doubt reflects his acute sense of isolation. The friendship nonetheless survived the tempest, and he was moved when, in February, Brod dedicated what was to become his most successful novel, *Tycho Brahe's Path to God*, to "my friend Franz Kafka." Ernst Weiss, whom he saw frequently, was of no help when it came to Felice; he had gone to see her in Berlin at Kafka's behest and come away with a fierce dislike of her in which he was never to waver (though late in life he seems to have somewhat revised his opinion). Felix Weltsch was about to be married, and in a letter to Grete, Kafka professed relief at the inevitable demise of this close friendship: "We formed a kind of bachelor fraternity which I, at least, at certain moments experienced as downright spooky. This has now been dissolved; I am free. Alone, everyone can be what he is and wants to be" (FEL, 2/19/14).

Grete, or rather his letters to her, thus became his most solid human contact. After five weeks of waiting for an answer to his latest proposal, he received a noncommittal postcard from Felice, again followed by a total blackout that finally drove him to try once more what had never worked before. Their meeting in Berlin on February 28 remained predictably inconclusive, as he described it to Grete: "F. rather likes me, but in her opinion this is not enough for marriage, not for this marriage."

Throughout the month of March, his attempts to see Grete, to arrange for at least a brief encounter somewhere midway between Prague and Vienna, became ever more insistent; they finally settled on April 12, Easter Sunday, as a likely date. Felice was still not heard from, and on March 25 Kafka told Grete that "the final, quite futile deadline" he had set was expiring the next day and that, unless he had a letter—"totally inconceivable"—both he and Felice "would be free."

Inconceivable or not, the letter arrived in the nick of time: Felice agreed to marry him.

Her abrupt about-face after months of equivocation and outright hostility came as a stunning surprise. And even had he been more adept at self-deception, Kafka would have had a hard time convincing himself that "the heart has its reasons" and that it was love, after all, that had tipped the balance. To Grete, who seemed somewhat perplexed, he affirmed that in essence nothing had changed between him and Felice.

True, as far as it went. But a drastic change had, in fact, taken place back in Berlin, seriously affecting Felice's family and her own life situation. The discovery of certain financial indiscretions had

induced her adored younger brother Ferdinand abruptly and unceremoniously to abandon fiancée, family, and *Vaterland* and, like
Kafka's hero, try for a fresh start in Amerika; he had left for the
United States in early March. The scandal was a devastating blow to the
Bauers. Felice, moreover, also faced the prospect of added burdens,
financial as well as emotional. It seems hardly unfair to suspect that,
in the circumstances, the idea of marriage and all it entailed, specifically
the chance of putting Berlin, the disconsolate family, and the inevitable
gossip behind her, would suddenly appear in a different and altogether
more appealing light.

Thus on Easter Sunday, instead of meeting Grete, Kafka went to
Berlin to settle the terms and conditions of his engagement. Tired,
distracted, and basically indifferent, as he himself admitted, he put up
little resistance to Felice's demands. He yielded to her preference for
the hideous bourgeois furniture he detested and even agreed to a religious
ceremony, to which he had been opposed on principle. The wedding
was scheduled for September, and announcements of the engagement
appeared in both the *Prager Tagblatt* and the *Berliner Tageblatt*.

The six weeks separating the unofficial from the "official" engagement merely provided further evidence that, aside from such technical
arrangements, nothing had fundamentally changed in the relationship
itself. Even while describing his engagement, Kafka insisted to Grete
that he felt "a very strong and real longing" for her and again proposed
a meeting, perhaps *à trois*—"I don't know if this is permissible to
people who are engaged. Those not engaged are much better off; they
are permitted to do everything and don't have to do anything" (FEL,
4/5/14). He assured her that neither engagement nor marriage would
make any difference in how he felt about her and refused outright to
heed her request for the return of her letters. But though he continued
to press for a meeting with at least a show of naïveté that seems
excessive, Grete quite sensibly would have no part of it and did not
show up in Prague even when Felice arrived there at the beginning of
May, mainly to be in on the search for suitable living quarters. Kafka
himself dutifully simulated prenuptial flutter, but in the end it was his
parents who found them a pleasant three-room apartment at Langegasse
(now Dlouha) 923, a few blocks from Kafka's office; the monthly rent
of 1,300 crowns amounted to slightly over one-fourth of his salary.
In commenting on this latest demonstration of parental competence,
he was to prove tragically prescient: "My parents seem to have found

a nice apartment for F. and myself, while I wasted a beautiful afternoon rushing about in vain. I wonder if they will also lay me in my grave, after a life made happy thanks to their solicitude" (DI, 5/6/14).

The official engagement was celebrated at a reception in Berlin on May 30, 1914, at the Bauer home in the presence of both families. The mutual sympathy that developed between the two mothers, an uncommon enough sentiment sedulously ignored by Kafka, was to survive many of the vicissitudes of his relationship to Felice. He himself described the festive occasion in terms that already anticipate the sequel: "I was tied up like a criminal. Had they stood me in a corner, put me in real chains, posted policemen around me, and only let me look on like that, it could not have been worse. And that was my engagement, with everyone trying to make me come alive and, since they didn't succeed, putting up with me the way I was. F., be it said, least of all, and for good reason, since she was the one who suffered most. What to the others was merely a matter of appearance was a threat to her" (DI, 6/6/14).

No sooner back in Prague, though, than he furiously began to rattle the chains. Among the June entries in his diary are three haunting and haunted stories, eerie visions of nameless dread. But in his letters to Grete Bloch he was much more explicit about what it was that haunted him, putting her in an extremely awkward position. Here was the man whose formal engagement to her girl friend she had just attended—and with whom she had herself become infatuated—marshaling once again all the arguments that spoke against his marriage, and countering her every doubt and objection with ever more damaging confessions that could leave her with only one final, unanswerable question: why, given the way he felt, did he want to marry Felice in the first place?

On June 27, Kafka went to Dresden, mainly to visit the garden suburb of Hellerau, founded five years earlier as an artists' colony and now a thriving center of avant-garde culture. He especially wanted to see the experimental school run by Émile Jaques-Dalcroze, whose eurythmics method and educational theories had aroused his interest. Greatly impressed, Kafka in later years tried vainly to persuade his sisters to send their children to what by then had become A. S. Neill's Hellerau International Institute, forerunner of Summerhill—"release them from the grownups' cage . . . where they have been raised in luxury . . . without physical activity, without physical culture . . . without exercising eyes, ears, and hands." He also inspected Hellerau's

German Craft Workshops, which, foreshadowing Bauhaus principles and ideas, were turning out precisely the kind of functional furniture that appealed to him and served to exacerbate his dread of the ornate monstrosities that Felice's bourgeois taste was about to inflict on him.

The following day, June 28, 1914, he met in Leipzig with Kurt Wolff, Werfel, Willy Haas, and a number of satellite literati. There is no record of their having discussed the morning's news from the little Bosnian town of Sarajevo, where the Austrian crown prince and his wife had just fallen victims to an *Attentat* by Serb nationalists. Strangely enough, Kafka's diary alludes to that day's "horror beyond horrors," but the reference is to the tremors and convulsions in his own soul rather than to the distant rumble in the entrails of hell.

On July 3, his thirty-first birthday, Grete Bloch—by now transferred back to Berlin—told him that her having so desperately worked toward his engagement as a prelude to a happy marriage burdened her "with a boundless responsibility to which I no longer feel equal." Grimly triumphant, he wrote back that "I could now say that I have convinced you at last" (FEL, 7/3/14).

*   *   *

She was convinced, all right, but it is doubtful if even Kafka was quite prepared for the consequences. Grete Bloch now felt driven to rescue Felice by whatever means; one may charitably assume that she experienced this compulsion as a moral obligation and remained unaware of the part that jealousy and guilt played in her decision.

On July 11, Kafka left for Berlin, intending to continue from there with both Felice and Grete to the North Sea resort of Gleschendorf, where the three of them were to spend part of their summer vacation together. Instead, the next morning he found his hotel room transformed into a courtroom, and himself the defendant in the dock.

Felice was the plaintiff, and she had brought Grete Bloch along as well as her sister Erna. Ernst Weiss was summoned as an attorney for the defense, although feeling as he did, he could only have been pleased with an outcome predictable from the start. For the evidence against Kafka was overwhelming and irrefutable. He had himself provided it with extravagant abandon in his many letters to Grete, from which Felice proceeded to quote a substantial number of incriminating passages.

Kafka refused to defend himself, remained silent, not—as Felice later charged—out of truculence, "but because I had nothing decisive to say. I realized that all was lost, realized also that I could still save it at the last minute through some surprise confession, but I had nothing surprising to confess" (FEL, 11/14).

Arguments nonetheless dragged on for some hours as Felice, goaded to open fury by his silence, kept unwrapping and displaying a whole hoard of grievances, "well-thought-out, long-nursed, hostile." Throughout the trial itself, Kafka kept feeling that it was Grete who sat in judgment over him; on later reflection, he came to realize that, as always, he had himself been judge as well as executioner.

The verdict was a foregone conclusion, the formal engagement formally dissolved.

* * *

He left Berlin the next day, traveling as far as Lübeck, where two days later Ernst Weiss and his companion, Rachel Sanzara, caught up with him; the three went on together to the Dutch seaside resort of Marielyst. How deep a wound the "trial" at the Askanischer Hof had struck is amply evident from its echoes in the fictional *Trial*; and yet, on the face of it, the defeat and betrayal had not only failed to crush him but, on the contrary, engendered a new sense of freedom. In a letter from Marielyst addressed jointly to Brod and Weltsch, he broke the news of his aborted engagement: "Actually, though, I am well aware that it is all for the best and, since I see the clear necessity of it, I am not nearly as upset about the matter as one might expect. . . . I have dispensed with the apparent stubbornness that cost me my engagement and eat here almost nothing but meat, which makes me sick, so that I wake up after bad nights with my mouth wide open and my abused and tortured body like an alien and disgusting presence in my bed" (L, 7/14).

The Berlin trial, however scarred it had left him, put a temporary end to his ambivalence. Honestly or dishonestly, he had tried and failed to enter the kingdom of marriage. But if the gate leading to manhood and mankind was barred to him, there was no further point in wasting his life impersonating the obedient son and conscientious employee. Ardently encouraged, no doubt by Ernst Weiss, who was little short of fanatical on the subject, he decided to give up his job, leave Prague, settle in Berlin, and support himself by his writing. On July 22, still in Marielyst, he drafted a letter to his parents explaining his decision at great length. He felt, so he told them, that in the stifling atmosphere of Prague he could never aspire to truly adult independence. Moreover, with the collapse of his marriage plans, his career as a bureaucrat with its prospect of lifetime security no longer made any sense. He had saved 5,000 crowns, enough to live on for two years in Germany while concentrating only on his writing. The stature and reputation he was bound to attain during that grace period would, he felt sure, make it possible for him to live thereafter from his literary work.

Whether or not he would ever have realized these plans must remain an open question. The decision seemed firmly grounded in growing self-confidence and maturity, but it was preempted by events to which Kafka, like most of his friends, like most of the world, had up to that point paid little if any attention. The very next day, on July 23, Austria presented Serbia with an ultimatum. Three days later, Kafka returned to Prague. On the twenty-eighth, Austria declared war on Serbia. Karl Hermann, Elli's husband, was immediately called up in the general mobilization and left his accursed asbestos factory in the incompetent hands of his resentful brother-in-law. On August 2, Kafka noted in his diary that "Germany has declared war on Russia. Swimming pool in the afternoon."

Twenty-one

Except for a handful of prophets and madmen, no one really believed that war was about to break out, or if it did, that it would last more than a few weeks. Even those who knew enough to see the lights go out all over Europe only feared darkness in their own time. For forty-three years, ever since the Franco-Prussian War of 1870–71, no armed confrontations had taken place on the Continent itself. England fought the Boers in Africa, the tsar's armies were routed by the Japanese in far-off Siberia, and Austria's Balkan intrigues had led to localized brief clashes in 1912 and 1913. There was some apprehension in the air, mixed with elation at the prospect of adventure or at least a break in the routine, but it was still universally taken for granted, in those early days of August, that Austria's moves against the "terrorist sanctuaries" in Serbia would end in another quick victory and go down in history as the Third Balkan War. Sigmund Freud, a far more sophisticated observer than Kafka and with considerable expertise in reality-testing, reported from Vienna on July 26 that "for the first time in thirty years I feel myself to be an Austrian and feel like giving this not very hopeful empire another chance. Morale everywhere is excellent."

Forty-three years of peace and progress had, by common consensus, made war between the advanced industrial nations of the West unthinkable, hence impossible. The destructive potential of modern arms, the interdependence of capitalist economies, and the solidarity of Europe's working class as embodied in the Socialist International with its over 4 million members had rendered military confrontations obsolete.

Common consensus, however, is the product not of thought but of wishful thinking. For over a decade, the economies of Western Europe, for all their interdependence, had been harnessed to the goal of national offense and been all but wrecked in the process, as evidenced by a deepening crisis and severe unemployment. As for the Socialist International, it had long since turned into a paper camel led by calcified bureaucrats who, even had they wanted to, could never have implemented their ritual threats against the imperialist warmongers.

This time, however, they didn't even deem it necessary to go through the motions. Meeting in emergency session at Brussels on July 29 and 30, they concluded—not without some notable dissent—that Austria's quarrel with Serbia was a purely local issue which did not warrant action on the part of labor, especially not within Austria proper, where immoderate opposition was liable to jeopardize the legal status of the Socialist Party. Preserving the party was clearly more important than living up to its principles.

Whereupon the socialist leaders went home, like Kafka, to take a bath.

Of the dissenters, Jaurès was assassinated the following day, Liebknecht and Luxemburg went to jail. Friedrich Adler—whose father, Victor, as titular head of the Austrian party, cast his vote in favor of the Austrian assault on Serbia—two years later was to assassinate the Austrian prime minister as a gesture of protest against the war and against his father. Yet even they, in their worst nightmares, could not have foreseen what lay ahead, any more than the criminals and imbeciles who played with matches and set the world on fire.

*   *   *

Returning home from Marielyst the day after the Austrian ultimatum, Kafka traveled clear across Germany, with a brief stopover in Berlin for a post-mortem with Felice's sister Erna. The country was girding for war, and even he, preoccupied as he was with his own battles, took note of the discipline, confidence, and enthusiasm with which the population seemed to be reacting to events. As always, he was impressed by the conspicuous manifestations of German efficiency, as compared to the perennial Austrian *Schlamperei* with which he was so intimately familiar. For months, and even years thereafter, he alone among his friends remained convinced of an eventual German victory—without, however, having much of a stake in the outcome either way.

At bottom, it wasn't really anyone's war where he came from; Prague was on a different planet from Vienna or Berlin. Max Brod in his memoirs has left a telling description of the attitudes prevailing in his native enclave:

> War to us was simply a crazy idea, of a piece with, say, the perpetual motion machine or the fountain of youth. . . . We were a spoiled generation, spoiled by nearly fifty years of peace that had made us lose sight of mankind's worst scourge. No one with any self-esteem ever got involved in politics. Arguments about Wagner's music, about the foundations of Judaism and Christianity, about Impressionist painting and the like seemed infinitely more important. . . . And now, overnight, peace had suddenly collapsed. We were quite simply stupid . . . not even pacifists, because pacifism at least presupposes a notion of there being such a thing as war, and of the need to fight against it. [Brod, St. L., p. 82]

Brod, however, unlike Kafka, did not go swimming. Shaken to his depths by Austria's declaration of war on July 28, he quite simply decided that something had to be done to save the world and repaired to the Café Arco for consultation with his fellow aesthetes and intellectuals. They unanimously agreed that of all men living and accessible, Tomáš Masaryk, champion of truth and justice, was the only one who possessed the moral authority, intellectual stature, and political wisdom to deflect the great powers from their collision course by a last-minute appeal to reason.

No sooner said than done. A three-man delegation was elected, consisting of Brod himself, the already mobilized Franz Werfel resplendent in his uniform, and the young professor Max Wertheimer, who later founded the Gestalt school of experimental psychology. The three emissaries set out to corner the great man in his dingy, cluttered office off Wenceslas Square, where he edited the small but influential newspaper of his Realist Party. Masaryk received them politely, listened to their proposals, but his only response was a piece of gruff advice: he urged them to see to it that their "compatriots"—meaning German-speaking Jews—stopped informing on Czechs supposedly disloyal to the Austrian cause; several such cases had been brought to his attention.

With that he dismissed them and, a few days later, vanished from the scene. Not until December, when he turned up in Paris as the leader of the Czech liberation movement, did it dawn on Brod and his idealistic friends that with the outbreak of the war, the head of the

Realists had realistically abandoned the idea of an Austrian federation and, unlike Freud, was no longer willing to give the empire another chance.

The episode illustrates the touching naïveté of even the few would-be activists in Kafka's circle and, beyond that, the ever-precarious position of Prague's Jewish community at large, a position whose inherent ambiguities were bound to be sharply exacerbated by the outbreak of hostilities. There was no doubt at all about how the Czech majority— 90 percent of Prague's population—felt about the Austrians, even though actual subversion was, at least initially, kept more or less in check by the usual repressive measures perfected through centuries of Habsburg rule. They included martial law, suspension of all civil rights, including trial by jury, censorship of all communications; fatuously benign measures compared to current practices, but draconian by the standards to which the First World War so effectively put an end. The Czech response was widespread passive resistance of the sort immortalized by Jaroslav Hašek's *Good Soldier Švejk*, the antithetical twin brother to Kafka's Joseph K., as Brecht was first to point out.

Prague's German Germans, on the other hand, made up in stiff-lipped arrogance and patriotic fervor for what they lacked in numbers, and the official voices purporting to speak for German Jewry surpassed them, if anything, in fulsome affirmations of loyalty. Many Jews were, in fact, ardently pro-German, enlisted at once, and gave their lives for the defense of Teutonic civilization. Many more, however, were not, the community as a whole being fragmented to the point where almost everyone's stance involved an individual choice of lesser evils. Yet collectively, the choices were nonetheless circumscribed by a set of harsh facts that affected all of them equally: the Czech nationalists, traditionally anti-Semitic, had become more hostile than ever; the tsarist government, at that time considered the greatest enemy of all Jews everywhere, was a partner of the Allies and thereby mooted their claims to moral superiority; the Habsburg regime, while far from perfect, had long assured a basic framework of law and order, including the physical protection of Jewish lives and property. Finally, and perhaps most important, the formative links of language, culture, and education predisposed the majority of Prague Jewry toward a preference for the German over the Allied cause.

More often than not, though, it was a distinctly lukewarm preference. The younger generation in particular, with ties to Czech culture and antagonistic to Prussian militarism, soon withdrew into broad opposition to war in general as the butchery continued, and both its futility and its unprecedented brutality made self-deception increasingly difficult. And when, in time, the inconceivable—a German defeat—became, first conceivable, and later, with America's entry into the war, all but certain, practical considerations also began to work on the older generation and motivated many among them to more or less subtly switch their allegiance, or at least to display public evidence of having done so, well in advance of the by now inevitable changes. Even so, it was widely feared that Czech independence would mean the end of Jewish life in Bohemia.

* * *

No sooner back in Prague, Kafka was caught up in the first tremors and convulsions that preceded the actual war, disrupting lives before destroying them. For the first time in his life he had to move out of his parents' house, to make room for his sister Elli and her two children; with her husband in the service, she was no longer able to support an independent household. For some weeks he lived in the vacant apartment of his second sister, Valli, whose husband had also been called up and who was spending the month in the country with her daughter. After her return, he settled into Elli's place until February 1915. It was not quite the sort of independence he had envisaged, but he made the most of this first step, cushioning the traumatic impact by taking all his meals at home. Even more onerous were his responsibilities at the asbestos factory, orphaned by the call-up of both Karl Hermann and his brother Paul.

But the forces shaping his life resided in depths inaccessible even to himself and, as always, bore only the most tenuous relationship to external circumstances. "Just the same," he noted on July 31, "I am quite indifferent to all this misery and more resolute than ever. I'll have to spend afternoons in the factory and won't be able to live at home, because E. and her two children are moving in with us. In spite of all this I am going to write, absolutely. It is my own struggle for self-preservation" (DI, 7/31/14).

Already two days earlier—on July 29—the diary had erupted, as it were, in a few brief fragments of fiction, his first after months of self-absorbed and self-tormented brooding. The die was cast, cast out for good. All decisions had been made and unmade, taken out of his hands, shelved for the duration, postponed indefinitely. His own defeat in the war with himself ushered in global disaster, but instead of despair, it roused him out of his lethargy and drift. If Brod was anxious to save the world, Kafka was determined to save himself, in the only way he knew—by writing.

On the other hand, the notion that the catastrophe left him untouched was a myth of his own making. Focused more sharply than ever on the enigma of human existence, of the only human existence with which he was intimately and hauntingly familiar, living in "the immense world that is within me," he was able to watch the outside world from a distance. "I detect in myself nothing but pettiness, indecision, envy and hatred of those who are fighting, and whom I passionately wish everything evil," he wrote on August 6. "From the viewpoint of literature, my fate is quite simple. The urge to depict my dreamlike inner life has thrust everything else into the background; my life has shrunk horribly and will go on shrinking. Nothing else can ever satisfy me. But the forces available for that task are wholly unpredictable; perhaps they have already vanished forever, perhaps they will grip me once again, although the circumstances of my life certainly don't favor their reappearance." And a glimpse outward, across the chasm:

> Patriotic procession. Speech by the mayor. Disappears, reappears, shouts in German: "Long live our beloved emperor. Hurrah." And I stand there with an evil look on my face. These parades are one of the most disgusting by-products of the war. Organized by Jewish businessmen, who are German one day, Czech the next, even admit it to themselves candidly enough but have never until now been given permission to scream their heads off about it. Naturally they sweep others along with them. It was certainly well organized and is supposed to be repeated every night, twice on Sunday. [DI, 8/6/14]

Thus, far from blinding him to what was going on, the distance provided perspective as well as protection. And if he felt himself untouched by events, the work he produced during the remainder of the year—one of the most productive phases of his life—argues otherwise.

* * *

By the second week of August, with all formalities completed, the reciprocal declarations of war signed, sealed, and delivered, friend and foe more or less clearly defined (though Italy was to take another half year to choose sides), and hostilities about to start in earnest, Kafka was writing with disciplined concentration. On August 15, he noted that "I've been writing for the past few days, may it continue. I am not quite as sheltered by the work and buried within it as I was two years ago. Still, I feel a sense of purpose; my monotonous, empty, insane bachelor's existence has acquired a certain justification. I can again carry on a dialogue with myself and don't just keep staring into a total void. This is the only way I can get better" (DI, 8/15/14).

As always when the spirit was upon him, he surrendered to it with total abandon, undeterred and seemingly unfazed by the mounting confusion and turmoil that greatly complicated his personal situation. Having embarked on a new novel, he put it aside some days later when it hit a snag—his usual method of composition—to work on the "Memories of the Kalda Railroad," a lengthy sketch reaching back to "The Judgment" and focusing on Georg's friend braving the solitude of outer Siberia. By August 21, however, he had turned back to the novel and for the first time referred to it by its title, *Der Prozess*.

The ramified connotations of the German *Prozess*, with its simultaneous implications of both "process" and "trial," have no precise equivalent in English. And though no practical alternative exists to the generally adopted compromise solution, it points up the insidious, often insoluble difficulties of translating Kafka's classically simple yet highly charged prose into another language, even by the most competent hands.

A mere week later, he had completed the first chapter.

* * *

The connections between Joseph K.'s trial and what Kafka himself referred to as his own trial at the Askanischer Hof are at once obvious and elusive. The obvious ones have been labored with pedantic fervor and finality, though controversy persists as to whether Fräulein Bürstner represents Felice—the majority opinion among literal-minded critics—or whether Grete Bloch served as the model, a dissenting view advanced by Elias Canetti. The case against Joseph K., however, is not the case history of Franz Kafka's "struggle for Felice," though they have roots in common. And what inspired *The Trial* was not the scene at the Askanischer Hof but everything in Kafka that led up to this pseudo-confrontation—actually a last-minute reprieve in the guise of a bruising defeat, contrived with pervasive though unconscious cunning by Kafka himself. It left scars. It also freed him, for the moment, from a crushing burden that had flattened him like his own tombstone. Able to breathe, to feel, and to write once again, Kafka in the first days of World War I, in the first summer of the twentieth century, wrote a novel that with blinding lucidity evokes the spirit of the new era in its very opening sentence: "Someone must have maligned Joseph K., for without having done anything wrong, he was arrested one morning."

A preview of the fate of millions, of a century in which doomsday came to be an everyday event. Yet prophecy was the last thing on his mind, and not only because every café already had its prophet and every prophet his café. Kafka's gift was insight rather than foresight, the obsessive self-scrutiny that drove him on relentlessly beyond the self into the murky depths inaccessible to reason, where truth dissolved into a nexus of ambiguities and the irrational gave birth to an inexorable logic of its own—the syllogism of paranoia.

In chronicling Joseph K.'s struggle to discover the nature of his guilt, the identity of his judges, the letter of the law, and his stubborn efforts to pit reason and common sense against the flawless logic of a sentence based on a verdict beyond rational comprehension, Kafka quietly, without fanfare, without stylistic extravagance or verbal excesses, demolished the solid, taken-for-granted certitudes of nineteenth-century realism with its black-and-white contrasts and sharply defined outlines, not unlike the way in which post-Newtonian physics had begun to dismantle the commonsense notions of matter and dissolved the familiar world of solid objects in a space-time continuum governed by forces of terrifying potential.

In fact, he all but demolished the structure of the novel itself as he pursued guilt into the realm of the universal without ever losing sight of the specific, of the most minute detail of gesture or appearance, until the evidence in the proceedings against Joseph K. sufficed to justify any verdict twice over, not only against the accused but, with at least equal force, against his judges. It is this dynamic ambiguity, the outgrowth of authentic and profound ambivalence rather than intellectual mystification, that opens the novel to a multiplicity of interpretations, while at the same time foreclosing any claim to one definitive reading.

There is no single solution to the enigma. There is, in fact, no enigma, but a dazzling interplay of multifaceted meanings whose unraveling becomes itself a vital first step along a road that has no end in human experience, as Kafka himself was forced to recognize when he finally had to abandon both Joseph K. and his novel to their fate. Pursuing the trial all the way to the court of last instance is beyond the strength and limits of any human life.

That our everyday world has caught up with Kafka's vision and far surpassed it in irrational brutality accounts for much of the novel's fame and current appeal; *The Trial* today can be read as a depressingly realistic if sadly understated description of life in many parts of the globe, nowhere more so than in Kafka's own hometown— where, for that reason, it is quite understandably banned. Yet even at this most superficial level, it casts a spell that transcends crude analogies, an intimation, however vaguely perceived, of the ineffable beneath the opaque surface of language.

For, in the final analysis, the novel is language, and language has been a matter of life and death among Jews ever since the errant desert tribe smashed its idols and enshrined instead the word as its God. To live and die as a member of the tribe meant strict observance of the word of God become law. Transgressors died a lone death in the desert, outcasts twice over, attended by vultures.

Obedience to the spirit of the law presupposes knowledge of its letter. But knowledge breeds doubt, and as the letter of the law began yielding up the infinite ambiguities of its spirit, interpretation became the task of a lifetime, an endless "process" to which each generation contributed its share, expanding and refining the interpretations of the previous ones, heaping comment upon commentary ad infinitum, a way of life by which reason seeks to justify faith.

This tension between faith and reason, the dynamic, ever-precarious balance between essentially irreconcilable opposites, is at the heart of Jewish tradition and a source of its enduring vitality. And the struggle of Joseph K., incapable of compromise like his creator, to reason his way to faith owes its inspiration far more to that heritage than it does to neurosis, literature, or politics. Writing *The Trial* was part of that endless quest; to read it is, in some small way, to participate in it.

*   *   *

In 1914 as in 1940, Germany had carefully prepared for a two-front *Blitzkrieg*, a knockout blow against the enemy in the west, followed by an all-out assault on Russia that would end the war before the onset of winter. But the decisive victory eluded the Kaiser's armies. And by the middle of September, as early as six weeks into the war, its final outcome had become ineluctable, though it took another four years and millions of dead before the bloodbath came to a temporary halt.

In the West, the German advance ran into desperate last-ditch resistance by the French and was stopped—for good, as it turned out—in the battle of the Marne. Far more devastating, though, from the Prague perspective, was the almost instant collapse of Austro-Hungary's military might in the face of what had always been dismissed as inferior if not downright insignificant foes.

For the Russians, however ill equipped and poorly led, made short shrift of an Austrian army that in terms of leadership and equipment was obviously in even worse shape. The Vienna military clique, whose machinations had finally accomplished their purpose, were apt conspirators behind the scenes but hopeless clowns in action on the battlefield. It was quite in character for them to have spent a lifetime scheming and dreaming of war while neglecting the most basic preparations. The huge budget allocations for national defense, which by 1914 had brought the country to the brink of bankruptcy, vanished in the morass of an endemically corrupt economy but left the armies bereft of essentials, to the point where many soldiers went off to war wearing armbands instead of uniforms.

Moreover, these corseted bedroom politicians were still living in the era of the Congress of Vienna and had based their strategy, such as it was, on notions that bore no relation to the realities of twentieth-century warfare. The crack Hungarian cavalry regiments in their conspicuous operetta costumes were thrown into battle in massed formation across open plains to spearhead the drive into Russia. But instead of scimitar-wielding Turks, they found themselves facing concentrated fire from British-made machine guns, a radically innovative addition to the technology of death that not only wiped out the flower of the Austrian army but put an end to the inane romance of cavalry charges. And the Russians were quick to follow up on their initial successes. Cossack units routed the demoralized Austrian infantry, and by the end of

August, the tsarist armies had occupied Galicia, the Bukovina, as well as parts of Moravia, and seemed poised for a drive on Budapest, Prague, and even Vienna. Strict censorship—the one phase of operations in which the military proved efficient—suppressed any and all mention of these disasters. But the arrival of thousands of—mostly Jewish—refugees from the east was bound to generate rumors in the heartland, and after the fall of Galicia in early September, the Austrian General Staff saw fit to issue its first communiqué of the war, a masterpiece of reverse double-talk. Such Austrians as still believed their armies to be headed straight for Moscow were now informed that "Lvov is still in our hands."

Even more humiliating, though, in their symbolic implications, were the Austrian defeats at the hands of tiny Serbia. Far from smoking out the "sanctuary of terrorists," the Austrians were beaten back with heavy losses all along the line. Again there was no official word about the fiasco, but large blank spaces on the front pages told part of the story, and even the most euphoric of patriots could scarcely fail to note the absence of victory bulletins. The Serbs had, in fact, beaten back no less than three major attacks on their capital. Belgrade fell in December, but Serbia held out until the German Balkan offensive in September of 1915, by which time its defeat no longer provided much of a morale booster.

The mood in Prague, however, changed much more rapidly than in either Vienna or Berlin. The unexpected victories of their fellow Slavs aroused understandable enthusiasm among the Czechs, though open manifestations were effectively squelched by the military command, which had assumed absolute authority and demonstrated considerably more martial spirit on the home front than against the enemies abroad. Courts-martial liberally meted out death sentences against defeatists, rumormongers, and provocateurs. The partisans of Austria, on the other hand, were badly shaken. Whether all-out patriots, lukewarm supporters, or lesser-evil advocates, they all had taken a quick victory for granted; and in this city, with its unique population mix, its tradition of skepticism, efficient grapevine, and proximity to the front, it soon became difficult to fool oneself about the true affairs of state: Austria was a lost cause. Enjoy the war, for the peace will be terrible. But by September, the war itself began to seem terrible enough, and massive gloom settled over the city, infesting even those who, like Kafka, believed themselves more or less inured to patriotism and politics.

He had successfully withdrawn from his surroundings and become, quite literally, a sleepwalker in the outside world, an early practitioner of that "inner emigration" that was to be the refuge of so many others trapped in the "kafkaesque" universe of totalitarianism. He went through the requisite motions of attending to his obligations: the office from eight to half past two (by 1915, the personnel losses made it necessary to extend the hours to 4 p.m. and to add frequent mandatory Sunday work), lunch at his parents' house, followed by two hours of reading, attending to correspondence or office business, a nap until around 9 p.m., supper again with his parents, then back to his room to write "as long as my strength or fear of the next morning, fear of the headaches in the office will permit me."

It was a spurt of total dedication, a stubborn resolve to shut out everything and anything—Felice, the office, the factory, the war—liable to get in the way of his writing. Even so, the world would not always let itself be ignored. On September 13, he complained about having been able to write "barely two pages. At first I thought that grief about the Austrian defeats and worries about the future (worries that seem to me basically ridiculous and reprehensible) would prevent me from writing altogether. But it wasn't that, merely an apathy that keeps coming back and has to be overcome time and again. For grief itself there is time enough when I'm not writing. The thoughts relating to the war resemble my old worries about Felice in the tormenting way in which they keep gnawing at me from many different directions" (DI, 9/13/14).

If the news from the front upset him, the war also, and in a much more fundamental manner, added its share to the already staggering burden of guilt with which he was wrestling in his novel about the trials of Joseph K. Nearly all his friends and acquaintances—with the sole exception of Max Brod, rejected on medical grounds—had already been drafted, but Kafka himself was deferred as "indispensable" at the request of the Insurance Institute, objective testimony to the importance which his superiors ascribed to his work. He was carried on the reserve rolls of the 28th Infantry Regiment, and his status reviewed in June 1915 and again a year later. Both times he was found fit for active service, and both times the institute rejected his plea to release him; that his eagerness to join the army derived from very mixed motives goes without saying. By 1917, his illness had already declared itself, and he was deferred on medical grounds. It was not until March 1934, however, ten years after his death, that the military records section of the Prague municipality began to look for the "reservist František Kavka, son of Herman," in order to deliver his final discharge.

At the beginning of October he took a two-week leave to bury himself altogether in his work—"I usually sat at my desk until about five in the morning, one time even till half past seven, then went to sleep until one or two in the afternoon; during the last few days of my leave I even succeeded in actually falling asleep" (FEL, 10/14). One of the by-products of this punishing regimen—and no doubt of the tensions it was designed to master—were the excruciating headaches which had now become the bane of his existence, a subject of constant apprehension even when he was not in actual pain, and regularly alluded to in his correspondence; they characteristically subsided after the onset of his frankly somatic illness.

But the creative results of this total immersion more than justified such superhuman heroics. In addition to making good progress on *The Trial*, he wrote the last chapter of *Amerika*—the "Oklahoma Open Air Theater"—as well as *The Penal Colony*, an outburst of self-hatred, sadism, and visionary rage so savage that in its time most readers reacted with either disgust or defensive indifference. Even Kurt Wolff had his reservations, to which Kafka replied that "your objections to the distressing aspects accord completely with my own opinion, though I feel that way about almost everything I have written so far. . . . By way of clarifying this latest story, however, let me merely add that it is not alone in being distressing, but that our times in general, and my own time in particular, have been and continue to be equally distressing" (L, 10/11/16).

The literary antecedents of *The Penal Colony* have been persuasively traced to *Le Jardin des Supplices*, a rather lurid 1899 novel by the French playwright Octave Mirbeau that combines a sado-anarchist assault on bourgeois morals with explicit sexual imagery. The German translation, published in 1901, was instantly banned, thereby acquiring a not altogether warranted reputation as a pornographic underground classic. In both stories, the narrators are European explorers whose strictly scientific curiosity precludes moral judgment or human emotions as they investigate the exquisitely fiendish brutalities being perpetrated by aging bureaucrats passionately devoted to the technology of torture and wholly oblivious to the humanity of their victims.

The obviously profound impression Mirbeau's ornate decadence made on Kafka is somewhat difficult to account for unless one assumes that its explicit sadism struck a sympathetic chord in normally latent recesses of his unconscious. And it may be significant to note that, from all the evidence at hand, he started writing *The Penal Colony* on October 15, the very day he received a letter from Grete Bloch. It was the first communication from Berlin since his abrupt flight, and it opened old wounds. The pain it caused, the pain it made him want to inflict on himself, and his feelings about both Grete and Felice—"thoughts so base I cannot even write them down"—erupted in a vision of violence stripped of all its extrinsic components, the very essence of evil in its naked, terrifying banality. Whatever the subconscious residue of Mirbeau's lubricious sadism, Kafka's own fantasies, running only a few decades ahead of his time, evoked the impersonal twentieth-century technology of torture with the same graphic precision with which he had described the intricacies of the mechanical planes and trimmers in his insurance reports. And the figure of the head torturer himself is a prescient portrait of Adolf Eichmann, drawn from life.

That this intuitive sense of the evil that links his time to ours seemed totally incomprehensible to most of his contemporaries is hardly surprising and accounts for the cool reception and almost universally hostile reviews the story received at preliminary readings and after its publication in 1919. The sole exception was Kurt Tucholsky, seemingly at opposite poles from Kafka as a writer, yet closely related to him by curious affinities of intuition. In the *Weltbühne* of June 3, 1920, he hailed *The Penal Colony* as a masterpiece,

> a work of art so great that it defies all labels. It is definitely not an allegory, but something altogether different. The officer in charge explains the precise mechanism of the torture machine and comments with pedantic expertise on the victim's every convulsion. Yet he is neither crude nor cruel, but something much worse: he is amoral. . . . This officer is no torturer, let alone a sadist. His delight in the manifestations of the victim's six-hour agony merely demonstrates his boundless, slavish worship of the machine, which he calls justice and which in fact is power. Power without limits. To be able for once to exercise power without any constraints—do you still remember the sexual fantasies of early adolescence? What stimulated them was not just sex but the absence of constraints. To be able to impose one's will, without any limits. . . . This is the dream that Kafka's

story is about, and the obstacles in the way of perfect wish fulfillment are part of it. For the torture is eventually cut short not because society, the state, or the law indignantly rise up in protest and put a stop to it but because the spare parts for the machine turn out to be defective; the apparatus, though still tolerated by the higher echelons of bureaucracy, no longer enjoys full support at the top. . . . And all of this told with incredibly understated, chilling detachment. . . . Don't ask what it means. It means nothing. The book may not even be of our time. It is completely harmless. As harmless as Kleist.

*   *   *

Having taken three days out to write *The Penal Colony*—he was not happy with the ending but never came up with a better one—Kafka again took up *The Trial*. But the letter from Grete Bloch had derailed his single-minded concentration; the spell was broken. "For two months I led a calm life without any actual contact with F. I dreamed of her as though she had died and could never come back to life. Now that I have a chance to get in touch with her, she has again become the center of everything. And she probably also interferes with my work" (DI, 10/15/14). That Felice's roundabout overture succeeded in rekindling his love, such as it was or ever had been, seems questionable, but it certainly revived the old confusion and ambivalence, to the immediate detriment of his work. The feverish pace began to slacken, the lapses of inspiration multiplied and left him open to the intrusion of a by now decidedly ominous reality—the steady stream of destitute refugees arriving in the city, the first casualty lists, trainloads of wounded soldiers, friends, and relatives back from the front with tales of grisly horror.

Excluded from the brotherhood of mud and misery, more than ever the alien and outcast, Kafka found himself once again confronted by the threat, blandishment, and guilt of bachelorhood. And if marriage represented the only road to redemption, it was also the road to inevitable ruin.

This, essentially, was also the import of a very long and rather legalistic letter with which, at the end of October, he resumed the correspondence with Felice. After assuring her that "as far as I am concerned, nothing whatever has changed between us in the last three months, not for the better and not for the worse," he reiterated his need for a life wholly dedicated to writing but, for the first time, formulated specific accusations of his own: her insistence on a religious ceremony, her disapproval of his idiosyncrasies (which, he acknowledged, made him stress them all the more in her presence—"One night, at dinner with your sister, I ate almost nothing but meat. Had you been there, I would probably have ordered a dish of almonds"), her taste in furniture and living quarters, and above all the constant fear he sensed in her, fear of an unpredictable future with an unpredictable husband, which she strove to overcome by sheer willpower rather than by love.

It was a cool, perceptive analysis that should have induced either or both of them to draw the self-evident conclusions. But the relationship had by now acquired a momentum of its own, with force of habit compensating for the loss of illusion. And since both of them, though for very different reasons, continued to see marriage as a desirable or at least necessary goal, they apparently came to believe—implicitly if not explicitly—that the very absence of passion would make it easier to reach the state of rational compromise and mature resignation that characterizes the institution at its least unbearable. A few days later, on November 5, Felice's father died of a sudden heart attack, for which Kafka naturally claimed responsibility, further evidence of the "ruin" he had brought upon a family from which he now felt "totally detached," even though he had begun to dream once more of "getting Felice back. I might even really try to, unless self-disgust prevents me."

In the end, self-disgust did not prevent him from agreeing to another meeting with Felice. Since wartime regulations greatly complicated travel, they chose to meet in the border town of Bodenbach on the weekend of January 23, 1915. The results were the usual: "No outward quarrel, we walk along peacefully side by side, but all the time there is a tension as though someone were continuously slicing the air between us with a sword." Kafka, moreover, felt that the lack of communication was no longer confined to the long, hostile silences of their personal encounters; everything that letters could possibly say had been said. Besides, the mail had become unreliable, subject to censorship and long delays. Summing up the fiasco of this meeting, which he blamed for the sudden drying up of his inspiration, he vowed to plunge once more into his work, which, he somewhat feebly assured Felice, "in a certain sense is also done for your sake, even though some devil made you tell me that I ought to try and make something of the asbestos factory. Why do you have more understanding for the factory than for me?" (FEL, 1/25/15).

Throughout the final month of 1914, he had found it increasingly difficult to focus on his work, even though on the last day of that fateful year he surveyed the results with something approaching satisfaction.

> Have been working since August, on the whole not little and not badly, though not to the limits of my capacity as regards either quantity or quality, which I should have done, especially since according to all indications (insomnia, headaches, weak heart) my strength won't hold out much longer. Worked on, but failed to finish, *The Trial*, "Memories of the Kalda Railroad," "The Village Schoolmaster," "The Assistant District Attorney," and started a few minor things. Finished only *The Penal Colony* and one chapter of *Der Verschollene* (*Amerika*), both during the two-week leave. I don't know why I am drawing up this balance sheet, it isn't at all like me. [DI, 12/31/14]

By January 1915, however, work had bogged down badly, and on the seventeenth, just before the Bodenbach meeting, *The Trial* ground to a definitive halt.

The "struggle for Felice" had entered an altogether new phase, one over which the dour ghost of the recently (1912) deceased Strindberg hovered as a patron saint of sorts. Kafka had begun to devour his novels and autobiography in late 1914 and, while not uncritical, evidently felt a distinct kinship with the misogynist side of the bleak Swede and with his paranoid fear of vampire females sucking him dry of his creativity—not all that different in substance from Kafka's own fear of being emasculated as a writer by a woman who threatened to tie him down to an office or factory and bury him under mountains of overstuffed furniture. "We've never had one single good moment together, one in which I could breathe freely," he confessed on the day of his return from Bodenbach. "Except in letters, I never experienced with F. the sweetness of a relationship with a beloved woman such as I knew in Zuckmantl and Riva" (DI, 1/25/15). A remarkably depressing insight which, however, merely seemed to further exacerbate the conflict, for at stake was no longer love but marriage, a state that others long before Strindberg had come to regard as love's natural antithesis.

Being in touch at last with the hoard of antagonism, resentment, and abrasive contempt that were part of his feelings for and against Felice—and, at a deeper level, part of what had motivated his choice in the first place—he now faced the prospect of marriage in its pure Strindbergian form as the joint martyrdom of two individuals chained together for life and for worse.

No doubt it was the recrudescence of these oft-fought struggles after a period of comatose emotional truce that drained his energies. After Bodenbach, he tried desperately to resume the earlier pace and routine but found himself almost totally blocked. Between February and April of 1915, he still managed to complete one story patently linked to the theme that preempted his imagination; it was posthumously published under the title "Blumfeld, an Elderly Bachelor." After that last, grim effort, however, he succumbed to a creative stasis that was to last until December 1916.

Nevertheless, it seems farfetched to ascribe this nineteen-month silence entirely, or even principally, to inner conflicts over marriage and Felice. In the long run, the war would simply not be ignored. It affected everyone's life, and once shaken out of his trance-like isolation, he had to face countless practical problems.

Some of these might have seemed minor irritants to anyone but Kafka. There was the factory, an "everyday reminder of Yom Kippur," source of constant clashes with his father. The place had already closed down for lack of raw materials, but bill collection and settlement with creditors took up many a precious afternoon. Another complication was the housing problem. After Elli reclaimed her own apartment in February 1915, he rented a room in his sister Valli's building, which he found unlivable because "people simply lack comprehension for the kind of quiet I must have." But moving out required giving notice, and the landlady happened to be a sweet old lady ready to do anything for him, so that it took days of soul-searing agony before he mustered the courage to risk breaking her heart. The next room, at the Golden Trout, a fifteenth-century building in the Old Town, turned out to be "ten times as noisy as the first one," but a stunning view of the Prague castle evidently made up for that drawback. Quite a few of his peers, one suspects, would have been more than happy to trade places and put up with the rasping cough of a tubercular neighbor, rather than with the whine of an incoming artillery shell. But awareness of his petulance merely heightened the guilt without reducing the discomfort; few problems in his life were ever trivial or loomed as less than insurmountable.

Objectively far from trivial, however, was his mounting work load at the office. The labor shortage caused by the draft forced the closing—temporary or permanent—of a great many industrial enterprises, necessitating extensive changes in the whole system of industrial accident insurance and its actuarial bases. Even more troublesome was the administration of welfare and medical benefits for disabled war veterans, an entirely new sphere of activity formally delegated to the institute in 1915, for which there were no precedents or applicable models. This whole area, in due course, became one of Kafka's chief responsibilities. It would be difficult, from his own eloquent silence on the subject, to deduce the efficiency and dedication with which he acquitted himself of an exceedingly complex and emotionally draining task; quite understandably, his superiors considered him absolutely indispensable, and the draft board consistently concurred in their judgment.

And for good reason. The situation of the thousands of ex-soldiers permanently disabled by loss of limbs, blindness, neurological or internal diseases and unceremoniously dumped in ever larger numbers on their home communities, kept deteriorating at an alarming rate. Of the roughly five thousand amputees on the institute's dockets in 1917, over two thousand were also suffering from advanced tuberculosis. Government funds provided less than bare subsistence, so that the institute found itself compelled to solicit private donations for such basic needs as prosthetic devices, hospital care, and occupational retraining.

An especially tragic problem arising directly out of the technology of modern warfare was the vast number of soldiers who had sustained severe emotional damage on the battlefield. Diagnosed as "shell-shocked," they were for the most part cursorily discharged to shift for themselves, mental and emotional cripples with no access to appropriate therapy or facilities. Thus by 1916, more than four thousand such cases were vegetating in Prague alone, with a single, hastily improvised neurological clinic struggling to cope with the plight of what progressive medical circles had begun to refer to as traumatic neuroses.

It may not have been altogether accidental that Kafka, the expert on nerves, was put in charge of the institute's mounting case load relating to the care and compensation of this new type of disability. But beyond his official duties, he also took an active part in a private initiative designed to overcome the critical lack of treatment facilities and drafted the original appeal for contributions which, in October 1916, led to the opening of a veterans' hospital for nervous diseases at Rumburk. In October 1918, in fact, the Veterans Administration recommended him for a medal: "Dr. Franz Kafka, assistant secretary of the Workmen's Accident Insurance Institute for the Kingdom of Bohemia, who in addition to his official duties in the field of insurance has also, since 1915, been responsible for the agenda of the Committee for

Therapeutic Treatment and the administration of sanatoria" merited recognition for his outstanding services on behalf of disabled veterans. The war and the Habsburg empire, however, came to an abrupt end long before the necessary papers had cleared the labyrinthine channels of bureaucracy. Dr. Kafka never got his medal.

Twenty-two

THE Russian sweep into Galicia triggered a panic among the population of the Jewish settlements. Desperate to save their women and children from the legendary bestiality of the Cossacks, they fled with little but the clothes on their back, whole villages heading for sanctuary behind the Austrian lines. By the end of 1914, well over fifteen thousand such refugees were stranded in Prague, straining all available resources, not to mentioned the already strained relations between Galician *Ostjuden* and their assimilated "German" coreligionists.

Scanty government funds as well as private donations were channeled and distributed via the Jewish community, which assumed full responsibility for the welfare of the refugees. Many prominent Prague Jews volunteered their services, no doubt with genuine enthusiasm and the best of intentions. But while it may be more blessed to give than to receive, it also tends to inflate one's sense of nobility and to engender furtive expectations of gratitude that are bound to be disappointed in any confrontation between private charity and mass misery. In this particular situation, the overt and often strident contempt of the *Ostjuden* for Germanized upper-middle-class do-gooders further confirmed and exacerbated the long-standing prejudices rampant in both camps.

To Kafka, however, who had long since shed the preposterous snobbism of his enlightened peers, the Galician refugees were the living embodiment of Jewishness. His biting sketch of a refugee relief center he visited in November 1914, shortly after the arrival of the first contingent, strikingly illustrates the contrast between the two worlds:

> Yesterday on Weavers' Lane, where they distribute old clothes to the refugees from Galicia, Max, his mother, Mr. Chaim Nagel. The intelligence, patience, affability, industry, openness, wit, dependability of Mr. Nagel. People who within their own sphere handle any task to such perfection that it seems as though they

would succeed at anything they put their hand to, yet part of their perfection is that it also keeps them from overreaching themselves and aiming beyond their grasp.

The bright, lively, proud, and modest Mrs. Kannegiesser from Tarnov. All she wanted was two blankets, but nice ones; what she got instead, despite Max's intercession, were old and dirty ones. The clean blankets were being kept in a separate room, along with all other items in good condition, reserved for the better class of people. Then again, she only needs them for two days, until her linen arrives from Vienna, and used articles cannot be taken back because of the cholera danger.

Mrs. Lustig, with many children of all ages, and her brash, self-assured, quicksilvery little sister. She spent so much time selecting a children's dress that Mrs. Brod finally yelled at her, "You either take this one, or you won't get any." Whereupon Mrs. Lustig, yelling even louder and concluding with a wild, expansive sweep of her arms, replied that "the mitzvah (good deed) is worth a lot more than all these shmattes (rags) put together. [DI, 11/24/14]

Drawing largely on its own resources and volunteer staff, the Prague Jewish community also organized, practically overnight, an entire school system for the younger refugees, which quickly outgrew its original scope and developed into a lively cultural institution offering a wide range of courses at all levels. Kafka himself frequently attended Brod's weekly lectures on world literature and became quite attached to one of the students, a bright and opinionated young girl from Lvov who joined him on several of his Sunday expeditions. He also took his nephew Felix to the Hanukkah celebration at the day-care center for refugee children. But he refrained from participating in any of the institutional activities, partly for lack of time, mostly because he could not abide the complacent sense of superiority that tainted the charitable efforts and spilled over into the whole notion of bringing culture to the ignorant masses from the East. To him, these masses possessed precisely what Western Jewry had long since lost—deep roots, a sense of belonging, and communal strength, infinitely more precious than the smatterings of Homer and Goethe which Brod and his well-meaning friends were attempting to purvey.

It was also his growing interest in this authentic strain of Judaism that led to Kafka's friendship with Georg, alias Mordechai, Langer, one of the more colorful eccentrics on the Prague scene. Langer was a medieval Jewish mystic born into the wrong century, as well as into the wrong, thoroughly assimilated family; his brother, František Langer, became a prominent Czech dramatist. Georg, on the other hand, left home in adolescence, spent years in a Hasidic community in Hungary, and finally, rather to the consternation of his respectable family, returned to Prague, a bearded Hasid in outlandish garb determined to devote his life to probing the mysteries of the Cabala. Supporting himself by Hebrew lessons, he wrote esoteric treatises and poetry in Czech, German, and Hebrew. Kafka later became one of his students, and one of Langer's last Hebrew elegies—he died in Tiberias in 1943—commemorates Kafka's death as the union of a pure soul with the infinite.

Langer, a disciple and follower of the Belzer rabbi, provided first-hand contact with an aggressively vital branch of Judaic tradition that instinctively appealed to Kafka. For the rest of his life, he felt strongly drawn to the antirational, mystical elements in Hasidism, whereas the petrified formalism of the traditional synagogue left him supremely unmoved. "The Hasidic tales in *The Jewish Echo*," he wrote to Brod in 1917, "may not be the best. But all these stories—I don't know why—are the only thing Jewish in which, regardless of my condition, I always and immediately feel at home. Everything else I merely drift into, and the first breeze whisks me out again" (L, 9/17).

But a vast gap separates *feeling* at home in that world from *being* at home in it. Langer took both Brod and Kafka to a dingy warren in suburban Žižkov, where the Grodeck rabbi was temporarily ensconced with his flock. Kafka was not altogether unimpressed: "According to Langer, all rabbis look like savages. This one wore a silk caftan, with his underwear showing. Hair on the bridge of his nose. A fur hat, which he keeps shoving back and forth. Dirty and pure, a peculiarity of people engaged in intensive thought. Scratches his beard, spits on the floor, reaches into the food with his fingers—and yet, when he lets his hand rest on the table for a moment, you see the whiteness of the skin, a whiteness such as you think you could only have seen in your childhood imaginings. In those days, however, the parents, too, were pure" (DI, 9/14/15).

The respectful conclusion seems forced. And Brod, who at the time was himself passing through a phase of quasi-revivalist religiosity, reports that throughout the evening—a "Third Meal" Sabbath celebration—Kafka remained decidedly distant and cool: "Though undoubtedly moved by the primordial strains of an ancient folk tradition, he said to me on the way home: Actually, it was rather like a visit to a tribe of African savages. Blatant superstition" (Brod, bio., 137).

The same struggle between head and heart, the ambivalent mixture of sympathy, faint respect, and intransigent skepticism again crops up in a long letter to Brod the following year from Marienbad, where Kafka participated with Langer in the daily constitutional of the vacationing Belzer rabbi and his disciples.

> He looks like the kind of sultan I used to admire as a child in the fairy-tale illustrations by Doré. But real, rather than just dressed up to look like one. And not just sultan but also father, grade-school teacher, high-school professor, and so forth. The sight of his neck, of his hand resting on his hip, of the sweep of his broad back, all of this inspires confidence. And the whole group has that look of calm, happy confidence that comes across. . . . He inspects everything, asks questions. . . . On the whole, the banal chatter and questions of idle monarchs, with perhaps a little more joy and kindness; in any event, they irresistibly reduce all thought processes of his retinue to the same level. Langer seeks, or suspects, a deeper meaning in all of this; I think the deeper meaning is that there is none, and this, in my opinion, is quite sufficient. [L, 7/16]

The sometimes civilized, often violent, but always tense confrontations between the two different worlds and different centuries of Judaism certainly helped to enliven an otherwise dismal scene that spring. The Zionist *Selbstwehr* preached Jewish national solidarity, the Bar Kochba student organization provided a forum for debates between East and West, Brod and Bergmann, among others, lectured to often contentious and critical audiences. Yet beneath and beyond the public discussions, private encounters led to many close personal ties between individual refugees and their hosts.

Kafka, who had been idealizing *Yiddishkeit* ever since his first exposure to the Yiddish actors, now had his chance to observe the lives of ordinary Jews from Eastern Europe at close range. And what he saw impressed him even more in its stark contrast to the rootless ambiguity of his own origins. To him, they were "a people," and years later, in a letter to Milena Jesenská, he told of watching a group of Russian-Jewish emigrants in transit through Prague, lodged temporarily in the auditorium of the Jewish Town Hall pending the arrival of their U.S. visas: "Had I been given the choice to be whatever I wanted, I would have chosen to be a little Eastern Jewish boy in the corner of that room, without a worry in the world" (MIL, p. 168).

It may not have struck him that, had he had his wish, he would have grown up in America to face much the same dilemma he had been wrestling with in Europe.

* * *

In Prague, the first spring of the war was a season of bleak despair. The winter's human losses had been enormous, there was no end in sight, food prices had doubled, the first shortages had set in. The Czech opposition was being more brutally suppressed than ever, their leaders jailed. In May 1915, Italy declared war on Austria, and the immediately ensuing battles claimed thousands of new victims, among them Kafka's old friend Oskar Pollak, killed on the Isonzo front on June 11.

He himself, after his return from Bodenbach, was perfectly in tune with the city's mood, plagued by excruciating headaches, refusing to see even the few friends still around, spending all his evenings at home, yet totally incapable of working. And though he at least inferentially blamed Felice and the office, these were in fact his strongest, if not his only, links to life on the outside.

> What the war does to one [he wrote to Felice in April] is something that in essence one cannot yet know. Outwardly it affects me because it ruined our factory, something I suspect rather than know because I haven't been there for a month. My brother-in-law's brother is getting his basic training here, and is therefore able to attend to things a little, for the time being. My older sister's husband is with the Quartermaster Corps in the Carpathian Mountains, hence probably not in any immediate danger. My other sister's husband was wounded, as you know, went back to the front for a few days, came down with sciatica, and is now being treated at Teplice. Aside from that, I mostly suffer from the war because I am not taking part in it. Which sounds rather stupid when you spell it out bluntly like that. Besides, it is not out of the question that my turn will still come. What prevents me from volunteering are certain decisive factors, though also partly again those things that always stand in my way. [FEL, 4/5/15]

In April, he chaperoned his sister Elli on a four-day trip to Hungary to visit her convalescing husband and returned in an even worse frame of mind. "Total indifference and dullness. A well run dry. Water in depths beyond reach, and uncertain even there. . . . Nothing, nothing. Emptiness, boredom, no, not boredom, just emptiness, senselessness, weakness" (DI, 5/3/15). Despair that made the age-old temptations of war—the security of mindless obedience, the risk of socially encouraged self-destruction—seem more appealing than ever. "Why can't you understand," he asked Felice a few days later, "that it would be a great good fortune for me to become a soldier, always provided my health was up to it, which I certainly hope. I'll be called up at the end of this month or the beginning of June. You ought to wish me what I wish for myself— that I'll be accepted" (FEL, 5/6/15).

He spent the Whitsuntide holidays at the end of May in the Bohemian mountains with Felice, who had brought Grete Bloch and another girl friend along by way of reinforcement or bodyguards. Partly perhaps as a result of this precaution, it seems for once to have been a pleasantly low-keyed interlude, and a month later the two again spent a weekend together at the Karlsbad spa. Relations between them were now guardedly polite and friendly; the all-encompassing reality of the war, with its day-to-day uncertainties and wholly unpredictable consequences, made the problems of their relationship and its future seem less pressing. Once again it was Felice who took the initiative, traveled to see him, complained about not receiving letters for weeks on end, while he in turn withdrew more and more into himself, racked by insomnia and by headaches so ferocious that right after the Karlsbad meeting he felt close to a complete breakdown. By June, his hopes for battlefield oblivion had again been dashed by the institute's steadfast refusal to release him. Blocked from seeking refuge in the army, he spent ten days in July at the Frankenstein Sanatorium in Rumburk, the very same which, one year later, he helped convert into the first veterans' clinic for nervous diseases. It seemed to him a despicable compromise— "fits my life perfectly, like the cover on the pot. . . . What ails me is impatience. Or patience. I don't know which" (FEL, 7/20/15).

Frankenstein, predictably, did nothing for what ailed him, either way.

> For weeks on end I dread being alone in my room. For weeks on end, fever is the only sleep I know. I go to a sanatorium, convinced ahead of time that to do so is crazy. What can I possibly expect to find there? A chance to escape the night? On the contrary, things are worse there: the days, too, are like

nights. I get back and spend the first week in a state of stupor. . . .
A kind of imbecility comes over me. . . . At the moment, there
appear to be only two remedies. . . . One is Felice, the other,
military service. Both are beyond my reach. [FEL, 8/9/15]

So paralyzing had his depression become that, for the remainder of
the year, he practically stopped writing to Felice altogether. "After all,
haven't I caused more grief by my writing than by my silence?" he asked
rhetorically, in August, anticipating her reproaches and urging her to
keep in touch just the same. She did; she even repeatedly offered to
meet him but was more or less politely rebuffed. "It would be nice to get
together, but we had better not," he wrote in December. "It would
merely be another improvisation, and we've suffered enough already
from such makeshift expedients. I could only bring you more disappointment, bundle of insomnia and headaches that I am. . . . My rare and
insipid answers cannot possibly convey how glad I am to hear from you"
(FEL, 12/5/15).

Yet even in the pit of depression Kafka apparently managed to live
up to the ever-expanding demands of his job. That it took a heavy toll
is self-evident; that it also enabled—or, more accurately, forced him to
survive, is a suspicion he himself resolutely but not altogether convincingly rejected:

> I am desperate like a caged rat, racked by headaches and
> insomnia; the way I spend my days beggars description. My sole
> hope of salvation, my supreme wish, is freedom from the office.
> There are obstacles: the factory, my alleged indispensability at
> the office, currently very busy (new office hours: from 8 to 2,
> and from 4 to 6), but all of this dwindles down to nothing
> compared to the overwhelming need for freedom, the ever
> steeper downhill slide. But I lack the strength; it isn't even up to
> lesser tasks. Not that I am afraid of life without the office; the
> fever burning in my head day and night is caused by lack of
> freedom. And yet, when my boss starts complaining that the
> department would collapse if I left (a crazy notion about whose
> absurdity I have no illusions), that he himself is ill, and so
> forth, I find myself simply unable to go through with it; the
> conditioned bureaucrat within me cannot do it. And so the
> nights, the days go on and on. [FEL, 3/16]

But if his correspondence to Felice was confined to a few laconic
notes, Kafka's literary output had stopped altogether, his sole more or

less creative achievement for the year being seventy pages of the Insurance Institute's 1915 annual report. On the other hand, his earlier work had begun to receive a measure of recognition that clearly gave him pleasure even if it failed to shake him out of his lethargy. "The Metamorphosis" finally appeared in print, first in the October 1915 issue of *Weisse Blätter*, a Leipzig literary monthly edited by the Alsatian novelist René Schickele, and in November as a handsome volume in Kurt Wolff's Doomsday series. Kafka had some last-minute misgivings about the artist chosen to do the cover drawing: "Since Stark is an illustrator, it occurred to me that he might actually want to draw the insect itself. Not that, please, not that. I don't wish to encroach upon his realm of competence but merely to plead with him, out of my own naturally more intimate knowledge of the story. The insect as such cannot be depicted. It cannot even be shown from a distance (L, 10/25/15).

In October, the prestigious annual Theodor Fontane Prize was awarded to Carl Sternheim, a dramatist and short-story writer (1878–1942) of experimental, expressionist tendencies, radical leanings, and independent wealth. Sternheim accepted the honor but passed the small cash award (800 marks) that went with it on to "the young Prague writer Franz Kafka as a token of appreciation for the *Meditations, The Stoker,* and 'The Metamorphosis.' " The gesture, baffling to Kafka, who had never met Sternheim, was probably inspired by Franz Blei, as head of the award jury; the resultant publicity motivated Kurt Wolff to reissue the *Meditations*.

It was not enough, however, to lift the heavy burden, a leaden apathy punctuated by brief bursts of wild agitation:

> Great state of excitement in the afternoon. Started with my trying to decide whether I should buy war bonds, and if so, how much. Twice went to the office to leave the necessary instructions, and twice returned without having gone in. Feverishly calculated the interest. Then asked my mother to buy a thousand crowns' worth of bonds, raised it to two thousand and, quite incidentally, found out that I already owned some three thousand crowns' worth of bonds which I knew nothing about. The discovery hardly touched me at all. There was no room in my head for anything except doubts about the war bonds, and even half an hour's walk through the busiest streets would not allay them. I felt myself directly involved in the war, tried to evaluate—at

least in the light of my limited information—the general financial prospects, kept calculating the interest that would someday be coming to me, etc. Gradually, however, the excitement underwent a transformation, my thoughts turned to writing, I felt up to it, wanted nothing more than a chance to write. [DI, 11/5/15]

The agitation abated, and with it—at least on that November day, and for nearly another year thereafter—the urge to write. How many Austrian war bonds he finally ended up with is not known, but it would have made no difference whatsoever unless he had wanted to paper his walls with them. The creditor firm, like his asbestos factory, went out of business.

*   *   *

The now more or less constant headaches and insomnia had, by the spring of 1916, thoroughly demoralized Kafka and begun to dominate every aspect of his life. He was, as his sister Ottla remarked in a note to her future husband, in really bad shape, and "one sometimes has to be patient with him." Ernst Weiss, who came to Prague in April, evidently lacked that patience. The two of them had a falling out whose precipitating cause is unclear but irrelevant, given Weiss's notorious paranoid tendencies and Kafka's labile state. In April, he even went so far as to consult a neurologist, who diagnosed a "cardiac neurosis" and recommended "electrotherapy," a suggestion Kafka chose to disregard. (The treatment, developed by the Hungarian physician Viktor Gonda, was being promoted at the time as a miracle cure for traumatic neuroses.)

A government directive of April 1916, which banned vacations for anyone deferred on occupational grounds, served as pretext for a petition which Kafka himself qualified as dishonest: if the war was to end by October, he wanted a long leave of absence without pay; if it continued, he wanted the institute to lift his draft exemption. "It was a total lie. It would have been only a partial lie had I asked for an immediate long leave and, in case of refusal, for dismissal. The truth would have been for me to give notice. I did not dare risk either, hence the total lie" (DI, 5/11/16).

Director Marschner, not unreasonably, assumed that all Kafka really wanted was his annual vacation in spite of the new rules, and he granted it at once. But when his valued employee kept on fantasizing about vague long-range plans, Marschner

> started talking like a psychiatrist. . . . Among other things, he told me that I, after all, didn't have to worry in the least about my position or career, whereas he himself in his early days had enemies attempting to saw this very limb off from under him. What limb? What tree? Where does mine grow, and who is sawing away at it? . . . I can handle the simplest practical task only by staging a major emotional scene, but how difficult that is. . . . When I want to turn right, I first turn left, then mournfully move toward the right. . . . The main reason may be fear: I am not afraid to turn left, because that is not really where I want to go. [FEL, 5/14/16]

Marschner certainly had no insight into Kafka's problems. But in responding to this confused and confusing request by urging him to take a vacation, he again displayed the sensible and quite unbureaucratic attitude that was to characterize his dealings with Kafka all through the years. Kafka himself later acknowledged that "what the institute put up with, in my case, transcends all the rules and regulations of bureaucratic officialdom." As usual, he gave himself no credit for that rather remarkable fact.

Shortly after this incident, a business trip took him for the first time to Marienbad. He found the spa so delightful that he decided to take Marschner up on his offer and arranged for a three-week vacation in July. Felice, on hearing of his plans, offered to join him, and this time he agreed.

* * *

They spent ten days together in Marienbad, occupying adjacent rooms at the exclusive Castle Balmoral Hotel. Years later, looking back on this one harmonious interlude with his fiancée, Kafka chose to remember it as even less unclouded than in fact it seems to have been. Felice was already waiting for him when he arrived on July 3, and he spent the first night in utter misery—"the well-known first night of despair." And three days later, he still noted in his diary: "Miserable night. Impossible to live with F. Unbearable living with anyone. This is not what I regret. Regrettable is the impossibility of not living alone" (DI, 7/6/16).

Quite suddenly, however, things between them took an abrupt and decisive turn for the better.

> We attained a human closeness such as I have never known and which in depth approached the relationship we had during the best period of our correspondence. Basically I have never been on intimate terms with a woman, except for two instances—the one in Zuckmantl (but there she was a woman, and I was a boy) and the one in Riva (and there she was a child, while I was totally mixed up and sick in every sense conceivable). This time, however, I saw the look of trust in a woman's eyes, and I could not deny myself. . . . After all, I never really knew her. Aside from other reservations, what also hampered me in the past was outright fear of the real human being behind those letters. [L, 7/16]

The doomsday fever and emotional pitch of life in time of war may have played a part in fostering this sudden idyll; so, no doubt, did Marienbad's gruesomely incongruous atmosphere of luxury and leisure. But more decisive, by far, was the distance they both had traveled in the nearly four years of what hardly qualified as a love affair; they emerged from it with a wistful readiness to accept one another as well as the constraints of reality.

It was an idyll of quiet tenderness rather than blazing passion, during which they achieved their first true emotional and—one assumes—physical intimacy. Kafka's health improved miraculously. His headaches vanished, and for the first time in months he slept well. In a joint letter to Felice's mother, they in effect announced their re-engagement, and even a visit to Kafka's mother, vacationing in nearby Franzensbad, went well beyond all expectations.

> Our contract, in brief, is as follows [he wrote to Brod]. We'll get married soon after the war, rent two or three rooms in some Berlin suburb, and each be responsible for our separate financial needs. F. will go on working as before, while I—well, that is too early to tell. True, if you try graphically to visualize the situation, you can see two rooms in, say, Karlshorst, in one of which F. gets up early in the morning, trots off to work, and returns at night exhausted and ready to drop into bed, while in the other room I lie on the couch feeding on milk and honey. . . . Nevertheless, for now it contains the promise of serenity and security, hence of a possible life. [L, 7/12/16]

The quiet contentment, the rare sense of being at peace with himself, evaporated almost immediately upon Felice's departure on July 13. Even the headaches returned as if on cue; the inner peace turned out to have been no more than a temporary truce, after all. Still, he was determined this time to stick to his decision, come what may, and resolutely fought his doubts and misgivings. The doubts and misgivings fought back, locked his head in a vise grip, kept him from sleeping, and once again drove him to the edge of madness. On August 18 he consulted an internist, who diagnosed an "extraordinary nervousness" and advised moderation in smoking, drinking, and in the consumption of meat. "My fits of despair," he wrote to Felice, "have a way of ending not with a leap out the window but into a doctor's office."

His hypochondria somewhat allayed by Dr. Mühlstein's essentially negative diagnosis, the "other foolishness" suddenly seized him again, and four days later he drew up yet another balance sheet for and against marriage, its muddled banality symptomatic of the effort to obfuscate the fundamental issues. Under the provocative heading "To Remain Pure," the brief credit column lists "Bachelor. I remain pure. I focus all my strength. Responsible only for myself. No worries, concentrating on work." The debit side contrasts this elysian vision with "To be married. Husband. Pure? You remain out of context, you become a fool, you fly off in all directions but don't make any headway, I draw from the circulation of human lifeblood the total of whatever strength I have available. All the more preoccupied with myself. (Grillparzer, Flaubert) Since my strength increases, I also carry more weight. Therein, however, lies a certain truth" (Fragments, "Wedding Preparations in the Country," p. 173).

But with the Marienbad meeting, his relationship to Felice had entered a new phase. For whatever reasons—and the emphasis on "purity" strongly suggests sexual intimacy and guilt as at least one of them—he now felt irrevocably committed to the marriage, a commitment that forced him to repress his continued ambivalence and let it fester in the subconscious.

In the meantime, he set out to guide and to reform Felice, now that he found himself faced with the real woman rather than an idealized or caricatured vision. In the Marienbad "contract," he had already extorted significant concessions from her, which ran counter to all bourgeois conventions and drastically altered the terms of their first engagement—a tiny flat in a bleak Berlin suburb instead of a spacious apartment

in the heart of romantic Prague, a business career instead of mother-
hood, and an impecunious freelance writer for a husband rather than a
respectable medium-level civil servant with pension rights. At his con-
siderately phrased but relentlessly insistent suggestion, Felice was made
to volunteer at the Jewish People's Home in Berlin, a residence and
educational institution for refugee children from the East sponsored by,
among others, Brod, Buber, and Landauer, and directed by the prominent Zionist educator Dr. Siegfried Lehmann. "I am desperately eager
for you to participate. It isn't the Zionist aspect that matters to me (nor
should it to you), but the thing itself, and what it may lead to" (FEL,
8/29/16).

What he evidently hoped it would lead to was her wasting less time
on what he judged to be idle distractions, and dedicating herself instead
to service in a socially useful cause. "This is a thousand times more important than the theater, Klabund, Gerson, and whatever else there may
be. Besides, it is one of the most self-serving of pursuits. One does not
help, but seeks help instead; there is more honey to be gathered from
this sort of work than from all the flowers in the Marienbad woods"
(FEL, 8/30/16). He expected this contact with authentic Jews to do
for her what it had done for him—help her overcome the prodigious
indifference to authentic Judaism which, in the light of his own growing
involvement with it, had seriously begun to trouble him.

> The values of Eastern Jewry can obviously not be conveyed in
> the Home . . . but perhaps—and therein lies the hope—they can
> be acquired, earned. And the volunteers have, so it seems to me,
> a chance to do just that. This involves Zionism (at least from
> my point of view, though not necessarily from yours) only in the
> sense that Zionism confers upon the work at the Home a youth-
> ful, vigorous method, youthful vigor in general, that it kindles
> national aspirations where all else might fail, that it invokes the
> immense and ancient past, albeit with the limitations without
> which Zionism could not exist. How you come to terms with
> Zionism is your business; any way you approach it (indifference,
> in other words, is out) will please me no end. It is still too early
> to discuss it. But should you ever feel yourself to be a Zionist
> (you once flirted with the idea, but it was a mere flirtation, not
> a serious commitment) and then come to realize that I myself am
> not a Zionist—as any close examination would probably estab-
> lish—I would not worry, and neither should you. Zionism is not
> something that divides people of good will. [FEL, 9/12/16]

Felice actually did get serious about her volunteer work at the Home. Ever conscientious and efficient, she taught classes several nights a week and took part in weekend outings, thereby evoking paroxysms of enthusiastic approval on Kafka's part. Educational theories and experiments—Dalcroze, Hellerau, etc.—had always held a special fascination for the child still suffering from the indignities inflicted upon him, and he bombarded Felice with detailed advice unconstrained by practical experience. He suggested and contributed books, even insisted on defraying her expenses, eager to feel that she was doing what he should be doing himself but considered beyond his strength. Her activities, moreover, seemed to promise a more substantial intellectual partnership, especially in the realm of Judaism.

> It will be up to you to direct [the children's] trust in you to matters other than religion and, where this cannot be done, to let the dark complexity of Judaism as a whole, so pregnant with impenetrable mystery, do its work. Which does not mean fudging anything, as people here, for instance, are in the habit of doing. That, I believe, would be altogether wrong. I myself would not dream of going to the synagogue. The synagogue is not something you sneak up on. I could not do this today any more than I could as a child; I still remember how I literally drowned in the terrifying boredom and pointlessness of the temple services. They were hell's way of staging a preview of my later office career. Those who crowd into the synagogue simply out of their Zionist convictions strike me as people trying to force their way into the temple in the wake of the Ark of the Covenant rather than entering quietly through the entrance meant for ordinary mortals. But your case, as far as I can judge, is different from mine. I would have to tell the children . . . that, as a result of my origins, my education, disposition, environment, I have nothing tangible in common with their faith. (The observance of the commandments is not an outward formality but, on the contrary, the very essence of the Jewish faith.) But while I would somehow have to confess this (and I would do so quite candidly; in the absence of candor, none of this makes sense), you, on the other hand, are perhaps not entirely bereft of some vestigial ties to the faith. They may well be no more than half-forgotten memories buried beneath the din of the metropolis, the press of business, the silt of thoughts and arguments accrued over the years. I am not suggesting that you lingered on the threshold, but perhaps somewhere you can still see the doorknob gleaming in the distance.

You might still be able to give the children at least a sorrowful answer to their question; I could not even do that. [FEL, 9/16/16]

*　　*　　*

There was now, however, another woman in Kafka's life, far closer to him in every sense of the word.

His little sister Ottla had always been a headstrong, bracingly rebellious child. And though it was the father she consistently set out to defy—by plotting against him with the servants, as he saw it, conspiring with the personnel in the store, and befriending "every kind of riffraff"—Kafka felt that she alone of the four children had inherited Herrmann's vitality and temperament. Despite the nine-year age gap, the special bond between them had survived the strains of adolescence and turned into an easy, undemanding intimacy. Beyond being brother and sister, the two had come to be friends. That any such relationship carries a heavy burden of psychic ambiguities is self-evident but says nothing about their particular resolution in the individual case; to ascribe Kafka's problems to an incestuous involvement with his sister or sisters— as has recently been done—merely points up the damage that primitive thinkers can do to complex thoughts. Kafka's own insight, on the other hand, was characteristically subtle: "Ottla at times seems to me just like the kind of mother I would have liked to have in my past: pure, truthful, honest, consistent, with humility and pride, receptivity and reticence, devotion and independence, shyness and courage in unfailing balance. I mention Ottla, because my mother is after all also part of her, though wholly beyond recognition" (FEL, 10/19/16).

Ottla at twenty-four was still headstrong and rebellious. She had worked full-time in the family store ever since leaving school, constantly at loggerheads with her father, whose blanket disapproval of everything she did and said provoked head-on collisions in which she proved more than a match for him; they ended, more often than not, with Herrmann clutching his chest, and Julie rushing in with the cold compresses. And as the relations between them continued downhill, she increasingly turned to her brother for support, affection, and strategic advice in the fight against the common enemy.

Franz had, in fact, always been the dominant influence in her life— inevitably so, given the family constellation. But it was not until Felice, rather perceptively, accused him of having "oppressed" his sister that he allowed himself to become aware of his role and began treating her as an adult whose love, devotion, and need entitled her to far more than she had thus far been receiving from him. And by 1916, Ottla's situation at home had become all but unbearable. One sore point was her budding romance with Joseph David, a Czech Gentile; her parents' apprehensions no doubt merely strengthened Ottla's resolve to follow her own instincts and counsel. At the same time, she was sick of the pointless drudgery in the family store. Inspired by a mixture of Zionism, bucolic romanticism, and plain orneriness, she had decided instead to seek redemption through labor, and to return to the soil by working as a farmhand or going to agricultural school, with a view to possibly joining a kibbutz in Palestine after the war. Nothing, needless to say, could have been better calculated to infuriate her father than this *mishegass* on the part of a crazy, mixed-up kid, this contemptuous repudiation of everything he stood for—and nothing could have elicited more enthusiastic support from her brother, who not only admired her spunk but also wholly identified with her aims.

The practical realization of her plans, however, took many months, and for the rest of the gloomy year brother and sister drew ever closer, forming an unholy alliance in the increasingly acrimonious confrontations at home. Ottla became Kafka's constant and only companion on their regular weekend outings. Moreover, her educational deficiencies— a result of the woefully inadequate schooling common to most young women of her day—challenged the irrepressible educator in him, and he made it his business to remedy them to the best of his ability by introducing her to Goethe, Schopenhauer, Hamsun, Plato, and Dostoevsky.

None of this, however, sufficed to cure his restlessness, headaches, and creative stasis. "Start seeing yourself for what you are, rather than trying to figure out what it is you are going to be," he admonished himself, concluding again with the obsessive notion that "the immediate task, without fail, is to become a soldier" (DI, 8/27/16). Kurt Wolff suggested a more appropriate way out—out of Prague, at any rate—by offering him an editorial position in Leipzig, which Kafka ruefully declined, pleading poor health; he obviously felt that a job in a publishing house was physically more demanding than service in the Austrian army. He did, however, use the opportunity finally to arrange for publication of "The Judgment" in book form; it appeared in October 1916 as a small, 22-page volume in the Doomsday Library.

As part of its series of literary evenings devoted to contemporary writing, the avant-garde art gallery Goltz in Munich invited Kafka in late fall to give a public reading from his works. He eagerly accepted, chose the as yet unpublished *Penal Colony* as his text, obtained—somewhat to his surprise—the requisite preliminary censorship approval, and, over the weekend of November 10, undertook the grueling round trip, which under wartime conditions took nearly eleven hours each way.

Felice came to Munich to meet him, but in the circumstances, they had time for little more than one brief quarrel in a pastry shop. The reading itself, from all accounts, was a calamitous failure. Max Brod, who had also been scheduled to read, was unable to attend, thus obligating Kafka to recite some of Brod's poetry in addition to his own story. Both offerings were poorly received by the audience and roundly panned by the critics, who quite unanimously damned the material and ridiculed the delivery. On the whole, Kafka agreed with their judgment. "I abused my writing by exploiting it as a ticket to Munich, a city to which otherwise I haven't the remotest spiritual ties, and after two years of not writing, I had the temerity to read in public, while for the past year and a half in Prague I didn't read a thing even to my best friends" (FEL, 12/7/16).

There was, however, one exception that more than made up for all the negative reviews put together. It is not entirely clear whether Rilke, who at the time happened to be in Munich, personally attended the reading, and whether Kafka actually met him. But a few weeks later he referred to the poet as having made "some extremely kind remarks about *The Stoker*, after which he said that in his opinion neither "The Metamorphosis" nor *The Penal Colony* had attained quite the same decisiveness. The remark is not easy to understand, but insightful just the same" (FEL, 12/7/16). Rilke's continued interest in Kafka also shows in a letter to Kurt Wolff of February 17, 1922, in which he requested the publisher to keep him posted "most particularly on anything new by Franz Kafka. I can assure you that I am among his most devoted readers" (Wolff, *Briefwechsel*, p. 152).

Kafka, rather paradoxically, rebounded from the fiasco with a surge of energy, though the Munich venture may itself already have signaled a turning point. Suddenly anxious to work but unable to do so in his noisy and unprepossessing room, he at last mustered the strength to look for more suitable quarters and enlisted the faithful Ottla in the search. Among the rental offerings happened to be one of the tiny, medieval row houses on Golden Lane, a street with fairy-tale magic high on the hill behind Hradčany Castle, currently a major tourist attraction. These curious dwellings were built in 1597 during the reign of King Rudolf II, a generously indiscriminate patron of science and quackery; legend has it that they were originally designed to house the monarch's resident crew of alchemists. If so, these must have all been dwarfs, perhaps shrunk in the process of transmuting base metals, for the entrances are barely five feet high, the windows diminutive, and the total floor space about six square meters.

The gangling Kafka rejected it out of hand, but Ottla instantly fell in love with the place and ended up renting it as a secret hideaway for herself, where she could escape from the tensions at home, a first step toward full independence. She turned what had been a filthy and neglected hovel into a cozy den, and when, by December, Kafka still had not unearthed anything to suit him—his "modest" requirements of total silence and a pleasant view at minimal expense were not easy to meet—she put her little house at his disposal. He could work there undisturbed every night in peace and quiet, using his own room in the Old Town only to sleep in until something better turned up.

It proved to be a brilliant interim solution.

> In the beginning, it had many shortcomings. . . . Now it suits me perfectly. Everything about it: the splendid climb up the hill, the silence up there. Only a thin partition separates me from my neighbor, but he is quiet enough. I carry my supper up there with me and usually stay until midnight. Then the advantages of the walk back to my own room: I simply have to make myself stop, and I can then cool my head on the way home. Also the life up there: it is quite something special to have a house of one's own, to lock the world not out of a room or an apartment but out of a whole house; to step from one's front door straightway into the snow of the peaceful lane. And all this for twenty crowns a month, with my sister taking care of all my needs, and a little flower girl [Ottla's pupil] doing what little cleaning is required, everything pleasant and in good shape. [FEL, 1/17]

It was here that he dug in for the winter, for a perversely contented hermit's existence that provided the order and routine on which he depended for his productivity, if not his inspiration. Working steadily between December 1916 and April 1917, he created a substantial body of work which, aside from the fragmentary "Guardian of the Tomb," his only attempt at a play, included the bulk of the short pieces published in his lifetime: "The Bridge," "The Hunter Gracchus," "The Bucket Rider," "Jackals and Arabs," "The New Attorney," "A Country Doctor," "In the Gallery," "A Visit to the Mine," "The Next Village," "A Fratricide," "The Neighbor," "The Great Wall of China," "An Old Manuscript," "The Knock at the Manor Gate," "Eleven Sons," "A Crossbreed," "Report to an Academy," and "The Worry of a Family Man."

* * *

It was a good winter for hermits.

Not so for the rest of Prague. The streetcars had stopped running, the theaters shut down, most lectures and meetings were canceled. Perhaps most painful were the nights of arctic solitude: the few cafés and restaurants that chose to remain open had nothing to offer beyond dim, unheated premises and infusions of home-brewed cynicism. The country was running out of food, out of fuel, and out of hope.

At that, 1916 had been another year of glory for the Central Powers, or at least for their generals, whose triumphs were enshrined in a permanent addition to the German language—the expression *sich zu Tode siegen*, to kill oneself by winning victories. Except that those who got killed were not the generals.

The massive Russian spring offensive against the Austrians, coordinated with Italian pressure from the south, had been halted, though at great cost. In August, Rumania declared war on the Central Powers but was quickly defeated in a series of battles that ended in December with the German occupation of Bucharest. In the west, the Germans had fought the Allies to a stalemate at Verdun. But the military situation bore scant relation to the global picture. Far more significant than the blood-soaked fields of Flanders or the banks of the Isonzo were the waters of the Atlantic and the Mediterranean, still the all but exclusive domain of the British navy. Despite the challenge of the German U-boats, the Allied blockade remained devastatingly effective, superimposed as it was on an economy already disrupted and strained to the limits. By 1916, with stockpiles nearing exhaustion and first priority given to the needs of the military, the civilian population experienced its first severe shortages of food and fuel. Already in October, Kafka's mother, in reply to Felice's New Year's greetings, wrote that "we observed the Jewish holidays like good Jews. On New Year's we closed the store for two days, and yesterday, on Yom Kippur, we fasted and prayed a lot. The fasting came easy, since we've been in training for it all year" (FEL, 10/8/16). If even the relatively affluent Kafkas felt the pinch, those less privileged were presumably in correspondingly more trouble.

It was the onset of winter, however, that brought real suffering. The food shortages grew serious, leading to widespread malnutrition and outright hunger. Almost as bad was the lack of coal. Despite rigorous conservation measures, including the suspension of most non-essential, i.e., not war-related, transportation, there was little coal left for civilian uses. In the circumstances, the dwarfish dimensions of Kafka's matchbox of a studio on Golden Lane proved a real boon; it took, as he discovered, just a manuscript and a few sticks of wood to heat it.

On the propaganda front, however, the Allies were winning hands down with their promise of independence for the national minorities of the Habsburg empire—a promise rendered all the more appealing by the oppressive terror with which the Austrians responded to it.

Prague was, as always, at the seismic center of the shock waves convulsing the monarchy, and no group felt more threatened by the impending cataclysm than Prague's Jews, exquisitely sensitive to every tremor. The first came on October 21, when Friedrich Adler, the son of Austria's socialist leader, shot and killed the prime minister, Count Stürgkh. Adler, though an atheist, was a Jewish atheist, and the news of the assassination caused grave concern in Jewish communities, mindful of past experience. The next blow, a month later, was the death of the octogenarian Emperor Franz Joseph. His 68-year reign—from 1848 to 1916—had spanned the entire period of Jewish emancipation and assimilation, and the generation of the Jewish "founding fathers" tended to venerate him with absurdly uncritical devotion. But even the sons, down to the militant Zionists around the *Selbstwehr*, generally regarded him as a fair-minded ruler who, while far from unbiased, detested demagoguery and had always striven to protect Jewish lives from mob violence. His successor, the Emperor Karl, on the other hand, was an unknown quantity whom plausible rumors linked to anti-semitic extremists.

As it happened, these particular fears proved groundless. Fritz Adler's brilliant defense at his trial made him the hero of the by then thoroughly war-weary Austrian working class and undercut all attempts to exploit his case for anti-Jewish propaganda. The bumbling new emperor didn't stay on his throne long enough to do much damage. But there were other, equally disquieting developments. The Russian "February" revo-

lution of March 1917 had not only raised the hopes and fired the imagination of their fellow Slavs in Prague but also enabled Masaryk to
organize a Czech Legion on Russian soil. Wholesale desertions from the
Austrian army became commonplace. And when, in April 1917, the
United States officially entered the war on the Allied side, no one could
have had any further doubts or illusions.

In Prague, the Czechs were—as yet secretly—jubilant, the Germans grimly defiant, the Jews apprehensive. By way of precaution,
Herrmann Kafka dropped the second "r" from his name, to become
what may have struck him as a less conspicuously Teutonic Hermann.

*   *   *

That the hermit on Golden Lane rode the tide in his dream capsule
without feeling the chill in his bones seems improbable, if for no other
reason than that he started every working day having to face the heartbreak and misfortunes of people mangled in the gears of the war machine. But as he carried his frugal supper up the castle hill every night
and immured himself in the house and in his work, he was certainly
more determined than ever to shut the world out of his life. Although
Max Brod and Oskar Baum dropped in on him for brief visits, he himself made no attempt to see any of his friends. Withdrawing even further,
he all but broke off contact with Felice. No letters of his dated between
January and September of 1917 have been preserved—"the until now
longest surcease in five years of suffering" (O, 8/29/17). Some few
have apparently been lost, but there clearly was a deliberate effort on
his part to avoid even thinking about the marriage, to simply plunge
into it eyes closed and teeth clenched, accept it like death itself as his
immutable fate in some distant future.

With the arrival of spring, however, the protective walls around
him began to crumble. Ottla finally carried out her threat and left home
in April to work on a 50-acre farm owned by her brother-in-law, Karl
Hermann, in the north Bohemian village of Zuerau (now Siřem). The
sanctuary on Golden Lane had to be given up, but in March Kafka was
able to move into the apartment of his dreams, for which he had been
negotiating since early in the year.

It was a rather improbable abode, in a remote wing of the eighteenth-
century Schönborn Palace, now housing the U.S. embassy in Prague—
two vast rooms with antechamber, morning light, a view of the immense

garden, and above all silence. "I have electric light, though no bathroom, no tub, but I can do without that." He was absolutely delighted with his find and even allowed himself to envisage it as an auspicious environment for the initial adjustment to life with Felice: "After the war, I am definitely going to try and get a year's leave, first of all. . . . The two of us would then have the most marvelous apartment I could dream of in all Prague, though only for a relatively brief time, during which you would have to do without a kitchen of your own, or even a bathroom. Still, it would suit me very well, and you could get a proper rest for two or three months. And that indescribable park, in spring, perhaps in summer (with the landlord's family gone), or in the fall" (FEL, 1/17).

Aside from the lack of plumbing, the apartment, as he was to find out, had another drawback—it was forever clammy and cold. The rooms of the drafty old palace, with their high ceilings and enormous windows, were difficult to heat in the best of circumstances; given the coal shortage, the task had become hopeless, and even the ascetic Kafka later admitted to having felt uncomfortable on occasion.

Even so, he was pleased with his new quarters, across the river from his haunts in the Old Town, providing not only seclusion but even an excuse for not going out at night: the palace gates, once shut, could not be opened from the outside. And as the inspiration began once again to give out in spring, he spent his evenings on a new and secret passion: studying Hebrew. Starting out all by himself, with the heroic pedantry with which he tackled all such tasks, he plowed through lesson after lesson of Moses Rath's venerable *Hebrew Grammar and Reader for Schools and Self-Instruction*, the classic—and classically indigestible— "modern" Hebrew textbook of his day, and slowly progressed from translating "My books, my copybook, and my pens are lying in my satchel" to "If it will not rain tomorrow, I shall go to the forest with my girl friends and pick flowers." He actually made good progress, nonetheless, stunning all his ardently Zionist friends by his advanced knowledge when, the following year, he joined them in taking a course with Mordechai Langer.

With the arrival of Felice in Prague early in July, however, this period of creative reclusion came to an end. They once again announced their engagement, this time without fanfare or ceremony, yet eager—if Brod's testimony is to be credited—to play by the rules: "Franz and conventions! It was a pitiful sight, yet he made every effort to conform to the conventions he accepted as valid. A different partner might, of course, have freed him from such compulsions by one mighty roar of laughter. Then again, it seems doubtful if Franz would have wanted or accepted such freedom. Oddly enough, the two of them even paid me a formal visit on July 9, 1917. There was something moving, and at the same time spooky, about the sight of the rather embarrassed couple, particularly of Franz in his unaccustomed high, stiff collar" (Brod, bio., p. 140).

Two days later, Kafka accompanied Felice on a visit to her sister Elise, exiled—by marriage—to Arad, a remote commercial center in the Hungarian boondocks. He survived, though it was "not a trip designed to promote rest or understanding," and returned by himself a few days later via Budapest and Vienna. He had a brief, less than happy reunion with his old friend Yitzhak Levi, settled in Budapest for the duration. Drug addiction, among other things, had turned the always cranky but once spirited actor into a ranting paranoiac who accused Kafka of having joined in the conspiracy against him. In Vienna, Kafka spent the evening with the Prague poet Rudolf Fuchs. Recollecting their meeting twenty years after the fact, Fuchs claimed that in the course of it Kafka "quite calmly" informed him that he had "just broken off with his fiancée." There is no other evidence to substantiate this assertion.

On July 19, he was back in a city seething beneath the still placid, in fact comatose surface. From his headquarters in Kiev, Tomáš Masaryk had issued a call for the immediate abdication of the Habsburgs.

Sauve qui peut. Just before his trip to Arad, Kafka had submitted thirteen stories, the bulk of his winter's work, to Kurt Wolff, who immediately offered to publish them. (Due to the unsettled circumstances, the actual publication of these pieces in a volume entitled *A Country Doctor* did not take place until 1919). In his reply of July 27, Kafka accepted the offer, leaving all technical details up to the publisher. For the time being, he stated, he was not even interested in the matter of royalties, but

> this is likely to change drastically after the war. I am going to quit my job (this step is, in fact, the strongest hope that sustains me), I am going to marry and leave Prague, possibly for Berlin. Even then, as I am still inclined to believe, I won't have to depend entirely on the income from my writing. Nonetheless I— or the deep-rooted civil servant within me, which amounts to the same—am obsessively frightened by the thought of what lies

ahead. I sincerely hope, dear Mr. Wolff, that when that time comes, you will not entirely forsake me, provided, of course, that I in some measure merit your help. In the light of all these uncertainties, both present and future, a word from you in that sense would mean a great deal to me at this time. [L, 7/27/17]

The word did come back at once; Kurt Wolff was not one to procrastinate. By return mail, he promised Kafka "steady material support" after the war.

And yet, it came too late.

Though he paid little attention to it at the time, Kafka during the first week of August had on several occasions spat up small quantities of blood. On the night of August 9, however, he suffered a massive pulmonary hemorrhage.

Twenty-three

Years later, in a letter to Milena Jesenská, he described the onset of his illness:

> I got up, excited by the novelty of it all . . . also somewhat alarmed, of course, leaned out of the window, went over to the washstand, walked around the room, sat down in the bed—the blood kept coming. At that I wasn't at all unhappy, because for some reason I gradually realized that, provided the hemorrhage stopped, I would be able to sleep for the first time after some three or four almost sleepless years. And in fact it did stop (it hasn't come back since), and I slept the rest of the night. True, in the morning the maid came in (I was living in Schönborn Palace at the time), a decent, almost self-sacrificing but extremely matter-of-fact girl, saw the blood, and said: "You're not long for this world, Doctor." Yet I felt better than ever, went to the office, and only later in the afternoon saw the doctor. [MIL, p. 12]

Dr. Mühlstein, the general practitioner, diagnosed a bronchitis, gave Kafka three bottles of medicine, and told him to come back in a month unless he had a recurrence. After a second hemorrhage the following night, the good doctor ("whom, by the way, I didn't like at all at that point") allowed that there might be some pulmonary involvement and finally succeeded in scaring Kafka by trying to reassure him: "All city dwellers are tubercular anyway, an inflammation of the lung tips (one of those figures of speech, like saying piglet when you mean big fat sow) isn't all that terrible; a few tuberculin injections will take care of it" (O, p. 39).

For two entire weeks he kept the secret to himself, reliving all the sins and transgressions that had brought him to this pass, while never doubting for one moment that resistance was futile, and that life as he had known it was about to come to an end, for better as well as for worse. It was not until August 24 that something like a surge of rebellion and common sense made him confide in Max Brod, who immediately took matters in hand: "Kafka's illness requires action," he noted in his diary. "Kafka sees it as psychogenic, his salvation from marriage, so to speak. He calls it his final defeat. But has been sleeping well ever since. Liberated? Tormented soul" (Brod, bio., p. 144).

Even so, it took another ten days of impassioned argument before Kafka let himself be persuaded to consult the eminent lung specialist Professor Friedl Pick.

> Without going into all the medical details [he informed Felice on September 9], the result is that I have tuberculosis in the apices of both lungs. The onset of an illness as such did not surprise me, and neither did the blood; after all, with my headaches and insomnia I have for years been asking for a major illness, until the maltreated blood finally burst out. But that it turned out to be tuberculosis, of all things, did come as a surprise, hitting me overnight like that, at age thirty-four, and without any known antecedents in the family. Well, I must accept it; moreover, the hemorrhage seems to have flushed away my headaches. The prognosis is still uncertain, the future course of the disease remains its own secret; my age may possibly help to slow it [FEL, 9/19/17]

By way of therapy, Pick recommended a sanatorium cure. Kafka, however, in not merely accepting but fully embracing his illness as both doom and salvation, seemed determined this time not to settle for any compromise measures. He applied for immediate retirement on grounds of disability, a request which Dr. Marschner refused to forward "in your own interest," granting him instead a preliminary three-month leave of absence. As for sanatoria, Kafka was familiar enough with their routine to reject the idea out of hand. "Now that I am really starting to be sick, I'll never again go near a sanatorium. Everything there is wrong" (L, 1918). What he felt he needed, most of all, was silence, a move to a distant planet infinitely remote from Prague, the office, the family, the war, the world—and with it the all-encompassing love and care of an understanding, totally devoted mother. On September 12, he left Prague to stay with Ottla in the village of Zuerau. He planned to spend his three-month leave with his sister, but the three months were to stretch, with brief interruptions, into what he later called the eight happiest months of his life.

* * *

Objectively his illness, though serious, was at this stage far from life-threatening, and Dr. Mühlstein's grudging attempt at reassurance had a sound basis in fact and experience. The great white plague of the nineteenth century, always endemic in the cities, had flared up again with particular virulence during the war, the result no doubt of extreme deprivation and widespread malnutrition. And although Koch had isolated the tuberculosis bacillus back in 1882 and even developed a vaccine—the "tuberculin" referred to by Mühlstein—whose only drawback was that it didn't work, the exact etiology and mode of transmission retained much of their mystery. In Kafka's case, it was the clammy apartment in Schönborn Palace that got blamed as the precipitating factor, further proof of the father's prescient wisdom, since Herrmann had been vehemently opposed to the move. No one, however, seems to have suspected the possibly baneful role of Kafka's food fetishes—his vegetarianism, which made him consume large quantities of milk, and his obsession with the "natural goodness" of natural foods, which made him insist on drinking his milk raw, un-pasteurized, and unboiled in a country where cattle inspection, a joke even in peacetime, had been suspended altogether for the duration of the war and where, in any case, milk from tubercular cows would not have been withheld from a market desperately short of food. In his rural retreat, Kafka obviously had ample opportunity to indulge this passion, and he made the most of it in the belief, fostered already by the ancient Greeks, that fresh milk was the cure for precisely what ailed him.

Which once again would tend to bear out the wisdom of the fathers and is ultimately of mere marginal relevance, the source of the infection being only one factor, and a far from decisive one, in the evolution of this particular disease. As the patch test, an outgrowth of Koch's unsuccessful vaccine, subsequently demonstrated, Dr. Mühlstein was absolutely right: most city dwellers in his day did indeed show evidence of a passing bout with TB at some point in their lives, as a rule with minimal or no clinical manifestations. In a relatively small though numerically significant number of cases, however, additional factors such as stress, genetic predisposition, or lowered resistance led to an infection that justified concern; throughout the war, and for years thereafter, tuberculosis accounted for 30 percent of all deaths in Prague.

Nevertheless, the diagnosis as such was certainly no death warrant. Already in Kafka's day, the majority of patients—and the overwhelming majority of middle-class patients—eventually recovered. The standard treatment involved rest, a mild climate, and a high-calorie diet. The physical benefits of this regimen, chiefly measured in terms of weight gained, were largely illusory. But for those who could afford a sanatorium cure, it meant escape from an often stressful home environment and a chance for the natural recuperative forces of body and soul to come into full play.

What complicated Kafka's case was that he so obviously welcomed the illness, at least in its initial stages, as a form of salvation.

On September 20, a week after he had settled in with Ottla, Felice came to see him. Nothing much was said between them during her two-day visit, nothing much needed to be said. But at the end of the month, Kafka wrote her a letter—the next to the last ever—that not only summed up their five years together but also defined the nature of his illness with an uncompromising lucidity that mere medical science could never hope to match.

> As you know, there are two of me at war with each other. That the better of the two belongs to you is something I have come to doubt less than ever in the past few days. By word and by silence, and by a mixture of both, you have been kept informed about the progress of the war throughout these five years, a torment to you more often than not. . . . Of those two struggling within me, or rather, whose struggle constitutes the essence of myself except for one small, tortured remnant, one is good, the other evil. At times they switch masks, which further confuses the already confused struggle. Yet despite setbacks I had finally come to believe that the most improbable . . . would happen after all, that I, grown wretched and miserable over the years, would at last be allowed to have you.
>
> Now it turns out that too much blood has been lost. The blood shed by the good one (he now seems good to us) on your behalf has served the enemy. . . . Because secretly, you know, I don't believe this illness to be tuberculosis, or at least not primarily tuberculosis, but my all-around bankruptcy. I thought it could

still go on, and it can't. It wasn't my lung that the blood came pouring out of, but a decisive stab wound inflicted by one of the two opponents. . . . The supposed tuberculosis . . . is a weapon compared to which the countless earlier ones, ranging from "constitutional frailty" all the way up to my "work" and back down to my "stinginess" stand revealed in all their primitive expediency.

And finally, let me tell you a secret which at the moment I myself still don't believe (though the darkness closing in on me from afar as I attempt to work or think might perhaps convince me) but which nonetheless is bound to be true: I shall never get well again. Just because what we are here dealing with is not a tuberculosis that can be nursed back to health in a deck chair but a weapon that remains absolutely indispensable as long as I live. It and I cannot both go on living. [FEL, 9/30/17]

They saw each other one more time, in Prague on Christmas. Felice made it clear that she would stand by him. He made it equally clear that he would not accept the sacrifice, would not dream of adding to the already unbearable burden of his guilt toward her. He would never marry—not her, nor anyone else. "What I have to do," he told Brod that afternoon, "I can only do myself. Get clear about the ultimate things. The Western Jew is not clear about them; that is why he has no right to marry. For him there is no marriage. Unless, of course, he is the kind that doesn't worry about such things. A businessman, for instance" (Brod, bio., p. 146).

The next day he bade Felice goodbye at the station, then went to Brod's office and broke down. "I cried more that morning," he wrote to Ottla, "than in all the years since childhood" (O, p. 47).

Felice returned to Berlin and, a year and a half later, married a businessman. According to Brod, Kafka was pleased when he learned of the marriage.

* * *

Flight into illness, but the first stop was paradise. Perhaps never before had Kafka felt so unpressured, at one with the seasonal rhythms of the isolated village still not electrified and many miles from Michelob, the nearest railroad stop. His sister knew how to take care of him without encroaching on his sense of privacy. "Ottla literally carries me on her wings through this difficult world. The room is excellent, airy, warm, and almost totally quiet; everything I am supposed to eat is piled up around me in abundance . . . and freedom in the bargain, freedom best of all" (L, 9/17). Ottla, in turn, reported that her brother dreamed of buying a house in the village after the war, with a plot just large enough for a garden to keep him occupied. "That is really all he wants, at this point. . . . I think that God must have sent him this illness, without which he would never have left Prague."

With no apparent help from him, the hemorrhage in a single night seemed to have washed away all the intractable problems—from marriage and job to insomnia and headaches—which reason, conscience, and a vegetarian diet had vainly struggled to resolve for years. "Sometimes it seems to me as though brain and lungs had communicated without my knowledge. 'Things just can't go on this way,' said the brain; and after five years, the lungs offered to help." Small wonder that at least in the beginning his attitude toward his illness was "that of a small child clinging to his mother's skirts." He luxuriated in his freedom, scrupulously observed the hallowed therapeutic ritual of long sunbaths in a homemade deck chair, occasionally lent a hand around the farm and in the vegetable garden, and spent long, lazy autumn evenings with Ottla by candlelight "in a good little marriage." He read a fair amount, "almost exclusively Czech and French, and nothing but autobiographies and collections of letters," as he informed Felix Weltsch, who kept him supplied with books from the university library. And by conscientiously forcing himself to eat three proper meals a day, with ample fresh milk in between, he managed to gain two pounds during the first month.

And yet, two pounds or twenty, he had convinced himself that he would never recover. And since at the same time he undoubtedly also wanted to be proven wrong, he had to find a way of living with death, not as an abstract notion, but as a concrete possibility. Life with tuberculosis was not unlike the life in the trenches he had yearned for, minus the mud, a precarious balancing act on the crumbling edge of mortality. And with the focus shifting onto "ultimate things," the proximate fears, worries, and obsessions lost much of their urgency, the more so since Ottla was always ready to defend and protect him.

Knowing that he dreaded nothing so much as having to go back to work, she tried to free him permanently from this nightmare. Early in November she went to see her parents, who had thus far been kept in the dark about Kafka's condition, told them the truth, and also arranged for an interview at the institute with Director Marschner in yet another attempt to obtain her brother's definitive retirement on disability. Marschner was sympathetic but firm in his refusal, though he readily agreed to an extension of the leave, with full pay.

What Ottla did not know, and what Kafka only discovered on his Christmas trip to Prague, was that the power over such decisions had already slipped from Marschner's grasp. By the end of 1917, with the Habsburg empire teetering on the brink, the Czech majority was beginning to assert its claims. At the front, well over ten thousand Czech soldiers deserted to join Masaryk's Czech Legion; at home, the army of subordinate Czech civil servants was getting ready for the take-over by sabotaging the Austrian administration at every turn and breaking aggressively into the top-level posts traditionally barred to them. The Workmen's Accident Insurance was one of their targets. When Otto Přibram, its president and Kafka's original sponsor, died suddenly in November 1917, only a legalistic subterfuge enabled the German minority on the Board of Directors to block the election of a Czech successor. The resulting stalemate was resolved in January 1918 by direct government intervention and the appointment of a provisional board, which did nothing to allay the murderous antagonism of the two factions. Marschner and his German top assistants, though still defiant, knew that their days were numbered, and moved, if at all, only with extreme caution.

In the meantime, however, Kafka had obtained his reprieve and could look forward to spending the winter and spring in Zuerau. "Once you get over the somewhat disconcerting sensation of living in the modern version of a zoo, in which the animals are given free run of the place, there is nothing more comfortable and, above all, more free than life in the village. Free in the spiritual sense, with the least possible encroachment on the part of either the surroundings or the past. This kind of life is not to be confused with life in a small town, which is probably horrible. I'd like to live here forever" (L, 10/17).

Initially, he did no writing at all and even kept his diary entries to the barest minimum. "I cannot concentrate on writing. If, like a bat, I could save myself by digging holes, I would dig holes." But in mid-October he began the series of aphorisms which, in his own later revision, were published posthumously in 1931 under the title *Meditations on Sin, Suffering, and Hope*, contrived by Brod. Meditations they certainly were, even if Brod's extreme unctuousness clashes with the terse rigor of the text itself. It marks Kafka's first attempt to deal with his situation in transcendental terms; the Hasidic undertones reflect not only his growing familiarity with actual texts but, more basically, his affinity for the ways of thinking and the type of argumentation which preceded and inspired that particular literature.

But the hours of daylight were brief and, during the winter, curtailed even his reading. Moreover, an infestation of mice sent him into hysterics and made it impossible for him to sleep or work in his room until he learned to keep a cat, a cure that struck him as scarcely preferable to the disease. "When it comes to mice," he wrote to Brod, "I am scared of them, plain and simple. Finding the reason for that is a job for the psychoanalyst. I don't happen to be one." And to Weltsch's well-meant counsel he replied, with some asperity, "You think you have nothing against mice? Of course not. You also have nothing against cannibals. But if, in the middle of the night, they came creeping out of all your closets and flashed their teeth, you would definitely stop being fond of them." When his "Report to an Academy" appeared in the November issue of Martin Buber's magazine *Der Jude*, Brod reported that "Werfel was enthusiastic about your monkey story, thinks you are the greatest German writer. This, as you know, has long since been my opinion as well." Kafka answered that "Werfel always gets effusive that way, and if you want to see it as proof of his good feelings, so be it."

He read Tolstoy and Herzen, but it was Kierkegaard, notably the Danish philosopher's autobiographical writings, that most captivated him by the striking parallels they revealed to his own quest and ambivalence, not least Kierkegaard's long, tormented, and ultimately aborted engagement to Regine Olsen. "Marry and you'll rue it; marry not, and again you will rue it" was the sort of proposition born of fear and trembling with which Kafka had no difficulty empathizing.

Its more general validity, however, was also at just that time being forcefully brought home to him. Both Max Brod and Oskar Baum were undergoing acute crises in their chronically problematic marriages, and Kafka, having just broken off his own engagement, found himself cast in the role of marriage counselor during his week in Prague. It was a task he disliked, not least because it threatened his own precarious equilibrium, but friendship compelled him to do what he could, and the surviving letters dealing with that episode exhibit an impressive combination of tact and candor. His insights were shrewd, sensitive, conveyed with a light touch and an abundance of that common sense so egregiously unavailable to him when wrestling with his own problems.

In essence, as he well knew and emphasized, outside advice was worthless to those not ready for it, and Brod certainly was not. He felt victimized by his wife's reaction to his extramarital affairs and wallowed in romanticized self-pity. Kafka's sympathies clearly were with Elsa Brod, but he remained loyal to Max, though his loyalty did not prevent him from skewering Brod's sanctimonious platitudes and confronting him with the sort of either/or choices that he himself had never been able to make. (Brod did not make them, either. He time and again wiggled through the cracks, remaining formally married and informally promiscuous.)

Oskar Baum was at least more forthright about his troubles. The handsome blind novelist loved his wife, in his fashion, along with half a dozen other women. Since none of them could live up to his standards of perfection, he had come to regard marriage itself as an impossible as well as intolerable institution. In his own case, however, guilt feelings, a dash of sentimentality, and, one suspects, some reservations relating to his handicap, kept him from leaving his wife and six-year-old son, a noble decision for which he felt entitled to Kafka's—and the world's— compassion. Kafka rather reluctantly took Baum back to Zuerau and put up with him for a week, "saying yes or no whenever I thought I heard him say yes or no, and my only contribution consisted of agreeing with what I thought I heard."

The trip to Prague, the break with Felice, and Baum's visit set him back for a while, but the wintry silence of the village and the resumption of his solitary life with Ottla—"actually we live together, or at least I live with you, better than with anyone else"—soon restored a measure of calm. He corrected the proofs of *A Country Doctor*, a collection of fifteen of his stories Wolff was about to bring out, and returned them on January 27, 1918, with the request for a flyleaf dedication worded "To My Father." That no irony was consciously intended seems clear from a letter, written two months later, in which Kafka asked Brod to intercede directly with Wolff so as to expedite "what presumably will be my last book. . . . Ever since I decided to dedicate the book to my father, I am anxious for it to appear as soon as possible. Not that I could thereby bring about a reconciliation between us; the roots of our enmity run far too deep for that. But at least I will have done something, not perhaps settled in Palestine, but at least traveled there with my finger on the map" (L, 3/18).

Palestine, the return to the source, communal life as an authentic Jew among Jews, now offered a glimpse of the Promised Land, and at precisely the moment when the dream was assuming practical reality. In mid-January, British troops had driven the Turks out of Jerusalem, and from a special issue of the *Selbstwehr* Kafka for the first time learned of the Balfour Declaration. As for himself, however, he feared that all he still had time and strength for was a book, dedicated to his father by way of defiance, self-justification, and a plea for understanding which he knew in advance to be futile.

In a journal entry of February 1918 he wrote that "it isn't indolence, ill will, or clumsiness . . . that account for my failures, or not even failures: family life, friendship, marriage, profession, literature. It is lack of soil, of air, of law. My task is to create them, not so as to make up for past omissions, but so as not to omit anything, because that task is as valid as any other. . . . I have not, like Kierkegaard, been led into life by the albeit already heavy drooping hand of Christianity, nor did I catch the last fringe of the vanishing Jewish prayer shawl, like the Zionists. I am the end or the beginning" (4th Octavo Notebook, 2/18).

It was during that same period that he drew up the program for a "Commune of Workers without Private Property," which, if one over-looks the heavy dose of utopian naïveté and monastic asceticism, could be read as a blueprint for the Israeli kibbutz. And in fact, the unmistakable bootprints of Tolstoy strongly point to Aaron David Gordon, prophet of Jewish "redemption through labor" and one of the founders of the kibbutz movement, as the inspiration for this curious document, often cited in evidence of Kafka's social conscience or socialist convictions. Gordon's ideas, with which Kafka must have been already familiar through the *Selbstwehr* (the two subsequently met in Prague), themselves owed much to Tolstoy and Kropotkin, though Gordon tempered their brand of anarchism by a grasp of practical reality as inaccessible to anarchist aristocrats as it evidently was to Kafka.

What this rather turgid manifesto suggests is probably both more and less. In his heart, Kafka stubbornly clung to the hope of eventually "making aliyah." Despite increasingly frail health, he continued till nearly the end of his life to fantasize about settling in Palestine, first as a bookbinder in Hugo Bergmann's Jerusalem library, later as a waiter in a Tel Aviv restaurant. And in a deeper sense, Gordon's religion of labor was one faith that had always appealed to Kafka. "The working life as a matter of conscience and a matter of faith in one's fellow man," as he put it in the manifesto, recalls his "writing as a prayer" and obviously transcends programmatic socialism.

Marriage as the victory over the father, Palestine as the conquest of death. In the spring of 1918, both goals seemed equally remote. Prague remained the center of gravity, and even Zuerau turned out to be locked in its orbit. On April 30, Kafka moved back in with his parents and resumed his job at the office.

* * *

Though somewhat loath to admit it, he was not unhappy to be back among the familiar landmarks of his life, in the city he professed to hate. Prague was eerily quiet in that last spring of the war, a battle-ground after the battle, haunted by haggard, careworn, and exhausted survivors. The food shortages, ever-mounting casualties, and brutal repression had sparked strikes and riots earlier in the year; the Czech masses demanded food, the Czech leaders demanded independence, the German-speaking bourgeoisie demanded protection and the rigorous suppression of all subversive elements. As late as March 1918, Kafka's superpatriot cousin Bruno Kafka, legislator and editor of the right-wing *Bohemia*, sent a sharply worded protest to Vienna denouncing the censorship board for having permitted the performance of a Czech opera—Leoš Janáček's *Jenufa* in Max Brod's translation—which in his opinion compromised "the German character" of the capital, at the Imperial Opera House. By May, however, the warring factions had retreated into their customary sullen, age-old enmity, waiting for the inevitable end; the Czechs with hope, hate, and confidence, the Jews and Germans with foreboding and resignation.

Except for Kafka, who, if he did so at all, contemplated the coming revolution with supreme indifference. His health had greatly improved in Zuerau. More important, and inextricably linked to this physical improvement, were the inner changes which the shock and gradual recovery had brought about. He had been given a second chance at childhood in those eight months with Ottla, and the world to which he was returning had lost much of its power to terrorize him. The mundane fears of long ago had assumed metaphysical dimensions, and having faced the prospect of dying, he found it a great deal easier to put up with his family, his job, and with what he perceived as his all-around failure. Wistful and bemused rather than depressed, he withdrew more than ever, avoided his friends, for some weeks even refused to see Brod, not so much out of despair this time as out of a need to listen to the silence within.

And he had stopped writing, had even given up on his diary. "The Judgment," he now felt, had marked not the initial surge but rather the high point and outer limits of his creative powers. Everything he had written since was merely a labored effort to delay the slide into insignificance.

Yet even this defeat he accepted with relative equanimity. His headaches were gone, his lungs were clear, according to Professor Pick, and he slept reasonably well in what had been Ottla's room. With only three adults left in the house, he now seldom had reason to complain of noise, the less so since he no longer spent nights at his desk. His father, though at bottom still convinced that everything was his son's own fault, was at least trying to be civil. Julie, tragically self-effacing as always, did what she could to make her child feel at home. More than anyone, certainly more than anyone was aware of, she suffered with him and for him, yet was as miserably dumbstruck by fear as she had always been by love. In any case, both parents were consumed by worries about food, money, business, the war, the future, the children, all subjects about which Kafka displayed a pronounced lack of interest that obviated most points of potential friction or even contact.

This same detachment was no doubt what inured him to the mounting tension at the office and enabled him to remain on good terms with both his Czech and his German colleagues when he reported back for duty on May 2. The institute had split into two fiercely hostile camps, the Czechs honing their knives against the day of reckoning, the Germans well aware that *Der Tag* was fast approaching but determined to hang in till the bitter end and defend every last post, power, and privilege. As institute Secretary, protégé of the late president, intimate of such top executives as Marschner and Pfohl, Kafka was automatically identified with the German faction. Moreover, his duties in 1918 mainly revolved around the Frankenstein Veterans Hospital for Nervous Diseases, which he had helped to found and which was supported exclusively by the German community in Bohemia.

In spite of this ambiguous position, he maintained good relations with the increasingly militant Czech contingent. He was, of course, fluent in Czech, had never manifested the least pro-Austrian or anti-Czech bias, and made no effort to ingratiate himself with either side. Another point in his favor was, ironically, the fact of his being Jewish; the token Jew under the German administration eventually became the token German under the Czechs, the nominal representative of a minority he didn't represent. On the other hand, he had always been well liked by everyone, from director to doorman, from secretary to cleaning lady. The apparent ease with which he managed to get along with everyone during this tense period no doubt owed more to his character and personality than to any extraneous factors.

It was a lonely but rather busy and not unhappy life he led that summer, swimming regularly, taking long walks, and resuming his Hebrew studies, which he had neglected in Zuerau. In early fall, together with Brod, Weltsch, and Irma Singer, he attended one of Georg Langer's Hebrew courses and apparently dazzled his friends by his knowledge, not as yet of the language as such but of Moses Rath's old warhorse of a textbook. From time to time he traveled on business, chiefly to the Frankenstein Sanatorium at Rumburk; and by way of keeping in touch with the soil and following Gordonian precepts, he volunteered his help with the fruit trees at the Pomological Institute in suburban Troja.

Ottla, too, needed help. The disastrous economic situation forced Karl Hermann to sell the Zuerau farm, and Kafka was commissioned to find an agricultural or gardening school where she could get advanced training. Conscientious as always, he went to great lengths to assemble the pertinent information; she was, after all, acting quite in his spirit, following his guidance, even to the point of having turned vegetarian herself. Beyond placing her in an appropriate school, Kafka also insisted on assuming the full cost himself. "Don't even think of talking to Father about it. I'll be happy to pay for it all; the money is worth less and less anyway, so let it be my investment in you, a first mortgage on your future farm" (O, p. 56). In November, Ottla enrolled for what turned out to be an extremely demanding but rewarding six-month course at the Friedland School for Agriculture.

A long moment of suspended animation, calm after the storm. The forebodings and premonitions seemed to have been ill founded, and though Kafka still fretted about his illness, he made no further concessions to it and seemed physically in quite good shape until the night of October 14, when he suddenly developed shortness of breath, a hacking cough, and a temperature of 105 degrees. The diagnosis posed no difficulty: nearly one out of every three people in Prague had either already caught the Spanish flu or was coming down with it.

Not only in Prague, of course. The butchery on the battlefield was about to end, but the dying had merely begun. Unlike bombs and bullets, the influenza pandemic of 1918, the Black Death of our time, made no distinctions among allies, enemies, or neutrals, between soldiers or civilians, though it displayed an anomalous preference for the young, the strong, the healthy, leaving most of its older victims enfeebled but alive. A matter of immunity, or of the devil bent on finishing what man had left undone. In its sweep around the globe, the Spanish flu eventually killed an estimated 20 million people, though the exact count will never be known.

In retrospect, it seems quite likely that Kafka, too, was one of its victims. He had, up to that point, made good progress toward full recovery from tuberculosis, and an arrested case was certainly no longer incompatible with a near-normal life span. But the initial assault had been far too recent for the scars to have healed. It still left him highly vulnerable, and the fulminating viral infection not only devastated his organism but also reactivated the disease in a much more virulent form.

He developed double pneumonia, and for some days his life hung in the balance. It took three weeks before he was able to get out of bed. When, on November 19, he finally reported back to work, the Workmen's Accident Insurance Institute for the Kingdom of Bohemia had changed its name, its auspices, and its management. For, on November 14, the Kingdom of Bohemia had become the Republic of Czechoslovakia. The war was over. Peace had broken out.

Twenty-four

FOR years, the end of Habsburg rule had been predicted as imminent. Yet when at last it came, the speed with which the empire collapsed, overnight, like a monumental tower rotten at the base and undermined by termites, stunned everyone caught in the wreckage.

Kafka himself was out of it all, his indifference carried—this time not out of his own volition—to the point of delirium as he lay in his parents' bedroom, struggling for every breath. The momentous events taking place on the outside passed him by, and more than once during those last two weeks of October it seemed as though he no longer had much of a chance ever to catch up with them.

On October 24, Austrian resistance ceased on the Italian front. On the twenty-eighth, the Czechs formed a provisional government in Prague, and on the thirtieth, the Austrian socialists took over in Vienna and concluded an armistice with the Allies. On November 9, armed workers and mutinous soldiers seized power in Berlin; the general armistice ending the war was proclaimed on November 11. One day later, the last of the Habsburgs abdicated; the multinational empire had finally come unglued, and what remained of Austria herself became a republic.

History outran all expectations and flattened those trapped in its path. Kafka himself was spared the panic into which the abrupt Czech takeover threw most of his fellow Jews. Even Brod, wholly in sympathy with the Czech cause, nonetheless feared a long winter of lawlessness and mob violence against Jews and Germans.

For the most part, these apprehensions proved groundless, largely because Masaryk and the Czech leadership moved swiftly and decisively to fill the power vacuum and assert the authority of the new government. On November 14, the Czech National Council proclaimed the Republic of Czechoslovakia and elected the still absent Masaryk as its first president. On the sixteenth, the new president returned in triumph to the capital from which he had fled four years earlier as a subversive ex-professor and newspaper editor, and four days later he moved into Hradčany Castle, the residence of Bohemia's ancient kings. On the whole, the professor of philosophy ruled far more wisely and successfully than any of his royal predecessors.

He was, of course, a rather unusual philosopher, gifted with a striking sense of realism that had nothing in common with *Realpolitik*. No end, in his view, justified corruption, terror, and injustice. He believed in goals moral as well as practical, his most immediate one being the need to weld a multitude of disparate, antagonistic minorities —Czechs, Slovaks, Ruthenians, Hungarians, Jews, Germans—into a modern nation capable of functioning as such. His government's first task was thus defined: to guarantee full protection and full representation to every ethnic group in the country. It was a task he tackled with great moral fervor and a refreshing absence of cant: "You don't necessarily have to love one another in order to live together in peace" was one of his characteristic early pronouncements on the subject, which he backed up by the integrity of the new judiciary and the organs of public safety.

Even so, the consolidation of power and the sway of Masaryk's moral authority took some time to make themselves felt, especially in the provinces, and the early years of the republic saw numerous incidents of rioting, looting, and assaults on individual Jews and Germans, both organized and spontaneous. Between 1918 and 1920, some six thousand Jews left Czechoslovakia for Palestine. After 1920, anti-Semitism receded markedly, and Jewish emigration to Palestine dropped correspondingly, to a total of about four thousand for the entire period between 1921 and 1939.

Under the new state constitution, the Jews were granted the status of a national rather than a religious minority, and entitled as such to representation in parliament. Resolute assimilationists "of the Mosaic faith" vehemently opposed this change, but a resounding majority identified with the Jewish National Council, founded on October 28. Max Brod, who was elected to the three-man executive committee, later represented the Zionist faction in parliament. The council's activities were undoubtedly instrumental in reducing tension during the transition period and contributed significantly toward the integration of the Jews into the new state. But the radical shift from demagogic anti-Semitism to a near-exemplary tolerance within the Czech community, which defied all dire predictions, was largely the achievement of Masaryk himself, as uncompromising in his moral commitment as he was in its implementation.

*   *   *

Whether under less trying circumstances Kafka would have taken a more active interest in these developments is hard to say. But as a result of his illness he was both physically and emotionally remote from the scene, and the final act of the drama, including the actual transfer of power, coincided with the most acute stage of his near-fatal illness. His first confrontation with the new order, therefore, did not come about until November 19, the day he reported back to work.

The Arbeiter-Unfalls-Versicherungsanstalt für das Königreich Boehmen in Prag had been renamed the Delnička úrazová pojištovna pro Čechy v Praze (Workmen's Accident Insurance Company for Bohemia in Prague), with Czech instead of German as the language of discourse both within the office and in all outside communications. Pending the nomination of a new director, the management was in the hands of an interim administrator who immediately fired all German top executives, including Kafka's superiors Marschner and Pfohl. All other non-Czech employees were subjected to a thorough background investigation, their fate decided on a case-by-case basis according to the extent of their known, suspected, or reported anti-Czech sentiments. Kafka, as already mentioned, was one of the very few to survive the purge, though he did not give himself much credit for it. A year later, in describing the institute's new Czech director, a former professor of sociology, he wrote: "Now as to the director: he is a very kind and friendly person. He was especially good to me, though political motives no doubt played a part in his conduct, which now allows him to tell the Germans that he had treated one of their people with exquisite consideration, while at bottom this particular German was merely a Jew" (L, 3/21). It was an accurate perception of future developments; for increasingly, as Nazism began to spread among the ethnic Germans, the Czechs turned to the Jews as the only democratic "German" element supporting the integrity of the state.

Whether as a result of this exposure to the chill winds of change, or of simply not having given himself time enough to recover fully, Kafka after a mere four days on the job suffered a relapse. He again ran a fever, and the medical certificate submitted with his request for a leave mentions dyspnea and night sweat, both common in tuberculosis, as the prevailing symptoms. The family doctor urgently advised another extended rest, and Kafka, *faute de mieux*, settled on a boardinghouse in the Bohemian mountain village of Schelesen, now Želizy, not far from what was to become the infamous Terezin concentration camp, through which all three of his sisters passed on their way to the gas chambers.

With Ottla away at school, it devolved upon his mother to make the necessary arrangements, and on November 30 she accompanied him to Schelesen and installed him at the Pension Stüdl.

*   *   *

Ottla's mounting problems, in the meantime, had become Kafka's major concern. Conditions at the agricultural school were harsh. Overworked, underfed, and homesick, she had to share a room with the only other girl in an all-male class. Her recently acquired vegetarian principles, to which she stuck with characteristic rigor, complicated things even further. And after nearly a decade out of school, the academic subjects loomed more forbidding than sheer physical labor.

Even before leaving for Schelesen, Kafka had still tried to be helpful: "I know your situation is not easy. Going hungry, not having a room of your own, being homesick for Prague, and at the same time having to learn a whole lot of things, is a great test; passing the test is, of course, just as great. . . . So the choice, dear Ottla, is between hanging in or coming home, between staying healthy or coming home. If you make it, I'll admire you. If you come back home, I'll comfort you" (O, 11/11/18).

He no doubt meant it. But the real choice facing Ottla, as he must have been well aware by then, was a great deal more complicated. For while it is not certain when he first learned of his sister's relations with Joseph David, their affair had, by the end of 1918, reached the point where David felt it imperative to pay a formal call on Ottla's parents. He did so on November 27, while Kafka was still in Prague.

It must have been a somewhat difficult move for a young man in his position. David, a law student before the war, had just been demobilized and was going back to a very modest job with the Prague

Municipal Savings Bank while studying for his law boards. Far more disturbing than his financial prospects, however, was the fact that, his two Old Testament names notwithstanding, Joseph David was Gentile, a Czech chauvinist, ultraconservative in his views, and with a hefty dose of that populist bias which Jews, in those more innocent days, used to shrug off as "healthy anti-Semitism," by way of distinguishing it from its more morbid varieties. Though intelligent and exceedingly articulate, David was far more interested in soccer scores than in abstruse matters of the intellect, and it would have been difficult for Ottla to find a man more radically different from her beloved brother in every conceivable way.

At the same time, David was warm and generous, with great charm and a lively sense of humor that dazzled even the senior Kafkas, despite all their misgivings. "He made the best possible impression on us," Julie reported to her daughter. "However, I must admit that he seemed very foreign to us and that we'll first have to get used to him. He is probably a very good and intelligent man, but Father has certain reservations, first about his small salary, and then about his religion. Well, let's hope that it all turns out for the best. After all, the only thing we want is to see you happy."

Father Kafka's reservations about David's "religion" in the end amounted to no more than token resistance, the mechanical reflex of a minimal Jew, further attenuated by supreme indifference. Ottla's own feelings in the matter were understandably far more complicated. As early as October 1918, in a chillingly prescient letter, she rebuked her future husband for some tactless remarks: "Some Jews, perhaps even a majority, may now be doing what they ought not to do. But that certainly does not apply to all of them. In any case, I don't wish to be treated as an exception. I could not accept that." It was this same sentiment that, in 1941, when her marriage to an "Aryan" would have saved her from deportation, made her divorce her husband and voluntarily register as a Jew.

The unconscious dynamics of the relationship between Ottla and her brother, the conflicting and complementary needs that evolved on either side, defy posthumous analysis; the few known facts permit at best some tentative hypotheses. For Ottla, the stark contrast between brother and lover personified the clash between disparate worlds, between identity and independence, between Palestine and Prague, which in the end even her marriage left unresolved. As late as March 1920 she was still planning to attend a *hakhsharah*, a training course designed to prepare her for farming in Palestine, and in a letter to Brod, Kafka told him of his silent vow to contribute a thousand crowns to the Jewish National Fund if Ottla went and was accepted: "What pleases me even more than the thing itself is that it so strongly appeals to Ottla." Yet a mere four months later, she married Joseph David—with whom, on the other hand, she had carried on an intense affair that probably went back as far as 1917, when, partially to elude parental supervision and obtain some privacy, she rented the fairy-tale cottage on Golden Lane which she let Kafka use as a refuge. If at the time he suspected as much, he never let on. But he certainly knew that the separation from David was a major cause of her Friedland miseries.

In the circumstances, jealousy would have been natural enough and could have been easily cloaked in pseudo-rational objections. How he really felt about it is something even he himself may not have known. Overtly, however, he not only accepted but spiritedly defended a relationship which, parents aside, was regarded as misguided and unfortunate even by many of his closest friends. Brod, for one, was frankly disapproving and expressed regret over the prospective loss to Jewry, a remark which Kafka urged Ottla to ignore:

> After all, this is the sort of thing you must have told yourself a thousand times over. You know that you are doing something out of the ordinary, and that to do it well is extremely difficult. If you never forget the responsibilities implicit in so hard a task, if you are aware that you are breaking ranks with as much self-confidence as that with which David, for instance, left the army, and if, despite this awareness, you retain faith in your strength to carry this matter to some sort of satisfactory conclusion, then —to end on a bad joke—you will have done more than if you had married ten Jews. [O, 2/20/19]

Although there is no doubt—and his "secret vow" merely confirms the obvious—that Kafka would have much preferred her choosing Zionism over marriage, the fact of David's not being Jewish seems to have troubled him least of all. On the contrary, it was, if anything, a cause for envious admiration: "He lives among his people, he is cheerful and healthy, in essence . . . rightfully satisfied with himself . . . rightfully (by the same right by which the tree stands in the ground) dissatisfied with others in some areas" (O, 5/1/20). The two did, in fact, become good friends, on the whole, although Kafka's somewhat romanticized notion of rootedness did not blind him to at least its more grotesque manifestations, from self-righteous know-nothingism and soccer mania to the boozy conviviality of professional patriots. The atypically playful and consistently teasing tone of his notes to "Pepa" may well have been a compromise between genuine fondness and smoldering hostility.

On his return to Prague at Christmas, he found the family in an uproar. Herrmann was now dead set against his daughter's marriage to a goy with no status, no money, and no future, nor did he approve of her wasting time and money learning how to shovel manure and raise pigs, in Friedland or anywhere else. With admirable tact, Kafka somehow managed to defuse the situation, calm the outraged Ottla, and ship her back to Friedland to finish her course. He himself, still in no shape to go back to work, applied for a three-month leave, but was granted only three weeks, though he later obtained two extensions. On January 22, 1919, he returned to Schelesen, where he remained until the end of March.

* * *

Among the guests—all mild TB cases—marooned in Stüdl's boardinghouse in the dead of winter was a shy, twenty-nine-year-old dressmaker from Vinohrady, a suburb of Prague. Julie Wohryzek, daughter of a shoemaker and synagogue sexton, seemed to him mousy and distinctly unappealing at first. But the heady mix of fear, fever, loneliness, and snow worked its own special magic, which began to trouble both of these grown-up children in some rather pathetically adolescent ways: "For several days we laughed whenever we met, continuously, at meals, on walks, sitting opposite each other. The laughter on the whole was not pleasant, it had no tangible cause, it was tormenting, humiliating."

Soon he began to see in her "a common and yet amazing apparition —not Jewish, not non-Jewish, not German, not non-German, crazy about movies, musicals, and comedies, wears makeup and veils . . . on the whole quite ignorant, more cheerful than sad . . . ethnically, she belongs to the race of shopgirls. And yet in her heart she is brave, honest, unselfish—great qualities in a creature physically not devoid of beauty but about as insignificant as the gnats hitting my lamp. Similar in this, as in other respects, to Miss Bl. [Grete Bloch?], whom you may recall with some aversion" (L, 2/6/19).

A rather snobbish though probably accurate description, in spite of which, for the first time in over a year, he had some sleepless nights: "I understand the threat." Understood, and embraced it wholeheartedly by beginning to court Julie in his customary fashion. He read to her, lectured her on Zionism—she had, it turned out, been engaged to a young Zionist killed in the war—and, by the end of her stay in mid-March, he had made it eloquently clear that "in a certain sense I considered marriage and children the most desirable goal on earth, but that I personally found it impossible to marry . . . and that therefore we had to part."

Part they did, for about three weeks. Right after his return to Prague, they "rushed as though driven toward one another" and became virtually inseparable throughout the spring and early summer. "There was nothing we could do about it, either of us." What had started as a short-lived *Magic Mountain* flirtation turned into a stolidly regular if still platonic and uncommitted relationship. Julie, modest in her expectations and, in any case, taking her cue from him, seemed satisfied or at least resigned to this state of affairs. It was Kafka who, in midsummer, abruptly changed his mind and insisted that they get married, after all.

Why the sudden about-face? Some months later, in a letter to Julie's sister, he himself rhetorically raised that question and attempted to answer it to his own satisfaction:

> Conditions seemed so much more propitious this time than on the earlier occasions; in fact, one could hardly have imagined them more favorable. I don't want to go into details, beyond saying that we were—and still are—closer to one another than even Julie herself is aware, that it seemed safe to assume that all the arrangements could be taken care of quickly and easily, and finally, that given the unfortunate relationship between my father and myself, his very resistance to the marriage strengthened me in the belief I was doing the right thing. [K, p. 116]

Of course, none of this adds up to a persuasive reason for this sudden desperate urge to marry, and chances are that he himself repressed the most likely one at hand: the affair between Ottla and David, with the two of them clearly headed for marriage.

However understanding and supportive, he must at the very least have experienced a great sense of loss, if not of betrayal. He was, after all, about to be deserted by the one woman who for years had both idolized and mothered him, and seeking someone to replace her would have been a plausible reaction. And Julie was in many ways the ideal candidate: a sensitive, self-effacing woman who worshipped him, accepted whatever he did—and did to her—without protest, though certainly not without pain, and who was willing to live with him on whatever terms he proposed. Beyond that, she was accustomed to poverty, undemanding, and in Kafka's view, at age twenty-nine well past a woman's innate desire for children.

The most stimulating obstacle to the marriage was, as he had pointed out, his father's furious opposition, and here, too, Ottla led the way. That Herrmann, already shaken by his daughter's self-willed plunge into a totally unsuitable liaison, would explode at being told of this latest family disaster was rather predictable. The prospect of his son—a shlemiel in many ways, but still, a doctor of jurisprudence and a scion of the House of Kafka—marrying the daughter of a petty *shammes* doubling as shoemaker was nothing less than a slap in the face, a direct assault on his own hard-won social status. What Kafka underestimated, however, was not so much his father's brutality as his own still exquisite vulnerability to it. Twenty years earlier, Herrmann had offered to teach his son the facts of life by taking him to a whorehouse. This time, informed of Kafka's marriage plans, his rage erupted in much the same pattern of crude imbecility: "She probably put on a fancy blouse for your benefit. Those Prague Jewesses are good at that sort of thing. And right away you have to marry her, of course. Immediately, if not sooner—in a week, tomorrow, today. I simply can't understand you. You are a grown man, you live in the big city, and you still can't think of a better way to handle the problem than to marry the first girl that comes along. Haven't you ever heard of other possibilities? If you're afraid, I'll make it my business to take you there myself" (*Letter to His Father*).

It was a vicious jab, and it hit a sensitive nerve, a whole bundle of them. "I doubt if you ever verbally humiliated me more profoundly," Kafka wrote a few months later, in the *Letter to His Father*, itself an act of retribution. "But you certainly were never more blatant in your show of contempt."

Yet it was true that Herrmann's rage strengthened Kafka's resolve.

Despite the appalling postwar housing shortage, he succeeded in finding an expensive but acceptable one-room apartment in a new building still under construction and supposedly available by November 1. All the arrangements were made, but in October, just two days before the date set for the wedding, they learned that a third party had topped their bid and snatched the apartment away from them. "That was the turning point. After that, the downward slide could no longer be halted. The grace period granted me this time had expired" (Letter to J. Wohryzek's sister, in WA/ro, p. 116).

Even though it conceivably might have been viewed as a case of common sense asserting itself in the nick of time, Kafka saw it as another defeat, and he went through almost the identical motions and emotions with which he had responded to the earlier trials. And yet it was not quite the same, after all. He had aged immeasurably in the meantime and grown weary. Julie, moreover, and his involvement with her, differed vastly from Felice and the struggles of his youth; she even agreed to go on seeing him on the same terms as before. But the failure hurt, just the same. He had meant this time to fling himself into marriage like a suicide diving off a bridge, and at the last moment he had opened his eyes, looked down, and backed off. It saved his life, but at the cost of having to live it, and in those final days of October he felt increasingly incapable of coping with that task. At Brod's urging, he took a two-week leave, and on November 9 the two of them together went back to Schelesen. "Why so many stops along the road to death," Kafka is said to have complained on the way; "why does it take so long?" (Brod, bio., p. 182).

*   *   *

Whereas with Felice he had constantly stressed writing as a major obstacle to marriage, Kafka scarcely even raised that point with Julie Wohryzek. For well over a year he had, in fact, written nothing at all, not even kept a diary, and it almost seemed as though, along with the hope for recovery, he had also abandoned all further literary ambitions and projects. A lapidary Last Will and Testament on the back of a calling card, which he had kept in his briefcase since mid-1918, instructed Brod, as his testamentary executor, to destroy all unpublished manuscript material.

But during his ten-day vacation at Schelesen he broke out of this silence, though the inspiration for the monumental—and, in the view of some of his closest friends, monstrous—letter to his father can hardly be regarded as creative in the conventional sense. The document, handwritten between the tenth and the twentieth of November 1919 and running to forty-five pages in its later typewritten version, was certainly not consciously intended as literature but rather as an effort to ease the strain between father and son. That Kafka could still, at this point in his life, believe his primitive, emotionally stunted, and intellectually underdeveloped father able or willing to follow the tortuous sophistry of this venture into self-exploration and into the origins of their mutual hostility is itself a clue to the true meaning of a letter which in the end was never mailed, because he to whom it was addressed had long since moved and left no forwarding address.

The line between God, the Father, and Father, the God, blurred to begin with and increasingly fuzzy with time, produced a split image of troubling contradictions. Kafka quite obviously hated his father, and for some very good reasons, all of them developed at great length in this letter purportedly meant as a love offering. In pursuit of this self-imposed goal, he opened his plea with the questionable observation that neither he nor his opponent could help being what he was, and thereupon proceeded to spell out in relentless detail just what he had in mind. The father, in this portrait drawn from life, emerges as a petty tyrant, crude, cruel, and opinionated, vicious toward his inferiors, a boss who treats his employees as "animals" and "paid enemies" but turns into a deferential bootlicker before those he deems socially superior, a father who tyrannizes the whole household by his constant ranting, raving, and obscene threats of violence—"I'll tear you apart like a fish"—and who insists on proper manners in his children while he himself behaves at the dinner table like an orangutan, a hysterical hypochondriac who, by means of his "heart seizures," constantly blackmails the family into compliance with his every whim and wish. And more. A great deal more.

There are some perfunctory attempts to dilute the venom, but once launched on his tirade, the defendant "in this terrible trial that has been pending between us" was clearly unable to stop himself until he had unloaded the bulk of his grievance collection. Accurate or not, this was the image of Herrmann Kafka as seen by his son. More accurate than not, one suspects, hyperbole and histrionics notwithstanding; Kafka Senior was, by most accounts, a fairly uncouth character, though outsiders often found him charming, as outsiders are apt to so long as they stay on the outside. Then again, such decorative traits as tact or aesthetic sensibility were not among the talents that enabled the little barefoot peddler from the Wossek ghetto to claw his way up into middle-class affluence, a struggle that left deep scars, among them an indiscriminate mistrust bordering on paranoia, and the defiant bluster of the self-made man masking a pervasive sense of inferiority.

Intellectually, Kafka was well equipped to appreciate his father's accomplishments; emotionally, they left him cold. "You were such a giant in every respect; how could you expect compassion from us, let alone help?" At issue, however, is not the objective truth of the portrait —no son can be objective or truthful about his father, though he may come to know him better than anyone else—but the uncanny power of the still raw emotions that drove the thirty-six-year-old to uncrate and exhibit his grievances all the way back to the emblematic trauma on the porch, suffered at age four, which split his world into three parts: "my own, that of the slave, ruled by laws invented solely for my sake and to which, moreover, I could never quite conform; then the second world, infinitely remote from mine, in which you reigned supreme, giving orders and being annoyed at the lack of compliance, and finally the third world, where the rest of mankind dwelled without orders or the need for obedience in happiness and freedom."

Neither the process nor its meaning seem unduly mysterious, less so, perhaps, than in fact they are. Even Kafka himself had no trouble discerning the Freudian triad and linking the resumption of oedipal hostilities to the clash over his intended marriage. Yet something went wrong with this self-analysis leading up to a symbolic parricide. For the squalling brat still being brutalized by an all-powerful father was also an incorruptibly lucid adult gifted with more than his share of reason and insight who—as the letter itself amply demonstrates—saw Herrmann as a weak bully whose very obsession with money and status was nothing but the ghetto fear of poverty and humiliation. The man whom he in effect accused of having ruled and ruined his life, and of still dominating all but one single aspect of it—his writing, sole sanctuary and means of escape—was, as Kafka must have been well aware, scared of him, a bumbling clod helpless against the icy contempt of the certified intellectual. In the opening sentence of the letter, Kafka quotes his father as having "recently asked why I maintain that I am afraid of you." Herrmann's real question, which remains unanswered along with the rhetorical one, was "How can *you* be afraid of me, when I am afraid of you?"

By the time Kafka wrote the letter, the gap between the father and the father image was as wide as the world. At one extreme stood the pathetic figure of Herrmann himself, and about the kindest thing his son could find to say about him was that he, too, was a victim, a prisoner of his time like all the founding fathers who broke their backs and their hearts transmuting faith into money. At the other extreme loomed the one to whom this letter was addressed, omniscient, omnipotent, but looking suspiciously like Herrmann Kafka on an off day and acting with the same capricious malevolence. A very Jewish God.

Kafka wanted to make peace with both. He wanted to love the father he hated, and to have faith in the God he didn't believe in. The purpose of the letter was to prove that the impossible was impossible, and to that extent it succeeded.

* * *

On November 21, he went back to work.

The institute was still in the process of reorganization, but with the election of Dr. Bedřich Ostrčil as the new director, things were generally beginning to fall into place. Earlier in the year, Kafka had put in a request for what he felt was a long overdue promotion, but received no response. He was, moreover, distinctly unhappy to be working under Jindřich Valenta, the venerable but less than competent Czech successor to the sacked Eugen Pfohl. He therefore resubmitted his request and, in January 1920, was appointed Legal Secretary, effective March 1. In his new position, Kafka headed one of the four departments into which the institute had been divided as part of the reorganization. It was his job to evaluate the legal aspects of all cases originating in the other departments, to delegate their execution, or to deal personally with the more delicate ones involving governmental bodies or major industrial concerns.

His elevation and expanded responsibilities, however, actually led to a significant reduction in his work load, a not uncommon peculiarity of hierarchic organizations. Though he may, as usual, have understated his contributions—"I did nothing at all during the past eighteen days, wrote a few letters, read a few, mostly stared out the window, picked up some letters, put them down again, had a few visitors, otherwise nothing"—he probably did work much less than before. What pleased him even more was that, as department head, he now reported directly to the new director. Relations with Ostrčil were less personal than they had been with Marschner and Pfohl, but the ex-professor, though a rather distant and authoritarian administrator, treated his deputy with a consideration and generosity qualified by Kafka himself as "extraordinary" and "unbelievable." He also greatly impressed and rather intimidated Kafka by his superbly literate and eloquent use of the Czech language, one reason why Kafka, during his subsequent extended leaves, always made it a point to have his letters to the director edited and corrected by the language-pedant Joseph David. Although his own spoken Czech was good, he never trusted himself— justifiedly so—with the fine points of Czech grammar and spelling.

But while less of a burden, the office also no longer afforded the compensatory gratifications that had helped to sustain him under the old regime. He had few social ties in the new organization and derived little satisfaction from the work itself, yet in view of his increasingly frequent absences and paid leaves, he felt duty-bound to do the best he could whenever his health permitted it.

It was a fallow period, a time of chronic depression punctuated by bouts of low-grade fever. The letter to his father, whatever its inspiration, had been his one creative effort for the year. After showing it to Ottla and to his mother, he buried it in his notebooks, whence Brod, years later, retrieved it for use in his 1937 Kafka biography. Although he had known of its existence and even discussed it with Kafka during their joint stay at Schelesen, the actual text shocked him. It not only offended his notions of filial piety but also clashed with his ardent belief in the saintly character of his late friend, which may tell more about Brod than about the character of saints. Not until the 1950s, still with considerable misgivings, did Brod bring himself to publish the full text as part of the first complete Kafka edition.

Early in autumn, Kafka had given two of his short pieces, "An Imperial Message" and "The Cares of a Family Man," to Felix Weltsch, who was shortly to take over the editorship of the *Selbstwehr*, where they appeared in September and December of 1919. Furthermore, the Kurt Wolff Verlag was at last able to resume normal peacetime production and began to catch up with its sizable backlog. *The Penal Colony* came out in May 1919, followed in December by the long-delayed *A Country Doctor*, with its dedication to Kafka's father, who acknowledged the gift with a memorably effusive—and never forgotten or forgiven—"Put it on the night table."

During the gloomy first six weeks of 1920, Kafka wrote the series of aphorisms now known under the title of *He*. Writing about himself in the third person was not an altogether novel device; he had repeatedly used it in letters to Felice. The literary depersonalization in the *He* series, however, represented a more conscious and consistent effort, not only to gain distance from himself, but to contemplate his own anguish against the wider background of human suffering and was, in that sense, a linear sequel to the quest begun at Schelesen. But where the narrow, obsessively personal focus of the letter to his father had ultimately led him into a dead end, he was now beginning to confront the monumental task of articulating its latent metaphysical implications.

Dread, depression, and anxiety were what inspired these few pages dense with the spirit of cabalistic mysticism, a pervasive sense of the paradox of human existence. He lived very quietly that winter, with almost no human contact. It was clear now that he had never really recovered from his bout with the Spanish flu a year earlier, and the condition of his lungs gave cause for grave concern. The severe Prague winter was no help, either; at the very least, it contributed to the acute flare-ups that nearly every couple of weeks incapacitated him for several days. On February 26, he went to see Dr. Kodym, the institute's medical consultant, who found "symptoms of significantly advanced infiltration of both lungs" and recommended an eight-week leave, which Ostrčil approved at once.

Kafka had originally intended to spend an extended spring vacation in Munich, preferably in the company of Julie Wohryzek. The two continued to see each other as before, and he still indulged in some feeble attempts at persuading himself that "we would see a different part of the world, some things might change a little, some weaknesses and fears might change their shape or direction." By February, however, it had become obvious that his condition required "a sick leave rather than a health leave," as he put it to Kurt Wolff. Apologizing for a long-delayed answer to Minze Eisner, an exuberant nineteen-year-old met at Schelesen with whom he conducted a sporadic correspondence full of avuncular advice, he explained that he had been ill—"It wasn't really a matter of being ill so much as of not being well. Rather, it belongs to that certain category of illnesses whose origin is not where they seem to be nesting and which therefore render the doctors even more helpless than usual. Of course it is the lungs; but then again, it isn't the lungs. Maybe I'll go to Merano, after all, or else travel to the moon, where there is no air at all and the lungs could get a real rest" (L, Spring 1920).

Merano seemed extravagant. Wolff had recommended a much less expensive sanatorium in the Bavarian Alps, but in the end Kafka was unable to get a German visa and decided to "scrape together all my money and go to Merano after all. I am not really happy about it, although it may be better for my lungs. The head wanted Bavaria, and since it is in charge of orchestrating the illness, Bavaria would somehow have been right" (L, 3/20).

He remained in Prague until the end of March, probably because of office business connected with his promotion and with the general reorganization of the institute, and only left for Italy in early April, still planning a fall vacation with Julie. Nothing, however, was to come of their plans. Only a month later, Kafka was deeply involved in what was perhaps the one true love affair of his life.

Twenty-five

MILENA JESENSKÁ was born in Prague in 1896 into a prominent family with age-old ties to the Czech cause; a tablet on Prague's Old Town Square still commemorates the martyrdom of her ancestor Jan Jesenius, beheaded on that spot in 1621 as one of the leaders of the Hussite rebellion. Two of Milena's paternal aunts, Marie and Ružena Jesenská, were popular novelists. Her father, Jan Jesenský, was a surgeon regarded as one of Europe's leading specialists in jaw reconstruction, but his choleric cruelty went far beyond the bounds of occupational sadism. A rabid nationalist and rigid, self-righteous conservative, he was unbending in his hatred of Jews, Austrians, and Germans; Jews above all. In 1894, he married a gentle and artistically gifted woman who bore him two children; the boy, three years younger than Milena, died in infancy. The mother came down with pernicious anemia and, after years of suffering, died when Milena was thirteen, leaving her martinet of a husband without a male heir. Apparently bent on making up for this disappointment, Dr. Jesenský treated Milena like the son of whom fate had cheated him. On the one hand, he beat her without mercy and at the slightest provocation; on the other, he enrolled her in the Minerva High School, a decision which he may have come to regret. The Minerva, founded in 1891 by a group of Czech intellectuals, was Bohemia's first academic secondary school for girls. Funded privately, and thus not subject to civil-service rules or other governmental constraints, it was able to provide an educational climate considerably more progressive and productive than the prison atmosphere in which the likes of Kafka and Brod were introduced to the rigors of classical scholarship. The Minerva alumnae—Masaryk's daughter Alice was a member of the first graduating class—became the nucleus of the Czech women's movement and played a major role in the political and intellectual life of the republic.

At the Minerva, the adolescing Milena came into her own. She also, as it later turned out, managed to learn a great deal. But while in school, she distinguished herself not as a student but as the leader and chief instigator of an exceedingly bright and high-spirited group of girls bent on challenging all adult limits and assumptions. Most of them came from wealthy homes, but none spent money with more reckless abandon than Milena, whose father was far too busy to keep track of household finances or petty cash. They shocked the stolid burghers of Prague by their outrageous dress and behavior, experimented with drugs Milena stole from her father's office, and, with the daring of utter innocence, went so far as to blithely cross the chasm that separated the Czech elite from the coffeehouse society of German-Jewish intellectuals, a near-sacrilegious defiance of deep-seated prejudices on either side.

Milena, in becoming a much-adored, much-fussed-over pet of Werfel's Arco circle, was of course also defying her own father and everything he stood for in a most profoundly personal way. The struggle between them assumed Homeric proportions, but it was not until she quit medical school after the first semester—he had always taken it for granted that she would follow in his footsteps, even forcing her to assist at operations when she was still a child—and began to scandalize café society as well as the Czech *haute bourgeoisie* by her affair with Ernst Polak that matters between them came to a head.

Polak, an already somewhat seedy sexual athlete, litterateur, and bank clerk, intimate of Brod and Werfel, was ten years older than his teenage lover. But his worst offense, in Jan Jesenský's eyes, was his being a Jew, and a German-speaking one at that. Determined to thwart this miscegenation, the irate father took drastic action: abetted by an obliging psychiatrist colleague, he had his daughter committed to the Veleslavin lunatic asylum.

Milena spent nine months, from June 1917 to March 1918, in this latter-day Bedlam, where brutal beatings, straitjackets, and solitary confinement were a routine part of the therapy. Her repeated escapes, stubborn resistance, and clandestine trysts with her lover, though severely punished, finally convinced Dr. Jesenský that further efforts were futile. He gave up, broke off all further contact, and vowed to cut his daughter out of his heart and his will. Milena, in turn, went ahead and married Ernst Polak, thereby inflicting upon herself a punishment compared to which the most exquisite cruelties devised by her father must have seemed benign.

Polak, whose intellectual acrobatics awed even the Arco crowd, was commonly referred to as "Kenner Polak"—wise guy Polak, or the all-knowing Polak, but either way an apt description of this polymath with a mind absorptive like a sterile sponge, and equally unproductive. Polak was also, however, a profligate psychopath who would not let his relations with Milena interfere in the least with his compulsive promiscuity. His main reasons for marrying her seem to have been snobbery and vengeance, the ego-gratifying public display of his powers of seduction, and the humiliation inflicted on a man who despised him.

Shortly after the wedding, the couple left for Vienna, where Polak spent the next few years as a worshipful hanger-on of the post-Machian positivists known as the Vienna Circle, studying philosophy in private seminars with Neurath and Schlick, and insisting on unconditional freedom for himself as a matter of positivist principle. He categorically refused ever to give Milena any money, thus forcing her to support herself as best she could, the very best by far being a frequent stint as baggage porter at the main railroad station. Malnutrition, however, had sapped her strength; she had recently begun to cough up some blood, and sheer desperation drove her to try and earn some money by freelance writing, and by translations from the German for Czech publications.

It was one of her first efforts along these lines that led her to Kafka. Writing to him in October 1919 from Vienna, she expressed her admiration for his work and requested permission to translate some of it into Czech. Kafka was evidently pleased, so much so that he showed the letter to Julie Wohryzek, and immediately gave the project his blessings, at the same time asking Wolff to send Mrs. Polak copies of all his books.

In his reply, he recalled having once met her personally at the Café Arco in Prague, an encounter so brief that even he, the obsessive eyewitness, "could not recall your face in any precise detail. Only how at the end you walked away between the tables, your figure, your dress, that I can still see" (MIL, p. 5). But however fleeting their personal contact, he could scarcely have been unaware of the gossip and lubricious outrage inspired by this troubling teenage enchantress, erstwhile queen of Prague's golden youth and middle-aged bohème.

Shortly after his arrival in Merano in early April 1920, he dropped her a friendly though noncommittal note inquiring after the progress of the translation. Having received no answer, he followed up with a second, less formal and more insistent letter, whose contents suggest that he was already quite familiar with her plight. (Few of the letters to Milena were dated; their order in the published edition is therefore based on internal evidence and remains tentative throughout. The sequence of the first two, however, is quite obviously reversed.) He concluded with an ultimatum of sorts: "I expect one of two things: either continued silence, meaning, 'Don't worry, I am quite well,' or else a few lines."

This time she replied at once, being in fact far from well, as she must have described in poignant detail, with that utterly unself-conscious candor that marked her style. Although her letters to Kafka are lost, enough of her writing survives—letters to Brod, the moving tribute to Kafka that was his obituary in the Czech press, and her many articles and feature stories, their limpid grace and wry humor turning dark and venomous as the barbarians started closing in—to convey a keen sense of her vitality and depth, both as a writer and as a woman. It makes the instant, shattering effect of her letters on Kafka easy to understand: for once the epistolary lover had met his match. This was no prim and prissy Berlin business executive, no grim "fortress to be conquered," but a "living fire," and within a matter of weeks, even days, he was close enough to the source of heat to get burned.

Milena at twenty-four bore the scars of a woman twice her age. Kafka, too, had in the face of death aged rapidly and way beyond his years, though he was still frequently taken for a teenager; he described one such comic episode to her with rather melancholy pride. She herself was totally beyond pretense, false pride, or bourgeois prejudices, and from the start never left him in doubt as to the state of her body and soul, no matter how chaotic. More important, she had what it took to see him as perhaps no one else ever had, certainly neither of his fiancées. Intuitively she sensed, perhaps before she ever met him, that he was not of this world, and not long for it, either. "I knew his fear before I ever knew him," she later wrote to Brod, "and I armed myself against it by grasping it. . . . Frank will never get well. Frank will die soon. Life for him is entirely different than it is for the rest of us. . . . His books are amazing. He himself is much more amazing" (Brod, bio., p. 201).

In her first letter, written in German, she gave him some unpathetic but devastating glimpses of her life as an exile and slave—exile in a dreary town full of dead people, enslaved by ties utterly beyond reason or argument to a scoundrel who treated her like dirt, spent his days philosophizing in neo-positivist cafés and his nights sleeping with whatever he could bed. She herself was near-destitute and ill; the doctor suspected the lungs.

It was the sort of honesty, self-critical but devoid of self-pity, that made posturings unthinkable, and Kafka responded in kind; the straight-edged and strikingly unambiguous prose of his letters to Milena provides a stark contrast to the metaphysical contortions and rhetorical excesses of the letters to Felice, a woman whom he desperately wanted to love but seldom even liked. "For almost five years I battered away at her (or, if you will, at myself). Fortunately she turned out to be unbreakable, a Prussian-Jewish mixture, tough and invincible. I wasn't nearly that tough. On the other hand, she only had to suffer, whereas I both battered and suffered" (MIL, p. 38). Moreover, Milena's translation of *The Stoker*, published in the April issue of the Czech literary monthly *Kmen* (*Tribe*), which she sent him toward the end of that month, must have disposed of any lingering doubts about her ability to enter into his world. It was, as he recognized at once, an astonishing feat, a flawless translation of what he had long since come to think of as a badly flawed original.

He urged her to henceforth write to him in Czech, "because Czech is what you are part of; that is where I can see Milena whole (the translation only confirms this)." And when she did so, a few days later—they subsequently carried on all their correspondence in both languages—he felt gratified:

> I have never lived among Germans. German is my mother tongue, hence comes to me naturally, but Czech is much closer to my heart. That is why your letter dispels many uncertainties. I see you more clearly, the movements of your body, your hands, so quick, so decisive, almost like a personal encounter. Yet when I try to lift up my eyes and look at your face, the letter bursts into flames, and all I see is fire. It could tempt one to believe in the law which, according to you, rules your life. . . . As for myself, I am willing to believe in your law, but I don't believe that it will forever mark your life with such blatant cruelty. It may be a piece of insight, but merely one along the way, and the way is infinite. . . . [MIL, p. 16]

There was, by this time—the end of April, three weeks into their correspondence—no more question about their feelings toward one another. Love, as always, robbed him of his sleep. He worried more about Milena's lungs than about his own. She wanted to know all about his engagements and rather imperiously demanded that he break off with Julie Wohryzek, though on second thought she had the good grace to feel guilty about it. But the symbolic and symptomatic meaning of her jealousy was not lost on Kafka.

His own feelings about her marriage, on the other hand, were less accessible, perhaps less primitive, though he was shocked by what she revealed of it:

> I must say that I had quite a different picture of your husband. In his coffeehouse circle he seemed to me the most solid, the most reasonable and calmest of the lot, almost excessively paternal, though at the same time also inscrutable, but not to the point of negating the above. I always respected him, though I never had the chance or ability to get to know him more closely. But friends, especially Brod, had a high opinion of him, a fact I was always conscious of whenever I thought of him. At one time I especially liked this peculiar habit he had of having himself called to the phone several times a night in every café. There was presumably someone who, instead of sleeping, always dozed the night away by the phone, head on the back of the chair, and who started up from time to time just to phone him. It is a condition I understand so well that this may be my only reason for mentioning it. [MIL, p. 21]

Sexual rivalry, however implicit, was hardly at issue; in that arena he obviously had no chance and no desire to compete.

> This whole world to him is and remains mysterious [Milena wrote]. A mystical secret, something he cannot cope with and tends to overestimate with touchingly pure naïveté because it is "efficient"—*geschäftstüchtig*. When I told him about my husband, who is unfaithful to me a hundred times a year, and who holds me and many other women under a kind of spell, his face lit up with the same kind of awe as it did when he talked about his director, who was so good at typing and therefore an excellent person, or when he talked about his fiancée, who was so *geschäfts-tüchtig*. [Brod, bio., p. 200]

Yet in other ways they had already reached an almost uncanny intimacy. At Kafka's insistence, she sent him some of her feature stories published in the *Tribuna*, and he was stunned. "She who wrote these is no ordinary writer. Having read them, I now have almost as much confidence in your writing as I do in your person. Given my limited knowledge, I am familiar with only one Czech speech melody, that of Božena Nemcova. This here is music of a different kind, yet related to the other in its decisiveness, passion, loveliness, and above all its clairvoyant wisdom" (MIL, p. 20).

At the same time, he was not nearly as ineffectual in matters practical as he liked to think, and as Milena seemed to believe. Early in June, he proposed that she leave her husband, at least for a while.

> Nothing new about it, after all; you already did it once before. The reasons: your illness, his nervousness (you'll be doing him a good turn as well) and finally, conditions in Vienna. I don't know where you want to go, the best would probably be some peaceful spot in Bohemia. It would also be best if I neither personally mixed in nor appeared on the scene. The necessary money you'll borrow from me (we'll come to some agreement about the repayment). I would myself derive an additional benefit from this arrangement in that it would make me do my work with downright enthusiasm. My job, by the way, is laughable; you can't imagine how pathetically easy. I don't know what I am getting paid for. [MIL, p. 24]

The next day he added: "If there be cunning in this proposition—and where isn't it, this monstrous animal that can make itself invisible—I'll keep it in check. Even your husband can trust me in this. I am beginning to exaggerate. Nonetheless: I can be trusted. I won't see you at all. Not now, not later" (MIL, p. 27).

It was presumably this unsolicited display of nobility on his part that infuriated Milena and prompted one of her characteristic outbursts. (She may, for some years, have been in thrall, sexually and emotionally, to her husband, but she had sharp claws, a hair-trigger temper, and was definitely not the only one who got hurt in this marriage.) She was far too much the flesh-and-blood woman to settle for a long-distance love affair and a place in Kafka's fantasy life, let alone accepting his financial support in return for this dubious role. By way of counterproposal, she urged him, first of all, to stop off in Vienna at the end of the month, on his way back to Prague.

The request threw him into the usual panic. And it was when he told her that he could not possibly come—not for any technical reasons but simply because he was what he was—that she asked him if he was Jewish.

* * *

It was not, perhaps, as blunt as all that, but a curious question just the same, given her background, and it understandably struck him as odd.

> You ask if I am a Jew. You must be joking. Perhaps what you are really asking is whether I am one of those anxiety-ridden Jews. At any rate, as a native of Prague you could not possibly be as innocent in this respect as Heine's wife, Mathilde. . . . However, you don't seem to be afraid of Jews. Which, considering the last, or next to the last, generation of urban Jews, seems rather heroic. . . . It also entitles you to reproach the Jews for their specific anxiety, although so generalized a reproach suggests a knowledge of human nature more theoretical than practical. Theoretical because, first of all, the reproach does not apply to your husband, as you describe him; second, in my experience it does not apply to most Jews. Third, it is applicable only to rare individuals, such as myself; but those it hits hard. That the reproach is generally unjustified happens actually to be a very strange fact. The insecure position of the Jews, insecure within themselves, insecure among mankind, would make it supremely understandable for them to believe that they can possess only that which they can grasp with their hands or teeth, that only tangible possessions give them the right to live, and that what they once lost is gone forever and can never be retrieved. Jews are threatened by dangers from the most improbable quarters— or, if for the sake of accuracy we leave out the dangers—threatened by threats. An example close to home. I may have promised not to pass it on (at a time when I still barely knew you), but I have no compunction about mentioning it, because it won't tell you anything you don't already know, it demonstrates your relatives' love for you, and I am not mentioning any names or details because I don't remember them. My youngest sister is about to marry a Czech, a Gentile. When he once mentioned his intention of marrying a Jewish girl to one of your relatives, she exclaimed: "Anything but that. Don't ever get involved with Jews. Look at what happened to our Milena . . ." etc. [MIL, p. 34]

Milena, who in her teens already had defied the laws of her own tribe and strayed across closed if unmarked borders, and who had all but killed her father by marrying a Jew, needed no introduction to the Jewish problem, though she no doubt failed to appreciate the depth and virulence of the emotions it aroused in Kafka. Of necessity, she saw it in starkly realistic terms and later, when it counted, acted on her convictions by sounding some of the earliest warnings of final solutions, risking her own life many times over to save potential Nazi victims, and ultimately sharing the fate of the overwhelming majority of Prague's Jews. But she was sensitized enough to read an accusation into his lecture, and in denying such intentions, Kafka let himself be provoked into what, in the context of subsequent events, proved a rather chilling metaphor: ". . . no trace of a reproach intended; rather, I could reproach you for having much too high an opinion of the Jews of your acquaintance (myself included); there are, of course, others. Sometimes I'd like to stuff them all into the drawer of my laundry chest, wait a while, then open the drawer a little to see if they've all been suffocated, and if not, close the drawer again, and so on to the end" (MIL, p. 43).

It was a fairly nasty sentiment even in his time, the human obverse of angelic meekness. That he harbored cosmic rages was certainly no secret to his readers, of whom he was himself one of the most astute. But seldom did these monsters break loose to roam the world in plain daylight. That he let them slip into a letter to Milena testifies both to his trust in her and to the mounting intensity of his inner conflicts as a man and as a Jew.

Nor was it the only example. A far worse display of Jewish self-hatred at its murkiest, a letter to Milena probably written during the second half of June 1920, has thus far been suppressed in its entirety, for reasons that bear looking into.

*   *   *

After Kafka's death, Milena carried out his instructions by turning all his manuscripts and diaries in her possession over to Max Brod, keeping only the letters personally addressed to her. But after the Nazi invasion of Czechoslovakia in 1939, she became active in the Czech underground, regularly harbored fugitives in her home, and had good reason to fear a Gestapo raid. She therefore gave the letters to her friend Willy Haas, who in turn hid them with relatives before fleeing abroad. He recovered them after the war and, in an amicable agreement with Brod, undertook to edit them for publication.

He seemed eminently qualified for the task. An editor both in his native Prague and later on in Germany, Haas was close to Milena, on friendly terms with Kafka, and intimately familiar with their respective circles. These personal links, however, also led to a conflict of interest to which he alludes in his editorial postscript:

> Unfortunately, certain parts of these letters had to be deleted out of consideration for persons still alive. The editor regrets this all the more since, of necessity, the deletions include passages in which his own name is repeatedly mentioned. Personally—let any future publisher be assured of this in advance—he has no objections to their publication, however farfetched and fantastic some of the conclusions which Kafka drew from a certain episode. One odd aspect of these love letters is that Kafka's jealousy, in the accepted sense, was directed not at Milena's male friends, but at the girl friends of her youth. Stranger yet is the fact that he evidently did not always fully recognize the sources of his hatred for certain persons. As a result, these letters contain literary portraits, or rather caricatures, which bear no resemblance to reality and cannot be published at this time. The gross inaccuracy of these portraits should be stressed here and now, also with a view toward any future—and, it is to be hoped, unabridged —edition. For equally obvious reasons, almost all references to Milena's family have been omitted. [MIL, p. 219]

What prompted these cryptic and conspicuously defensive remarks on the editor's part was his own role in a scandal involving Milena's closest Minerva pal and lifelong intimate, Jarmila Ambrozova, whose first husband committed suicide, ostensibly because of her affair with Willy Haas. Haas quit his studies, and the guilt-stricken pair left Prague under a cloud whose lingering toxicity no doubt helped to poison their own subsequent marriage. In the circumstances, it would have taken a truly inhuman detachment for the editor not to let himself be swayed in his judgment, consciously or otherwise, by his personal views of people and events referred to in these letters. A certain bias is, in fact, apparent, even though many of the cuts were indeed unavoidable, or at least defensible at the time on legal grounds.

(An unexpurgated edition is being prepared but may not be forthcoming for some time. It will be published as part of a "text-critical" edition of Kafka's collected works, which is currently engaging the zeal of an impressive slate of text-critical academics.)

It happens that the letter Haas chose to delete in its entirety dealt with the Haas-Ambrozova scandal. Aside from the obvious parallels to his own relationship with Milena, Kafka saw it as an emblematic reenactment of the "Hilsner affair," the 1899 case of alleged ritual murder that led to a wave of anti-Semitic violence throughout the country. But to him, Haas was a Hilsner who had in fact committed the deed, its intrinsic monstrosity undiminished by the victim's seemingly willing surrender. What was more, Haas merely retraced a pattern paradigmatic of all relationships involving Jewish men and Gentile women. Its horror was the inevitable if symbolic rape which, misunderstood, had given rise to the blood libel, counterbalanced by the Jew's tragically inescapable need to destroy himself as well as his victim.

Personal feelings aside, one can hardly fault Haas, in the immediate wake of the Holocaust and the emotional climate of postwar Europe, for having exercised his editorial judgment, although in the long run censorship rarely serves the truth. The full text of the letter is muddled and scurrilous, even if its complex chain of strictures and reservations ultimately turns the accusation into a plea for the defense. But to read this document as a reasoned comment on the Jewish question—or on anything else, for that matter—is to ignore the crisis that spawned it, while giving its manifest content far more weight than it deserves.

Kafka's volcanic self-hatred scarcely requires additional documentation. Nor is it surprising that his relationship with a Gentile woman, in which he felt himself rapidly losing control, should have dredged up its specific Jewish component, the contempt for himself as the quintessential Western Jew. The terror, torment, passion, and flicker of hope that Milena inspired were to fuse two years later in a supreme creative effort; *The Castle* reaffirms the remorseless lucidity of his vision as an artist.

His vision as a man in love or in hate, however, was fallible and often clouded. What offends in these passages are not so much the sentiments expressed—genuine to a fault—but the arguments invoked to justify them, the strident neo-Wagnerian strain that infests the hysteria. Kafka was basically of far too sound a mind to succumb to the marsh-gas mythologies of blood, sex, and race rising in dense cloud formation from the ideological swamps of Europe. Yet even he took some of its exponents, both Jews and Germans—the romantic mythomaniac Hans Blüher, the demented prodigy Otto Weininger, and self-styled prophets such as Karl Kraus, Anton Kuh, and Otto Gross—far more seriously than was warranted by the specific gravity of their ideas. And while he did not, as a rule, agree with them, he too believed in the fundamental antagonism between Jews and Gentiles and, in moments of extreme distress, borrowed from their droppings to indulge his self-disgust. That he hated himself, not for being a Jew, but for not being enough of one, marks one essential difference.

* * *

Milena was shocked by these splutterings, and not shy about letting him know, with a pointed vigor which, quite uncharacteristically, made him retract or at least soften some of his more morbid formulations.

He was now totally under her spell, physically still in Merano but as indifferent to his surroundings as he was to his food and his fellow patients, the body laid out on the sundeck each day for the prescribed number of hours, and entombed at night for an unrestful bout with nightmares and insomnia. "One thing bothers me about your letter," he wrote to Brod in mid-June, "the passage where you talk about my getting well again. No, since last month there can no longer be any question of that" (L, 6/20).

Heart and soul, in the meantime, were preempted by Milena around the clock. They wrote to each other at least once a day, and the mounting tension she fueled in him between fear and fantasy may well have contributed to the therapeutic failure of this rest cure. Though he had gained a couple of pounds, his cough was worse than ever, and the lungs obdurately refused to show any improvement. Moreover, he began to have scruples about Milena's husband, in spite of what he now knew about him. "Perhaps—I cannot think about this—I am doing him a terrible wrong, but almost equally strong is the sense of my now being tied to him, ever more firmly—in life and in death, I was almost going to say. I wish I could talk to him. But I am afraid of him, he is much superior to me. You know, Milena, when you went with him, you took a huge step down from your level. But if you come to me, you'll be leaping into the abyss. Do you realize this?" (MIL, p. 43).

The thought of her risking that leap no doubt frightened him a great deal more than it did her. That he could not only dare to think but actually utter it, that for the first time in his life he wanted a woman —another man's wife, at that—to share his life, and for no reason more complicated than that he was in love with her, revealed a kind of desperate courage he would never have suspected in himself and which, in his sober view, verged on madness. It was he himself who, perched on the brink of darkness, was ready to risk a literally death-defying leap into the abyss.

But sobriety, however troubling, never prevailed for long against the image of Milena.

> Your interpretation of my "you must get out of Vienna" is not entirely correct. I did not toss it off lightly, nor did I fear any material burdens (I don't earn much, but I think it should be adequate for us both, provided of course no illness interferes). Furthermore, I am sincere to the full extent of my powers of thought and expression (always have been, though you are the first to have a helpful awareness of it). No, what I fear, with my eyes wide open . . . is only this inner conspiracy against me (which you will better understand when you read the letter to my father, though again not entirely, because it was meant to serve a specific purpose). What it more or less comes down to is that I, far from even being a pawn of a pawn in the great game of chess, now intend to break all the rules and muddle the entire game by occupying the place of the queen . . . and after that perhaps also the place of the king himself, or even the whole board, and that, if I really wanted this, it would have to happen in a different and other than human way. That is why the proposal I made you means so much more to me than to you. It is, at the moment, real beyond any doubt or sickness, and it makes me absolutely happy. [MIL, p. 55]

Absolute happiness was a novel experience for Kafka, and bound to wake sleeping demons. His leave, twice extended, was ending on July 5. Long-standing plans called for his leaving Merano the last week of June and spending a few days at Karlovy Vary (Karlsbad) with his parents and Julie Wohryzek. But Milena was now urging him to return to Prague via Vienna. He refused; seeing him in the flesh would, he felt sure, mean the end of her love for him. She insisted, he agreed, then definitely turned her down, only to change his mind again at the last moment, wiring Julie to call off their meeting and instead taking the train to Vienna, where on Sunday evening, June 27, he checked into the Hotel Riva, a run-down fleabag near the railroad station.

It took him until Tuesday morning to screw up his courage and send Milena an express letter asking her to meet him the following day in front of the hotel. "Please, Milena, no surprises. No sneaking up on me from the side or from behind."

*   *   *

There were no surprises. Milena was what she was, what she had been in her letters, was everything he had dreamed she would be. And a great deal more. She knew how to disarm his fears, make him forget self-consciousness, mortality, and guilt, and give him, for the first time in his life, a sense of being loved, and of being able to love in turn. "Your life-giving strength, Mother Milena . . ."

They spent four days together in Vienna and surroundings. In those four days, Milena later wrote to Brod, Kafka lost his fear.

> We laughed about it. I know for certain that no sanatorium will ever succeed in curing him. He will never recover, Max, as long as he has this fear. And no effort to strengthen his psyche will overcome this fear, because the fear itself prevents his growing strong. This fear does not refer to me alone, but to everything that lives without shame, such as the flesh, for example. The flesh is too exposed; he cannot bear to see it. That was what I was able to dispel at the time. Whenever he felt this fear, he would look into my eyes, we would wait for a moment as though to catch our breath, or as though our feet hurt, and after a while it would be gone. Not the slightest strain was involved, everything was clear and simple. I dragged him all over the hills outside Vienna, running ahead because he walked slowly. He trudged along after me, and I only have to close my eyes to still see his white shirt and tanned throat and the effort he was making. He hiked all day, up and down, walked in the sun, and didn't cough once. He ate an awful lot and slept like a log. He was quite simply in good health, and his illness during those days seemed to us like nothing more than a slight cold. [Brod, bio., p. 203]

There was one fear of his she did not try to overcome but handled with guile, discretion, and the instinctive tact of one who, as he put it, "is simply unable to make others suffer." However close, emotionally and intellectually, they stopped short of complete physical intimacy. More precisely, it was he who stopped short. For her part, she never forced the issue, but instead of coyly ignoring it, she brought it out into the open, made him face his fear of sex, accepted it as she accepted everything else, and, for a start, sought to reassure him. They had, she insisted, "already been one." And, for good measure, added a contemptuous remark about "men's business—that half hour in bed."

She was persuasive enough to reassure even Kafka for a little while. He returned to Prague on Sunday, July 4, in a state of ecstasy. "Since I love you, I love the whole world."

*   *   *

Had I gone back to Prague with him at that point [Milena later wrote], I would have remained to him what I had been. But I had both feet firmly planted on this earth, I was incapable of leaving my husband, and perhaps I was too much the woman to find whatever strength it would have taken to submit to his way of life, a life I knew would have meant the strictest asceticism. There is in me an irrepressible longing, a raging desire for a life altogether different from the one I lead and probably shall always be leading, a life with a child, a life close to the soil. That, probably, is what in the end won out over everything else—over my love, over my wish to soar with him, over my admiration, and over my love once again. [Brod, bio., p. 203]

Milena was all of twenty-four, high-strung, emotionally labile, but conscious of her gifts and just beginning to come into her own. She may even have been sincere in her ostentatious disdain of "that half hour in bed," but she could hardly have ignored the deeper implications of Kafka's attitude which, far beyond sex as such, involved nothing less than a denial of life itself. That she did not trust herself to either change or accept it shows a remarkable maturity and self-awareness.

In the first days following their meeting, however, things between them seemed better than ever. Kafka got back to Prague, still walking on air, quite certain that Milena would join him in a matter of weeks. "He, always so reticent in the past, talked about his days in Vienna with such rapturous exuberance and happiness that I scarcely recognized him," Brod remembered.

The momentum helped him sail with near-insouciance through the mass of unpleasant tasks and mundane aggravations awaiting him on his return—cosmic disasters, every one of them, in his mere normal state. The first and most difficult was to break off his quasi-engagement, as he had promised Milena—"a hangman's job" which he was so anxious to get over with that he went to see Julie the very afternoon of his arrival. She took it very hard, even insisted on writing to Milena directly, but he was far too callously happy to feel more than perfunctory guilt or compassion.

On July 5, he reported back to work, and neither the cordial welcome nor the case load on his desk deterred him from first answering the two letters he had already received from Milena. "Tomorrow I'll send you the letter to my Father. Please take good care of it; I may yet someday want to give it to him. And try to understand all the lawyer's tricks it contains; it is a lawyer's brief" (MIL, p. 61).

The following day he had to vacate his room and move in with his sister Elli. Ottla was getting married on July 15, the apartment was in a state of siege, and Uncle Alfred, arriving from Madrid for the wedding, had to be put up. But even this break in his routine, his uncle's demands on his time, and the turmoil in the house left him quite unfazed: "Of course I'd like for things to be different, and I'd like the office to disappear altogether. Then again, I deserve a slap in the face whenever I express wishes beyond the present moment, this moment that belongs to you" (MIL, p. 67).

The euphoria did not outlast the week, this time for reasons substantive rather than neurotic. Milena, while loving as ever, obviously had second thoughts about rushing to join him in Prague. She brought up the matter of her husband, wanted to talk things over with her old schoolmate Staša Jílova, failed to react to his impetuous wire assuring her that "your home is here. How shall I send you money?" Still buoyed by hope and unwonted self-assurance, he argued that Polak was not his friend, hence "I did not betray a friend . . . and you, again, did not betray him, because you love him, whatever you may say, and if the two of us get together . . . it will be at a different level, not in his domain" (MIL, p. 70). Yet human relations, as he was well aware, are not susceptible to such neat geometric triangulations. Moreover, he was troubled by Milena's turning to her schoolmate for advice and emotional support. He had met Staša, a bright but conventional young woman, herself married to a Jew, and suspected her of intriguing against him.

With the foundations of his dream castle suddenly springing large cracks, Kafka was far too preoccupied to mourn his sister's marriage. Rather, it was Ottla herself who seemed to have trouble coping with her feelings. In May, when she notified him of the wedding date, he wrote to her from Merano: "Why should a July wedding come as a surprise? I had already expected it at the end of June. You sometimes talk as if you were doing me an injustice by getting married, when in fact just the opposite is true" (O, 5/20). He came through the ordeal with only minor damage, as he reported to Milena right after the event: "A myrtle pinned to my lapel, halfway rational despite a splitting headache (separation, separation!), I managed to finish the wedding meal seated between my brother-in-law's good sisters. Now, however, I feel drained. How easy life will be once we're together" (MIL, p. 81).

However, the stubborn resolve with which he still clung to this thought grew increasingly desperate as his own doubts began to surface. The institute's physician, who examined him on his return to duty, found no perceptible improvement. But Kafka—the very man who, at the first suspicion of TB, had immediately broken off his engagement to Felice and who, a mere month earlier, had given up all hope of recovery—now argued that "although the doctor considers the cure a fiasco, I regard it as rather successful; what would I now look like if I had spent that time in Prague? Also, he thinks I did not gain any weight, but according to my calculations I gained about 2 kgs." (MIL, p. 78). And a few days later: "I am not all that sick, and if I manage to get a little sleep, I feel as well as I hardly ever did in Merano. Lung diseases as a rule are, after all, more amiable than most, especially during the hot summer months" (MIL, p. 82).

But the chief obstacles, as both of them well knew, were not external ones, and the rift that opened up between them revealed far deeper conflicts. Oblique reproaches and recriminations began to creep into their letters, blunted as yet by tenderness but already barbed enough to smart. "Look, Milena, if in Vienna you had been *absolutely convinced by me* . . . you would no longer be there, in spite of everything; or rather, there would be no 'in spite of everything' " (MIL, p. 86). She had indeed not been convinced, and now felt constrained to tell him why. But it was her abiding love for Polak, "in spite of everything," that she put forward as the main cause of her doubts and hesitations. Given her unsparing honesty, one must assume that she sincerely believed this to be true, and that she had some trouble distinguishing between masochism and conjugal love. Furthermore, Kafka's devotion had the not uncommon result of briefly rekindling Polak's own interest in her, and for a while he decanted his private brand of charm.

But, as Kafka quite accurately observed, "it isn't your husband and I who are fighting over you; the fight is taking place only within yourself" (MIL, p. 84), and her real choice lay not between Polak and Kafka, but between living her own life and sharing it with someone she knew to be incapable of living.

He still kept urging her to come to Prague. She refused; her husband was sick, she could not possibly leave him at this point. But she wanted Kafka to come to Vienna; she desperately needed him to help her sort out her feelings. His turn to refuse. He did not have the nerve to ask for more time off, nor could he make up a plausible excuse. "I couldn't come because I cannot lie in the office. I can also lie in the office, but only for two reasons. One is fear (fear is an office matter, it belongs there, and in such cases I am able to improvise lies with inspired spontaneity), the other is dire need" (MIL, p. 105). The mounting tension between them, the daily—often twice daily—letters back and forth, were bound to take their toll. Brod, frantic about Kafka's visibly worsening state, the by now often hour-long coughing spells, the eyes darker than ever with passion and pathos, felt constrained to intervene on his own and wrote to Milena directly, laying out the true facts of Kafka's illness and pleading for her help and understanding; their friend badly needed a rest, both physically and emotionally. It was an "act of friendship" well meant, about which Brod never seems to have had any misgivings, even though it most certainly did not improve matters. Until then, Kafka had quite deliberately underplayed his illness and led Milena to believe that what ailed him, physically, was merely an acute exacerbation of a very common disease, generally self-limited but nearly always curable; she even seemed to have a touch of it herself. Thanks to Brod, she was now made to realize that her intuition had been even more tragically prescient than she had suspected; "Frank" was not only incapable of living; Frank was, in fact, quite literally moribund.

For Kafka, life and the world beyond Milena had shrunk to near-total insignificance. He was pleased when the *Tribuna*, to which Milena contributed fashion reviews, printed several of his stories in her translation. He also managed to read Brod's about to be published magnum opus, *Paganism, Christianity, Judaism*, and his cautiously restrained critique is of some relevance. He thought the book "splendid" on the whole, even making allowances for the unavoidable bias on his part, "which does not mean that I agree with you. . . . When you speak in your own voice, I feel very close to you; when you start polemicizing, I get the urge to do likewise (to the best of my ability, of course). Actually, I don't believe in 'paganism' in your sense of the word. . . . Nor did you prove that the Greek soul was in despair, but merely that you yourself would be desperate if you had to be a Greek" (L, 8/7/20). It was an observation apposite to Brod's interpretation of Kafka's own work, in which he contrived to discern the very uplift, salvation, and faith that he himself would have felt "if he had had to be Kafka."

The tone of Kafka's letters to Milena remained passionate; they exchanged flowers by wire, asked for comfort, reassurance, love. But the undercurrents of doubt, fear, and jealousy erupted with increasing frequency. Her sense of guilt made her lash out at him, exacerbating the guilt and crushing him in the process, turning trivial misunderstandings into acrimonious quarrels. "Actually, we keep writing the same things over and over. First I ask you if you're ill, then you ask me. First I want to die, then it is your turn. First I want to cry in your lap like a little boy, then you in mine like a little girl. And once and ten times and a thousand times and always I want to be with you, and you say so, too. Enough, enough" (MIL, p. 113).

The results of another medical examination during the first week of August gave him little cause for cheer; the doctor urgently recommended a rigorous cure, this time in a sanatorium specializing in pulmonary diseases, "one of those institutions rocked to their foundations day and night by cough and fever, where they make you eat meat, where retired hangmen dislocate your arms if you try to resist injections, while Jewish doctors stand by and stroke their beards, looking on with no mercy toward Jews and Christians alike" (MIL, p. 120).

Milena finally declared outright that she could not leave her husband because he needed her, an argument that infuriated Kafka, who saw it as a shallow rationalization. He proposed a weekend meeting at Gmünd, the Austrian border station midway between Prague and Vienna, for August 14, which she accepted with an alacrity that immediately roused his apprehension; nothing between them was simple anymore.

The apprehension proved justified; unlike their Vienna idyll six weeks earlier, Gmünd was a confrontation full of tormenting silences, recriminations, and grotesque misunderstandings. She remained utterly beyond reach, diffident, and distracted. "I remember your asking me if I had been faithful to you in Prague—half joking, half serious, and half indifferent, three halves just to confirm the impossibility. You had my letters, and still you asked. . . . That day we talked and listened to one another, long and often, like two strangers" (MIL, p. 157).

It marked the beginning of the end, an inward break they still refused to acknowledge. He raved about her translation of "The Judgment," still to him the summit of his powers; he wrote to her every day, all resolutions to the contrary notwithstanding, sent her an article on Bolshevism in Russia: "What the author criticizes is precisely what for me constitutes the highest possible praise" (MIL, p. 169). But by mid-September his strength gave out, he could no longer bring himself to play the game. "Few things are certain, but one of them is that we shall never live together, in the same apartment, body to body, at the same table, never, not even in the same town" (MIL, p. 179).

The letters slowed to a trickle. Milena spent several weeks recuperating in a St. Gilgen sanatorium—the cure made possible by a partial reconciliation with her father—while Kafka's steadily deteriorating health so alarmed Ottla that in October, on her own initiative and without consulting her brother, she obtained an extended leave for him from the institute. He was still trying to arrange for a stay at the Grimmstein Sanatorium near Vienna when, on November 16, Prague erupted in a three-day orgy of anti-Jewish and anti-German riots. The mob sacked the offices of German-language newspapers, attacked "Jewish-looking" victims in the streets, broke into the German National Theater and the Jewish Town Hall, destroyed the archives and burned ancient Hebrew manuscripts in front of the Old-New Synagogue, an act which the city's mayor hailed as a "manifestation of national consciousness."

> I've spent all afternoon out in the streets [Kafka reported to Milena] bathing in Jew-hatred. *Prašive plemeno*—filthy brood— is what I heard them call the Jews. Isn't it only natural to leave a place where one is so bitterly hated? (That doesn't even take Zionism or feelings of national pride.) The heroism involved in staying put in spite of it all is the heroism of the cockroach, which also won't be driven out of the bathroom. I just looked

out the window: mounted police, a riot squad ready for a bayonet charge, the screaming mob dispersing, and up here in the window the ugly shame of always having to live under protection. [MIL, p. 184]

He began to have serious misgivings about Grimmstein because of its proximity to Vienna.

> You say, Milena, that you can't understand it. Try to understand it by calling it an illness. It is one of the many manifestations of illness which psychoanalysis prides itself on having uncovered. I don't call it illness, I regard the therapeutic application of psychoanalysis as a hopeless error. All these ostensible illnesses, sad as they may seem, are matters of faith, the efforts of a human being in distress to sink roots into some maternal soil. Thus psychoanalysis also perceives the origin of religion as nothing more than what, in its view, also causes the "illnesses" of the individual. . . . Such roots, however, sunk into real soil, are not, after all, man's individual and interchangeable property but preformed in his nature and, in turn, continuing to form it (as well as his body) further in this direction. And this is what they mean to cure? [MIL, p. 188]

In the course of a sleepless night, early in December, he decided against going to Austria: "I don't have the strength it would take to go. Even ahead of time I can't bear the thought of standing before you, can't bear the pressure on my brain." A few days later, they agreed to stop writing to each other. "I won't say goodbye. There will be no goodbye, unless the force of gravity that lurks in the wings pulls me down all the way. But how could it, when you are alive?" (MIL, p. 195).

Thus ended their love affair, but not their friendship. Though intermittently and at a distance, they kept in touch. In 1921, Milena had the first of a series of reconciliations with her father and spent the last three months of the year in Prague. Kafka was by then already more or less confined to the house, and she paid him four visits— rather formal calls that nonetheless stirred deep emotions. In October, he went so far as to give her all his diaries, which up to then no one had been allowed to read, with instructions to pass them on to Max Brod after his death; it is difficult to conceive of a more persuasive tribute. She again came to see him the following spring, on April 27 and May 8, 1922, apparently for the last time, when he gave her the manuscript of the *Amerika* novel, of which she had translated the first part.

* * *

What if she had followed him to Prague?

The question came to haunt her, though she might have found the answer in his very diaries: "That which is possible will surely happen. Only that which happens is possible" (DI, 1/5/14).

Milena finally left Polak in 1924, shortly after Kafka's death, and for some years lived with Count Schaffgotsch, an aristocratic German Communist who introduced her to Marxist thought and left-wing circles. She returned to Prague a year later as a regular contributor to both the *Tribuna* and its conservative counterpart, the *Národný Listy;* three collections of her work were eventually published in book form. In 1927, she married the architect Jaromir Krejcar, but the birth of their daughter in 1928 was complicated by a near-fatal sepsis that left Milena crippled with arthritis and addicted to morphine. She eventually overcame the addiction, joined the Communist Party in 1931 but was expelled in 1936, an experience invaluable to her career as a political journalist, in which her lack of illusions and party commitments gave her a formidable edge over most of her colleagues.

What she had foreseen and vainly warned against came to pass in 1939, when the Germans invaded Czechoslovakia. Milena's satirical attacks on the Nazi occupation were often Aesopian—or Švejkian— enough to get past the censors, but at the same time her apartment became the hub of an underground rescue operation in which even her eleven-year-old daughter participated as a courier. Ever outspoken, refusing to curtail her public contacts with Jews and instead demon- stratively wearing the yellow star herself in the hope of inducing other Czechs to do likewise, she was singularly ill suited to clandestine conspiracies and soon ran afoul of the Gestapo. She was arrested in the fall of 1939 and, after a year in Prague and Dresden prisons, transferred to the Ravensbrück concentration camp. It was there that Margarete Buber-Neumann met her in October 1940.

Buber-Neumann, herself a woman of unflagging courage who had already survived three years in Soviet gulags, only to be turned over to the Gestapo during the Stalin-Hitler pact, was being ostracized by the Communist inmates for the same reasons for which they sought to persecute Milena. The friendship between these two extraordinary women ended with Milena's death at Ravensbrück on May 17, 1944. *Kafka's Friend Milena*, the biography Buber-Neumann published in 1963, bears witness to that friendship as well as to the heroism of both the author and her subject. (An English translation was published under the absurd title *Mistress to Kafka.*)

Thanks to an SS camp doctor who had once studied with him, Dr. Jesenský received permission to claim his daughter's body for burial in Prague. Milena's own daughter survived and became a writer in turn. She has since died in an automobile accident in Czechoslovakia.

Twenty-six

" " A FEW days ago I resumed my 'war service,' " Kafka wrote to Milena on August 26, 1920, ten days after the defeat at Gmünd. "Or more precisely, the 'maneuver life' which, as I discovered years ago, suits me best during certain periods. In the afternoon, I go to bed and sleep as long as possible, then take a two-hour walk, and after that I try to stay awake as long as possible. But this 'as long as possible' is the crux of the problem: it is not possible for very long, not in the afternoon and not at night, in spite of which I am totally worn out when I get to the office in the morning. The real treasures lie buried in the depths of the night, in the second, third, and fourth hours, but nowadays, if I don't get to sleep, or at least to bed by midnight the latest, the day and the night and myself are lost. Still, none of this matters; just being back in service feels good even if there are no results. Nor are there likely to be any; I need half a year like this just to 'loosen my tongue,' at which point I'll find that it's all over, that the service leave has expired. But as I said, it is good in and of itself, even if the cough tyrannically interferes, in the short run or in the long" (MIL, p. 159).

After a silence of well over two years in which Kafka had not just stopped writing but, at times, stopped thinking of himself as a writer—he had convinced himself that *A Country Doctor* would be his last book—the Milena crisis forced him once again to come to terms with himself and his fate in the only way he knew. Conditions militated against any major project, nor was his remark about needing half a year just to "loosen his tongue" a mere figure of speech. The night was unfathomable, the treasures buried deep in silt, and bringing them to the surface took time and patience. All he had, as it turned out, were four months—to the middle of December—before another setback forced him to leave Prague again and cut short his attempts to retrieve some points of reference in the desert of his solitude. During those four months, however, he worked away quite steadily at the preliminary sketches of an inner nightscape, most of which he evidently discarded. The fragments that survived suggest an exploratory foray into neo-cabalistic realms; a number were later published by Brod, who provided the titles (cited here from the currently available English edition): "The City Coat of Arms," "The Problem of Our Laws," "The Vulture," "The Test," "At Night," "The Conscription of Troops," "The Helmsman," "The Top," "Home-Coming."

* * *

On December 18, Kafka left for what was billed as a sanatorium for pulmonary diseases at Matliary, in the High Tatra Mountains, a predominantly Hungarian border region now part of Czechoslovakia. Like most such institutions, Mrs. Forberger's "sanatorium" actually amounted to little more than a boardinghouse; its large dining room, open to the public, was favored by the officer-patients of the nearby military hospital. However, the local doctor—"A good doctor? Yes, a specialist. Would that I had become a specialist; how splendidly a one-track mind can simplify the world"—resided on the premises and, for a modest retainer, agreed to see Kafka at least once every day. For a starter, he prescribed five glasses of milk, plus two glasses of heavy cream daily between meals, and offered arsenic injections at twelve crowns a shot. Kafka refused the injections, and Dr. Strelinger, diffident and unpretentious, was not one to insist; he seems to have had unprofessionally modest expectations of medicine's power to heal, part of his pervasive, melancholy skepticism. When Kafka, bloated with vegetarian guilt, complained about having had to eat anchovies, the doctor's only comment was, "Better you them than they you."

The thirty-odd regular guests were for the most part in fairly advanced stages of the disease. And as a patient among patients, busy all day long resting, drinking milk, collecting his sputum, getting weighed, taking his temperature seven times a day, and keeping a chart of the results, Kafka for the first time found himself face to face with the specter of the illness as such—not a metaphorical eruption of his own inner conflicts, but a sinister bacterial invasion, a monstrous enemy in its own right, whose potential for evil was depressingly evident all around him and deserved to be taken seriously. He began to worry about his family, especially now that Ottla was pregnant. "For my part, I still don't believe it to be infectious, but the most sincere belief is of no help when contradicted by the facts; and for someone with this disease to kiss small children in particular, or let them eat from the same plate, is an abominable wrong" (O, p. 107).

Socially it was an ill-assorted group, babbling away in three languages—German, Czech, Hungarian—mostly middle-aged and middle-class, about equally divided between Jews and anti-Semites whom common boredom and routines quickly welded into a family of sorts. Even Kafka, who at first made strenuous efforts to keep his distance, soon found himself drawn into the circle, the residual anti-Semitism manifesting itself merely by a shade more conspicuous cordiality on the part of its proponents toward their Jewish fellow sufferers. There were, he assured Ottla, no females young enough to cause problems for him. But in February 1921 a new patient arrived, an orphaned twenty-one-year-old Jew from Budapest who soon adopted Kafka as his mentor, and whose fiercely possessive devotion proved at times almost as troublesome as a love affair. In the end, however, Robert Klopstock turned out to be an angel in disguise.

*   *   *

A most unusual disguise, in fact, although the young Klopstock could on occasion look downright cherubic, in stark contrast to his usually morose appearance. He had been studying medicine in Budapest until illness forced him to leave school—"very ambitious, bright, also very literary, outwardly resembles a cruder version of Werfel, starved for human contact in the manner of a born physician, anti-Zionist, Jesus and Dostoevsky are his leaders" (L, 2/21). But tuberculosis, as Kafka soon came to realize, was the least of what ailed his young friend and admirer: "That hapless medic. Never yet have I seen so demonic a spectacle from close up. Hard to tell whether the powers at work in him are for good or evil, but uncannily strong they are in either case. In the Middle Ages, he would have been regarded as possessed. A young man at that, all of twenty-one, tall, broad-shouldered, strong, apple-cheeked, extremely intelligent, truly unselfish, sensitive" (O, p. 115).

The demons glimpsed by Kafka were to haunt Klopstock all his life, a life in perennial exile of which Matliary was merely the first and perhaps least painful stage. Politics—the Red Terror, followed by the White Terror—and a doomed passion for a married cousin kept him from ever going back home, or so he claimed. As neurotic as he was gifted, ill at ease in any language other than Hungarian, he for some time entertained literary ambitions. But Kafka, to whom he clung right from the start with the consuming jealousy of a fatherless child, sensed that Klopstock's choice was to become either a good doctor or a bad writer. With much patience, tact, and practical help, which involved mobilizing contacts in Prague and Berlin, he eventually succeeded in steering and coaxing his filial friend back into medical school.

Klopstock completed his studies in Berlin after Kafka's death and had already gained a reputation as a specialist in pulmonary diseases when he was forced to leave Germany in 1938. He came to the United States, spent seven years at Massachusetts General Hospital on research involving the development of segmental resection for pulmonary tuberculosis, obtained his New York license in 1950, and went on to become chief of thoracic services at the Veterans Administration Hospital in Brooklyn, as well as a professor at Downstate Medical Center. His dedication not only to his calling but to his patients was legendary; at the same time, he remained an enigmatic and impenetrable personality, fiercely private, kindly yet aloof to the point of resisting any effort to socialize, or even to make contact with him outside a professional setting. He was married, but the couple had no children, and few of his colleagues ever got to meet his wife; their universally fond and respectful recollections evoke the image of both a brilliant surgeon and a deeply troubled, unhappy man living in self-imposed exile. Dr. Klopstock died in New York City in 1972.

But at Matliary in 1921, his ardent solicitude was welcome and vexing at once. Kafka quickly grew fond of this big, volatile, sentimental teddy bear of a man and slipped rather effortlessly into the unaccustomed paternal role. Klopstock, moreover, took expert care of him during the repeated episodes of acute illness that plagued him—bronchitis, furunculosis, a severe intestinal infection—and could be excellent company. But even the best of companions seemed a burden much of the time. And while the pent-up force of Klopstock's intrinsically unmeetable needs may not yet have been apparent at that point, the emotional distress signals he sent out must have been picked up by Kafka long before they attained their full volume of pathetic urgency.

There was, in any case, little he could or would have done about it. His stay at Matliary had turned into an extended hibernation, a state of suspended animation from which he seemed increasingly disinclined and unable to rouse himself. Twice—in March and in May—his leave expired. Both times he got ready to go home simply because he could not bring himself to apply for an extension, and both times Ottla, by now the mother of a baby girl, obtained it for him by appealing on her own initiative directly to Dr. Ostrčil. The simple truth was that Matliary had done absolutely nothing for his health, although by mid-March he had gained over six kilograms, a significant improvement by the criteria to which medical science subscribed in his day. He himself knew better. Leaden fatigue, the ever-worsening cough, the constant boils, hemorrhoids, and abscesses that refused to heal, all indicated a steadily declining resistance to infection. In any event, the fulminating gastroenteritis in April all but wiped out the weight gain as well. His always morbid sensitivity to noise had become an excruciatingly painful obsession—"though it isn't the noise here that plagues me but the noise of the world, and not even that noise but my own not making any noise" (L, 5/21).

He did no work, initially read the Bible, then stopped reading altogether, and even the letters to Brod and the family seemed at times to exceed his strength. The fatigue increased. "I spend hours in the deck chair, in a sort of twilight stupor such as I used to marvel at as a child, watching my grandparents" (L, 3/21). He was clearly losing touch with Prague, and the depth of his isolation alternately pleased and frightened him. "You are going to see Milena," he wrote to Brod in May. "I won't ever have this joy again. When you speak to her about me, speak as you would of someone dead" (L, 5/21). In April, the weather improved, and so, to some extent, did his mood. He showed a lively interest in his new niece, Ottla's daughter Vera, born on March 27, and mentioned having done some reading, including Jonathan Swift, whose authority he invoked in offering Elli Hermann some unsolicited advice on how to bring up her ten-year-old son. With a passion born of filial hate and self-contempt, he implored Elli to send Felix to the International Boarding School at Hellerau, to get him out of Prague, away from parents and family, whose generic selfishness —according to Swift—disqualifies them *a priori* from raising their own offspring. "But, I repeat, all this is merely Swift's opinion (who was, by the way, himself the father of a family). My own opinion tends in the same direction, though I don't dare to formulate it quite so decisively" (L, 1921. The dating of "Fall 1921" in the *Collected Letters* is obviously in error; Kafka was by then back in Prague).

Once again, though, his own irrepressible sanity somewhat spoiled the effect: "Here I go giving advice to others on how to raise their children, when I wasn't even capable of advising myself on how to have children of my own." What he did not know was that the qualifications of his expert witness were equally suspect: Swift, with a love life considerably more muddled than Kafka's, kept his marriage a secret, had no known progeny, and his expertise in child-rearing was most convincingly demonstrated in "A Modest Proposal." In any event Elli, who felt that a ten-year-old was too young to leave home, trusted her own instincts more than those of either the gloomy Dean or her no less gloomy brother. And to Kafka's profound disappointment, his sister Valli soon came to the same conclusion about her own oldest daughter, though she went so far as to visit Hellerau for a conference with its new director, A. S. Neill.

By August, he was in good enough shape to do some hiking, though it seemed to him that what had improved was the weather rather than his health. Dr. Strelinger agreed. He saw no point in any further extension of the treatment, and on August 26, Kafka reported back to work.

* * *

It was a heroic effort, inspired by his civil-service conscience and a sense of obligation toward the institute, but it brought the almost immediate realization that he was no longer physically able to live up to even the most minimal demands of the job—"If I didn't go to bed as soon as I get home from the office, I could not survive." He continued to run a temperature and, already within the first few weeks, repeatedly had to stay home with infections, so that by mid-September the institute's own physician recommended another rest cure.

His halfhearted attempts, after a ten-month absence from Prague, to ease back into the flow of social life were hardly more successful. Brod was largely unavailable, melodramatically torn between his wife in Prague and his lover in Berlin, shuttling back and forth between women and cities while writing a novel, *Franzi, A Second-Class Love*, about his plight. Old friends came to see Kafka—Ernst Weiss, Otto

Pick, Franz Werfel, Minze Eisner, Georg Langer—but their visits tired and depressed him. He had also been adopted by a young man just out of his teens, the would-be poet Gustav Janouch, son of an eccentric office colleague who, after a messy divorce, later committed suicide. "He came to see me at the office, weeping, laughing, screaming, brought me a pile of books which I am supposed to read, then apples, finally his girl friend, a nice little forester's daughter; he lives out there with her parents. He professes to be happy but makes an at times frighteningly mixed-up impression, also looks very bad, wants to get his high-school equivalency diploma and then study medicine ('because it is such quiet, modest work') or law ('because it leads into politics'). What devil feeds this fire?" (L, 9/21).

This is the same young man who, some twenty-five years later, claimed to have kept a verbatim record of his *Conversations with Kafka* extensive enough to fill two entire volumes. Whatever devil may have fed the fire, it was Kafka who fed Janouch after World War II.

Even more trying, however, were the encounters with Milena in October, which robbed him of his sleep and added to his physical as well as emotional distress. The basic harmony between them, her vast compassion and understanding, which moved him to a confessional act without precedent—the surrender of all his diaries—merely accentuated what he now saw as an ineluctable finality. "Ehrenstein . . . lately said something to the effect that in Milena, life held out its hand, and that I had the choice between life and death. That was somewhat too grandiloquently put, but true in essence just the same. Stupid was only his belief that I had a choice in the matter. If there still were a Delphic oracle, I would have consulted it and been told: 'The choice between life and death? How can you hesitate?' " (L, 5/21).

He did not hesitate. On October 15, after an interruption of nearly two years, he again began to keep a diary, distinct from the earlier ones he had just turned over to Milena in that it ignored the passing scene and focused instead on the heart of the matter—"I am a memory come alive. Hence also the inability to sleep" (DI, 10/15/21).

By the end of October, it had become painfully evident that Kafka was no longer up to the physical demands of his job, and on the twenty-ninth he was granted another leave of absence. Unable or unwilling this time to face up to the formidable expense of yet another sanatorium, he decided to stay in Prague instead and to submit to a regimen supervised by Dr. Hermann, the family physician. "I've started to be one of those people who never have time," he reported to Klopstock in December. "The day is so carefully divided into segments for resting, walking, and so forth, that I don't even have time or strength left for reading. After a few fever-free days, the fever has now come back. All the doctor gave me was a special tea which, if I understood him correctly, contains silicic acid. He read somewhere (not in a humor magazine, I hope) that this promotes scarring" (L, 12/21).

Klopstock, with an ego as fragile as a raw egg, was not about to accept any excuses from his dilatory correspondent. Even while involving Kafka in his myriad personal and practical problems—he was forever unhappily in love, suicidally depressed, trying to acquire Czech citizenship, to matriculate at Prague University, to find living quarters, and to obtain a stipend or a job—he constantly felt neglected, accused Kafka of having betrayed their Matliary brotherhood, and bombarded him with near-paranoid reproaches followed by abjectly hysterical apologies. It was a tribute to his then still boyish charms and touching devotion that Kafka seldom lost patience with him, or at least did not have the heart to show it. Moreover, in spite of his own troubles, Kafka took an active hand in straightening out Klopstock's legal and financial tangles and finally arranged for him to resume his studies in Prague.

The turn of the year and the first gloomy weeks of January 1922 drove Kafka into ever more barren regions of dread.

> Last week I suffered something like a total breakdown. The only one that even came close was that night, two years ago; otherwise I've never known anything like it. Everything seemed finished, and even today it does not really look any different. One can interpret it in two ways, both no doubt equally correct: first, a breakdown, making it impossible to sleep, impossible to stay awake, impossible to endure life, or more precisely the sequence of life. The clocks are out of synch, the inner one racing at a hellish or demonic or at any rate inhuman pace, while the outer one ticks away at its usual speed. . . . Second: The chase drives one outside humanity. The loneliness, largely imposed from the outside but also sought by me—though this again was compulsion—has now emerged quite unequivocal and is approaching ultimate limits. Where will it lead? Madness seems the inevitable end; nothing further can be said about that, the chase passes right through me and tears me apart. . . . "Chase" is a figure of speech; I could also call it "assault on the outermost

temporal limits." . . . All of this writing is an assault on the limits, and if Zionism had not intervened, it might easily have developed into a new secret doctrine, a Cabala. [DI, 1/16/22]

He was in so obviously desperate a state that his doctor, about to take his own family to the mountain resort of Spindlermühle (Špindlerov Mlýn) near the Polish border for a four-week winter vacation, urged him to come along and arranged for another three-month extension of his leave. Exposing a tubercular patient to the rigors of winter at high altitudes was daringly unorthodox medicine and suggests either uncommon wisdom or a sense of futility on Dr. Hermann's part. But the shock treatment seemed to work, although Kafka's own inner forces of resistance had already begun to consolidate and come into play: "The strange, mysterious, perhaps dangerous, perhaps saving consolation of writing, a leap out of murderers' row, the observation of action . . ." he noted, on the day of his arrival, along with an eerie coincidence: "Although, in making my reservations, I had quite legibly spelled out my name, and although the hotel had already correctly addressed two letters to me, the desk clerk had me down as Joseph K. Should I enlighten them, or should I let them enlighten me?" (DI, 1/27/22).

The snow and the mountain air had an exhilarating effect. He went hiking, sleigh riding, even tried skiing, and his fear of pneumonia—"fear not so much of the illness itself as fear for and of my mother, my father, the director, and all the rest"—proved groundless. He stopped taking his temperature and, except for the fatigue and insomnia, felt physically better than he had in a long time. And although the depression, the sense of utter loneliness and isolation, refused to lift, he at last found the strength to fight them with the only weapon at his disposal. At the end of February, shortly after his return to Prague, he wrote to Klopstock: "In order to save myself from what is commonly referred to as 'nerves,' I have lately begun to write a little. From about seven at night I sit at my desk, but it doesn't amount to much. It is like trying to dig a foxhole with one's fingernails in the midst of battle, and next month that, too, will cease and the office begin once more" (L, Spring 1922). A few months later, already in the midst of a creative phase, he was even more explicit: "The existence of the writer is truly dependent on his desk. If he wants to escape madness, he really should never leave his desk. He must cling to it by his teeth" (L, 7/5/22).

The initial results of these driven efforts to burrow into his solitude were four brief but striking parables of alienation—"First Sorrow," "The Departure," "Advocates," and "A Hunger Artist," perhaps already conceived at Spindlermühle and probably all written in February 1922. By the end of that month, at any rate, he had embarked on the most daring and desperate of his voyages into the night of self and the world.

* * *

The Castle is Kafka's most elaborately autobiographical work, replete with references not only to the crises in his own life that inspired it but also to the passions and pathologies of those on whom he drew as models for his supporting cast; aside from Milena and Polak, they include family, friends, teachers, colleagues, and superiors. His initial impulse, in fact, had been to tell the story in the first person altogether, a radical departure from his usual self-protective device; the later substitution of the transparently pseudonymous "K." forced him to revise the first two chapters but adds no measurable distance to that between himself and his protagonist, the surveyor in spite of himself, denied admission to a territory whose nature and boundaries resist surveying.

But if flagrantly autobiographical components supplied the bricks for *The Castle*, they don't yield up the keys to the interior. Here again, the sedulous efforts to identify the putative real-life originals thought to have inspired the novel's characters provide few meaningful clues to the author's complex intent, let alone his actual achievement. The exegetical literature on *The Castle* already runs into hundreds of articles and books in dozens of languages, and although the approaches cover every angle of the compass, they may be roughly divided into a few broad categories.

Brod's editorial preface to the posthumous first edition of the novel in 1926 authoritatively proclaimed *The Castle* a symbolic quest for divine grace. The specifics of his theology soon came under fire, not so his basically allegorical interpretation of the novel, which long continued to dominate and led to a host of derivative readings of *The Castle* as an allegory of bureaucracy, of secular Judaism, of power, alienation, or the road to Christ, among many others.

The Freudians, by contrast, eschewing larger perspectives, tended to focus on the analysis of specific symbols, while the sociologists in turn attempted to anchor the novel in the context of its time. With the postwar surge of existentialism, Sartre's comments on *The Castle* as dramatizing the existential crisis of modern man in a world without fixed values colored a wide range of critical studies in the West, but it was Simone de Beauvoir who recalled the initial impact of Kafka's works on her generation of French intellectuals in more perceptively personal terms: "Our admiration for Kafka was instantly radical, without our quite knowing just why we felt that his work concerned us personally. Faulkner, all the others, told us remote stories; Kafka spoke to us about ourselves. He revealed to us our own problems, confronted by a world without God and where nonetheless our salvation was at stake. No father had embodied the Law for us, but the Law was inflexibly engraved in us just the same. No universal reason could hope to decode it. It was so singular, so secret, that we ourselves could never succeed in spelling it out; yet we knew that if we failed to obey it, we were lost."*

In the East, Georg Lukács's outright condemnation of Kafka's work as decadent avant-gardism had the authority of a Party verdict and, as such, was beyond argument, until the all-too-brief period of liberalization in Kafka's homeland encouraged a measure of dissent culminating in the 1963 Liblice Conference on Prague's German-language writers, which legitimized Kafka as the prophet of alienation and went so far as to acknowledge the continuing pertinence of his views even in a socialist society.

Other contributions have yielded valuable insights. W. H. Auden and the perceptive French critic Marthe Robert persuasively argued the influence of Western literary tradition and the quixotic elements of K.'s quest, while the structuralist school, textual and linguistic analysis, and other disciplines and subdisciplines are merely beginning to mine what to them promises to be a rich lode.

The range and intensity of these responses bear witness to the phenomenally allusive potential of the stimulus, quite regardless of the extent to which they help to elucidate or obfuscate the multilayered meanings of a novel whose very title—*Das Schloss* being either castle or lock—imposed ambiguous choices, or a choice of ambiguities. Common to nearly all such essentially rational approaches, however, is the concomitant assumption of an equally rational plan, a teleological grand design cunningly, or at best unconsciously, shrouded in a series

* *La Force de l'Age,* p. 193.

of mystifying symbols whose decoding will reveal one final and definitive meaning. It is an assumption not warranted by anything known about Kafka or his working methods—themselves, of course, a quintessential expression of his tortured and driven personality, whose morbid ambivalence rendered him hypersensitive to the ambiguities inherent in the human condition. He worked when, and only when, the spirit was upon him, guided strictly by its dictates rather than by any preconceived ideological road map, translating the dilemmas of his life into the paradoxes of his fiction.

* * *

On February 18, 1922, Kafka got back to Prague, determined to make the most of his remaining leave, and by sticking close to his desk was able to read Brod the entire first part of *The Castle* one month later. In a letter to Milena, written during this flight into work, he pleaded with her never to write to him again: "All the misery in my life was caused by letters, so to speak." She was still sufficiently involved to be devastated by his request, and though she promised to heed it, she nonetheless came to see him at least twice during her next visit to Prague. "M. was here, won't come again; probably being wise and true, yet there may still remain a possibility, whose locked door we both guard lest it open, or rather lest we open it, for of itself it surely will not open" (DI, 3/15/22).

His leave was up on April 27, his health worse than ever, and rather than ask for yet another extension, he took his annual five-week vacation starting on that date. But in the meantime, it had become all too obvious that hard decisions could no longer be postponed and that Kafka, who on February 2 had been promoted to Senior Secretary, was never going to recover sufficiently to return to active duty. Professional optimism or etiquette still constrained the institute's doctor to hold out hope for an eventual cure, but even he was now talking in terms of years rather than months. On June 7, therefore, Kafka formally requested "a temporary transfer to the inactive status," with rights to a disability pension. His retirement was approved, effective July 1, 1922.

Kafka's salary as Senior Secretary would have been just under 30,000 crowns annually, an adequate if far from munificent income. His pension, on the other hand, initially fixed at 884 crowns a month and later raised to an even thousand, i.e., 12,000 crowns a year, barely supported a marginal existence to begin with. The rampant postwar inflation, however, soon zoomed out of control altogether and, within the brief remainder of his life, reduced his real income to a pittance.

Poor, perhaps, but free at last to come and go as he pleased, he joined Ottla and her baby in a tiny summer cottage at Planá, in the Bohemian Forest, on June 23. It was a cozy but somewhat cramped setup, especially during July, when Ottla's husband came up to spend his vacation with them. Moreover, even in the midst of the most peaceful countryside, the demons of noise continued to conspire against Kafka's sanity. No Ohropax earplugs could keep the sound of hammers. saws, horses, wheels, children, and even a plangent stray piano from drilling straight into his brain.

In all, though, it was a relatively peaceful period, thanks once again to the indefatigable Ottla, self-sacrificing as ever when it came to looking after his comfort and well-being. And while he still preferred being alone with her, he got along remarkably well with his easygoing and undemanding brother-in-law, whom he somehow never seems to have taken seriously enough to regard as a rival. During the first few weeks he continued to work on *The Castle*; he even considered the sections written at Planá much superior to the earlier chapters. The outside world loomed remote and ever more irrelevant: "Political news now reaches me . . . only in the truly excellent capsule form of the *Prager Abendblatt*. If you read nothing else, you'll know about as much of what goes on in the world as you once learned about the progress of the war from reading the *Neue Freie Presse*. According to the *Abendblatt*, the whole world is now as peaceful as the war used to be. They chase away your worries before you ever have them" (L, 6/30/22).

But so labile was his emotional state that the merest trifle sufficed to upset the balance. A planned visit to his blind friend, Oskar Baum, triggered a wild panic, sleepless nights, a spate of hysterical letters and telegrams, ending with the cancellation of the visit and a flood of self-recriminations. A few days later, on July 14, a frantic telegram from home made him rush back to Prague, where his father had undergone emergency surgery for a strangulated hernia—"a seventy-year-old man, after all, still weak from his recent and possibly related illness, and suffering from a heart condition besides" (L, 7/16/22). Herrmann, in critical condition for a day or two, made a miraculous recovery and soon was his old obnoxious self again. "His affection for me shrank by the day. . . . Yesterday he already couldn't get rid of me fast enough, while he forced my mother to stay with him. . . . And as the in my opinion wonderful nurse was leaving the room, he made a gesture behind her back that in his language could only mean 'you bitch'" (L, 7/20/22).

A week later, Kafka was back in Planá, increasingly edgy, plagued not only by illness but also by health, though health was hardly what he himself would have associated with the distracting temptations of carnal desire. After again spending a few days in Prague, at the beginning of August, he confessed to Brod: "This routine, a few days in the city, a few months in the country, might be ideal for me, although four summer days in the city approaches the limit. It would be impossible, for instance, to resist the half-naked women who parade around there; in summer you really first get to see that curious sort of flesh in massive quantities" (L, 8/22).

Brod, in turn, free from such scruples, had troubles of a different kind, and Kafka suffered for him vicariously and with evident gusto. Emmy Salveter, Brod's Berlin lover, now graduated with Brod's help from chambermaid to aspiring actress, had taken up—or threatened to take up—with a man not only younger and more attractive but straight-backed and Gentile in the bargain. Kafka's quasi-logical analysis of Brod's predicament led him to recommend a defiantly open *ménage à trois* as the only honest solution. Brod eventually came up with a solution of his own, less honest but more practical.

At the end of August, Kafka abandoned *The Castle*—"evidently for good. I was not able to pick up the thread again after the 'break-down,' which began a week before my trip to Prague, even though the parts written at Planá are not quite as bad as the ones you know" (L, 9/11/22). Ottla's decision to return to Prague at the end of August and let him fend for himself through September brought on another fit of hysteria so violent that she found herself compelled to change her plans. The true nature of that "fear of total loneliness" to which he ascribed his utterly disproportionate reactions, bewildering even to himself, is not difficult to fathom, given the relentless progress of his illness. But his troubles with *The Castle*, one suspects, were literary rather than psychogenic, inherent in the transcendental scope of a novel that defies plot and progression and instead unfolds in concentric and potentially infinite ripples of paradox. From several tentative drafts of further chapters in his notebooks it seems clear that the novel's growing complexity had outrun the author's power to control it—as suitable a conclusion to this extraordinary work as any that could be imagined.

On September 18, he returned to Prague, constrained now to settle into the routine of an invalid. With the approach of winter, he found himself increasingly confined to his room in the parental apartment on Old Town Square, his virtual imprisonment made somewhat more bearable by the fact that Ottla and her family lived in the same building. During the first two months, still able to do a certain amount of work, he wrote "The Married Couple," "Give It Up," "On Parables," and undertook an extensive revision of the "Investigations of a Dog." By the end of the year, however, a severe intestinal infection lasting several months forced him to abandon further efforts and spend much of his time in bed, with Kierkegaard and a Hebrew grammar as his main companions.

Brod dropped in from time to time, other friends occasionally came to visit, including Werfel, who invited him to Venice even though Kafka felt impelled to criticize his latest play with rather acrimonious severity. But visitors for the most part drained him and merely exacerbated his sense of isolation. A year earlier, in a brief testamentary disposition, he had appointed Brod his executor and instructed him simply to destroy all his writings. Now, after a relatively creative period, he was somewhat more discriminating in his self-destructive fury. A revised will, drawn up around this time, exempted "The Judgment," *The Stoker, The Penal Colony,* "The Metamorphosis," *A Country Doctor,* and "A Hunger Artist" from this sweeping verdict; all other writings of whatever kind were to be cremated as before.

Brod, as is known, later disregarded these instructions. In so doing, he not only invoked the immeasurable loss to literature but also quite persuasively argued that Kafka, by appointing as his executor a man whom he knew to be incapable of carrying out this wanton destruction of his work, was in effect sanctioning its publication without compromising his self-critical stance.

The infection kept him shut in through much of the winter and, despite gradual improvement in the spring of 1923, left him severely debilitated. Moreover, his insomnia, a scourge to which he should by now have been inured, tormented him to such an extent that he even overcame his naturopathic principles and resorted to sleeping pills— which, since he didn't expect them to help, failed to do so.

In any case, his insomnia would probably have resisted therapy of whatever kind; there is no cure short of murder or suicide for the fear of death, reflected in the mind's frenzied refusal to surrender to even temporary oblivion. Something of the sort gradually dawned on him also: "I realized that if I somehow wanted to go on living, I had to do something quite radical, and so I decided to emigrate to Palestine. I probably would not have been able to do so; I am also quite unprepared in Hebrew and in other respects, but I simply had to have hope of some kind to latch on to" (O, 10/23).

It was not quite as unrealistic a project as it appeared, and it certainly provided the glimmer of hope he so desperately needed in order to keep up the struggle. His fascination with many aspects of Judaism had steadily intensified over the years, and in this late period, in particular, he read a great deal of both fiction and non-fiction relating to Jewish history, lore, and religion. Nevertheless, his familiarity with the field has probably been much overrated, and to interpret the evolution of his religious beliefs in terms of a late-life conversion to traditional observance is a daring leap back into banality.

Thus Brod, in his diary reconstructed from memory after the war (the original was lost in Prague), claims that Kafka asked for *tefillin*—phylacteries—toward the end of his life. Beyond their romantic appeal, such deathbed gestures, whether or not accurate or accurately reported, help to confirm the faithful in their faith. This is not to say that Brod himself did not believe the story to be true, or even that it was not. But in the absence of any substantiating evidence whatsoever, it permits no sweeping conclusions concerning Kafka's attitudes toward a rabbinically approved brand of Judaism. On the other hand, he as late as January 1923 chided his friend Oskar Baum for not having notified him of the exact date of his son's bar mitzvah: "I just happened to hear about it by chance a few days ago but assumed it to be on Sunday the sixteenth. Only yesterday I learned what I should have known all my life—another of those things I was not informed about on time, but in this you're innocent—that this particular ceremony can only take place on a Saturday" (L, 1/23). Given this rather startling ignorance concerning one of the most common rituals of Jewish life, it seems hard to imagine what Kafka, a few months later, would have done with phylacteries even if he had in fact asked for them.

Yet ever since his first contact with the Yiddish players back in 1911 he had been conscious of his identity as a Jew, not in the religious, but in the national sense. He consistently saw, vilified, pitied, and condemned Western Jews as a people whose misguided attempts at assimilation had trapped them in a deadly impasse that had also helped to ruin his own life, and to which there was only one solution: a Jewish nation with its own language in its own land. Skeptical of ideologies, leery of chauvinism, and repelled by the petty politics of organizations large and small, he remained on the sidelines and never officially joined any Zionist body, but he left no doubt—in letters, diaries, personal contacts, by his collaboration with the *Selbstwehr* and attendance at Zionist meetings and lectures—as to his basic sympathies and orientation. Especially in the postwar years, following the Balfour Declaration, the Prague riots, and the consolidation of Czechoslovak Jewry as a recognized national rather than religious minority, he became quite unequivocally enthusiastic about the Jewish national revival in Palestine. It was therefore rather natural for him, *in extremis*, to grasp at this last great hope and expect from it a miracle, not only for the Jewish people, but for himself as well.

*   *   *

Language, to Kafka, was the essence of being. And if, in later years, he felt that by writing in German he had betrayed his very identity as a Jew, "snatched the stranger's child out of the cradle" and passed it off as his own, it is easy to understand why the revival of Hebrew as the living language of the Jewish people struck him as the most vital aspect of an authentic national renewal.

He had been studying it for a number of years, first with the aid of Moses Rath's antiquated grammar and later with teachers of varying competence, none really conversant with the idiom that was evolving in the settlements of Jewish Palestine. The transformation of biblical Hebrew into a modern vernacular rests to a large extent on the labors of one man, Eliezer Ben-Yehudah, a Lithuanian Jew born in 1858 who settled in Jerusalem in 1881 and carried his fierce, initially quixotic struggle for the secular acceptance of the holy tongue to a wildly successful conclusion. He compiled the first complete dictionary of modern Hebrew, a project that was completed after his death in 1922. And it was in the fall of that very year that one of his pupils, herself a first-generation Palestinian Jewess speaking modern Hebrew as her native tongue, arrived in Prague.

Puah Ben-Tovim was born in Jerusalem in 1903 and grew up in

a Hebrew-speaking household; her father, the writer Zalman Ben-Tovim, was a Hebraist in his own right who also happened to be Ben-Yehudah's friend and neighbor. Precocious and gifted, Puah was enrolled in a German Lutheran Gymnasium in Jerusalem after completing her elementary education, since no Hebrew secondary schools existed under Turkish rule. It was her bilingual fluency that brought her to the attention of Kafka's old schoolmate Hugo Bergmann, when he arrived in Palestine in 1920 and needed help in organizing the library of the newly founded Hebrew University. Her zeal and knowledge proved a major asset, but Bergmann quickly recognized that, intellectually, Puah was vastly overqualified for the job and arranged for her to stay with his parents in Prague and study mathematics at Prague University; he assured her that she would have no problem supporting herself by Hebrew lessons.

As indeed she did not. The arrival of what Bergmann announced as "the first native Hebrew-speaking bird from the old-new land of Israel" created a sensation among Prague's Zionists, and in the Jewish community at large. She was swamped with requests for Hebrew lessons, but the very first student she took on was the friend whom Bergmann had most emphatically commissioned her to seek out at once.

Kafka lived just a few blocks from the Bergmanns, and from the fall of 1922 through the spring of the following year, Puah twice a week faithfully went to his home to initiate the invalid and would-be immigrant into the subtleties of her native tongue. And of all her students, she maintains, none could match Kafka's drive and passionate dedication.

"Passionate, and also pathetic at the same time," recalled the now octogenarian Dr. Puah Menczel. One of Israel's outstanding educators, long since retired, she still exudes a vitality that belies her age. "In advance of every lesson, he used to compile long lists of words he wanted to know. But his lungs kept giving out. Every so often he'd have a painful coughing spell that would make me want to break off the lesson. And then he'd look at me, unable to speak, but imploring me with those huge dark eyes of his to stay for one more word, and another, and yet another. It almost seemed as if he thought of those lessons as a kind of miracle cure. He was living with his parents, and every so often his mother would quietly open the door and motion for me to let him rest. But he was insatiable, and he made good progress; toward the end we were reading a novel by Brenner."

The exoticism of Puah's provenance may have enhanced her charms in the eyes of Prague's ardent young Zionists, but she was far more than a mere fledgling bird of paradise and harbinger of Zion reborn. Nineteen years old, attractive, vivacious, enormously bright and dauntingly self-possessed, she had come to Europe at great sacrifice to acquire an education in science. The sexual mores of the Prague bourgeoisie were not part of the lesson plan, and though far from priggish, she was shocked by the crudely aggressive propositions she constantly was forced to fend off.

Kafka, too, was not insensitive to either the mystique or the natural endowment of what he called his "little Palestinian." She embodied the spirit of the new generation he had dreamed about, and their lengthy chats and growing closeness evidently gave rise to a few furtive illusions about Puah's becoming, if nothing else, his guide and mentor in the new land.

Illusions were not something Puah ever cared to nurture. "I soon came to realize that, emotionally, he was thrashing about like a drowning man, ready to cling to whoever came close enough for him to grab hold of. And I had my own life to live. I had neither the will nor the strength to be a nursemaid to a very sick man some twenty years older than I—not even if I had known then what I now know about him."

Spoken some sixty years later, but her whole life and subsequent career bear witness to the terrifyingly clear-eyed realism that even at nineteen must have enabled her to see the relationship in exactly those terms.

In April 1923 Kafka's still rather nebulous emigration plans received a sudden boost with the arrival of Hugo Bergmann himself, who briefly visited Prague on a mission for the Jewish National Fund. Bergmann urged him to forget about the risks and simply head for Palestine as soon as possible. More important, in practical terms, he offered Kafka hospitality in his Jerusalem home, and material help for as long as it took to get his bearings. The offer gave a solid base to what, until then, had been mostly wishful thinking, and it was agreed that Kafka would be in Jerusalem by October—subject, of course, to the vagaries of health or illness.

The prospect buoyed Kafka sufficiently to make him want to "test his transportability" by risking a few short trips, a daring enough enterprise, after six months of near-total confinement. In May he took a short train ride to Dobřichovice and, encouraged by the results, agreed to accompany his sister Elli and her children to the seaside resort of Müritz, on Germany's Baltic coast.

Along the way he planned to visit Puah, who in the meantime had left Prague at the end of the spring semester. Having discovered that her gifts were not, after all, up to the demands of pure mathematics, she had decided to study biology instead at the University of Berlin and taken a summer job at nearby Eberswalde, in a camp for under-privileged children, pending the start of the fall semester.

And so, during the first week of July, Kafka in the company of Elli and her three children set out for Müritz.

Twenty-seven

Elli and the children went straight on to Müritz, while Kafka stopped off in Berlin for a day, intending to visit Puah. He had also, however, promised Brod to meet Emmy Salveter, who much to his surprise turned out to be a charming and delightful young woman. Fast friends, they set off together for Eberswalde, but Kafka had underestimated the distance and gave up along the way, settling for a brief walk in rural Bernau and returning to Berlin in time to continue his journey.

It was ten years since he had last seen the sea, and for the first few days, the air and the view from his balcony combined to induce a "moderate sense of well-being." But what immediately caught his attention and cheered him far more than the spectacular Baltic tides was a summer camp for Jewish refugee children from Poland, sponsored by the same Jewish People's Home in Berlin where he had once induced Felice to volunteer. "Through the treetops I can see the children at play. Cheerful, healthy children full of spirit, Eastern European Jews, saved by Western Jews from the perils of Berlin. They fill the house, the forest, and the beach with their songs through much of the day and night. When I am among them, I am not exactly happy, but on the threshold of happiness" (L, 7/23).

Contact was quickly established. He must have presented a rather startling appearance, seated for hours in the high-backed, roofed wicker chair on the beach, his dark and melancholy eyes intently watching the children as they built their sand castles by the water's edge, and it did not take long for one of the counselors, a teenage Berlin girl more brash and inquisitive than the rest, to come wandering over and strike up a conversation. The very things about him that tended to frighten smaller children such as his nieces—the piercing look, his grave and formal manner, and the close attention he paid their every move—

seemed to captivate adolescents. The uncannily youthful appearance he preserved until the last few months of his life may have helped, but more important was the total absence of pretense and of adult pomposity. And he, in turn, was at ease with young people; young girls, in particular, quickly brought out in him the adored older brother. Tile Rössler, at any rate, developed an instant crush on the mysterious foreigner, and Kafka responded with candy and some very cordial notes. (She later became a prominent Israeli choreographer, and a romanticized account of their relationship appeared in Tel Aviv in 1943 under the title *Dina and the Writer Kafka.*) But her greatest service to him was an invitation to an *Oneg Shabath* (Sabbath Delight) celebrating the eve of the Sabbath at the children's camp—"Today I am going to celebrate Friday evening with them, for the first time in my life, I think" (L, 7/13/23). It was on that Friday the thirteenth— to which no onus attaches in Jewish lore—that he met Dora Diamant.

At nineteen, Dora was not much older than Tile, but light-years separated her in every other way from the flirtatious German-Jewish middle-class girl. Raised in Galicia in a Hasidic family, fluent in Hebrew as well as in Yiddish, she had broken out of the ultra-Orthodox, sectarian ghetto and, like so many of her young contemporaries, made her way, first to Breslau, later to Berlin and Dr. Lehmann's Jewish People's Home, where she now worked as a counselor. Nor did her ardent nature brook any halfhearted flirtations. Dora was uncompromisingly passionate in everything she did, with energy to match the tempestuous intensity of her emotions. She was also very lonely, a stranger in a strange land. Kafka's quiet presence, his suffering looks, his grave demeanor touched both the child and the mother in her. She not only fell in love with Kafka but came to worship him as her teacher and master, inscrutable in his wisdom, and endowed in her eyes with an authority no less absolute than that of the *Gerer rebbe* who had dominated the world of her childhood.

Kafka for his part was fascinated by the vivacious and pretty young girl, an Eastern Jewess of—to him—exotically romantic background, intimately familiar not only with the languages of authentic Judaism but with the universe to which they held the key. Puah's perception of him as a drowning man thrashing about and ready to cling to whoever came close enough for him to grab hold of was unquestionably accurate. (Puah herself finally came up to Müritz for a one-day visit in early August.) But ultimately it must have been Dora's limpid candor, her utter lack of artifice or calculated reserve that overrode Kafka's constitutional ambivalence, defeated the conspiracy of ambiguities, and enabled him—with Ottla's ardent encouragement and support—to risk a step of literally death-defying courage—"a deed of reckless daring, given my condition, the equal to which you can only find by turning back the pages of history to, say, Napoleon's invasion of Russia" (L, 9/26/23).

Whether, in the three weeks with Dora at Müritz, their relationship had already reached the point where they contemplated living together in Berlin—as a trial stage on the road to Palestine—is not known. But on August 7, he left for Berlin, where he spent two exhausting days in utter misery, went to see Schiller's *The Robbers* "without taking in more than my own fatigue," and even refrained from seeing Emmy Salveter because, on reflection, he was unsure of how she really felt about him. On August 9, he was back in Prague, a six-foot skeleton weighing 118 pounds—"less than I ever weighed in my entire life"—and on the point of complete physical collapse. The ocean air and the emotional turbulence had obviously done nothing to arrest the progress of his illness, and the indomitable Ottla, determined to keep him from lapsing even further into his customary Prague-induced depression, quickly whisked him off to Schelesen along with her other two children —a second, Helene, had been born in May.

Kafka's letters to Dora have not been preserved, but it was evidently during his month at Schelesen that the two of them reached their final understanding. The promise of Dora's reassuring presence gave him the strength at least to envisage the realization of a dream that had obsessed and defeated him for well over a decade, ever since he had first met Felice—escape from Prague, escape from the family, and the start of a new life in Berlin. "Berlin is the antidote to Prague."

On September 13, he was still vacillating. "Palestine would in any case have been utterly beyond my strength," he wrote to Klopstock, "and is now no longer urgent, in view of the possibilities that Berlin offers. On the other hand, Berlin, too, is almost beyond reach. (My temperature keeps shooting up, quite aside from other problems.) There remains the danger of the journey to Palestine shrinking down to a journey to Schelesen. May it at least shrink no further; may it not, in the end, turn into a trip by elevator from Old Town Square up into my room" (L, 9/13/23). But Ottla went all-out in encouraging him to take the plunge, and the example of Puah's stiff-backed courage may also have helped to firm his resolve. On September 22, he went back to Prague for a day, just long enough to pack his things, and after a painful confrontation with his parents and a cruel night, in the course of which he again resorted to sleeping pills, decided to cancel all his plans, and suffered agonies of anticipatory guilt and self-abasement, he left for Berlin on September 24.

* * *

There is a special irony in Kafka's having found peace and serenity of sorts precisely in what was probably at that moment the least peaceful and serene of cities, germ cell of a malignancy which, ten years later, would turn out to be fatal. Militants of the right and left were battling it out nightly in the streets. Strikes paralyzed the public sector. Monarchist death squads murdered with impunity. French troops had just occupied the industrial Ruhr Valley, and the German currency was on the point of total collapse. In fact, the mark went into free fall at just about the time Kafka arrived. "The room," he wrote to Ottla on October 2, "unfortunately no longer costs 20 crowns as agreed, but about 70 for September and at least 180 in October. Prices here have been climbing like the squirrels do in your part of the world" (O, 10/2/23).

The Weimar Republic in 1923 seemed about to crumble under the combined onslaught of its enemies at home and abroad. But the absurd incident in Munich on November 9, where an Austrian ex-corporal led a handful of crazies, ex-officers, and other thugs in a coup to overthrow the government was something Kafka would not have been likely to notice; he seldom could afford to buy a paper. People by then were carting their day's wages home in wheelbarrows. On November 15, the mark finally hit bottom with a splash. The old mark was dead, replaced by the new one conceived by a con man of genius, one Horace Greeley Hjalmar Schacht; one billion old marks bought one of the new ones. The inflation abated—not soon enough to do Kafka any good—and turned into a ten-year depression that gave the Austrian corporal his second chance.

Kafka did his best to remain aloof from it all. But a remark of his, in a letter to Brod, can be made to seem uncanny in its foresight or foreboding: "Yesterday I looked at a local paper, something I've been avoiding for days. Bad, bad. But there is a certain justice in our being tied to Germany's fate, like you and me" (L, 10/2/23).

And yet, though aware of it all, it did not really touch him where it mattered. Even the inflation, which soon reduced him from poverty to misery, was merely an external threat to his existence, and those he could still cope with. Dora and he found a small furnished apartment in the Steglitz borough, at that time still an outlying suburban district with an almost country-like atmosphere. Stunned by his own daring, still not quite able to believe it himself, he settled into a domesticity and peace such as he had never known, not even in Zuerau with Ottla.

Zuerau, in fact, struck him as the closest analogy. But Dora was not his sister. Dora, with all the fierce, possessive passion of her being, dedicated herself exclusively to him, to his care, welfare, and comfort. True, at first her domestic skills left much to be desired. Puah, who in the first few weeks repeatedly dropped in on them, tried to teach her the rudiments of sewing and even did their laundry a few times. Dora was not yet much of a cook, either, but Kafka's peculiar diet and the sky-rocketing food prices made that a largely irrelevant problem. In any case, their gas and electricity were cut off in November because they were unable to pay the bill. Instead, they acquired a kerosene lamp—"a masterpiece of both lamp-making and of purchasing knowhow"—that did triple service as light source, heater, and kitchen range. And whatever Dora may have lacked in culinary sophistication, she more than made up for by ingenuity and adaptability; whenever they ran out of money for kerosene, she used old candles to heat the food.

One is tempted to romanticize this *vie de bohème* by an authentically Bohemian *poète maudit* and his tempestuous child-mother. They spent much time reading to each other, mostly in Hebrew; with Dora's help, Kafka tackled the Torah, a novel by Brenner—which he disliked—and even the Rashi commentaries on the Torah and Talmud. He also introduced Dora to many of the German favorites he had once read to his sisters. Above all, they clung to the dream of a new life together in an old land—next year in Jerusalem. Or in Tel Aviv, where they were going to open "a little restaurant," with Dora in the kitchen and Kafka waiting on tables. As Puah put it, Dora didn't know how to cook, he would have been hopeless as a waiter, but why not? "In those days, you know, most restaurants in Tel Aviv were run by couples just like them."

For Dora, a healthy nineteen-year-old accustomed to hardship and unfazed by privation, life with Kafka was the ultimate epiphany. That she sensed the impending tragedy is more than likely. But death's shadow merely quickened the radiance of life. In the world of her own childhood, a woman's happiness had always been the fleeting moment wrested from pain.

* * *

A fugitive from the shtetl, Dora Diamant—or Dymant, as she later came to be known—had fled to the urban jungle of the West in search not of enlightenment or riches but of the freedom to live her own life. Like thousands of other bright and determined young women whom the patriarchal straitjacket of Jewish Orthodoxy cut off from even such spiritual sustenance and compensation as the ghetto may have offered to the doubly chosen males, she opted for the uncertain risks of independence over the certain miseries of lifelong servitude to a man of her father's choosing. Nostalgia has sanctified the "world of our fathers" and restored it as a plastic shrine. Whoever bothers to remember the world of our mothers, the world of unremitting toil and struggle, of pain and suffering, of childbed agonies and early death, while the lords of creation argued the fine points of Mishna and Gemara on hallowed premises barred to the tainted daughters of Eve?

And yet, even in 1920 it could not have been easy for the teenage daughter of an Orthodox family to leave home, to break with the customs and traditions in which she had been reared, and to strike out on her own. Sensitive and warmhearted, full of inchoate yearnings and passionate intensity, Dora found herself very much alone in a cold and hostile universe. Until she met Kafka.

He was everything she had been longing for: a man with the mind and manners of an educated Western European, and a heart as Jewish as her own. A man who was gentle and sweet, who cared for her deeply, who formed her mind and guided her steps. A man who, above all, needed her desperately. His need became her whole reason for living, a challenge that aroused primordial instincts.

She loved the man.

That the man also happened to be a writer, and a great one at that, was of no interest to her in his lifetime, but it became an issue and a threat to her after his death. He belonged to her alone, and she did not propose to share him with anyone else. These possessive sentiments first surfaced in her protest against the posthumous publication of Kafka's novels, and it took all of Brod's tact and diplomacy to make her see—though probably not feel—the error of her ways. In a 1930 letter to him, she quite candidly explained that

> as long as I was living with Franz, all I could see was him and me. Anything other than his own self was simply irrelevant and sometimes ridiculous. His work was unimportant at best. Any attempt to present his work as part of him seemed to me simply ridiculous. That is why I objected to the posthumous publication of his writings. And besides, as I am only now beginning to understand, there was the fear of having to share him with others. Every public statement, every conversation I regarded as a violent intrusion into my private realm. The world at large does not have to know about Franz. He is nobody else's business because, well, because nobody could possibly understand him. I regarded it— and I think I still do so now—as wholly out of the question for anyone ever to understand Franz, or to get even an inkling of what he was about unless one knew him personally. All efforts to understand him were hopeless unless he himself made them possible by the look in his eyes or the touch of his hand. And this, of course, he can no longer do. All well and good what I am saying here, but also very petty, as I have recently come to realize. [Brod, St. L., p. 113]

Despite this belated insight, however, Dora apparently continued to conceal a number of Kafka manuscripts and letters, while steadfastly denying that she had done so. The sentiment or sentimentality that moved this otherwise recklessly truthful woman to persist in her lie, even in the face of tenacious prodding by Kafka's editors and friends, may somehow be touching, but it led to a tragic loss.

Some time in the late 1920s, Dora married a prominent leader of the German Communist Party, with whom she had a child. Days after the Nazi takeover in February 1933, her husband fled abroad, just in time to evade the Gestapo dragnet. The agents, however, raided his home and confiscated every scrap of paper they could lay their hands on, including all the Kafka material. Dora, disconsolate and hysterical with remorse, confessed her folly and appealed for help to Brod, who immediately mobilized the Prague poet Camill Hoffmann, at the time cultural attaché at the Czech embassy in Berlin. Hoffmann, himself one of Kafka's friends, did what he could, but was informed by the Gestapo that the mountainous stacks of paper confiscated in those first days of Nazi rule had already reached such monstrous proportions as to defy all rational attempts at locating a specific document. For all we know, those mountains are still there, as indestructible as the secret police itself, being sifted, indexed, and filed in the bowels of some bomb-proof archives beyond the Berlin wall, and may yet disgorge further incriminating evidence in the trial of one Franz Kafka.

Shortly thereafter, Dora and her child left Germany and eventually reached Moscow, where the family was reunited. The idyll in the workers' paradise, however, was short-lived. The husband was arrested, sentenced, tried, shipped to Vorkuta, and never heard from again. Their little daughter, in the meantime, had come down with a kidney disease curable, in the opinion of Soviet specialists, only by treatment and medication not yet available in Russia at the time. But if it took a miracle to cure the child, it took more than a miracle, at the height of the Stalin purges, for the Polish-born Jewish wife of a convicted German Trotskyite saboteur to be allowed to leave the Soviet Union with her six-year-old daughter. What it took was Dora. Mother and child were able to get out in 1938 and reached England just before the outbreak of World War II. The daughter, in and out of hospitals for years, now lives in England. Dora herself developed progressive kidney failure after the war and died in 1952.

*   *   *

The very fact that for once Kafka did not agonize over the relationship but simply surrendered to Dora as to a force of nature and positively exulted in his total dependence suggests the depth of his own attachment to her. In earlier years, the manifest disparities between them, of which the age gap was probably the least important, would have caused problems. At this point, the illness had stripped life bare of the ambiguities and reduced it to basics.

Kafka—so Brod reports—wrote to Dora's father, presented himself as a Jew not yet observant but in quest, and formally asked for Dora's hand. The father is said to have submitted the letter to the *Gerer rebbe*, God's local representative, who read it, shook his head, and said no. Brod cites the inscrutable decision as proof of the wonder rabbi's gift of prophecy; that it might have been the spiteful reaction of an old man whose authority had been challenged by a mere female's rebellion does not seem to have occurred to him.

In early fall, Kafka was still able to take long walks and, on occasion, to travel into the city, though the trips invariably sapped his strength and morale. Despite his determination to stay on the sidelines, remain outside history and outside time itself, he could not shut out the evidence of widespread suffering, and he dispatched numerous appeals to Prague with long lists of needy people he either knew personally or had heard about. The food packages he himself received from home probably made the difference between hunger and starvation; money, on the other hand, was for some time being mysteriously withheld: "Today is already the sixteenth, and so far I've received a total of sixty crowns for the month. Did the institute fail to remit it, did a letter get lost, or are they trying to teach me a lesson in how to earn money? If so, they should have started a whole lot sooner" (O, 10/16/23). Their prissy landlady, increasingly paranoid about the disreputable *Ausländer*, became so obnoxious that in November they moved to another apartment nearby. On moving day, Kafka left the house in the morning, attended a lecture, and had lunch in the city. By the time he returned, Dora had already settled them into their new place.

He toyed with the idea of a gardening school in preparation for making deserts bloom but had to give it up as impractical. During the first two months, however, he attended courses at the Berlin Academy for the Science of Judaism—"an oasis of peace in wild Berlin and in the wild regions of the inner self. . . . An entire building, beautiful lecture halls, a large library, peace, warmth, few students, and everything free of charge. Of course, I am not a regular student . . . but even so, the school exists and is splendid, and then again not splendid at all but rather odd to the point of being grotesque and, beyond that, something unfathomably delicate (the liberal-reformist tone of the whole thing, that is, and the pretensions to scientific objectivity)" (L, 10/19/23).

He also began to write again. Failing health and hardship notwithstanding, he seems to have produced a considerable volume of work between October and the turn of the year, when his physical condition made further creative efforts all but impossible. Much, perhaps most, of this material was lost. Dora later told of having had to burn many manuscripts on Kafka's orders, including one dealing with the Beilis ritual murder in Kiev. In fact, only two stories from this period have survived, one of which—"The Burrow"—is incomplete. Since the manuscript ends in mid-sentence at the bottom of a page, and since Dora affirmed that Kafka had finished the story, the ending must be presumed lost. The fragment nonetheless remains a brilliant self-portrait of the underground man, so far below ground that he is a man no longer, the recluse "immured in the innermost room of a vast, locked cave" who has tunneled into an underground shelter that at last affords the precarious illusion of safety. "A Little Woman," on the other hand, was obviously inspired by the desiccated witch from whom they had rented their first apartment, hate personified in search of a victim—a chilling preview of the Jew-killer who hates the Jew even for being dead.

Some time toward the end of 1923, Brod put Kafka in touch with a new publishing house, Die Schmiede (The Smithy), founded by a group of left-leaning intellectuals who agreed to publish Kafka's works on relatively more favorable terms than Wolff. Kafka made the switch, and a first volume, *A Hunger Artist*, came out a few months after his death. Aside from the title story, it contained "First Sorrow," "A Little Woman," and "Josephine, the Singer," Kafka's last story, written in March 1924. His contract with Die Schmiede netted him a small but most welcome advance. The publishers, in turn, acquired the rights to all his subsequent—and, as it turned out, posthumous—work, but only *The Trial* appeared under their imprint in 1925. Sectarian dissent soon wrecked the enterprise, so that *The Castle* (1926) and *Amerika* (1927) were again published by Wolff.

Late in November, Ottla breezed in for a personal inspection tour and, with her usual decisiveness, moved heaven and earth on the couple's behalf after her return home. She saw to it that they received several food packages a week, arranged for regular money remittances, and sent them whatever linen and household necessities she and her sisters could spare.

By the end of the year, however, Kafka's condition had taken an alarming turn for the worse. He ran an almost continuous high fever, was seldom able to leave the house, and more often than not spent the day in bed. "What I am leading here is a somewhat shadowy life," he wrote to Klopstock in January 1924, although the steady stream of visitors certainly made for the illusion of a rather active social whirl. Emmy Salveter frequently dropped in to complain about her lover. Brod himself, of course, made regular trips to Berlin, many other Prague literati came to the metropolis on business, and there were Berlin friends such as Ernst Weiss and Tile Rössler.

But the disease was gaining on him now with terrifying speed, and even Dora's heroic devotion and somewhat forced good cheer proved no match for it. In January, he had to call a doctor—"One hundred and sixty crowns for a simple visit; D. later haggled him down to half that amount. Since then I've been ten times as worried about getting sick. A second-class bed in the Jewish Hospital costs 64 crowns a day, which only pays for bed and board but does not cover medical care and service" (L, 1/24). Despite the currency stabilization, prices continued their relentless climb. By January, his 1,000-crown-a-month pension had become hopelessly insufficient, and although his parents and sisters made up the deficit with more than good grace, the idea of his once again relapsing into a state of dependency depressed him profoundly.

The "impecunious and insolvent foreigners" apparently upset their second landlady as much as the first, so that in January they again had to move. This time they found shelter in the Zehlendorf district with the widow of the German poet and novelist Karl Busse. But throughout most of February, Kafka was unable to leave his bed. Alerted by Brod, the family finally delegated Uncle Siegfried, the country doctor from Triesch, to pay a house call on his nephew. Dr. Löwy refrained from disclosing his diagnosis, but he conveyed sufficient concern to convince even his understandably reluctant patient of the urgent need for treatment in a properly equipped institution and suggested either Vienna or Davos. Kafka agreed in principle but insisted on first stopping off in Prague.

On March 14, Brod came to Berlin to attend the premiere of Janáček's opera *Jenufa*, for which he had translated the libretto, and on the seventeenth he accompanied Kafka back to Prague. Dora was to remain in Berlin until further notice; Kafka was determined not to expose her any more than necessary to the poison fumes of his father's house.

It was the saddest journey of his short life.

Six months earlier he had set out to challenge gods, father, and fate. He had succeeded beyond his wildest dreams, only to be betrayed in the end by his body, his past, and his time. The prodigal son was made to come crawling home, heartbroken and barely able to crawl.

* * *

He spent three miserable weeks at what was no longer his home. Brod stopped by every day, and Klopstock, now back in medical school, assumed full responsibility for the day-to-day care. And, miraculously, Kafka once more mustered the strength to defy death and madness by "clinging to his desk": "Josephine, the Singer" was his last prayer, the last story he ever wrote. The crackling tension in the land of mice between Josephine, would-be master in the artless art of whistling, and her rootless people, condemned to eternal exile, touches with great subtlety and wit on the nature of art, artists, and society; that it was also a many-faceted and prophetic allegory of Jewish exile and redemption had already been pointed out by Brod.

But Josephine, the Singer, did not actually sing. What she produced instead was a wheezing sound which only her faith in herself raised to the level of art. And it was, of course, no mere coincidence that Kafka himself had begun now and then to lose his voice and come out with similar weird noises. "One evening," Klopstock reports, "when he had finished the last page of the story, he said to me: 'I think I may have started the investigation of animal squeaking at the right moment. I've just finished a story about it.' I didn't have the courage to ask him to let me read it. That same evening, he told me that he felt a strange burning sensation in his throat whenever he drank certain beverages, especially fruit juices, and he expressed worries about his larynx being affected" (L, p. 521).

Dora arrived in Prague at the end of March, and on April 7 she took Kafka, now weighing less than a hundred pounds fully clothed, to the Wiener Wald Sanatorium in Austria, where his worst suspicions were confirmed. The burning sensation in his throat was due to tubercular lesions of the larynx.

Tuberculosis of the larynx secondary to long-standing pulmonary involvement was, at the time, a far from uncommon complication. No effective prevention or treatment existed as yet for this most exquisitely painful of afflictions, a protracted martyrdom only partially relieved by such palliative measures as anesthetizing lozenges and alcohol injections into the laryngeal nerves.

While reasonably stoic about the diagnosis itself, Kafka was frantic about the prospective cost of the treatment. "Max, this is going to cost, and might well cost a terrifying amount of money," he wrote to Brod immediately upon admission. "Josephine will have to help out a little, there is no other way. Please offer her to Otto Pick. . . . If he takes her, send her to Die Schmiede later; if he doesn't, ship her off to Die Schmiede right away." The story actually appeared in the Easter Sunday issue of the *Prager Presse*, but the royalties could scarcely have made much of a dent in Kafka's medical expenses.

They were mounting rapidly. Within days it became apparent that what ailed him required more professional skill and medical facilities than were available at the Wiener Wald, and on April 13 he was transferred to the University Clinic in Vienna. Professor Hajek, the specialist in charge, was a ruthless autocrat who ran his ward like an army stockade, but he knew his business, and within days his treatment, though purely palliative, had enabled Kafka at least to swallow again. Dora, however, was appalled at the atmosphere in the clinic and outraged by Hajek's crude arrogance. She got in touch with Klopstock, who quite simply dropped his studies and rushed off to join her in Vienna. On April 19, the two of them, over Hajek's strenuous objections, took Kafka to the small Kierling Sanatorium in a rural setting near Vienna, where he was at least assured a large and pleasant room of his own, and where Dora and Klopstock could take full charge of his care.

They did so with truly saintly devotion and self-sacrifice, surrounding their patient day and night with a love and attention far more effective than the paltry efforts of medical science in easing the agony of his final days. Thanks to them, Kafka was still able to enjoy moments of happiness—the view from the window, the hillside turning green, the spring flowers that filled his room. Dora, the self-taught cook, outdid herself trying to come up with dishes bland yet tasty enough to tempt his appetite and coax him into eating. He did not need much coaxing; as long as the pain would permit it, he forced himself to eat. The would-be suicide of long ago had become a model patient who desperately wanted to live. When a Viennese specialist, one of several whom Dora insisted on consulting, assured him that his throat seemed improved, he wept with joy. The doctor was merely being kind; in private he agreed with his colleagues, who gave Kafka anywhere from one to three months. They unanimously advised Dora to break off the expensive and useless sanatorium treatment and take him back home, but she categorically refused. To do so, she insisted, would have robbed him of the last shred of hope.

The throat lesions made speaking as well as swallowing progressively more difficult. Urged to spare his vocal cords as much as possible, Kafka began to communicate with his "little family" by means of written notes. Many of these conversation slips were saved by Robert Klopstock; the incontrovertible authority with which they convey Kafka's own words sets them apart from the customary accretion of pious apocrypha orally transmitted by witnesses of bad faith or unwitting mendacity. They document the courage, the unsparing lucidity, self-transcendence and love of life with which Kafka faced his death: "To think that I was once able to manage a big sip of water."

On May 11, Brod came for what he knew would be his last visit, pretending merely to have stopped off on his way to a lecture in Vienna so as not to alarm his friend. Kafka, by then quite unable to eat, was wasting away, dying of starvation—and immersed in the galley proofs of *A Hunger Artist*. Fate lacked the subtle touch of Kafka's art.

The effort drained him. "Kafka's physical condition at this point," Klopstock later wrote, "and the whole situation of his literally starving to death, were truly ghastly. Reading the proofs must have been not only a tremendous emotional strain but also a shattering kind of spiritual encounter with his former self, and when he had finished, the tears kept flowing for a long time. It was the first time I ever saw him overtly expressing his emotions this way. Kafka had always shown an almost superhuman self-control" (L, p. 520).

The erosive invasion of the upper larynx was now causing such excruciating pain that every bite and every sip became pure torture. "The worst is that I cannot drink a single glass of water. But the craving itself gives me a little satisfaction." He no longer had any illusions about the outcome: "If it is true—and it seems probable— that my present food intake is insufficient for the body to heal itself, then there is no longer any hope, except for miracles."

Thirst, though, became a plague far worse than hunger. The craving for liquids swamped his memory with the hallucinatory recollections of past pleasures, so lightly taken for granted at the time—a glass of water, wine, beer, lemonade. And as though not yet tried sufficiently, he contracted an intestinal infection at the end of May that further accelerated his dehydration. About four days before his death, he wrote a long, chatty, and supremely cogent letter to his parents, designed both to reassure and to dissuade them from any thoughts of a visit. But even here, the specter that now haunted him day and night flashed its caustic grin: "The current heat spells frequently remind me of how Father and I used to drink beer together, many years ago, when he took me to the Civilian Swimming Pool." And, referring to the cut flowers in his room: "How marvelous that lilac, isn't it? Even dying it still goes on drinking, guzzling." As opposed to himself: "A dying man drinking, that doesn't exist."

Above all, there was pain, constant pain, barely dulled by the in themselves painful twice-a-day alcohol injections directly into the upper laryngeal nerve. Klopstock had long ago promised him morphine if the pain ever got to be altogether unbearable; why Kafka's doctors were being so conservative or moralistic about the use of opiates at this terminal stage is unclear. But in addition to his own suffering, Kafka also had to bear the full knowledge of what he was inflicting upon Dora: "Of course the pain is made worse by your being so good to me. In this respect, the hospital is better."

Yet it was Dora's presence, and her presence alone, that turned the trials of Job into a triumph of human grace: "Put your hand on my forehead for a moment, to give me courage."

* * *

On Monday, June 2, Kafka seemed somewhat improved. He was able to spend much of the day working on the galleys of the book and still made several changes. But around four o'clock the next morning, Dora noticed his labored breathing. She alerted Klopstock and the attending physician, who administered a camphor injection.

Kafka became extremely agitated and began to rage at Klopstock, demanding the long-promised morphine: "You've always promised it to me. For four years you've been promising it, you're torturing me, you've always tortured me. I am not going to talk to you anymore. So be it, I'll die without it." He was given two shots, but he still persisted: "Don't try to fool me. You're giving me an antidote." And in one final spasm of lucidity, he challenged the friend become father, judge, and God: "Kill me, or else you are a murderer."

As the sedative began to take effect, he confused Klopstock with his sister Elli and apparently worried about infecting her: "Don't come so close, Elli, not so close . . . yes, this is better." He died at noon on Tuesday, June 3, 1924.

Dora, heartbroken and utterly past reason, refused to leave the body until Klopstock gently forced her to get some rest. "Only he who knows Dora can know the meaning of love," he wrote to Brod a few hours later, in an outpouring of his own savage grief.

It took only a week this time to bring Kafka back to Prague, where he was buried on June 11. About a hundred mourners attended the funeral. Brod delivered the eulogy, and as the casket was being lowered, Dora had to be restrained from flinging herself into the grave.

* * *

In the tiny world-within-worlds in which he had spent most of his life, Kafka's death was noted and mourned. The *Prager Presse* of June 4 published Brod's moving tribute to his friend. The rest of the German-language press ran lengthy obituaries, and some five hundred people filled the auditorium of Prague's German Chamber Theater on June 19 for a Kafka memorial service. In the world at large, even among his Czech fellow citizens, Kafka's death went all but unnoticed.

There were exceptions. The Communist editor Stanislav Kostka Neumann, who had brought out the Czech translation of *The Stoker*, wrote on Kafka for the Prague *Communist Review*. Three Czech papers published obituaries. One was perfunctory, the second misspelled Kafka's name. The third, however, was Milena Jesenská's farewell, which appeared in the conservative *Národný Listy* of June 5, 1924; it more than made up for the rest:

> Dr. Franz Kafka, a German writer who lived in Prague, died the day before yesterday in the Kierling Sanatorium at Klosterneuberg near Vienna. Few knew him, for he was a loner, a recluse wise in the ways of the world and frightened by it. For years he had been suffering from a lung disease, which he cherished and fostered even while accepting treatment. . . . It endowed him with a delicacy of feeling that bordered on the miraculous, and with a spiritual purity uncompromising to the point of horror. . . . He wrote the most significant works of modern German literature; their stark truth makes them seem naturalistic even where they speak in symbols. They reflect the irony and prophetic vision

of a man condemned to see the world with such blinding clarity that he found it unbearable and went to his death.

*   *   *

Kafka was buried in Prague, as he had known and feared he would be; the claws of the "little mother" held on to him to the bitter end. Prominent markers in five languages now guide jet-age pilgrims to his grave in the Jewish section of the Strašnice cemetery. Nor did he escape his parents, even in death; they share his grave and his tombstone.

The irony is somehow fitting, compounded by the fact that, in his native city, Kafka's grave is honored but his work is banned.

And for good reason.

The world that Kafka was "condemned to see with such blinding clarity that he found it unbearable" is our own post-Auschwitz universe, on the brink of extinction. His work is subversive, not because he found the truth, but because, being human and therefore having failed to find it, he refused to settle for half-truths and compromise solutions. In visions wrested from his innermost self, and in language of crystalline purity, he gave shape to the anguish of being human.

Bibliography

THE literature dealing with Kafka and his work currently comprises an estimated 15,000 titles in most of the world's major languages. (The last comprehensive bibliography, Harry Järv's *Die Kafka Literatur,* was published in Malmö, Sweden, over twenty years ago and at that time already contained over 5,000 titles.)

The following selection emphasizes material published in book form and available in English; many important contributions, however, have never been translated. An effort has also been made to cover as broad a range of criticism and interpretation as possible.

THE WORK

The publication history of Kafka's works—both in his lifetime and after his death—is immensely complicated. (For details, see Binder, *Kafka Kommentar,* and Unseld, *Franz Kafka.*) In 1933, when his books were burned and banned by the Nazis, Zalman Schocken acquired the copyright to Kafka's works and continued to publish them, first in Czechoslovakia and later in the United States. Schocken Books still holds the rights to Kafka in the original as well as to those English versions it has published.

In postwar Germany, the thus far most complete edition of the works was published by S. Fischer Verlag under license from Schocken. A "scientific, text-critical" German edition of the collected works edited by a number of renowned Kafka hands has been in preparation since 1974. The first volume, *Das Schloss,* together with the critical apparatus in a separate volume, appeared in 1982. At this rate, completion of the project may well extend into the next century. In his day Max Brod, working largely by himself, was able to prepare a virtually complete posthumous edition of the Kafka corpus within less than a decade.

Unfortunately, however, in his will Brod left the original Kafka manuscript material he owned—including the manuscript of *The Trial*—to his longtime secretary, Esther Hoffe. Mrs. Hoffe, who for some years now has been disposing of these manuscripts in a haphazard but profitable way through auctions and private sales, refused even to make copies of the material available to the editors of the text-critical edition. Her refusal adds further complications to an already complicated project.

The following English translations of Kafka's works are currently available in the United States in the Schocken edition:

The Trial
The Castle
Amerika
The Complete Stories
Letter to His Father
The Metamorphosis
Description of a Struggle
The Penal Colony
The Great Wall of China
Letters to Felice
Letters to Milena
Diaries I and II
Letters to Friends, Family, and Editors
Letters to Ottla and the Family

(The contents of several of the volumes overlap to some extent.)

THE LIFE

Bemporad, Jules. "Franz Kafka: A Literary Prototype of the Depressive Character." In: Silvano Arieti and Jules Bemporad. *Severe and Mild Depression.* New York: Basic Books, 1978.

Binder, Hartmut. *Kafka-Handbuch.* Stuttgart: Kröner Verlag, 1979.

———. *Kafka in neuer Sicht.* Stuttgart: Metzler, 1976.

Brod, Max. *Franz Kafka.* New York: Schocken, 1960.

———. *Der Prager Kreis.* Stuttgart: Kohlhammer, 1966.

———. *Streitbares Leben.* Munich: Herbig Verlag, 1969.

———. *Über Franz Kafka.* Frankfurt: Fischer, 1974.

Buber-Neumann, Margarete. *Mistress to Kafka.* London: Secker & Warburg, 1966.

Canetti, Elias. *Kafka's Other Trial.* New York: Schocken, 1982.

Demetz, Petr, ed. *Franz Kafka a Praha.* Prague: Vladimir Žikeš, 1947.

Hayman, Ronald. *Kafka.* New York: Oxford University Press, 1982.

Janouch. Gustav. *Conversations with Kafka.* New York: Praeger, 1953.

———. *Kafka und seine Welt.* Vienna: Deutsch, 1965.

Louzil, Jaromir. *Dopisy Franze Kafky Delničke Urazove Pojištovne* (Letters to the Insurance Institute). Prague: People's Museum, 1963.

Nordlicht, Stephen. "Franz Kafka's Struggle to Survive." In: *New York State Journal of Medicine,* Volume 78, Number 1, January 1978.

Robert, Marthe. *As Lonely as Franz Kafka.* New York: Harcourt Brace Jovanovich, 1982.

Steiner, Marianne. "The Facts about Kafka." In: *The New Statesman,* February 8, 1958.

Urzidil, Johannes. *There Goes Kafka.* Detroit: Wayne State University Press, 1968.

Wagenbach, Klaus. *Franz Kafka. Eine Biographie seiner Jugend.* Bern: Francke Verlag, 1958.

————. *Franz Kafka.* Hamburg: Rowohlt, 1964.

Weltsch, Felix. "The Rise and Fall of the German-Jewish Symbiosis: The Case of Franz Kafka." In *Leo Baeck Yearbook.* London, 1956.

————. *Religion und Humor in Leben und Werk Franz Kafkas.* Berlin, F. A. Herbig, 1957.

BACKGROUND AND CONTEXT

Baedeker, Karl. *Oesterreich-Ungarn.* Leipzig: Baedeker Verlag, 1913.

Bauer, Johann. *Kafka and Prague.* New York: Praeger, 1971.

Bergmann, Hugo. *Faith and Reason.* New York: Schocken, 1961.

Bezzel, Chris. *Kafka Chronik.* Munich: Hanser Verlag, 1975.

Cipolla, Carlo M., ed. *The Fontana Economic History of Europe.* Glasgow: Collins Sons & Co., 1973.

Clough, S. B., ed. *Economic History of Europe: Twentieth Century.* New York: Walker, 1968.

Eisner, Pavel. *Franz Kafka and Prague.* New York: Arts, Inc., 1950.

Frynta, Emanuel. *Kafka and Prague.* London: Batchworth Press, 1960.

Gay, Peter. *Freud, Jews and Other Germans.* New York: Oxford University Press, 1978.

Gold, Hugo, ed. *Max Brod—Ein Gedenkbuch.* Tel Aviv: Olamenu, 1969.

Grunfeld, Frederic V. *Prophets without Honor.* New York: Holt, Rinehart & Winston, 1979.

Haas, Willy. *Die Literarische Welt.* Frankfurt: Fischer, 1983.

Hays, Carlton J. H. *A Political and Cultural History of Modern Europe.* New York: Macmillan, 1916.

Hermann, A. H. *A History of the Czechs.* London: Allen Lane, 1975.

Herrmann, Ignat, *et al. Das Prager Getto.* Prague, 1903.

Janik, Allan, and Stephen Toulmin. *Wittgenstein's Vienna.* New York: Simon & Schuster, 1973.

Johnston, William M. *The Austrian Mind.* Berkeley: University of California Press, 1972.

Kestenberg-Gladstein, Ruth. *Neuere Geschichte der Juden in den Boehm-ischen Ländern.* Tübingen: Mohr, 1969.

Kohn, Hans. *Karl Kraus, Arthur Schnitzler, Otto Weininger.* Tübingen: Mohr, 1962.

Macartney, C. A. *The Habsburg Empire, 1790–1918.* New York: Macmillan, 1969.

Mahler, Raphael. *A History of Modern Jewry.* New York: Schocken, 1971.

Masaryk, Tomáš G. *The Meaning of Czech History.* Chapel Hill: University of North Carolina Press, 1974.

Muneles, Otto. *Bibliographical Survey of Jewish Prague.* Prague: Orbis, 1952.

Riff, Michael A. *Czech Anti-Semitism and the Jewish Response before 1914.* London: Weiner Library Bulletin, 1976.

Scholem, Gershom. *Major Trends in Jewish Mysticism.* New York: Schocken, 1963.

————. *On Jews and Judaism in Crisis.* New York: Schocken, 1976.

————. *Sabbatai Sevi.* Princeton: Princeton University Press, 1973.

————. *Walter Benjamin Briefwechsel.* Frankfurt: Suhrkamp, 1980.

Schorske, Carl. *Fin-de-Siècle Vienna.* New York: Knopf, 1980.

Selbstwehr Verlag. *Das Jüdische Prag.* Essays collected on the publication's tenth anniversary. Prague, 1917.

Society for the History of Czechoslovak Jews. *The Jews of Czechoslovakia.* Historical Studies and Surveys. Philadelphia: Jewish Publication Society, 1968.

Stölzl, Christoph. *Kafkas Böses Boehmen.* Munich: Text + Kritik, 1975.

Tapie, Victor L. *The Rise and Fall of the Habsburg Monarchy.* New York: Praeger, 1971.

Tramer, Hans. "Prague—City of Three Peoples." In: *Leo Baeck Yearbook.* New York, 1964.

Wechsberg, Joseph. *Prague, the Mystical City.* New York: Macmillan, 1971.

Wolff, Kurt. *Briefwechsel eines Verlegers.* Frankfurt: Fischer, 1966.

CRITICISM AND INTERPRETATION

Amann, Jürg. *Franz Kafka.* Munich: Piper, 1983.

Anders, Günther. *Franz Kafka.* New York: Hillary House, 1960.

Barthes, Roland. *Critical Essays.* Evanston, Ill.: Northwestern University Press, 1972.

Beck, Evelyn Tornton. *Kafka and the Yiddish Theater.* Madison, Wisconsin: University of Wisconsin Press, 1971.

Beicken, Peter U. *Franz Kafka—Eine kritische Einführung in die Forschung.* Frankfurt: Athenaeum, 1974.

Benjamin, Walter. *Illuminations.* New York: Harcourt Brace Jovanovich, 1968.

———. *Benjamin über Kafka.* Frankfurt: Suhrkamp, 1981.

Benson, Ann Thornton. *The American Criticism of Franz Kafka, 1930–1948.* Knoxville: University of Tennessee Press, 1958.

Binder, Hartmut. *Kafka Kommentar* (2 volumes). Munich: Winkler, 1976.

———. *Motiv und Gestaltung bei Franz Kafka.* Bonn: Bouvier, 1966.

Borchardt, Alfred. *Kafkas zweites Gesicht.* Nürnberg: Glock & Lutz, 1960.

Bridgwater, Patrick. *Kafka und Nietzsche.* Bonn: Bouvier, 1974.

Carrouges, Michel. *Kafka versus Kafka.* University, Alabama: University of Alabama Press, 1968.

Cohen, Arthur A., ed. *Arguments and Doctrines.* New York: Harper and Row, 1970.

David, Claude, ed. *Franz Kafka. Themen und Probleme.* Göttingen: Vandenhoeck and Ruprecht, 1980.

Dietz, Ludwig. *Franz Kafka.* Stuttgart: Metzler, 1975.

Emrich, Wilhelm. *Franz Kafka.* New York: Ungar, 1968.

Fauchery, Pierre, *et al.* "Faut-il brûler Kafka?" In: *Action,* May-August 1946.

Fischer, Ernst. *Von Grillparzer zu Kafka.* Frankfurt: Suhrkamp, 1976.

Flores, Angel, ed. *Franz Kafka Today.* Madison: University of Wisconsin Press, 1958.

———. *A Kafka Bibliography, 1908–1976.* New York: Gordian Press, 1976.

———. *The Kafka Debate.* New York: Gordian Press, 1977.

———. *The Kafka Problem.* New York: Octagon, 1963.

Fraiberg, Selma. "Kafka and the Dream." In: *Partisan Review,* Number 1, 1956.

Garaudy, Roger. *D'un realisme sans rivages.* Paris: Plon, 1963.

Goldstücker, Eduard, ed. *Weltfreunde* (the 1965 Liblice Conference on Prague German literature). Prague: Luchterhand, 1968.

Goodman, Paul. *Kafka's Prayer.* New York: Vanguard, 1947.

Gray, Ronald D. *Franz Kafka.* Cambridge: Cambridge University Press, 1973.

Greenberg, Martin. *The Terror of Art: Kafka and Modern Literature.* New York: Basic Books, 1968.

Hall, Calvin S., and Richard E. Lind. *Dreams, Life and Literature: A Study of Franz Kafka.* Chapel Hill: University of North Carolina Press, 1970.

Heller, Erich. *Franz Kafka.* New York: Viking, 1974.

———. *The Disinherited Mind.* New York: Harcourt Brace Jovanovich, 1975.

Heller, Peter. *Dialectics and Nihilism.* Amherst: University of Massachusetts Press, 1966.

Hughes, Kenneth, ed. *Franz Kafka: An Anthology of Marxist Criticism.* New England University Press, 1981.

Kafka Symposium. Contributors: Paul Raabe, Malcolm Pasley, Klaus Wagenbach, Ludwig Dietz, Jürgen Born. Berlin: Wagenbach, 1965.

Kafka Symposium. (Papers from a Kafka Conference at Temple University, Philadelphia, 1974, ed. Maria Luise Caputo-Mayr.) Berlin: Agora, 1978.

Kuna, Franz. *Literature as Corrective Punishment.* London: Elek, 1974.

————. ed. *On Kafka: Semi-Centenary Perspectives.* New York: Harper and Row, 1976.

Lukács, George. "Franz Kafka or Thomas Mann?" In: David Craig, ed. *Marxists on Literature.* Harmondsworth, England: Penguin Books, 1975.

Nabokov, Vladimir. *Lectures on Literature.* New York: Harcourt Brace Jovanovich, 1980.

Nagel, Bert. *Franz Kafka.* Berlin: Schmidt, 1974.

Neesen, Peter. *Vom Louvrezirkel zum Prozess.* Göttingen: Kuemmerle, 1972.

Neider, Charles. *The Frozen Sea.* New York: Russell & Russell, 1962.

Pazi, Margarita. *Max Brod.* Bonn, 1970.

Philippi, Klaus-Peter. *"Das Schloss": Reflexion und Wirklichkeit.* Tübingen: Niemeyer, 1966.

Politzer, Heinz. *Franz Kafka, Parable and Paradox.* Ithaca, N.Y.: Cornell University Press, 1966.

Richter, Helmut. *Franz Kafka.* Berlin: Ruetten & Loening, 1962.

Robert, Marthe. *Kafka.* Paris: Gallimard, 1968.

————. *The Old and the New: From Kafka to Don Quixote.* Berkeley: University of California Press, 1977.

Rolleston, James. *Kafka's Negative Theater.* University Park, Pa.: Pennsylvania State University Press, 1974.

Sokel, Walter. *Franz Kafka.* New York: Columbia University Press, 1966.

————. *Franz Kafka: Tragik und Ironie.* Munich: Langen, 1964.

————. *The Writer in Extremis.* Stanford, Cal.: Stanford University Press, 1959.

Spann, Meno. *Franz Kafka.* Boston: Twayne, 1976.

Spilka, Mark. *Dickens and Kafka.* Bloomington: Indiana University Press, 1963.

Stern, J. P. *The World of Franz Kafka.* New York: Holt, Rinehart & Winston, 1980.

Sussman, Henry. *Franz Kafka: Geometrician of Metaphor*. Madison, Wisc.: Coda Press, 1979.

Thorlby, Anthony. *Kafka: A Study*. London: Heinemann, 1972.

Tiefenbrun, Ruth. *Moment of Torment*. Carbondale, Ill.: Southern Illinois University Press, 1973.

Tucholsky, Kurt. *Gesammelte Werke*. Reinbeck: Rowohlt Verlag, n.d.

Unseld, Joachim. *Franz Kafka: Ein Schriftstellerleben*. Munich: Hanser, 1982.

Walser, Martin. *Beschreibung einer Form*. Munich: Hanser Verlag, 1961.

Weinberg, Helen. *The New Novel in America: The Kafkan Mode in Contemporary Fiction*. Ithaca, N.Y.: Cornell University Press, 1970.

Weitzmann, Siegfried. *Studie über Kafka*. Tel Aviv: Olamenu, 1970.

Wessling, Berndt W. *Max Brod*. Stuttgart: Kohlhammer, 1969.

Wolff, Kurt. *Autoren, Bücher, Abenteuer*. Berlin: Wagenbach, 1973.

MAP OF PRAGUE'S OLD TOWN AROUND THE TURN OF THE CENTURY

1. *Kafka's birthplace*
2. *Herrmann Kafka's business, Celetná Street 12 (1882)*
3. *Apartment, Václavské Náměstí 12 (1885)*
4. *Apartment, Dušná Street*
5. *Apartment, Niklas Street 6 (1887–88)*
6. *Apartment, Celetná Street 2 (1888–89)*
7. *Apartment, Old Town Square (House "Minuta") (1889–96)*
8. *Elementary School, Meatmarket (1889–93)*
9. *Gymnasium, Kinsky Palace (1893–1901). Herrmann Kafka's business was later located on the same premises*
10. *Apartment, Celetná Street 3 (1896–1901)*
11. *Carolinum, the University of Prague*
12. *Assicurazioni Generali, where Kafka had his first job (1907–8)*
13. *Apartment, Niklas Street 36 (1907)*
14. *Workmen's Accident Insurance Institute*
15. *Golden Lane*
16. *Schönborn Palace*

Index

Adler, Friedrich, 153, 154, 316, 354
Adler, Viktor, 183, 316
"Advocates" (Kafka), 421
"Aeroplanes of Brescia, The" (Kafka), 200, 201, 202
Aktion, Die (pub.), 295
Altstädter Gymnasium, 46–50, 53, 59, 101, 129
Ambrozova, Jarmila, 398, 399
Amerika (Kafka), 94, 169, 231, 254, 255, 257, 261, 271, 277, 278, 327, 331, 410, 441
Amethyst (pub.), 161
anarchism, 69, 151, 152, 153, 368
anthroposophy, 144, 221
anti-intellectualism, 204–5
anti-Semitism, 22, 31, 32, 39–44, 55, 58, 60, 61, 115, 129, 149, 150, 151, 203, 205, 377, 399, 414
Arco Café (Prague), 142, 143, 317, 391
Arkadia (pub.), 271
Ascher, Ernst, 251
Assicurazioni Generali, 175, 177, 178, 182, 191
assimilation of Jews, 54–5, 288, 354; failure of, 98–9, 428
"Assistant District Attorney, The" (Kafka), 331
"At Night" (Kafka), 413
atheism, 69, 70, 74
Auden, W. H., 422
Auschwitz concentration camp, 88, 199
Austrian Socialist Party, 61, 62
Austro-Hungary, 5, 7, 19, 20, 21, 22, 23, 29–30, 31, 32, 33, 36, 37, 38, 39, 41, 42, 61, 95, 98, 105, 122, 148–9, 178, 183, 298, 318, 354; strains and stresses within, 149–50; in World War I and subsequent disintegration, 314, 324, 325, 326, 335, 339, 353, 354, 369, 373
Avenarius, Ferdinand, 90

"Bachelor's Ill Luck, The" (Kafka), 253, 265
Badeni, Kasimir, 149, 150
Baeuml, Max, 193
Bailly, Mlle, 18
Bakunin, Mikhail A., 151
Balfour Declaration, 368, 428
Bar Kochba, 107, 247, 338
bar mitzvah, 55, 59–60, 61, 427
Bassermann, Albert, 217
Bauer, Carl, 266, 330
Bauer, Erna, 292, 312, 316
Bauer, Felice, 238, 262, 265–71 *passim*, 274, 275, 278, 279, 281–94 *passim*, 297–304 *passim*, 307–12 *passim*, 329, 330, 331, 340, 341, 344, 346, 347, 349, 355, 356, 357, 362, 363, 382; Kafka's letters to, 265, 266, 267–8, 280, 283–4, 285–6, 288, 291, 300, 301, 304, 329, 393; as plaintiff vs. Kafka, 312, 313; as volunteer at Jewish People's Home (Berlin), 347, 348
Bauer, Ferdinand, 310
Bauhaus principles, foreshadowing of, 312
Baum, Oskar, 124, 128, 131–2, 139, 141, 168, 223, 248, 251, 271, 298, 355, 366, 367, 424, 427; quoted, 124, 132–3
Baxa, Karel, 43
Beauvoir, Simone de, 422
Beck, Evelyn Tornton, 240n., 242
Beck, Matthias, 33, 34
Benjamin, Walter, 112, 113, 273, 299
Ben-Tovim, Puah, 428–9, 430, 431, 433, 435, 436
Ben-Tovim, Zalman, 429
Ben-Yehudah, Eliezer, 428, 429
Bergmann, Else, 221
Bergmann, Hugo, 33, 49, 50, 63–70 *passim*, 73, 76, 88, 101, 106, 130, 145, 146, 152, 241, 247, 290, 368, 429, 430; quoted, 104–5

Berlin, 180, 201, 214, 216, 220, 244, 266, 291, 292, 295, 296, 299, 304, 307–16 *passim*, 325, 328, 347, 373, 415, 432, 433, 434, 435, 442; University of, 431
Berlin Academy for the Science of Judaism, 440
Berliner Tageblatt, 295, 310
Besant, Annie, 221
Bies, Oscar, 135
Bismarck, Otto von, 183
Blavatsky, Mme, 144
Blei, Franz, 161, 194, 342
Bleschke, Johanna (Rachel Sanzara), 299, 313
Bloch, Grete, 104, 303–13 *passim*, 321, 328, 329, 340
"blood-and-soil" romanticism, 90
Blüher, Hans, 400
"Blumfeld, an Elderly Brother" (Kafka), 332
Bohemia, 7, 8, 13, 21, 22, 24, 25, 31, 32, 37, 39, 40, 61, 69, 86, 89, 103, 105, 108, 119, 139, 183, 184, 187, 189, 191, 220, 319, 370, 389, 395
Bohemia (pub.), 108, 137, 201, 213
Bondy, Max, 108
Brecht, Bertolt, 318
Brentano, Franz, 119, 130, 143, 144, 145, 146, 221
"Bridge, The" (Kafka), 353
Broch, Hermann, 150
Brod, Elsa Taussig, 195, 248, 263, 367
Brod, Max, 46, 47, 59, 61, 68, 70, 73, 75, 83, 86, 90–97 *passim*, 107–14 *passim*, 121–9 *passim*, 134, 143, 145, 146, 147, 156–70 *passim*, 174, 178, 180, 187–97 *passim*, 200, 201, 202, 220, 223, 227–33 *passim*, 237, 240, 247, 255, 257, 258, 262, 263, 267, 271, 274, 285, 288, 305–6, 308, 309, 317, 336, 337, 338, 360, 363, 366, 367, 373, 374, 382, 386, 392, 394, 397, 406, 407, 409, 417, 421, 424, 425, 426, 427, 438, 439, 442, 443, 445, 447; as Kafka's biographer, 110, 111, 112, 114, 126, 173–4, 202, 305, 386; quoted, 133–4, 157, 173–4, 201–2, 306, 316–17; and Zionism, 99, 108, 110, 288, 290, 308
Brod, Otto, 199, 200
Brod, Sophie, 283
Buber, Martin, 290, 291, 347, 366
Buber-Neumann, Margarete, 410, 411
Budapest, 244, 325, 357, 414
"Burrow, The" (Kafka), 441
Busse, Karl, 442
Byron, Lord, 127

Cabala, 337
Canetti, Elias, 321
Cantor, Georg, 147
"Cares of a Family Man, The" (Kafka), 353, 386
Caruso, Enrico, 138
Castle, The (Kafka), 111, 120, 139, 180, 189, 220, 255, 399, 421–2, 423, 424, 425, 441
Castle Norrepygge (Brod), 192*n.*
Catholic Church, 20, 21, 46
Chinese Ghost and Love Stories (Buber), 291
Christianity, 151, 317, 368; and anti-Semitism, 40; Jews converted to, 61
"City Coat of Arms, The" (Kafka), 413
Claudel, Paul, 216
Collected Letters (Kafka), 417
Comedy of Errors, The (Shakespeare), 217
Comenius, John Amos, 22
"Commune of Workers without Private Property" (Kafka), 368
Communism, 69, 410; *see also* Marxism; socialism
Communist Review (Prague), 447
"Conscription of Troops, The" (Kafka), 413
Conversation with Kafka (Janouch), 71, 418
Cooper, James Fenimore, 158–9
Country Doctor, A (Kafka), 290, 353, 357, 367, 386, 412, 426
"Crossbreed, A" (Kafka), 353
Czech Legion, Masaryk's, 355, 365
Czech National Theater, 140
Czech nationalism, 22, 31, 32, 37, 42, 105, 150, 151, 204, 317, 318, 366, 369
Czech Social Democratic Party, 38, 44, 61, 62, 71
Czechoslovakia, 39, 43, 108, 372, 373, 374, 411, 413; Nazi occupation of, 87–8, 397, 410

D'Annunzio, Gabriele, 251
Darwin, Charles, 65, 69
Darwinism, 74, 75
David, Joseph, 350, 376–7, 378, 386, 424
David Copperfield (Dickens), 231
Death unto the Dead (Brod), 165*n.*
Deml, Ferdinand, 74
"Departure, The" (Kafka), 421
"Description of a Struggle" (Kafka), 160, 161, 162, 163, 166, 255
Diamant, Dora, 259, 433, 434, 436–47 *passim*; quoted, 438

Dickens, Charles, 100, 159, 160, 231, 256
Dickens and Kafka (Spilka), 231
Dina and the Writer Kafka, 433
Dollfuss, Engelbert, 226
Don Giovanni (Mozart), 137
Doomsday series, Wolff's, 276, 279, 295, 342, 350
Doré, Gustave, 338
Dostoevsky, Feodor, 53, 100, 159, 231, 300, 350, 414
Doyle, Conan, 158
Dresden, 155, 259, 311, 410
Dreyfus case, 42, 61, 226

Edict of Toleration (1792), 23, 24
Ehrenfels, Christian von, 144
Ehrenstein, Albert, 295
Eichmann, Adolf, 328
Einstein, Albert, 145, 147
Eisner, Minze, 387, 418
Eisner, Paul, 136
"Eleven Sons" (Kafka), 353
England, 315, 439; in World War I, 353
eurythmics, 311
existentialism, 422
Eyewitness, The (Weiss), 299

Fackel, Die (pub.), 225, 226, 228
"Fackel Neurosis, The" (Wittels), 226
faith and reason, tension between, at heart of Jewish tradition, 323
Fanta, Berta, 144, 145, 146, 147, 221, 222
Faulkner, William, 422
Feigl, Friedrich, 168
Feinmann, Siegmund, 242, 243
Ferdinand-Karls University, 101, 105
Fichte, Johann Gottlieb, 147
Fieger, Franz, 33
Figaro (pub.), 216
"First Sorrow" (Kafka), 421, 441
Flaubert, Gustave, 98, 159, 167, 214, 300, 346
Fletcher, Horace, 208, 224
Fontane, Theodor, 159, 342
Forberger, Mrs., 413
Force de l'Age, La (Beauvoir), 422*n.*
France, 140, 214, 215–16, 299; in World War I, 324
Franco-Prussian War (1870–71), 315
Frank, Philipp, 145
Frankenstein Sanatorium, 340, 371
Franz Joseph, Emperor, 12, 33, 98, 149, 150, 298, 354
Franzi, A Second-Class Love (Brod), 417

"Fratricide, A" (Kafka), 353
Frederick II (King of Prussia), 20
Free School Association, 69
Frémaux, Paul, 287
French Revolution, 5, 35, 36, 233
Freud, Sigmund, 7, 53, 81, 82, 88, 120, 121, 150, 180, 203, 226, 271, 272, 298, 315, 318; *see also* psychoanalysis
Freund, Ida, 144
Freytag, Gustav, 251
Friedland School for Agriculture, 371, 379
Fromer, Jacob, 245
Fuchs, Rudolf, 142, 357

Gablonzer Zeitung, 211
Galicia, 21, 325, 335, 433
Galley, The (Weiss), 298, 299
Garrigue, Charlotte, 43
Gegenwart, Die (pub.), 161
General Education Act (1774), 21
German Authors League Concordia, 137
German Craft Workshops, 312
German Gymnasts' Association, 205
German-Jewish schools, 24, 29, 33, 106
German language, and Kraus, 225, 226, 227
German National and Civic Elementary School, 19, 25, 26, 27
German National Democrats, 108
Germany, 30, 31, 33, 36, 90, 103, 105, 153, 183, 258, 295, 304, 316, 398, 415, 431, 436; in World War I, 314, 316, 324, 325, 353
Gestalt psychology, 143, 317
Gestapo, 268, 296, 397, 410, 438, 439; *see also* Hitler, Adolf; Holocaust; Nazism
"Give It Up" (Kafka), 426
Gmünd (Austria), 407, 408
Gobineau, Joseph Arthur de, 149
Goethe, Johann Wolfgang von, 74, 100, 104, 155, 159, 199, 216, 251, 258, 259, 336, 350
Goldfaden, Abraham, 242, 247
Golem (Meyrink), 156
Gonda, Viktor, 343
Good Soldier Švejk (Hašek), 111, 151, 318
Gordin, Jacob, 242
Gordon, Aaron David, 368, 369
Gottwald, Adolf, 74, 75, 146
Grace and Freedom (Weltsch), 129, 130
Graetz, Heinrich, 245
"Great Wall of China, The" (Kafka), 353
Grillparzer, Franz, 300, 346
Grimmstein Sanatorium, 408, 409
Gross, Hans, 119, 120, 121
Gross, Otto, 120, 121, 400

"Grotto" (Kafka), 139
Gruen, Nathan, 59
Gründerjahre, Europe's, 38
Gschwind, Emil, 50, 72–3
"Guardian of the Tomb" (Kafka), 139
Gypsy Synagogue, 60

Haas, Willy, 145, 197, 253, 271, 312, 397–8, 399; quoted, 398
Habsburg, House of: *see* Austro-Hungary
Hadlik, Karel, 3
Hadwiger, Victor, 156
Haeckel, Ernst Heinrich, 69
Hajek, Prof., 444
Hamlet (Shakespeare), 217
Hamsun, Knut, 104, 158, 159, 350
Handbook for Investigative Judges, Policemen, and Gendarmes (Gross), 120
Hanukkah, 336
Hašek, Jaroslav, 111, 151, 152, 318
Hasidism, 337
Hauptman, Gerhart, 138, 251
He (Kafka), 387
Hebbel, Friedrich, 159
Hebrew Grammar and Reader for Schools and Self-Instruction (Rath), 356
Hebrew language, 356, 371, 428, 429
Hebrew University (Jerusalem), 63, 65, 129, 429
Hecht, Hugo, 71, 78, 287
Hedin, Sven, 63, 158
Hegel, Georg, 147
Heine, Heinrich, 99, 226, 228
Heine, Mathilda, 396
Heller, Erich, 266
Hellerau International Institute, 311
"Helmsman, The" (Kafka), 413
Henry, W., 287
Herderblätter (pub.), 232, 253
Hermann, Dr., 418, 420
Hermann, Karl, 217, 234, 235, 236, 237, 238, 314, 319, 355, 371
Hermann, Paul, 238, 319
Herzen, Alexander, 153, 366
Herzl, Theodor, 61, 151, 226
Hesse, Hermann, 159
Hilsner, Leopold, 42, 43, 44, 203, 399
Histoire de la Littérature Judéo-Allemande (Pines), 245
History of the Jewish People (Graetz), 245
Hitler, Adolf, 42, 150, 204, 226, 230, 299, 435; *see also* Gestapo; Holocaust; Nazism
Hitler, Alois, 25
Hitler-Stalin pact, 410

Hoffmann, Camill, 156, 296, 438
Hofmannsthal, Hugo von, 159, 160, 251
Holitscher, Arthur, 256
Holocaust, 399; *see also* Gestapo; Hitler, Adolf; Nazism
"Home-Coming" (Kafka), 413
Homer, 336
homosexuality, 91, 92
House Minuta (Prague), 13, 27
Hruza, Agnes, 42
Humanistic Gymnasium, 35, 51
Hungary, 337, 339, 357, 441
"Hunger Artist, A" (Kafka), 421, 426, 441, 445
"Hunter Gracchus, The" (Kafka), 353
Hus, Jan, 39, 43
Husserl, Edmund, 143
Hussite rebellions, 38, 387
Hyperion (pub.), 160, 161, 194, 197

Ibsen, Henrik, 138
Iliad, 73
Illový, Rudolf, 71
"Imperial Message, An" (Kafka), 386
impressionism, 317
"In the Gallery" (Kafka), 353
Industrial Revolution, 36
industrialization, 21, 22, 36, 40, 148, 149
inflation in Germany (1923), 435
influenza pandemic (1918), 372
"Investigations of a Dog" (Kafka), 426
Iphigenie (Goethe), 200, 216
Israel, 290, 429; National Library in, 65, 368, 429
Italy, 232, 233, 301, 304, 388; in World War I, 339, 353

"Jackals and Arabs" (Kafka), 353
Janáček, Leoš, 111, 369, 442
Janouch, Gustav, 71, 72, 152, 188, 227, 305, 418
Japan, 315
Jaques-Dalcroze, Émile, 311, 348
Jardin des Supplices, Le (Mirbeau), 327
Jaurès, Jean Léon, 316
Jenufa (Janáček), 369, 442
Jerusalem, 368, 428, 429, 430, 436
Jesenius, Jan, 389
Jesenská, Marie, 389
Jesenská, Milena, 389, 390, 391, 392, 397, 399, 400, 403, 404, 406, 408, 409, 410, 411, 416, 418, 421, 423; Kafka's letters to, 52–3, 84–5, 204, 268, 338, 359, 391–2, 393, 400, 402, 404, 406, 407, 408, 423;

Kafka's love for, 394, 401, 402, 403, 407;
at Ravensbrück, 410, 411
Jesenská, Ružena, 389
Jesenský, Jan, 389, 390, 411
Jewish Echo, The, Hasidic tales in, 337
Jewish National Council (Czechoslovakia),
374
Jewish National Fund, 378, 430
Jewish Orthodoxy, 437
Jewish People's Home (Berlin), 347, 348,
432, 433
Jewish State, The (Herzl), 61
Jewry, Austro-Hungarian, 5, 7, 8, 10, 11,
22–3, 31, 32, 54–5, 98
Jílova, Staša, 404
Jones, Ernest, 120
Joseph II, Emperor, Edict of Toleration
issued by (1782), 23
"Josephine, the Singer" (Kafka), 6, 441,
443, 444
Journal of Philosophy, Czech, 130
Joyce, James, 54
Judaism, 22, 24, 31, 54, 55, 56, 57, 60, 61,
65, 108, 129, 130, 226, 240, 241, 243,
245, 248, 251, 289, 290, 338, 347, 348,
421, 427, 433, 440
Jude, Der (pub.), 366
"Judgment, The" (Kafka), 168, 213, 219,
239, 255, 269, 270, 271, 272, 273, 276,
278, 281, 284, 321, 350, 370, 408, 426
Jung, Carl, 120
Jungborn Sanatorium, 259, 260–1

Kafka, Anton, 152
Kafka, Bruno, 107, 108, 109, 119, 369
Kafka, Elli (Elli Hermann), 25, 45, 71, 77,
86, 87, 217, 234, 263, 319, 332, 339, 404,
416, 417, 431, 432, 447
Kafka, Franz: birth of, 3, 12; childhood
of, 3, 13–19 *passim,* 25, 26, 27, 28, 29;
psychoanalytic insights into work and
character of, 7, 15, 19, 81, 384; exotic
heritage of, 9; in conflict with father, 15,
18–19, 58, 80, 81, 96, 102, 164, 219, 234,
239, 274, 300, 383, 385; rage spawned
in, 15, 63; at German National and Civic
Elementary School, 19, 25, 26, 27; at
Gymnasium, 35, 45, 46–49, 51, 52, 53,
54, 59, 72–6, 101, 106; self-deprecation
by, 53, 95, 172, 190, 203, 204, 205, 213,
293–4, 399, 400; and Judaism, 55, 56, 57,
240, 241, 243, 245, 248, 251, 289, 290,
347, 348, 427, 440; as omnivorous
reader, 63, 158–9, 251; adolescence of,
64–5, 67, 69, 74, 75, 77, 80; in debates
with Bergmann, 65–6; Bergmann's por-

trayal of, 67–8; in "Prague circle," 68;
Free School Association joined by, 69;
employed by Workmen's Accident Insurance Institute, 70, 135, 181–2, 184–93,
194, 199, 206, 210, 211, 220, 288, 326,
332–3, 341, 343–4, 370–1, 375, 385–6,
417; and socialism, 71, 72; and Jewish
middle-class values, 72; and fairy tales,
fondness for, 74, 158, 159; and sexuality,
77–80, 82, 83, 84–6, 118, 122, 133, 135,
171–2, 179–81, 203, 302, 403; sisters of,
relationships with, 86, 87, 88, 349, 350;
writing defined by, 97; as hypochondriac,
104, 190, 200, 206, 223; at university,
105, 109, 114–23, 143–4; and Hall of
Lecture and Discourse for German
Students (Prague), 106, 107, 109, 110,
121; at Zuckmantl Sanatorium, 121, 122,
165, 331, 345; awarded degree of Doctor
of Laws, 122, 165; unworldliness of, 125,
135, 175, 282; appearance of, 130, 176,
202, 204, 285, 433; humor in work of,
131; intellectual independence of, 157;
as lover of books, 158; curiosity of, about
other people's lives, 159; as law clerk,
164–5, 166; at twenty-four, 169; and
purity of writing, 174; employed by
Assicurazioni Generali, 175–9; in
allusions to suicide, 179, 236; recurrent
depressions of, 190, 191, 192–3, 195,
341, 420; physical frailty of, 202;
masturbation by, 203, 204; bodily
infirmities of, 206; authority mistrusted
by, 207; converted to body-building
program, 207–8; as vegetarian, 208, 209,
285, 361, 364; and self-imposed
starvation diet, 209; tuberculosis of lungs
incurred by, 209, 358–64 *passim,* 400,
405, 406, 407, 420, 442; diaries of,
212–13, 418; at twenty-eight, 219; and
flight into illness, 223–4, 363; and Prague
Asbestos Works Hermann & Co., 234–6,
237, 238, 274, 319; and Yiddish theater,
239, 240, 242–8 *passim,* 250; and
Zionism, 241, 288, 290, 308, 347, 380,
420, 428; on Yiddish language, 248; as
alienated Western Jew, 249, 399; tenacity
of, in pursuit of writing, 252; at
Jungborn Sanatorium, 259, 260–1;
fascination of, for young girls, 259,
301–2, 433; manuscripts of, confiscated
by Gestapo (1933), 268, 438–9; at thirty,
296; during World War I, 325–6, 332–4,
339–40, 355; afflicted with headaches,
327, 339, 340, 343, 346; at Frankenstein
Sanatorium, 340, 371; Golden Lane

studio of, 351, 354, 355; at Schönborn
Palace, 355–6, 359, 361; and
Frankenstein Veterans Hospital for
Nervous Diseases, 370; at Matliary
"sanatorium," 413–17; at Spindlermühle,
420, 421; critics' views of work of, 422;
insomnia of, 426; at Wiener Wald
Sanatorium, 443, 444; tuberculosis of
larynx incurred by, 443, 444, 445, 446;
at University Clinic (Vienna), 444; at
Kierling Sanatorium, 444–5; death of,
447; buried in Prague, 448; *see also*
Bauer, Felice; Bloch, Grete; Brod, Max;
Diamant, Dora; Jesenská, Milena; Kafka,
Herrmann; Kafka, Julie Löwy; Kafka,
Ottla; *titles of Kafka's works*
Kafka, Georg, 16
Kafka, Heinrich, 16
Kafka, Herrmann, 4, 5, 6, 7, 8, 11, 12,
14–19 *passim*, 32, 35, 42, 46, 58, 64, 65,
66, 80, 87, 107, 164, 165, 169, 172, 174,
234, 235, 245, 246, 272, 273, 300, 349,
350, 355, 361, 377, 379, 381, 383, 385,
424–5; in conflict with son, 15, 18–19,
58, 80, 81, 96, 102, 164, 219, 234, 239,
274, 300, 393, 385
Kafka, Jakob, 4–5, 6
Kafka, Joseph, 107, 108
Kafka, Julie Löwy, 8–15 *passim*, 17, 64,
80–81, 82, 165, 237–8, 274, 297, 370, 377
Kafka, Morits, 107
Kafka, Ottla (Ottla David), 45, 86, 87,
104, 263, 290, 343, 349, 350, 352, 355,
365, 370, 371, 376, 377, 405, 414, 426;
and Franz Kafka, 87, 270, 349, 350, 351,
352, 360, 362, 363, 364, 367, 369, 371,
376–81 *passim*, 405, 408, 416, 424, 425,
434; marriage of, 378, 404, 405
Kafka, Valli, 45, 86, 87, 253, 263, 319,
332, 417
Kafka and the Yiddish Theater (Beck),
240*n*., 242
Kafka's Friend Milena (Buber-Neumann),
411
Kant, Immanuel, 143, 145, 147
Karl, Emperor, 354
Karlsbad spa, 340, 401
kashrut, 209
Kerr, Alfred, 228
kibbutz movement, 290, 368
Kierkegaard, Søren, 100, 159, 160, 230,
366, 368, 426
Kierling Sanatorium, 444, 447
Kirchner, Margarete, 259
Kisch, Egon Erwin, 98, 142, 174
Kisch, Guido, 49, 118

Klabund, 347
Kleist, Bernd Heinrich Wilhelm von, 74,
100, 159, 160, 229, 276, 300, 301, 329
Klimt, Gustav, 150
Klopstock, Robert, 414, 415, 419, 420,
434, 441, 443, 444, 445, 446, 447; as
distinguished physician in United States,
415
Kmen (pub.), 393
"Knock at the Manor Gate, The" (Kafka),
353
Koch, Robert, 361
Kodym, Dr., 387
Kohn, Hans, 49, 247, 296
Kokoschka, Oskar, 150
Kowalewski, Gerhard, 145
Krasnopolski, Horaz, 119–20, 143
Kraus, Karl, 99, 142, 225–7, 228, 229, 400
Krejcar, Jaromir, 410
Kropotkin, Prince, 69, 151, 153, 368
Kubin, Alfred, 234, 251
Kuh, Anton, 400
Kunstwart (pub.), 90, 157

Landau, Ezekiel, 24
Langer, František, 337
Langer, Mordechai (Georg), 336–7, 338,
356, 371, 418
language rights, struggle for, 39
Last Days of Mankind, The (Kraus), 227
Latteiner, Josef, 242
Laurenziberg hill, 162
Lehmann, Siegfried, 347, 433
Leipzig, 257, 258, 312, 342, 350
Leppin, Paul, 110, 155, 156
Letter to His Father (Kafka), 15, 18, 26–7,
28–9, 51, 55–6, 58, 78–9, 103, 202–3, 381,
383, 384, 385
Levetzow, Ulrike von, 259
Levi, Yitzhak, 240, 241, 244–5, 246, 247,
248, 250, 273, 357
Liebknecht, Karl, 316
Literarische Blätter (pub.), 240
Literarische Welt, Die (pub.), 145
"Little Ruin Dweller, The" (Kafka), 213
"Little Woman, A" (Kafka), 441
Lodz ghetto (1941), 87
Löwy, Alfred, 10, 115, 175, 264, 404
Löwy, Jakob, 9, 10
Löwy, Joseph, 10
Löwy, Julie: *see* Kafka, Julie Löwy
Löwy, Richard, 10, 164, 264
Löwy, Rudolf, 10
Löwy, Siegfried, 10, 116, 170, 264, 442
Loos, Adolf, 150

Lord Clive of India (Macaulay), 127, 165
Louvre Café (Prague), 142, 143, 144, 145, 146
Lueger, Karl, 150
Lukács, Georg, 422
Luxemburg, Rosa, 316

Macaulay, Thomas B., 127, 165
Mach, Ernst, 74
Madrid, 10, 115, 175, 264, 404
Mahler, Gustav, 150
"Man Who Disappeared, The" (*Der Verschollene*) by Kafka, 231, 255, 261, 331
Mann, Heinrich, 160, 161
Mann, Thomas, 159, 299
Mareš, Michal, 152
Maria Theresa, 20
Marienbad, 338, 344, 345, 346
Markert, Hans, 33
"Married Couple, The" (Kafka), 426
Marschner, Robert, 184, 185, 186–7, 188, 301, 343, 344, 360, 365, 370, 375, 386
Marty, Anton, 143
Marx, Karl, 99
Marxism, 61, 151, 410; *see also* Communism; socialism
März (pub.), 288, 295
Masaryk, Alice, 389
Masaryk, Jan, 39
Masaryk, Tomáš, 29, 32, 43, 44, 317, 355, 357, 365, 373, 374, 375
Matliary "sanatorium," 413, 414, 415, 419
Mautner, Fritz, 49
Meditations (Kafka), 160, 275, 276, 288, 295, 342, 365
"Memories of the Kalda Railroad" (Kafka), 321, 331
Merano (Italy), 388, 391, 400, 401, 405
"Metamorphosis, The" (Kafka), 167, 272, 274, 278, 279, 285, 342, 351, 426
Meyrink, Gustav, 110, 156, 157, 158, 161
Milan Cathedral, 232
militarism, German, 204, 229
Minerva High School (Bohemia), 389, 390
Mirbeau, Octave, 327, 328
"Modest Proposal, A" (Swift), 417
Molière, 217
Moment of Torment (Tiefenbrun), 273
Moravia, 7, 8, 22, 24, 25, 37, 325
Mozart, Wolfgang Amadeus, 137
Mueller, Jens Peter, 207–8
Mühlstein, Dr., 346, 359, 361
Munich, 116, 155, 201, 214, 232, 288, 305, 351, 435
Müritz (Germany), 431, 432, 433, 434

Musil, Robert, 150, 276, 295
mysticism, 155, 221, 337, 387

Napoleon Bonaparte, 214, 233, 286, 287, 434
Národný Listy (pub.), 410, 447
nationalism, rise of, in early nineteenth century, 21
Nazism, 41, 111, 199, 204, 229, 268, 296, 304, 375, 397, 410, 438; *see also* Gestapo; Hitler, Adolf; Holocaust
"Neighbor, The" (Kafka), 353
Neill, A. S., 311, 417
Netuka, Karl, 33
Neue Freie Presse (pub.), 226, 296, 424
Neue Rundschau (pub.), 295
Neue Weg, Der (pub.), 194
Neumann, Angelo, 138
Neumann, Stanislav Kostka, 447
Neurath, Otto, 391
"New Attorney, The" (Kafka), 353
"Next Village, The" (Kafka), 353
Nielsen, Carl, 111
Nietzsche, Friedrich, 65, 69, 83, 90, 110, 126, 144, 149, 157, 159
nihilism, 61
Nostitz, Count von, 137
Novak, Willy, 251

occultism, 144, 221
Odyssey, 73
"Oklahoma Open Air Theater" (Kafka), 257, 261, 327
"Old Manuscript, An" (Kafka), 353
Old Town Square (Prague), 4, 10, 11, 12, 13, 27, 35, 39, 145, 164, 188, 308, 332, 356, 389, 426, 434
Olsen, Regine, 366
"On Parables" (Kafka), 426
Oneg Shabath, 433
Opale, Die (pub.), 161
Organism of Jewry (Fromer), 245
Ostjuden, 245, 335, 338
Ostrčil, Bedřich, 385, 386, 387, 416

pacifism, 317
Paganism, Christianity, Judaism (Brod), 406–7
Palestine, 65, 67, 84, 129, 132, 241, 262, 269, 290, 301, 304, 305, 350, 368, 369, 374, 378, 427, 428, 429, 430, 434
pan-German nationalism, 31
Pan-German Nationalist Union, 149
pan-Slavism, and Sokol, 204
pantheism, Spinoza's, 69

Paris, 10, 214, 215, 216, 217, 233, 244, 299, 317
Path of the Lover, The (Brod), 168
Penal Colony, The (Kafka), 187, 275, 327, 328, 329, 331, 351, 386, 426
Perception and Concept (Weltsch), 129
Pfohl, Eugen, 188, 190, 301, 370, 375, 385, 386
phenomenology, 143
phylacteries, 427
Piaristenkollegium, 46, 47
Pick, Friedl, 360, 370
Pick, Otto, 142, 251, 295, 296, 417–18, 444
Pines, Meyer, 246
Planá (Czechoslovakia), 424, 425
Plato, 73, 350
Platowski, Franziska, 5, 6
Polak, Ernst, 390, 391, 394, 395, 400, 404, 405, 406, 410, 421
Poland, 39, 432
Pollak, Oskar, 88–9, 90, 91, 92, 95, 96, 107, 109, 114, 115, 119, 124, 157, 158, 160, 162, 195, 339
Pollak, Wilhelm, 176
Porias, Amschel, 9
Porias, Esther, 9
Porias, Nathan, 9
Porias, Sarah, 9
positivism, 391
Powderpuff, The (Blei), 194
Prager Abendblatt, 424
Prager Presse, 444, 447
Prager Tagblatt, 98, 110, 122, 137, 138, 180, 247, 296, 310
Prague, 3, 8, 10, 11, 12, 13, 29, 30–1, 32, 35, 39, 43, 44, 54, 71, 84, 86, 90, 103, 105, 106, 119, 123, 125, 130, 136, 137, 138, 141, 144, 151, 153, 155, 156, 163, 168, 192, 196, 201, 203–4, 205, 214, 216, 221, 251, 290, 295, 296, 316, 369, 372, 410, 411, 434, 447, 448; Altstädter Gymnasium in, 46–50, 53, 59, 101, 129; anti-Austrian riots in (1913), 298; anti-Jewish riot in (1897), 42, 60; anti-Jewish and anti-German riots in (1920), 408; coffeehouses in, 141–2; German-Jewish artists and intellectuals of, 151; illegitimacy rate in (1912), 180; Institute of Technology in, 184, 187; Jewish population of (1900), 98, 136; Liblice Conference in, on German-language writers (1963), 422; literary cafés in, 142–3, 144, 145, 146; literati of, 98, 109; as musical center, 138; Nazi occupation of, 132; prostitutes in, 179, 180, 181; theater in, *see* theater in Prague;

University of, 105, 119–20, 129, 143, 145, 419, 429; during World War I, 318, 325, 333, 335, 336, 339, 353–4, 369; Young vs. Old Guard, 153, 154, 156, 228
Prague Asbestos Works Hermann & Co., 234–6, 237, 238, 274, 319
"Prague circle," 68
Pravo Lidu (pub.), 71
Příbram, Ewald Felix, 70, 71, 121, 134, 135, 162, 181
Příbram, Otto, 135, 181, 210, 365
"Problem of Our Laws, The" (Kafka), 413
prostitution, 80, 179–80, 181
Prussia, 19–20
psychoanalysis, 120, 409; and Kafka's character and work, 7, 15, 19, 81, 384; *see also* Freud, Sigmund
Purple Death (Meyrink), 157

Rachilde, 251
Racine, Jean Baptiste, 216
Rath, Moses, 356, 371, 428
Ravensbrück concentration camp, 410, 411
Realist Party, 44, 317, 318
Realschule, 35
reason and faith, tension between, at heart of Jewish tradition, 323
Religion and Humor in the Work of Franz Kafka (Weltsch), 129
Renaissance, 199
"Report to an Academy" (Kafka), 353, 366
"Resolutions" (Kafka), 253
Respektspersonen, 29, 33, 87
Reubeni (Brod), 111
revolution of 1848, 5
Richter, Moses, 242
Riddle of Laughter, The (Weltsch), 129
Rilke, Rainer Maria, 150, 154, 155, 156, 160, 351
Rimbaud, Arthur, 155
Riva (Austria), 122, 199, 202, 210, 301, 302, 303, 308, 331, 345
Robbers, The (Schiller), 434
Robert, Marthe, 422
Robitschek, Selma (née Kohn), 83; quoted, 83
Rohling, August, 41
Rössler, Tile, 433, 442
Rowohlt, Ernst, 257, 258, 261, 262, 271, 275
Rudolf II, King, 352
Rumania in World War I, 353
Russia, 273, 315, 434; in First World War, 314, 318, 324, 325, 335, 353; revolution in, 354–5; *see also* Soviet Union

Salus, Hugo, 110, 153, 154
Salus, Wolfgang, 154
Salveter, Emmy, 425, 432, 433, 442
Sanction of Ethics (Brentano), 130
Sanzara, Rachel (Johanna Bleschke), 299, 313
Sarajevo, 312
Sartre, Jean-Paul, 422
Sauer, August, 105, 114, 115
Savoy Café (Prague), 239, 242, 244
Schacht, Hjalmar, 435
Schafftgotsch, Count, 410
Schelesin (Bohemia), 376, 379, 382, 386, 387, 434
Schickele, René, 279, 342
Schiller, Johann Christoph Friedrich von, 155, 258, 434
Schlick, Moritz, 391
Schmiede, Die, 441, 444
Schnitzer, Moritz, 224, 234
Schnitzler, Arthur, 138, 150, 217
Schocken, Walter, 305
Schocken, Zalman, 267, 268
Schönberg, Arnold, 150, 153
Schönborn Palace, 355–6, 359, 361
Schönerer, Georg Ritter von, 149, 150
Schopenhauer, Arthur, 110, 350
Selbstwehr (pub.), 130, 205, 227, 241, 247, 296, 338, 354, 368, 386, 428
Sentimental Education (Flaubert), 167
Serbia, 314, 315, 316, 325
Shakespeare, William, 103, 127, 217
Sharkansky, Abraham, 242
Shaw, George Bernard, 127
Singer, Irma, 290, 371
Slaviček, Karel, 151
socialism, 38, 44, 61, 62, 67, 71, 72, 183, 227, 316; *see also* Communism; Marxism
Socialist International, 315, 316
Sonnenfels, Josef, 20–1
Soviet Union, 439; gulags in, 410; *see also* Russia
"Speech on the Yiddish Language" (Kafka), 248
Spilka, Mark, 231
Spinoza, Baruch, 65, 69, 174
spiritualism, 144, 145, 156
Stalin, Joseph, 39, 145, 146, 439
Stalin-Hitler pact, 410
Steiner, Karl, 101
Steiner, Rudolf, 144, 221, 222, 223, 224
Sternheim, Carl, 342
Stoker, The (Kafka), 231, 255, 271–7 *passim*, 295, 296, 342, 351, 393, 426, 447
Strelinger, Dr., 413, 417
Strindberg, August, 138, 331

Stürgkh, Carl, 354
"Sudden Walk, The" (Kafka), 253
Swift, Jonathan, 416, 417
Switzerland, 183, 196, 233, 234

Talmud, 24, 97, 98, 174, 199, 264, 281, 436
Talmud Jew, The (Rohling), 41
Taussig, Elsa (Elsa Brod), 195, 248, 263, 367
Tel Aviv, 201, 369, 433, 436
Terezin concentration camp, 87, 116, 132, 376
"Test, The" (Kafka), 413
Tetschen-Bodenbacher Zeitung, 185
Teweles, Heinrich, 137, 138
theater in Prague, 137–8, 139, 140; Yiddish, 239, 240, 242–8 *passim*, 250
theosophy, 144, 222, 223
Thieberger, Friedrich, 4
Tiefenbrun, Ruth, 273
Tiszaeszlar (Hungary), 41, 43
Toleranzpatent (1782), 23, 24
Tolstoy, Leo, 69, 138, 151, 366, 368
"Top, The" (Kafka), 413
Torah, 23, 24, 59, 98, 174, 436
Treblinka concentration camp, 244
Trial, The (Kafka), 105, 111, 120, 139, 180, 189, 216, 232, 242, 255, 265, 275, 313, 321, 322–3, 329, 331, 441
Tribuna (pub.), 395, 406, 410
Triesch (Moldavia), 115, 116, 170–1, 172, 264, 442
Trieste, 175, 176, 177, 301
Tshissik, Mania, 243, 244
Tsvey Prager Dikhter (Levi), 240
tuberculosis of larynx, incurred by Kafka, 209, 443, 444, 445, 446
tuberculosis of lungs, 361–2, 415; incurred by Kafka, 358–64 *passim*, 400, 405, 406, 407, 420, 442
Tucholsky, Kurt, 99, 228–9, 230, 328 quoted, 328–9
Tycho Brahe's Path to God (Brod), 111, 309

Ulbrich, Josef, 118
"Unhappiness" (Kafka), 213
United States in World War I, 354
"Unmasking a Confidence Trickster" (Kafka), 253
"Urban World, The" (Kafka), 213, 219
Utitz, Emil, 69, 71, 75, 101, 146

Valenta, Jindřich, 385
Venice, 301, 426

Venture of the Middle, The (Weltsch), 129
Verdi, Giuseppe, 138
Verdun, 353
Verlaine, Paul, 155
Verne, Jules, 159
Verschollene, Der ("The Man Who Disappeared") by Kafka, 231, 255, 261, 331
Vice King, The (Feinmann), 242, 243
Vienna, 7, 8, 31, 36, 38, 43, 86, 98, 120, 131, 150, 155, 172, 188, 214, 225, 244, 295, 296, 298, 301, 307, 315, 316, 325, 357, 369, 373, 391, 395, 401, 402, 407, 444; Jewish population of (1900), 98; University of, 172; University Clinic in, 444
Vienna Circle, 391
Vienna Psychoanalytic Society, 226
"Village Schoolmaster, The" (Kafka), 331
"Visit to the Mine, A" (Kafka), 353
Vltava River, 48, 168, 195, 201
Voltaire, 199
Vrchlický, Jaroslav, 251
"Vulture, The" (Kafka), 413

Wagenbach, Klaus, 146
Wagner, Richard, 138, 144, 149, 317
Warsaw, 244, 245
Weber, Alfred, 165
Weber, Max, 165
"Wedding Preparations in the Country" (Kafka), 122, 165, 166, 167, 189, 264, 346
Wedekind, Franz, 88, 138, 251
Weiler, Hedwig, 171, 172, 173, 177, 179, 181, 193
Weimar, 258, 259, 269
Weimar Republic, 258
Weininger, Otto, 400
Weiss, Emil, 127
Weiss, Ernst, 49, 298–9, 301, 309, 312, 313, 343, 417, 442
Weissberger, Arnold, 176, 178
Weisse Blätter (pub.), 279, 342
Weltbühne (pub.), 229, 328
Weltfreund (Werfel), 196, 197
Welträtsel, Die (Haeckel), 69
Weltsch, Felix, 75, 127–32 *passim*, 134, 145, 196, 205, 224, 251, 290, 298, 309, 364, 371, 386

Weltsch, Lise, 290, 301
Werfel, Franz, 7, 46, 61, 86, 95, 110, 111, 121, 145, 156, 157, 168, 196, 197, 228, 251, 298, 312, 317, 366, 390, 418, 426
Werner, Marie, 17, 169
Wertheimer, Max, 317
Wiener, Oskar, 156
Wiener Wald Sanatorium, 443, 444
Winicky, Otokar, 156
"Wish to Be a Red Indian, The" (Kafka), 213, 253
Wittels, Fritz, 226
Wittgenstein, Ludwig, 150
Wohryzek, Julie, 379, 380, 381, 382, 387, 388, 391, 394, 401, 404
Wolff, Kurt, 160, 258, 272, 275, 276, 277, 279, 295, 298, 312, 327, 342, 350, 351, 357, 358, 367, 386, 387, 388, 391, 441
women: fear of, 82, 180; Kafka's attitude toward, 83–4, 88, 180, 281, 286; traditional Jewish attitudes toward, 283, 290
women's movement, Czech, 389
World War I, 36, 39, 89, 143, 188, 226, 227, 290, 299, 314–19 *passim*, 322, 324, 325, 326, 329, 332–6 *passim*, 339, 343, 353, 354, 355, 369
World War II, 72, 267, 304, 439
World's Mysteries, The (Haeckel), 69
"Worry of a Family Man, The" (Kafka), 353, 386

Yiddish theater, 239, 240, 242–8 *passim*, 250
Yiddishkeit, 240, 338
Yom Kippur, 240, 332, 353
Young Czech movement, 42, 43, 106

Zigeunersynagoge, 60
Zionism (Zionists), 61, 65, 66, 67, 99, 104, 107, 108, 110, 130, 151, 154, 205, 227, 240, 241, 246, 247, 288, 290, 301, 308, 338, 347, 350, 354, 380, 420, 428, 429, 430
Zionist Congress, Eleventh World (1913), 301
Zionist Jewish Girls' and Women's Club (Prague), 290
Zola, Émile, 44
Zuckmantl Sanatorium, 121, 122, 165, 331, 345
Zuerau (Bohemia), 133, 355, 360, 365, 367, 369, 371, 436